LAUMBACHS IN NEW MEXICO
And Those Who Went Before
In Germany, Iowa and New Mexico

By Jan Girand

Edited by Jan Girand

Research by Charles O. Sanders

And contributions by several others

WHO WERE THEY?

THEREFORE, WHO AM I?

*Knowing his genealogy
roots a person in history,
giving him a place and a time,
and a reason for being.
jg*

First Edition. Copyright © 2015 by Jan Girand All rights reserved.

Except for brief quotations in a review, no part of this book may be reproduced in any form or by any electronic or mechanical means including information storage and retrieval systems without permission from the publisher at
publisher@yellowjacketpress.com

Any historical errors or opinions are the authors' and the editor's.

For information contact author Jan Girand at jan@yellowjacketpress.com or editor at editor@yellowjacketpress.com

Library of Congress Cataloging-in-Publication Data
Girand, Jan: Laumbachs in New Mexico And Those Who Went Before

ISBN: 978-0-578-16677-3
Barcode:

Roswell New Mexico
2015

www.yellowjacketpress.com

Cover design by Stephanee Killen, with Integrative Ink in Ohio.

Venita Laumbach Ames, daughter of Pedro and Lily Laumbach of Roy, took the 2015 photograph of the gate that graces this book's cover.
The Peter J. Laumbach family's private La Cinta Cemetery gate was a team effort by the children of Eleanor and Alfred Laumbach. Rose and her husband designed the wrought iron portion; Michael was the wrought iron *artisano* and, with help, the master mason who built the stone gate pillars with rock quarried on what had been the P.J.L. ranch. It reflects the family's love and respect for all who slumber within this *camposanto*.

AUTHOR'S/EDITOR'S PREFACE

For *Laumbachs in New Mexico* I've worn many hats: author, editor—which includes choosing the book's content—and publisher. Publisher adds its own unique tasks. This has been a major project, with years in the process. I have learned much about our family history as this book evolved. Sometimes the process was frustrating because it took so long, but I loved the journey. My family history has been a life-long love.

The story of Bibiana especially fascinated me and over the years, I've written (thus far unpublished) several stories based upon her amazing life and times, including a full-length historical fiction novel. Bibiana was born December 1827 and died October 1897 at almost 70. Her life spanned a large portion of the 1800s during New Mexico's formative years. She touched or was touched by many important events and people. She lived in New Mexico under the jurisdiction and flag of Spain, then Mexico, and finally the United States. I've always loved and admired her—my independent great-great-grandmother—born long before women sought equality. She deserves her own book. *Bibiana and Her Children* follows this one, one of three family history books. The *Bibiana* book will include an extensive court transcript of the dispute between two branches of her family that spanned decades, a timeline spanning many hundreds of years with family births and deaths set in context with national and New Mexico events, as well as an expanded genealogy and paper trail by Charles "Butch" Sanders, and many other things.

Any errors or wrong conclusions in this book are mine.

ACKNOWLEDGEMENTS

Charles O. "Butch" Sanders of Delaware has rendered immeasurable assistance for this book. Thus far, he has never visited New Mexico, yet knows more about its geography and history than most of us whose families have lived here for countless generations. He is a self-taught genealogist and history researcher, finding significant data no one else can. He is a stickler for accuracy. With just a few clues—like a dog with only a sniff or two of a worn sock—he follows complicated and indistinct trails and soon knows who's who, despite diverse locations and weird spellings and errors on census and other documents. On census records he not only seeks the subjects, he takes note of all of their neighbors and their locations, even the census-takers. From his remote position, he sees clearly what leaves me cross-eyed and confused, and soon knows who begat whom for generations. He found many pertinent photos and maps and enhanced the quality of most of our families' vintage photos and documents for this publication. He has been faster than anyone responding to my email queries. We have worked together for years on my several history gathering and book projects. I will always be indebted to him, and to his wife Barb for tolerating his long hours spent at his computer through countless nights.

When this Laumbach book was at its end and being prepared for publication, I learned that some of my conclusions—particularly those expressed in the final chapter—do not reflect his or Karl's. Those are primarily about who lived where and when in the Mora area. Butch's additional documentations and conclusions and maps will be presented in the forthcoming *Bibiana* book.

Karl Laumbach, of Las Cruces, New Mexico has been gathering family history and copying family photographs and documents from various family most of his adult life. Formerly director of research and public education, he is now its associate director as well as the principal investigator with Human Systems Research. HSR is a non-profit corporation involved with research in archaeology, anthropology and historical discovery and preservation of sites, especially in southwest and south-central New Mexico. For more than 30 years, Karl has been the lead archaeologist on hundreds of projects, and also gathers and preserves oral regional histories. Although physically involved, long hours and days out in the field on digs as well as in the office, he took time to respond to my requests. He lent his gathered knowledge as well as many images of photos and documents. Three chapters in this book are Karl's.

Danny Chaves of Mora was my tour guide of that area and responded to my email queries despite his busy schedule as Mora Public Schools principal and part-time employee at the Allsup Ranch at Buena Vista. He has spent much of his life working part time for the various owners of the ranch that was first established by Andreas and Elionor. He began working there when he was young. He and some of his extended family who had also been neighbors of Henry Laumbach—son of Andreas and Elionor—are probably more familiar with the history of the property than anyone now living in the Mora area. I am also indebted to the Allsup Family, current owners of the ranch; they encouraged Danny and Ned Walker, their ranch manager, to extend their gracious hospitality to my daughter and me when we visited for research. I appreciate all of the property's owners, past and present, for preserving many physical aspects of the original buildings and property.

Ned Walker, the manager of Allsup's Ranch at Buena Vista, extended his own and his employer's hospitality when we visited. He gave us a tour of the ranch and shared what knowledge he had about the place. That visit brought back for me very early nostalgic childhood memories of what had once been the childhood home of my grandfather and his siblings, and their parents' home-place.

Chick Burney, manager of the Abel family's Buena Vista Ranch, has always been gracious and interested in helping me gather information whenever I called or visited, even when he was in the midst of round-up. The Abel family owns this ranch founded and established by Frank Metzger, and then owned by Metzger's daughter, Juanita, and her husband, Henry Korte. That was where Frank and Apolonia lived the last years of their lives, where they died and were buried in their nearby private family cemetery on the property. Our family will always be grateful to the Abel Family, as well as previous ranch owners, for their historic preservation of many of its features. That includes what had once been the Buena Vista post office, blacksmith shop and store on the ranch. The original Metzger-Korte home no longer exists. It burned about 1975 when the Thompsons, the ranch's then-owners, were away from home. The Thompson family rebuilt the headquarters buildings in a more modern style.

Anna Marie and Albert Ortega of Taos arranged for my 2013 visit to the Allsup and Abel ranches; they introduced me to Ned Walker and Chick Burney. They enabled me to visit the Metzger-Korte family cemetery and the Abel Ranch for the first time in my life. Anna Marie's mother, a daughter of Henry Laumbach, was raised by our Aunties and lived many of her childhood years at the Laumbach Ranch, where Anna Marie feels a strong connection.

Pete Laumbach of Las Lunas traveled to Germany with his wife, Ophie, in 2005, to visit their son, then based there, and his young family. In the limited time he had, Pete located the repository of our family's archived history. His subsequent research pushed further back in time our knowledge of our Germanic roots—history and genealogy. Pete cut a CD and he and Ophie designed and created a huge chart tying together both lines of our genealogy—in Germany and in northern New Mexico. Unfortunately, that chart is too large and extensive to be included—even considerably reduced—in this book. After he compiled it and wrote the text covering his findings, Pete generously shared those with his extended family. A few years later, he consented for his material to be included in this book.

The family has many Petes, Pedros and at least one Petra Laumbach. To clarify, this Pete grew up in Las Vegas, New Mexico. He is a son of Rudolph and Leona, and grandson of their family's patriarch, Peter Joseph "Pete" Laumbach.

José Antonio Esquibel extracts, translates and transcribes data from archived sacramental documents that are hundreds of years old. From that, he painstakingly compiles family genealogies of early New Mexico families, picking up and continuing the task begun by Fra Angélico Chavez. José shares his knowledge in various publications and with the state's genealogical societies. Without the exhaustive works of Chavez and Esquibel, families with deep roots in New Mexico would not know their early histories. José kindly took time from his busy schedule to proof several chapters of this book for accuracy of early New Mexico history, and he provided a chapter about our forebear, Bernardo Martín, with information few of us knew. In it, some of his provided documentation was from research by his cousin, **Amanda Maestas Freiberg**. I am honored to include José's contribution.

Dallas Laumbach was someone we in New Mexico did not know until after I had begun research for this book. Karl found him on the Internet and reached out to him by phone. Thus began our acquaintance. Since then Dallas and Rosalie have twice come from Texas to New Mexico to visit members of their new-found family. He was our first opportunity to meet an "Iowa Laumbach." Connecting with him was of even greater significance. His great-grandfather was the same Henry several generations of our family had thought was lost. That Henry was the brother of our great-grandfather, Andreas. It was said that Henry disappeared from the New Mexico and Iowa family after his brief visit to New Mexico in late 1879 or soon thereafter. Dallas was surprised to learn our New Mexico branch had lost him; the Iowa branch had not, at least not then. Some years later, however, the Iowa branch also lost him, as mysteriously. Read Dallas' chapter about this Henry Laumbach.

Trent Shue is the great-great grandson of Fritz Eggert, whose early life remains a mystery to all of us. Fritz was an adopted member of our family because he played an important role in our family's stories about our great-grandfather, Andreas. The two young men were friends. Fritz and his family continued to be connected to the Laumbach family by association for generations afterwards. I met Trent at an extended family gathering at Fort Union to celebrate the arrival of Andreas 2nd in New Mexico 150 years earlier. Trent was interested in his own family history. He was invited to include a chapter about Fritz in this book. His knowledge of Fritz was limited to his life after arriving in New Mexico. Trent's chapter also provides an excellent overview of historical goings-on in northern New Mexico. It gives us a valued glimpse of the setting in which our forebears lived.

Jane Anglin, neighbor and friend, has worked with me for several years on writing projects, sometimes doing data entry but more often proofreading. So doing, she became well acquainted with our family's early history. She repeatedly proofed at least the first half of the book so many times, she could probably recite some of it from memory. **Kathy Cook** and her husband, **Ed**, scanned some images and vintage photographs, and took photos of memorabilia. Kathy sometimes also helped with layout of images on pages. **Pam Garlinger** came over to help me set up pages one weekend when I was particularly frustrated about delayed progress. **Bianca K. Cheney** helped format some photos and proofed several chapters. **Boo Reynolds** proofread a few chapters, too.

Stephanee Killeen of Integrative Ink in Ohio has been wonderfully patient and supportive, helping me in my last stages of book development. She designed the book's cover.

Tracy Ikenberry, my daughter, was my "designated driver" when medications affected my vision. I could not have made several trips to northern New Mexico without her taking me to gather much needed additional information and provide me a more intimate feel for that land of my grandfather's childhood.

Dan Girand, my husband, may be listed last but he is Number One.

He was my designated driver for a nostalgic journey in 2010 to visit the ranch of my grandparents, where my mother and her siblings grew up on the Canadian River Gorge.

The first year of our marriage, mid-1985 to mid-1986, was filled with multiple adventures while we both worked at demanding jobs and were physically involved with building our adobe home that we designed. Those adventures included—but were not limited to—Dan doing sports car pro-rallys on rugged mountain logging roads of Colorado, and both of us serving as ground crew for a small sport parachute club that briefly involved all three of our sons, but mostly Devin, who jumped every opportunity that year. We had several harrowing experiences and runs to the hospital E.R. That led to my "forever" dedication:

TO DAN: Without whom my life would be like a holey parachute, without purpose, containing nothing.

Andreas Detlef Laumbach
1833-1904

Born in Jagel, Schleswig
Came to America in 1856
Arrived in northern New Mexico
October 29, 1859

Elionor Eberle Laumbach
1849-1933

Born in Mora, New Mexico

Family faces are magic mirrors.
Looking at people who belong to us,
we see the past, present and future.

Gail Lumet Buckley, American writer/journalist

LAUMBACHS IN NEW MEXICO

Table of Contents

Section I, Introduction   1

Chapter 1   Faith of our Fathers and Mothers 3
Images:
- Santa Biblia page with Elionor's signature
- Inside pages, reduced, of 1871 Lutheran Bible study book in German text (2 images)
- The Last Supper, with German caption, from 1871 Lutheran study book
- Crucifixion and Lord's Prayer in German, from 1871 Lutheran study book
- "1895" maps of Schleswig area, including three close-ups (5 images of maps)

Chapter 2   Overview 16
Images:
- Archived 1864 Marriage record of Elionor & Andreas Laumbach
- Deutchland 1866 manifest—Peter Henkens passage (2 images)
- Peder Claus Henkens painting
- John Herman 1856 manifest—Andreas Laumbach passage

Section II, Germany   29

Chapter 3   German Documents 31
Images:
- Three German Documents and Wax Seal
- Mrs. Katz's Translations of 3 Documents

Chapter 4   Journey to Germany 40
Images:
- Jagel (3 photos)
- Der Holm (2 photos)
- St. Johannis Kloster (5 photos)
- Church of Haddeby (3 photos)
- Geltorf (2 photos)

Chapter 5   More History 57
No images

Chapter 6 Trip to Jagel by Pete Laumbach 61
Images:
- Cover Letter to Pete from Frau Jessen
- Pete's spreadsheet listing all family documents archived at the Petri Dome (2 pages)
- Death of Detlef Koos archived entry
- Birth of Anna Koos, 1811 archived entry
- Birth of Marx Heinrich Lauenbach, 1840 archived entry
- Birth of Anna Christina Lauenbach, 1848 archived entry

Section III, Iowa and Nebraska   75

Chapter 7 Goose Lake 77
Images:
- German letter written by Anna Henkens "before 1879" with translation (4 images)
- Envelope for letter from Peter Henkens to A.D. Laumbach family in NM
- German letter written by Peter Henkens "before 1879" with translation (5 images)
- Collection of calling & greeting cards from Henkens family and friends in Nebraska, and Laumbach family and friends in New Mexico (multiple cards)
- Laumbach family in New Mexico holiday cards (multiple cards)
- Emma Henkens' autograph book, begun 1899; image of cover & her entry
- Hausfrau, print of a German girl

Chapter 8 Search for Henry by Dallas Laumbach 102
Images:
- Lillian Kral Laumbach
- Justus Theodore Laumbach
- John Andrew Laumbach
- Alvina Greve Laumbach

Chapter 9 Iowa & Nebraska, by Verna L. Sparks... 109
Images:
- Studio portrait of Anna and Peter Henkens
- Emma Henken's 1876 German christening doc. in Clinton Iowa (certificate in 2 parts)
- Studio portrait of Henkens brothers: Edwin, Claus, Herman, August, John
- Studio portrait of Henkens sisters: Emma, Emilie, Caroline
- Studio portrait of Emma's brother, August, and his family

Section IV, New Mexico   119

Chapter 10 History 101-Grolet 121
No images

Chapter 11 Mora Private Land Claim 124
No images; transcribed portion of Mora Private Land Claim, Number 32

Chapter 12 Potrero, Mora, etc. 136
  Images:
  - Santa Cruz, 1882
  - Santuario de Chimayo (2 photos)
  - Santa Cruz, 1915
  - Apolonia photo, cropped
  - Bernardino Martín's 1792 christening, image of archived entry
  - Bernardo & Polonia Martín's January 1827 marriage, image of archived entry
  - Maria Viviana Martín's December 1827 christening, image of archived entry
  - *Bulto* of San Rafael, by Eulogio and Zoraida Ortega, *santeros* de Velarde
  - *Retablo*, Nuestra Senora de la Joya by Eulogio and Zoraida Ortega
  - Maria Marta Ebel's February 1856 baptism, image of archived entry
  - Santa Gertrudes parish church circa late 1800s
  - Santa Gertrudes de Mora plaza, photo courtesy of Ann Cassidy
  - Interior of Santa de Gertrudes church circa late 1800s
  - Santa Gertrudes church, photo of painting by Freddie Olivas
  - Apolonia's metate
  - Bernardo's brass candlesticks
  - Bibiana's kerosene lamp
  - Laumbach family memorabilia representing 5 generations
  - Apolonia's gold filigree lavaliere
  - Daniel's pocket knife
  - Elionor's pin with photo of her husband Andreas
  - Reverse of Andreas' pin & Elionor's cameo with JSC stamp
  - Laumbach family vintage jewelry collection
  - Carved Pink Rose, ivory or shell, with handmade chain
  - Gold filigree & emerald pendant
  - Silver filigree pin
  - Mother of pearl doves pin
  - Enamel flowers pin
  - Silver filigree with diamond pendant
  - Black beadwork
  - White & pink beadwork

Chapter 13 James Bonney: A Bonney on the Santa Fe Trail 161
  Images:
  - Santiago "Bone" Grant land description, court document (2 pages)
  - Santiago Bone Grant Sketch Map
  - Cover of petition document for Case #62 Bone Grant; Petition of M C (Maria Cleofas) Bone, regarding her father's grant
  - #62 Bone Grant Report (2 pages)
  - James Bonney's 1840 archived letter to Manuel Alvarez, U.S. Consular (2 pages)
  - Bonney Ditch 2001 photo

Chapter 14 More Bonney History 179
  Images:
  - Bonney Grant, 3 court documents
  - Maria Cleofas Bonney Lopez Burial Marker

- Cleofas Bonney & Trinidad Lopez ruin
- Feliciana Jimenez & Santiago Bonney Jr. photo
- Feliciana Jimenez Bonney ap. for military grave marker for husband
- Santiago Bonney & Felicia Jimenez ruin
- Rafaela Bonney & Bernardo Salazar ruin
- Fieldstone burial markers (2 photos)
- Jesuit mission ruin
- Karl Laumbach & Herman Weisner at 1991 BTK symposium at Ruidoso
- Herman Weisner, Verna Sparks & Karl Laumbach in Roswell
- Trinidad Lopez, young soldier
- Fernando Nolan (2 photos)
- Newspaper clipping, 1863, NM Volunteers
- Newspaper clippings, 1876: Maclovia & Fermin Nolan marriage announcement in English and Spanish
- Newspaper clipping, 1878: Mora County Republican Party Convention, Fernando Nolan & Trinidad Lopez, legislators

Chapter 15 Santiago Bonney grant, 1887 testimony 200
No images, only transcriptions

Chapter 16 A Bonney Ballad 206
Images:
- Billy Bonney tintype, enhanced
- Cañon Overlook From Ramon's Cabin, Verna Sparks painting
- Bonney's cabin remnants, 2010 photo

Chapter 17 U.S. Mil. Ser. Bernardo Martín, 1848, by Jose A. Esquibel 215
Images:
- Ancestry chart for Bernardo Martin
- Bernardo Martin's 1848 U.S. Military Service record preserved in a bounty land warrant application filed in 1857 and 1858, obtained from National Archives in Washington DC by Amanda Maestas Freiberg (5 pages)

Chapter 18 Ancestors, by Verna L. Sparks 223
Images:
- Bibiana's gold filigree butterfly pin

Chapter 19 Andreas 1 & 2 238
Images:
- Bibiana's grave marker, 2 photos taken about 25 years apart
- Buena Vista home of Elionor Ebel and Andreas D. Laumbach; water color by Verna L. Sparks
- The home established by Elionor and Andreas Laumbach, now owned by the Lonnie Allsup family, 2013 photo
- Vintage photo of the place at Buena Vista, probably taken in the 1880s
- The backside of vintage photo
- Once the Laumbach home, photo taken around 1953
- Old log and rock stable once behind Laumbach place, photo taken in 2013. Could this have been the structure built by Andreas 1st?

- Another view of little stable
- LaCueva grist mill, est. by Vicente Romero; water color by Verna L. Sparks
- Document, Natl. Archives, Washington DC, perhaps dated in July 1862, shows Andreas Laumbach resident of Precinct 5, Mora County, Territory of NM (images of document)
- Andreas Laumbach, May 12, 1903 preemption claim for 40 acres at the Carruco on the Canadian River Gorge
- Andreas' 1900 naturalization document
- Memorial cards for Andreas Laumbach November 1904
- Portrait of Andreas Laumbach 2nd and his eldest child, Margaret
- Portrait of Elionor Laumbach and her sons

Chapter 20 Fritz Eggert by Trent Shue 258
Images:
- Fritz Eggert and Juanita Le Blanc portrait
- La Placita at El Monton Del Los Alamos
- La Capilla de Nuestro Santo Nino church
- Charles Ilfeld letter
- Ancon near Cañon Largo
- Inside church ruin at Cañon Largo
- Juan Carlos "Charles" Eggert
- Juanita Le Blanc's gravesite in Cañon Largo
- Children of Fritz Eggert & Juanita Le Blanc
- Bacharach Brothers' sign painted on brick building on Old Town Plaza

Chapter 21 Children of Andreas & Elionor 283
Images:
- Margaret as a young woman
- Margaret about 90 years old
- Estefanita & Crestina as young women
- J.S. Candelario & Estefanita
- J.S. Candelario & Estefanita & baby Alice
- Alice Candelario, girl
- Henry & Natividad Laumbach on their wedding day
- Henry Laumbach portrait
- Henry on horse at Buena Vista
- Anna, young woman
- Anna with young Rosa
- Daniel
- Daniel with his niece, young Alice Candelario
- Crestina, as a young woman
- Crestina, middle-age
- Mary, young woman
- Mary as a girl
- Mary in apple orchard
- Mary, large cameo portrait
- Leonor, young woman
- Leonor, young woman with book
- Mary & Leonor with horses at Buena Vista

- Leonor
- Mary, Anna & Leonor with young Adelina
- Rosa Duran, her niece Adelina, Aunt Anna and Adelina's small children
- Anna, Mary & Leonor with their flowers at Buena Vista
- Five Aunties at Las Vegas: Margaret, Leonor, Mary, Crestina & Anna
- House where Aunt Crestina once lived on Valencia, Las Vegas
- House where Aunties once lived on Hot Springs Boulevard, Las Vegas

Chapter 22 Metzger & Korte 299
Images:
- Korte Cowboys Branding Scene
- Group Family Korte portrait
- Henry & Sito at J.S. Candelario's well
- Sito & Arthur Weeks at J.S. Candelario's well
- Laumbach well shaft, 2014 photo
- Frank Metzger's marker at Metzger-Korte cemetery
- Henry Korte portrait from family album of Daniel & Emma Laumbach
- Henry Korte's marker at Metzger-Korte cemetery
- Juanita Metzger Korte's marker at Metzger-Korte cemetery
- Juanita Metzger's artwork, blue flowers in colored pencil
- 1880 Letter from Henry & Juanita Korte to Andreas & Elionor Laumbach (2 pages)

Chapter 23 Henry Korte Civil Lawsuit 314
No images; transcribed court documents

Chapter 24 Aunts and Uncles by Verna L. Sparks..321
No images

Chapter 25 Ramon Bonney et al, by Karl Laumbach 327
Images:
- Ramon & Anastacia Lucero Bonney with their family
- Amada Bonney Campos with 2 children
- Anastasia with 2 daughters, including Amada

Chapter 26 Sunset, Uncle Bonney by Verna L. Sparks..341
Images:
- Bonney standing in front of Rock House at Dan & Emma's ranch
- Bonney with the goats

Chapter 27 Never a Road, Aunt Marie, by Verna L. Sparks 346
Images:
- Canon de Agua, large oil painting by Verna L. Sparks
- Bibiana's gold filigree earring, given to Maria Marta, who later sold to Emma Laumbach, who made a pin with this one

Chapter 28 The Letter, by Verna L. Sparks 351
  Images:
  - Manuel Antonio Sanchez portrait
  - Photo of children Tony and Adelina Sanchez

Chapter 29 J.S. Candelario 357
  Images:
  - J.S. Candelario, curio man, postcard
  - J.S. Candelario, young man
  - Estefanita, young woman
  - Postcard from Sito to Sra. Laumbach
  - Gold's Old Curiosity Shop
  - J.S. Candelario's Original Old Curio Shop, postcard
  - Young Johnny Candelario at La Fonda
  - J.S. Candelario with Taos Indian Council, post card
  - Johnny Candelario, college boy
  - Johnny Candelario, professional photographer
  - John Candelario, middle-age
  - J.S. Candelario Curio Shop memorabilia
  - J.S. Candelario advertising envelope
  - Estefanita's letter to Verna

Chapter 30 Sabinoso Wilderness by Karl Laumbach 378
  Images:
  - Canadian River Gorge, modified BLM map
  - Canadian River Gorge looking toward Ancon & Sabinoso
  - Canadian River Gorge from west rim

Chapter 31 U.S. Census Records 390
  Images:
  - 1850 US Census, No. Div. Taos, Terr. NM, Maria Juana Mascarenas & Bonney children.
  - 1860 US Census, Santa Gertrudes, Mora Terr. NM, with Apolonia and family
  - 1860 US Census, La Cebolla Precinct, County of Mora Terr. NM with Bernardo, Bibiana & family
  - 1900 US Census, Precinct 14, Armenta, Mora Co. Terr NM; Families of: Ramon Bonney, Felipe Esquibel, Andres Ebell, Pedro Laumbach, Conrado Andrada, Casimiro Andrada, Nieves & Isabel Ebell Gallegos (3 pages)

Chapter 32 Peter Joseph Laumbach by Karl Laumbach 403
  Images:
  - Cropped group photo at Buena Vista: Margaret & Jose Cruz, Ramon Bonney, Peter & Mrs. Knaur
  - Vintage photo of Laumbach place at Buena Vista, perhaps 1880s
  - Andreas & Elionor Laumbach & family: Margaret & Jose Cruz, Anna, Leonor, Andreas (father), Leonor (mother), Christina Laumbach
  - Peter J. Laumbach, between age 14 & 16
  - Andres Ebell & 3 young sons
  - Peter J. Laumbach, perhaps his wedding photo in 1900
  - Fort Union receipt for 1 bay mare pony
  - Making Cider at Buena Vista; photo includes "old man" Wissler

- Fidelia, pretty girl. Wedding photo?
- Peter J. Laumbach, brother-in-law Leopoldo Andrada & friend
- Fidelia Laumbach with 2 small children, 1905
- The first Alfredo, young boy (photo on a kind of tintype)
- Family and friends with carriage at Buena Vista
- Peter J. Laumbach family, 1912
- Peter J. Laumbach family, 1926
- Luther Raines School House
- Peter J. & Fidelia Laumbach with their 4 older sons, mid-1920s
- Peter J. Laumbach with 6 sons 1937
- Laumbach brothers, cowboys on horseback
- Peter J. & Fidelia Laumbach grave marker

Chapter 33 More Pete..........428
Images:
- La Cinta ranch house
- Peter J. Laumbach ranch
- Peter J. Laumbach & family, 4 sons, 3 daughters
- 4 Laumbach brothers and sister Petra, 1980
- Cousins: Tony Sanchez, Christina L. Foxall & husband Frank & John Candelario
- Laumbach family, 6 brothers & 2 sisters, 1983
- 4 Laumbach brothers at Roy, 2003
- La Cinta Ranch
- Al & Pete

Chapter 34 Papa & Mama by Verna L. Sparks..........433
Images:
- Dan & Emma on their wedding day
- Front gate to Dan's ranch
- Round-Up at Dan's
- Dan & Emma's Cedar Springs Ranch, with pond
- Dan & Emma's young family
- Dan's first car
- Mabel's medallion from Allison-James
- Laumbach furnishings
- Emma Laumbach's kitchen cabinet & memorabilia
- Emma and Daniel at the ranch, snapshot
- Emma and Daniel "portrait" made from above snapshot

Chapter 35 To Buena Vista by Wagon, by Verna L. Sparks..........457
Image:
- Verna, college girl, about 1928

Chapter 36 Presbyterian Mission Schools..........462
Images:
- Allison Mission School 1889
- Allison Mission School 1906

Chapter 37 Tony 466
Images:
- Tony portrait in oil pastel, by Betty Sparks
- Mission bell in tower at Tony's ranch
- Tony's home at ranch
- Tony, age 2 & Adelina, baby
- Tony & Adelina, children
- Tony
- Tony's letterhead, NM Representative
- Tony's business card, director, The Bank of NM

Chapter 38 Emma's & Daniel's Ranch 2010..474
Images:
- Alfredo at La Cinto
- Uncle Bonney's pines
- View of Canyon behind Ramon's Cabin
- Uncle Bonney's cabin remains
- Alfredo at Uncle Bonney's cabin
- Laumbach's bath house ?
- The Old Rock House
- Food Cellar
- Log Cabin
- Ranch house, 2010
- Barns, 2010
- Horse-drawn wagon
- Cistern
- Looking up the Spring Trail, 2010

Chapter 39 Buena Vista and Mora 2013...496
Images:
- La Cebollita view from road to Ledoux
- 1908 Newspaper article, demolition of building near Metzger's store
- 2 abandoned historic buildings on Mora Plaza
- Frank Metzger store ruin
- Santa Gertrudis Entrance
- Henry Laumbach's children
- Gate to the Laumbach cemetery at Buena Vista
- Laumbach cemetery at Buena Vista
- Allsup Ranch headquarters at Buena Vista, once the Laumbach home
- Riner Lake
- Metzger-Korte Cemetery gate
- Broken grave marker at Korte cemetery
- Abel's private road to their Buena Vista Ranch
- Buena Vista Ranch entrance
- Buena Vista Ranch headquarters
- Chick Burney's home at Buena Vista Ranch
- Prison Wagon, *True Grit* movie prop
- *True Grit* movie setting

- Doorway showing thickness of adobe walls
- Buena Vista's old Post Office, Store & Blacksmith shop, rear view
- Buena Vista's old Post Office, Store & Blacksmith shop, front view
- Old Apple Cider Press
- Old Billows in Blacksmith Shop
- Chick Burney
- Buena Vista Ranch bunkhouse
- Inside Buena Vista Ranch bunkhouse
- A few of the Ortegas' collection of Santos
- Large framed print from Aunties' at Buena Vista, now at Ortegas'
- Old rock & log stable behind Allsup's Ranch
- Vigas in wall abutments of Allsup ranch house that was once Laumbachs'
- Debris from old homestead site east of Abel's Buena Vista Ranch
- Evidence of that homestead east of Abel's headquarters
- Cebollita valley, evidence of a homestead near road to Ledoux
- Is this the site of the vintage Korte Cowboy Branding Scene?

Chapter 40 Finale 526
Images:
- 1875 Court Document (2 images)
- Transcription of above 1875 Court Document (2 pages)

Appendices   539

Appendix I Newspaper Articles, Laumbach 541
    Part B Metzger/Korte/Naeglin Newspaper Clippings 570

Appendix II Genealogy Chart, Martin-Serrano 578
    Part B Genealogy Chart, Laumbach 584

Appendix III Bios & Photos of Major Contributors 633
Images:
- Charles O. "Butch" Sanders
- Karl W. Laumbach
- Peter James "Pete" Laumbach
- José Antonio Esquibel
- Trent Shue
- Dallas Laumbach
- Verna Sparks
- Jan Girand

LAUMBACHS IN NEW MEXICO
And Those Who Went Before
In Germany, Iowa and New Mexico

WHO WERE THEY?

THEREFORE, WHO AM I?

Section I
INTRODUCTION

*Every generation enjoys the use of a vast hoard
[of knowledge] bequeathed to it by antiquity,
and transmits that hoard,
augmented by fresh acquisitions, to future ages.*

*Lord Thomas Babington Macaulay
1800—1859*

SECTION I: INTRODUCTION

Chapter 1: Faith of Our Fathers and Mothers
by Jan Girand

The faiths of our fathers and mothers played important roles in their combined histories.

Germany

In the sixteenth century, the Reformation begun by the German Catholic monk Martin Luther led to a religious schism in Germany. His teachings became the basis of the Lutheran Church. The northern portion of Germany was then predominately Lutheran, while the southern portion mostly remained Catholic. That religious division of Germany continues today.

Lutheran was the faith of the Lauenbach family from Schleswig. Andreas Detlef Lauenbach (*pronounced LauENbah*) was born at Geltorf on November 25, 1802. His wife Anna Koos (*pronounced Kohss*) was born at Jagel (*pronounced YAHgl, rhymes with toggle*) on August 9, 1811. By the time of their marriage on November 4, 1832 in the Protestant church of Haddeby, Andreas was also living at Jagel where Anna and her parents lived. Andreas was 30; Anna was 21.

Today Geltorf, Jagel and Haddeby are villages in the German state of Schleswig-Holstein, south across the Schlei firth from the small city of Schleswig and part of its suburbs. In the Lauenbachs' time, this area was the southernmost part of the independent Duchy of Schleswig, whose duke was the King of Denmark. Most of the people living in southern Schleswig, including the Lauenbachs, considered themselves German rather than Danish, and German was the language used in their communities. Later, tensions between the Danish Crown and the German populace led to a series of wars. Those wars were probably a major reason the Lauenbachs left for America.

Geltorf, Jagel and Haddeby are now tiny villages of 100 to 400 people and may have been even smaller 200 years ago. They are part of the *Amt* of Haddeby, a municipal collective centered by Haddeby's St. Andreas Church (Andreas is translated as Andrew). Haddeby itself is part of the larger town of Busdorf and is situated about a mile from its center.[i] They form a triangle with Haddeby-Busdorf on the Schlei, directly across from Schleswig, and Geltorf and Jagel just to the south. None of the three were more than six kilometers (under four miles) from the others—an hour's walk—and were part of a broader community of about 2,000 people sharing the same churches and schools. It is likely the families of Andreas and Anna knew each other all of Anna's life (Andreas was nine years older).

Until recently, most of what was known about Andreas and Anna, their families and life in Germany, came from three documents: their birth certificates and their marriage certificate. Data in the documents had been copied from entries—probably first written in a registry at the Protestant Church of Haddeby and then at Skt. Johannis kloster vor Schleswig (*St. Johannis Cloister, or the Priory of St. John the Baptist, in the city of Schleswig*). All three of those documents were written in old German script at St. Johannis on March 31, 1856 and given an official seal. (Photocopies of these original documents and seal are at the beginning of chapter 3.) Andreas and Anna probably had these documents made immediately before leaving for the United States. Those fragile documents have endured.

In 2005, Pete Laumbach (son of Rudolph and Leona Laumbach) learned the sacramental records housed at St. Johannis were moved in the 1850s to St. Peter's Cathedral at Schleswig. Pete's research also extended our knowledge of the family further back in time.

Both Andreas and Anna had been baptized and also married in the Haddeby pastorate of Busdorf in what was the 12th century Romanesque church of Haddeby. All three of those events were ultimately recorded at St. Johannis Cloister, then in the seat of the Duchy of Schleswig, an independent state. In those documents, the original family name was spelled Lauenbach.

The St. Johannis Cloister was founded in the 13th century by Benedictine nuns. In 1542, following the Reformation, it was converted to a convent to shelter unmarried noblewomen.[ii] It was a wealthy institution that owned large estates in the vicinity of Schleswig. At the time Anna was born, the village of Jagel was owned by the priory of St. Johannis, which still operates as a Protestant women's collegiate foundation and continues to admit unmarried daughters of the Schleswig-Holstein knighthood.

St. Johannis is located in the oldest part of the city of Schleswig, sitting just across the Schlei from Haddeby.

Inside the adjacent museum within the St. Johannis complex is a wooden replica of the first Johannes Gutenberg printing press. In the Rhine Valley in 1440, Johannes Gutenberg invented what was to be the world's first printing press with moveable letters. He is also credited with printing the world's first book using movable type. His invention and revolutionary printing of the Gutenberg Bible led to the Bible and all other books becoming available and affordable to the common man. It also enabled, in the 1500s, the printing of quantities of inexpensive pamphlets, which played an important role in the Reformation Movement—its members called Protestants because they protested against the Catholic Church. As a result, Protestantism became the primary faith of northern Europe. The largest of those Protestant churches was Lutheran.

The Lauenbach family—Andreas, Anna and seven of their eight children, some very small—traveled across the ocean in a stifling and confining ship in 1856. They probably began their journey in early April of that year. We can only imagine how difficult and frightening were the conditions on board, how they must have clung to their faith and prayed for safe passage. Their eldest, also named Andreas, followed them to America soon thereafter, departing in July of that same year.

Iowa

Their pre-selected destination in America was Goose Lake, Iowa. Family tradition says they chose it because Andreas and Anna already had family or friends established in that Germanic settlement in the northern central United States. Apparently that connection was friends; we found no evidence of family preceding them. The majority of the settlers there spoke their same Germanic language and dialect and shared their Lutheran faith.

About three months after Andreas, Anna and all but one of their children arrived at Goose Lake, their eldest son, Andreas 2nd, joined them. The parents and their younger children quickly settled in there, but soon after he arrived, son Andreas—and family tradition says also his good friend, Frederick "Fritz" Eggert—headed west.

New Mexico

Long before the younger Andreas Detlef Laumbach arrived in New Mexico:

"Those who went before" including the Anasazi—and various Indian tribes and pueblos with their own spiritual beliefs—were the first inhabitants of southwestern America, until Spanish colonists arrived in the 1500s and 1600s, bringing with them from Europe their Catholic faith, which then dominated all aspects of Southwestern culture for the next several hundred years.

European Spaniards began immigrating to the American southwest a century after Columbus landed in 1492. Spain entitled their Catholic Christians to free ship passage.[iii] Thereafter came multiple explorations of North America by various Spaniards in the name of God and their country. In 1598, a large group of people from Nueva España settled New Mexico. In 1680, the Pueblo Indians revolted and drove out the Spanish settlers. Between 1690 and 1697, the Spaniards retook New Mexico and re-colonized it. In September 1692, their appointed governor, Diego de Vargas, entered Santa Fe with *Nuestra Senora del Rosario* (Our Lady of the Rosary, also called Our Lady of Peace), now best known as the state's beloved *La Conquistadora,* a priceless *santa* [iv] that has endured for 320 years. She resides in the Cathedral Basilica to the Rosario Chapel in Santa Fe, near its plaza.

Soon thereafter, Spaniards began to give land grants to established settlers on the lands. Mexico, formerly known as Nueva España, took New Mexico from Spain in 1821. As a means of populating the isolated area, the custom of land grants continued throughout the Mexican rule. In 1846—just 168 years ago—New Mexico became the possession of the United States of America.

Bibiana/Viviana Martín/Martinez, destined to become the mother-in-law of the younger Andreas D. Laumbach, was a Catholic. She had three separate family-type relationships—some called them marriages—that produced children. First was with an English immigrant, James Bonney, with whom she had a son, Ramon Bonney, born in the spring of 1846, a few months before James was killed by Indians that fall. The faith of James Bonney is unknown. Next, Bibiana was with Daniel Eberle—name once written on the translation of a document as Garlien Ebarley. That first name is an error of translation; the last name is a spelling variation due to mispronunciation. That name error has unfortunately been repeated at least once. Eberle, known by the family to have been a Swiss-German immigrant, enlisted in the U.S. Army in Missouri in June 1846 as part of the almost all-German Company B, Battalion of Light Artillery of the Missouri Volunteers. Most of the men of this company were Germans recruited by Woldemar Fischer, a Prussian who became captain of Company B under the command of Col. Alexander Doniphan. This company entered Santa Fe in September 1846. The soldiers of Company B were stationed at Santa Fe and helped construct Ft. Marcy.

When his 12-month enlistment ended, Daniel Eberle remained in New Mexico and settled in the Las Vegas, where he married or entered into a common-law marriage-type relationship with Maria Bibiana Martín. Her father was one of the 76 original grantees of the Mora Land Grant.[v]

Bibiana and Daniel had three children, including Elionor/Eleanore or Eleanora Eberle/Ebel, who would marry the second Andreas Detlef Laumbach. Their other two children were Juan Andres Eberle/Ebel and Maria Marta Eberle/Ebel. Daniel Eberle was killed, most of the family agrees, because of the gold he carried. There are several versions of his death, which will be related later. Bibiana's third relationship, with Prussian immigrant Frederick "Frank" Metzger, produced three daughters: Dolorita "Lola," Josefita and Isabellita. In the 1860 U.S. census, the enumerator gave everyone in the family's La Cebolla household the same last name as its head of household: Bernardo Martinez. In other records these three daughters' names were recorded as Metzger.

We do not know the faith of Eberle or Metzger. Some have said Metzger was Jewish, which is likely. If not, both were raised as Lutheran or Catholic, depending on their specific places of origin.

~~

On his journey west, the younger Andreas eventually stopped near the valley of lo de Moro (also known as St. Gertrudes/Gertrudis de Mora) in northern New Mexico. Some sources say that valley's earlier name, Moro, may have come from an early family living in the area. Its later briefer name, Mora, translates to "mulberry." Mulberries grew wild in the valley.

Only 13 years before Andreas 2nd arrived, New Mexico had become a U.S. territory instead of a possession of Mexico, and before that, of Spain. According to New Mexico historians, the Hispanic Mora Valley settlers had been living in the area at least since 1818.[vi] They were late settling the area because of danger presented by the Indians who had first settled there.

This Andreas 2nd settled at La Cebolla (la sayBOYah, "the onion"), an established Hispanic settlement in the smaller fertile valley near lo de Moro in the fall of 1859. Andreas' friend, Fritz, however, did not tarry long in the land of Moro. He moved on, but not far. He first settled at La Junta/Watrous, and later at Cañon Largo, a canyon of the Canadian River gorge. (Trent Shue relates the story of his great-great-grandfather, Frederick "Fritz" Eggert, in his chapter later in this book.)

Elionor Ebel/Eberle was born to Bibiana Martín and Daniel Eberle in June 1849, probably at La Cebolla, in what would become Mora County. (The first counties created by the Territory of New Mexico in 1850 were Bernalillo, Rio Arriba, San Miguel del Bado, Santa Ana, Santa Fe, Taos and Valencia. The county of Mora was not created until 1860.)

On various permanent records, Elionor's first name had several spellings, including Eleanore. To be consistent in this book, I mostly spell her name the way she herself wrote it in her personal *Santa Biblia*.[vii] Others spell it differently in their chapters in this book.

Andreas, a Lutheran, and Elionor, a Catholic, both lived at La Cebolla when they married in April 1864. Andreas had to promise the officiating priest that the couple would raise their children as Catholics. *(A copy of Elionor and Andreas' actual marriage entry and translation accompany Chapter 2—An Overview.)*

Karl Laumbach (*son of George and Margaret Laumbach*) remembers seeing our great-great-grandmother Bibiana's *patrona santa*. Cousin Tony Sanchez (son of Crestina Laumbach and Manuel A. Sanchez) had a priceless old *santos* collection, some of them centuries old, upstairs at his mother's home in Las Vegas. Karl had seen Bibiana's *santa* at Sanchez, Tony's ranch. Unfortunately, Tony's *santos*, like all of his priceless collections at his mother's home and at his ranch, passed from the family after his death.

This is the story Karl told about Bibiana's *santa*: "Tony Sanchez showed me the *santa* when my parents and I visited the Sanchez headquarters [*ranch near Sabinoso*] in the early 1970s. As the story goes, Bibiana had the *santa* at the *'casita de abuela'* where she lived before her death near the [*Andreas and Elionor*] Laumbach home at Buena Vista. The Laumbach children often went to see her, perhaps even stayed with her for short periods. Henry Laumbach [*her grandson*] was visiting when a tremendous storm ensued. The thunder and lightning were intense, and Bibiana didn't like it. She prayed to the *santa* to stop the storm, but her prayers were not answered. The storm intensified. Bibiana became angry with the *santa* and picked it up, intending to throw it in the fire. Henry interceded, begging her not to burn the *santa*. She thrust it at him, told him to take it. He had it for many years. Then, curiously, it disappeared. He thought it was lost. Sometime later, perhaps after Henry's death, Tony was in Santa Fe visiting his Uncle Sito Candelario's Curio Store on West San Francisco Street. Looking around, he saw and recognized the *santa*. Tony acquired and preserved it until he died. When he showed it to me, he had it in one of the rooms off of the store at Sanchez [*his family ranch*]. It was wrapped with cloth and stored in a trunk. Unfortunately, I did not have a camera and took no photographs of it. It was lost to the family when his estate was settled."

This is a story Mary Louise Maestas (great-granddaughter of Maria Marta Ebel Esquibel) told me years ago: When Maria Marta was born (1856), the famed Padré Antonio José Martinez of Taos (1793-1867) personally took a blessed rosary to Bibiana for her baby. Mary Louise ultimately inherited that rosary.

Mary Louise also said she had heard that the archbishop of Santa Fe excommunicated Bibiana, but she did not know why. I wish I knew Mary Louise's source of that story. She had a wealth of fascinating information she had gathered about our family history, much of it lost at her death.

In the late 1800s, the Presbyterian Church began to establish Hispanic Presbyterian missions in northern New Mexico, bringing to its isolated villagers the coveted opportunity of education. Especially desired was the ability to read and write. Several children of Elionor and Andreas 2nd and their spouses became Presbyterian missionaries. (There is more on this in a later chapter.)

Elionor was a practicing Catholic until the latter years of her life when she converted to Presbyterianism like some of her children. Subsequently, some of their family and descendents also became Presbyterians. Others remained Catholic or Lutheran.

~~

In the last hundred years, a few unsubstantiated rumors in New Mexico claimed an ethnic Jewish heritage for at least one family branch. I had heard that Frederick Metzger and Henry Korte—Metzger's son-in-law, friend and business partner—both Prussians, were Jews. The New Mexico Laumbachs, myself included, are not descended from Metzger and/or Korte, but some Bibiana and Apolonia descendents are. Apolonia Martín was the mother of Bibiana.

The Internet Wikipedia says the Ashkenazi Jews, an ethno-religious group, settled along the Rhine in Germany and Alsace around the Middle Ages. It says "the main centers of Jewish learning" were in Germany, and those who migrated to America were most likely of Ashkenazi heritage from western and central Europe.

Certain illnesses and diseases are predominately found among groups that, over the centuries, married within their ethnicities. That kept some traits undiluted, which led to genetic disorders for a few. I recently became interested in Jewish DNA about ten years ago when a Laumbach relative developed a rare autoimmune blistering disease most often found among Jewish people. David is a cousin. For three years, his problem was misdiagnosed because he is Hispanic and did not fit the genetic profile. He said he had an epiphany after reading an article published in the *Smithsonian* magazine[viii] about certain diseases common to Jewish people. The article said research found an unusually high incidence of people with a rare illness, symptoms like his, among Catholic Hispanics not known to be Jewish, living in certain areas of southern Colorado and northern New Mexico—where both sides of his family had lived for generations. That article led him to insist on having a biopsy to test for that disease. That finally gave him a correct diagnosis after three years of trial and error medical remedies that did not help his symptoms and aggravated his health. That *Smithsonian* article caused David to recall an unusual top he had played with as a child that he, years later, learned was typical of a toy Jewish children played with called a *dreidel*—a four-sided top—gifted at Hanukkah.

Numerous articles and books have been written about Sephardic Jews and Crypto-Jews, whose families centuries ago settled in the southwest, including northern New Mexico. (For further information, use an Internet search engine and go to "Crypto-Jews in New Mexico.")

After David's diagnosis several years ago, I had my DNA tested for genealogical purposes, but my results were too generalized to be useful.

In spring 2012, I, too, was diagnosed with an autoimmune blistering disease, even rarer but oddly similar to David's in initial symptoms, name and remedy. Mine is not known to be genetic.

We thought a Laumbach Jewish heritage unlikely because we know much about our genealogical history, which does not reveal it. However, we have not traced our lineage back 2,000 years.

In addition to a general interest in, even a fascination of, family history, these recent medical events provide yet another compelling reason to want to know our heritage and family's genealogy.

~~

In this book for consistency, I usually spell my great-grandmother's name Elionor, the way she herself wrote it in her *Santa Biblia,* but it also appears herein with different spellings.

Elionor's signature as it appears in her Santa Biblia: Elionor E. Laumbach. Sometimes she also wrote it "Elionor N. Laumbach" or "E.N. Laumbach of Buena Vista." The "N" represented her middle given name.

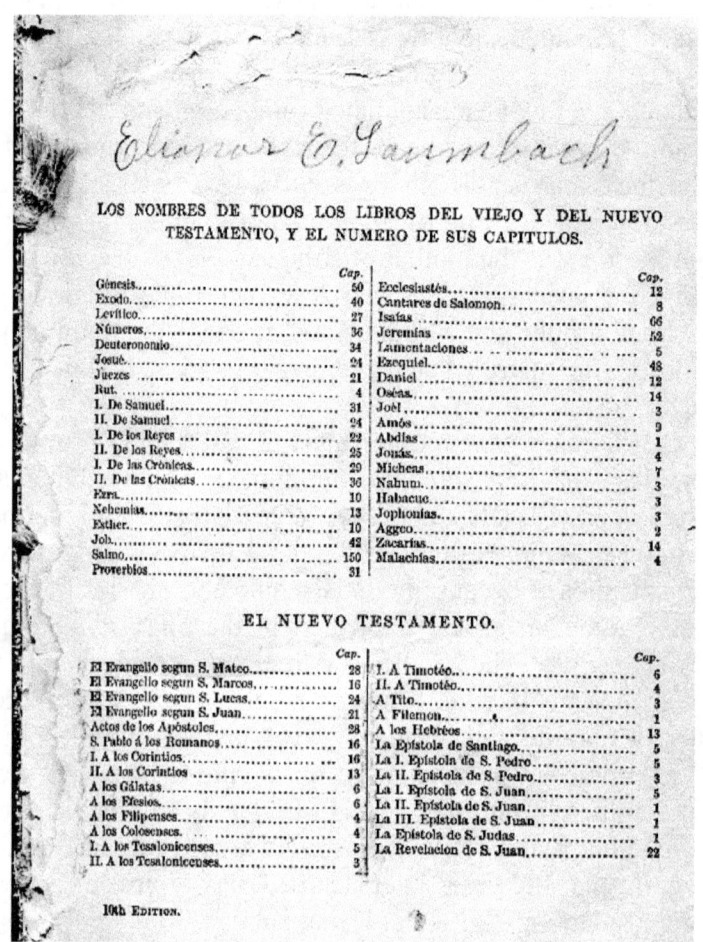

Additional image explanations:

I inherited a first edition 1871, Saint Louis, Missouri book, with German-text, of Lutheran teachings. I do not know who originally owned this book, likely Andreas 1st and Anna K. Laumbach, or Peter and Anna Henkens. Either Andreas or Emma Henkens brought it to New Mexico from his or her German Lutheran family and community. A published physical description found on the Internet: "Concordia Publishing House, St. Louis, 1871, hard cover, Illustrated with engraved portrait Frontis (illustrator); over 9¾" - 12" tall. First Edition/First Printing. 22 x 28cm. hard cover. 404pp." Sanders found C.F.W. Walther's biography in the 1898 and 1902 *Encyclopedia Britannica*. Excerpt: "WALTHER, Carl Ferdinand Wilhelm, German-American theologian; born in Saxony, Oct. 25, 1811; graduated …University of Leipsic in 1833; pastor at Braunsdorf in 1837. With Reverend Martin Stephan and [*others*] immigrated to United States in 1839…settled in Missouri…pastor of a congregation of Lutheran Saxons in St. Louis…became recognized leader [*of* …] [*who*] settled in large numbers in Missouri. In 1846 organized the synod of Missouri…largest Lutheran synod in America…author of numerous works [*including*] Amerikanisch-LutherischeEpistel-Postille and Amerikanisch-Lutherische Evangelien-Postille (1871) … [*He*] died in St. Louis, May 7, 1887."

The following condensed images are two inside pages of the 1871 American Lutheran book mentioned above.

Loose inside the book were two colored pictures: the Last Supper, with a German caption, and the Crucifixion surrounded by the Lord's Prayer in German, with an apple, snake and human skull embossed at its base. The Crucifixion is in white relief on a gold-leaf background. These two pictures, changed to black and white for this book, follow.

Three pages of old German topographical maps of the Lauenbach homeland follow. The first provides a larger view, encompassing more of the area to the north of Schleswig. The second provides a more close-up view of our family's pertinent communities and provides a portion of the information that had been in the lower margins of all of the old regional maps in this series. It tells us these are 1895 editions of maps published in 1881 from surveys made in 1877. On the third page are three close-ups of the specific communities from where the Lauenbachs and their families came.

The first two maps are to show the close proximity of St. Johannis Kloster, Haddeby, Busdorf, Geltorf, Jagel and Gross Rheide—named places on the family's 1856 documents, all of which still exist. An additional purpose of the second map is to show the edition, initial publication and survey dates contained in the margins of the two original maps used to create these. Researcher Charles "Butch" Sanders carefully spliced (aka merged or stitched) together the southern edge of the Schleswig regional map and the northern edge of the Rendsburg regional map. Schleswig and Haddeby are in the Schleswig region, while Busdorf, Jagel and Geltorf are in the Rendsburg region.

Of the two 1895 edition regional maps used (Schleswig regional and Rendsburg regional), Sanders found an earlier version of only one of them—the Schleswig regional published in 1881. That's why he used the 1895 editions rather than the 1881 initial publications. Comparing the 1895 edition of Schleswig regional with its predecessor published in 1881 and surveyed in 1877, he found them identical—with no changes in the depictions of topography, fence lines, roads, streets and structures. Thus, these 1895 edition maps show the area as it was surveyed in 1877—just 20 years after the Lauenbachs left. It is unlikely much changed in those years since. Members of our family would have actually lived in some of the structures indicated on these maps.

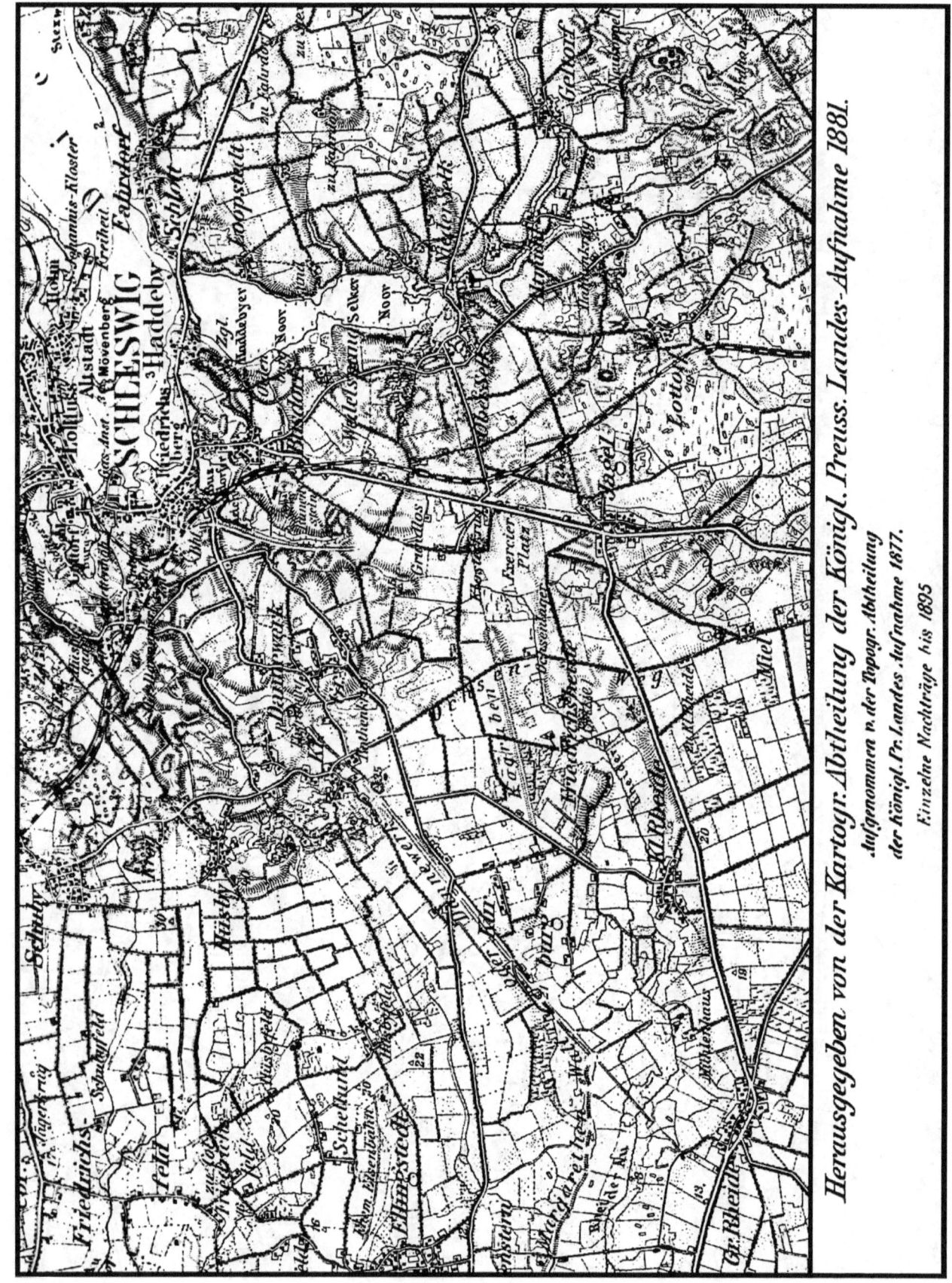

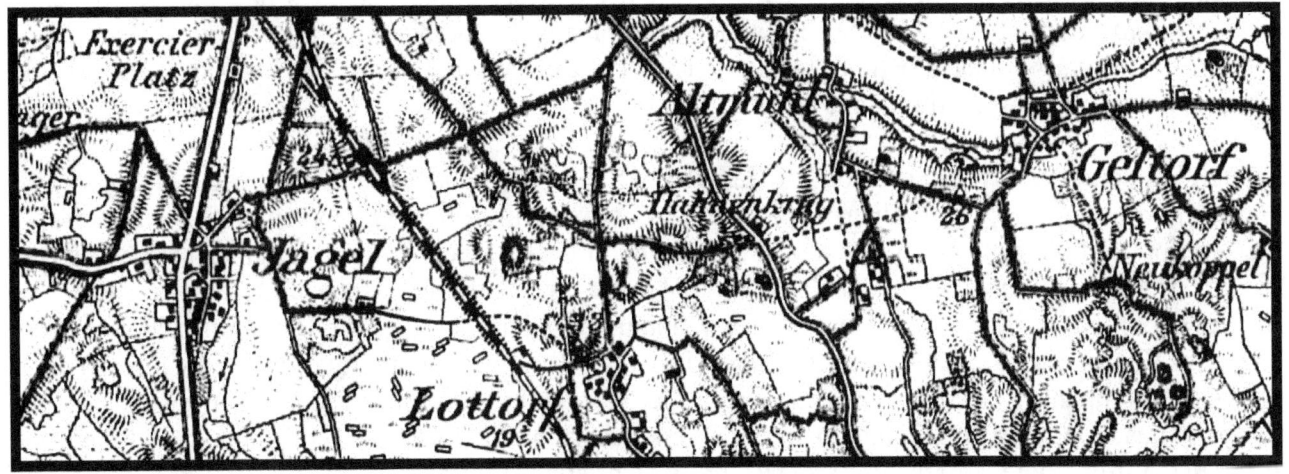

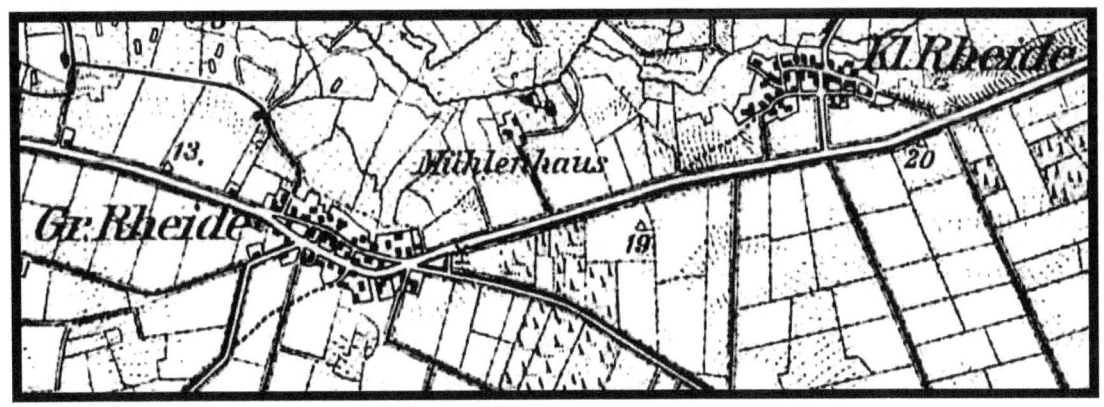

[i] Information found in chapter by Pete Laumbach.

[ii] Information provided by my son, David A. Ikenberry, who had lived and worked for several years in Bremen, Germany. In addition to holding a PhD in physical chemistry, he is a lifelong scholar of European history.

[iii] New Mexico Blue Book, 2012 Centennial issue, page 36: "1492 SPAIN…Almost immediately a liberal Spanish immigration policy to America is enacted: Catholic Christians are eligible for free passage, exempt from taxes… granted title of all lands they cultivate for four years…supplied with stock and grain from the Royal Treasury …no tax on imports or exports."

[iv] *Santas* and *santos* are valued forms of indigenous folk art and religious artifacts produced by New Mexican *santeros*—the earliest ones primarily from isolated northern New Mexico villages. *Santeros* carved and created them from native woods, using local *jaspe* (gypsum) and painted them with natural dyes. They depict religious figures, *Jesu Cristo,* Maria or favorite saints in the form of *bultos* (three-dimensional) and *retablos* (painted on flat wooden panels). Depending upon the village of origin or the *santero*, some are gentle and benevolent, others sad and suffering. The people of those early Hispanic villages were (and still are) deeply religious but then had no access to priests, churches and religious images. Their own hand-crafted *santos* filled that need. Most humble abodes had their own beloved resident *santos,* and villages their patron saints. After places of worship were built, *santos* were depicted on *tablas* or *reredos*—panels behind the alters. Life was difficult and hazardous for people in early New Mexico. Santos eased their living and dying.

[v] Butch Sanders recently found record of Daniel Eberle in *Doniphan's Expedition*, the *Conquest of New Mexico and California*, by William E. Connelly, published in 1907. (Coincidentally, I'd inherited the first edition of that book from my mom, but we hadn't seen Daniel Eberle's name in it until Butch brought it to my attention.) At the back of that book are "official rosters and records." Roster for Artillery Company B, of St. Louis, under Captain Woldermar Fischer, Battalion Light Artillery, Missouri Volunteers: accepted for service to U.S. for 12 months, from June 21, 1846; muster-in roll shows the company at Ft. Leavenworth. From October 31 to December 31, 1846, the roll shows the company headquartered at Santa Fe. Number 73 entry is Daniel Eberle, private. Whether or not pertinent to us, listed immediately after him, number 74, is "Christian Egertt," private. On this same muster roll, the third officer listed is 3rd Corporal Chr. (Christian?) Aug. (Augustus or August?) Lamsbach (Christian and August were common names among early German families); number 91 is Godfried Metzger, private. Many of those muster rolls have additional personal information about the individual soldiers, but none is provided for Daniel Eberle, "Egertt," "Lamsbach" or Metzger. Karl Laumbach did some additional research and found a little more military information about Daniel Eberle, which he shares in one of his chapters in this book.

[vi] The New Mexico Historian, "Lo de Mora, A History of the Mora Land Grant on the Eve of Transition," by Michael Miller.

[vii] "Elionor E. Laumbach" is how she wrote her name in her Santa Biblia, or as "E.N. Laumbach." I have also seen it elsewhere, at least once, with a middle initial N. The Biblia's edition page is missing; that

would have told us the Bible's version as well as age of book. Printed on an inside page is "10ᵗʰ edition." Loose inside, used as a book mark, is a small November 1890 calendar page. Written with pencil inside the back cover are names, written in Spanish, of various books of the Bible in Elionor's handwriting. She didn't speak English, but she had some education in Spanish, or was self-taught. Perhaps she learned with her children when they studied. Her notes and the signs of wear in her *Santa Biblia* show she used—read and studied—it.

[viii] The *Smithsonian* magazine published articles about Jewish gene variants that inexplicably showed up as diseases also among modern-day Hispanic Catholics of southern Colorado and northern New Mexico. Studying DNA, researchers traced some lines back more than 2,000 years to the late Middle Ages when Ashkenazi Jews of Spain were forced to convert to Catholicism. Some of those Sephardic (Spanish origin) Jewish people, known as crypto-Jews (those who kept their Jewish heritage secret to avoid persecution) migrated to the American southwest. In little remote cemeteries in northern New Mexico, including the old cemetery at Ledoux (formerly called La Cebolla), are grave markers with both Christian and Jewish symbols for families who lived in the area for generations.

SECTION I: INTRODUCTION

Chapter 2: An Overview
by Jan Girand

Early Background German History

Because Schleswig-Holstein was the Lauenbachs' (Laumbachs') area of origin until they left Europe in 1856, we will briefly focus only on the history of the duchies of Schleswig and Holstein, which eventually became one duchy. After that date, our focus is on America.

The Danes dominated the area's early history because of its geographic location. Schleswig-Holstein is within that arm of present-day Germany that reaches up to touch Denmark. Through several centuries, that area had been a Denmark possession.

The religious diversity between what would eventually become northern and southern Germany caused conflict for centuries.

The Thirty-Year War in the 17th century between religious factions left a third of the people dead and cities destroyed. By 1789, the area was split into 350 small independent principalities and free cities, partly because of the Germanic rule of dividing territory among all sons of the ruler. Without the security of national unity, the people clung to local customs and traditions. Then Napoleon Bonaparte took control of what was then Prussia in the early 1800s.

People, believing that unifying their states would help guard against bullies like Napoleon, caused some unification, reducing the number of independent principalities to about 39.

After 1815, the Danish duchy of Holstein became part of the German Confederation, thrusting both Schleswig and Holstein into several military conflicts with Denmark.

Claus Peder Henkens (grandfather of Emma Henkens, wife of Dan Laumbach) probably lived during and participated in at least one of those conflicts between Denmark and Prussia.

Per manifests found by "Butch" Charles O. Sanders (researcher and genealogist, see the Appendix for his bio and photo), Peter Claus Henkens (father of Emma Henkens Laumbach) came to America on the Deutschland, departed Hamburg 15 April, 1866 bound for the port of New York.[i] Arriving in New York May 22, he was on shipboard for 37 days. Peter Henkens brought with him an oil painting of his father, Prussian officer Claus Peder Henkens, depicted in full regalia and plumed hat, sitting on a rearing horse with both front legs in the air. Traditionally, statues of officers on horses—I'm uncertain if this applies also to paintings—depicted with both front feet off the ground indicate the officer died in battle; one of the horse's feet uplifted means the officer ultimately died of battle injuries; both front feet on the ground indicate the officer died of natural causes. Did that painting tell the fate of Claus Peder Henkens, Emma's paternal grandfather? Decades ago, a descendant of his, then living in Nebraska, gave a photograph of the original painting[ii] to my mother, Verna L. Sparks.

Denmark was able to hold onto Holstein in the war of 1848 to 1851 against the Kingdom of Prussia. When the Anna and Andreas Laumbach family left in 1856, the duchies of Holstein and Schleswig were still part of Denmark. In the Second War of Schleswig, in 1864, about eight years after the Laumbach family left, the king of Denmark lost both Schleswig and Holstein to Prussia. Andreas and Anna fled to America between those two wars.

In 1866, Austria lost any claim to the region by losing the Austro-Prussian War. Schleswig-Holstein, which included the duchy of Lauenburg in 1876, became a Prussian province and free-state from 1868 to 1946. Therefore, ever since 1868—12 years after the departure of Andreas and Anna and their family—the two duchies became one Prussian province, Schleswig-Holstein, until after World War II.

Andreas and Anna in Schleswig

The city of Schleswig surrounds the Schlei—a small inland sea fed by the Baltic. From family stories and for other reasons, for years I had believed the family's point of departure by ship had been Kiel Bay. That journey would have been from there to the Baltic Sea, then up over the top of Denmark to the Atlantic Ocean, before heading for the American continent. I was likely wrong.

A diligent search by Butch Sanders found no ship's manifest for Andreas and Anna and their family, although they traveled with documentation.

Sanders said economics was the primary reason the majority of Germans departed via Hamburg rather than other ports. He said: "The Port of Hamburg was older, bigger, better, and its ships were headed in the right direction—westward, directly to the North Sea. And if they left at high tide, it would have been downhill to the sea about 66 miles to the west. Heading east via Kiel Bay would have added several hundred miles to a voyage to America, and those waters were probably more treacherous than floating along the Elbe." Sanders believed most of those who headed east through Kiel Bay for America went via Copenhagen where they had to change to a ship heading west to America. For centuries, Hamburg has been the center/hub for commercial trade in Central and Eastern Europe. "The reason is her inland tidal port," said Sanders.

From http://www.hafenhamburg.de/en/content/history-hamburg-port: "From 1850 onwards the Hamburg flag could be encountered on all the world's oceans!"

And from http://www.portofhamburg.com/en/content/geographic-position: "The Port of Hamburg is located the farthest east of the German North Sea ports, giving it an advantageous position in Central Europe. The port serves as an important transit port, especially for cargo to and from Central and Eastern Europe. Good land and inland waterway connections to the hinterland make Hamburg an important logistics hub for Northern Europe. The port's advantage of location helps reduce transportation costs."

Sanders provided this explanation for possibly why no manifest has (yet) been found for Anna Koos and Andreas Detlef Lauenbach and most of their family: "They might have left from Bremen, Hamburg's chief competitor port, [but] no Bremen passenger manifests have been preserved from that era."

An excerpt from http://www.progenealogists.com/germany/articles/hambpl.htm: "As people were leaving Germany for the New World in the latter half of the 19th century, most took one of three routes"—Hamburg, Bremen or La Havre.

"Hamburg: Those from Schleswig-Holstein and other parts of Northeastern Germany, Eastern Prussia, Brandenburg, Silesien and even northern parts of the Russian Empire left by way of Hamburg. Many Swedes and Danes also left by way of Hamburg, traveling by ship from Gothenburg, Copenhagen or other Scandinavian ports to Kiel, Germany and then taking a train to Hamburg (especially in the period before steam boats became more common, pre-1870).

"Bremen: Germans from northwestern Germany and central Germany largely left from Bremen on the Weser River, which was the other major German port for emigrants to America.

"La Havre: Germans from southern Germany, notably Baden, Wurttemberg and Bavaria, often took a train to the port of La Havre and left from there for the new world.

"Although as many or nearly as many Germans probably left from the port of Bremen as left from Hamburg, until the 20th century there are no preserved passenger lists from this port. The early 20th century passenger lists are being indexed by the genealogy society there and a few books of passengers from Bremen have been compiled based upon arrival lists in US ports from the 1850s and 1860s, but otherwise there are no records available for the thousands of Germans who left from Bremen. Likewise there are no passenger lists from the port of La Havre, France."

~~

At their European departure with their three documents, probably in early April 1856, Andreas was 54 and Anna was 45. Of their eight children, seven—ranging in ages from 4 to 20, all daughters except one son, Marx Heinrich, 16—traveled with them. Only one of their children did not go with them. The departure of their first-born, age 22, also named Andreas Detlef Lauenbach, born December 2, 1833 in Jagel, was delayed because, according to family lore, he had been, reluctantly, conscripted into the Prussian army and was required to serve three years. Probably because economic conditions and political upheaval in their homeland directly affected them, perhaps also to avoid their second son, Heinrich, from being drafted into the military, the Lauenbachs felt driven to leave when they did, even without son Andreas. They hoped he would soon be able to join them in America.

Those three documents had been the extent of our family's knowledge of Lauenbachs in Germany. That is, until Peter James "Pete" Laumbach (son of Rudolph and Leona Laumbach) and his wife Ophelia went to Germany in 2005 to visit their son stationed there, and—with copies of these documents in hand—researched and extended the family's knowledge of Lauenbachs in Germany further back in time. Pete's valued findings are included in this book. It was from Pete's extended genealogy that we learned the names and ages of all the children of Andreas and Anna who came to America with their parents, including Marx Heinrich.

The German port of departure and American port of entry for the Anna and Andreas Lauenbach family is unknown, having no ship's manifest record of their crossing. According to the Internet site, *Germans to America*, inbound Prussians-Germans arrived at several major U.S. ports: New York, Baltimore, Boston, Philadelphia and New Orleans. Logic says the Lauenbach family departed from Hamburg and landed at Castle Garden, New York, as we now know their son did soon thereafter.

Years after she was grown, Anna, one of the Lauenbach children who made that journey at the age of 8, related some of its frightening details to her own family.

Andreas 2nd left within three-and-a-half months after the date on his parents' documents. That is confirmed by a ship's manifest found by Sanders. Andreas was a listed passenger on the John Hermann's manifest that departed Hamburg for New York 15, July 1856.[iii] Sanders carefully searched all four pages of that manifest, finding no other Lauenbach/Laumbach or any Frederick "Fritz" Eggert listed on it with any various spelling. That might negate our family's oral tradition that Fritz traveled from Germany with his friend, the younger Andreas, but perhaps Fritz had been an undocumented stowaway, as our family believed for more than 100 years that both men had been. While we cannot prove Fritz Eggert had known Andreas in Schleswig or that they traveled together to America, we believe the two spent time together during their first years in the USA, if not earlier.

Laumbachs in Goose Lake, Clinton, Iowa

The spelling of the family's last name changed soon after they arrived in America. We don't know exactly where, when or why, but changes of names and their spellings commonly occurred with incoming immigrants.

After the Laumbach family's long, anxious ocean crossing, and their probably stressful processing at the port of entry, they still had to travel a distance overland to reach their chosen settlement in the middle of this large country. The entire course of their journey was difficult and frightening. A language barrier was just one of their many difficulties. Only a worse situation behind them would have driven them to an uncertain future. Like all immigrants and early pioneers to a new land, they were a brave and resilient people.

Upon their arrival at Goose Lake, they were relieved to be welcomed into an established farming community of Germans who had shared those hazards and fears when they, too, came from the same region of Europe—which was then part of Denmark, as was often recorded as their place of origin in U.S. Census records.

After landing in New York's Castle Garden—before an Ellis Island port of entry for immigrants was established—the younger Andreas traveled to Goose Lake, Clinton, Iowa to see his family. He arrived there about three months after they did.

Soon after going to Goose Lake, he—and family stories say accompanied by his friend Fritz—headed west. They had adventures along their way. According to my mother (Verna Laumbach Sparks, daughter of Daniel and Emma Laumbach), they stopped a while to search the streams for gold in the area that would be Denver.

Laumbachs in New Mexico

The younger Andreas ended his journey in northern New Mexico in the Hispanic settlement of La Cebolla, near the community of lo de Moro, also known as St. Gertrudes de Mora, New Mexico. New Mexico had become a USA territory only 13 years earlier. People of the isolated mountain settlements of north central New Mexico retained their Spanish heritage, their Castilian language, faith, mores and folkways for generations. They still do.

A handwritten entry in the family's German Bible states Andreas 2nd arrived in New Mexico on October 29, 1859. That Bible, with handwritten entries recording births and deaths of Laumbachs in New Mexico, had been with the family at Buena Vista, New Mexico until the family ranch sold in 1948. Then Aunties—our maiden aunts—Anna, Mary and Leonor (daughters of Andreas and Elionor) brought the Bible with them to Las Vegas. In her last years, the remaining Auntie, Leonor[iv], gave it to her nephew Tony Sanchez (son of her sister Crestina Laumbach and Manuel A. Sanchez), who gave it to me (daughter of Verna Laumbach Sparks). I delayed taking possession of it. After Tony's death when his estate was settled, that Bible, like Tony's other family keepsakes, was lost to the family.[v]

According to local tradition, the Laumbach families in both New Mexico and Iowa lost track of Henry, brother of Andreas 2nd, after his brief visit west. One New Mexico Laumbach branch said he had come from Iowa with his brother, Andreas, when he arrived in northern New Mexico in late October 1859. Another branch said Henry came with his father Andreas 1st a very few years later. In both versions, Henry did not tarry long in New Mexico; he headed north to Colorado, perhaps to search for gold. Thereafter, local family lore said he was not heard from again by family in Iowa or New Mexico. We now know that was not totally correct, according to census records and Dallas Laumbach.

Karl Laumbach (son of George and Margaret Laumbach) had located via the Internet, and contacted, a fellow residing in Texas named Dallas Laumbach. Soon after that, researching the Laumbach family, Karl, Pete (son of Rudolph and Leona Laumbach) and I met and became acquainted with Dallas and his wife Rosalie. After comparing notes, we were all convinced Dallas descended from our "missing" great-great-uncle Henry Laumbach. In the process of our acquaintance, Dallas learned more about his own Laumbach family, and we learned more about Henry. A chapter in this book, by Dallas, provides his conclusions about his great-grandfather Henry—who we are now convinced was Marx Heinrich (the second), born in 1840, brother of Andreas 2nd. (Andreas 1st also had a brother named Marx Heinrich Lauenbach who remained in Germany.)

After Andreas 2nd had lived in La Cebolla for about four-and-a-half years, he married Elionor Ebel (Eberle) on April 10, 1864 at the St. Gertrudes parish church in Mora, New Mexico.[vi] For a while, Elionor and Andreas continued to live at La Cebolla.

In New Mexico, Elionor's last name, of Germanic origin, was recorded with various spellings, first as Eberle, but also Ebel, Ebarley and sometimes Evil or Ebell.

Elionor Eberle/Ebel was born to Bibiana Martín (Martinez) on June 10, 1849, in the Mora area, probably at La Cebolla. We have found no record of her birth or christening, or that of her brother, Juan Andres Eberle/Ebel. We only found a birth record for their younger sister Maria Marta Eberle/Ebel that indicates she was legitimate. Subsequent records for all three indicate Bibiana and Daniel never married. Little is known about Elionor's father, Daniel Eberle. Verna L. Sparks said he was a Swiss immigrant of German heritage who settled in or near Las Vegas, New Mexico until his death. She said he was a wealthy Las Vegas merchant with ranch holdings in the area. Karl Laumbach and his cousins believe Bibiana lived with Eberle at Las Vegas.

Butch Sanders has found a Daniel Eberle, private, who came into New Mexico, probably from Missouri, with Doniphan's Expedition, Artillery Company B that mustered in at Ft. Leavenworth June 21, 1846, headquartered in Santa Fe in October, November and December 1846.[vii]

Laumbach family branches tell different versions of Eberle's murder; those will be related in later chapters, including one by Karl Laumbach.

Sanders found an April 2001 post on an Internet genealogy forum by an apparent descendant of Eberle. John Ebel stated in that post that Eberle was a German who landed in New York about 1880 (incorrect date). This John Ebel said Eberle "traded goods along the Santa Fe Trail," had three children with Bibiana, and was robbed and murdered about 1830. (John's dates are obviously confused.) We know Bibiana was with Eberle/Ebel sometime after James Bonney was killed in the fall of 1846. Dates of birth of Bibiana's and Eberle's children confirm the years they were together: Elionor, born 1849; Juan Andres, born 1852; and Maria Marta, born 1856.

~~

Elionor's mother, Maria Bibiana Martín, was born December 1, 1827 at Potrero, Chimayo, New Mexico. Bibiana's father, Bernardo Martín, was born at Potrero on May 20, 1792 to a family that had resided there for generations. Bibiana's mother, Apolonia Gutierrez de Solano, was born April 11, 1811 in Santa Fe, also to a family long established there, but when she was small, her parents moved to Potrero. (At the end of Chapter 12—Potrero, Mora, etc. is data extracted from historically archived microfiche entries recording baptisms of Bernardo, Apolonia, their marriage, baptisms of Bibiana and of Maria Marta Eberle/Ebel—daughter of Bibiana and Daniel Eberle—and others, as well as images of some of those actual entries, courtesy of Nancy Anderson with the New Mexico Genealogical Society.)

Contrary to tradition passed down among various branches, the families of both Bernardo and Apolonia lived in New Mexico for countless generations. Their lines of ancestry were painstakingly traced in New Mexico from the earliest surviving Catholic Church's sacramental records. One of their lines was traced to Juan de Oñate's 1598-1604 expedition, another line to the exploration by Frenchman La Salle—Rene-Robert Cavelier, Sieur de La Salle—of the Great Lakes area of the U.S. and Canada. He also explored the Mississippi River and the Gulf of Mexico. LaSalle's land-claim for France ultimately resulted in America's Louisiana Purchase that doubled the size of the United States of America.

On LaSalle's last trip, in the 1680s, at least two of his ships wrecked at Matagordo Bay. Two shipwreck survivors became forebears of some early New Mexico families. (An overview of how that event related to Bernardo Martín is in Chapter 10—History 101, Grolet.)

We credit much of the family's very early genealogical information in New Mexico to the availability of sacramental records of the Archives of the Archdiocese of Santa Fe and the seminal works of Fray Angelíco Chavez. Sacramental Records and the Preservation of New Mexico Genealogies from the Colonial Era to the Present, a chapter written by José Antonio Esquibel, published in *Seeds of Struggle, Harvest of Faith*, edited by Thomas J. Steele, S.J., Paul Rhetts and Barb Awalt, tells how those records survived and were painstakingly translated and transcribed, then preserved for posterity. Included in Esquibel's chapter of that book is a genealogical chart showing the forebears of both of Bibiana's parents: Apolonia Gutierrez de Solano and Bernardo Martín. (An overview of Esquibel's chapter is addressed later in this book and will also be in the Bibana book, a publication to follow this one. Esquibel also wrote Chapter 17 in this book relating to Bernardo Martín's U.S. military service.)

---

[i] Images of pertinent pages of manifests. The Deutschland departed Hamburg 15 April 1866, bound for the port of New York: Peter Claus Henkens is passenger number 236 on page 7 of that 14-page manifest (the form in German). Sanders said that manifest, written in Hamburg, was left on file there. A manifest was also submitted upon ship's arrival at the port of New York May 22, 1866 (form in English). There Henkens is still passenger 236, but that entry is on page 5 of 11 pages of the manifest. These records were found and described by researcher, Butch Sanders. Sanders shortened the list of neighboring entries of Peter's fellow passengers, and rotated the New York manifest, where width was a limiting factor, to provide a readable image for this book.

District of New York—Port of New York.

I, **F. Hoven**, Master of the **Minot Ship Dudlelland**, do solemnly, sincerely and truly swear that the following List or Manifest, subscribed by me, and now delivered by me to the Collector of the Customs District of New York, is full and perfect list of all the passengers taken on board of the said **Steamer** from which port said **Ship** has now arrived; and that on said List is truly designated the age, the sex, and the occupation of each of said passengers, the port of the vessel occupied by each during the passage, the country to which each belongs, and also the country of which it is intended by each to become an inhabitant; and that said List or Manifest truly sets forth the number of said passengers who have died on said voyage, and the names and ages of those who died. **So help me God.**

F. Hoven

Sworn to this 22 May 1866
Ellerslie

Before me — **Manet Ship Dudlelland** whereof **Hoven** is Master, from **Hamburg**

first or Manifest Of all the Passengers taken on board the ___ burthen ___ tons.

No.	NAMES	Age Years	Months	SEX	OCCUPATION	The country to which they severally belong	The country of which it is their intention to become inhabitants	Died on the voyage
114	Paul Hanghaus	28		Male	Clergyman	Germany	United States	Wisconsin
115	Anna H.	22		Female	his wife			
116	Carl H.	18		Male	Steam			
117	Carl Ellinghoff			Male	Farmer			
118	Carl do	16		Male	Farmer			
119	Christ do	13		Male				
120	Carl do	11		Male				
121	Carl do	1		Male				
122	Eugene do	4		Female				
123	Guthel Lorenzen	20		Male	Farmer - Children			
124	August Christiansen	21		Male	Farmer			
125	Johann Hartmann	29		Male	Farmer			
126	Peter Hanfling	25		Male	Farmer			
127	Steppan John	27		Male	Farmer			
128	Heine do	27		Male	Farmer			
129	Marie Hanfling	24		Female	his wife			
130	Ruth Hister	40		Male	Farmer			
131	Peter Boye	40		Male	Farmer			
132	Greggi Whitney	24		Female	his wife			
133	Adolph do	16		Male	Children			

[ii] Photo of painting of Claus Peder Henkens, Prussian officer, father of Peter Claus Henkens, who was father of Emma Henkens Laumbach. This photo was given to Verna Sparks by a Henkens cousin in Nebraska. Image was enhanced by Butch Sanders.

Information Sanders provided about this painting:

"Insignias on saddle blankets/saddle cloths were sometimes called cyphers. What I'd initially thought was a large R with a crown on top was actually a stylized "FR"—one letter superimposed over the other. FR stood for 'Fredericus Rex' (King of Prussia). That was the monogram of Frederich I and Frederich II, both of Prussia. I found many examples of its use. Long after Frederich I and II passed into history, this insignia appeared on the breast of the Prussian eagle, but not on the Imperial German eagle. Otherwise, the two eagles were almost identical for a time. The saddle blanket/saddle cloth was a 'shabraque' placed over the saddle with the insignias/cyphers displayed on the front and rear panels. The one on Peder's front panel is likely the above described 'crowned FR' as it is often called now days. I have not found anything elsewhere resembling the arrowhead-like insignia on the rear panel of Peder's shabraque. It may represent the tip of a lance; could that mean (a wild guess) that he was a lancer? Whatever it represents, it is rare; I've looked at hundreds of images of old paintings and drawings of Prussian cavalry and none display anything like that. Among those, several are similar to Peder's, but the differences are fascinating. Only Peder's painting displays the lance-like insignia; only Peder's displays what looks like his bedroll (or whatever) tipped up and over, almost on end behind the saddle; only Peder's displays what I think are reins (tow reins?) forming a loop in front of his horse. In addition to the 'tow rein,' Peder is using a double rein system, which was common. That brings us to what I believe was intended to represent an 'X' just above the crowned FR. The portion of this 'X' that extends from just below Peder's left hand, down and just above the left half of the crowned FR and across the fringe of the shabraque, may be a continuation of the lower rein depicted from the bridal bit, but not visible along the horse's lower neck in the painting. The other half of the 'X' extends from further up the shabraque fringe downward, just above the right half of the crowned FR—perhaps a portion of the same rein—the end portion looping from the top of Peder's hand. Assuming both halves—of what I think is a deliberate X—are the lower rein, it's possible the artist drew it in this manner to avoid encroaching on the crowned FR. But my guess is that the artist intended to form an X, reins or not, to convey the rider was deceased. The tipped blanket roll and third rein (what I call a tow rein) might have also intended to convey the same message. It also looks as if his scabbard is empty; his sabre/sword is missing. And unless it's a flaw in the painting (or the photo of it), the artist highlighted the empty scabbard with the explosion of white where the handle/hand guard should be. There is also something hanging off Peder's back that I cannot find in any other painting or drawing.

"A Prussian military history expert should be able to say what this all means, as well as Peder's unit, rank, the time period, etc. I cannot see details in the uniform but an expert might identify the shapes and patterns. This is a very interesting and seemingly unique painting!" [*Editor's Note: Sanders was able to considerably enlarge an electronic image of this painting in his computer and zoom in on details.*]

[iii] Image of pertinent manifest page listing Andreas Detlef Lauenbach (2nd) as a passenger on the John Hermann that departed Hamburg for New York 15, July 1856. This manifest record was found by Butch Sanders. He wrote: "…a nightmare to work on the images of 1856 manifest with Andreas because of relatively low resolution and all the lines running across the heading portion of Andreas' entry." But Butch was able to clean up and made readable the pertinent entry, which we never expected to see because we (still) believe Andreas traveled without documentation. He was passenger number 55. Note that entry shows him to be age 26; in fact he was a quarter past 22. (Butch found males were often listed on manifests as older than they actually were.) Andreas' listed origin was Holstein; perhaps that reflected the location of his military unit when he left.

Verzeichniss
der Personen, welche mit dem Hamburger Schiffe _John Hermann_
Capitain _Bernholdt_ nach _New York_
zur Auswanderung durch Unterzeichneten engagirt sind. _15. Juli 56_

№	Zu- und Vorname und Familie.	Geburts- und Wohnort.	Landes.	Gewerbe.	Alter	Geschlecht		Total	Recapitulation.		
						männl.	weibl.		Erwachsene und Kinder über 8 Jahr.	Kinder unter 8 Jahr.	Kinder unter 1 Jahr.
55	Andreas Launbach	Rendsburg	Holstein		26	1		1	1		

[iv] Leonor herself, and her sisters, spelled her name both ways—Leonor and Leonore—with and without an "e" and the end.

[v] Die Bibel, the Laumbach family's German Bible. Inside its front page is a handwritten signature or entry in German script dated 1848. Printed in the Bible is copyright date 1853, New York, which makes the 1848 inscription confusing. The date of copyright might indicate this Bible had been brought by the Andeas Detlef Laumbach family when they came from Schleswig in the spring of 1856, but apparently not because it was published in New York. It ultimately belonged to our maiden Aunties, the last to live at the home place at Buena Vista. When they sold the place and moved to Las Vegas, they took it with them. The last surviving Auntie, Leonor, gave the Bible to their nephew, Tony Sanchez. He gave it to Jan, but it remained in his possession until his death and probate of his will. It then passed away from the family. Handwritten in it was registry of many of the New Mexico Laumbach family's births and deaths. That data, which I copied from Die Bibel and later typed, is provided below:

Die Bibel
The German Family Bible
Hand-written Registry of Family Births and Deaths:

"Our father Andreas Laumbach was born in Germany December 2nd, 1833, come [sic] to New Mexico in fall of October 29, 1859. Died November 4, 1904. Mother Elionor E. Laumbach was born in N.M. *Jaun* [Sp.] 10, 1849.

Margarita Laumbach Born March 21, 1865
Peter Laumbach Born June 29, 1867
Estefanita Laumbach Born Jan. 28, 1870
Daniel Laumbach Born Jan. 28, 1872
Henery (sic) Laumbach Born Sept. 29, 1874
Alexander Laumbach Born Dec. 28, 1876
Anna Laumbach Born July 11, 1878
Crestina Laumbach Born Aug. 30, 1881
Mary Laumbach Born Jan. 22, 1884
John A. Laumbach Born May 23, 1886
Lionor A. Laumbach Born Aug. 10, 1888
Cordelia Laumbach Born Nov. 20, 1891

Deaths:
Father-Andreas Laumbach died Nov. 4, 1904
Mother Elionor E. Laumbach died June 27, 1933
Henry Laumbach died Sept. 20, 1929
Estefanita L. Candelario died May 2, 1938
J.S. Candelario died July 30, 1938
J.E. Cruz died Jan. 25, 1931
Anna Laumbach died May 10, 1958
Margareta L. Cruz died June 16, 1958
Mary Laumbach died Nov. 5, 1965"

Following are additional "entries" on a loose notepaper inside the Bible, which Tony Sanchez later indicated in a letter that he had written:

"Deaths:
Alice Candelario died April 18th, 1928
Mabel Laumbach died 1920
Alfredo Laumbach died Aug. 29, 1918
Eleanor E. Cruz died Aug. 18, 1933
Adelina C. Sanchez died Jan. 26, 1921
Juan A. Cruz died Jan. 26, 1908"

[vi] Following transcription, translation and image of archived entry recording marriage of Andreas Detlef 2nd and Leonor Ebel in 1864 are courtesy of the New Mexico Genealogical Society.

Roll 94 Mora
St. Gertrudes
Frame 194
SRCA
28
Andreas Lombach
Y
Maria Leonor Ebel
Abril 10 de 1864.

Case a Andreas Lombach soltero hijo de Difto. (difunto) Andreas Lombach y de Ana Caus (Koos) nacido en Alemania y residente en la Cebolla, el dicho Lombach es protestante y se oblige delante de los testigos abajo afirmando de dar libertad a su mujer para que eduque a los hijos (sitiene?), en la religion catolica—con Maria Leonor Ebel Solta. (soltera) hija de Difto. Daniel Ebel de Viviana Martin de la Cebolla.

Jn Grosstete
Vicente Romero
Miguel Mascarenas

Provided translation:

April 10 of 1864

I married Andreas Lombach unmarried son of the deceased Andreas Lombach and of Ana Caus (Koos) born in Germany and residing in La Cebolla, said Lombach is protestant and binds himself before the witnesses below vowing to give liberty to his wife to educate the children if he has any, in the Catholic religion—to Maria Leonor Ebel unmarried daughter of the deceased Daniel Ebel by Viviana Martin of La Cebolla.

Jean Grosstete
Vicente Romero
Miguel Mascarenas

(Note: Editor marked in bold above, the <u>incorrect</u> name applied, by the transcriber, to the presiding priest.) Following is image of actual entry:

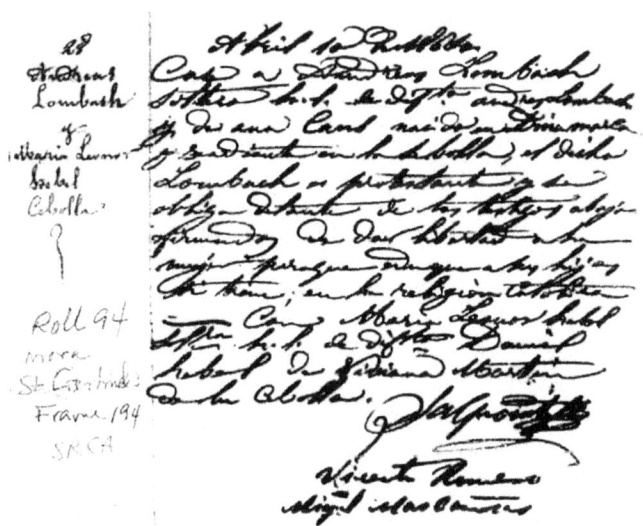

Butch Sanders wrote: "The translator misidentified the person who performed the ceremony and signed the document as 'Jn Grosstete'. The priest who married them that day signed it with only his surname—which was good enough to identify him: 'Salpointe' as in 'Jean-Baptiste Salpointe.' At that time he was the priest at the Mora parish. Not too long after this marriage ceremony, Bishop Lamy assigned him as 'the first Bishop of Arizona.' After that, he would become 'the second Archbishop of Santa Fe.'"

In his pursuit of accuracy, Sanders collected images of five Salpointe's signatures from various documents archived in Arizona. In one, probably the chronologically last of those, he signed only his last name like he did on Andreas and Elionor's marriage entry. Sanders electronically enhanced—lightened, applied higher contrast and cleaned up the dark background—the image provided here.

Note the named witnesses to Andreas and Elionor's marriage: a.) Vicente Romero, who became rich and powerful in the Mora area after the 1850s by buying or otherwise procuring property from original Mora land grantees until he held nearly 33,000 acres, and built a huge home, store, grist mill, and an irrigation system still in use at La Cueva today. b.) Miguel Mascarenas, one of the Mora Land Grantees and the justice of peace at Mora, was often cited in early documents of legal proceedings. He was father of Juana Maria Mascarenas, with whom James Bonney had three children.

vii Doniphan's Expedition, Conquest of New Mexico and California, by William Elsey Connelley, copyright 1907. Within the official rosters and records, on page 579 of that book, is entry #73 Daniel Eberle, private.

LAUMBACHS IN NEW MEXICO
And Those Who Went Before
In Germany, Iowa and New Mexico

WHO WERE THEY?
THEREFORE, WHO AM I?

Section II
GERMANY

"In all of us is a hunger, marrow deep
to know our heritage—to know who we are and where we came from.
Without this enriching knowledge, there is a hollow yearning."

Alex Haley, Roots

SECTION II: LAUMBACHS IN GERMANY

Chapter 3: German Documents & Translations
by Jan Girand

Ördtliche St. Johannis Klö-
sterliche Kirchenfreiheit. —

Geburts- und Taufschein.

Im Jahre achtzehn hundert und elf (1811) den neunten
(9) August ist geboren und den elften (11) ejusdem men-
sis & anni getauft:

Anna Kroos, des Käthners in Hagel Detlef
Kroos und seiner Ehefrau Anna Christina geb.
Rindt eheliche Tochter. —

Gevattern bei der Taufe waren

Catharina Margaretha Lauenbach
Maria Hagge
Hans Hinrich Greve

Haddebyer Pastorat zu Busdorf
den 31 März 1856.

In fidem.
S. B. Schmidt

Geb. 3 ß 3 ß Rm.

Adeliche St. Johannis Klosters dichte
Hungelfreiheit.

Trauschein.

Im Jahre achtzehnhundert und zwei und dreißig
(1832) den vierten (4) November ist in der Haddebyer Kirche getrauet worden das Brautpaar:
Andreas Detlef Lauenbach in Jagel, ehelicher
Sohn des Christian Rudolph Lauenbach, weil. Häuerling zu Geltorf und der Catharina Margarethe
geb. Bahr, mit seiner erlobten Braut
Anna Koos, eheliche Tochter des Detlef Koos
weil. Käthner zu Jagel und der Anna Christina
geb. Bindt.

Zeugen 1. Jürgen Rohwer } aus Jagel.
2. Claus Stricker }

Haddebyer Pastorat zu Busdorf
den 31 März 1856

Geb: 13/Rm.

In fidem
S. B. Mau.

This seal on all three original documents made them official. This photograph of the seal taken by Karl Laumbach with special lighting allows us, for perhaps the first time, to see its details.

The pages that precede this chapter are copies of the three original 1856 German documents frequently referenced in this book. Accompanying them is an image of the wax seal that certified each of the three a legal document. (Seal was on all three documents, including the marriage document, not seen on the copy included here.) As with most images and photos in this book, Butch Sanders spent considerable time improving their quality.

Following is the "Chain of Custody" of the original German documents, hand-recorded March 31, 1856 at St. Johannis kloster vor Schleswig:

Andreas Detlef Laumbach 1st and his wife Anna Koos Laumbach went from Jagel to St. Johannis Cloister to request their pertinent birth and marriage data—recorded there probably in a ledger—to be copied onto official documents on March 31, 1856. We believe they requested them just prior to their premeditated departure for America. Andreas and Anna hand-carried them on shipboard across the ocean and overland to Goose Lake, Clinton, Iowa. Within a short time after their arrival there, it was probably Andreas 1st who brought them to the Mora area of northern New Mexico when he joined his son Andreas Detlef Laumbach 2nd in the very early 1860s. After Andreas 1st was killed in New Mexico prior to April 1864 in what was then Mora County, New Mexico *(the area later became Colfax County)*, the original documents passed to his son, Andreas Detlef Laumbach 2nd. Records show that at the time of his father's death, Andreas 2nd still lived at La Cebolla, within the greater Mora Valley of New Mexico. Sometime after the death of the second Andreas Detlef Laumbach at Buena Vista, New Mexico in 1904, the documents passed from his wife Elionor Ebel Laumbach at Buena Vista, to their son Daniel Laumbach and his wife Emma Henkens Laumbach while they lived at their Cedar Springs Ranch at Enciero on the Canadian River Gorge in San Miguel County.

In nearby Roy, where they lived their final years, the documents passed after their deaths—Daniel died in 1947 and Emma died in 1956—to their eldest son, Joyce Laumbach, who had a ranch, previously a portion of his father's, in the TV country southwest of Roy. After Joyce sold the ranch, he lived briefly in Roy, then moved to Las Cruces for his final years. There, at his death in 1991, the original documents passed to his daughter, Vera Jane Laumbach Morris of Las Cruces. She recently donated them, for purpose of archival preservation, to the New Mexico Farm and Ranch Heritage Museum at Las Cruces. They are fragile but have endured. *(Verna L. Sparks, in a later chapter in this book, describes how her parents had presumed those documents, in their keeping, were lost. When preparing to move to Roy, they found them behind a desk drawer at their Cedar Springs Ranch. Most of those years, the documents had been kept loosely rolled like scrolls to prevent them cracking on fold lines.)*

While Joyce had the documents in Roy, his sister Verna made copies, which she shared with cousins.

~~

Following are my basic translations of the three certified Laumbach family's German documents. They were translated[i] years ago by Margaret Katz, wife of a German Jewish merchant in Las Vegas, New Mexico.

I. Legitimate son Andreas Detlef Lauenbach was born November 25, 1802 to parents Christian Rudolph Lauenbach from Geltorf and Catharina Margaretha Busch *(Mrs. Katz had mistranslated Busch as Buhite)* from Gross-Rheide. The Haddebyer clergyman of Bustorf christened Andreas on November 28. In addition to his parents, present were two witnesses from Geltorf—Detlef Rohr and Peter Koll—and a witness from the parish of Huttener—Margaretha Maardt. Written at the top of the document was "St. Johannis Cloister" and "nobility, no stamp (or fee) necessary." Written at the bottom center, "Haddebyer Clergyman of Bustorf," and the date March 31, 1856. At the bottom left hand side: "Fee 3 Thalers, 3 Imperial Marks," and on the right, "In faith, S.B. Lindt" and the official wax seal.

My remarks:

- Why the notation of nobility? Were families of either or both of Andreas' parents—Christian Rudolph Lauenbach and/or Catharina Margaretha Busch—aristocratic landowners? In 1802, was one or both of the provinces of their origin, Geltorf and/or Gross-Rheide, then just a walk apart, small independent principalities or free cities? Which parent (or both?) was considered to be of noble birth?
- The original record of Andreas' christening was probably first written at the church of Haddeby, and then entered in a ledger at the Protestant St. Johannis Cloister.
- The data was hand-copied at St. Johannis 54 years later, on March 31, 1856, onto a document certified legal with a wax seal.
- This document was probably hand-written by "S.B. Lindt," a Lutheran cleric.
- Per the notation at the top, the usual fee stated at the bottom of the document was waived.

(In 2005, Pete Laumbach, son of Rudolph and Leona, discovered that Christian Rudolph Lauenbach had been a widower with three children when he married Catharina Margaretha Busch.)

II. Legitimate daughter Anna Koos was born August 9, 1811 in Jagel to Detlef Koos and his wife Anna Christina (born Bindt). Witnesses at her baptism on August 11 were Catharina Margaretha Lauenbach, Maria Hagge and Hans Heinrich Grene. Written at the top of the document was "St. Johannis Cloister" and "nobility, no stamp (or fee) necessary." Written at the bottom center: "Haddebyer clergyman of Bustorf," and the date March 31, 1856. Written at the bottom left corner of the document: "Fee 3 Thalers, 3 Imperial Marks," and in the right-hand corner: "In faith, S.B. Lindt," with the seal below, certifying it a legal document.

My remarks:

- Were families of either or both parents—Detlef Koos and Anna Christina Bindt—landowners? In 1811, the population was class-conscious. Which parent(s) was considered to be of noble birth?
- This document, or its translation, gives few place names; there might be one following the names of Anna's parents that is not included in the translation. The church at Haddeby, the place of Anna's baptism, was just a brief walk or ride from where her parents resided at Jagel.
- The original entry of Anna's christening would have first been written at the church of Haddeby, and then recorded in a ledger at the Protestant St. Johannis Cloister.
- It was re-recorded there on March 31, 1856 onto a document certified with a wax seal.
- Catharina Margaretha Lauenbach witnessed Anna Koos' christening nine years after the birth of her own son Andreas. The families lived within an hour's walk from each other and also from the protestant or Lutheran church at Haddeby where both families probably worshipped. Their families' friendship led to the marriage of their children Andreas and Anna.
- The usual fee, written at the bottom of the document, was waived because of the family's status.

III. On November 4, 1832, in the church of Haddeby in the Haddebyer pastorate of Bustorf, were married Andreas Detlef Lauenbach from Jagel, son of Christian Rudolf Lauenbach of Geltorf and Catharina Margaretha (born Busch), and his bride Anna Koos, daughter of Detlef Koos of Jagel and Anna Christiana (born Bindt). Witnesses at the marriage were Jurgen Rohwer and Claus Stricker, both of Jagel. Written at the top of the document was "St. Johannis Cloister" and "nobility, no stamp (or fee) necessary." At the bottom center: "Haddebyer clergyman of Bustorf," with the date March 31, 1856. Written at the bottom left corner of the document: "Fee 3 Thalers, 3 Imperial Marks" and on the right-hand corner: "In faith, S.B. Lindt" with the seal below that certifying it a legal document.

My remarks:
- Were parents of Andreas Detlef Lauenbach and Anna Koos landowners, or were they themselves landowners? Were the provinces of their origins, and/or Jagel, still small independent principalities or free cities in 1832?
- When this marriage took place at the church of Haddeby, in the pastorate of Bustorf, Andreas lived in the small community of Jagel, as did his bride and her parents and two witnesses.
- These documents already showed us that the Lauenbach and Koos families had known each other a long time, and were friends.
- The official entry of their marriage would have been first written in a ledger at the church of Haddeby, and then recorded at the Lutheran St. Johannis Cloister.
- The data was hand-copied at St. Johannis more than 23 years later, on March 31, 1856, onto a document certified with a wax seal.
- St. Johannis, Jagel, Geltorf, Gross-Rheide, Bustorf and the Haddeby church at Busdorf were within an hour's walk of each other, at least at that time before growth of city, population and the autobahn.[ii]
- Our family does not know why all three documents have "nobility" and "no fee/stamp required" written on them. That implies an aristocratic designation for families of both Andreas and Anna, which waived the usual fee written at the bottom of the documents.

I have learned that in old German script (perhaps also modern), a large flourished "f" is an "s" as in Bustorf; and a "ẞ" is a double "s" as in Gross Rheide. Like in English, in German "gross" means large. Detlef, like Dieter, means David, depending upon the locality. A place-name ending in "torf" or "dorf" means small community.

When I asked for meaning or literal translation of our name's suffix, Bob Figge, a retired Albuquerque high school teacher of European history, said "bach" means brook or creek, and "berg" means hill or mountain, not community as I had thought. "Added to a name, they indicate where one came from," Figge said.

Within the state of Schleswig-Holstein is a town named Lauenburg—also known as Lauenburg an der Elbe—situated on the north bank of the Elbe River, east of Hamburg. According to Wikipedia, it was founded in 1182 by an ancestor of the Dukes of Lauenburg. Its castle burned down in 1616, but a small portion of the ruins remains. After the Napoleonic Wars, Prussia ceded Lauenburg to Denmark. Saxe-Lauenburg was a duchy until July 1, 1876, when it became part of the Prussian province of Schleswig-Holstein. Was Lauenburg the origin of the Lauenbach name?

The Duke of Lauenburg—Otto Eduard Leopold, Prince of Bismarck—was known as the father of Germany for uniting numerous independent Germanic states in 1871 into what became the German Empire. That was about 15 years after our family left.

In the 1980s, I showed copies of our documents to German nationals temporarily assigned to the research and development shop at the manufacturing company where I worked near Roswell. They said they could not read or translate them because they were written in old Germanic script.

---

[i] Following are copies of translations of the three documents by Margaret Katz, wife of a German Jewish merchant in Las Vegas, New Mexico. Copies of translations were reduced for this book, two are on one page.

[ii] See Schleswig Rendsburg 1895 maps end of chapter 1.

KATZ 5c & 10c STORE
BRIDGE STREET
LAS VEGAS, NEW MEXICO

Nobility St Johannis Monastery
No Stamp Necessary
Birth Certificate

In the Year 1802 on the 25 of November was born and baptised on the 28 of November Andres Detlef Lauenbach son of Christian Rudolf Lauenbach from Geltof and his wife Catharina Margaretta (Born) Buhite from Grohs-Rheide legitimate John

Witness Detlef Rohr from Geltof
" Peter Kohl " "
" Margarethe Haardt from Huttener Parish

Haddelsyer Clergyman from Buhtorf

38

KATZ 5c & 10c STORE
BRIDGE STREET
LAS VEGAS, NEW MEXICO

Birth Certificate and
Baptist Certificate

In the Year 1811 on the 9 of August was born
and on the 11 of August was baptized a Daughter
Anna Koos
Daughter of Detlef Koos and his Wife Anna
Christina born Bindt eje.   Daughter

Wittness at the Baptis. where the following
Catharina Asoy ore the Laumbach
Maria Hagge
Hans Heinrich Greve.

KATZ 5c & 10c STORE
BRIDGE STREET
LAS VEGAS, NEW MEXICO

Nobility St Johannis Monastery
No Stamps Necesary
Marriage Certificate

In the Year 1832 the 4 of November in the
church of Hadeby this Couple was married
Andres Detlef Lauenbach from Jagel
the son of Christian Rudolph Laumbach
and the : Catherine Margaretha
born Buhte and his Bride Anna Koos
Daughter of Detlef Koos and his Wife
Anna Christina born Bindt

Wittnesses 1 Juegen Rohwer
          2 Claus Stricker from Jagel

Haadebyer Clergyman   from Buhtof
         the 21 March 1856

SECTION II: LAUMBACHS IN GERMANY

Chapter 4: Journey to Germany
by Jan Girand

In the late summer of 1993, when I thought Mama (Verna L. Sparks) should no longer live alone, I designed and, with help from a few laborers, built an adobe efficiency apartment for her onto our adobe home. In essence, she lived with us almost three years.

In 1996, I planned a trip to Germany when my son, David, lived there. Our journey was arranged while we thought Mama was in good health, but we still intentionally planned our trip short-term because of her. We did not want to be gone long, although I'd made arrangements for someone to stay in our home with her.

I had bought advance non-refundable tickets for my husband, Dan, my grandson, Brandon, and me to travel in early July. Then my mama was suddenly ill, hospitalized, and in ten days was gone at half-past 86, on May 23, 1996. Being nonrefundable tickets, we were unable to increase the duration of our trip without doubling the cost for the three of us. Therefore, our travel itinerary was unchanged.

It had seemed wrong for us to travel just six weeks after Mama died. But with introspection and encouragement, it seemed right.

From her childhood, she had listened to the "old ones," born in or before the mid-1800s, talk; she took notes on anything handy, even flattened envelopes, and remembered. When she was in college at New Mexico Normal in Las Vegas in the late 1920s and early 1930s, she lived with her Aunt Crestina Sanchez and continued to listen to family stories told by the old ones still living, including her grandmother Elionor, her great-half-aunt Isabel Metzger Gallegos (Elionor's half-sister), her daughter Isabel, and a distant cousin, Eduardo Korte. She took more notes. She, in turn, became the family's storyteller. She wrote many of those as complete stories, including for college classes.

In October 1933, she wrote—which was published in the *New Mexico Historical Review*—an extensive piece: <u>Las Vegas before 1850.</u> An article and some of her poetry were also published in the *New Mexico Magazine*.

Mama, born in 1909, was my bridge spanning back into the 1800s and early 1900s. She enabled me to cross over to the past. Now my life—which began at the end of 1940—spans forward into yet another century. It was because of her lifelong fascination with her family histories, and her love for the people in her stories repeatedly told to me, that loaned me a personal acquaintance with them.

Soon after my 1996 trip to Germany, I wrote a booklet compilation of family history, *The Story of Andreas and Elionor*.

In this chapter, I'm including a portion of that booklet describing our visit to Germany. Other portions of it and my mother's *In Search of Springs,* and her written family history, are in subsequent chapters of this book.

My journey of a few thousand miles began with copies of those three old German documents inherited by Daniel Laumbach and his wife, Emma. They recorded his grandparents' births and marriage. They were also the records of Emma's family. Emma's mother, Anna Laumbach, married Peter Claus Henkens in Clinton, Iowa.

The history in those documents reaches back in time more than 200 years. I never dreamed I'd someday walk the cobblestones walked upon by my great-grandfather, his parents and his grandparents, even generations before them, but I now have.

Come with Me to Haddeby by the Schlei

By lucky providence, my son David then resided and worked in Bremen, Germany, a day's drivable distance to all the places named in those documents—places I had doubted still existed. What a once-in-a-lifetime opportunity to visit now, before his employment transferred him to England or elsewhere in the next year or so. We acquired our passports and burned our bridges (*we thought*) with nonrefundable flight tickets. When Mama suddenly became ill and died, those bridges were inconsequential. However, the two events—my mother's death and this scheduled trip—seemed indelibly inked together. The cost of the flight ticket for my grandson, Brandon, who would begin high school in the fall as an honors student, was a gift from his Uncle David. I could not disappoint him by postponing it.

In early July 1996, we—husband Dan, 14-year-old Brandon, and I—traveled to northern Germany. We went, we saw and I was thrilled to find that those places, every one of them, still exist. For Brandon and Dan, it was just a fine adventure.

My journey to Schleswig began with the basic information in those three early German documents dated 1856.

About 50 years after they were made, the documents passed from their son, Andreas 2nd to his wife, Elionor, then to their son, Daniel and his wife, Emma. Apparently there was no document for Andreas 2nd, who was also German-born and grown. Based on family stories, we believe that was because Andreas and Anna had made an orderly and sanctioned departure from Germany, but their son did not. However, we found no ship manifest for Andreas and Anna and most of their children, but researcher Butch Sanders found one for the undocumented son Andreas.

At the beginning of my 1996 journey east across the Atlantic, 140 years after that of Andreas and Anna and their children and their young adult son Andreas coming west, I was uncertain where to begin my ancestral search. All I really knew was that Lauenbachs had come from a northern part of Germany. Mama and her brother Joyce said they had come from the area around Kiel Bay. Long ago, family might have chosen Kiel as a referenced point of departure because it was a well-known German seaport and easy to find on a map. But Kiel is in Holstein; our ancestors came from nearby Schleswig.

I had a copy of a section of an old map sent to me in the 1970s by a cousin newly awakened to the joys of sleuthing family history. I think Louise Laumbach Luft (daughter of George and Margaret Laumbach, sister of Karl) said it was a pre-World War II map; I had hoped it was much older than that. The map, depicting a small square of Germany, looked like pieces of a jigsaw puzzle. I assumed those many pieces were German provinces or states. Uncertain then, as I still am, how old that map was, I imagined each marked section was a pre-Bismarck free sovereign state or principality. Of course, they might have been states within a more modern Germany, but they seemed small. (I should not use the United States for size comparison.)

I knew it was not yet a united country named Germany when Andreas and Anna lived there. Otto von Bismarck did not unite all the sovereign states into one country until 1871.

What did the notation "nobility, no stamp necessary" written in 1856 on all three documents mean? The transcriber probably copied forward that notation on the three original entries of 1802, 1811 and 1832, but it may have still been applicable in 1856. On that subject, our family now knows no more than it ever did.

Peter Joseph, the grandfather of Louise, Karl, Pete and many others, and my grandfather, Daniel, were brothers. That map had interested Louise because on it she had located Jagel and Geltorf; they appeared to be small areas rather than towns. There I also found the area of Gross ("Groß") Rheide. On it and other maps I since found, Jagel, Geltorf and Gross Rheide are loosely across from each other, not far below the city of Schleswig. Before my trip, the documents and that map from Louise were all I had. Before we left on our trip, I tried to study modern maps of Germany, but I had none detailed enough to show those small places. Also, on most of the maps I had, inexplicably the topmost portion of Germany was cut off—that left arm reaching up to touch Denmark—which was most important to me. Oh well; I expected to find better maps when I reached Germany. I took a list of places—Schleswig and Kiel, which I knew I could find—plus the small places named in the documents that I did not expect to find. After all, since 1856 much had happened, including two obliterating world wars to change the face of Europe.

The Journey Begins

Early Monday morning, July 8, 1996, Dan, Brandon and I flew from Albuquerque to Atlanta, Georgia, our chosen place of U.S. departure despite the impending World Olympics soon to be held there. My son, Devin, met us at the airport. We traveled with him by car from Atlanta, Georgia to Anniston, Alabama to visit his worksite, American Ikarus. We then drove 30 miles further to view his home in a gorgeous wooded setting on the edge of a lake near Mumford, Alabama. There we ate a rushed bite and returned to the Atlanta airport—all within six hours. Then Dan, Brandon and I flew all night via Delta to Frankfurt, Germany.

Mid-morning Tuesday, David, arriving from a business trip in England, met us at the Frankfurt airport. There we were surprised to see armed guards walking in pairs carrying machine guns in-hand. After passing through customs together, we four took a fast-moving train to Bremen. We traveled through thick woods, brilliant green meadows, large cities and picture-perfect towns. From Frankfurt, we went through the industrial city of Fulda where autos are produced, the university town of Gottingen, the large city of Hanover, to Bremen. We arrived late Tuesday afternoon, walked all over the heart of the fairy-tale city, and enjoyed our first authentic German meal.

I wanted to do as much as possible in what little time we had in Germany. We had just six days, most of which David prophesied would be affected by jetlag. We surprised ourselves. We weren't jetlagged. We slept when we were supposed to sleep and were mostly awake and alert during the daytime. Besides having to adjust to the eight-hour time difference, during that time of year, German daytime hours are long and darkness is brief. It stayed light until nearly 11:00 p.m. and the sky lightened about 5:00 a.m. Likewise, our days' activities were long, our sleeping hours brief. Because of David's large, sun-captivating windows, Brandon chose to sleep in what had been designed as a broom closet. It was confining for the long, lean Brandon, and his feet stuck out of the doorway, but he liked it in there. David had adapted the broom closet to a small walk-in library, lined with shelves filled with books. Brandon read himself to sleep each night—what little night there was.

On Wednesday, we wandered on foot seeing the awesome sights of Bremen, the site of many things, including the "Musicians of Bremen" tale by the Brothers Grimm. The musicians—a stacked up donkey, dog, cat and rooster—are depicted in many art forms all over the city, including in small souvenir versions in most shops. In some of those places we were amazed to also see souvenir Roswell New Mexico aliens!

Bremen, like all of the Germany we saw, was an immaculate and wonderful place. I felt as if I had stepped into a fairy tale, not by the Brothers Grimm but by Hans Christian Andersen. Since the purpose of this chapter is to record my visit to Germany and pursuit of family history, I will say little of Bremen itself except that I can understand why, but for the high cost, David was pleased to live there.

Visiting there, one can't help being apprehensive of Germans in their natural habitat after being repeatedly told of their mass cruelty or indifference under Hitler. I could not understand how the awful things in Germany, a civilized "first-world" country, and the land of my gentle ancestors, could have happened there little more than 50 years ago. After visiting Germany, even more I cannot. Witnesses, many then youthful, still live there. What terrible Nazi war-time experiences did they witness or did parents tell their children and grandchildren? That surely impacted many of its current residents.

To their credit, modern Germans do not try to bury that part of their history under their cobblestones. They are open and frank. The ugliness of concentration camps is preserved for public viewing. They direct visitors to them in their guidebooks. David said one is near Bremen and we could visit if we wished. (We did not wish.) British soldiers were the first to liberate that camp and forced the Bremen people to view it. So close by, residents must have known what was happening there. How could the German people, as well as millions of Jewish and Christian victims, allow such a thing to happen? Weren't the Nazis only a small portion of the populace?

While we were there in early July, the weather was cool. We wore light jackets, the sky was overcast, and, unlike in Alabama, we did not feel humidity. We found it a comfortable climate. David said it rarely freezes or gets too hot in Bremen.

No water fountains, no glasses of water with meals, no iced tea or other iced beverages. You are expected to drink beer. When in Germany, do as the Germans do. Drink beer.

Writers are told to never make generalized statements, but I did generalize because I thought that completed the picture of a first-time visitor to Germany. My impressions and those brief generalities of Germans and Germany are not included in this chapter but are available upon request.

Sashay to Schleswig

"Schleswig" refers to southern Schleswig in Germany. Northern Schleswig is in Denmark. Schleswig-Holstein—that is, southern Schleswig and Holstein combined into one state—includes Lauenburg and what had been the independent city of Lubeck.

The night before we headed for the city of Schleswig, I studied David's map booklets of Germany. One of those was particularly helpful. Each page was a small close-up section or a detailed city map. On his maps and on one we picked up the next day when we bought gas near Schleswig, we located every one of the place names on our documents.

Early Thursday morning, in David's car, we headed north via the Autobahn. David navigated; Dan drove. From the back seat, I saw the speedometer needle mostly on 120 or 140 km, but autos passed us with ease. I believe Dan, an experienced and still wishful race car driver, enjoyed himself except for being dependent upon David to keep him out of trouble. Knowing no German, he had to rely on David for directions, to read maps and road signs and know traffic laws.

Before arriving in Germany, I had never seen so much or such a vivid green—except when we had briefly visited Alabama. There, like here, unless it is carefully and regularly cultivated, vegetation crowds in upon you. We often saw thick woods a few feet from the roadway. It reminded me of what a homesick Fritz had said days earlier in Anniston, Alabama. Fritz, a coworker of Devin's there, and before that, of mine and Devin's near Roswell, said, "Soon you OD [*over-dose*] on green. It reaches out and touches you, makes you claustrophobic. The other day, they cleared an area behind us and we discovered a house and a neighbor we never knew we had! I long for the wide open spaces of New Mexico where you can see!"

Being from arid southern New Mexico, only visiting Alabama and now Germany, I delighted in the green, the beauty and visual perfection. My only complaint: We went too fast. I had too little time and so much I wanted to see. I was given only one day to travel to and visit all those important places, which had been my sole reason for visiting Germany.

Leaving Bremen, we got on Autobahn 1 to Hamburg. At Hamburg, a huge port city, we passed over a bridge close to majestic tall ships in the harbor, went through the Elbe Tunnel under the Elbe River, and took Autobahn 7, bypassing Lubeck, heading for Schleswig. Our picturesque journey took us past verdant meadows where spoilt Holstein and Jersey milk cows grazed. You'd expect to see cows in Holstein that lent its name to a breed of cattle, and we did. In Germany, a few cows, golden brown or black and white, stood out against the brilliant green meadows, whereas herds of beige cattle disappear on the beige prairies of New Mexico. In Germany, all colors are bright and beautiful, even on the cows.

We passed rivers and lakes, thick woods and forests, meadows sprinkled with wild flowers, quaint villages of gingerbread houses with peaked, sometimes thatched hip roofs, artful gardens and yards with multicolored splashes of geraniums and other bright flowers.

Near a road marker directing drivers to Bustorf, we turned off 7 to 77 onto a fast moving two-lane paved road to Jagel. *(Ja is pronounced Yah in German. We later heard someone say the name Jagel; it rhymes with "toggle.")* My first thrill was seeing Jagel announced on a sign. From what I could see as we flew past, Jagel is a small village, a few blocks long mostly lining the roadway, with a few houses and businesses. Like all I saw in the Deutschland, there everything was perfect. Every inch could be proudly depicted on a postcard for the world to see. Because the roadway had no shoulder and traffic was fast, it was difficult or impossible to slow down, pull over, and stop without risking a collision. I begged to stop, was frustrated when we did not, but grateful for the opportunity to at least pass it by. As we did, David leaned out the window and snapped pictures for me from the moving car.[i]

(Jagel: Residence of Anna's Detlef Koos family, in 1811 and 1832, AND residence of two 1832 marriage witnesses, AND residence of Andreas prior to his marriage, AND his and Anna's residence during their lives together in Germany, AND where their son Andreas and his siblings were born, AND except probably for his hitch in the local military, that was where Andreas 2nd lived until he went to America.)

Jagel was an important place in our family's history, but regrettably I had no opportunity to walk its streets.

From Jagel, we crossed 77 to Schleswig. Within Schleswig, situated on and around the Schlei, we traveled over city streets towards the wharf in search of St. Johanniskloster vor Schleswig, which David had easily found on a city map. We drove along the wharf-side road searching for a place to park. The spaces in the two or three parking areas were filled with small autos and compact motor homes. The sparkling Schlei—reflecting the mighty green-spiraled cathedral of St. Peter across the way, and filled with rowboats, sailboats, motorized boats, steamers and seabirds—was spectacular. At last, we found a place to park.

A map shows the Baltic Sea feeds the Schlei, which begins at the city of Kappeln. It is a long, downward reaching arm of water, like a wide river, until it becomes like an inland sea, roughly shaped like a butterfly, around which the city of Schleswig grew.

We walked the short distance from the Schlei-side to the idyllic ancient Viking fishing village of Schleswig-Holm.[ii] It was a snug inner community of tightly spaced homes encircling a small private church and churchyard (*kirche* and *kirchegarden*) of tiny cultivated family burial plots.

(St. Johannis Cloister: Where Andreas' and Anna's 1802, 1811 and 1832 major life events were recorded, and, per their request, where all three documents were made on March 31, 1856.)

A short walk beyond Der Holm stood the centuries-old large stone, thick-walled St. Johannis Cloister (Skt. Johannes Klosteret).[iii] Being able to actually see it was my next thrill. I had imagined St. Johannis no longer existed or would be so small and insignificant or isolated that we could not find it. In fact, it is large and a Schleswig landmark. On the church was a plaque with a German inscription. David translated it. He said this was a cloister for women, where families sent their unmarried noblewomen to reside. David said St. Johannis was Lutheran, like all northern Germany cathedrals and churches. The Christian faith in the northern half of Germany changed from Catholic to Lutheran in the mid-1500s. The "faith of our fathers," like Andreas, was Lutheran and remained Lutheran among those who stayed within German settlements in America.

We Americans, citizens of a relatively young country, tend to forget Europe's antiquity. High up on the wall of the cloister church itself were the dates 1639 and 1735.
It was noontime and the church, other stone buildings and the inner courtyard seemed nearly deserted.

We noticed a posted bulletin welcoming visitors to Bible study classes and a museum up a flight of stone steps. A woman stood in the open doorway beckoning us. Inside, in a place of honor in the room, was a wooden replica of the first Johannes Gutenberg printing press. A sign reminded me that mass-produced duplication of the printed word was born in Germany about 1450. Before Gutenberg, and long after his invention of movable type, writings were still meticulously copied by learned men in cloisters such as this, writings like the beautifully handwritten documents copied here in 1856 that brought us across the ocean in 1996.

David had taken a short walk, so we had to rely upon the woman's broken English. We learned she was a Bible teacher, new to the job, and she knew almost nothing about the place. I said I had come seeking information about old birth and marriage records that had been kept here. She suggested we knock on a certain apartment door across the inner courtyard and speak to "an old lady, a nun" who lived there many years, who best knew the cloister's history. We said we did not want to intrude. We were urged to do it.

Through the woman's broken English, the purpose of her urgency was clear. The old lady would happily be intruded upon to provide us information in exchange for generous donations for premises restoration, which was on their agenda in the near future.

The day had begun early. Our repast of Jacobs' coffee and butter-cake at David's Bremen apartment was most satisfying but long ago. It was past noon, we were starved, and we still had miles to go and important places to see before we slept. Regrettably, David had promised Brandon a castle on this already overloaded, very important day—probably my one and only lifetime opportunity to visit the places of my family's origin.

We entered no building at the cloister except that room at the top of the steps to talk to the teacher. Leaving there, we stopped at a café and sat at one of the outdoor tables covered with a heavy oilcloth. David helped us make selections from the menu and give it to the waiter, who spoke no English.

After eating, we wandered to a tiny one-room shop a block or so from St. Johannis, where souvenirs and postcards were sold. There was little specifically on St. Johannis, but I chose a few brochures and postcards. With David's help, I asked the proprietor if the family names from our documents seemed familiar. I showed him a photocopy of a German document, pointing to the handwritten names of Andreas Detlef Lauenbach and Anna Koos. He noted St. Johannis written at the top and the date, and nodded, "*Ja.*" He seemed interested and tried to be helpful, but he was not familiar with the name Laumbach or Lauenbach. At David's suggestion, he got out a phone book with listings of the Schleswig area. Together, he and David searched for family names, including Koos, but found none. We thanked the man and departed with our few purchases.

We returned to our car and drove down winding streets in search of the castle. David encouraged me to visit it, saying, "All of your family's places were in this vicinity. They were probably invited to Schloss Gottorf, the nearest castle. Nobles hung at the castles. Who knows, some of them may still hang there. Paintings, that is." This was said with wry amusement. His teasing words were not what steered me briefly away from my family-seeking mission. I, too, had promised Brandon a castle; who knew if he'd ever see another.

Schloss Gottorf was easy to find. It sat on and nearly filled a small island in the Burgsee, a dam-made lake from the Schlei that provided the castle a natural moat. I was disappointed with it and, I think, Brandon was, too. Although it was large, it was less ornate than many buildings I saw from a distance and in books about Germany. The part open to the public was bare except for displays of centuries-old religious art. Those only interested me because they closely resembled the priceless collection of *santos*—*retablos* and *bultos*—owned by my mother's cousin, Tony Sanchez, in northern New Mexico.

When we arrived at the Schloss, it was nearly closing time. In German, David asked a curator to let us view the private quarters. That curator conferred with another curator, a woman, who looked us over and reluctantly agreed, leading us across an open auditorium-size room. With much ado and with jangling keys, she unlocked double doors and threw them open for us. We stepped inside. These cozier rooms were furnished with china, silver, still-life art, scenes and portraits hanging on the walls, and fine pieces of furniture. She walked quickly through the rooms, expecting us to follow at her pace, so it was a fast tour. As we passed portraits of nobles, my son with his droll humor asked, "See any family resemblances?"

None of us was inclined towards staying more than an hour at the Schloss.

(Bustorf: Location of the church of Haddeby and, therefore, also the Haddebyer clergyman in 1802, 1811, and 1832. By finding Bustorf we would locate Haddebyer and Haddeby.)

We backtracked through and saw some additional parts of Schleswig and drove around the Schlei to the other side—through what I thought was an extension of Schleswig but maps show to be Friedrichsberg—in search of the little church of Haddeby. It was easy to pinpoint on the Schleswig city map, after we found Haddebyer Noor, dam-made from the Schlei, a much larger lake than the Burgsee. On it was a small area marked Haddeby, and even "St. Andreas kirche zu Haddeby," which had to be OUR church!

(Church of Haddeby: The Lutheran church where Andreas Detlef Lauenbach and Anna Koos had each been baptized in 1802 and 1811, and where they were married in 1832. A clergyman from Haddebyer, not necessarily the same man, officiated at all three events that spanned 30 years.)

We found and I saw the actual church in which both Andreas and Anna Lauenbach had been christened at birth, and married. Until we visited it, I did not know the church of Haddeby[iv] was named St. Andreas. Were our two Andreas men named for that patron saint, or were they named for this church that played an important role in their lives?

The building was locked, and there was no one around. We only viewed it from outside. The small stone Haddeby church seemed ancient. However, where we stood in the well-tended graveyard surrounding it, the markers reflected modern times and burials. I had noticed the same in the tiny Holm *kirchegarden:* markers for graves of only modern-day people. How odd. A possible explanation was that in our limited time without guides, we stood in newer portions of those cemeteries and did not see older sections. We spent little time studying the markers but saw no familiar names. I wanted to know where the older burials were, but no one was available to question and we had to push on.

Off we went. We turned onto 76 and eventually turned off of it, taking small lanes and roads leading to Selk. We passed through Selk in search of Geltorf. We made several backtracks, nearly gave up, but at last we found it.

(Geltorf: Place of residence in 1802, 1811 and 1832 of Christian Rudolph Lauenbach and family AND residence of two 1802 witnesses at Andreas' baptism.)

Geltorf [v] was a small rural village, a lane or two of stone houses—some quite large, some with thatched hip roofs—and a few commercial buildings. There we did stop and get out of the car for a few minutes.

We watched a woman, with a white bib-apron over her dress, step out her door and walk purposefully past us, without greeting, to her neighbor's yard. Her neighbor was outside. The two women talked together, a picture of domesticity. That scene reflected life here nearly 200 years ago: friendly neighbors chatting. We watched them a while. I wanted to question them but knew language would be an impossible barrier, at least for me, a one-tongue American. Besides, 1802, 1811 and 1832 was a long way back for recollection, and these reserved Germans likely were not interested in queries from a nosey tourist. I let the questionable opportunity pass.

We had parked near an illustrated map, displayed under glass, of Geltorf, and took a photo of it. Within a few yards was a phone booth that seemed totally out of place. It spoiled the ambiance but was handy for searching its directory for family names. We found none. I was tempted to tear out the one Geltorf page and take it with me as a souvenir. Voicing my inner temptation, David dryly suggested I practice restraint instead of vandalism. For the record (in case my humor missed its mark), I have no directory page of Geltorf. And, for the record, I regret it.

In one rushed day, we made a 200-year journey. Although they were nearby, the only places named on the three documents we did not visit were Gross Rheide and the parish of Huttener. We had just run out of day.

(Gross Rheide: Original residence of Catharina Margaretha Busch Lauenbach. Parish of Huttener: Residence of an 1802 baptismal witness.)

From Geltorf, we headed back to Bremen. Our already full day was not yet over. Even on the high speed Autobahn, Bremen was hours away. About halfway there, the only hitch to our otherwise perfect day began. It became a big hitch in our get-along.

The Autobahn was four and sometimes six lanes wide, with no shoulder on either side. The day was getting late and traffic, coming and going, was bumper to bumper. Suddenly, the infamous high speed of the Autobahn was not possible. Soon, no speed was possible. All traffic came to a complete halt. We and hundreds of others in compact cars and motor homes and transport trucks sat at a standstill smelling each other's exhausts. It was stifling, and we had to keep our windows down. For the first and only time since our arrival in Germany, I was aware of pollution.

With nothing else to do, the delay provided ample time to observe our surroundings. Unfortunately, our surroundings on all sides were stopped vehicles. According to their printed numbers, logos and languages, the large transport trucks, like foreign ships in harbors, were from many countries. One does not see that on highways of America, especially inland New Mexico, except on very rare occasions, vehicles from Canada or Mexico. A huge semi had something printed on it that made me giggle. I had lived through the Cold War when bomb-shelters were common design options with construction of American homes and schools. I, too, well remember the chilling threat of Russian's leader, Khrushchev: "Someday we will bury your children." We were visiting (West) Germany in 1996, just a few years after the Berlin Wall came down; world brotherhood was still tenuous. (And still is.) On the truck, my giggle-factor was printed in English, in large letters: "FROM RUSSIA WITH LOVE." I had thought Russians had no sense of humor and lacked a love-thy-neighbor attitude. They had adopted the title of a James Bond movie.

After a frustrating wait, traffic slowly began to move and then picked up speed. It soon slowed to a halt again. We had another frustrating wait. Dan and David's patience was admirable. Late daylight turned to dusk hours past what would have been our sundown in New Mexico.

At last we arrived in Bremen, drove to David's apartment building, into his basement garage, parked his small car in its tight electronic space and, with the touch of a button, watched it lift to its upper berth. We wearily climbed his marble stairs. Too late and too weary to go out to eat, we ordered pizza that was soon delivered, along with a complimentary bottle of wine, by what seemed to be a couple of Russian gypsies determined to please. "Nice chaps but not very good business people," David commented. German pizza is different from American; I liked it. It had no red sauce but was blanketed with melted cheese. Ours were paprika pizzas. David said in Germany paprika means peppers; those were sweet peppers, not the *chile* kind we are accustomed to in New Mexico.

The meal was a relaxing comedown to a very long, exciting, eventful day. I hoped it was as much of an adventure for everyone else. For me it was an exceptional day, a once-in-a-life-time dream come true.

While we enjoyed our pizza and wine, David told Brandon what he really needed was a trip to Berlin, which he thought we should do the next day, Friday—short hours away. Dan and I looked at each other and privately wished David would not put ideas in Brandon's receptive head. Berlin did not beckon Dan or me. A weary Dan, who had spent a very long day driving a considerable distance at high speed and then a long time at no speed in a foreign-language country, truly lacked enthusiasm, especially knowing he would again be the designated driver. Berlin was also even further than Schleswig. We effectively discouraged the trip.

The next evening, even David was glad we did not go. On his television, we saw we had missed participating in the great "Berlin Love In." That day, Berlin was a sea of humanity. It was filled, head-to-head and body-to-body, with tens of thousands of uninhibited hippy-types, many nude, French kissing and more. Not the thing we staid old-foggy Americans considered interesting. Can you imagine the traffic jams? We might have been stuck in Berlin for days. We thought it was hilarious, but only because we had not experienced it.

Instead of joining the wild Berlin Love-In, we spent a pleasant, leisure Friday roaming sedate Middle-Ages Bremen and taking a ferryboat down the Wesser.

———————————

[i] Jagel

ii Holm by the Schlei

iii St. Johannis Cloister (SKT Johannes Kloster)

iv Church of Haddeby

ᵛ Geltorf

SECTION II: LAUMBACHS IN GERMANY

Chapter 5: More History
by Jan Girand

Some of this chapter is also an excerpt from the booklet I wrote in 1996 following our trip to Germany.

In 1990, after 14 years of intensive research, work and a trip to Germany, Mary Lou Stoltenburg Orr completed, and the National Genealogical Publishers published, *From the Probstei of Germany to the Prairies of America*, a genealogical study of Antje and Hans Heinrich Stoltenburg and their descendants. Antje and Hans were Mary Lou's forebears from Holstein, who later settled in Pleasant Valley, Nebraska. One of her family lines joined my mother's. Mary Lou's great-grandmother Margaretha Henkens was Peter Henkens' sister.

Mary Lou Orr wrote in a letter to my mother on October 16, 1978: "Once upon a time a long time ago, about 200 years to be more exact, a baby boy was born in Germany, near the Danish border. His name was Peter Henkens and when he grew to manhood and married, he had a son named Claus Henkens, born in 1807. Claus Henkens married Catharina Margaretha Thiessen. Some of their children were Peter [*Verna's line*], Thiebka, Christina, Margretha [*Mary Lou's line*], and … Claus and John …" Mary Lou's great-grandmother Margretha Henkens married "Thomas (Tona) Thomsen in Germany in 1858. They came to America in 1881. Her father and some brothers and sisters came earlier. … [*They settled in*] Dodge County, Nebraska." Some of Mary Lou's letters to my mother give this additional Henkens lineage information.

When Mary Lou was researching and writing her huge book, she reached my mom, Verna Sparks, seeking Henkens genealogy and history.

Orr's forebears, Antje and Hans Stoltenburg, came to America in 1870 from the Probstei in Holstein via the steamer Saxony out of the Hamburg Port to New York. Published in her book is a letter (with translation), written by Hans when he still lived in Germany. I found it poignant, and it fits our family's German history in area and era.

"In the year 1845 there was a failed harvest of potatoes in Holstein and other regions. There were soon no usable potatoes at all suitable to eat. They all had bruises, spots, marks, and blue spots and they stank. But they were usable for feed for hogs and cattle. They ate them up and were not harmed by them." In another letter, written in 1847, Hans wrote: "In the year 1847 there were expensive times. A barrel of wheat cost 36 thalers and a barrel of rye 30 thalers and so on. Everything came very dear. In this year many people had to learn what they did not know before and got into a great deal of trouble." His letters described some of the many troubles the Laumbachs and others probably shared in Schleswig and Holstein, propelling them to America. There were then enormous German exoduses.

Some of our Laumbach and Henkens families, including my grandmother Emma Henkens before she came to New Mexico Territory in January 1902, had settled in Pleasant Valley, Nebraska, like Mary Lou's predecessors.

~

In the fifteenth century, in the independent duchies of Schleswig and Holstein under the King of Denmark, the population of Schleswig was a mixture of Danes and Germans; Holstein was predominately German. Both duchies were bound to Germany by trade and commerce, and people mostly spoke German or a German dialect.

When Napoleon occupied western Germany, the two duchies were still nominally independent but ruled by the Danish king. During the Industrial Revolution, 1810-1870, both duchies had more in common with Germany than with Denmark. Population became more concentrated in the cities. After Waterloo in 1815, the German Confederation consisted of 39 states. The confederation was loose politically; most states were still independent monarchies.

In 1848 were minor rebellions all over Europe. Denmark unsuccessfully tried to incorporate Schleswig and Holstein. Later, the two were again under control of the Danish crown but kept their nominal independence. The German Confederation was reestablished in 1850, again including Holstein but not Schleswig. From 1849 through 1864, Schleswig and Holstein remained separate duchies. It was in that time period, in 1856, that our Lauenbach family left.

Our family came from southern Schleswig. In the nineteenth century and earlier, the duchy of Schleswig extended further north. Part of it is still in Denmark today.

When exploring an area for his roots, one would typically search for his family name or anything resembling it: names of towns, valleys, rivers, streets, buildings, parks, pubs, and in local directories. Since ours had been a whirlwind tour of only one day on my visit to Germany, I had limited opportunity to do that.

I was interested in the root or literal meaning of the name Lauenbach and wondered if it might have derived from a common word in Germany. I learned "bach" means spring or stream and "lau" means tepid or lukewarm. In Germany, like elsewhere, spellings and pronunciations of words and names varied depending upon the local dialect, and could be arbitrarily changed.

Searching maps and brochures of Austria and Germany, we found Laufenbach, Lautenbach, Lauterbach, Leombach, Laimbach and Lambach. In Schleswig-Holstein, I found Lauenburg, which seemed closest to the original spelling of the family's root name.

I bought a postcard with an illustrated map of Schleswig-Holstein with the name Lauenburg and an image of a turreted castle on it.

Before and after 1880, the younger Andreas and other New Mexico Laumbachs told U.S. census takers that the senior Andreas was born in Denmark or in Germany. Whoever was at home at Buena Vista on June 15, 1880 when the federal enumerator knocked said Andreas' father was born in Wurttemberg. At any rate, that was what the enumerator recorded. Because of its distance from Schleswig-Holstein, we had assumed that notation was an error. However, with an Internet search engine, Pete Laumbach found "Lauenbach, a farm" in Baden-Wurttemberg. If Lauenbachs had originated from there, it must have been generations before our known family history. It remains an unexplained mystery why Wurttemberg had once been listed as Andreas' place of origin. It is remotely possible the enumerator was familiar with Wurttemberg having a place called the "Lauenbach farm" and independently noted that name on the census that day.

More mysteries are discovered when researching genealogy than are solved. A researcher should consider data from multiple sources, not just one.

My children's last name Ikenberry—also German—literally means oak forest. Their paternal grandfather's people were known as high German, darker complexioned (not Scandinavian), from southern Germany, at a higher elevation, thus "high" German. Their name was originally Ikenburg or Eichenburg. Hixenbaugh (*HIX-en-bah*), also German, was their paternal grandmother's maiden name. Same suffix pronunciation as ours, but different spelling. Comparing those and ours is an interesting study of German names.

I wanted to know what it was like to live in the area of Schleswig during the first half of the eighteen hundreds—from 1800 until early 1856. I wanted a credible explanation, which eluded me, for the "nobility" notation on all three earlier referenced documents. Also, why did Andreas and Anna, at their age, depart this lovely, long-established place where they, at least locally, still enjoyed a certain social standing, to venture with their children across the forbidding Atlantic to an unknown and recently settled foreign place? Were they, perhaps, caught between two German classes, belonging to neither?

By that time, their nobility, whatever it might have been, probably had no meaning or value. Perhaps they believed future taxes or changing politics would remove their remaining assets, maybe even their lives, or their sons' lives. Those were drastic, war-torn times requiring drastic, evasive action.

In 1996, I found the Atlantic forbidding just flying over it for eight or nine hours. I was then just two years older than Andreas when he and Anna and their children crossed the cold Atlantic by slow ship in 1856. Unlike mine, theirs was a difficult and frightful crossing with an unknown future. Like all immigrants, they were brave.

We know of no family member who preceded them to America, but they must have had at least good friends who beckoned them, whose word they trusted, who had previously made that journey and successfully settled in America—a more tranquil place than the one they were leaving. Those people must have convinced them that the traumatic upheaval to their lives would eventually be worthwhile, if not for themselves, then for their children.

I studied materials I purchased in the Schleswig area, but much of it was written in German, which might as well have been Greek. From the small portion that had translation, I read: "Schleswig, metropolis of the Viking age, was known by the Scandinavian name Haithabu. One thousand years ago, the Vikings built the small settlement, favorably located for traffic in the Schlei, into the most significant trading center in Northern Europe. The blossoming town was in demand…inhabitants of Haithabu resisted numerous conquerors until the town was finally razed to the ground by Slav invasions in 1066. The survivors left the ruins of Haithabu…built a new settlement on the other bank of the Schlei, where the old town of Schleswig stands today…Schleswig, first mentioned in 804 AD…is one of the oldest towns in Northern Europe…once a significant trading center, then a cathedral town and a blossoming seat of the court until 1713. From 1868 to 1945, the Prussian province of Schleswig-Holstein was governed from Schleswig."

The only information I found in English leaped over that era of history I most wanted to know.

After I returned home, I poured over books from my shelves trying to learn more German history. I especially sought anything that included the area of southern Schleswig.

~~

From Pete Laumbach's extended genealogy research, we learned Christian Rudolph Lauenbach had three children—Wiebke, Peter and Margaretha Lauenbach—from a prior marriage to Anna Margaretha Ehlert of Geltorf. From Pete we learned that Christian's first wife died. With his second wife, Catharina Margaretha Busch of Geltorf, he had four children: Anna, Jurgen, Henrich and our elder Andreas Detlef Lauenbach (born in Geltorf in 1802).

The elder Andreas and Anna probably sold their property, animals and other non-portable possessions to friends and kinfolk. On March 31, 1856, they went to St. Johannis Cloister to have documents made to carry with them. Then they and their children traveled to a port city, probably Hamburg, and purchased passage on a steam ship for America, taking with them only what possessions they could carry.

I suspect each passenger, including the smallest child, age four, had to carry on board ship his own sleeping gear and eating utensils. At any rate, Aunties had at least one plate and cup brought from

Germany. They said the plate they gave me had been carried from Germany by my grandmother's mother, Anna, who was then only eight. They said a cup they gave me had also come from Germany.

Their son Andreas left via the Hamburg port in mid-July 1856, and landed at Castle Garden, New York. He probably took few possessions with him.

My mother's eldest brother, Joyce Laumbach, believed their grandfather, Andreas 2nd, and Andreas' friend Fritz Eggert, had found a sympathetic ship's captain who accepted them on board without legal documentation. The captain was short of crew and hid them until they were out to sea, and let them work for their passage to America.

A year or two ago, Butch Sanders found a ship's manifest with the younger Andreas on board. Andreas was listed when the ship left the Hamburg harbor. (*See Chapter 2 end note.*) He was not hiding. Sanders searched the four-page list of passengers but did not find any other Laumbach or Lauenbach. He also found no Frederick "Fritz" Eggert.

We, and Eggert's family, cannot prove exactly when Fritz came to America. Because of lingering family stories, Fritz may have been an unlisted stowaway on that ship, and the two friends did come to the USA together. We know the two were friends and connected for a while. There is more about Fritz in subsequent chapters, including one written by his descendant, Trent Shue.

SECTION II: LAUMBACHS IN GERMANY

Chapter 6: Trip to Jagel
by Pete Laumbach

In June and July of 2005, my wife, Ophelia, and I made a trip to Europe. Our primary purpose was to visit our son, Rudy, and his family who were living in Ansbach, Germany, which is about 30 minutes southwest of Nuremburg. Rudy had returned to Ansbach in March after a year in Iraq with the Apache Gunship Battalion attached to the 1st Infantry Division. Another objective on this trip was to see the area from which the Laumbachs immigrated to the United States in the 1850s.

On Monday, June 27, Ophie and I left Ansbach early in the morning and traveled by train to Kiel. The trip took us through Wurzburg, Frankfurt, a train change in Hamburg and on to Kiel, which is a seaport on the Baltic Sea and the seat of government for the state of Holstein. The city was an important naval base during WWII, so it was heavily bombed and almost completely destroyed. The present city was rebuilt with less emphasis on restoration than in most German cities, and the result is that the city centrum is mostly modern. Our hotel was in the Neumühlen District across the Kieler Förde estuary from the centrum. It was a university and residential area and very pleasant. We found there was a dock about half a block from the hotel where we could catch a water taxi that would take us to the city centrum in about 20 minutes.

The villages our family came from are near the town of Schleswig, situated at the end of the Schlei Estuary, which opens to the Baltic. Schleswig has a population of about 25,000. It's very old, and the old Viking port of Haddeby, where the church that was used by our family is located, dates back at least to 802 AD.

On Tuesday, Ophie and I took the train from Kiel to Schleswig, about an hour's ride. From the Schleswig train station we took a bus to Jagel, which is about six kilometers south. Jagel, the birthplace of my great-grandfather, Andreas Detlef Laumbach, who was the father of Margarita, Estefanita, Peter Joseph, Daniel, Henry, and all the Aunties, is a small town, comparable in population, I would say, to Wagon Mound. Although there are a few older houses of the traditional German farmhouse type, with the residence and barn in a single structure, most of the houses are modern. It is obvious from the surrounding country that Jagel was a farming village, now a bedroom community for military and civilian personnel who work at the German Air Force base that bounds the town on the north. When we were asking for information at the train station in Kiel, we said we wanted to know the best way to get to Jagel, and the woman at the information desk asked why we would want to go to Jagel.

A few years ago, Uncle Ike had given me copies of documents, which were hand transcripts of the birth and baptismal records and the marriage record of Andreas Detlef Lauenbach* and Anna Koos, the parents of Andreas Detlef Laumbach* of Buena Vista, New Mexico. (*These will be referred to as Andreas Detlef I and Andreas Detlef II.) Apparently, the spelling of our surname changed when the family entered the United States. This was not uncommon—immigration officers recording foreign names spelled what they heard, and immigrants, who feared angering anyone who could hinder their entry to the country, were not inclined to argue about such details. The hand transcript documents were made in 1856, at a monastery [*cloister*[i]] named St. Johannis Cloister, attributed to the Haddeby Pastor. Along with the transcriptions from Ike were copies of the translations to English, made by Mrs. Margaret Katz, wife of a German Jewish merchant in Las Vegas, New Mexico. These translations were very helpful. However, I found one point on which I believed she was mistaken. She had taken the German cursive "s" for "h," which is understandable, since they are similar. I noticed that the combination of "ch" was always accompanied by a superscript flourish. For example the "ch" in Lauenbach has a flourish. [*Editor's Note: Images of these 1856 documents and Mrs. Katz's translations accompany Chapter 3.*] Mrs. Katz also identified what I was convinced was the town of Busdorf as "Buhdorf." As a result, I believe my great-great-great-grandmother, identified by Mrs. Katz as Catharina Margaretha Buhite, was really Catharina Margaretha BUSCH. This turned out to be correct.

Ophie and I walked around the village of Jagel, which didn't take long. We pretty well covered it in about an hour. For the most part, the town looked like a modern subdivision, but we could find no sign of a church, let alone a monastery. We went into an establishment named Zum Norde, a hotel, restaurant and bar. Seeking information in a tavern was made more pleasant by the fact that Germans know a few tricks about beer making.

In the larger German cities, we found most people we dealt with spoke English. This included ticket agents, desk clerks, waiters and waitresses, and practically everyone dealing with the transportation systems. In small rural towns, this is not the case. My German is barely functional at the written level and almost non-existent at the spoken level.

There was a young woman at the bar who spoke no English. We were able to order beer, and she was kind enough to call out the cook, named Raymond, who spoke English more than adequately. We told him we were looking for information about our family. Raymond said his family was originally from Lübeck and he had only lived in Jagel since the mid-1970s. We asked him if there were any churches in the town, and he told us that the parish church for the Lutherans was in Busdorf, at the south edge of Schleswig. Then he remembered he had a book about the town of Jagel that was made sometime in the 1980s. The book was somewhat like a yearbook. It gave some of the history of the town, had a lot of pictures, and listed some of the resident families. None of the family names shown in the documents from Uncle Ike were included.

By chance, Ophie found a reference to St. Johannis Cloister in the book. Raymond had to translate for us, but it turned out that, historically, the Lutheran residents of Jagel were annually assessed certain goods, meats, produce, or their equivalent value, for the support of the cloister located in Schleswig. For example, each family might be required to provide one goose every year or, failing that, *x* kroners in its place. (Until the end of the Prusso-Danish war in 1864, the duchies of Schleswig and Holstein were under the sovereignty of the kingdom of Denmark. After that war, it was ceded to Prussia. When our family emigrated in the mid-1850s, they were technically Danish subjects.)

In the middle of this conversation, a man named Walter came in, and when he was told what we were doing, he became very interested. He spoke no English, so Raymond had to translate for us. Walter said that he was 74 years old, and his family had lived in Jagel for as long as anyone knew. He asked for the family names that were in the documents. We gave him the surnames Lauenbach, Busch, Koos, and Bindt. The only one he recognized was Koos (pronounced kohss). He told me it was a "*grosse familie*," large family, with "*viele menschen*," many people. He said that if we were going to be in the area beyond that day he would make some phone calls to see if he could find anyone who recognized the surnames. We agreed to meet at the Zum Norde the next afternoon.

Ophie and I caught the next bus back to Schleswig, and then the train back to Kiel. Shortly after we reached our hotel, our son, Rudy, his wife, Kristin, and our grandchildren, Lillian and little Rudolph, joined us, after driving up from Ansbach, to spend the rest of the week. It was decided that the trip to Schleswig and Jagel that we planned for the next day would be difficult for the little kids, so Ophie, Kristin, and the kids would spend the day sight-seeing in Kiel, while Rudy and I would drive to

Schleswig to see what we could learn. Early the next morning, we decided to first try to locate St. Johannis Cloister to find the source of the documents. This we did.

At some time after the 1850s, the cloister was closed after being in existence since the 11th century. It was converted into a home for indigent women. The site draws many tourists to see the buildings and grounds. We were directed to the *Kirchkreisamt* or district administrative offices of the Lutheran Church at the Petri Dom or St Peter's Cathedral where the church records had been transferred from St. Johannis. It is an impressive building with a large complex of offices and residences. We had been told to ask for Frau Jessen, a nice lady in charge of the church records. She told us the records had been catalogued by computer, so we requested a search for any entries concerning Christian Rudolph Lauenbach, Catharina Margaretha Busch, Detlef Koos, Anna Christina Bindt, their parents and their children. There was a fee for each 30 minutes of computer time. We paid for an hour of search time and added what we thought would be ample for copies and postage to Los Lunas, New Mexico.

Then, Rudy and I set out to visit the villages of Gross Rheide and Geltorf, which the documents indicated were the homes of Catharina Margaretha Busch and Christian Rudolph Lauenbach. Both were smaller than Jagel and off the beaten track. Again, both were farming villages. It is very pretty country with rolling hills, forested where it hasn't been cleared for farming or grazing, and very, very green.

After driving around and viewing the area for a while, we turned back to Jagel and the Zum Norde to meet Walter. He showed up right on time, and told us he had called several people, but none had any knowledge of any surnames, except several knew the Koos family. He called a woman he knew who was a widow of one of the Koos family. She told him that her husband had told her little about his family, and their children had all left the area. She doubted they would know much.

There were other people in the bar who became interested after learning what we were doing there. One woman spoke good English, and she translated for us. Everyone was friendly. We sat and talked to them for a while, and told them about our family in the United States, and then we said goodbye and started the drive back to Kiel.

We spent a couple more days there before Rudy, Kristin, and the children drove back to Ansbach, and Ophie and I continued to visit more of northern Europe before returning home to await the results of the computer search of the church records.

The New Documents

As usual, I wish I had known then what I know now. After studying the map more carefully, I saw that Haddeby Church, where all the marriages, baptisms, and funerals had taken place, was just off the highway that we took into Schleswig. The church is shown on the map as a site of interest, but, unfortunately, we overlooked it while we were there. Also, I did some searching on the Internet and found that, although there were no listings for the name Lauenbach in the Schleswig area, there were three listed in Kiel, and a great many in the town of Heide—especially in Husum, which are near the west coast of the Jutland Peninsula, opposite Kiel. If I had checked on this before the trip, I would have tried to locate some of them.

We received the documents from Frau Jessen in late July, and the results exceeded my expectations. It pushed the threshold of my information back a couple generations. Detlef Koos, the great-grandfather of Anna Koos, wife of Andreas Detlef Lauenbach I, died on January 1, 1770, at the age of 86. That would have made his birth year 1683. The documents included the entries for births and baptisms, marriages and deaths from the record books from Haddeby Church or Kirch. I have tried to find someone who could fully translate the documents. I contacted Tomas Jaehn, the Librarian at the Angelico Chavez Library at the Palace of the Governors in Santa Fe, who is a native of Stuttgart. I showed him the documents. He said he was unfamiliar with the script, and many of the descriptive words were no longer in use. Using the translations by Mrs. Katz, my German-English dictionary, and my sparse command of German, I was able to figure out what the records were, generally. There are many descriptive words not in the dictionaries due to obsolescence. I hope that someone will be able to improve on what I have done. [*Editor's Note: The villages named in the documents can be seen on early maps with Chapter 1. The maps show how close the places were to each other.*] The following is a summary of the documents or entries from the Haddeby Church, which are also summarized in the spreadsheet. The copies made from microfiche are not very clear.

1. Cover letter from Frau Jessen.
2. Document Spreadsheet.
3. Death of Johann Krögers, born 1711, died December 8, 1769, buried December 11, husband of Margaretha Haggen. (Great-grandfather of Anna Koos.)
4. Death of Detlef Koos, born 1684, died January 1, 1770, buried January 6. (Great-grandfather of Anna Koos.)
5. Marriage on October 24, 1773 between Marx Koos, son of Detlef Koos of Stexwig, and Lencke Meggers of Borgwedel, to Anna Krögers, daughter of Johann Krögers and Margaretha Haggen of Fahrdorf. (Grandparents of Anna Koos.) This record was unsuitable for copy. Typed transcription.
6. Birth of Detlef Koos, on September 12, 1774, baptized on September 18, son of Marx Koos and Anna Krögers at Fahrdorf. (Father of Anna Koos.)
7. Birth of Anna Christina Bindt, on March 31, 1777, baptized on April 6, daughter of Johann Jacob Bindt and Anna Peters at Jagel. (Mother of Anna Koos.)
8. Death of Johann Jacob Bindt, died March 9, 1780, buried March 12. (Maternal grandfather of Anna Koos.)
9. Death of Marx Koos, 42, died March 11, 1780, buried March 14, left three children, Detlef, Johann and Marx. (Grandfather of Anna Koos.)
10. Marriage on October 24, 1790, between Christian Rudolph Lauenbach, son of Johann Jacob Lauenbach of Ascheffel, and Anna Margaretha Ehlert, daughter of Peter Ehlert of Geltorf. Typed transcription.
11. Death of Anna Margaretha Ehlert Lauenbach, 35, died June 7, 1796, buried June 11, wife of Christian Rudolph Lauenbach, and mother of three children: Wiebke, Peter, and Margaretha.
12. Marriage on April 28, 1797, between Christian Rudolph Lauenbach, a widower of Geltorf, and Catharina Margaretha Busch, daughter of Andreas Petersen Busch of Jagel, and Anna Petersen of Alsen. Typed transcription.
13. Birth of Andreas Detlef Lauenbach, on November 25, 1802, baptized on November 28, son of Christian Rudolph Lauenbach and Catharina Margaretha Busch of Geltorf.*
14. Marriage on November 18, 1808, between Detlef Koos, son of Marx Koos and Anna Krögers of Loobstedt, and Anna Christina Wasmuth (nee Bindt), daughter of Johann Bindt and Anna Peters of Jagel. Typed transcription.
15. Birth of Anna Koos on August 9, 1811, baptized on August 11, daughter of Detlef Koos and Anna Christina Bindt at Jagel.*
16. Death of Christian Rudolph Lauenbach, 69, died July 11, 1820, buried July 13, left two children from his marriage to Anna Margaretha Ehlert: Wiebke and Peter (no mention of Margaretha), and four children from his marriage to Catharina Margaretha Busch: Andreas Detlef, Anna, Jurgen, and Heinrich.
17. Death of Anna Christina Koos (nee Bindt), 52, died June 16, 1829, buried June 20, wife of Detlef

Koos, left four children: Marx, Anna, Margaretha and Anna Christina.
18. Death of Detlef Koos, 56, died November 6, 1830, buried November 10, husband of Anna Christina Bindt, left four children: Marx, Anna, Margaretha, and Anna Christina.
19. Marriage on November 4, 1832 between Andreas Detlef Lauenbach, son of Christian Rudolph Lauenbach and Catharina Margaretha Busch of Geltorf, and Anna Koos, daughter of Detlef Koos and Anna Christina Bindt of Jagel. (This record was not included in those sent by the Kirchenkreisamt in 2005, but was one of the hand transcriptions of 1856.)*
20. Birth of Catharina Margaretha Lauenbach, on March 2, 1836, baptized on March 8, daughter of Andreas Detlef Lauenbach and Anna Koos, at Jagel.
21. Birth of Margaretha Lauenbach, on March 1, 1837, baptized on March 20, daughter of Andreas Detlef Lauenbach and Anna Koos, at Jagel.
22. Death of Catharina Margaretha Lauenbach (nee Busch), died December 17, 1838, buried December 22, wife of Christian Rudolph Lauenbach, left three sons: <u>Andreas Detlef</u>, Jurgen, Heinrich Friedrich, daughter-in-law Anna Koos, two grandchildren: <u>Andreas Detlef</u> and Catharina Margaretha. (No mention of grandchild Margaretha, who should have been 21 months old.)
23. Birth of Marx Heinrich Lauenbach, on March 26, 1840, baptized on April 14, son of Andreas Detlef Lauenbach and Anna Koos, at Jagel.
24. Birth of Christina Margaretha Lauenbach, on July 6, 1841, baptized on July 18, daughter of Andreas Detlef Lauenbach and Anna Koos, at Jagel.
25. Birth of Anna Margaretha Lauenbach, on September 15, 1843, baptized on September 21, daughter of Andreas Detlef Lauenbach and Anna Koos, at Jagel.
26. Birth of Anna Christina Lauenbach, on March 13, 1848, baptized on April 2, daughter of Andreas Detlef Lauenbach and Anna Koos, at Jagel.
27. Birth of Catharina Lauenbach, on May 11, 1852, baptized on June 13, daughter of Andreas Detlef Lauenbach and Anna Koos, at Jagel.

These were the 1856 hand transcribed documents brought to America by the family.

It becomes obvious looking at these records and those that appear with them that people in that area didn't have a lot of originality when naming their children.

The father of Christian Rudolph Lauenbach was listed as Johann Jacob Lauenbach from Ascheffel, a village southeast of Geltorf. The typed transcription says the church record book from Ascheffel was not at the Petri Dom.

A glaring omission in these documents is the birth record of Andreas Detlef Lauenbach II. He was born December 2, 1833, according to his gravestone at Buena Vista, which would have made him about 27 months older than his sister, Catharina Margaretha. They are both listed as surviving grandchildren of Catharina Margaretha Busch in her obituary notice (Entry no. 22). The record of marriage between Andreas Detlef Lauenbach I and Anna Koos was also missing from the documents we received from Frau Jessen, although it is among the hand transcribed documents of 1856. It is possible that these entries were mistakenly omitted from the computer database.

One U.S. census record stated that Andreas Detlef Lauenbach II was born in Wurttemburg; a few other people repeated that. I find this doubtful. Schleswig is the northernmost state in Germany bordering on Denmark, while Wurttemberg borders on Switzerland at the opposite end of the country. It is difficult to imagine Andreas Detlef I and Anna Koos being married while residing in Jagel in November 1832, moving to Wurttemberg sometime after, remaining in Wurttemberg during the period Andreas Detlef II was born, returning to Jagel before Catharina Margaretha was born in March 1836, and remaining there for the births of the next 6 children.

For one thing, country people in Germany are extremely sedentary, even today. Most people to whom I spoke said their families had lived in the same place since beyond memory. It took conditions of extreme instability for people to pull up roots. In the 1850s there was conflict between the Danes, the Prussians and the Palatine States over who was going to own Schleswig and Holstein, which eventually led to war. That, possibly along with economics, was the likely reason our family emigrated. For another thing, travel in Germany was difficult at that time. The first railroad line in Germany wasn't built until 1835, in another part of the country. It is unlikely they moved to Wurttemburg for the stated period.

Except for that one census, I do not know a source for the story that Andreas Detlef was born in Wurttemburg. *The Lost Gold Mine of Juan Mondragon: A Legend from New Mexico Performed by Melaquías Romero*, edited by Charles L. Briggs and Julián Josué Vigil, quotes Johnny (Gallegos) White as saying that Andrés (sic) Laumbach was a native of Wartenberg (sic).[ii] It also quotes him as saying his grandfather, Frank Metzger, was from "Metz, Germany." Metz is actually in Lorraine, was then and is now part of France. It was ceded to the Prussians after the Franco-Prussian War in 1871, after the Metzgers and Laumbachs were already settled in New Mexico. Alsace and Lorraine were given back to France after WW I.

There may be some reason the birth of Andreas Detlef II isn't in the database. We know the marriage of his parents was in the record book—we have the hand transcription from 1856—but that record is not in the database either. It could be a case of simple omission in both instances. The only way to find out is for someone to have the Haddeby book itself examined for the entries of November 1832 and December 1833. I tried to have this done by long distance. I wrote back to Frau Jessen in December 2005, requesting the records be searched specifically for these two entries, but I suspect what I subsequently received was the result of another computer search, yielding duplicates of records we had already received. Perhaps the next family member to visit Schleswig will be able to pursue the matter in person.

The records reveal that Andreas Detlef Lauenbach I and Anna Koos had eight children.[iii] I have heard that Andreas Detlef II did not come with the rest of the family, that he was in the army when they left, that he traveled to the United States separately and rejoined the family in Iowa. Which army? I also heard that the Eggert family was a neighbor in Germany,[iv] and an Eggert immigrated with the Lauenbachs to Iowa and then to New Mexico with Andreas Detlef I or Andreas Detlef II.

My question is, "What happened to Anna Koos?" I have never seen or heard any mention of her in New Mexico.[v] We know we still have relatives in Iowa and Nebraska, and some have scattered over many states and Canada. How did Andreas Detlef I and II come to split off from the rest of the family, and come down the Santa Fe Trail?

I hope this information is of some interest to the family, and that it contributes somewhat to the general knowledge of our history. I have developed a great deal of curiosity about it. I know many of you know more than I do. My hope is that some of the many gaps can be filled, and that the information will be shared among us all.

---

[i] Editor's Note: According to Pete, St Johannis was "established in 1192 as a Benedictine Monastery by the Catholic Church. It was converted to a women's cloister 'frauenstift' after the reformation."

[ii] Editor's Note: I believe any subsequent statements to that effect resulted from that one 1880 U.S. census erroneous entry indicating, for whatever reason, that Andreas 2nd, his father and mother were from "Wurtenberg."

Editor's Additional Note: The cited publication of an Hispanic ballad of northern New Mexico by Briggs and Vigil contains several genealogical or family history errors, including in its genealogical chart. The authors' primary informant of our branch of family history was John (Gallegos) White, son of Isabel Metzger Gallegos, daughter of Bibiana Martín and Frederick Metzger. John said he changed his last name from Gallegos to the Anglo-sounding White to find a job.

[iii] Editor's Note: All eight children came to America; seven with their parents after March 31, 1856; the eldest, Andreas 2nd, departed Europe mid-July 1856. Pete's research provided us with the names of all of these children. Previously we only knew of son Andreas, a son Henry and daughter Anna, but believed there were others.

[iv] Editor's Note: This is a long-time family tradition among New Mexico Laumbachs and Eggerts, but we have not found anything to substantiate that the families knew each other and lived nearby in Germany. The Eggerts only seem to know their family history beginning with Fritz in New Mexico. We and they have been unable to find a ship's manifest documenting Fritz Eggert coming to America, including on the manifest that lists his friend Andreas. Andreas 2nd was listed on the manifest of the John Herman even as it left the Hamburg harbor on July 15, 1856. Apparently Andreas was not hiding, as most of our family had believed. His friend, Fritz, may have been the only stowaway and the basis for this family tradition.

[v] Editor's Note: Pete wrote this piece, a valuable chapter in this book, soon after his return from Germany. At that time he knew little about Anna Koos; afterward, he too found her burial record in Clinton County Iowa. The question then and still is among all of us: Why did Andreas 1st leave his wife and children behind in Iowa to come alone to New Mexico so soon after he had arrived in the U.S.? Family tradition says he came to New Mexico to join his son Andreas 2nd in the ranching business. We can only assume he intended for the rest of his family to join him after he was settled, but he was killed before that happened.

Editor's Note: Results of Pete's trip to Germany extended our knowledge of the Lauenbach family history in Germany further back in time. He found records from the church of Haddeby that were recorded at St. Johannis Cloister were ultimately archived at the Kirchkreisamt of the Lutheran Church at the Petri Dom or St Peter's Cathedral at Schleswig. At Pete's request, those many archived records pertinent to our family were sent to him, which he shared. At end of this chapter are: Pete's spreadsheet listing and describing those pertinent records archived at the Petri Dome; copies of some of the actual entries preserved on microfiche, some of which Pete translated and typed for readability. He has many more pieces of documentation besides those included here.

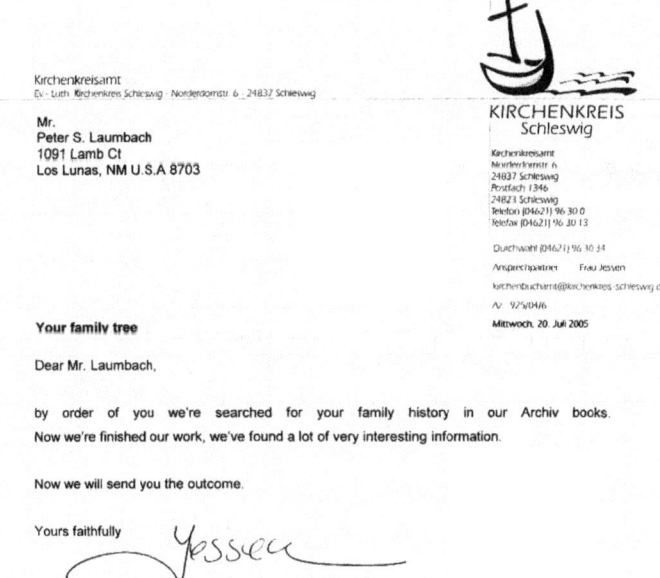

Record	DATE	DESCRIPTION	NAME	PARENTS	NOTES
3	DECEMBER 8, 1768	DEATH	JOHANN KRÖGER, AGE 57		BORN 1711
4	JANUARY 1, 1770	DEATH	DETLEF KOOS, AGE 86		BORN 1684
					5 CHILDREN
					?
					?
					?
					MARX
					JURGEN
					2 GRANDCHILDREN
					DETLEF
					MARX
5	OCTOBER 24, 1773	MARRIAGE	MARX KOOS	DETLEF KOOS OF STEXWIG	TYPED TRANSCRIPTION
				LENCKE MEGGERS FROM BORGWEDEL	
			TO		
			ANNA KRÖGERS	JOHANN KRÖGERS FROM FAHRDORF	
				MARGARETHA HAGGEN	
6	SEPTEMBER 12, 1774	BIRTH/BAPTISM	DETLEF KOOS	MARX KOOS	
				ANNA KRÖGERS	
7	March 31, 1777	BIRTH/BAPTISM	ANNA CHRISTINA BINDT	JOHANN JACOB BINDT OF JAGEL	
				ANNA PETERS	
8	MARCH 9, 1780	DEATH	JOHANN JACOB BINDT OF JAGEL		
9	MARCH 11, 1780	DEATH	MARX KOOS, AGE 42		BORN 1738
					3 CHILDREN
					DETLEF
					JOHANN
					MARX
10	OCTOBER 24, 1790	MARRIAGE	CHRISTIAN RUDOLPH LAUENBACH	JOHANN JACOB LAUENBACH	TYPED TRANSCRIPTION
			TO	OF ASCHEFFEL	
			ANNA MARGARETHA EHLERT	PETER EHLERT OF GELTORF	
11	JUNE 7, 1796	DEATH	ANNA MARGARETHA LAUENBACH		3 CHILDREN
			NEE EHLERT, AGE 35		WIEBKE ?
					PETER
					MARGARETHA
12	APRIL 28, 1797	MARRIAGE	CHRISTIAN RUDOLPH LAUENBACH	JOHANN JACOB LAUENBACH	WIDOWER
			TO	OF ASCHEFFEL	TYPED TRANSCRIPTION
			CATHARINA MARGARETHA BUSCH	ANDREAS PETERSEN BUSCH OF GELTORF	
				ANNA PETERSEN OF ALSEN	
13	NOVEMBER 25, 1802	BIRTH/BAPTISM	ANDREAS DETLEF LAUENBACH	CHRISTIAN RUDOLPH LAUENBACH	
				CATHERINA MARGARETHA BUSCH	
14	NOVEMBER 18, 1808	MARRIAGE	DETLEF KOOS	MARX KOOS OF LOOBSTEDT	TYPED TRANSCRIPTION
				ANNA KRÖGERS	
			TO		
			ANNA CHRISTINA WASMUTH BINDT	JOHANN BINDT OF JAGEL	
				ANNA PETERS	

#	Date	Event	Name	Parents/Spouse	Notes
15	AUGUST 9, 1811	BIRTH/BAPTISM	ANNA KOOS	DETLEF KOOS OF JAGEL	
				ANNA CHRISTINA BINDT	
16	JULY 11, 1820	DEATH	CHRISTIAN RUDOLPH LAUENBACH		2 CHILD. W/ ANNA EHLERT
			AGE 69		WIEBKE ?
					PETER
					3 CHILD. W/ CATHARINA
					ANDREAS DETLEF
					ANNA
					JURGEN
					HEINRICH
17	JUNE 16, 1829	DEATH	ANNA CHRISTINA KOOS, AGE 52		BORN 1761
			nee BINDT		4 CHILDREN
					MARX KOOS
					ANNA KOOS
					MARGARETHA
					ANNA CHRISTINA
18	NOVEMBER 6, 1830	DEATH	DETLEF KOOS, AGE 56		4 CHILDREN
					MARX KOOS
					ANNA KOOS
					MARGARETHA
					ANNA CHRISTINA
19	NOVEMBER 4, 1832	MARRIAGE	ANDREAS DETLEF LAUENBACH	CHRISTIAN RUDOLPH LAUENBACH	AT HADDEBY KIRCH
				CATHARINA MARGARETHA BUSCH	**HAND TRANSCRIPTION**
			TO		**FROM 1856**
			ANNA KOOS	DETLEF KOOS	
				ANNA CHRISTINA BINDT	

There is no entry for birth of Andreas Detlef Lauenbach II, who was born Dec. 2, 1833.
He is listed as a surviving grandson of Catharina Busch Lauenbach below.

#	Date	Event	Name	Parents/Spouse	Notes
20	MARCH 2, 1836	BIRTH/BAPTISM	CATHARINA MARGARETHA LAUENBACH	ANDREAS DETLEF LAUENBACH	IN JAGEL
				ANNA KOOS	
21	MARCH 1, 1837	BIRTH/BAPTISM	MARGARETHA LAUENBACH	ANDREAS DETLEF LAUENBACH	IN JAGEL
				ANNA KOOS	
22	DECEMBER 17, 1838	DEATH	CATHARINA MARGARETHA LAUENBACH		3 CHILDREN
			NEE BUSCH		ANDREAS DETLEF
					JURGEN
					HEINRICH FRIEDRICH
					DAUGHTER-IN-LAW
					ANNA KOOS
					2 GRANDCHILDREN
					ANDREAS DETLEF
					CATHARINA MARGARETHA
23	MARCH 26, 1840	BIRTH/BAPTISM	MARX HEINRICH LAUENBACH	ANDREAS DETLEF LAUENBACH	IN JAGEL
				ANNA KOOS	
24	JULY 6, 1841	BIRTH/BAPTISM	CHRISTINA MARGARETHA LAUENBACH	ANDREAS DETLEF LAUENBACH	IN JAGEL
				ANNA KOOS	
25	SEPTEMBER 15, 1843	BIRTH/BAPTISM	ANNA MARGARETHA LAUENBACH	ANDREAS DETLEF LAUENBACH	IN JAGEL
				ANNA KOOS	
26	MARCH 13, 1848	BIRTH/BAPTISM	ANNA CHRISTINA LAUENBACH	ANDREAS DETLEF LAUENBACH	IN JAGEL
				ANNA KOOS	
27	MAY 11, 1852	BIRTH/BAPTISM	CATHARINA LAUENBACH	ANDREAS DETLEF LAUENBACH	IN JAGEL
				ANNA KOOS	

Death of Detlef Koos

| 11. | 9. Jan | 9. b. Jan. | Detlef Koos, Abschiedsmann zu [illegible] alt [illegible] 88 Jahre; hinterläßt 5 Kinder, Jürgen, [illegible], Ilsen, v, Antje i. 4. Marg. ух Jürgen. [illegible] juengsten Sohn sind 2 Kindeskinder Detlef u. Marg. [illegible] |

Birth of Anna Koos

Taufprotokoll 1811

Num.	Natal.	[illegible]		
28	[illegible]	4. Aug	Catharina Margaretha Bock des Hufschmann in Fahrdorf Jürgen Bock und s. Ehefr. Christina Schröders ehel. Tochter. Gev. Margaretha Schröder — Margaretha [illegible] — Jürgen Oye.	Fahrdorf m. [illegible]
29.	9 Aug.	11 Aug	Anna Koos, des Käthners in Jagel Detlef Koos und s. Ehefr. Anna Christina geb. Biedl ehel. Tochter. Gev. Catharina Margaretha Lauenbach — Maria Hagg — Hans Hinrich Greve.	Jagel m. d. 1814.32 1819.12.
30.	8 Aug.	11 Aug	Anna Margaretha Döns des [illegible] in Fahrdorf Hermann Döns und s. Ehefr. [illegible] Maria geb. Peters ehel. Tochter. Gev. Margaretha Peters — Anna [illegible] — Detlef Döns.	Fahrdorf m. J. Cauf. 1809 n. 26. - 1814.36.
31.	5 Sept.	8 [illegible]	Anna Catharina Stensen des Käthners in [illegible] Detlef Stensen und s. Ehefr. [illegible]	[illegible] Mädch. [illegible] 1805.18.

Birth of Marx Heinrich Lauenbach

Birth of Anna Christina Lauenbach

		3, Hinrich Henning	
		5, Gübige	
29,	21 März	21 März	Hans Greve, ehel. Sohn des Hinrich Jagel in Jagel Jürgen Greve und das Margareten geb. Gudeck. — Gev. 1, Jürgen Greve 2, Catharina Greve 3, Johann Greve
30,	13 März	13 März	Anna Christina Lauenbach, ehel. Tochter des Hufners in Jagel Andreas Detlev Lauenbach und der Anna geb. Coos. — Gev. 1, Christina Jöns 2, Anna Claushorst Jagel 3, Hinrich Matthies
31,	12 März	Schul	Anna Catharina Saß, ehel. Tochter des Hausmannes Joh. Detlev Saß in Selkow und des Weibes Catharina geb. Lüth. Gev. 1, Anna Jebe 2, Catharina Möler 3, Ludwig Schacht

Zeit: 16.00-17.00

Anfragesteller: Lauenbach

Suchfrage: Lauenbach

Kirchenbuch Haddeby
Siehe Kopien

Kirchenbuch Auszug: Haddeby

1773 24 Oct. Der Geselle Marx Koos, des gewesenen Abnahmemannes Detlef Koos zu Stexwig und Lencke geb. Meggers aus Borgwedel ehel. Sohn; mit Jungfer Anna Krogers aus Fahrdorf, des gewesenen Hauerinsten Johann Krogers zu Fahrdorf und Margaretha Haggen ehel. Tochter

1790 d 24 oct. Der Geselle Christian Rudolph Lauenbach des weyl. Johann Jacob Lauenbach Hauerinste zu Ascheffel nachgel. Ehel. Sohn und Jungfer Anna Margartha Ehlert des weyl. Halbhuf. Peter Ehlert zu Geltorf nachgel. Ehel. Tochter.
Testes 1 Johann Frahm aus Geltorf
       2 Peter Sauer aus Esprem
(Anmerkung Kirchenbuch fUr Ascheffel ist nicht hier im Kirchenarchiv)

1797 d 28 April Der Wittwer: Christian Rudolp Lauenbach, Hauerinste zu Geltorf, und Jungfer Catharina Margartha Busch, des weyl. Andreas Petersen Busch gew. Hauerinste zu Jagel und Anna Petersen aus Alsen nachgel. ehl. Tochter.

1808 18Nov Der Gesell Detlef Koos, des weil Marx Koos in Loobstedt und seiner Ehefrau Anna geb. Krogers ehel. Sohn, mit Anna Christina Wasmuth geb. Bindt des weil. Johann Bindt Katner in Jagel und seiner Ehefrau Anna geb. Peters ehel. Tochter.

Bemerkungen:

Fur einige Jahre sind keine Kopien auf Fisches vorhanden. Kopien aus den Kirchenbuchem durfen nicht gemacht werden. Einsicht in die Originale sind nUTmit Genehmigung moglich!

Bearbeitet: 17.07.2005

Richardsen

LAUMBACHS IN NEW MEXICO
And Those Who Went Before
In Germany, Iowa and New Mexico

WHO WERE THEY?
THEREFORE, WHO AM I?

Section III
IOWA AND NEBRASKA

"If you cannot get rid of the family skeleton,
you may as well make it dance."

George Bernard Shaw

SECTION III: LAUMBACH IN IOWA

Chapter 7: Goose Lake, Clinton County, Iowa
by Jan Girand

We believe Andreas 1st and wife, Anna Koos Lauenbach, and seven of their eight children departed Europe by steam ship just days after March 31, 1856, and probably—like their son, Andreas soon thereafter—landed at Castle Garden in New York, on the southern tip of Manhattan, where for more than 60 years, ten million immigrants entered the United States. The better-known port of entry, Ellis Island, did not open as the primary immigrant port of entry until 1892.

Castle Clinton, then known as Castle Garden and now again called Castle Clinton, was a large circular building of red brick, built as a fort to defend New York harbor from the British before our nation's War of 1812. It was converted into our country's official immigration center about 1830.

Castle Garden was probably a far less traumatic, more welcoming port of entry for our ancestors than Ellis Island was for later immigrants. In those earlier decades, America encouraged emigrants to come settle its still vast undeveloped lands.

An unnamed female steerage passenger wrote of passing through Castle Garden; her experiences were published by *The New York Times* in 1866. She described how, after getting off the ship, she and the others were seated inside the building. Staff members asked for their names and destinations and helped them arrange for their travels and settlements in America. They were told: for price of a ticket a steam ship or railroad could take them east, west, north or south; how they might be able to communicate with friends or family in America; how to exchange their currency; and how to find employment. That writer believed the government's "Intelligence Department" tried to protect the incoming vulnerable immigrants from exploitation. Based upon her description, I believe she and our family were more fortunate than many who came later.

I read on a bio that a traveler from Hamburg to New York in 1866—also ten years after our family came—was on shipboard for seven weeks. On another bio, I read people on a ship crossing the Atlantic sighted multiple icebergs in one day. What frightening experiences and dreadful conditions our family and tens of thousands of others encountered coming to America.

Somewhere, sometime between their departure from Schleswig and their arrival in Clinton Iowa, the spelling of our family's last name was changed from Lauenbach to Laumbach, which became the common family spelling in America. That probably happened at the port of entry. We do not know how nine members of the Laumbach family—two adults and seven children ranging in age from 4 to 20—traveled overland to Clinton, Iowa, how long it took them, or who, already settled there, had beckoned them to come. We also do not know how the son Andreas traveled there overland.

We only know that Andreas Detlef Laumbach 1st, age 54; his wife Anna Koos Laumbach, age 45; daughters and one son: Catharina Margaretha, born 1836; Margaretha, born 1837; Marx Heinrich "Henry," born 1840; Christina Margaretha, born 1841; Anna Margaretha, born 1843; Anna Christina, born 1848; and Catharina, born 1852, eventually arrived in the area of Goose Lake, in what is now Clinton County, Iowa.

We know son Andreas Detlef 2nd, born 1833, departed the Hamburg port when not yet 23, on July 15, 1856 and entered the United States through Castle Garden, traveled overland, and joined his family in Iowa. We think he arrived there about three-and-a-half months after they did.

Who or what attracted the family to Goose Lake, Iowa?

~~

Wolfe's History of Clinton County Iowa, Volume I—published by B.F. Bowden & Company, Indianapolis, Indiana, 1911, by P. B. Wolfe, Editor-in-Chief (herein called Wolfe's History)—provided information about that area's early history. It began with a physical description of Deep Creek Township, organized in 1841, the first of six townships, all rich farming lands beside the Elk River. Wolfe described the area as mostly rolling prairie, earlier with some areas of old timber the first settlers used for construction and fencing. Wolfe wrote that Goose Lake was in the center of the valley, then no longer a lake that attracted ducks, geese and other water fowl except after run-off from heavy rains. Goose Lake, fed by springs, and perhaps occasional overflow from two creeks, had been drained by earlier settlers for irrigation and to create hundreds more acres of rich grazing pasture lands.

Most of the earliest settlers near Goose Lake were Irish and German immigrants. The permanent settlers acquired their land from the government—claims in increments of 600 to 1,000 acres—by going to a high place and staking all the land within their sights. Wolfe said those settlers were seldom bothered by land speculators or claim jumpers.

The Midland Railway was built in 1870, crossing the northern portion of Goose Lake over an embankment.

Wolfe wrote, "…The township is now mostly German," but there still remained some Irish settlers.

In his history, among those Wolfe named who platted the town of Goose Lake in 1889, were the familiar names of Christ (Christian) Eggert (*perhaps kinsman of Fritz Eggert; see chapter by his descendant Trent Shue*) and Peter Kruse, perhaps the grandfather of my great-aunt Wilhelmina Kruse who married Edwin Henkens, my grandmother Emma's brother. Goose Lake had a population of 125 in 1909. Other early established townships in the area were Boone Springs, named after an early settler, nephew of Daniel Boone; Bryant, platted in 1871; Waterford Township, organized in 1854; and Charlotte, established in 1853 and platted in 1871. These townships provided the area with three churches: Catholic, Methodist and German Lutheran. Wolfe wrote that August Petersen had been an early rural mail carrier for Charlotte when that route was established in 1904. Quigley, later called Petersville, was platted within the Waterford Township.

In *Wolfe's History*, Volume II, Wolfe profiles Claus Kruse, beginning page 924, who was father of one named Peter Kruse. Born in 1835 near Kiel, province of Holstein, son of Paul and Margaret (Shombarger) Kruse of Holstein, Claus' father came to America in 1853, settled in Iowa, was a life-long Lutheran and died at age 80. Claus married Catherina Petersen, born in Schleswig 1841 to parents Hans and Catherina (Neave) Petersen of Germany.

Wilhelmina Kruse, wife of Edwin Henkens, was born at Goose Lake, Iowa to parents Peter and Anna Kruse on August 26, 1883. She died December 15, 1974, buried in Greenwood Cemetery in Chadron, Nebraska.

I knew, admired and loved Wilhelmina, my great-aunt Minnie. In fact, I had intended to live with her while I attended college in Chadron, beginning 1959-1960, but did not. (Instead, I attended UNM in Albuquerque, New Mexico.) When I visited her the summer of 1959, she was still a delightful, energetic lady. She flew around in her son Earl's two-seater airplane. She scampered nimbly over rugged, steep rock embankments to climb onto their rocking motorboat to go out onto a huge lake to give me an adventure. It became more adventure than either of us expected when that motorboat died and we had to climb from it—in the middle of what seemed like an ocean—onto a rescue boat rocked by stormy sea-sized waves. Minnie was fearless. I was not. (I do not swim; I wonder if Minnie did?) She and her son Earl also took me to Mount Rushmore. A few years later, in early 1965, she and some of her family visited with my family and me in northern New Mexico, soon after my third child, Devin, was born.

For genealogical purposes, a woman named Annette Lucas listed burials at the Center Grove (Ingwerson Center Township, Clinton County, Iowa) Cemetery—located about five miles north of Elvira. I do not know what date she created this list or how complete and current it is. It can be found on ancestory.com. I have found it useful.

On it are many people named Clausen and Claussen. Among those listed is Dierk Clausen, born July 31, 1835, died October 17, 1919. He is likely the same Dierk Clausen who added his salutation at the bottom of Peter Henkens' letter "written before 1879" from Charlotte, Clinton Iowa to the Andreas Detlef Laumbach family in Buena Vista, New Mexico.[i] According to the letter from Peter Henkens, Dierk Clausen was his brother-in-law. He also mentions "Aunt Christina," who had recently arrived from Germany in Clinton County with her husband and adult children. *(Peter and Anna Henkens were the parents of my grandmother, Emma Margaretha Henkens Laumbach.)*

There are two Kleppiens on this cemetery's list of burials: Matilda, who died April 7, 1871, and Thomas, who died October 6, 1867—but no Theodore Kleppien, who added his salutation to the bottom of this same letter from Peter Henkens to the Laumbach family. *(See copies of letters at the end of this chapter.)*

On Lucas' cemetery listing are several people with the last name of Dierks; one is Emma, maiden name Kruse, born May 24, 1892.

There are 13 Eggerts on this Clinton County cemetery listing, including Adolph, born February 23, 1822, died February 3, 1892; and Christine Wiebke Eggert, no birth date given, who died May 22, 1888. Trent Shue found a record of the young couple Adolf and Christine Eggert, emigrating from Holstein to Clinton County in 1857, the year after Laumbachs arrived. They had a son named Christian. *(See chapter Fritz Eggert by Trent Shue.)* I believe Adolph and Christine were the first Eggerts to settle in Clinton County. The other Eggerts on that cemetery listing were probably their children and grandchildren. Pete Laumbach (son of Rudolf Laumbach Sr.) had heard that an Eggert who visited Germany decades ago found evidence that Fritz and his family had come from the Schleswig-Holstein area, but that has not been confirmed.

On this same Clinton County cemetery listing is a Wilhelm P. L. Henkens, who died March 7, 1877. He was probably a kin to Peter Henkens. Several Jepsens are listed; Jepsen is a name we've seen several times on family memorabilia.

Marx Koos, born August 7, 1809, was born in Jagel like his sister Anna Koos Laumbach. He died August 28, 1864 in Clinton County, Iowa. *(Note: Butch Sanders found images of Anna's and Marx's stone burial markers in this cemetery on ancestry.com.)*

On Lucas' Center Township cemetery listing are more than 50 entries for people named Kruse, including several named Claus, Peter and Anna.

Therein are three listed Laumbachs: Anna, born February 7, 1904; Jurgen, born December 11, 1898; and Anna, born August 11, 1811—she died August 24, 1868. This second named Anna buried in this cemetery was our great-great-grandmother Anna Koos Laumbach, widow of Andreas Detlef 1st. It was her birth and marriage documents that were recorded at St. Johannis in Schleswig in 1856, hand-carried to America, that are shown in this book.

LAUMBACH, Anna	07 Feb 1904	
LAUMBACH, Jurgen	11 Dec 1898	
LAUMBACK, Anna	09 Aug 1811	24 Aug 1868

Butch Sanders believes these two younger listed Laumbachs—Anna, born 1904, and Jurgen, born 1898—were related to Jurgen Laumbach, brother of Andreas Detlef 1st. He thinks they were Anna Koos Laumbach's nephew and his wife, who was also named Anna.

There are 45 listings for people named Petersen.

I scanned this list for other names I might recognize. Those include some I've seen in salutations in Emma Henkens' (my grandmother's) autograph book, which she began May 21, 1899 when living in Clyde, Nebraska. Was that book with personal greetings, perhaps, begun in anticipation of her marriage and eventual move to remote New Mexico, a way to keep family and friends with her? Besides in her autograph book *(some images of it at the end of this chapter)*, I also searched Lucas' list for familiar names I saw printed on many "greeting cards" given to Laumbachs by members of the Henkens family and their friends who lived in that area of Iowa and Nebraska in the late 1800s. There are also greeting cards exchanged among those in New Mexico. (*Many of these images are at the end of this chapter.*[ii])

There are likely many names listed on this cemetery record pertinent to various members of family, by marriage or association, that I do not recognize. However, Lucas' list has been useful.

Peter Claus Henkens, farmer, born "in Denmark" Nov. 6, 1840, emigrated from Schleswig, Denmark to America in 1866. (*See image of his ship manifest entry at the end of chapter 2.*) About one year later, on December 3, 1867, he married Anna Christina Laumbach, who had been born at Jagel, Schleswig on March 13, 1848. Anna had come to America with her family in 1856 at age 8; she lived in Clinton County, Iowa with her family prior to and after her marriage to Peter. Sometime between 1885 and 1900, Peter and Anna Henkens and their family moved to Colfax County, Nebraska. Anna (died November 26, 1908) and Peter Henkens (died February 13, 1916) are buried in Ridge Cemetery, Dodge County, Nebraska.[iii]

Their children[iv] were as follows: Caroline "Carrie," who married Robert H. McCann; August Henkens (born February 15, 1871), who married Emma Grantz; William (died in infancy); John, a blacksmith living in Waterford, Clinton, Iowa, who married a woman named Wilhelmina "Minnie"; Peter Henkens, died in infancy; Emma Margaretha Henkens, born 1879 at Goose Lake, Iowa, raised in Nebraska, came to New Mexico to marry Daniel Laumbach in January 1902, died in Roy New Mexico April 17, 1956; Emelia "Melie" Henkens (born January 20, 1881), who married Roy Petersen; Herman Henkens, who married Mayme Parsons; Edwin Henkens (born June 11, 1884 in Chadron, Nebraska), who married Wilhelmina "Minnie" Kruse—they and their children Earl, Lester and Bernice Henkens Chamberlain lived in Chadron, Nebraska, Edwin died at Chadron February 22, 1949; and Claus Henkens (born February 9, perhaps in 1886), who married Bertha.

My mother, Verna L. Sparks, kept in touch with most of them and their children.

---

[i] Images of letters follow. They were written in German in Clinton, Iowa "before 1879" by Anna and Peter Henkens to the Andreas Detlef (2nd) Laumbach family in Buena Vista, New Mexico. Their translations are included. Anna enclosed with her letter two swatches of hair—one blonde, one red—with a dried flower. I believe hers was the blonde. Was the red hair Peter's? These letters passed from Andreas and Elionor Laumbach in Buena Vista, New Mexico to Daniel and Emma Laumbach, then to their son Joyce, then to his daughter, Vera Jane Laumbach Morris. VJ donated them to the New Mexico Farm and Ranch Museum near Las Cruces for archived preservation. Butch Sanders improved the sharpness of images of these letters for this book.

Lieber Bruder

jetz ergreife ich die Feder um dir ein
paar Zeilen zu schreiben wie es uns
geht wir sind Gotz [Gott] lob bei gesundheit
wir den ~~4~~ letzten Brief von dir noch
erhalten ~~haben~~ haben wir zwei Kinder
varloren ~~ein Sohn und Tochter~~
baide Söhnen der eine 4 Jahr alt
und einer 4 ~~Mot~~ Monat. Lieber
Bruder ich habe zu langen auf ein
Brief gewartet aber kein erhalt
ich möchte doch gern Mal ein Par
Ein ab die geht ich wolte ich könte
dir mal sehen und mit dir sprechen
aber es ist ja zu weit wen ich wolte
die Kinas mal besuchegst da könt
wir mal recht sprechen Meine
baide alte Kinder die fragten immer
Mama schreibe mal und Natal
Julch sie wollen dir kosten mit
ihr namen darauf schiben noch

üvren beiden Ältestnen Lieber
Bruder Jetz möchte ich dir bitten doch
bals Mel wieder zu schreiben dann
ich denke es werry Mel an dich
Aber weil ich so schlecht schreiben
kan habe ich immer das schreiben
fein her laßen Jetz muß ich
schlißen und hoffe das diese
Zeile euch Mögen bei
guter Gesundheit untrefen
Viele Grüße von mir und
Mann und Kinder an dir und
Frau und Kinder deine dich
liebende Schwester Anna
Gentrub

Charlotte Clinton Co
Iowa

Dear Brother

I am taking my pen to write to you a few lines how we are getting along. We are all right again, since we received your last letter. We lost two children two boys one 4 years old and the other one month old. Dear brother I have been waiting a long time to hear from you, but no reply. I would like to know you are getting along. I wish I could see you in person and talk to you but it is too far away. I wish you would pay us a visit than we can talk together. My two oldest children always say, Mamma write once to uncle Detlef. they want two cards with their name on it, of the two oldest children. Dear brother now I beg of you to write again than I think of you quite often but as I write so poorly I can quit writing. now I want to close and hope that these few lines will reach you in the best of health. best regards from me, my husband and children for you and wife you loving sister

Anna Henkens
Charlotte Clinton Co
Iowa

Envelope for letter from Peter Henkens.
Address: "Mr. Detlef Laumbach, Lo de Mora, County of Mora, New Mexico."

Lieber Schwager

Jetzt ergreife ich die Feder um
euch zu schreiben Wir sind Gott
Lob sind gesund und munter
und hoffen dass euch von euch
so sind Jetzt schon 5 Jahren das wir
nichts von euch gehört haben und
wissen nicht mer ob Ihr gestorben
seid oder böse seid oder ob Ihr
uns vergessen habt. Wir möchten
doch gern mal wieder was die
Ursache ist das Ihr unsre
Briefe nicht beantworten thut.
Wir haben die Schneiderei
verkauft vor 2800 Taler und
haben uns einen Farm wieder
gekauft nämlich hundert und 4
Acker für 3100 Taler Es ist drei
Meilen von Charlotte Wir haben
3 Kinder 2 Söhne und 1 Tochter.

Tante Kristina und ihr Man
sind auch von Deutschland gekommen
mit ihre 2 Töchter die eine ist
schon Verheiratet nemlich Eure
Vrent Brieder Hinrich und
Schwager Diart Klauß... haben
sie Rübner komen lassen. Der
Weitzen kostet hier 70 bis 75 Cent zur
Bushel Gersten 125 bis 130 zur bushel
Hafer 50 Cent, Korn 55 bis 60 Cent zur
bushel. Schweine kosten 620 lebendig
750 geschlacht zur 100 ℔ Jetz weil ich
schließen dann ich weiß nicht unnd
mehr zu schreiben. Und hoffen das
mein schreiben euch bei guter
gesundheit antrefen Möge.
Viele grüße von mir und meine
Frau. Und zuletz einen Herzlichen
gruß an euch hallen lieben
Schwager und Schwägerin.
Von Eueren Schwager
Peter Henkens

bezahlt
die Adressen ist an Peter Henkens
Lyhnn ? Clinton C° Pos Charlotte

Schreibet bald mal Kinder

Richtig
die Adressen ist an Peter Henkens
Charlotte Clinton C° Jowa
Id Theodor Kleppien
Dierk Claussen

Before 1879

Dear Brother-in-law

I am writing to you to let you know how we are. we are well and happy and hope the same from you.
It is now 5 years since we heard from you and we dont know if you are mad or if you forgot us. we would like to know the reason why you dont answere our letters.
we sold our Machine shop for $2,800. and bought a farm 104 acres for $3,100. it is three miles from Charlotte.
we have 3 children 2 boys and daughter. Aunt Cristina and her husband arrived from Germany with two daughters one is married with Anna Jans brother Heinrich and brother in law Dierk Claussen got them over here.
wheat is worth 70 to 75 cents a bushel

> Barley $1.25 to $1.30 oats 50 cents corn 55¢
> hogs cost live weight $6.20.
> Killed $7.50 per 100 pounds.
> Now I am going to close I dont
> know any other news and hope
> my writing will reach you in
> good health and spirit
> regards from me and my wife
> and heartest regards for you
> Dear brother-in-law and sister-
> in-law from your brother-in-law
> Peter Henkens

[ii] On the next pages are some greeting cards from the end of the 1800s. Daniel Laumbach and his sisters in New Mexico, and Emma Henkens and her siblings and German friends in Iowa and Nebraska, exchanged these with each other, their families and friends. Apparently it was a period custom among some to exchange these little cards, with senders' names preprinted. The small ones seem to be "all-occasion" greeting or calling cards.

At the end of this chapter are a few images of pages in Emma Henkens' autograph book. Most entries are not included here. Many entries were in German script. Most were written in Nebraska, but some entries were added later, after Emma lived in New Mexico. She began with her own entry in the book, inside the cover: "Clyde, Nebr May 21th 1899 Oh how sweet it will be in that beautiful land so free from all sorrow and pain; with songs on our lips and harps in our hands to meet one another again. Miss Emma M. Henkens." The last dated entry in this little book, "Roy, N Mex. Dec. 31, 1917" was by Mary McNeilly. She was one of the home-school teachers who lived on the ranch, hired to teach the Laumbach children. Apparently, when Emma began this autograph book in the spring of 1899, she already anticipated going to New Mexico to marry Daniel. She arrived in the west, got off the train in Trinidad, Colorado, and they married January 24, 1902. Many entries written in Nebraska prior to that date indicated the writer knew she would be living far away. All of the entries in German script were written by family and friends while she still lived in Nebraska, prior to 1902.

"Emilie Henkens"

Ornate envelope with printed card inside:
"John Henkens Forgotten thou will never be!"

"Have kind thoughts of me"
John Tichata

2-ply card that opens:
"Claus P. Henkens"

"God's blessing   Emma M. Henkens"

"Mr. & Mrs. R. H. Mc Cann"

"M. L. Laumbach"

"Annie Laumbach" (2)

Ornate little envelope with printed card inside:
"Crestina Laumbach"

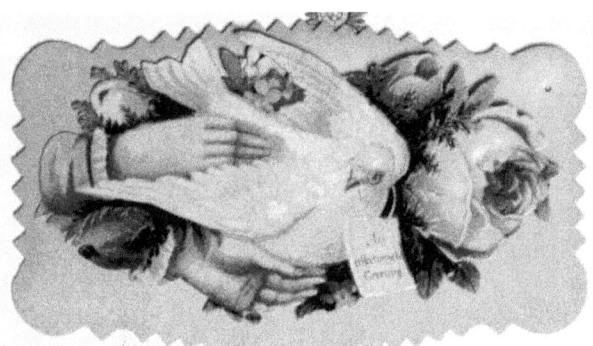

"Dan Laumbach"

Cristina Laumbach

"Daniel Laumbach"

"Many Joys to you Mary Laumbach"

"M.E. Fraker"

"Friendship Tie   Love Sincere
Emma D. Grantz"

"You know that I love you,
and love you right hard,
or why should I trouble
to give you my card
Affection's offering
Emma M. Henkens"

"Lizzie D.W. Moeller"

"With Love's blessings" Mary Kleppien

"With Love's blessings" Mary Kleppien

"Clara Kleppien"

"With my love   Mary Laumbach"

Eddie T. Henkens

This card originally had a decorative piece on top: "Clara C.W. Kleppien"

"Many joys to you" Henry Stultenburg

"Remember me"   Dora Goettsa

"Deep as the sea is my love for thee John B. Filen"

"Love grown your way George Burch"

love and best wishes
to my little cousin
Verna from
Rosa
Verna Laumbach
Roy, N.M.

with lots of love
and kisses from
your Aunt Mary
Miss Vernie Laumbach
Roy, N.M.

Hallow Dearie
How do you like
this old fellow
To Vernie
From Aunt Anna

Love and
a Kiss to my
Sweetheart
Vernie
From Your
Madrina

A merry Christmas
To Little Ruth
From Aunt
Anna

Vernie Laumbach
from Aunt
Christina

"Hallow Dearie. How are you Getting along? I suppose you are getting ready for Santa Claus. I hope he will get there with plenty pretty things to make you all happy and cheerful. With love from Aunt Anna"

Handmade greeting card from: "Mary Laumbach 1911"

Valentine card, No name to or from

On reverse is printed the Lord's Prayer Handwritten at top: "Mabel Laumbach" This was probably a card expressing condolence when Mabel died.

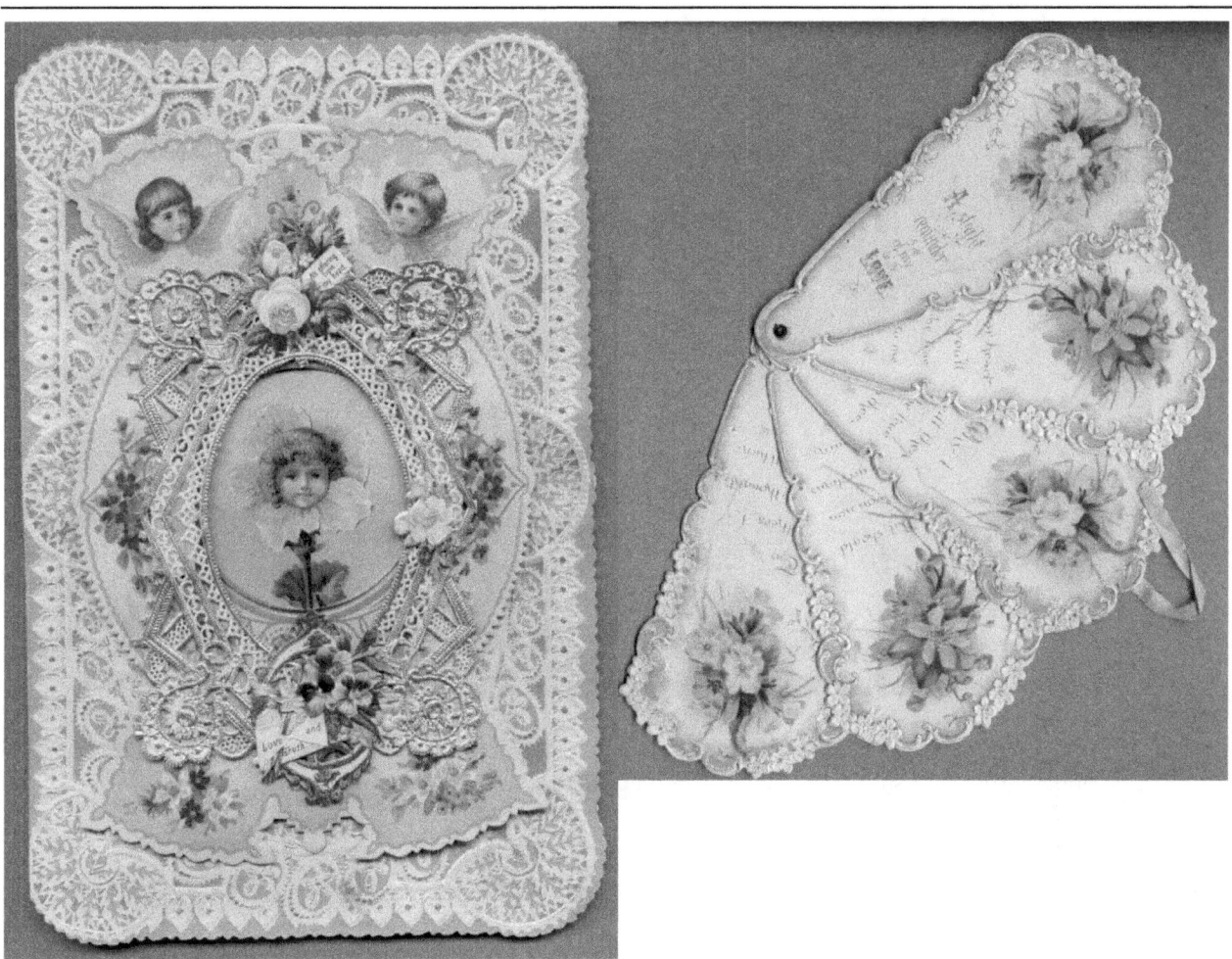

Large ornate 3-dimensional valentine
No name inside

A valentine card, unfolds (strings attached) like a fan with words printed on each of 5 panels.
"A slight reminder of my love"   Unsigned

Cover of Emma's Autograph album (made in Germany), which she began in Clyde Nebraska in 1899, apparently when she already anticipated going to live in far away New Mexico.

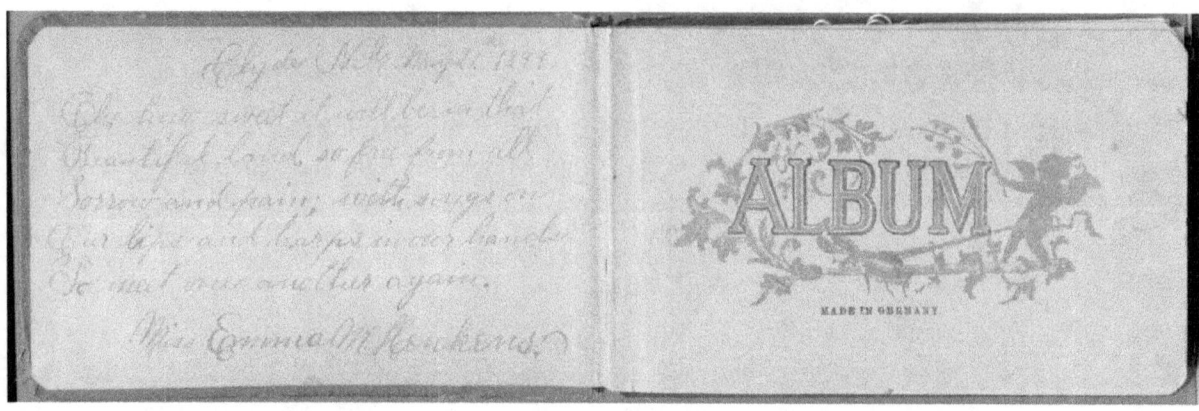

Emma wrote inside front cover: "Clyde Nebr. May 21th 1899, Oh how sweet it will be in that Beautiful land, so free from all Sorrow and pain, with songs on our lips and harps in our hands To meet one another again. Miss Emma M. Henkens"

The entries in this album are not in chronological order. People wrote on various inside pages out of order, beginning in 1899 in Nebraska, and ending 1917 in Roy New Mexico. The entries in German script were written when she still lived in Nebraska, before she came to New Mexico on January 25, 1902 to marry Daniel Laumbach.

Hausfrau
I do not know if the print of this charming German girl predates Buena Vista;
it ultimately passed from there to my grandparents and then to my mom.

SECTION III: LAUMBACHS IN IOWA

Chapter 8: Search for Henry Laumbach
by Dallas Laumbach

On May 28, 2009, out of the blue, I received a call from Karl Laumbach, whom I had never met. He said he and two of his cousins, Jan Girand and "Pete" Peter James Laumbach, were working on Laumbach family genealogy. He had heard that I visited some of his family in Albuquerque back in the '60's and wondered if we might have some pertinent family data we would be willing to share to help them fill in some of the blanks.

A blank spot concerned a Henry Laumbach. According to their oral history, that Henry had left the family and was never heard from again. They thought he had headed west from Iowa in search of gold.

This Henry Laumbach is the Marx Heinrich Laumbach on Peter James Laumbach's family tree diagram (Reference 6) born in 1840 in Jagel in the state of Schleswig, which at that time was a sovereign state of Denmark.

My paternal great-grandfather was named Henry Laumbach, but before our recent contact with the New Mexico Laumbachs, I knew little about him and did not know he had left his family and headed west, probably in search of gold.

My wife, Rosalie, had an appointment with a local Wimberley, Texas doctor two days after I had received that call from Karl. While she waited in one of the small examining rooms, she picked up something to read. It happened to be the spring 2009 edition of *American Archaeology*. In the middle of this journal on page 29 was a picture of Karl Laumbach (see Reference 13) at a dig he was heading up at Canada Alamosa, New Mexico. Rosalie was amazed and couldn't wait to tell me about it. She offered to buy the copy of *American Archaeology*, but one of the doctor's staff told her she could have it. When she got home and showed me the article, I said, "This is too much of a coincidence. We've got to meet these folks." I mean, how many doctor's offices have copies of archaeology publications—let alone one in Texas with an article about Karl Laumbach!

I told Karl when I had talked to him on the phone that I had little family data, but my sister, Lois, had done some family genealogy work when her husband, Bob Ives, had been stationed with the U.S. Army in Germany. I got her into the loop, and we both exchanged a number of emails with Karl, Jan and Pete. Pete sent us his well-researched family tree; his comprehensive tabulation of birth, marriage and death certificates; and his documentation of his family's trip to Jagel in 2005 (see References 6, 7 and 8). All of this family data is included in his chapter in this book. Note that the original family name was "Lauenbach" on all the early German documents.

I've found no Lauenbachs listed on the Internet living in the U.S. It appears that virtually all of them had the spelling of their surname changed to Laumbach when they came here. You can see how this might have happened since all of the documents were handwritten in German script.

My sister, Lois, was pleased to learn about the "Lauenbach" spelling because she thought the "Laum" portion of the name was not truly German. When she went back and looked at the family historical documents we now have, she said it is "Lauenbach" in the old Germanic script on all of them. There is a small town in southwestern Germany about 25 miles east of Strasbourg named Lauenbach, but we do not know if it has any relevance to our family's origin.

The fact that there is a large number of "Laumbachs" and virtually no "Lauenbachs" in the U.S. suggests very few "Lauenbachs" immigrated to the U.S., or government officials consistently changed the spelling. Otherwise, one would think some of the Lauenbachs would have retained the original spelling of their surname.

In July 2009, Rosalie and I traveled to New Mexico to meet Karl, Jan and Pete. We first met with Jan and her husband, Dan Girand, in Artesia, New Mexico for lunch on July 7th. The three hours we had allowed for lunch turned out to be too short—we had many interesting things to talk about. In particular, we learned that Jan and Dan had gone to Germany in 1996 and also visited places named in the original family documents. In addition, Jan provided us with a copy of some of the results of valuable census and other document research by Charles O. Sanders. (See Reference 12.)

On the evening of July 7th, Rosalie and I joined Karl, his wife Toni and their son Kristopher for dinner in Las Cruces, New Mexico at the Mesilla Plaza in Old Town. After getting acquainted, Karl regaled us with many vintage family pictures, and stories to go with them.

Rosalie and I had lunch with Peter James Laumbach, his older brother, Rudy, and their Uncle Ike (Casimiro) on July 8, 2009. (Pete and Rudy are the sons of Rudolph and Leona Laumbach; Rudolph was Ike's brother.) This was a great get-together and very entertaining. Pete and Rudy had interesting tales to tell, but their Uncle Ike topped them all. He was 96 years old at the time, but his memory was still keen. We also talked about Pete and Ophelia's trip to Germany in 2005 and all the data they assembled so Pete could generate the family tree diagram and a comprehensive table of marriage/birth/baptismal/death certificates. Pete's contributions are with his chapter in this book.

Alice Lillian Kral Laumbach (1908-1989), born in Crawford County, Iowa. She was Dallas' mother.

Justus Theodore Laumbach (1906-1993), born in Sac County, Iowa. He was Dallas' father.

Karl had sent Jan an email before he called me on May 28, 2009. She later forwarded that email to me prior to our meeting with the "New Mexico Laumbachs." In that email, Karl said some Laumbachs from Iowa had lived in Albuquerque in the sixties. They had connected with his Uncle Red (Andreas Detlef Laumbach 3rd) for a brief visit. Red said the older fellow (who was my dad, Justus) told him that his grandfather, Henry Laumbach, abandoned his grandmother's family in Iowa and came west, never to be heard of again. Or something like that.

From census and other data, we have since concluded that Henry actually left Iowa sometime after 1885.

Rosalie and I were the Laumbachs from Iowa who came to live in Albuquerque. While we lived there from 1962 to1966, my folks, Justus and Lillian Laumbach, came to visit us. Other than Lake City, Iowa, where Rosalie and I were both born and raised, we had never lived where there were other Laumbachs in the phone book. I thought, while we were there, it would be interesting to meet some of those who lived in Albuquerque. And we did. (We had no subsequent contact with any of them until Karl called me in 2009.) I didn't hear Dad tell Red about his grandfather, Henry Laumbach, abandoning his family. In fact, *I never heard about it* until I saw Karl's email, but it does explain my great-grandmother, Augusta Grantz, marrying for the second time.

So two distinct Laumbach "branches" had tales of a Henry Laumbach who headed west, presumably in search of gold, and then lost contact with the rest of his family. Could those two Henry Laumbachs be the same person?

It had not been certain that the Marx Heinrich Laumbach, born in Schleswig in March 1840, son of Andreas Detlef Laumbach 1st (ADL 1st)—shown on Pete Laumbach's family tree diagram—was my great-grandfather, but I now think he was. In the following I will: (1) Show that Marx Heinrich Laumbach (call him "Mark Henry") was the same age as my great-grandfather, Henry Laumbach (call him "Henry"); (2) Show that they were in the same place (a sparsely populated Iowa township) about the same time; and (3) Show that they were then both known as Henry Laumbach. Therefore, they are likely the same person.

We know my great-grandfather Henry married Augusta Grantz. This marriage is substantiated by: (1) family records; (2) an IGI Individual Record on my grandfather, John Andrew Laumbach (Reference 5); (3) a Grantz Forward Lineage Chart; and (4) the obituary for Henry and Augusta Laumbach's oldest daughter, Elsabea Laumbach Miller (Reference 11).

Researcher Charles Sanders has worked with Jan for several years on this and her other writing projects. His extensive research on the Laumbachs is included in this book. He found a considerable amount of relevant census and genealogy data (see the summary of Sander's research in Reference 12).
In the 1860 Deep Creek Township, Clinton County, Iowa, U.S. Census data, a portion of the family of ADL 1st is still at home, including Mark Henry (listed as "Mark"). Mark Henry's age is given as 21; his age was actually 20 according to Pete Laumbach's family tree and comprehensive birth/ marriage/death certificate documentation.

On the 1870 Deep Creek Township, Clinton County, Iowa, U.S. Census data, the family of ADL 1st is no longer shown; we don't know why. *[Editor's Note: the father, Andreas, had left Iowa for New Mexico soon after the 1860 census. The mother, Anna, died in Deep Creek, Clinton County in 1868. We don't know why none of the other children were listed in the 1870 census, but all except Andreas and Henry were girls and probably changed their names by marriage. We know at least some of the family had moved to other Iowa locations and other states.]* However, a Henry Laumbach is listed and he is the same age as Mark Henry Laumbach. This Henry is clearly my great-grandfather because Augusta "keeps house" for him. The term "keeps house" was commonly applied in early census records, regardless of the age of the couple living together or their marital status. *[That designation was also*

104

applied to teen-age daughters in the family household.] So over the ten-year time frame, from 1860 to 1870, Mark Henry Laumbach "disappears" and Henry Laumbach "appears" in the same Deep Creek Township where the only town is Goose Lake, with less than 250 people. Thus we conclude that Mark Henry and Henry are the same person.

I said above that Henry was the same age as Mark Henry. In the 1870 Deep Creek Township census data, Henry's age is given as 32, which would make him a year older than Mark Henry. However, if we follow him a short distance west to Waterford Township in Clinton County (immediately west of Deep Creek Township), we find him listed there in the 1880 census. His age is given as 41, which is consistent with the age Mark Henry claimed on the 1860 census data ten years earlier. Moving forward in time, the 1885 Waterford Township data shows him to be 46. Thus, in two out of three censuses, Henry's age is shown as the same age claimed by Mark Henry, and the third is only off one year. Perhaps, before he was 20, Mark Henry/Henry thought he was one year older than he actually was, or that was what the household person reporting to the census taker thought.

A different Henry Laumbach shows up in the 1880 U.S. Census for Elk River Township, Clinton County, Iowa. That Henry was married to Martha Peters, and his obituary and census data (see References 4 and 12) indicate he was born in 1847. He was probably the son of ADL 1st's brother, Heinrich. (See Pete Laumbach's Family Tree, Reference 6). In a category titled "Emigration from Schleswig-Holstein," Rootdigger (see Reference 2) lists a Hinrich Laumbach, born in 1847, son of Hinrich Friedrich and Weibke Utermann Lauenbach.

The Andreas and Anna Koos Laumbach family came to America in 1856 (see Reference 10) and settled in Iowa, where many of them remained. Their son, Andreas (ADL 2nd) arrived in the States separately and soon thereafter settled in New Mexico. According to the New Mexico family's Bible, ADL 2nd arrived in New Mexico in the fall of 1859. Not long afterward, according to the New Mexico family, his father ADL 1st came to join him in his ranching operations.

Census data found by Charles Sanders indicates that ADL 1st left Clinton County, Iowa sometime after 1860 and before 1870. IRS Tax Assessment Lists (see Reference 12) indicate he had left Clinton County before 1865. According to stories told by the New Mexico Laumbachs (see, e.g., Reference 3), not long after he had joined his son, ADL 2nd, in New Mexico, he was killed by Indians east of Springer. The 1864 marriage record for his son, ADL 2nd, and Elionor states his father was then no longer living. Therefore, ADL 1st came to New Mexico after 1860, and was killed there before the spring of 1864. ADL 1st was probably in New Mexico no more than three years. Perhaps ADL 1st intended the separation to be temporary when he left his family behind in Iowa.

When he went to New Mexico, his wife, my great-great grandmother, Anna Koos Laumbach, and the rest of their family remained in Iowa. Anna passed away just 12 years after she came to America, at the age of 57 on August 24, 1868 (see References 9 and 12). She was buried in the Center Grove (Ingwerson) Cemetery in Center Township in Clinton County, Iowa. From bits of published data, we conclude that her husband, ADL 1st, lived in America no more than eight years.

If it is true that Henry came to New Mexico, even briefly, as the New Mexico stories say, that must have been with his brother Andreas in late 1859 or with his father after 1860. When the New Mexico family lost track of him, the Iowa family did not. Apparently, he returned from New Mexico to Iowa, and didn't leave there again for many years, after which the Iowa family also lost track of him.

Whether or not my great-grandfather, Henry Laumbach, went to New Mexico between 1859 and 1864, he appears in the Clinton County censuses from 1860 through 1885 but disappears from the Clinton County census after 1885. He apparently left Clinton County (and probably Iowa) sometime after 1885 and before 1890, which puts his age at the time he left at somewhere between 45 and 50.

Some family data documented by my father's oldest sibling, Alma Margaret Laumbach, states that my great-grandfather, Henry Laumbach, died in Sonora, California, a town that lies within what had been the California gold rush country. She gives no date for his death. Perhaps he left his family on a "temporary" basis in search of gold and never returned, but one wonders why he never kept in contact with his family. Did he meet with foul play or just did not keep in touch?

Knowing what I do about my grandfather, John Andrew Laumbach, and my father, Justus Theodore Laumbach, I would guess that my great-grandfather, Henry Laumbach, was a risk-taker, an adventurer, an outdoorsman, a pioneer, a person looking for a better way of life—the kind of person who typically settled the land west of the Mississippi. Perhaps he wanted to achieve a certain level of success before contacting folks at home or returning, or—considering the risks of life in the early west—he didn't live long after leaving Iowa.

Henry and Augusta Laumbach had six children: four girls—Elsabea, Anna, Mathilda and Josephene; and two boys—my grandfather John Andrew, and his younger brother, Henry Albert. According to a Grantz Forward Lineage Chart, my great-grandmother, Augusta, married a second time; this time to Ferdinand Lassen and they had one child, Helen Lassen Clausen, born in 1890. Augusta Grantz Laumbach Lassen passed away in 1933 and was buried in the same cemetery in Clinton County, Iowa as my great-great-grandmother, Anna Koos Laumbach (see Reference 1). It is interesting to speculate whether Anna Koos Laumbach knew [her daughter-in-law] Augusta. Anna passed away at the young age of 57 on August 24, 1868, and Augusta and Henry's first child, Elsabea, was born December 24, 1869. It is likely she did.

My Aunt Alma Laumbach, in her documentation of family data, concluded by saying, "I am hoping this material will be the means of knitting the Laumbach family closer together—and in many cases, be the instrument which will lead to new acquaintances and friendships." With this intent, foresight and understanding, she would have appreciated the benefits of documenting the Laumbach family genealogy in a book such as this.

In closing this contribution to the Laumbach book, I would like to say that meeting the New Mexico Laumbachs has greatly enriched our family's life. Jan's connection with Charles Sanders resulted in his thorough, comprehensive census research. Pete's family tree and family documents extended knowledge of our family in Germany. The May 28, 2009 call from Karl brought me and my family into the loop. Without their efforts and especially Karl's email about the discussion between Red and my dad, it is unlikely this chapter of the Laumbach book would have been written. I also would not know nearly as much as I do now about my great-grandfather, Henry Laumbach, his predecessors and relatives.

John Andrew Laumbach (1873-1956), born in Clinton County, Iowa, son of Henry and Augusta Grantz Laumbach. He was Dallas' grandfather.

Alvina Catherina Greve Laumbach (1879-1939), born in Schleswig-Holstein, Germany, daughter of Hans Henry and Catherina F. Greve. This picture was taken on her wedding day, January 26, 1899, when she married John Andrew Laumbach. They spent their married life in Sac County and Calhoun County, Iowa. This lovely lady was Dallas' grandmother.

References

1. Lassen, Augusta Grantz Laumbach (1933), Burial in Cemetery, Center Grove (Ingwerson) Center Twp, Clinton, Iowa, http://files.usgwarchives.net/ia/clinton/cemeteries/cent.txt.
2. Lauenbach, Hinrich (2009) Emigration from Schleswig-Holstein, http://www.rootdigger.de/Emi.htm.
3. Laumbach, Andreas Detlef 1st, Death by Indians, http://www.nmfarmandranchmuseum.org/oralhistory/detail.php?interview=116.
4. Laumbach, Henry (1921) Obituary, http://boards.ancestry.com/localities.northam.usa.states.iowa.counties.crawford/1185/mb.ashx.
5. Laumbach, John Andrew (1899) IGI Individual Record http://www.familysearch.org/Eng/Search/IGI/individual_record.asp?recid=100422625106&lds=1&region=11&regionfriendly=North+America&frompage=99.
6. Laumbach, Peter James (2005) Laumbach Family Tree.
7. Laumbach, Peter James (2005) Tabulation of Laumbach Historical Certificates.
8. Laumbach, Peter James (2005) The Trip to Jagel.

9. Laumback, Anna Koos (1868) Burial in Cemetery, Center Grove (Ingwerson) Center Twp, Clinton Iowa, http://files.usgwarchives.net/ia/clinton/cemeteries/cent.txt
10. Launbach, Andreas (2009) Emigration from Schleswig-Holstein (in 1856), http://www.rootdigger.de/Emi.htm.
11. Miller, Elsabea A. (1961) Obituary, http://archiver.rootsweb.ancestry.com/th/read/US-OBITS/2004-03/1079236641.
12. Sanders, Charles O. (2009) Research of Census/Government Records Data.
13. Tessier, Denise (2009) Life on the Frontier, American Archaeology, vol.13, No.1, 26-32.

SECTION III: LAUMBACHS IN IOWA

Chapter 9: Mama's Life in Iowa and Nebraska
by Verna Laumbach Sparks   1909-1996

"Studio Portrait" of Peter and Anna L. Henkens

Editor's Note: Verna took notes on anything handy while growing up on her family's ranch, and on frequent visits to Buena Vista to visit her grandmother Elionor, and Aunties. She also noted conversations when she stayed with her Aunt Crestina while attending college at New Mexico Normal in Las Vegas in the late 1920s and early 1930s. When she spent a summer at Boulder, Colorado in 1956 to further her education as a teacher, she compiled her many family history notes and began writing them into a cohesive family history. In October 1991, her daughter, Janet, typeset those for her, and spiral-bound the pages into a booklet presented to her for her 82nd birthday on October 8th. Jan titled the booklet <u>The Story of Andreas and Elionor</u>.

Following is an excerpt of Verna's story about her family in Iowa and Nebraska.

Before going into the story of my parents' married life in New Mexico, I want to give some information about my mother's early life in Iowa and Nebraska before she came west and married my father.

Both of my mother's parents came from [Schleswig] Germany. [We wonder: Did their families, Laumbach and Henkens, know each other there?] Her mother, Anna, came over as an eight-year-old child, and she well remembered the long voyage over on the ship. Her mother's family settled in a mostly German community at Goose Lake, Iowa.

My mother was born Emma Margaretha Henkens in Clinton County, Iowa.i When she was two years old, her folks moved to Boone County. When five, they left Iowa for Chadron, Nebraska.

My grandfather, Peter Henkens, farmed and leased most of the places where they lived. In his family were the following children: August, Caroline, John, Emma, Herman, Edwin, Emilie and Claus,ii all fair and blonde,iii and they grew up to be tall and handsome. My mother, the only small one, was pretty with a lovely complexion and fine, naturally curly blonde hair.

Emma's mother told about a neighbor who could not believe Mama's ringlets were natural. He accused her of curling them. So one morning, when the man was plowing, my grandmother took Mama, a small child at the time, out to the field and dampened her hair in front of the man, and then sat her down on the edge of the field. Grandmother told the man that he could plow once around the field, and watch to see that the child remained sitting there alone. When he got back to her he would find her short hair dry and in a cluster of ringlets. This experiment satisfied the neighbor.

Mama and Aunt Emilie started school in Chadron. It was an English school—the teacher spoke no German. The children spoke no English; only German was spoken at home. They developed a good system in the school: the teacher and pupils taught each other.

After they lived in Chadron for five years, they moved to Pleasant Valley, Nebraska, a rolling plain with dirt hills that could be plowed. Woods grew along the creeks and rivers, with many wild berries and fruit like elderberries, plums, and raspberries. They made good wine from the elderberries.

The farms had lots of trees and orchards, and everybody raised geese, ducks and chickens. Their principal crops were wheat, oats and corn. The farmers depended upon rain for their crops and usually had more than they needed.

It really was a pleasant valley. My mother liked it there. The farmers were nearly all of German origin and neighborly. They joined together to husk, thrush, and shell the corn and other grains, and together they built a house for anyone who needed it. The people of the close-knit community worked and played together.

The women organized quilting bees, which gave them a chance to catch up on the valley news. The children played games like London Bridge and Hide and Seek while their mothers sewed.

Both young and old enjoyed barn dances. Girls nearly always first wore a new calico dress to a dance. "Miller Boy" was one of the popular songs at dances.

The men gathered together at harvesting time, working one farm then moving on to the next. All of the women cooked. Each farm furnished the food while its fields were being harvested. The food was good and plentiful.

First came a very early breakfast and the men went into the fields while it was still cool. They worked until 9:00, when the women brought them a mid-morning "snack" of freshly baked bread, great slices of ham or fried chicken, coffee and sweet rolls. At noon a huge meal was served in the house or under the shade trees on elevated planks in the yard. At 3:30 in the afternoon another lunch was taken out to the fields and a big supper was served rather late, about 7:00.

Eating late gave the men more time in the fields and then to take care of the horses and washing up. At harvesting time, the women and older children took care of regular chores like milking and feeding the pigs and chickens. Besides chores, the women took care of the smaller children, did the tremendous job of cooking and baking, washed mountains of dishes and in-between, visited.

All in all, harvesting time was enjoyed, but it was a lot of work for both men and women. Hearing about it, it seemed to me that the meals were a continuous glorified picnic and gab fest. And hearing about the dishes they served always made me hungry: baked goose, ham, fried and baked chicken, vegetables from the garden served with fresh butter or cream sauces, pickles, fresh-baked bread, pound cakes, pies, cream puffs, melons and homemade ice cream. The hard work made large meals necessary. Girls were taught at a young age how to make good light bread.

Mid-morning and mid-afternoon snacks were only served to the men on harvesting days, but the women nearly always stopped for a few minutes in the afternoon to drink tea or coffee and eat a piece of cake. Mama still had that habit at the ranch. There was almost no day that she did not stop her work for a coffee break.

The women were good housekeepers as well as good cooks. They carefully made the beds, with feather mattresses or "straw ticks" shaken and fluffed out daily. My grandmother insisted on hand-scrubbing her kitchen floor every morning.

Women wore corsets then, at least two slips, and ruffled or full skirts. They wore their hair in different ways, sometimes in little curls around their faces.

Girls seldom dated boys alone. A crowd went along on sleigh rides or in the wagons to dances. Parents usually accompanied the young people to parties. Occasionally a young man called on his girl on a Sunday afternoon, and they went for a short ride in his buggy. I've heard that a horse could walk along pulling the buggy without guidance, leaving the young man's arm free for courting.

Mama attended a German school for a few years, where she became a good speller, reader and writer. Her teacher also taught her students good posture, making them stand straight for their singing exercises. "Chest out, stomach in," he would say. Mama went as far as the sixth grade and then had to stop to help at home, but she still had nice penmanship and she liked to read. When she was older and had more time for reading, she subscribed to many magazines and read them.

Mama's self-reliance and courage later exhibited at the New Mexico ranch began when she was young. Once, she and her younger brothers and sister were left alone on the farm while their parents went somewhere and were gone overnight. The first night a sudden blizzard arrived that was so fierce no one could travel. The children were left alone for days. They had to take care of the newly born animals and keep fires going in the house.

Their biggest problem was lack of fuel; they were unprepared when the blizzard struck. Mama knew she had to keep the cook stove going or they would freeze. They had to burn the precious ears of corn. It made good fuel but was almost like burning money. To keep from becoming ill, because they had to venture out in the howling wind to take care of the chickens and stock, Mama opened her mother's elderberry wine, and they all had a drink every evening. When the children's parents were finally able to come home, they were relieved to find everyone alive and well, thanks to corn fuel and elderberry wine.

A favorite tiny dog, Frisky, belonged to Mama's youngest brother. Claus taught him to sit up and beg, and sit in a high chair to eat popcorn. Frisky preferred to lie in Grandfather's favorite rocking chair. If Grandfather got there first, sometimes Frisky ran to the window and barked. When Grandfather got up to see who was coming, Frisky ran and jumped into his rocking chair.

My Aunt Carrie, the oldest in the family, married when Mama was still quite young. After Aunt Carrie had small children, Mama often went to Fremont to help take care of them.

Later, Mama wanted to earn some money. She worked in some of the well-to-do households in Fremont. She worked for several families; some she liked and some she didn't. It is amazing the amount of work required of a hired girl in those days, and the small amount of salary she was paid. But Mama was able to save some money, which later came in handy for her hope chest.

Mama's younger sister Emilie, or "Melee," was the joy of the family. She had high spirits, always laughing, singing and joking.

Mama never tired of listening to her own mother [Anna] talk of her early days and her family. It would take a book to tell all the stories about Mama's parents, her siblings and her own early life.

~~

Editor's Note: Years later a traveling photographer came by, when Verna's parents lived at their ranch above the Canadian Gorge. Emma—terribly homesick for her old home and family—gave the photographer two small photos of her parents, Peter and Anna Henkens, for him to make into a large studio-type portrait. As often done then, the photographer merged the two photos into one, making it appear that the couple sat together when the photograph was originally taken. Emma asked him to make it a large oval portrait with glass and frame and tint it.[iv] When it arrived, she proudly hung it on a prominent wall of their ranch home.

Daniel was jealous when he saw it hanging there. He wanted one like it of his parents. He also provided the photographer with two small photos of his parents, Andreas and Elionor. We don't know if Daniel requested that his parents' portraits be two large individual oval framed pictures, each the same size as the one of Emma's parents together, instead of merging the two into a large portrait like hers. Those portraits of Andreas and Elionor are the front-pieces of this book. The one of Emma's parents, Peter and Anna L. Henkens together, begins this chapter. These photos—taken of the large oval glass portraits—were enhanced by Butch Sanders for publication in this book. (They could not be removed from their frames and glass. When photographing them in their frames, the oval glass caused distortions and reflections, requiring extra effort by Sanders.)

After her parents died, Ruth E. Laumbach (sister of Verna) inherited all three of these large oval framed portraits, one of Peter and Anna Henkens together and the two of Andreas and Elionor Laumbach. Towards the end of Ruth's life, she gave them to her niece, Vera Jane Laumbach Morris of Las Cruces, New Mexico.

Apparently someone else in the Laumbach family, perhaps Daniel's brother Henry, had identical small original studio prints of Andreas and Elionor that he gave to a photographer to combine into one "studio portrait." Henry's daughter, Clara, in California, had a tinted print of this version. Butch Sanders—while enhancing Emma's large "coupled" portrait of Peter and Anna Henkens (image at beginning of this chapter), and also while working on a copy of Clara's—discovered that Clara's photograph of Andreas and Elionor together was made the same way. The original photos used to create Daniel's two large portraits of his parents were the same small studio prints used to make Clara's group portrait. Butch also found that the original photos used in the two "grouped" portraits—Emma's of Peter and Anna Henkens, and Clara's of Andreas and Elionor—had been separate individual photographs taken at different times, perhaps even by different photographers. Those grouped portraits had been early-day results of what we now call computerized "photo shop."

My cousin, Vera Jane Laumbach Morris, loaned me a "studio portrait" of our grandparents, Emma and Daniel, together when they were middle-aged. That picture was created the same way. But for that one, the photographer used a snapshot of Dan and Emma standing in their yard by their windmill, placed them closer together as if they sat indoors together, and tinted the photograph. The "photo shopper" also made other changes to that image. That tinting was not done well; Sanders tried to repair the poorly done colorization.

Vera Jane had loaned me some of her father's collection of family snapshots. It included the one of Emma and Dan that her father, Joyce, had loaned the photographer for that "studio portrait." His instructions are on the back of the snapshot. In the original, Daniel's hat sits tipped back on his head. For Joyce's commissioned "studio portrait" of his parents, probably made after Daniel died, the photographer also changed Dan's straw hat to felt, and placed it squarely on his head. That "studio portrait" and its original snapshot will appear later in Chapter 34, Papa and Mama.

---

[i] Image of Emma Margaretha Henkens' 1879 German christening document follows. The original is in color and twice page-size. It is shown in black and white on the next two pages.

[ii] Studio portraits of Emma's brothers, and of Emma and her sisters. Photos were probably taken end of 1800s in Nebraska, before Emma came west to marry Daniel in January 1902. In order as seen in two photos: Brothers: Edwin, Claus (the youngest), Herman, and seated, August and John. Sisters: Emma, Emilie, and the oldest, Caroline "Carrie."

[iii] Family of August Henkens, Emma's brother. Photo courtesy of Anna Marie Ortega, granddaughter of Henry Laumbach. This photo had belonged to our Laumbach Aunties who lived at Buena Vista and later at Las Vegas, New Mexico.

[iv] At the beginning of this chapter is the "studio portrait" of Anna and Peter Henkens.

LAUMBACHS IN NEW MEXICO
And Those Who Went Before
In Germany, Iowa and New Mexico

WHO WERE THEY?
THEREFORE, WHO AM I?

Section IV
NEW MEXICO

Es necesario conocer el ayer antes que pueda ver el mañana.
You must know yesterday before you can see tomorrow.

Los que olvidan su pasado no tendrán future.
Those who forget their past have no future.

Old Spanish proverbs

SECTION IV: LAUMBACHS IN NEW MEXICO

Chapter 10: History 101, The Grolet Connection
by Jan Girand

(Most of this piece was first published several years ago in the Roswell Web Magazine)

This chapter is dedicated to Mary Louise Maestas of Las Vegas, New Mexico.[i]

Mary Louise was the first to share with me some of the following vignettes of history over long telephone conversations, beginning in the last decades of the 1900s, sharing our joint family history. It was from her I first heard about José Antonio Esquibel[ii] and some of the valued genealogy he provided people searching for traces of their early New Mexico families. I believe it was he who first told her about the shipwreck near Corpus Christi, Texas related in this chapter. Karl Laumbach gave me a copy of Esquibel's genealogy chart on our family, as well as a copy of the book, *Seeds of Struggle, Harvest of Faith*. Coincidentally, about the same time, my friend, author and historian, Don Bullis, published a piece in his *New Mexico Historical Notebook* about L'Archèvèque and Grolét.

In other coincidences, my mother, Verna L. Sparks, knew Franciscan priest Fray Angelico Chavez[iii] and his family—mother and sister—in the 1930s when he was a handsome young priest assigned to the Peña Blanca Diocese. That was when, in their very early married years, Mama and Daddy lived for a while beside the Domingo trading post when Daddy worked on the Santa Fe Railroad's extra-board. A couple named Archibeque, who became their friends, were running the trading post. Mrs. Archibeque had bright red hair; I met her once at the trading post, many years ago.

Fray Angelico was later assigned to Santa Fe and appointed as that Archdiocese's archivist. His meticulous extractions and translations of early Spanish sacramental records and documents led to his publication of *Origins of New Mexico Families: A Genealogy of the Spanish Colonial Period*. José Antonio Esquibel continued and considerably enlarged Fray Angelico Chavez's works. Their efforts considerably broadened the knowledge for all of us with forebears in early New Mexico. *(In his later life, Fray Angelico stopped placing accents on his name.)* Most of the following information originated with José Antonio Esquibel.

~~

In 1595, Don Juan de Oñate organized a large expedition of soldiers, settlers and clergy to colonize lands for Spain and the Catholic Church. A portion of that land to be colonized, now known as New Mexico, was then only inhabited by tribes and pueblos of American Indians.

That era—called the colonial period—when those Europeans came to the New World to colonize these lands for God and king, is New Mexico's earliest recorded history. During the initial years of that period, the Catholic Church recorded marriages, christenings, sometimes last rites and wills or last wishes. However, many of those earliest records did not survive. Most were lost during the Pueblo Revolt of 1680.

The Spaniards, who had been ousted by the Indian revolt, returned to New Mexico in late 1693. They again established church communities within the pueblos and Indian settlements. The church again recorded marriages, births and deaths. Some of those early records survive. Enduring records began to be more complete in the 1700s. For an extended time, beginning in the 1600s, the convent at the Santo

121

Domingo Pueblo became the archival place of those records for the entire colonial area of New Mexico. However, an 1886 flood and poor record-keeping caused further loss.

In 1954, Fray Angelico Chavez, with the Church's blessing, began the awesome and tedious task of extracting, deciphering handwriting and archaic spellings, translating into English, cataloging and filing the entire collection, those that miraculously still existed, of sacramental records that spanned 300 years of New Mexico history. From the exhaustive efforts of Chavez, and later also by José A. Esquibel who continued this work, we can trace early genealogies of many of New Mexico's long-time Hispanic and some Indian families.

Thanks to those two men, two branches of our family tree can be traced back to the earliest European settlers of New Mexico who arrived in the late 1500s with Oñate's expedition.

Our family's genealogy spanning nine generations, from 1660 to 1827, is shown on a chart in a chapter written by José Esquibel in *Seeds of Struggle, Harvest of Faith, The History of the Catholic Church in New Mexico*. The LPD Press published this book, edited by Thomas J. Steele, S. J. Paul Rhetts and Barbe Awalt, in 1998. On Esquibel's chart on page 33, the family lines of Bernardo Martín and Apolonia Gutiérrez de Solano begin with a common ancestor, a woman named Anna (Ana). The chart ends nine generations later with the marriage of Bernardo and Apolonia, and the 1827 birth of their daughter, Maria Viviana Martín. In life, their genealogy continues. Viviana/Bibiana, my maternal great-great-grandmother, has hundreds of descendants, including Esquibel.

A line can also be traced from one branch of that genealogy to a Frenchman, Jacques Grolet. Therein is a story from the history books.

Frenchman René Robert Cavelier de La Salle made more than one expedition to the New World in the 1600s. He explored the Great Lakes and the Mississippi River. In 1684, he claimed a large portion of what is now the continental USA for his king, Louis XIV. When the United States purchased that vast land from France in 1803, it was named the Louisiana Purchase for that king.

But back to LaSalle's expedition:

With four ships and almost 300 people, including soldiers, settlers and servants, La Salle set off on another expedition, returning to the area to search for the mouth of the Mississippi. That would be his final journey. They landed, perhaps accidentally, at Matagorda Bay, Texas, on the Gulf of Mexico in 1686. There, La Salle planned to establish a colony. Conditions were difficult and their efforts failed.

Some of the settlers mutinied. La Salle, an arrogant, unpopular man, and some of the others, were killed. Early Catholic Church records in New Mexico trace two survivors of that final, fateful La Salle expedition: 20-year-old soldier/sailor Jacques Grolet and 13-year-old servant, Jean de L'Archèvèque. Unlike La Salle and most of his entourage, those two survived and ultimately settled in New Mexico—but not without encountering serious difficulties along the way. Their subsequent adventures are too much to detail here.

Jacques Grolet was born in La Rochelle, France to Ybon Groleé—his father's name according to one of his enduring records. Jacques, or those who recorded his history, changed his name to the Hispanic spelling and pronunciation, Santiago Gurulé, sometime after he became a New Mexico resident.

This Grolet/Gurulé Frenchman married New Mexico native, Elena Gallegos, who was probably born around the time of the 1680 Pueblo Revolt. Hers is another story from the history books.

In 1716, sometime after the death of her husband, Elena Gallegos de Gurulé (Grolet) purchased or otherwise acquired—some records say she inherited—a large tract of land from Diego de Montoya, her husband's longtime friend. Some of her descendants speculate whether Montoya willed that land to her, instead of to his legitimate sons, because they were lovers. By the mid-1800s, that land became known as the Elena Gallegos Land Grant. Because of unpaid taxes, her heirs ultimately lost that land that spanned from the Rio Grande to the Sandia Crest. Today, most of the city of Albuquerque sits upon the Elena Gallegos Grant, and a large public open lands area, named for her, lies in the Sandia foothills. Elena Gallegos, the first New Mexico woman known to inherit a large expanse of land, lives on through her heritage and history.

To fast-forward: In 1995, the remains of a shipwreck were discovered under just twelve feet of water in Matagorda Bay, north of Corpus Christi, Texas. This 1686 wreck, La Belle, was lauded as the most significant underwater archeological find in North America because of its treasure-trove of artifacts. It was the smallest of the four ships of LaSalle's final and ill-fated adventure. The reclamation crews built a cofferdam in the Bay to excavate, retrieve and ultimately reconstruct this ship. The recovery work alone took a year, from 1996 to 1997. Reconstruction work continued long afterward in Matagorda Bay.

---

[i] Mary Louise Maestas was a daughter of Faye Romero of Roy and later of Springer. Faye was daughter of Florencio Esquibel, son of Maria Marta Ebel Esquibel. Mary Louise, a retired mid-level public school teacher in Las Vegas, was always interested in her family history, and gathered a considerable amount of data and stories from various sources. I "met" her through Karl Laumbach, who had known her years longer than I. She and I—like she and Karl—spent long hours on the phone sharing family history. When Mary Louise Maestas died at home in Las Vegas in 2005, we lost a valued source of history.

[ii] José Antonio Esquibel's genealogy: Juan Andres Eberle/Ebel was the full brother of Elionor Eberle/Ebel Laumbach and Maria Marta Eberle/Ebel Esquibel. Andres' daughter, Nicanora Ebel, married Conrado Andrada. Their daughter Inez Andrada, and Juan Isidro Esquibel, were grandparents of José Antonio Esquibel. José is an author and renowned researcher and genealogist of early Hispanic families of New Mexico. He extended our family's knowledge of our early forebears in New Mexico seven generations before Bernardo and Apolonia.

[iii] Fray Angelico Chavez—born in Wagon Mound, New Mexico in 1910, died in Santa Fe in 1996—was a Franciscan priest. He received his primary education at the Loretto Academy in Mora; at age 14 he went off to study at a seminary in Ohio. He served on the battlefield as a World War II chaplain and continued his military service during the Korean War. He was assigned to the Archdiocese of Santa Fe to serve as its archivist. His work not only benefited families seeking their early New Mexico genealogy, extending their knowledge many generations back in time, his findings also corrected some New Mexico history. With his research and book, *But Time and Chance,* Chavez redeemed the tarnished reputation of Father Antonio José Martinez (1793-1867). Fr. Martinez had been long discredited by authors, historians and Bishop Lamy. Among other things, they and historians wrongly accused Fr. Martinez of being involved with the 1847 Taos Rebellion.

Fray Angelico Chavez was an artist, poet, esteemed author and historian. The New Mexico Museum in Santa Fe named its History Library for him, and his larger-than-life bronze statue stands near the Palace of the Governors. (Source: Various, including Wikipedia, and book *But Time and Chance* by Fray Angelico Chavez.)

SECTION IV: LAUMBACHS IN NEW MEXICO

Chapter 11: Mora Private Land Claim, Number 32

The following document series was found by Charles O. Sanders. He wants us to note that he found the English translations somewhat incomplete when compared to the Spanish ones immediately preceding them. He said they are that way in every congressional series he looked at, no matter what year the publication. There may be important data in the Spanish versions that the translator omitted or misinterpreted in his translation. Those of you wanting to confirm accuracy should compare the actual Spanish version against the translations.

Note: This book's editor removed some of the spacing that had been in the documents. Also note that the below text is not a true copy. Sanders transcribed the data from source he found and he cautioned, when he learned it would be added to this book, that his transcription could have errors. For accuracy of this Congressional Hearing, refer to the original documents.

[*Congressional Serial Set-Issue 1047-1860-pages 180-192*]
EXECUTIVE DOCUMENTS
PRINTED BY ORDER OF THE
HOUSE OF REPRESENTATIVES
DURING THE
FIRST SESSION OF THE THIRTY-SIXTH CONGRESS,
1859-'60.
IN FIFTEEN VOLUMES.

WASHINGTON:
THOMAS H. FORD, PRINTER.
1860.

36TH CONGRESS HOUSE OF REPRESENTATIVES Ex. Doc. 1ST Session No. 14.

NEW MEXICO—PRIVATE LAND CLAIMS.

LETTER
FROM
THE SECRETARY OF THE INTERIOR,
COMMUNICATING

Documents in relation to private land claims in New Mexico.
FEBRUARY 10, 1860. Referred to the Committee on Private Land Claims, and ordered to be printed.

DEPARTMENT OF THE INTERIOR,
Washington, February 3, 1860.

Sir: I have the honor herewith to transmit, for the action of Congress under the eighth section of the act approved July 22, 1854, the transcripts of nineteen private land claims in New Mexico, designed for the House of Representatives, as indicated in the letter of the Commissioner of the General Land Office, of the 30th November last, of which a copy is now enclosed.

Similar documents, submitted by the Commissioner in the same letter, for the Senate of the United States, have been this day transmitted to the presiding officer of that body.

Very respectfully, your obedient servant,

J. THOMPSON,
Secretary.

Hon. W. Pennington,
Speaker of the House of Representatives.

GENERAL LAND OFFICE, November 30, 1859.

Sir: I have the honor to transmit herewith, in duplicate, the documents in relation to nineteen private land claims, numbers 20 to 38, both inclusive, in New Mexico, with the request that they may be laid before the ensuing Congress for their final action thereon. These claims have been investigated and approved by the surveyor general of New Mexico, with the exception of number 26, which has been rejected by him.

The foregoing documents are put up in two separate packages, marked "U. S. House Reps.," and "U. S. Senate," and each of the nineteen claims is accompanied by a schedule of documents specified in the exhibit "A" herewith.

I have the honor to be, very respectfully, your obedient servant,

S. A. SMITH,
Commissioner.

Hon. J. Thompson,
Secretary of the Interior.

[*Pages: 180 – 192*]

CLAIM No. 32.
TOWN OF MORA.
Documents composing claim No. 32.

1. Notice.
2. Grant, Spanish.
3. Grant, translation.
4. Receipt for deed, Spanish.
5. Receipt for deed, translation.
6. Testimony.
7. Report.

NOTICE.

UNITED STATES OF AMERICA,
Territory of New Mexico.

To the surveyor general of New Mexico:

José Ma. Valdez and Vincente Romero, on behalf of themselves and the other inhabitants, settlers of the valley of Mora, and those claiming under or deriving title under the original grant, respectfully represent to you that they are the claimants and legal owners in fee of a certain tract of land lying and being situate in the county of Taos, in said Territory of New Mexico, and known as the valley of Mora, and bounded on the north by the Rio de Ocate, on the east by the Aguage de la Llegua, on the south by the mouth of the Sapello, where it empties into the Rio de Mora, and on the west by the Estillero, all of

125

which points and boundaries are well-known landmarks in the said county of Taos. And the said claimants claim a perfect title to said lands by virtue of a grant made on the twenty-eighth day of September, A. D. 1835, by Albino Peres, political chief of the Territory of New Mexico, but which said grant has been lost or destroyed, as also by virtue of being placed in actual legal possession of said lands, and occupying and cultivating said lands from said twenty-eighth day of September down to the present time, which said grant and occupation was made according to the laws, usages, and customs of the republic of Mexico, which were declared and recognized to be in force and effect at that time in the republic of Mexico, for which power and authority see Collection of the Decrees and Orders of the Cortes of Spain, published in Mexico by Martin Galvan, in 1829, page 56, and from pages 91 to 101; see also the decrees of Mexico of June 4 and September 18, 1823, pages 123 and 180 of 2d vol. of Galvan's Decrees; see Ordenanzas de Pierras y Aguas, and 8th Peters's Reports, 436, 15th Peters, 130, 1 Howard, 24, 6th Peters, 691, Holcomb's U. S. Digest, 358 to 363.

The present claimants cannot show the quantity of land embraced in the said grant except as therein set forth, as within the above well-known metes and boundaries, nor can they furnish a plat of survey, as no survey has ever been executed. Claimants know of no adverse claim to said grant, and further state that the original grantees, under whom the present claimants claim, were legally put in possession of said lands, and have held the undisturbed possession down to the present time.

Claimants file this their said claim under the 8th section of the act of Congress approved 22d July, 1854, entitled "An act to establish the offices of surveyor general of New Mexico, Kansas, and Nebraska, to grant donations to actual settlers therein, and for other purposes," and respectfully ask confirmation by you of this their said claim.

M. ASHURST,
Attorney for Claimants.
JACKSON, for Claimants.

Note.—The present claimants hereby relinquish all right and interest they may have in and to a grant made to John Scolly and others, made on the 7th day of May, 1846, and approved on the 15th of August, 1859, by the surveyor general of New Mexico, so far as the said grant conflicts with this grant.
M. ASHURST, for Claimants.
JACKSON, for Claimants.

Surveyor General's Office,
Santa Fe, New Mexico, August 20, 1859.
The above is a true copy of the original on file in this office.
WILLIAM PELHAM, Surveyor General.
GRANT—SPANISH.
Sello Tercero. [SEAL.] Dos Reales.
Para los años de mil ochocientos cuarenta y mil ochocientos cuarenta y uno.
VALE UN PESO EL PLIEGO.

En veinte de Octubre de mil ochocientos treinta y cinco, yo Manuel Antonio Sanches alcalde constitucional de la jurisdicción de San José de Las Trampas, con los testigos de mi asistencia con quienes actuó por receptoría; en cumplimiento al superior decreto del Sor. gefe politico del Territorio Don Albino Pérez, fecha 28 de Septiembre de este mismo año, pase al punto de lo Demora jurisdicción de mi cargo, con el fin de repartier este sitio baldío según lo dispuesto en el referido superior decreto; y estando en el presentes los interesados pobladores que son en numero de setenta y seis cuídanos, se le puso por ubicación al valle de abajo, valle de Santa Gertrudes, y al de arriba valle de San Antonio: y en el nombre de la nación Mejicana y de esta municipalidad se brizo el señalamiento de plasas en uno y otros valles, siendo la de Santa Gertrudes de norte a sur al decientas varas, y de oriente a poniente ciento y cincuenta varas, dejando treinta varas afuera para chorreras y pisos de todos, y la veja para beneficio común con sus entradas y salidas libres la plaza de San Antonio es de norte a sur de decientas varas, y de oriente a poniente ciento y cuicuenta varas quedando la ciénega para beneficio común de los pobladores, con las entradas y salidas por el norte la cañada de los Comanches, por el sur el Rio de la Casa y al valle de la Sebolla. En requida se procedió al repartiemento de tierra para labor, y tirado el cordel de oriente a poniente se midieran en el valle de Santa Gertrudes a la banda del sur, cuatro mil cien varas de tierra, y a la banda del norte que nirra al tulquillo, se midieron mil sebecientas varas de tierra, las cuales fueron repartidas a los agraciados pobladores por el orden que abajo quedan alistados. A continuación el dia siguiente pasamos al valle de San Antonio, yestando en el tirado el cordel de la orilla de la canega al rumbo del Poniente, se midieron y repartieron, según el orden de la lista como dicho es, dos mil ochocientas varas de tierra en el valle; quinientas sesenta varas de tierra en la Lagunita: y dos cientas cincuenta varas de tierra enfrente de la plaza al sud—Veshe de ella, según consta en la citada lista. Siendo los linderos generales de este sitio, para beneficio de los agraciados y pásteos comunes al ellos, por el norte el Rio de Ocate: por el sur donde desemboca el Rio del Sapelló, por el oriente el Aguaje de la Slequa, y por el poniente el Estillero. Y de haberze tomado esta posesión quieta pacificamente y sin contradición de persona alguna, los agraciados de ella en demostraciones de alegria arrancaron yerbas, tiraron piedras, esparcieron puñadas de tierra, e hicieron otros actos posesorios dando vivas a dios ya la nación.

En testimonia para constancia perpetua y obligatoria en todo tiempo de lo ahora estipulado, se estendio este titulo de mercenacion, y las particulares escrituras de cada uno, las cuales con este acto, la petición, y superior decreto a ella estampado quedan protocoladas en el archivo de la gefactura política en Santa Fe: y copia en esta de mi cargo de solo lo actuado por mi el citado alcalde.

La lista de los agraciados que se anotan y el numera de tierra que á cada uno toco es del tenor siguiente, valle de Santa Gertrudes, banda del sur, medida de oriente á Poniente; José Tapia, cien varas; Carmen Arce, ciento cincuenta varas; Juan Lorenzo Aliso, docientas varas; Juan Antonio Garcia, ciento cincuenta varas; Carlos Rinto, docientas varas; Mateo Ringinel, decientas varas; Manuel Suhazo, cien varas; Gerónimo Martin, cien varas; Francisco Sandobal, cien varas; Francisco Loré, cien varas; Francisco Conen, docientas varas; José Mestas, cien varas; Ramón Archuleta, cien varas; Antonio Aba Trujillo, cien varas; Juan de Jesús Cruz, cien varas; Maria Dolores Romero, docientas varas; Faustin Mestas, cien varas; Maria Dolores Sanches, docientas varas; José Miguel Pacheco, cien varas; Yldefonso Pacheco, cien varas; Manuel Sanches, cien varas; Juan Trujillo, docientas varas; Felipe Carbajal, cien varas; José Maria Garcia, cien varas; Miguel García, cien varas; Gabriel Lujan, cien varas; Manuel Arguello, cien varas; Ygnacio Gonzales, docientas varas; José Guadalupe Ortega, cien varas; Felipe Arguello, cien varas; Manuel Gregorio Martin, cien varas; Juan Cristóbal Trujillo, cien varas; Banda del norte que mira al Tulquillo medida de oriente à Poniente; Tomas Encarnación García, ciento cincuenta varas; Carlos Salazar, ciento cincuenta varas; Francisco Arguello, cien varas; Francisco Sena, cien varas; José Ygnacio Madrid, cien varas; Miguel Paez, cien varas; Manuel Paez, cien varas; **Miguel Mascareñas**, docientas varas; Cecilio Montano, cincuenta varas; Cruz Medina, cien varas; **Bernardo Martin**, cien varas; Miguel Arguello, ciento cincuenta varas; Ramón Amado, ciento cincuenta varas; Pedro Aragón, ciento cincuenta varas; Esteban Valdez, cien varas.

Valle de San Antonio, banda del Sur medida de Oriente á Poniente, Manuel Sanches, cien varas; Juan Ygnacio Sanches, cien varas; Francisco Sarracino, cien varas; Albino Chacón, cien varas; Damasio Chacón, cien varas; Teodocio Quintana, cien varas; José Garcia, cien varas ; Rafael Paez, cien varas; Nepomoceno Gurule, cien varas; José Vigil, cien varas; Néstor Armijo, trecientas varas; Andrés Órnelas, cien varas; Mateo Montoya, cien varas; Juan de la Cruz Trujillo, cien varas; Juan de Jesús

Lujan, cien varas; Francisco Trujillo, cien varas; Andrés Trujillo, cien varas; Juan Andrés Archuleta, cien varas; Ramón Abreu, cien varas; Jesus Maria Alarid, cien varas; Vicente Sánchez, cien varas; Mateo Sandobal, cien varas; Juan López, cien varas; Pedro Chacón, cien varas; Miguel Antonio Mascareñas, cien varas; Antonio Arguello, cien varas; <u>Lagunita de San Antonio, medida de Oriente á Poniente</u>, José Silva, docientas ochenta varas; Juan José Vigil, docientas ochenta varas; <u>Frente á la plaza de San Antonio punto al Serrito que divide á la Lagunita</u>; Miguel Olguin, docientas cincuenta varas. Los individuos anotados han quedado unánimes conformes y posesionados del terreno de lo Demora, Valles de Santa Gertrudes y de San Antonio; á los que con el fin de que sepan lo que poseen y con quien lindan se les da copia de sus particulares escrituras, y hechoseles saber la estencion del terreno y sus egidos, según la generalidad del sitio. Lo que para constancia, perpetua de la legalidad de esta posesión, la antoriozo y firmo con los testigos referidos, de que doy fe. Manuel Antonio Sánchez. Ynstrumental, Teodocio Quintana. Ynstrumental, Néstor Armigo. Testigos de asistencia, Albino Chacón. Testigo de asistencia, Rafael Paez. Copiado, Agasto 12 de 1842.

TERRITORIO De NUEVO MÉJICO,
    Condado de Taos.

Yo Manuel Antonio Sánchez uno de los jueces de paz en y por el Condado de Taos. Certifico que un documento igual y conforme en todas sus partes al que antecede (y del que este es una correcta y legal copia) fue trabajado con autoridad competente en lo Demora los dias mes y año que en el mismo se mencionan y depositado entonces con los adjuntos documentos que se citan, en Santa Fé en el archivo del gefe político. Y yo ademas certifico que el abajo subscrito juez de Paz ahora, fue en aquel tiempo el mismo alcalde que con autoridad de las leyes de Méjico actuó el dicho documento en todas sus partes.

Firmado y sellado de mimano y sello privado por no haberlo publico en el precinto del llano numero 7 en la oficina de mi despacho hoy 3 de Febrero, A. D. 1857.

                      MANUEL ANTONIO SÁNCHEZ, [L. S.]
                                     Juez de Paz.

        SURVEYOR GENERAL'S OFFICE, TRANSLATOR'S DEPARTMENT,
               Santa Fe, New Mexico, September 10, 1859.
The above is a true copy of the original on file in this office.
        DAVID V. WHITING, Translator.

                GRANT—TRANSLATION.
               Seal Third. [SEAL.] Two Reals.

For the years one thousand eight hundred and forty and one thousand eight hundred and forty-one. [SEAL.] Its value is one dollar per sheet.

On the 20th of October, one thousand eight hundred and thirty-five, I, Manuel Antonio Sanchez, constitutional justice of the jurisdiction of San José de las Trampas, with my attending witnesses, with whom I act by appointment, in compliance with the superior decree of Don Albino Perez, political chief of the Territory, dated the twenty-eighth day of September last past, I proceeded to the place called Demora, within the jurisdiction under my charge, for the purpose of distributing this public land, as is provided in the aforementioned superior decree, and being there, and the settlers interested, amounting to seventy-six citizens, being there also, <u>the lower valley was called "Valle de Santa Gertrudes," and the upper one "Valle de San Antonio,"</u> and in the name of the Mexican nation, and of this municipality, the <u>town site was marked out in both valleys</u>, the one at Santa Gertrudes being two hundred varas from north to south, and one hundred and fifty varas from east to west, leaving thirty varas outside for drippage and a common road, and the meadow for the benefit of all, with its entrances and exits free. The site of the town of San Antonio contains two thousand varas from north to south, and one hundred and fifty varas from east to west, leaving the meadow for the benefit of all settlers, with the following entrances and exit: On the north the Canon of the Comanches, on the south of Casas river, and in the direction of the Cebolla. Thereupon I proceeded to distribute the land suitable to cultivation, and drawing the line from east to west, on the south side of the valley of Santa Gertrudes, there were measured four thousand one hundred varas of land, and on the north, in the direction of Tulquillo, there were measured one thousand seven hundred varas of land, which were distributed among the settlers in the order in which they are arranged on the list. On the subsequent day we proceeded to the valley of San Antonio, and being there, we drew the line from the edge of the Ciénega towards the west, another was measured and distributed according to the list aforementioned; two thousand eight hundred varas of land in the valley; five hundred and sixty varas at the Lagunita; and two hundred and fifty varas of land opposite the town, towards the southwest thereof, as will appear by the aforementioned list; the general boundaries of this tract, being for the benefit of the grantees and for common pasturage; on the north, the Ocate river; on the south to where the Sapéyo empties; on the east the Aguage de la Yegua, and on the west, the Estillero, and as having taken possession thereof quietly and peacefully, and without opposition from any person whatsoever, the grantees, in token of joy, pulled up weeds, threw stones, scattered handsfull of earth, and performed other acts of possession, giving thanks to God and to the nation.[i]

As a perpetual and binding evidence in all time to come of what has now been transacted, this title deed of grant was executed, and also the particular deeds to each one, which, together with this act, the petition, and the superior decree thereto attached, are deposited in the archives of the office of the political chief at Santa Fé, and a copy of only what has been done by me is deposited in this office under my charge.

MANUEL ANTONIO SANCHEZ.

Instrumental: TEODOCIO QUINTANA.
NESTOR ARMIJO.
Attending witnesses: ALBINO CHACON.
RAFAEL PAEZ.

Copied August 12, 1842.

TERRITORY OF NEW MEXICO, *County of Taos*:

I, Manuel Antonio Sanchez, one of the justices of the peace within and for the county of Taos, certify that a document in all respects alike to this (and of which this is a correct copy) was executed by competent authority, at Lo de Mora, on the day, month, and year therein mentioned, and then deposited with the accompanying documents referred to in the archives of the political chief at Santa Fé. And I further certify that the undersigned, now a justice of the peace, was at that time the same alcalde who, by virtue of the authority of the laws of Mexico, executed the said document in all its parts.

Signed and sealed with my hand and private seal, there being no public seal, at No. 7, of El Llano, at my office, this 3d day of February, 1857.

MANUEL ANTONIO SANCHEZ,
Justice of the Peace.

SURVEYOR GENERAL'S OFFICE, TRANSLATOR'S DEPARTMENT,
Santa Fé, New Mexico, September 19, 1857.

The foregoing is a correct translation of the original on file in this office.

DAVID V. WHITING,
Translator.

SURVEYOR GENERAL'S OFFICE,
Santa Fe, New Mexico, August 20, 1859.
The above is a true copy of the original on file in this office.
WM. PELHAM,
Surveyor General.

RECEIPT FOR DEED—SPANISH.

Recivi del alcalde anterior del año de 1835 una merced constante de cuatro foyas la que existe en poder del C. Miguel Mascareñas residente de este punto de lo Demoro, cuya merced nos entrego el C. Manuel Antonio Sánchez, accompañado con un decreto del sor gefe politico, Don Albino Pérez, fecha 10 de Octubre del año anterior, y para su resguardo ledi este delante del Juez territorial del punto de lo Demora, la que firmo yo y dos testigos de asistencia y para su resguardo lo firmamos hoy dia de la fecha.

Valle de lo Demora, 16 de Agosto de 1836.

MIGUEL MASCAREÑAS.

Juez territorial, JUAN LORENZO ALIRE.
(Testigo) JOSÉ MIGUEL PACHECO.
(Testigo) JOSÉ ESTRADA.

Trampas, Agosto 19 de 1836, de hecho me hago cargo del anterior recivo lo firme en dicho dia mes y año.

JÜAN DE JESÚS CRUZ.

SURVEYOR GENERAL'S OFFICE, TRANSLATOR'S DEPARTMENT,
Santa Fe, New Mexico, September 10, 1859.
The above is a true copy of the original on file in this office.
DAVID V. WHITING, Translator.

RECEIPT FOR DEED—TRANSLATION.

Received of the former justice of the year 1836 a grant, consisting of four pages, which is in the hands of citizen Miguel Mascarenas, resident of this place of De Mora, which grant was delivered to us by citizen Manuel Antonio Sanchez, accompanied by a decree of the political chief, Don Albino Perez, dated on the tenth of October of the previous year, and for his protection I gave him this before the territorial justice of the place of De Mora, which I sign, with two attending witnesses, and for his protection we sign on the day of the date.

VALLEY OF DE LO DE MORA, *August* 16, 1836.

MIGUEL MASCARENAS.

Territorial justice, JUAN LORENZO ALIRE.
Attending: JOSE MIGUEL PACHECO.
JOSE ESTRADA.

TRAMPAS, *August* 19, 1836.

I have taken charge of the foregoing receipt I signed on the date above mentioned.

JUAN DE JESUS CRUZ.

SURVEYOR GENERAL'S OFFICE, TRANSLATOR'S DEPARTMENT,
Santa Fe, New Mexico, *June* 29, 1859.

The foregoing is a translation of the original on file in this office.
DAVID V. WHITING, Translator.

SURVEYOR GENERAL'S OFFICE,
Santa Fe, New Mexico, *August* 25, 1859.
The above is a true copy of the original on file in this office.
WM. PELHAM,
Surveyor General.

TESTIMONY.

MANUEL ANTONIO SANCHEZ sworn:

Question. Have you any interest in this case?
Answer. I have none.
Question. Where do you reside?
Answer. In Santa Barbara, Taos county.
Question. Did you divide out the lands at Mora as stated in the document here presented, purported to have been made by you?
Answer. I did.
Question. When you divided out the land, did you have in your possession the original grant made by Albino Perez?
Answer. I did.
Question. To whom was the original grant made by Albino Perez?
Answer. To the persons referred to in the document made by me, and of which the document previously shown me is a copy.
Question. In what year was this land distributed?
Answer. In 1835.
Question. What did you do with the copy of the original grant which you made?
Answer. It was delivered to Miguel Mascarenas, who was one of the original grantees.
Question. Have the two valleys of Mora been settled and occupied and cultivated from that time up to the present?
Answer. They have been continuously occupied from that period up to this time.
Question. Do you know what became of the copy you gave to Mascarenas?
Answer. I do not know.
MANUEL ANTONIO SANCHEZ.
Sworn and subscribed before me this 1st July, 1859.
WILLIAM PELHAM, Surveyor General.

VICENTE ROMERO sworn:

Question. Have you at any time seen the copy of the original grant made by Albino Perez to the town of Mora; and if so, when, where, and at what time did you see it last?
Answer. I saw it in the archives of Mora while Thomas Lalande was alcalde. I saw it last in 1846.
Question. What became of the archives of Mora in the alcalde's office?
Answer. The archives of Mora were burned in the beginning of 1847. The United States troops set fire to the house during the revolution of January 1847.

Cross-examined by United States.

Question. Do you know what became of the copy of the Mora grant, which you saw in the archives?
Answer. I know it was burned up, from my own knowledge.
Question. Were you in charge of the archives when they were burned?
Answer. I was not.
VICENTE ROMERO.
Sworn and subscribed before me this 1st July, 1859.
WILLIAM PELHAM, Surveyor General.

RAFAEL PAEZ sworn:

Question. Have you any interest in this claim, and do you live upon it?
Answer. I have not, and do not reside there.
Question. Were you present in the years 1835 and 1836 as a witness when Manuel Antonio Sanchez placed the parties in possession of the Mora grant?
Answer. I was.
Question. Did you see the original decree made by Albino Perez?
Answer. I did see it, in the hands of Sanchez, who was an alcalde at that time.
Question. What were the contents of that decree?
Answer. That the land of Mora should be divided out between the parties who had asked for it, upon condition that they would break up the land and cultivate it.
Question. Did Sanchez place the parties in possession and distribute the lands among the petitioners in conformity with that decree?
Answer. He did.
Question. When was that possession given?
Answer. In October 1835. They have occupied it from that time up to this.
Question. How many settlers are there in the two valleys of Mora?
Answer. About one thousand souls.
Question. Were the parties placed in possession by Sanchez the sole grantees under the decree of Perez?
Answer. They were the only ones at that time.
Question. Do you know of any other grant made to the same land besides the one made as above?
Answer. I do not. Other parties have been placed in possession since, under the decree of Perez. I do not know of any documentary evidence of such possession. They were placed in possession by the authorities of Mora and Taos.
RAFAEL PAEZ.
Sworn and subscribed before me this 1st July, 1859.

WILLIAM PELHAM, Surveyor General.

DAVID V. WHITING sworn:

I hold the office of chief clerk and translator in the office of the surveyor general of New Mexico. I have examined all the papers composing the archives of the former government at Santa Fé, and selected there from all the grants, and papers having reference to grants, to lands in this Territory. I did not find the grant to Mora made by Albino Perez in 1836.

DAVID V. WHITING.

Sworn and subscribed before me this 1st July, 1859.
WILLIAM PELHAM,
Surveyor General.

SURVEYOR GENERAL'S OFFICE,
Santa Fe, New Mexico, August 20, 1859.

The above is a true copy of the original on file in this office.

WILLIAM PELHAM, Surveyor General.

REPORT.
THE TOWN OF MORA vs. THE UNITED STATES.

This case was set for trial on the 1st of July, 1859, and the parties and witnesses being present, the case was taken up and acted upon on the day fixed for the investigation. On the 20th October, 1835, Manuel Antonio Sanchez, constitutional justice of the jurisdiction of San José de Las Trampas, certifies that in compliance with an order issued to him by Albino Perez, political chief of the Territory, dated the 28th of September, 1835, he placed the parties in possession of the vacant and unoccupied lands referred to in said decree, to the petitioners therein mentioned.

The document containing the above purports to be a copy made on the 12th of August, 1842, of the original proceedings had in the premises, which is certified by Sanchez, who became a justice of the peace under the government of the United States on the 3rd of February, 1857, to be an exact copy of the original made by him in 1835. The case was argued by Messrs. Jackson & Ashurst on the part of the claimants, and R. H. Tompkins, esq., United States district attorney, on the part of the United States.

The principal objections made by the counsel for the United States, as submitted in his brief are that there is no evidence other than the testimony of Sanchez, that a grant was ever made or that it was ever seen at Santa Fe, the place of deposit, and that no evidence is shown that Albino Perez had any authority to make the grant.

That the witness Romero testified to the destruction of the order of Perez when it was not in his possession, nor could he have any certain knowledge that the grant was in the archives when they were destroyed.

That no evidence has been produced to show that Albino Perez actually executed the order for the distribution of the land, and that the witness testifies that lands were granted by the authorities of Mora and Taos within the limits granted to the original grantees by Perez, showing that the Mexican authorities did not consider the grant to have been made in fee.

That the failure of the petitioners to prove the execution of a grant to said lands by the competent authorities at Santa Fe, with the necessary formalities to sever the land from the public domain, and the failure to prove that any such document ever existed in the archives at Santa Fe, and the evidence that no such document was found among such archives, and the failure to prove the destruction of the archives or any portion of them at Santa Fe, at any time subsequent to 1835, tend strongly to prove that no such grant was ever made, and consequently that the lands in question were never severed from the public domain.

The evidence of Sanchez, a justice of the peace, and one of the constituted authorities under the Mexican government, acting within the scope of his authority, is deemed to be good evidence of the existence of the grant, and it is presumed that he would not arrogate to himself the authority of distributing the public domain without directions from the granting power of the country. Neither would the petitioners, who were going to remove there and expend large sums in improving the lands, be satisfied with the action of a subordinate executive officer alone, unless he was acting by authority and within the scope of his duties, knowing that all their improvements would be forfeited by this action of the justice if illegal and contrary to law.

The fact of the grant never having been seen at Santa Fé is not proven in evidence, and even if it were could have very little weight, as it was not the business of the grantees to look after the preservation and safekeeping of the original after they had received a copy duly certified to by a legal authority. That was a matter entrusted to the executive authorities at the seat of government. The original must have existed or a copy of it could not have been delivered by the alcalde of the previous year to Miguel Mascarenas, as is shown by Mascareñas' receipt.

It has been clearly proven in other cases before this office that authority was vested in the political chief to make grants of land, and the fact of Albino Perez having occupied that position is a matter of history, and it is well known that he was beheaded in one of the many unfortunate insurrections so prevalent in the country at that time.

The witness Romero testifies that he saw the copy of the Mora grant in the archives at Mora, while Thomas Lalande was justice of the peace in 1846. This he knows from his own knowledge; and as the archives of Mora was the proper place for it to be deposited in, and as it was to the interest of the parties interested to keep it, then the presumption is very natural that it was there when the United States troops set fire to the building, and that it was destroyed with the archives.

In granting lands to a number of persons for a town site, the land embraced within the limits of the grant, even under the control of the constituted authorities of the town, who, under the law, had the right to partition out such of the vacant land as might be asked for by other parties desiring to be incorporated in the town. This partition was of course made with the consent of the original grantees, and the granting of lands to others than the original grantees by the authorities of Mora and Taos was proper, and does not prove in any manner that the grant was not made in fee.

The failure to prove that the original grant ever existed at Santa Fé has no bearing on the case whatever, as it was not the business of the grantees to look after the original when it had passed from their hands to that of the justice, who was directed to place them in possession. It was sufficient for them that they were placed in possession under the original grant, as certified by the justice. Again, it is well known that the archives at Santa Fé were not then, neither are they at the present day, under the particular care or custody of any particular officer of the government, especially after the change of sovereignty, and it is believed that important documents have been taken from the archives at Santa Fé on more than one occasion; therefore the fact of the grant not being found in the archives is no evidence that no such grant existed; and it is hardly to be expected that the grantees should be held responsible for it after it had been returned to this place and deposited in the archives under the custody of the proper officer, whose business it was at the time to look after its safe-keeping.

The evidence also shows that the town or towns embraced within the limits granted have been settled upon and occupied by the original grantees and their assigns from the date of the grant up to the present time, and large and well-established settlements are growing up and flourishing there. It is not to be presumed that the government would allow the richest and most fertile portion of its territory to be usurped and taken up by a party of men without the color or shadow of law. Such was not the policy of the Mexican government at the time. There certainly was a grant, or they would not have been allowed to remain unmolested from 1835 to 1846, when the United States took possession of the country.

The grant made to John Scolly and others is acknowledged by the parties before this office to have been made with their consent and approval, given at the time their grant was made. Claimants, in their petition, refer to certain statutes and decisions, a large portion of which are not in the office, neither can they be had here ; therefore, no reference is made to them.

The instructions to this office provide that when the existence of a town is proven at the time the United States took possession of the country it is to be considered as prima facie evidence of the existence of a grant to said town or to the persons under whom they claim.

This fact also having been established in evidence, the grant is deemed to be a good and valid one, and the land embraced within the metes and bounds set forth in the act of possession severed from the public domain, and is, therefore, approved and ordered to be transmitted to Congress, with the request that it be confirmed to the original grantees and those claiming under, through, or from them, excepting that portion granted to John Scolly et al., and reported from this office on the 30th September, 1857.

WM. PELHAM, Surveyor General.

SURVEYOR GENERAL'S OFFICE,
Santa Fe, New Mexico, July 9, 1859.

SURVEYOR GENERAL'S OFFICE,
Santa Fe, New Mexico, August 25, 1859.
The above is a true copy of the original on file in this office.
WM. PELHAM, Surveyor General

---

[i] Note: Editor bolded two pertinent names of grantees and underlined land descriptions and locations in the above document that may provide insight and be pertinent to subject of this book.

SECTION III—LAUMBACHS IN NEW MEXICO

Chapter 12: Potrero, Mora, Bernardo, Apolonia & Bibiana
by Jan Girand

Santa Cruz de la Canada church[i] photo, taken by William Henry Jackson around 1882 or 1883

The land-locked villages founded by Spanish[ii] colonists in the sixteenth and seventeenth centuries still exist in northern New Mexico. Except for some venturing away for a period of time to seek employment, for generations many residents don't leave from birth to death. Their communities, Castilian Spanish language and ways of life are little changed.

The first established Hispanic community, which Spanish colonists called San Gabriel, was at an abandoned Tewa Indian village near another Tewa village, San Juan, which is now called Ohkay Owingeh. Because Spaniards were prohibited from living within close proximity to Indian communities, San Gabriel existed only a little more than a decade before the Spanish residents had to relocate. Hundreds of years later, archaeologists confirmed the site of San Gabriel near present-day Espanola.

Santa Fe was the first continually existing villa in New Mexico established by Spanish colonists in 1610. The second was Santa Cruz de la Canada in north central New Mexico. The much longer, original name, Villa Nueva de Santa Cruz de los Españoles Mexicanos, was shortened to Santa Cruz de la Canada. The "Españoles Mexicanos" portion of the original name signifies that those earliest colonists were Spanish people from Mexico City. There was then no country named Mexico. Santa Cruz translates as Holy Cross and "de la Canada" translates as "a small river's valley." That small river is the Santa Cruz River in the Galisteo Basin, at an elevation of more than 5,500 feet. Like traditionally in early New Mexico, settlers in Santa Cruz built their homes in a community plaza around their church, and along the banks of the river valley toward the Sangre de Cristo Mountains.

Santa Cruz de la Canada was founded in 1695 by Spanish colonists, decades after the founding of Santa Fe. There had been at least one older church structure at Santa Cruz; the current church, pictured at the beginning of this chapter, was built beginning in 1733 and took nearly 15 years to complete. It houses historic religious artworks, including priceless *santos*, from the colonial era. Santa Cruz is near El Potrero and Chimáyo,[iii] located on land owned by the Martín Serrano family since at least the mid-1600s.

The property and houses of the Luis Martín Serrano family at Chimayo were directly affected by the Pueblo Revolt of 1680. Descendants of Luis reclaimed their familial land in 1695 and continued to reside in the area into the 1800s. (This information is courtesy of Jose A. Esquibel.)

For generations, sacramental events at El Potrero and surrounding areas, and their records, were kept at the parish church of Santa Cruz de la Canada.[iv]

Perhaps for a hundred years, tradition among descendants and all branches of the family, including mine, said both Bernardo Martín and his wife, Apolonia (Polonia) Gutiérrez de Solano, were of European Spanish heritage. That tale was even more specific, saying they had both come from Isabella, Spain as adults. Versions said Bernardo came to New Spain with a Spanish expedition, coming up through what is now Mexico, liked what he saw in what became northern New Mexico, and returned to Spain for his family. He had already married Apolonia—or he married her after his return to Spain—and their child, Bibiana, was born there, too, before they came to the New World and settled in the Mora Valley. That detailed, embellished tale of unknown source was very wrong.

We have learned the factual origins of those two family lines from genealogist researcher José Antonio Esquibel[v], descendant of Juan Andres Ebel—son of Bibiana Martín and Daniel Eberle/Ebel. Esquibel took up and continued Fray Angelico Chavez's extensive research of early Hispanic families in New Mexico. For years he has been actively involved with New Mexico's genealogical associations.

Esquibel wrote the following in his chapter, <u>Sacramental Records and the Preservation of New Mexico Family Genealogies from the Colonial Era to Present</u>, published *in Seeds of Struggle, Harvest of Faith*, edited by Thomas J. Steele, S.J., Paul Rhetts and Barbe Awalt: "…faith that was nurtured through the colonial, Mexican and territorial eras of New Mexico history endured through the transition of three governments." Some early New Mexico family names "can be found in surviving record books of sacraments," he wrote. He said that is because Catholic colonists brought with them from Spain in 1521 to New Spain the custom of recording marriages, baptisms and burials. Those early records for period 1598 to 1680 were lost, most during the Pueblo Indian Revolt of 1680 when structures and symbols of Catholicism were destroyed. After colonists returned to New Mexico, these primary family events were again recorded, but some of those records are incomplete. The convent at the Santo Domingo Pueblo was selected by Franciscan missionaries in the early 1600s to be the repository of all Catholic sacramental records, but a major Rio Grande flood in 1886 swept away that church and many of its records.

Eventually the Catholic Church began the awesome task of translating, transcribing and preserving the records that endured. Fray Angelico Chavez took up the project, approved by Archbishop Byrne, in 1954. From his efforts, and subsequent work by José Esquibel, some of the long-time Hispanic New Mexico families can now trace their genealogies in New Mexico many generations backwards in time. That includes the families of Bernardo Martín and Apolonia Gutiérrez de Solano.

Included in Esquibel's chapter in the above mentioned book is a genealogical chart that spans 167 years in New Mexico—beginning in 1660 with Ana Velasquez/Velasco, an Apache Indian woman, and ending with Bibiana Martín, born in 1827. The chart shows both of Bibiana's parents—Bernardo Martín and Apolonia Gutierrez de Solano—descended from Ana Velasquez.

From José Esquibel's chart we learn the following:

Captain Jose Dominguez de Mendoza, son of Ana Velasquez, was born in New Mexico in 1666. His first marriage was with Juana Lopez Sambrano in April 1682. Their daughter, Maria Dominguez, married Dimas Jiron (born 1685). They had a son named Antonio Dimas Jiron, who married Lucia de Ortega in February 1744 in Santa Fe. Their daughter, Maria Rosa Jiron, married Antonio Solano y Castro in May 1763 in Santa Fe. Their son, Andres de Jesus Solano (born December 1785 in Santa Fe) married Feliciana Valdes (baptized January 1770 in Santa Fe). Their daughter, Maria Inez Solano, was baptized in December 1797 in Santa Fe. To Inez Solano and Antonio Gutierrez y Alire was born Apolonia Gutiérrez de Solano, baptized April 1811 in Santa Fe.

Captain Jose Dominguez de Mendoza had a second marriage, this one with Geronima Varela de Losada (she died in Santa Fe on April 1727). Their daughter, Ana Maria Dominguez, married Antonio Martín Serrano in May 1717 in Santa Fe. Their son, Salvador Martín, married Maria Manuela Trujillo in February 1756 at Santa Clara. Their son, Jose Guadalupe Martín, married Maria Juliana Vasquez Borrego in December 1786 at Santa Cruz. (Jose Guadalupe Martín died and was buried at Santa Cruz in May 1827.) Born to Jose Guadalupe Martín and Maria Juliana Vasquez Borrego was Bernardo (original name Bernadino) Martín, who was baptized in May 1792 at Santa Cruz. He married Polonia Gutiérrez de Solano (christened, and probably also born, in April 1811, at Santa Fe). *(Apolonia was about 15 years old when she married Bernardo, age 35, a man about 20 years older.)*

Their first born child was Maria Viviana Martín, born December 1 and baptized December 4, 1827 at Santa Cruz. Their son, Manuel Gregorio Martín, was born November 14, 1830 also at Potrero. Esquibel's research shows the families of both Bernardo and Apolonia[vi] lived in New Mexico for many generations, with the paternal lineage of Bernardo reaching back to Hernan Martín Serrano, who came to New Mexico in 1598 with don Juan de Oñate. It shows that Apolonia's family had lived in Santa Fe since the late 1600s, if not earlier. Bernardo's family also originated in Santa Fe with Captain Jose Dominguez de Mendoza, who died in Santa Fe. By 1756, records show Bernardo's family lived in or near El Potrero, west side of the Sangre de Cristo Mountains.

The following is written in the introduction of the New Mexico Genealogical Society's published book on *New Mexico Marriages 1726-1826, Santa Cruz de la Canada Church,* extracted and compiled by Henrietta Martinez Christmas and Patricia Sanchez Rau: "Santa Cruz de la Canada was the second villa in New Mexico. Marriages were performed here for all the surrounding communities. As was the tradition, the bride's residence was the usual place where the marriage ceremony was held…. Santa Cruz is made up of several plazas, such as Nuestra Senora de Dolores, San Pedro, Guadalupe, San Ysidro and N.S. [*Nuestra Señora—Our Lady*] de la Luz."

In the above captioned publication is the following marriage record of Bernardo's parents: "November 5, 1786, Jose Martín, s/ [*son of*] Salbador Martín and Maria Manuela Trujillo, with Maria Juliana Vasquez Vorrego [*Borrego*] d/ [*daughter of*] Diego Vasques Vorrego and Francisca Gurule, Wit [*witnesses*]: Francisco Gonzales and Juan Antonio Archuleta, all *españoles* from this parish."

The following transcripts are courtesy of genealogist Nancy Anderson of the New Mexico Genealogical Society, with data translated, transcribed and compiled from microfiche of original sacramental records from the Archives of the Archdiocese of Santa Fe:

"Bernardino Martín, of Potrero, bap 24 May 1792, b. 20 May; son of Jose Guadalupe Martín and Juliana Borrego; godparents, Pedro Martín and Ygnacia Garcia." (Margaret Langham Olmsted, transcriber, Margaret Leonard Windham and Evelyn Lujan Baca, compilers, *New Mexico Baptisms, Santa Cruz de la Canada Church, Vol. 1, 1710-1794*, Albuquerque: New Mexico Genealogical Society, 1994, p. 271. AASF #13, frame 709.)[vii]

"Maria Polonia Gutierres, bap 13 Apr. 1811, ae 2 day; d/ Antonio Gutierres & Ynes Solano; ap/ [*paternal grandparents*] Bartolo Gutierrez and Maria Alire; am/ [*maternal grandparents*] Andres Solano

& Feliciana Baldez; gp/ [*godparents*] Josef Manuel Gonzales & Maria Sandoval." (Ella Louise May, extractor, Margaret Leonard Windham and Evelyn Lujan Baca, compilers, *New Mexico Baptisms of Santa Fe, Parroquia de San Francisco de Asis, Volume II,* 15 August, 1796 to 30 December, 1822. Albuquerque, New Mexico Genealogical Society, 2002, p. 149, AASF #15, frame 1064.)[viii]

Apolonia's family had moved from Santa Fe to El Potrero when she was a child. She and Bernardo Martin married some years later at Chimayo on January 8, 1827.

"8 January, 1827 Bernardo Martínes, native from this villa, leg. s/ [*legitimate son of*] Jose Guadalupe Martínes and Juliana Borrego, with Polonia Gutiérres, native from this villa, leg. d/ [*legitimate daughter of*] Antonio Gutiérres, deceased and Ma Ynes Solano. Wit: Francisco Gonzales and San Juan Martínes and Maria Ygnacia Vexil." (Patricia Sanchez Rau and Henrietta Martinez Christmas, compilers. *Santa Cruz Marriages, 1826-1849 and Roots Ltd, Addendum*. Albuquerque, NM; New Mexico Genealogical Society, June 2013. AASF #30, frame 696.)[ix]

Less than a year after Apolonia and Bernardo married, Maria Bibiana was born to them at El Potrero.

"Maria Viviana Martín, born at Potrero *Republicade Nuevo Mexico*, bap 4 Dec. 1827 [*at Santa Cruz*]; [*daughter of*] Bernardo Martín & Polonia Gutierres; ap [*paternal grandparents*] Jose Guadalupe Martín & Maria Borrego; am [*maternal grandparents*] Ant [*Antonia*] Gutierres & Ma [*Maria*] Ynes Solano; gp (*padrinos/godparents*) Mariano de Aguero & Dolores Sanches." (*New Mexico Baptisms, Santa Cruz de la Canada Church, Volume III, 1827 to 1856,* transcribed by Virginia Langham Olmsted, compiled by Margaret Leonard Windham and Evelyn Lujan Baca, published by New Mexico Genealogical Society. Frame 274.)[x]

About three years later, their son Manuel Gregorio Martín was also born at El Potrero.

"Manuel Gregorio Martín, Potrero, bap 21 Nov. 1830, ae 7 da; a/ Bernardo Martín & Polonia Solano; ap/ Jose Guadalupe Martín & Juliana Borrego; am/ Francisco Solano & Ygnes Torres; gp/ Manuel Trujillo & Guadalupe Abrego of Santa Fe." (Virginia Langham Olmsted, transcriber, Margaret Leonard Windham and Evelyn Lujan Baca, compilers, *New Mexico Baptisms, Santa Cruz de la Canada Church, Vol. 3*, 1827-1856; Albuquerque: New Mexico Genealogical Society, 1997, p. 31. AASF #14, frame 352.)

El Potrero means "the pasture" in Spanish; Chimayo is located at Potrero. The Sanctuario de Chimayo is a well-known place often written about, painted and photographed. It was built between 1810 and 1816, so it did not yet exist when Bernardo was born. He and Apolonia married there in 1827.

I believe it was not long after Manuel was born (in 1830) that Bernardo moved his family to the other side of the Sangre de Cristo Mountains to La Cebolla ("the onion"), located on the outskirts of the Mora Valley. My belief is founded upon records that say Gov. Perez granted the Mora lands to 76 existing residents of the area in 1835.

There have been various meanings applied to the name Mora, or lo de Moro. Some say *mora* means to procrastinate. The Internet says the Spanish noun for *demora* means a camp or stop-over or delay.

Nancy Anderson, of the New Mexico Genealogical Society, said, "When the soldiers came in and started establishing a presence on the east side of the mountain, it curtailed the Indian raids and families were able to build homes and raise their families and livestock in relative peace. Some families had topped the mountain and grazed their sheep and started establishing a presence as early as 1830, but not enough to start a church."

The Hispanic settlers in the area were isolated, including from formal religious practices—like places to worship, to receive the sacraments and to access symbols of their faith. To fill that void, *los Hermanos de Penitentes,* or *Hermanos de Luz,*[xi] an Hispanic men's lay religious order or society of flagellants, became active in northern New Mexico in the second half of the 1800s. It was a secret society because it was unsanctioned by the Catholic Church. Also, lacking any, villagers began to create religious images—*bultos*[xii] and *retablos*[xiii]—of Jesus, his mother Mary and various patron saints to hang on their walls, or place in *nichos* or small, make-shift alters for places of worship in their homes and outdoors.

Some sources say it was because settlers wanted a church: They petitioned as early as 1818 for a grant. Settler families[xiv] petitioned Albino Perez, governor or *jefe politico* (the political chief of New Mexico), for a grant of land. Because Governor Perez wanted to establish settlements for security along the frontier's outskirts, he sanctioned their grant request in 1835. He traveled with Manuel Antonio Sanchez, the *alcalde mayor* of San Juan de las Trampas, across the Jicarita peaks to the valley of Mora in October 1835. It was Sanchez's responsibility to divide the land into sections of personally owned land for the grantees' homes, and also large parcels to be used in common, for the equal benefit of all. Most of the cited boundaries were ambiguous, nondurable surface landmarks; some of the cited boundaries were neighbors' invisible land-lines. More durable landmarks (but also prone to some change over time) of the grant were: the Rio Ocate marked the north-side, the Rio Sapello and the Agua Negra (Mora River) marked the south boundary; the Aguaje de la Llegua marked the east side; and the Estillero marked the west side. Basically the grant extended from the Sangre de Cristo Mountains to the plains near Wagon Mound. A survey showed the Mora Land Grant comprised 827,620 acres, or nearly 1,400 square miles.

As part of the grant process and ceremony, the grantees were required to do certain physical acts, like pulling up weeds and dirt and shouting thanks to God. To finalize it, grantees had to live on the land and work it, to protect their properties, families, livestock and crops. They were given no outside assistance to do that. It was a huge, impossible undertaking for the 76 families to nurture and cultivate, as well as protect, such a vast land. Marauding bands of Indians—that stole livestock and children— roamed the valley that had been theirs long before the Hispanic settlers moved in.

The name "Manuel Antonio Sanchez"—*alcalde mayor* of San Juan de las Trampas, who laid out the common lands on the plazas and on the vast open lands, and distributed the grantees' personally held portions of the grant—was also the name of the father of cousin "Tony" Antonio A. Sanchez (son of Crestina Laumbach and Manuel Antonio Sanchez). His father and grandfather, and finally he, too, owned the Sanchez ranch at Largartijas near Trementina and Sabinoso.

"Dec 3, 1887 Manuel Antonio Sanchez, soltero hijo legitimo de Antonio Sanchez y de Candelaria Cortez, con Rosa Felicita Eggert, soltera hija legitima de Frederico Eggert y de Juana Le Blanc, De Alamitos. Padrinos: Jose Aguilar y Juana Cisneros, tambien, D.F. Allen y Firenna Ceroa."

(The first wife of Tony's father was Rosa Eggert, daughter of Fritz Eggert.)

Was that *alcalde mayor* who platted the Mora Land grant a forebear or kin of our cousin Tony Sanchez? We do not know.

~~

I personally believe, but not all agree, that Bernardo's privately owned portion of grant land was at La Cebolla where—after he left Potrero—he lived the remainder of his life, as shown by census records. The only exception was that brief period when he served in the U.S. military. *(Chapter 17, by Jose Antonio Esquibel, provides Bernardo's 1848 U.S. military record.)* His daughter, Bibiana, and her children lived with Bernardo at La Cebolla. All of her children, except Ramon, may have been born at La Cebolla, where they also grew up.

The Santa Gertrudes Church of Mora was the parish church for villagers of the Mora Valley, and for generations was where sacramental events, and records, of the residents of the many surrounding villages in Mora Valley and beyond were held. In the 1860s, Santa Gertrudes was the major parish church for a huge area of northern New Mexico and southern Colorado.

According to Nancy Anderson of the New Mexico Genealogical Society, "The church in Mora did not begin until 1855—before that, people were baptized in Las Vegas, Picuris or Taos if they lived in the Mora area. The jurisdictions of churches for that time period were San Miguel del Bado, Las Vegas and Taos/Picuris. Also people were migrating to that area from all parts of New Mexico—San Miguel del Bado, Santa Cruz, San Juan, Albuquerque, Santa Fe, etc." Anderson also wrote: "Las Vegas did not even have a church until 1853." And, "The Watrous church did not start until 1873 … it contains the marriage [record] of Juan Andres "Evel" and his two daughters, Maria Isabel and Nicanora."[xv]

We have the image of the christening record for Maria Marta Ebel[xvi], third child of Bibiana and Daniel Eberle, born at La Cebolla February 1856, which indicates ("hl") that she was legitimate. That convinced Karl Laumbach that Bibiana and Daniel Ebel were married and lived together in Las Vegas. As she was their third child, logic says they would have also been married when the first two were born. Karl thinks Bibiana went to La Cebolla to be with her mother, Apolonia, for the birth. I think, and Nancy Anderson agrees, that the priest may have just concluded the parents were married. Karl's and Pete's belief that Bibiana and Daniel had lived in Las Vegas is also based upon a story Pete (son of Rudolph Laumbach) had heard about Bibiana and Eberle when they lived together in Las Vegas.[xvii] Verna also wrote that they lived at Las Vegas during their time together.

Based on census records and some stories told by Verna Sparks, I think Bibiana mostly lived at La Cebolla with her father and first born son Ramon Bonney. I believe that was where her three Ebel children were born: Elionor/Leonora, born 1849; Juan Andres, born about 1852; and Maria Marta "Ebarley," born February 1856. It is possible the two older Eberle/Ebel children were just not recorded on the ten-year census taken at La Cebolla or Las Vegas for 1860. For whatever reason, we have found no record of Elionor's and Andres' births or christenings; we only have Maria Marta's. There are, however, other records, some of which say Andres and Elionor were illegitimate.

According to Verna Sparks, Bibiana and Daniel Eberle separated before he was killed. He had told Bibiana that she had to choose between his money (he was a wealthy store and property owner) and their children; she chose the children. Verna said Bibiana had to appear in court to legalize their separation. *(Apparently Bibiana twice experienced that situation; the second time was the conflict between her and Frank Metzger.)* We have various family versions of Eberle/Ebel's death, which Verna and Karl address in later chapters. They all say he was murdered, only the details differ, but we do not know the date of his death. We can only guesstimate that based upon birth dates of his children with Bibiana, and other records, including Elionor's 1864 marriage entry that stated her father was deceased.

I believe Bibiana never formerly married the three men in her life. Those were monogamous relationships, what we call "common-law," which was a common practice in that era of scarce priests. We had to use the same method to establish approximate dates of death for Andreas Detlef Laumbach 1st and Apolonia Gutierrez Martín and—until Alvin Korte found his death record—for Bernardo Martín.

Alvin Korte found this transcription of a death record for Bernardo in the New Mexico State Archives and Records Center in Santa Fe: "1873 December 18. Death of Bernardo Martín. 80 años esposo de Poloñia Dif y enterro en la Cebolla [*Ledoux*] el dia 18 de Dic [*December*] 1873." (Source: Guide to the Archive of the Archdioceses of Santa Fe. 95 Roll 95 Frame 197 Mora St. Gertrudes, New Mexico State Archives and Record Center Santa Fe, New Mexico.)

Translation: "1873 December 18. Death of Bernardo Martín. 80 years old husband of Polonia, dead [*difunto*] and buried at La Cebolla cemetery [now Ledoux]. (Guide to the Archive of the

Archdioceses of Santa Fe. Roll 95 Frame 197. Mora St. Gertrudes, New Mexico. State Archives and Record Center Santa Fe, New Mexico.)

---

[i] Santa Cruz de la Canada, at one time the largest and most important mission church in New Mexico, is located in the Santa Cruz River valley in the Galisteo Basin about 25 miles northwest of Santa Fe. The image of the church, photo taken about 1882 or 1883 by William Henry Jackson, is at the beginning of this chapter. Butch Sanders located that and the next photo of Santa Cruz, also taken by William Henry Jackson. Sanders calls Jackson the nation's finest photographer of that era. He spent considerable time cleaning these images, removing smudges and fingerprints.

[ii] In the 16th and 17th centuries, the colonists/settlers, of what became Nuevo Mejico, were Spanish citizens who came with don Juan de Oñate. Those who originated in Nueva España (what is now old Mexico) were not "Mexicans." In the colonial era, there was no Mexican nation. Then "Mexican" only referred to the people from Mexico City. "Mexican Indians" (Indios Mexicanos) refers to Indians from Mexico City. The settlers from both Spain and New Spain (Nueva España) were Spanish colonists. The majority of those who came in 1598 were born in the Spanish Americas. The settlers of Santa Cruz in 1695 were called (in the settlement's original name) Españoles Mexicanos because they were mainly Spaniards from Mexico City. José Antonio Esquibel provided this clarification and early New Mexico history.

[iii] Santuario de Chimayo is a picturesque setting in northern New Mexico that draws artists and photographers, as well as the faithful because it is a designated holy place. Santo Niño de Atocha is Chimayo's patron santo. Chimayo is in Potrero. The following photos of Chimayo were located by researcher Charles Sanders.

Photo by Aaron B. Craycraft, taken between 1904 and 1917.

Photo taken by Willard Ames Van Dyke.

[iv] Santa Cruz Church 1915 photo by Le Baron Bradford Prince.

[v] José Antonio Esquibel is a renowned researcher and genealogist of early Hispanic families of New Mexico. He extended our family's knowledge of our early forebears in New Mexico seven generations earlier than Bernardo and Apolonia.

[vi] Apolonia's photo was among Aunties' collection of family photos, given to Mary Louise Maestas, great-granddaughter of Maria Marta Eberle Esquibel. José A. Esquibel and Karl Laumbach both made copies of Mary Louise's photo but because this is a copy of a copy, the quality is poor. Butch Sanders did the best he could to improve the quality. Aunties had told Karl there never was a photo of Bibiana.

[vii] Image of original 1792 entry recording christening for Bernardino (Bernardo) Martin, courtesy of Nancy Anderson, New Mexico Genealogical Society.

Santa Cruz
AASF #13, frame 709 - baptismal record of Bernardino Martin

[viii] Image of actual January 1827 entry recording marriage of Bernardo Martin and Apolonia Gutierrez, courtesy of Nancy Anderson, New Mexico Genealogical Society.

AASF #30, frame 696
Marriage of Bernardo Martin to Polonia
Gutierrez - 8 January 1827

[x] Image of actual December 1827 entry of christening of Maria Viviana Martin at Potrero.

Santa Cruz - AASF #14, frame 274
Baptismal record of Maria Viviana Martin
4 December 1827

[xi] Los Hermanos de Penitentes or Hermanos de Luz was an unorthodox form or "society" of the Catholic Church practiced by men in northern New Mexico. Archbishops Jean Baptiste Lamy and Jean Baptiste Salpointe tried to end their practice of self-flagellation without success, so its members kept their association secret, even from neighbors and friends. There are still a few practicing Penitentes in northern New Mexico. The ruins of their *moradas* (windowless buildings of worship, usually adobe) are still visible in some places. Many old, valuable *santos* that still exist were made by Penitente *santeros*. Those include some in Tony Sanchez's collection.

xii *Bultos* are three-dimensional images of saints, usually carved of wood, often painted, by *santeros*. The *santeros* who created this *bulto*—the archangel San Rafael—were Eulogio and Zoraida Ortega, renowned santeros of Velarde, New Mexico. The Ortegas—husband and wife—were the parents of Albert Ortega, husband of Anna Marie Espinosa Ortega, daughter of Adelina Laumbach Espinosa, daughter of Henry Laumbach.

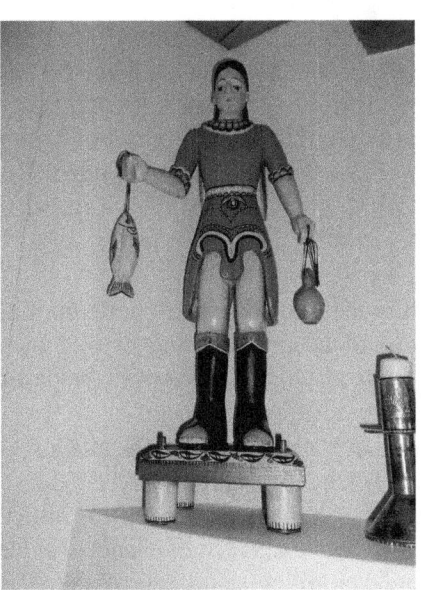

xiii *Retablos* are images of saints painted on flat pieces of wood—wooden tablets. The following *retablo*—*Nuestra Senora de la Joya*, Our Lady of La Joya—was painted by *santera* Zoraida Ortega of Velarde, mother of Albert Ortega, who is the husband of Anna Marie Espinosa Ortega. Anna Marie's mother, Adelina, was raised by Aunties.

xiv There were 76 original Mora Land Grantees. The Internet names only 42. For a list of all 76 grantees, see the Spanish version of the Mora Grant transcription in chapter 11 of this book. Several names on this list, in addition to Bernardo Martin and Miguel Mascarenas (they were named on both lists), are familiar. Those include Manuel Sanchez; was that grantee the *alcalde mayor* of San Juan de las Trampas who laid out the Mora Grant's physical boundaries and distributed the personal lands? Was a named grantee, Geronimo Martin, a brother of Bernardo? Was named grantee, Manuel Gregorio Martin, a brother of Bernardo for whom he named his son, born in 1830? Many grantees and other area settlers were related to each other. Bernardo's sister, Rosa, also an early settler of Mora, was the forebear of another genealogical line.

[xv] Source: Courtesy of genealogist Nancy Anderson, New Mexico Genealogy Society; data translated, transcribed and compiled from microfiche of original sacramental records from the Archives of the Archdiocese of Santa Fe: Luis Gilberto Padilla y Baca, compiler, *New Mexico Marriages, La Junta* (Watrous), September 1873 ~ April 1908 (Albuquerque, NM: Hispanic Genealogical Research Center of New Mexico, ca 2002; p. 5, p. 73, p. 84).

- "Today the 26th of January of 1874, I married Juan Andres Evel, single, natural son of the deceased Daniel Evel and of Viviana Martin, with Maria Ubalda Lopez, single, daughter of Demetrio Lopez and Maria Pastora Mestas from Ancon de Armenta. Witnesses: Jose Ramon Boney and Eulogia Lopez." (*The term natural means the parents were not married.*)
- "September 15, 1894, I presented the matrimony in a solemn mass of Conrado Andrada, widow [sic] of Leonires Chaves, legitimate son of Casimiro Andrada and of Carmen Romero, with Nicanora Evel, single, legitimate daughter of Andres Evel and of Maria Ubalda Lopez from Armenta. Witnesses, Nicolas Esquibel and Barbarita Andrada, Jose Tafoya."
- "March 10, 1897. I presented the matrimony of Jose Nieves Gallegos, single, legitimate son of Jose Gallegos, deceased, and of Dolores Chavez, with Maria Isabel Evel, single, legitimate daughter of Andres Evel and of Maria Ubalda Lopez from Armenta. Witnesses, Julian Gallegos, Antonio M. Romero, Andres Evel and Manuela Sanchez." (Source: Courtesy of Nancy Anderson, New Mexico Genealogy Society: Data translated, transcribed and compiled from microfiche of original sacramental records from the Archives of the Archdiocese of Santa Fe: Luis Gilberto Padilla y Baca, compiler, *New Mexico Baptisms, La Junta* (Watrous), August 1873 ~ September 1905, Albuquerque, NM; Hispanic Genealogical Research Center of New Mexico, 2006, p. 70; p. 160; p. 270; p. 314.) This Isabel Evel/Ebel Gallegos lived to age 108; she died in Santa Fe.
- "Today the 2nd of August of 1878, baptized Isabel Evel born in El Encierro on the 3rd of June, legitimate daughter of Juan Andres Evel and Maria Eduarda [*Uvalda*] Lopez. Padrinos, Ramon Bonney and Maria Concepcion Padilla."
- "Today the 12th of November of 1886, baptized Ana Maria Ebel born in El Rio Colorado on the 6th of May of this year, daughter of Andres Ebel and of Maria Ubalda Lopez from Rio Colorado. Padrinos, Roman Montoya and Teofora Vigil. Note on Record: This baptism made with the permission of the Church of Rio Colorado."
- "March 10, 1896, baptized Andres Evel born on the 30th of November [1895?], legitimate son of Andres Evel and Ubalda Lopez from Armenta. Padrinos, Pastora Maestas and Demetrio Lopez."
- "Maria Viviana Ebel born in Armenta on September 19 of 1898 and baptized February 20 of 1899, daughter of Andres Ebel and of Maria Nobalda [*Uvalda*] Lopez from Armenta. Padrinos, (blocked) [*probably Felipe*] Esquibel and Marta Ebel."

[xvi] Following is an image of an entry of Maria Marta Ebel's 1856 baptism. The priest and/or transcriber mistranslated the name of her father, Daniel Eberle, as Garlien Ebarlern. You can see his last name had been written in this record as Ebarley, and the transcriber misspelled it.

148

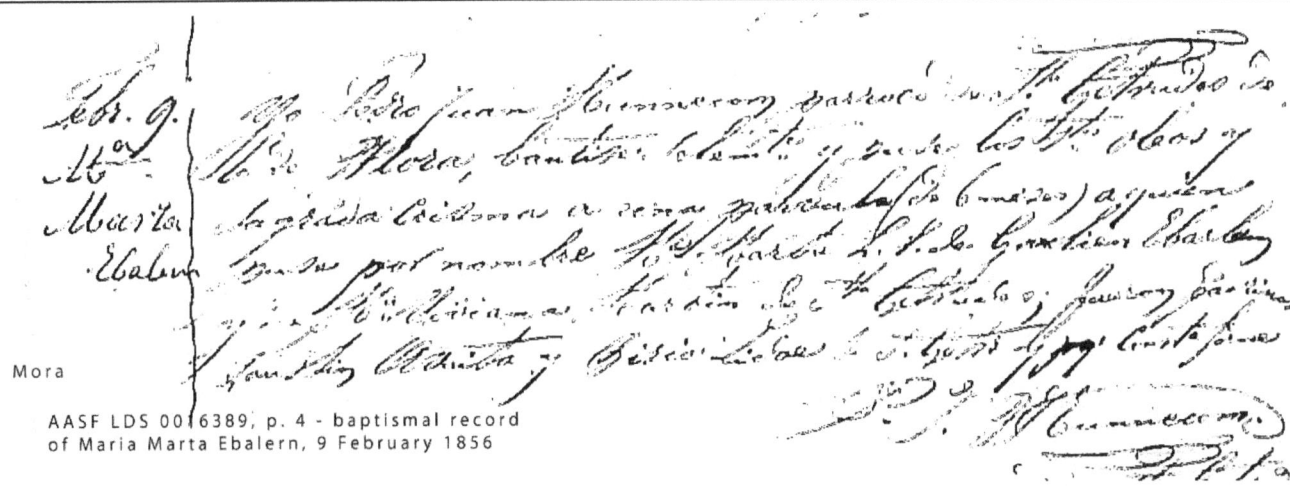

Mora

AASF LDS 0016389, p. 4 - baptismal record of Maria Marta Ebalern, 9 February 1856

[xvii] The story Pete Laumbach tells came from Andres Ebel, born about 1852, told by Doña Carmel, grandmother of Pete's wife, Opie: When Bibiana lived with Daniel Ebel in Las Vegas, they learned that the United States decreed slavery was unlawful. They released their two female Indian slaves. For more about this story, read the chapter written by Karl. Bibiana died in the fall of 1897.

Unless otherwise indicated, the following images of The Santa Gertrudes Church were provided by Danny Chavez of Mora. This early parish church burned around 1960, replaced with a more modern type building. In this older church occurred many of the family's sacramental events and was where their records were kept.

This image of the Saint Gertrudes Church is from an album of Danny Chavez's mother-in-law, Maria Concepción Maes-Esquibel. She is the older sister of Roque Maes, who married Fidelia Laumbach, granddaughter of Peter Joseph Laumbach. Fidelia's father was Pete Laumbach of Roy. She was named for her grandmother.

Photo of the Mora Plaza, circa 1890s, posted on Facebook by Anne Cassidy. Santa Gertrudes is on the far left.

Interior of the Santa Gertrudes Church photo hangs on the wall at the Cleveland Roller Mill Museum in the Mora Valley.

Painting of the Santa Gertrudes Church by Mora artist, Freddie Olivas; reprinted with his permission. Seen on the right is the Loretto Convent.

~

Additional images on the following pages are of historical items that had belonged to Apolonia, Bernardo and Bibiana.

Apolonia's metate was carbon-14-dated in the 1950s or early 1960s by archaeologists from the Museum of Natural History of Denver. They had been excavating a prehistoric site on Tony Sanchez's ranch when Verna told them about the *metate*. On their return to Denver, they stopped by our home in Springer and carbon-dated it with their equipment. Only organic matter can be carbon dated; therefore, it must have still held bits of grain and corn on its rough basalt surface, ground long ago with a *mano*. I recall hearing that they dated it at 1,000 years old! Finding that nearly unbelievable, I hope it will again be carbon-14-dated, if any organic matter remains.

It is unusually large and very heavy, uniquely designed with four feet, one end of *metate* higher than the other to aid the chore of grinding grains.

Before my mother died, she gave the *metate* and the two shown *manos* to my brother, Jerry, who later lived on the Oregon coast. When he died in 2006, he willed them to me. I wanted the *metate* brought back to its place of origin, New Mexico. Making that happen took some time and effort by Betty, Jerry's wife, still recovering from cancer. She was eventually able to send it home. It will be donated to the New Mexico Farm and Ranch Museum near Las Cruces. This photo was taken by my brother Jerry in Oregon. Ruler across *metate* gives an idea of its size.

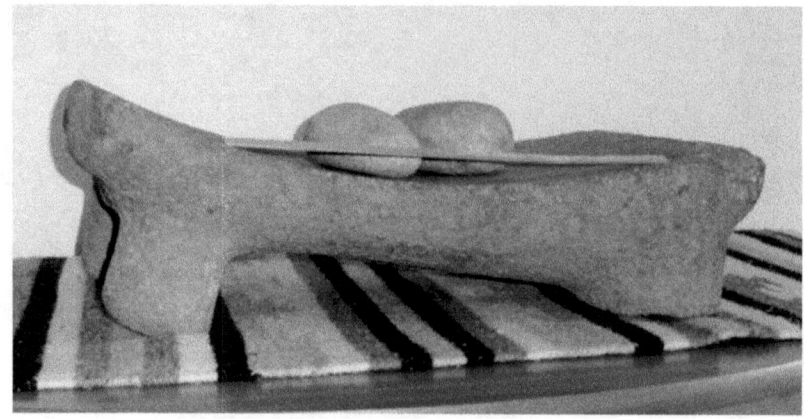

Bernardo's brass candlesticks: Verna said they had belonged to Bernardo Martín. They eventually passed from her brother Joyce to his daughter Fay Ann Laumbach Bush. His daughter, Vera Jane, had heard that they had belonged to Apolonia. Bernardo and Apolonia were married. However, if they had first belonged to Bernardo, that might make them even 20 years older. I wish we knew their history.

Bibiana's kerosene lamp: When Aunties gave it to me in the late 1960s, they said it had belonged to Apolonia. However, we believe she died before 1873—Karl heard from one source that she had died in 1862 or 1863. The date cut into the glass among the grapes at its base reads "Patent Aug. 29th 1876." Therefore, it probably belonged to Bibiana. In this photograph, it sits on the oak bench in front of the oak Windsor pump organ that had belonged to my grandmother, Emma Henkens Laumbach, at the ranch and later at Roy.

~~

Next is a collage of jewelry, etc. that represents 5 earlier-than-me generations.
1. Apolonia's little fine gold filigree lavaliere, set with turquoise. Apolonia was born in 1811. It was probably crafted by gold *artisans* in Las Vegas.
2. Bibiana's gold filigree earring, this one made into a pin. It is featured in Verna's story, Chapter 27 in this book, Never a Road. A photo of it in that chapter shows greater detail. Bibiana was born December 1827.
   Also pictured is Bibiana's gold filigree butterfly, given to her granddaughter, Estefanita. The story of this butterfly is related in another chapter of this book, with a close-up photo showing its delicate details.
3. Elionor's cameo pin set in gold filigree. On its reverse is stamped JSC. The gold filigree was made by J.S. Candelario's *artisans* at his store in Santa Fe. Elionor was born in 1849.

Also pictured is Elionor's broach with photo of her husband, Andreas Detlef Laumbach, set in gold filigree. On its reverse is stamped JSC. The filigree and pin was hand-made by J.S. Candelario's *artisans* at his store in Santa Fe.

4. Daniel Laumbach's pocket knife made when he still lived at home at Buena Vista (official address, La Cueva, as shown on knife). It predates 1900; he lived and worked at various ranches before he married Emma in January 1902. Daniel was born in 1872. Verna gave this knife to her son, Jerry. He willed it to Jan's son, Devin. It is his.
5. Verna's little silver cross presented when she was christened at Buena Vista in October 1909 shortly after her birth. Her *padrinos* were her uncle Henry Laumbach and aunt Anna Laumbach.

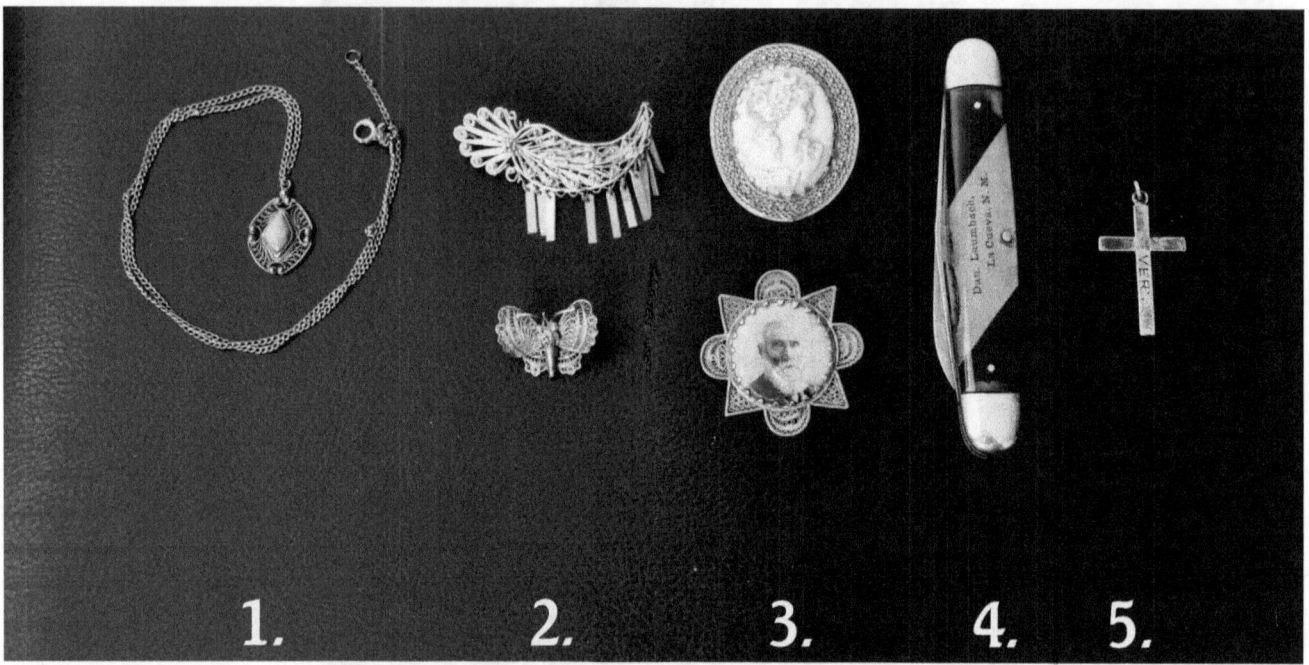

Details of Apolonia's little lavaliere: delicate gold filigree with turquoise in center. Apolonia died before 1873. This and other old pieces might have been made by the Las Vegas gold filigree *artisan* named in one of Verna's stories within this book.

154

Showing both sides of Daniel's pocket knife; one side has his photograph and a Hereford steer representing his livelihood. Daniel was born in 1872. This knife was custom-made for him while he still lived at home at Buena Vista—its postal or formal address was nearby La Cueva. He later hired out as a cowboy at several ranches in New Mexico and southern Colorado before he married Emma in January 1902.

Elionor's pin with her husband's photo. The celluloid of the photo had cracked; Butch Sanders applied photographic cosmetic surgery for this image, removing the cracks.

Reverse sides of the Andreas photograph pin and the cameo to show details of workmanship and the JSC imprint on them.

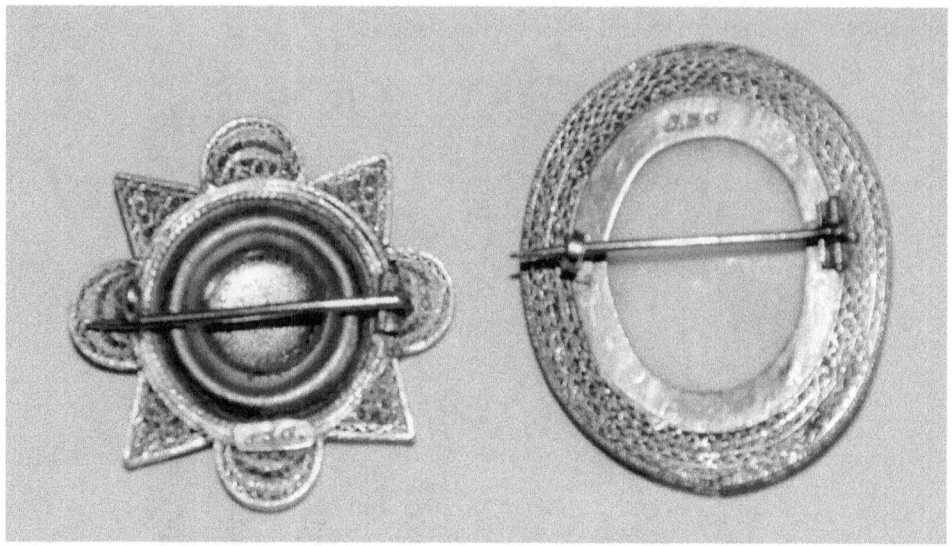

With the exception of Devin's knife and possibly Verna's little cross, this generational collection is donated to one of the New Mexico history museums: the historical museum in Santa Fe already has Sito's extensive collection of ledgers, etc. as well as John Candelario's photography. The Farm and Ranch Museum already has a number of Laumbach memorabilia. Some items shown in this book will be donated to both of these museums.

Following are additional pieces of family jewelry. I do not know to whom some of them belonged, but all are from earlier generations; all predate the 1900s and belonged to Laumbachs or Henkens families. These images would show better in color. Most are given to family, including extended family.

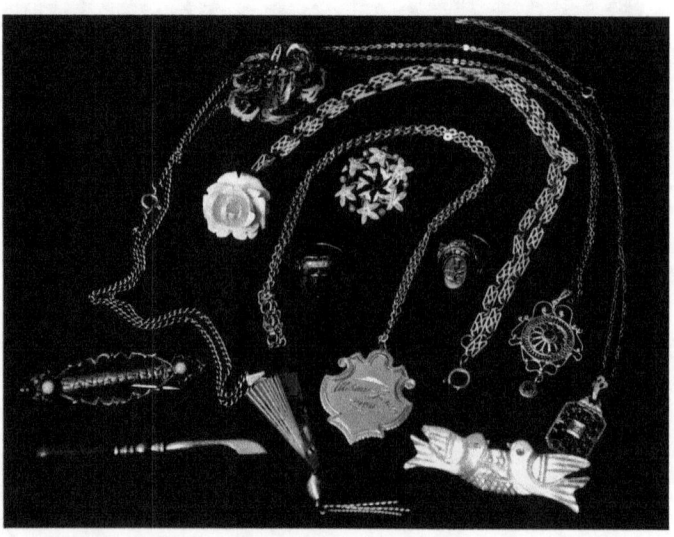

Carved rose pendent and chain. This sweet rose, carved from ivory or mother-of-pearl, is a soft pink. Even links of the chain appear to be hand-made of fragile shell.

Gold filigree pendent with green emeralds.

Silver filigree pin

Emma's hand-carved mother-of-pearl doves pin. She wore it when she sat for a portrait with her sisters about 1898 in Nebraska.

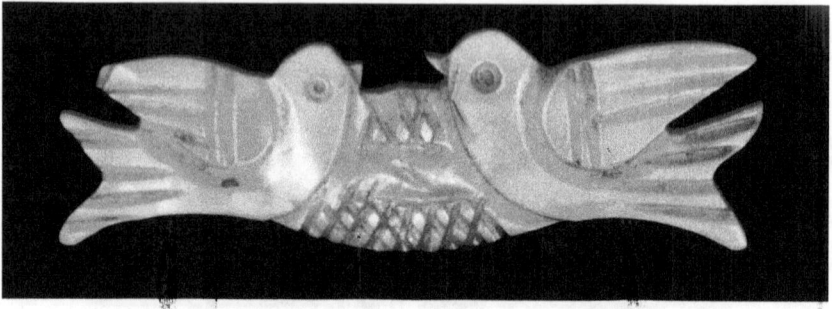

Pink floral pin with pearls. It might be cloisonné enamel.

Silver filigree with small diamond. These older pieces of gold and silver filigree and other materials were probably made by Las Vegas *artisans* for Apolonia and Bibiana. They were made many years before Jesus Sito had his curio shop in Santa Fe with his own employed *artisanos*.

Black hand-beadwork collar.

Pink and white hand-beadwork; this piece had once been several feet long. I saw it and additional broken pieces of it in a box when I was a small child. I believe it and the black beaded collar had come from Aunties. A newspaper clipping dated 1890, giving instructions for beadwork, was found, like a place-mark, in one of their old books.

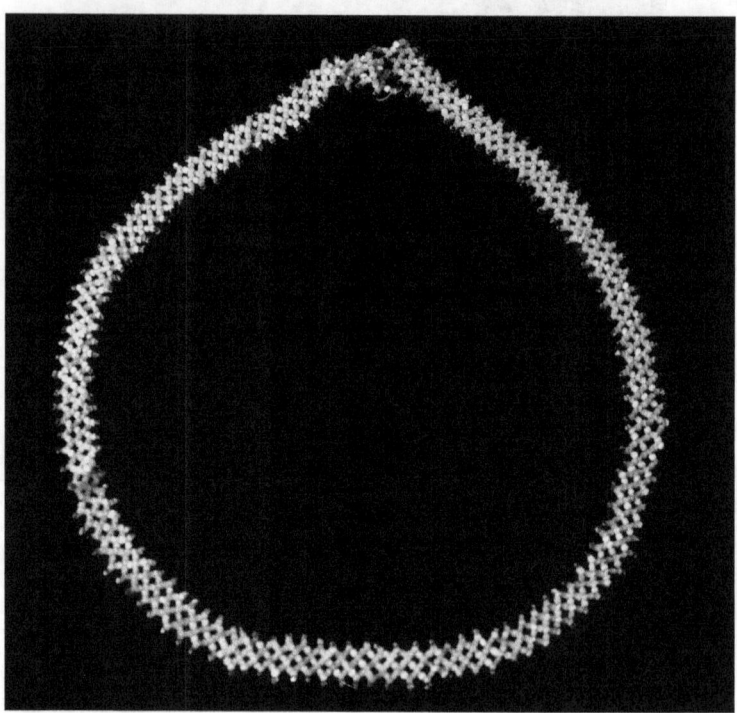

SECTION IV: LAUMBACHS IN NEW MEXICO

Chapter 13: James Bonney on the Santa Fe Trail
by Jan Girand

(Portions of this piece first published in roswellwebmagazine)

When the Spanish empire owned that then even vaster land known as Nueva España, they discouraged outsiders' visits. In fact, non-residents and non-Hispanics—especially Americans—entering its borders were usually arrested and imprisoned. A major change in hospitality occurred in 1821 when Mexico gained its independence from Spain. That new possessor of the land encouraged free trade between themselves and the United States.

That same year, American William Becknell and a handful of men and mules laden with goods left Franklin, Missouri and entered New Mexico from the east, over what became known as the Cimarron Cut-Off.[i] They intended to just trade with the Indians. However, when they entered Santa Fe, Mexican officials and residents—starved for goods—welcomed them.

Becknell found trade with New Mexico to be highly profitable. He returned to New Mexico again with goods over that route less awesome than the Raton Pass, but one no less treacherous because of Indian attacks. Near Dodge City Kansas, the Trail crossed the Arkansas River at three different places. The middle route, or the Cimarron Cut-Off, was near Cimarron, Kansas, the one most often used for commerce. It cut across a corner of the Oklahoma panhandle and entered the northeastern corner of New Mexico just above what is now Clayton and the Kiowa National Grasslands. From there, it crossed the Canadian River—known by early local settlers as the Red River or Rio Colorado—at the Rock Crossing.[ii] That Trail passed what is now Springer, then headed south between the distinctive basalt formations jutting up out of the prairie at Wagon Mound (once called Santa Clara or Santa Clara Springs). At Valmora, north of La Junta (now known as Watrous), the two trails—the Mountain Branch and this Cimarron Branch—converged into one and continued on to Santa Fe.[iii]

An informal agreement was made in 1829 between the two republics—the United States and Mexico—that each would provide, along their own portions of the Santa Fe Trail route, troops to protect the travelers. It was that Trail that caused the United States to begin to covet that land known as New Mexico. It brought U.S. General Stephen Watts Kearny and his Army of the West, which included Alexander Doniphan and his Missouri Volunteers. It also brought Jedediah Smith, U.S. topographical engineer James William Abert, American traders James Josiah Webb and Josiah Gregg, some soldiers with the American Army of the West and others who kept journals as they traversed the Trail during those eventful times.

When they marched over land at La Junta del Rios along the Sapello River, James Bonney marched—briefly and unmemorably to all but a few who cared—into recorded history.

His descendants and those various early-day journalists and historians who described him, said James Bonney was an Englishman. This was also recorded on various censuses and other documents. A few said he was a blue-eyed Irishman with red hair from the British Isles. He was described as handsome and generous. He was more likely English than Irish. That he was handsome, had red hair and blue eyes has never been disputed. Those blue eyes, apparently a dominant gene, passed down for generations among many of his descendants, and still prevail among some. Among others, Joe Lopez[iv] of Watrous, a descendant of Bonney and Maria Juana Mascareñas, has blue eyes.

James immigrated to the United States; some early family stories say a brother named Henry came with him. He settled in Missouri where and about when the Santa Fe Trail had begun in 1821. Family lore, and my mother, Verna, said Henry Bonney was not heard of again, until it was said that he had settled in the Denver area and Ramon, son of James and Bibiana, briefly met him.

According to Verna and his descendants from Juana Mascarenas, James had his first family in Missouri.

For a while, family stories say, James ran a successful freighting business over the early Trail between Missouri and Santa Fe. By or before 1825, according to Joe Lopez, he stopped freighting and settled down at what was then called La Junta del Rios because of the fertile valley made by the joining of two rivers—the Mora and the Sapello.

There in northern New Mexico, a few miles from the Mora Valley, and within the Mora jurisdiction, James began what we believe was his second family. Family tradition, and also historian Herman Weisner, said he had left his first family in Missouri. Bibiana Martín and his descendants from Juana Mascareñas knew about his family in Missouri. Bibiana herself knew about his Missouri family, according to Verna. She may have heard this from her uncle Ramon.

James Bonney's first relationship in New Mexico was with Maria Juana (I have also seen her name written as Juana Maria) Mascareñas. They produced three children: Maria Cleofas (born 1838), Santiago (born 1842) and Maria Rafaela (born 1845). Juana was the daughter of Miguel Mascareñas, the 42nd (of 76) listed Mora land grantee. According to Joe Lopez—descendant of James through Cleofas Bonney Lopez—James' father-in-law, Miguel, let him choose a piece of his own Mascareñas allotted Mora grant land. The portion Bonney chose was on the lower plaza, near La Junta, close to the junction—in addition to the rivers—of the two Santa Fe Trail branches.

Records show James Bonney was also given his own private grant. (A private, as opposed to a community grant, was given to an individual or family rather than a group of people, and had other differences.) On September 28, 1835, Albino Perez—the *jefe politico,* Mexican governor of Nuevo Mejico—gave "Santiago Boné" a private grant of 6,000 acres the same year he granted the much larger Mora Grant. This "Santiago Boné" grant within the Mora Grant overlapped the Las Vegas Grant and the Scolly Grant.[v]

The following translation of the "Bone grant" document[vi] in Spanish was made and filed with the U.S. court on October 7, 1856, after ownership of the property was disputed:

"Being in the Valley of Lo Demora, jurisdiction of Las Trampas, the Constitutional Alcalde thereof, with attending witnesses, with whom he acts by appointment, on the twenty-ninth day of the month of December 1837, declared that whereas Santiago Vone, an Anglo-American and citizen of England, belonging to the United States of the North, now resident of this place under my charge, solicited a grant of land and pasturage of his animals, cultivating a piece of the land, and he may enjoy the same as a citizen according to the decree of the governor. Dated the 9th day of August of the present year, in which it is ordered to give said property quietly and peaceably as being legitimately his own, and it being just to this community, I donate to him three hundred and fifty varas of land for such use as he may please to make of the same, and the boundaries of said land are, on the north the foot of a hill covered with thicket; on the south, the edge of the plaza; on the east vacant land; and on the west lands of Juan Antonio Garcia, and in sign of legal possession I entered hand in hand with said Santiago Vone upon and led him over said tract and he plucked up weeds, scattered handfuls of earth, and performed other ceremonies of possession without objection from any person, and having taken possession quietly and peaceably he requested a duplicate of this instrument for his security, which I gave him in due form;

and for perpetual evidence of this grant, and that his children, heirs and successors may hold, sell or alienate the same in the way they may choose, the said grantee therein does and did obligate himself to cultivate and hold the land for the time fixed by law, to which end, and for binding evidence of the stipulations of this instrument, the Alcalde and witnesses signed the same, to which I certify.
Juan Nepomoseno Truxio (Rubric)
Attending: Juan Jose Cruz (Pubrico)
                  Calletano Sandoval (Pubrico)"

~~

Perez, and other Mexican and earlier Spanish governors, rarely granted lands to newcomers or Americans. They granted land to established Hispanic settlers. Perhaps the unusual case of Perez giving Englishman James Bonney a private grant reflects that he knew Bonney was married (even if common law) to a native-born woman, and that he was already an accepted settler of the area.

That small private Santiago Boné[vii] grant had been a deliberate subdivision within the huge Mora Land Grant that also included the community grants/villages of Santa Gertrudes de Moro, San Antonio (now Cleveland) and Agua Negra (now Holman). Gov. Albino Perez knew he was granting the small private "Bone" grant within the confines of the Mora Community Grant.[viii] The sketch map, filed by James Bonney's adult children when ownership of their land was disputed, is at the end of this chapter in end notes.

Those smaller community grants were subdivisions of the vast Mora Land Grant. The 820,000-acre Mora grant was far too great an area for 76 grantees and their families to use, cultivate and protect from land-grabbers. Simply described, the Mora lands extended from Agua Negra (the Mora River) to the area near Wagon Mound.[ix]

Many Mexican land grants of northern New Mexico overlapped. Descriptions of their boundaries were ambiguous, citing indistinct and impermanent land descriptions. Most records of earlier land grants, those made during the Spanish era, were destroyed during the Pueblo Indian Revolt of 1680. More than 150 years later, records in Mora were again destroyed during the 1847 Taos Revolt when Indians and Hispanic settlers rose up against the American occupation. U.S. Military retaliated by laying siege to Mora.

The Mexican government's purpose of the Mora Land Grant and other large grants in New Mexico was to slow the progressive immigration of non-Hispanics—Americans and Europeans—and their acquisition of land in New Mexico.[x]

Dates of durable records, including Bonney's 1835 private grant, show James Bonney was the earliest Anglo settler in the area, despite what some historians have written. John Scolly, grantee of his own private land grant, and three other Anglo regional settlers—Samuel B. Watrous, William B. Tipton and the German, William Kroenig—arrived in the La Junta area several years after Bonney. Samuel Watrous did not settle in La Junta until around 1849.[xi] Watrous' eldest daughter, Maria Antonia, married William B. Tipton in Boone, Missouri when she was 12.[xii] Those two men became business partners in freighting merchandise in New Mexico. William Kroenig arrived in La Junta in 1848.[xiii] Kroenig also married a Watrous daughter, Louisa, and he later became a business partner of Charles Illfeld in a company that supplied ice to Fort Union.

Published description of James Bonney's grant: "Grant name: Santiago Boné (Maria Cleofas Boné); Sources: SG F 206 (30/956) PLC 62 (40/163); Bowden: 770-775; Grantee: Santiago Boné; Date 9/28/1835; Type Grant: Hispano private; Grantor: Gov Albino Perez; County: San Miguel & Mora; Claimed Acres: 6,000."

Much of this grant, and also the land given to Bonney by his father-in-law that James carefully chose to be the site for his trading post strategically near the Santa Fe Trail to take advantage of the commerce rolling past, was basically the same land. His chosen site for his trading post, home and headquarters was where two of the Trail's branches—the Mountain Branch and the *Jornada* or Cimarron Cutoff with the Ocate Crossing—joined and became one before it went on to Santa Fe. It was also beside the trail that went west, up over the mountain to the upper valley of lo de Moro where a settlement—one of the early non-Indian settlements in New Mexico—was already established. Most of those 76 Hispanic families, named as grantees of the Mora Land Grant in 1835, were already living in the region of lo de Mora by 1818.[xiv]

In the early fall of 1840, American Joseph Pulsiphur, a Mormon peddler, entered the Mexican territory of New Mexico from the north with a horse-pulled wagon loaded with goods. He camped one night at La Junta on Bonney land and then disappeared. His disappearance furthered racial tension in New Mexico.[xv] Charles Bent of Taos and Bent's Fort wrote a letter to Manuel Alvarez, the U.S. Consul, to advise him of the probability that the American trader had been murdered. Alvarez asked James Bonney, an "American" living at La Junta, to investigate, which he did to a large extent. He learned residents of lo de Moro had noticed the oddity of a resident selling goods from his home. Bonney's investigation implicated several suspects. Bonney's letter[xvi] to Consul Manuel Alvarez, in a beautiful script, shows he was an educated man for the day. (Image of Bonney's archived letter is at the end of this chapter in end notes.)

Probably in early 1845—when Maria Cleofas was about seven, Santiago was about three, and Maria Rafaela was a baby—Juana left James Bonney, taking the three children with her.

If the 1850 census that listed her as 28 was accurate (cited ages on census records often were not), she would have been 14 when her first daughter Cleofas was born, and in her early twenties when she left Bonney. Joe Lopez said James had tired of her, trumping up a charge against her of infidelity, and told her to leave. Whether or not Joe's cited reason was why, Juana returned to the upper plaza, to lo de Moro and her father's home. Miguel Mascareñas must have been partial to James Bonney. He was disgusted with her for causing a rift and he refused to take her in, said Joe Lopez. He said she had no choice: She and her children had to go live with the man with whom Bonney accused her of unfaithfulness. The 1850 Taos census (Mora was then in that jurisdiction), shows "Maria Juana Mascarinas" age 28, and Cleofas Bonne age 12, Santiago Bonne age 8 and Rafaela Bonne age 5 living in Rio Arriba County with Rafael Garcia de Noriega, age 60, a man more than twice Juana's age. A record shows that Juana and Rafael married. They had one daughter, Estefaña Garcia, born about 1852. Joe Lopez emphatically said Estefaña was not Bonney's child. Census records indicate this Estefaña later married Nerio Casados; they were forebears of Joe's mother.

It is indefinite exactly when Juana moved out and when Bibiana moved in with James Bonney at La Junta, but from records we can make a good guess. The New Mexico Historical Archives in Santa Fe has on microfiche a baptismal record showing that James Bonney and Juana Mascareñas baptized an adult Indian servant, "Jos de Jesus Bonney," on February 13, 1845. And records show José Ramon Bonney was born at La Junta to Maria Bibiana Martín and James Bonney on May 20, 1846. Based upon the dates of those records, Juana had probably left James by March or April 1845, and Bibiana joined him no later than the late summer of 1845.

("Santiago Bone" baptized, at Santa Gertrudis, a seven-year-old purchased Navajo Indian boy they named Juan Antonio "Bone" on February 14, 1861. Source: <u>Mora's Native American Heritage: Captive Indians in the Mora Valley 1861-1878</u> by Virginia Sanchez and Danny Martinez; published in the April 2014 issue of *Herencia*, the Quarterly Journal of the Hispanic Genealogical Research Center of New Mexico. In 1861, the senior James aka Santiago Bonney had been deceased for 15 years. This baptism record pertained to his son Santiago, a young man who had purchased and baptized this Indian boy.[xvii] At that time, this Santiago Jr. (son of James) was probably still living in the Mora area, hadn't yet returned to live at the lower plaza of La Junta on lands inherited from his father.

Soon after Juana's departure, Bibiana Martín came into Bonney's life and dwelling. She was about 18 in 1845, living with her father, Bernardo Martín, at La Cebolla. We do not know how the two met, but La Junta, in the lower plaza, was just a few miles below the Mora Valley that was in the upper plaza. A road of just a few miles connected the two. It is likely they already knew each other. We do not know whether she had her father's blessing when she began living with Bonney at La Junta. Bibiana was known, among her descendants, to have been a beautiful, fair-complexioned, strong-willed woman. Some family said her parents, especially her mother Apolonia, had forbidden her from marrying Bonney, so she declared, therefore, she would never marry. She never did.

The summer of 1846, U.S. Brigadier General Stephen Watts Kearny and his Army of the West passed through New Mexico and, without firing a shot, successfully claimed it from Mexico for the United States. When the battalions led by Kearny—including Col. Alexander W. Doniphan's First Regiment Missouri Volunteers—marched or rode over the Santa Fe Trail that had begun 25 years earlier, they passed through the "civilized valley" of La Junta. The soldiers considered it civilized because, their journalists wrote, it had plentiful water, fine grass, flocks of sheep, droves of horses, and large herds of cattle. They described James Bonney's settlement. The dugout dwelling, trading post and other structures, livestock, garden, *acequia* and animal pens those early journalists wrote of were his.

A few years earlier, Bonney had hired laborers to dig an irrigation ditch from the junction of the two rivers to the higher ground where he built his settlement and trading post. That *acequia*, still functioning in the new millennium, is called the Bonney Ditch[xviii] nearly 175 years after it was dug.

"The first settlement we had seen in 775 miles," wrote Lieutenant Emery, a journalist with the Army of the West. He also wrote, "Mr. Boney (sic) … has been some time in this country, and is the owner of a large number of horses and cattle which he manages to keep in defiance of wolves, Indians and Mexicans. He is a perfect specimen of a generous, openhearted adventurer, and in appearance what, I have pictured to myself, Daniel Boone of Kentucky must have been in his day. He drove a herd of cattle into camp and picked out the largest and fattest, which he presented to the Army."

Another early-day journalist who met Bonney wrote that he had red hair and beard and was English. He probably had a British accent distinguishing him to visitors as an Englishman.

The battalions led by Kearny were welcomed guests of James Bonney. Kearny and his soldiers camped beside the Sapello River on the night of August 13, 1846. While there, perhaps for two days, R. H. Weightman,[xix] captain of Company A, horse artillery unit under Doniphan, presented Kearny with his commission of Brigadier-General.[xx] Kearny's army may have still been there when the U.S. Army battalion, the Missouri Volunteers, commanded by Col. Alexander William Doniphan, arrived from the direction of Ocate. Either Weightman had arrived a day earlier with the commission, or he was with Doniphan's battalion when they arrived.

Early-day journalists confirmed the lore from descendants of James Bonney and Bibiana Martín that those two American armies had camped on Bonney land, and James had fed them his choicest beef.

Col. Doniphan commanded the First Regiment, Missouri Mounted Volunteers with 856 men, comprised of eight companies: A, B, C, D, E, F, G and H.[xxi] His First Regiment Company A was under leadership of Captain Weightman. His Company B light artillery was from LaFayette County, Missouri, under Captain Woldemar Fischer; it was known as the German regiment. Company B volunteers were "accepted into service for 12 months" at Fort Leavenworth, according to their muster-in roll, dated June 21, 1846.

Listed (in alphabetical order) on that muster roll is number 73 Private Daniel Eberle. He was destined to be the second man in Bibiana's life, the father of Maria Elionor Eberle/Ebel, Juan Andres

Eberle/Ebel and Maria Marta Eberle/Ebel. If our forebear mustered into that army at Fort Leavenworth on June 21, 1846, he was likely with Fischer's company under Doniphan almost two months later when they spent that August 14, 1846 night at La Junta. If so, that might have been when Daniel Eberle and Bibiana Martín first glimpsed each other. Or perhaps it was just an amazing coincidence that they were nearby that evening but unaware of each other.

Thanks to the amazing research abilities of Butch Sanders, we only recently learned that Daniel Eberle was listed on that muster roll, conveniently placing him in New Mexico at the right time, in 1846. That group bivouacked and remained in Santa Fe through December 1846. Karl learned that Daniel Eberle mustered out in Santa Fe in December of that year instead of at Fort Leavenworth on August 19, 1847 with most of that company. Before Sanders' discovery of Daniel Eberle on a roster of Doniphan's Regiment, the family knew little about the man, where he came from, except for the family tradition that he was a German Swiss immigrant.

The year 1846 was memorable for the young Bibiana. She had, just months earlier, in 1845, begun life with James Bonney. Her son, José Ramon Bonney, was born May 20. In August, armies of American soldiers, the first she had ever seen, briefly bivouacked nearby. In October, James Bonney was killed by Indians not far from home. (Another version of his death is that he was killed by his adult Indian servant.)

According to Joe Lopez, Indians had stolen some of Bonney's horses. The next morning, while the signs were still fresh for tracking, James went after them, taking an Indian servant for translation and a bag of freshly baked tortillas for barter.

His arrow-studded body was found beside Dog Creek[xxii] beyond Valmora. Joe Lopez and family tradition say he was buried in what later became the Tiptonville cemetery. Some think they can identify the location of his unmarked grave.

Defenseless, Bibiana, with her baby, Ramon, had to return to La Cebolla, leaving James Bonney's considerable property and assets unprotected. Verna said Bernardo took friends with him to La Junta, and then to Las Vegas to report to the militia stationed there, the Indian attack and the need of protection for the large Bonney estate. However, Verna said, "Bonney's acquisitive, well-known and powerful, neighbors" had taken possession of his property. This was confirmed by others.

Bibiana again lived with her father Bernardo at La Cebolla, where she lived most of her life.

New Mexico had only just become a possession of the United States. At that time, no American forts existed along the Santa Fe Trail. Soon there would be many.

~~

In 1851, the U.S. government began building Fort Union at its first location, below and southeast of the bluffs that overlooked what became known as the Fort Union Valley. Some years later, as a boy, my grandfather Daniel Laumbach (born in 1872) sat on his horse on the mesa above, watching the soldiers do horseback maneuvers in that valley below.

The first Fort Union was not far from what had been James Bonney's trading post. It, and/or the fort built at its secondary location in that valley, may have been built on Bonney's grant land. At any rate, years later, Bonney's grown children by Juana told presiding officers at Fort Union that the U.S. owed their family rent.[xxiii]

Bonney's adult children petitioned the U.S. Court of Private Land Claims to reclaim their father's grant land. Their charge was led by Trinidad Lopez, an attorney, the educated and intelligent husband of Cleofas. Frank Springer, a well-known attorney in New Mexico history, and for whom the town of Springer was named, became involved in this case behind the scenes. He provided legal advice to the United States attorney on how to undermine the Bonney heirs' claim.[xxiv] Recorded evidence says the Bonney heirs withdrew their claim. However, Joe Lopez said they eventually won their suit, which also appears to be true. Those three Bonney children with Juana did acquire, own and possess their inherited La Junta lands where they lived the rest of their lives. What seems likely, from looking at court documents, is that they lost or gave up their suit concerning James' 6,000 acres of land granted by Mexican Gov. Albino Perez in 1835. But they won their suit regarding that portion of the Mora grant land their maternal grandfather, Miguel Mascarenas, gave to their father, James Bonney. The land Bonney had chosen for his settlement and trading post at the fertile junction of two rivers, alongside the Santa Fe Trail, is ultimately the same land where his adult children settled. Comparing maps and other documents, the majority of the two parcels of land disputed in both cases—Bonney's grant and that portion of the Mora Grant given to him by his Mascareñas father-in-law—was basically the same land. The only difference seems to be that the 6,000-acre grant was a larger parcel.

In New Mexico are many descendants of James Bonney. Most come from his three children with Maria Juana Mascareñas: Cleofas Bonney and husband Trinidad Lopez, Santiago (James Bonney, Jr.) and his wife Feliciana Jimenez, and Rafaela Bonney and her husband Bernardo Salazar.[xxv] Their parents' liaison was recognized as a marriage in some early New Mexico court documents, but in others it was called common-law. There was also a matter of his prior marital relationship in Missouri, but perhaps that one, too, was common-law, common in those days. If that first one in Missouri had been a sanctioned marriage, a divorce was unlikely.

James' descendants also come from Ramon, son of Maria Bibiana Martín, the daughter of Apolonia and Bernardo Martín, the 40th (of 76) listed grantee of the Mora Land Grant.

I am not descended from James Bonney, but he has long fascinated me because of his brief relationship with Bibiana Martín, my great-great-grandmother, which produced Ramon, my mother's memorable great-uncle Bonney. Most of all, James Bonney is a fascinating facet of our family history.

---

[i] *Wagon Tracks*, Vol. 28, Number 2, February 2014. Page 16, article by Karla French, "The road to Santa Fe … leaves the Arkansas River at three different crossings. The … Lower Crossing … Then Middle Crossing or Cimarron Crossing near Cimarron, Kansas … Commercial traffic mostly used the Middle Crossing." She also wrote that Harry Meyers and Michael Olsen showed that Becknell did not use the Raton Pass: *Wagon Tracks* November 1992. Entering New Mexico from the northeast through the Oklahoma panhandle, the Cimarron Crossing avoided the treacherous Raton Pass.

[ii] It was at or near the Rock Crossing—where the Trail crosses the Canadian River by what was later Taylor Springs east of Springer—where Andreas Detlef Laumbach 1st was killed by Indians in the early 1860s. In most places, the river bed was loose sand and mud, where cattle, horses and wagons bogged down. In this place, however, the river bed was solid flagstone, providing a safe crossing for early travelers of the Trail.

[iii] "Journey to Cimarron" by Jan Girand, in the first issue of *PastWord, Access the Era of Billy the Kid*, published by Yellow Jacket Press in 2012.

[iv] Joe Lopez is an interesting story teller and has been a good source of information, but one should not rely exclusively on him for family history. He sometimes gets his facts wrong, especially when he talks about the other Bonney branch and Laumbach history.

[v] *Land Grants & Law Suits in Northern New Mexico*, by Malcolm Ebright, published 1994 UNM Press, page 193.

[vi] Thomas B. Catron collection at the University of New Mexico Libraries. MSS 29 Series 301, box 11, folder 6. Description: Santiago Bone Grant - Maria Cleofes Bone - Case 62 1893-1895. Publisher: Center for Southwest Research, University Libraries, University of New Mexico. http://elibrary.unm.edu/cswr/

Following is one of the documents in that collection pertaining to the dispute over ownership of the lands of the "Santiago Bone" private grant. This public domain collection was found by Butch Sanders.

Estando en el valle de lo Demora jurisdicion de las Tranpas el Alde. constitucional de ella y testigos de asistencia con quienes actuo por resetoria a los veinte nueve dias del mes de Dbre. de 1837 dijo a que por cuanto Santiago Vone angulo americano vesino de la Yngalatera correspondiente de los Estados Unidos del norte residente en este puesto de mi cargo solicito posesion de terreno para mancomun de su animales cultivando un pedaso para labor y puede gosala como suidadano segun el decreto del Ser. Govor. fecha 5 de Agosto del ano propio, en el qual se dice qe. qe de quiela y pacificamente como muy suya tal propiedad vien alqerida se le dono por gusto de esta comunidad trescientas cinquenta varas de tierra para los fines que le convengan, y son sus linderos de dha tiera por el norte el pie de una loma montosa por el sur la linea de la plaza y por el oriente tierras valdias y por el poniente tieras de Juan Anto. Garcia y en senal de verdadera posecion le entre de la mano al espresado Santiago Vone al sitio referido le pacie en contorno del aranco llevas esparecio punadas de posesion sin contradicion de persona alguna tiera yso otros actos, y de averla tomado quieta y pacificamente pi pidio testimonio de este instrumento pa. su resguardo el cual le di en debida forma para constancia perpetua desta posesion y qe. sus yjos crederos y susecsores puedan posela vendela enagenala en la manera que mejor les convenga, el referido agraciado en ella se obliga y obligo a cantivala y posela el tiempo determinado por las leyes a cullo fin y pa. constansia obligatoria de lo estipulado por esta escritura lo firmo el alcalde y testigos de qe doy fee

Juan Nepomoseno Truxillo (Rubrica)
Assa. Juan de la Cruz (Rubrica)
Assa. Calletano Sandoval (Rubrica)

P. Dt. Que los doqumentos primeros que al interesado Vone se le dicron fue despojado de ellos por Ramon Arellano se tomo la facultad qe. malos vale lo mismo.
(Rubrica)

[vii] James translates as Santiago in Spanish. In most early documents and records, the name Bonney was written as Bon, Boné, Von, Voné and Boney. Just as his first name was usually written in Spanish in New Mexico, his last name was said with a Spanish pronunciation and spelled phonetically: "Boné." In Spanish a B and a V are interchangeable in pronunciation and spelling.

[viii] On October 20, 1835, Gov. Albino Perez granted James Bonney the smaller private grant within the confines of the Mora Community Grant, according to University of New Mexico's Thomas B. Catron Papers collection. The following sketch map was drawn and filed with a claim by James Bonney's adult children years later because of disputed ownership of the land.

Note: I do not see Bonneyville marked on this map. Toward the top, a little to the right, the cluster of boxes represents dwellings in Tiptonville. Bonneyville was established by Trinidad Lopez, when he was an adult, after he had served as a U.S. soldier, stationed at Fort Union.

The documents that follow the sketch map are also from the Thomas B. Catron collection in the University of New Mexico Historical Library Archives. Source: "MSS 29 Series 301, box 11, folder 6." Description: Santiago Bone Grant - Maria Cleofes Bone - Case 62 1893-1895. Publisher: Center for Southwest Research, University Libraries, University of New Mexico. http://elibrary.unm.edu/cswr/ This public domain archived collection can also be found elsewhere.

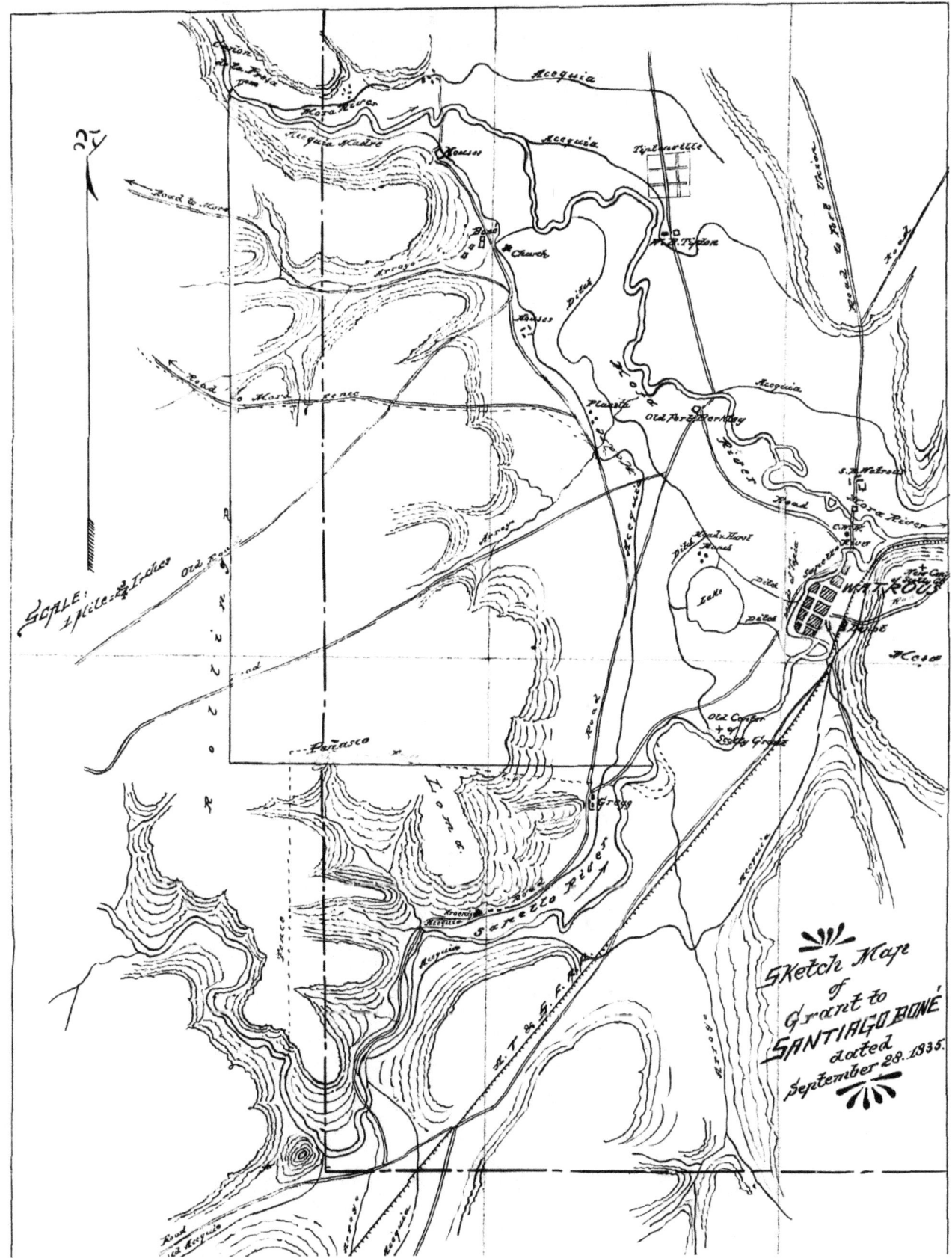

CASE No. **62**

FILE No. ....

Maria C. Bonneval,

   Plaintiff**S**

-vs-

THE UNITED STATES,
   Defendant.

"*Bone*" *Grant*

Exhibit D

Report

~~ANSWER~~

The town of Mora
vs.
The United States

Matt. G. Reynolds,

   U. S. Attorney.

UNITED STATES)
)   vs.
OF AMERICA   )

           In the Court of Private Land Claims,
             Santa Fe District, 1895.

Maria C. Bone et al.   )
    Plaintiffs.   )
)
   vs.   )   No. 62 Bone Grant.
)
United States   )
    Defendants.)

REPORT.

To the Attorney General,

    Washington, D. C.

Sir:

    Under the provisions of section nine (9) of the Act creating the Court of Private Land Claims, I have the honor to submit the following report in the case of Marie C. Bone, et al. vs. the United States, No. 62 for what is commonly known as and called the Bone Grant.

-2-

On January 19, 1893, petition was filed for confirmation of this claim alleged to contain about 6,000 acres.

On June 26, 1894, an answer was filed on behalf of the government; the case was set for trial February 6, 1895, and after thoroughly preparing the case, when it was called for trial, the United States announced itself ready, plaintiff applying for continuance which was denied whereupon plaintiff voluntarily dismissed the suit.

I have the honor to be,

Your obedient servant,

U. S. Attorney.

Santa Fe, N. M.
Feby. 18, 1895.

[ix] Office of the State Historian, Lo de Mora, *A History of the Mora Land Grant on the Eve of Transition* by Michael Miller.

[x] Page 197, Volume II [of five volumes], 1912 first edition, *Leading Facts of New Mexico History*, by R. E. Twitchell.

[xi] Per New Mexico Office of the State Historian, New Mexico History.org, piece written by Shirley Cushing Flint and Richard Flint: Samuel B. Watrous came to NM in the 1830s, worked a while at Taos and other northern New Mexico areas. He did not settle in the La Junta area until 1849, when he bought a half-interest in the Scolly Grant.

[xii] Maria Antonia Watrous, eldest daughter of Samuel Watrous, married William B. Tipton in Boone, Missouri when she was 12, according to familytreemaker.genealogy.com.

[xiii] William Kroenig arrived in La Junta in 1848 according to the oral history given by his descendant, Dogie Jones, for the New Mexico Farm and Ranch Museum.

[xiv] Office of the State Historian, on the Internet, *Lo de Mora, A History of the Mora Land Grant on the Eve of Transition,* by Michael Miller. And Volume II of V, first edition 1912, *The Leading Facts of New Mexico History,* by R.E. Twitchell.

[xv] *Murder and Justice in Frontier New Mexico, 1821-1846,* by Jill Mocho, published in 1997 by UNM Press. A chapter in this book gives extensive information about Bonney's involvement in the "missing peddler case." It has a few incorrect pieces of information concerning Bonney's earliest history in New Mexico.

[xvi] James Bonney's 1840 letter to the U.S. Consular. Collection 1959-179, Benjamin M. Read Collection, series 1, manuscripts-Read Numbers." Citation number: series 1, folder 95, Date(s) of creation 11/17/1840 Serial #8418, on microfiche in the New Mexico State Archives in Santa Fe.

Vegas 17th November 1840

Nº 95   Mr Manuel Alvarez
                                                    Sir

I left the Vegas for the Mora on the 13th inst. and on my arival Mr Slover told me he was going to the higher town to buy the riffle and some tobacco from a Sertain Cristobal Armijo and on telling me that, I toley him to wait a while as I had business [with him] and immediatly proceded up to take them but he was not there and was told he had gone to the Vegas, I then made some enquires about the goods and found he had sold some few articles and to loss not time I proceded to the Vegas and I thare was informed he had gone to the Buffalo, So with that I made some inquiry respecting the goods and offered a small reward to any one who would give me any information respecting the goods, on which I was informed that one Juan Angel Aboonca was selling goods I then immediatly applied to the Alcalde for assistance and proceded to whare he lived and tuck him and also searched his house and found the articles which you will see in the dispach sent to by the Alcalde and a coppy of the same also goes to the Governor. The Juan Angel Aboonca Confises that thare ware three Concerned in the affare, namly him self Juan Cristoval Armijo and Concion Montoya Servent of Juaquin Montoya of the peña Blanco which if he be there you will procede and have him takeing up – among the articles we found a small Pocket Book Containing a few receipts and a not of thirty dollars in favor of Joseph Pulsipher which appears to be the name of the person missing – the Pocket Book I will send it to you the first oppertunity that occurs or take it my self, I leave to day for lo de mora to Collect the articles that are there and open and Search a house that belongs to Said Armijo, which is Supposed to Contain Som of the property, and will Send you an account of the Same as Soon as posible — Juan Angel Apodaca Says that they left the wagon in a Cañada on this Side of the Crosing but Suspect that Armijo has don Something with it by this time — the person of Mr Pulsipher he denies all Knowledg of Saying they found the wagon alone but I will without delay go and Search for it — No more at present from your Obe.t Servent.

James Bonney

Editor's typed transcription of James Bonney's letter to U.S. Consular Manuel Alvarez dated November 18, 1840:

I left the Vegas for the Mora on the 12 instant [*past*] and on my arrival Mr. Slover told me he was going to the upper town to buy a riffle [sic] and some tobacco from a certain Cristobal Armijo and on telling me that, I told him to wait a while after I had business with him and immediately proceeded up to take him but he was not there and was told he had gone to Las Vegas. I then made some inquiries about the goods and found he had sold some few articles and to __[?] not time I proceeded to the Vegas and I thane [sic *then*] was informed he had gone to the [*hunt?*] buffalo, so with that I made some inquiries respecting the goods and offered a small reward to any one [sic] who would give me any information respecting the goods—on which I was informed that one Juan Angel Apodaca was selling goods. I then immediately applied to the alcalde for assistance and proceeded to whare [sic] he lived and tuck [sic *took?*] him and also searched his house and found the articles which you will sea [sic] in the dispatch sent to by the alcalde and a copy of the same also goes to the governor.

This Juan Angel Apodaca confi__ [*confirmed?*] that there [*they?*] were [?] concerned in the affare [sic], namely himself, Juan Cristoval Armijo and Asuncion Montoya servant of Joaquin Montoya of the Peña Blanca, which if he is there you will proceed and have him taking [sic] up. Among the articles we found a small pocket book containing a few receipts and a note of thirty dollars in favor of Joseph Pulsiphur which appears to be the name of the person missing—the pocket book I will send it to you the first opportunity that occurs or take it myself. I leave today for lo de Moro to collect the articles that are thare [sic] and open and search a house that belongs to said Armijo which is supposed to contain some of the property and will send you an account of the same as soon as possible. Juan Angel Apodaca says they left the wagon in the *canada* in the side of a crossing but suspect that Armijo has done something with it by this time. The person of M. Pulsiphur he denied all knowledge of saying they found the wagon alone but I will without delay go and search for it. No more at present from your Obe't Servent [sic]

/s/ James Bonney

    Editor's notes regarding the subsequent legal proceedings:
- The Juez de Paz de Mora (Mora Justice of the Peace) was Miguel Mascareñas, father of Maria Juana Mascareñas.
- Otros (others, i.e. witnesses) included "Santiago Bone" (James Bonney)

[xvii] Researcher Sanders found at least one Bonney man in the Mora area listed on census records whose ancestry he was unable to track. I think he was or descended from an adopted Indian given the Bonney name.

[xviii] Bonney Ditch, as it is still called today, was dug by laborers for James Bonney more than 150 years ago, an *acequia* to bring water from the river to irrigate his orchards and garden. (Photo by Jan Girand.)

[xix] Richard Hanson Weightman was Captain of Battery A, Missouri Light Artillery of Doniphan's First Regiment, according to *The Military Occupation of New Mexico, 1846–1851* by Ralph Emerson Twitchell, published 1909. Also in *Doniphan's Expedition* by William Elsey Connelley, published in 1907. Several years after the war, Weightman settled in Santa Fe and owned a newspaper. One day in the Exchange (Fonda) Hotel, Weightman stabbed F.X. Aubrey to death over a perceived slight. Francis Xavier Aubrey was a noted adventurer who may have led the way for the idea of the Pony Express by hard riding great distances in record times. F.X. Aubrey believed he had found a new, better route to California from Santa Fe.

[xx] *Leading Facts of New Mexican History* by Ralph Emerson Twitchell.

[xxi] Doniphan's First Regiment Missouri Mounted Volunteers were from Lafayette County, Missouri, according to *Doniphan's Expedition* by William E. Connelley, first edition, published 1907.

[xxii] Aunties told Karl that Bonney was killed in *Cañon del Perro*, which is close to Wagon Mound.

[xxiii] During a visit to Fort Union around 1996, comment made to Jan by Harry Meyers, then Superintendent of the Fort Union National Monument supported by the National Parks Service.

[xxiv] Among the extensive Thomas B. Catron collection of papers donated to the University of New Mexico, also archived elsewhere, is a letter from Frank Springer to the attorney representing the U.S. on the 1895 Claim #62, "Boné Grant." He begins that letter saying: "Referring to our previous correspondence on the subject of the Santiago Bone claim, No. 62, I have the following suggestions to make which I think may be of some use to you in resisting the claim. Please treat my communication, for the present at least, as confidential, and do not mention my name in connection with this case." Researcher Butch Sanders, who found the extensive Catron collection at two different locations, said: "Frank Springer then goes on to lay out his suggestions in great detail, and in a rather brilliant fashion (from a legal standpoint). I haven't closely read all 98 pages of these Catron Papers, but from those portions I have read, it appears to me that the United States' case against the Santiago Bone Claim proceeded, following every one of Frank's suggestions."

[xxv] A family in Lincoln County named Salazar claims kinship to Billy the Kid Bonney. That possibility is tenuous. Much of the following documentation was provided by researcher Butch Sanders.
- The modern headstone in the Lincoln Cemetery reads: "Ygenio Salazar, born Feb. 14 1863, died Jan. 7, 1936, 'Pal of Billy the Kid,' & Isabel Salazar born Sept.3 1868, died May 15, 1935." The Lincoln census recorded on July 3, 1860 shows "Higinio Salazar" as three years old in his parents' household. Subsequent census records also confirm Billy's pal was five or six years older than his burial marker says. Isabel's christening record states she was baptized in Tome, Valencia County NM on June 21, 1864. Other records also show her as about four years older than her burial marker indicates. The same slab that supports this marker also indicates "Francisco Salazar, 29 Jan. 1868-5 Sept. 1935" is buried beneath it. (It is doubtful all three were buried under that slab. Most likely there only lies Francisco.) This Francisco Bonney Salazar (husband of Sara Baca), was son of Bernardo Salazar and Maria Rafaela Bonney—daughter of James Bonney and Juana Mascarenas.
- Joe Salazar of Lincoln claims kinship with Billy the Kid. He said his grandparent visited her/his aunt Catarina in Silver City. He concluded that aunt in Silver City was Billy's mama.
- The four great-grandmothers of Joe Salazar of Lincoln are: Maria Rafaela Bonney (wife of Bernardo Salazar), Juana Chavez (wife of Saturino Baca), Maria Paula Chavez (wife of Teofilo Salazar), and the mother of Isabel Paniague (Ygenio Salazar's last wife). Joe's mother, Margarita Salazar (wife of Bernardo Baca Salazar) was not a daughter born to Ygenio Salazar and Isabel Paniagua; she was adopted. Census records say Ygenio and Isabel were childless. Joe's mother, Margarita, born 22 Feb. 1901, was recorded as their niece.

- Most of Joe Salazar's great-grandmothers, or their families, had a place in Lincoln County history. However, the only apparent Bonney connection—whether that connects to Billy remains debatable—was Rafaela Bonney, daughter of James Bonney. When I asked Joe Salazar if his claimed connection to Billy was through Yginio, Billy's pal, he said no. Catherine, mother of Billy, was his grandmother's aunt. He did not add details or give specifics. Another person on that family branch said Francisco Bonney Salazar (son of Rafaela Bonney and Bernardo Salazar) used to go to Silver City to visit his Aunt Catalina. She said his family never learned who that aunt was, or heard the rest of her name, but several on that family line concluded that aunt was Billy's mom. However, no genealogy or other substantiation has been found.
- Apparently there is no kinship between Ygenio and Bernardo—both named Salazar.

SECTION IV: LAUMBACHS IN NEW MEXICO

Chapter 14: More Bonney History
by Jan Girand

The history of James Bonney would not be complete without mentioning that an early newspaper article showed he had once resided at San Miguel del Bado[i], one of New Mexico's earliest settlements. However, Butch Sanders found nothing to substantiate that. Karl Laumbach said the 1835 article indicated he was then "running with a rough bunch." Karl and Butch both found that newspaper article saying an Englishman named "Santiago or James Bonney," who "with six other foreigners traveled to the Apaches to exchange powder and other effects." Karl said, to do that, Bonney traveled far from home to an area of Santa Rita. (Source: El Noticioso, August 21, 1835.) This was at a time when Apaches were enemies of Hispanic and Anglo settlers.

~~

In the middle of the year 2001, I traveled back more than 150 years in one hour of one day. What transported me was standing upon the site of James Bonney's dugout dwelling,[ii] possibly also the store and trading post that he established along the Santa Fe Trail in the early 1800s. Who transported me was 76-year-old Joe Lopez, a Hispanic man with startlingly blue eyes, like his father's, Benjamin (pronounced Ben-ha-MEEN) Lopez.

At age 21, Benjamin's blue eyes were cited in his World War I 1917-1918 draft record. We can assume Cleofas, and her son, Manuel Lopez—father of Benjamin and grandfather of Joe Lopez—also had blue eyes. Those same blue eyes were recorded on the World War I draft records of James' son, Santiago, and his sons Amado and Ricardo. Ricardo's record, and also a description of Santiago, showed they had red hair. It would be interesting to know how many of James Bonney's descendents inherited his blue eyes. Some years ago, Ray John de Aragon, author of *Padre Martinez and Bishop Lamy*, was a teacher in the Las Vegas public schools. He had a student named Bonney. De Aragon said that boy's father, who came to school to pick him up, was the spitting image of Billy Bonney, blue eyes and all. Also, he said, the father's name was James Bonney. It is likely the man de Aragon saw was a descendant of the Englishman James Bonney through his son Santiago (son of Juana) because his line had several named Santiago or James.

Blue eyes, often also red hair, are Laumbach family traits. The second Andreas Detlef, presumably also the first Andreas Detlef, had blue eyes, passed on to many of their children and grandchildren. Several of their descendants had red hair.

Joe and his children own some of James Bonney's land, including the site of the trading post where we stood that day. The only evidence of a structure still visible is an indented, subtly square-shaped area on a small grassy knoll surrounded by *vega*. Joe said Bonney's dwelling and trading post had been partially below-ground. (That could also have been a basement of a home built above it. Butch Sanders found an archived journal, a first-person account describing James Bonney's above-ground buildings.) That dugout was confirmed by at least two early journalists, including American trader Josiah Webb, who met Bonney in 1844. He described Bonney as a naturalized Mexican citizen from Kentucky. Webb said Bonney's home had been a partial dug-out, with a roof of poles (*vigas*) covered with sod. It is possible Webb gave Kentucky as Bonney's origin because another journalist, Lt. Emery with the Army of the West, had compared James Bonney to Daniel Boone of Kentucky.

179

In *Murder and Justice in Frontier New Mexico, 1821-1846*, Jill Mocho said James Bonney was living with his common-law wife, Maria Juana Mascareñas, and three or four children, the oldest a teenage son, in the Las Vegas or Mora area, and that he was not yet settled at La Junta when the peddler disappeared in 1840. That statement and some of Bonney's early history in New Mexico that Mocho wrote of in her chapter about the missing peddler may be at least partially incorrect. In 1840, James was living with Juana Mascareñas, and for at least 15 years, he probably lived at La Junta. His descendants believe he was living on a portion of Mora Grant lands given to him by his father-in-law Miguel Mascareñas. He may have had possession of his lands at La Junta, as required, but it is possible he lived with his family in their earlier years in a more populated area because of the continued Indian threat. Indians kept the area of La Junta—which had long been their own trading or gathering place—too dangerous for anything more than a temporary settlement until later. That "oldest, a teenage son" Mocho wrote of was probably an Indian servant. Records show James and Juana had baptized at least one, giving him the Bonney name, as was then commonly done.

Joe Lopez said that years after James Bonney's death, the adult Bonney-Mascareñas descendants legally fought for and regained ownership to his lands assumed by local Anglo settlers, Samuel B. Watrous, William Tipton and Kroenig. Evidence shows that, as adults, they did legally fight for the return of his lands. James' children—primarily Santiago Bonney and Trinidad, husband of Cleofas—were involved in two different legal battles to regain lands that had been their father's. Butch Sanders found the archived public domain Thomas B. Catron collection[iii] that includes interesting details about the Santiago Bone (James Bonney) grant. Copies and transcriptions pertaining to that disputed grant are found in Chapter 13. Chapter 15 is an excerpt of court testimony taken decades later concerning the Santiago Bone grant.

We also have copies of court proceedings, dated 1859, involving the dispute over many properties within Mora, including James Bonney's estate: "Vicente Romero et al Vs Carmen Arce et al, Cause #632."[iv] That one involved Santiago, the son of James Bonney, in a legal dispute over Mora Grant lands inherited from his grandfather, Miguel Mascareñas. Some information and images of those court documents are in end notes.

Near that settlement of La Junta in northeastern New Mexico had been two other settlements. The better-known of the two, and still sometimes shown on contemporary maps, was Tiptonville, named after the local settler Col. William B. Tipton, who married Samuel Watrous' young daughter. The other, lesser known settlement was Bonneyville, sometimes shown as Boneville on early census records. That community must have not lasted long; the homes of James Bonney's three children, at the same physical location, were later listed on Tiptonville census records. The community of Tiptonville also no longer exists. When my husband, Dan, and I stood that day at the site of James Bonney's dugout, Joe Lopez pointed towards the northeast, not too far distant, where he said Barclay's fort had once been.

Trinidad Lopez, husband of Cleofas Bonney, established Bonneyville after he, his wife and her siblings—the three Bonney heirs—legally regained their father's lands. When Trinidad had gone to nearby Fort Union to ask for protection, the officers recommended that he—who had earlier been a soldier stationed there—establish a community to protect himself and his family from Indian attacks. The adage of "safety in numbers" was critically important. The officers also suggested he "re-up" to gain the Fort's protection and receive a rank promotion. He did re-enlist. During the Civil War, if not earlier when assigned to Fort Union, Trinidad was an officer with the rank of lieutenant, Company A, First Infantry, as shown on his grave marker in the private Bonney family cemetery near Bonneyville, beside the grave of his wife, Cleofas Bonney Lopez.[v]

Trinidad was born September 10, 1835 in Rio Arriba County, New Mexico, and died August 31, 1898 in La Junta, Mora County, New Mexico. His father had been born in Spain. Trinidad was an attorney and, in later years, a Mora County deputy sheriff.

The 1880 census for La Junta Precinct No. 11 shows seven households listed on June 1, 1880 for "Boneville" (Bonneyville): Household #1: Lopez, Trinidad, white, male, age 45, lawyer, born NM, father born Spain, mother born NM; Lopez, Ma Cliofes [*Maria Cleofas*] white, female, age 38, "keeping house," born in NM, father born in England, mother born NM [*Cleofas was daughter of James Bonney and Maria Juana Mascareñas*]; Lopez, Manuel, white, male, age 12, son, laborer, NM, NM, NM [*he was father of Benjamin Lopez, who was father of Joe Lopez*]; Lopez, Manuela, white, female, age 16, daughter, keeping house, NM, NM, NM. Household #2: Nolan, Fermin, white, male, age 21, farmer, NM, NM, NM; Nolan, Monclovia, white, female, age 21, wife, keeping house, NM, NM, NM [*Maria Maclovia, daughter of Trinidad and Cleofas Bonney Lopez, married Fermin Nolan*]. Household #3: Bone, Santiago, white, male, age 35, cattle herder, NM, Eng, NM [*this is Santiago Bonney, son of Maria Juana Mascareñas and James Bonney*]; and Bone, Feliciana, white, female, age 28, wife, keeping house, NM, NM, NM [*Santiago's wife*], with six children listed, including apparently a set of twins. The other households were Ballejos, Fiborcio, a family of five; Gurule, Solome, husband, wife and one child; Armijo, Eujenio, husband, wife and two children; Segura, Ricardo, husband, wife and two children. The enumerator was Fernando Nolan. (Source: *La Junta Precinct No. 11 and the Area Surrounding Fort Union, Mora and San Miguel Counties, New Mexico, 1860, 1870. 1880*, Federal Census Enumeration, transcribed and edited by Harry Meyers, published by the New Mexico Genealogical Society.)

Cleofas,[vi] Santiago[vii] and Rafaela[viii] and their families, some relatives and a few others built their adobe and rock homes in the fertile La Junta valley not far from where James had built his trading post and dwelling. His children built their homes, not close beside each other but mostly within each other's view, on their own portions of their father's Bonney (Boné) land. The settlement of Bonneyville itself was a tighter cluster of a few rock and adobe dwellings built on Bonney land. (The other families only owned their homes, not the Bonney lands they sat upon.) The ruins of the three separate adobe and rock Bonney abodes remain, but only small portions of one or two dwellings within what had once been Bonneyville remain. Still, if you look closely and know what to look for, you can see foundations and indentations, stones and adobe rubble—the earthly remains of Bonneyville.

Near the ruins of Rafaela's home one can see flat and also upended natural, uncut field-stones, a few with subtle scratched etchings still visible, marking long-ago burials.[ix] There is also a Bonney/Lopez family cemetery on Lopez private land. On what is now Joe Lopez's *rancho* where he raised sheep and some crops had once been a church and convent[x] founded by Cleofas, near her home, on a portion of her land that she donated to the Jesuits. At that church some local sacramental events were held, and the records of those births and marriages, perhaps also of some burials, were kept there for a while. Joe Lopez gave me a copy of those records, which I will offer to the state genealogical societies if they don't already have them.

All former Bonney land and ruins are on private posted land. Only a portion of what had once been James Bonney's property, that piece once owned by Cleofas and Trinidad Lopez, still belongs to his descendants: Joe Lopez and his family.

My husband, Dan, and I enjoyed visiting with Joe on several occasions. On one of those, when we were in our little RV, he invited us to hook up to his electricity and use his pure well water at his little *rancho*, beside his sweet-smelling irrigated alfalfa fields. That night lying in our RV bunk, we heard coyotes howl and slept peacefully aware that we were close to the site of James Bonney's trading post, where Bibiana had lived with him for less than a year, and where my mother's great-half-uncle,

Ramon Bonney, was born. We were also a stone's throw from what had been the home of Trinidad and Cleofas and within sight of the site of the Jesuit mission church and convent, what little of it remained.

Joe regaled us with many stories. I wish I had had a tape recorder. One of those he told was about "Prim" Amado Leon Bonney, son of Santiago Jr. According to his draft record, found by Butch Sanders, Prim was born June 2, 1887. His father, Santiago, fought at Glorieta in the Civil War, and that experience left lastingly bad impressions. Later, he repeatedly cautioned his children to never join the military.

The army drafted Prim during World War I at age 30, according to his 1917-1918 draft record. After Prim completed boot camp in California, Joe said, he was to board a departing troop ship. Panicked, Prim and a New Mexico friend deserted, stowing away in freight trains and wooden barrels on transport trucks. They eventually found their way back to New Mexico. The rest of his life, Prim feared being arrested, or worse in his mind, forced to become a soldier. He lived many of the ensuing years—and he lived a very long life—in a cave at Cañon Largo in the rugged Canadian River Gorge. Two lifetime residents of Watrous told my husband, Dan, and me that they remembered seeing Prim, then an old man who always wore a black silk scarf tied around his neck, riding his horse into town. They and Joe Lopez said he remained wary of strangers in town, and kept out of sight of all but people he knew, even while he lived with his maiden sister Vicintita in the little adobe home of their father, Santiago, where they had been born.

Prim hung around in the local bars, and carelessly bragged that he carried a bag of gold. Locals teased him, asking about his bag, whether he was carrying his big one or his little one that day. He was known as an eccentric, an interesting character. Locals in the small community knew his story. However, as shy as he was with strangers, he was careless when drinking in bars. In the 1970s, a man, perhaps two, from the nearby community of Tecolote, offered him a ride home from the bar, intending to rob him. Somewhere on highway I-25, between Las Vegas and Santa Fe, they shoved Prim out of their moving vehicle. Passersby found him and transported him to the hospital in Santa Fe, where he died from injuries.

~~

According to Verna Sparks, when her Uncle Bonney (Ramon, DOB May 20, 1846) was a young man, he worked for a freighter transporting merchandise between northern New Mexico and Denver. On one of those trips to Denver, he met an Englishman named Henry Bonney. Because of their shared last name, Ramon and the older man spent time comparing information. They discovered that Henry and Ramon's father, James Bonney—who died when he was a baby, so he never knew him—were brothers. Henry was a wealthy man, perhaps a successful Denver businessman or property owner, who had no children of his own; therefore, he had no heirs. He wanted to adopt Ramon, but he drove a hard bargain. His Uncle Henry expected him to settle down with him in Denver, and traipse around no more. Ramon was also expected to forget about his family in New Mexico, including his mother, Bibiana.

After Ramon left Denver, he might have pondered Henry Bonney's proposal and decided he could not accept his rigid terms. Perhaps Ramon told his uncle that his deal was unacceptable. For whatever reason, they never saw each other again. That was Ramon's only encounter with and connection to his father's family, according to Verna.

I do not know her source for this story. It may have come from Aunties. More likely she heard it directly from her Uncle Bonney, perhaps when he was an older man on his nomadic visits to hers and the other families' ranches. It might have been said later still, one of the many stories he frequently told her family when he spent time at their ranch when he lived nearby in his rustic cabin.[xi] It was from Ramon that Verna probably also heard that James' brother, Henry, had initially come west with him from Missouri.[xii]

Years later, the mention of a brother of James named Henry caused speculation among a few that he was the same man as one settled in the Taos area named Henry Bonney, of about the same era. However, a descendant of that Taos man effectively quieted that possibility with a piece he wrote, published in *La Herencia*. In his article, "Henry Vaughn becomes Enrique Bone," Luis E. Madrid wrote that the Vaughn name had become Hispanicized to Von or Boné. That is believable because the same thing happened to James Bonney's name in New Mexico. Sanders also found census records that show parents of that Henry Bonney were named Vaughn.

Bibiana's family knew about James' earlier relationship or marriage in Missouri that produced children. When asked, Verna Sparks said Bibiana herself had known about that Missouri family.

Hearing that James had come from Missouri captured the attention of Billy the Kid Historian Herman Weisner, who became even more interested when he heard that Verna had said James had a brother named Henry in Denver. That was because Weisner had found records showing Billy and his mom visited an aunt in Denver.

For decades Herman Weisner had been a resident of Organ, New Mexico, near Las Cruces. He worked as an electrical technician for White Sands Missile Range. In those years, he was an avid researcher of early history and characters of New Mexico. He wrote and published numerous historical articles and wrote a book, *The Politics of Justice: A.B. Fall and the Teapot Dome Scandal, a New Perspective.* Unlike most history writers, his research was not limited to reading what others wrote. His was hands-on. He interviewed still-living witnesses of early events, and dug into boxes in dusty courthouse basements for long forgotten or lost records. He found many historical treasures. One was the original handwritten court transcript of the trial of Wayne Brazel, the man accused of killing Patrick Garrett. An affidavit by a county clerk attested that transcript had been lost for decades. (I have a copy of that transcript. It will be published in a later book.) Herman also found other missing court records, including warrants for Billy.

Those many dusty and moldy documents and artifacts Herman found damaged his lungs and overall health. To prolong his life, he and his wife, Augusta Kay, left arid New Mexico and moved to the more humid climate of Walnut Cove, North Carolina. Because of his failing health, in July 2001, they returned to New Mexico to be closer to their adult children. He died about two and a half years later, in January 2003, at Williamsburg, New Mexico at age 81.

Weisner believed he had found documentation of our James Bonney and his Missouri family. Into that family, said Weisner, was born a daughter named Catherine. Weisner died believing she was the Missouri-born mother of Billy the Kid Bonney. Whatever documentation he found was confirmed in his mind by coincidences or links that he learned of between bits of Billy's little-known early history and the oral traditions of New Mexico Bonneys, and my mother.

As Bob Boze Bell had written in his book, *The Illustrated Life and Times of Billy the Kid*, "Two-thirds of the Kid's life is unknown. Legend and myth have filled in the gaps." The unsubstantiated myths of Billy continue to be repeated or "newly discovered" today. The purpose of most of that has been to give publicity to the "tale tellers."

In his last years, Weisner's failing health and heart medication, which affected his memory, rendered him unable to satisfactorily prove his theory to other Billy historians, most of them skeptical.

Weisner publically told a group of BTK experts and forensic anthropologists at a Billy the Kid Symposium at Ruidoso in 1991[xiii] that he believed he had discovered Billy's origin, a fact that had eluded historians for more than a century. Billy was not from New York; that was a piece of Billy lore repeated by historians for decades without substantiation, said Weisner. Billy was from Missouri. In fact, Billy Bonney himself told the 1880 U.S. census enumerator that he was from Missouri.

Before Weisner moved to Walnut Cove, North Carolina, he searched for a worthy recipient for his extensive collection. He became unhappy with the State's and universities' history libraries and archives because they seemed indifferent to the valuable pieces of New Mexico history, many unique documentations, he possessed. He said many expected him to pay them to archive his collection. He believed none of them valued it. He ultimately donated his sizeable collection of papers, photographs, taped interviews and other historical memorabilia to the New Mexico State University archives, but he emphatically told me he did not give them his pertinent Billy Bonney research collection. He kept those boxes with him when he moved to Walnut Cove. From there by phone, he told me he wanted to give me all of his Billy material and records, hoping I would carry on his Billy research. That did not happen because of his failing health and frail condition. Presumably, his boxes of Billy collections came with him when he returned to New Mexico. When I visited his widow, Kay, and also in a phone call, she told me she had still not opened his many boxes of papers, after their move back to New Mexico.

Contemporary writers of western history knew his name and relied upon the integrity of his research. Many used data Weisner found, but not all credited him. He and Kay showed me at least one example where a published writer had repeated his exact words without crediting him.

~~

I first met Herman Weisner in the 1990s when Karl Laumbach brought him[xiv] to Roswell to visit my mom and me. That was not long before illness and medications affected his health and memory, and he had to leave arid New Mexico. Karl, anthropologist and historian, had known Herman Weisner long before I met him. Weisner came seeking confirmation for his theory about Billy. Before my mother and I met him, it had never occurred to us to consider a link between Billy and James Bonney. Mom had said Ramon visited Billy because of their name in common during Billy's brief incarceration in Las Vegas (he had said Fort Union, but history dictates it must have been Las Vegas). Still, she never gave a possible connection any more thought until Herman Weisner's visit.

No documentation exists that shows Billy was born in New York. For years, Butch Sanders searched for a record of Billy and his mother anywhere there. In fact, it was that search for Billy years ago that sparked Sanders' interest in genealogy, to disprove the public's long-held traditions of some of the early western characters. An early writer one time wrote and published that Billy was from New York. Thereafter, it was so often repeated that the public accepted it as fact. Some honest historians will tell you his New York origin is unconfirmed. No Billy historian has provided a credible reason why he adopted the Bonney name in the last years of his life, after he lived in New Mexico.

Some James Bonney descendants will tell you that the reason Catherine, with her two young sons, came to New Mexico with Antrim was to search for her father.

When Billy—a young man known as Henry McCarty and William Antrim—had warrants for his arrest, he adopted his mother's maiden name for anonymity. Thereafter he became widely known as Billy Bonney.

Without the efforts of Herman Weisner, New Mexico might have missed many other valuable pieces of history, in addition to Billy's. And without the efforts of his typist-wife, Augusta Kay, we might have never known what we might have never known.

Billy's origin—that which was discovered by Weisner—remains unproven.

---

[i] San Miguel del Bado is in San Miguel County, southwest of Las Vegas, New Mexico. It was the first large community grant for Spanish settlement on New Mexico's eastern frontier, made in the late 1700s by the area's Spanish governor.

[ii] Other records and early journals say James Bonney's home, perhaps also his trading post, in addition to the dugout, had been a more substantial one made of logs. The James Bonney settlement had more than one structure. He developed a major irrigation ditch, and journalists said he had gardens and crops, cattle, horses and sheep.

[iii] Thomas B. Catron collection is archived at both the Rocky Mountain Archives and also the Center for Southwest Research, University of New Mexico Libraries.

[iv] The 1859 Mora court proceeding, "Vicente Romero et al Vs Carmen Arce et al, Cause 632," includes dispute over the estate of James Bonney. Those documents are archived in the New Mexico Center & Archives, 604 Montezuma, Santa Fe New Mexico.

Cause 632: A civil suit, apparently begun in 1859, was brought before the County of Mora court, by Vicente Romero, T.B. Catron, Stephen B. Elkins, Thomas B. Veeder and others, against Carmen Arce and many other Mora Land grantees, who defended the unlawful taking of their grant lands. One of those defendants was Santiago Bonney, son of James Bonney and Maria Juana Mascareñas. The Bonney land in that dispute was not James Bonney's "Santiago Bone" private grant land. It was a portion of land inherited by descendants of Miguel Mascareñas, one of the original 76 Mora Land grantees, that he gave to James Bonney.

The Union Land and Grazing Company filed claim against Carmen Arce and others, wherein Elmer E. Veeder intervened and asked relief against Santiago Boney, Appelle, case number 632 on the civil docket. The last-named suit was a partition suit, filed to ascertain the owners of the Mora grant and of partitioning that property among them, which the court called the "principle suit." The grantees' appeals were called the "intervention."

The Union Land and Grazing Company, Elmer E. Veeder, et al filed in the principle suit petition to intervene, claiming Bonney land, an undivided one-twentieth of one-seventy-sixth interest in the Mora grant, requiring Santiago Boney to respond. He filed his answer on October 13, 1914, saying only he and his family, not the claimants, had proper title.

Santiago Boney inherited from Miguel Mascareñas, the 40th grantee in the Mora grant, a 1/20 of 1/76 interest in that grant. The claimants purported that on June 25, 1877, Santiago Boney and his wife deeded that land to Pedro Valdez, who passed it on (sold or inherited) to Pablo Valdez; the claimants presented in court a deed confirming that transaction on December 2, 1911.

Santiago Boney and his wife Feliciana Jimenez de Boney testified to deny they ever signed that document to give up interest in his portion of the Mora grant. In fact they never even knew about it until perhaps 1912. Manuel Lopez, a witness, confirmed that.

On October 22, 1914, the trial court found: That on and prior to the 25th day of June, 1877, Santiago Boney was the owner and had good title to an undivided one-fourth of one-fifth of one-seventy-sixth interest in the tract of land and real estate known as the Mora grant, being a portion of the interest of Miguel Mascareñas, one of the original grantees therein. In essence, Elmer E. Veeder's "proof" of Santiago Boney assigning his portion of grant land to Pedro Valdez on June 25, 1877 was not made, executed, or delivered by Santiago Boney or his wife, Feliciana Jimenez; they did not sign it nor agree to it. That land still legally belonged to Santiago Boney. Elmer E. Veeder had no right or title to that land, or any portion of it.

John D. W. Veeder and Elmer Veeder, both of Las Vegas, continued to argue their case.

~~

Following are a few examples of those court records.

Termino de Enero A.D. 1859

años hijo natural de María de la Cruz Martín la cual según la ley y por la examinación de dos testigos aparece á la satisfacción de de esta Corte que es una persona incompetente para cumplir con los deberes de Guardian y siendo juzgada incompetente é incapaz por esta Corte para poder ser guardian de su hijo Juan de Jesus Trujillo arriba dicho, es por este

Ordenado en y por la Corte que letras Credenciales le sean conferidas al referido Ygnacio Trujillo Constituyendolo, autorizandolo y nombrandolo Guardian y Curador de la persona y bienes de dicho Juan de Jesus Trujillo menor, y residente de este Condado de Taos, para lo cual dará una fianza por la suma de cien pesos con dos fiadores buenos y abonados condicionada por el fiel desempeño de su oficio durante el tiempo que lo tenga.

La Corte se prorrogó á las dos de la tarde deste dia.

Sesion de la tarde.

A las dos de la tarde presentes Juan de Jesus Valdez Juez de Pruebas, Pedro Valdez Escribano y Gabriel Vigil Alguacil Mayor y Colector la Corte se instaló según la prorroga.

Miguel Mascareñas administrador del Estado del finado James Bonney á quien cuyas letras le fueron concedidas por esta Corte con la fecha 28 de Diciembre A.D. 1849 comparecio ahora ante esta Corte para hacer el arreglo final de dicha administracion y pareciendo á la vista de dicha Corte que la tal administracion ha sido concluida se hace constar aqui que termino

Vicente Romero vs. Carmen Arce #632

In the District Court for the 4th Judicial District sitting within and for the County of Mora, Territory of New Mexico.

Stephen B. Elkins et al.,)o(
)o(
            vs.   )o(Chancery
)o(
Carmen Arce et al.,   )o(

VICENTE ROMERO et al Vs. CARMEN ARCE et al
Cause #632
Court testimony of Antonia Maria Romero,
daughter of Maria Dolores & Vicente Romero
(an original Mora Grantee)

Testimony taken before W.E.Gortner, Special Examiner appointed by the Court, on Tuesday July 8th, 1890.

Present, T.B.Catron Esq., Solicitor for complainants.

----------o------------

ANTONIA MARIA MOLINA being first duly sworn according to law deposes as follows, being examined by T.B.Catron Esq.,

My name is Antonia Maria Molina, I do not know what my age is, but I am about fifty years old. My mother was Maria Dolores Romero, one of the grantess in the Mora Grant. My father was Vicente Molina. My mother is dead; she has been dead over fourteen years. My mother only had one child by marriage, myself being that child.

I am acquainted with Rafael Romero and I know Jose Maria de la O. I have known Rafael Romero and Jose Maria de la O for more than twenty years. Before the month of March in the year 1880 I conveyed one-half of my interest in the Mora Grant to Jose Maria de la O. At the time of doing so I was sick from child birth and could not go before an officer and acknowledge the deed in favor of Jose Maria de la O. A short time after I had conveyed to Jose Maria de La O, and sold to him one-half of my interest in the Mora Grant, Rafael Romero came to me and desired to purchase all of my interest in the Mora Grant. I informed him at the time that I had sold one-half of my interest to Jose Maria de la O. He stated to me that that made no difference, that he would take all chances and all risks. Mr Catron paid me for the interest which I conveyed to Jose Maria de la O. Rafael Romero paid my husband a small sum of money, but he did not pay me anything. I did not sign any deed or other paper for Rafael Romero. I did sign a

Also a deed from Maria de la Luz Lucero and Teodoro Ortiz to T.B. Catron, dated the 6th day of August 1879, and marked Exhibit No. 32.,

-----0-----

Also a deed from of Antonia Maria Lucero and Francisco Salazar, her husband to Thomas B. Catron, dated the 29th day of November 188, and marked Exhibit No. 33.,

-----0-----
-----0-----

Also a deed of Marcelino Mascarenas to Pedro Valdez, dated the 18th day of March 1878., and marked Exhibit No. 34.

-----0-----

Also deed of Jose Rafael Martinez and Doloretas Aguilar, his wife to Pedro Valdez, dated the 22nd day of January 1878, and marked Exhibit No. 35.,

-----0-----

Also a deed of Jose Rafael Aguilar and Paula Padilla his wife to L. Sulzbacher, dated the 22nd day of August 1878, and marked Exhibit No. 36.,

-----0-----

Also a deed of Jose Ygnacio Pais to T.B. Catron, dated the 22nd day of August 1879, and marked Exhibit No. 37.,

-----0-----

Also a deed of Louis Sulzbacher and wife to Thomas B. Catron, dated the 17th day of September 1879, and marked Exhibit No. 38.,

-----0-----

Also a deed of Pedro Valdez and wife to Thomas B. Catron, dated the 10th day of September 1879, and marked Exhibit No., 39.

-----0-----

Also a deed from Thomas B. Catron to Stephen B. Elkins, dated 5th day of August 1874 and marked Exhibit No. 40.,

-----0-----

Also a deed of Stephen B. Elkins, to Thomas B. Catron, dated 15th dday of December 1879, and marked Exhibit No. 41.,

[v] Cleofas Bonney Lopez burial marker in private family cemetery, near what was once Bonneyville. Photo by Jan Girand.

[vi] Ruins of home of Trinidad Lopez and Maria Cleofas Bonney, daughter of James Bonney and Maria Juana Mascareñas. Photo by Jan Girand.

Feliciana Jimenez and her husband Santiago Bonney Jr., son of James Bonney and Maria Juana Mascareñas. Santiago's Civil War draft record said he had red hair and blue eyes, apparently like his father. Photo courtesy of Pete Laumbach; quality considerably improved by Butch Sanders.

Feliciana Bonney's application for a military headstone for her husband, Santiago Bonney. Document found by researcher Butch Sanders.

[vii] Ruins of the home of Feliciana Jimenez and Santiago Bonney, son of James Bonney and Maria Juana Mascareñas. This Bonney couple raised 14 children in this little house. Their single daughter, Vicintita, here lived her entire life, which was long—more than 100 years. This was also the home of "Prim" Amado Leon Bonney, where he resided when he wasn't hiding in a cave at Canon Largo. It was still occupied in the 1970s. Photo by Jan Girand.

[viii] Ruins of the home of Maria Rafaela Bonney and Bernardo Salazar. A portion was rock, a portion adobe. Photo by Jan Girand.

[ix] Natural fieldstones, some still upended, some fallen, some places sunken, mark early burials near the rock and adobe home of Rafaela and Bernardo Salazar (to the left, out of the photo). Cattle now freely roam in this field that was once a *camposanto*. The building seen in the background was Santiago's home. You can see the roof of the family's separate small bath house. Photos by Jan Girand

Etching on a rock that had been used as a burial marker. Photo by Jan Girand.

[x] Only evidence remaining of what had once been a Jesuit mission and convent on land donated by Cleofas Bonney Lopez, near her home. Photo by Jan Girand. Joe Lopez and his son used most of the material from this structure to build the son's home nearby.

[xii] James Bonney's descendants from Juana Mascarenas also say he had come from Missouri.

[xiii] Karl Laumbach and Herman Weisner at the 1991 Billy the Kid Symposium at Ruidoso, where Weisner presented his findings. Weisner told Jan that many in the history community discounted his research simply because he did not hold college degrees like they did. Photo courtesy Karl Laumbach.

[xiv] Herman Weisner, Verna L. Sparks and Karl Laumbach in the 1990s in Girand home at Roswell, New Mexico. Photo by Jan Girand

TRINIDAD LOPEZ AND FAMILY

This very handsome young man in uniform, below, is Trinidad Lopez, who would become husband of Cleofas Bonney. His father was born in Spain. He was a formally educated man, an attorney, a U.S. officer commissioned lieutenant stationed at Fort Union, then an appointed officer, commissioned as captain, for the Union with the New Mexico Volunteers during the Civil War. In his later years, he was a deputy sheriff of Mora County. When James Bonney's children were adults, they legally sought to gain back their father's grant lands at La Junta. Trinidad was their team leader and attorney of that endeavor. Butch Sanders found these wonderful images posted on the Internet by the Nolan family on their family tree.

In their early married life, Jose Fermin Nolan and his wife Maclovia, daughter of Cleofas and Trinidad, briefly lived in the tiny settlement of Bonneyville at La Junta. They later settled in the small farming community of Miami, New Mexico, west of Springer, where they raised their children. I knew many of their descendants, not knowing they descended from James Bonney.

Trinidad Lopez

Fernando Nolan with his daughters Clara and Dolores. Fernando was father of Fermin Nolan, who married Maclovia Lopez, daughter of Cleofas Bonney and Trinidad Lopez.

Fernando Nolan in his later years.

October 10, 1863. Item published in *Las Vegas Gazette* June 24, 1876. This article was also published in Spanish.

Officers for the New Volunteer Regiment.

Gov. Connelly has appointed and commissioned the following officers for the New Regiment of New Mexican Volunteers. They will rank from the date of their muster into the service.

Colonel, HENRY R. SELDEN.

Captain, Nicolas Quintana, of Santa Fé.
" Antonio Maria Vigil, of Rio Arriba.
" Ricardo Branch, of Taos.
" Trinidad Lopez, of Mora.
" John Brossee, of San Miguel.
" William Ayres, of Bernalillo.
" Francisco Montoya, "
" Bonifacio Romero, of Santa Ana.
" George W. Cook, of Santa Fé.
" Northrop Rockwell Kemp, of Doña Ana.

The Majors and other officers have not yet been appointed, but we presume they will be before the regiment is fully organized.

All the above appointments, so far as we are acquainted with the appointees, are good, and the officers will be efficient in the discharge of their duties.

Don Fernando Nolan of Santa Clara was in town during the week. We learn from him that a wedding will take place at the residence of Don Trinidad Lopez at La Junta Monday evening next, in which the principals are Miss Maclovia Lopez and Mr. J. F. Nolan, son of Don Fernando. A large number of invitations have been issued for the occasion.

Don Fernando Nolan, de Santa Clara, estaba aposado en la plaza durante la semana. Sabemos de el que el lunes proximo, en la tarde se verificara un casamiento en la residencia de Don Trinidad Lopez, en La Junta, del cual los novios son la senorita Madovia Lopez y el senor J. F. Nolan, hijo de Don Fernando. Se ha espedido un gran numero de invitaciones para la ocasion.

Item published in the *Las Vegas Gazette* October 19, 1878

The ticket was unanimously adopted.

Hon. Fernando Nolan then addressed the convention in an eloquent discourse approving the resolutions and ratifying the nominations. Hon. Trinidad Lopes likewise took the floor and spoke in favor of the Republican party and denounced the Democratic party of Mora county. He was followed by Don Antonio Armijo who confirmed the assertions of Messrs. Nolan and Lopes.

On motion it was adopted that these proceedings be published in the Las Vegas GAZETTE and in the *New Mexican*.

On motion the convention adjourned.

DANIEL MARTINES.
   President.

DAVID DE LUNA,
BERNAVA ARCHULETA,
   Vice-presidents.

Geo. W. Gregg,
Jose Ledux,
   Secretaries.

SECTION IV: LAUMBACHS IN NEW MEXICO

Chapter 15: Santiago Bone Grant Testimony, March 1887

While searching for documentation on James Bonney, Butch Sanders found the extensive archived Thomas B. Catron collection of papers (public domain). It includes 103 pages of material concerning the legal dispute over James Bonney's land granted to him in 1835, called "Junta de los Rios," which he settled in the early 1840s according to this testimony. This suit was brought years after his death by his adult children, primarily Trinidad Lopez—husband of Cleofas Bonney. Below is Sanders' transcription of pages 75 to 85, folder 5, of that collection.

These are transcripts of the 30 March, 1887 testimonies of Jose Ignacio de Luna and Juan Pomoceño Mora regarding their recollections of Santiago Bone (James Bonney). This testimony indicates Bonney's wife Juana Mascarenas, and children did not leave Junta de los Rios until after his death. However, records show Bibiana lived there with James about a year before he was killed in October 1846. They had a child, Jose Ramon, born in May 1846, just months before his death. These testimonies were taken years after the period of time in question; therefore, some portions could be honestly mistaken. Regardless, they provide interesting insight.

Folder 5, pgs 75-85 transcribed:

Santiago Bone Grant
Thomas B. Catron Papers
MSS 29 Series 301, box 11 folder 5

Pages: 75-85

Transcript of testimony of Jose Ignacio de Luna
Mch 30, 1887, since deceased:

In the matter of the investigation of Private Claim, file NO. 206, in the name of Santiago Bone, for the "Junta de los Rios" tract - testimony was taken at the Office of the Surveyor-General for New Mexico, in Santa Fe, on the 30th day of March A. D. 1887.

There were present, Fernando Nolan, Attorney for the claimants; and Will M. Tipton, the translator of the Surveyor-General's Office, who appeared for the Surveyor-General and also acted as interpreter.
Jose Ignacio de Luna being first duly sworn after his oath declares in answer to questions:
Questions by Mr. Nolan, Attorney for claimants:
Q.-- What is your name, age, occupation and place of residence?
A.-- My name Jose Ignacio de Luna, my age, about 68 years, my occupation is farming and I live at the Rancho de los Lunas, in Mora County.
Q.-- Were you ever acquainted with Santiago Bone?
A.-- Yes, sir, I knew him at Mora, I heard of him as long ago as the year 1837, but I was personally acquainted with him in 1842, when he was placed in possession of his land at the dam on the Mora river where the river comes out of the canon.

Q.-- Who put him in possession of that land?
A.-- Juan Antonio Garcia, my father-in-law.
Q.-- What was his official position at that time?
A.-- He was Captain in the rural Militia - and Justice of the Peace or Alcalde.
Q.-- State the boundaries of the land of Santiago Bone, if you know them?
A.-- Yes, sir, I know them, on the North, the Mora river; on the East, the junction of the Mora and Sapello rivers; on the South, a high rock una pena alta, close to the Sapello river; on the West, the hills, where they are the highest. The dam is a principal boundary, and is on the Mora river - and from there the line runs South.
Q.-- State whether or not Santiago Bone had possession of the land and if he did; for how long?
A.-- I know he was there about 1842, for I went there with two of my brothers to take up some land and found that he was living there in a "dug-out" and had all the good land taken up under the possession given him by my father-in-law. I am not certain how long he remained, but I afterward heard that the Indians had killed him close to where he had lived.
Q.-- To whom was this property recognized as belonging by the people of Mora and that vicinity?
A.-- To Don Santiago Bone, and to no one else in the world.
Q.-- Were there any other settlers within the boundaries of the tract as given by you at the time you were there, than Santiago Bone?
A.-- No, sir, not a soul.
Q.-- Was Santiago Bone married or single, and if married, who was his wife?
A.-- He was married to Juana Maria Mascarenas.
Q.-- Did he have any children by that marriage, if so, state their names if you know them?
A.-- As I recollect he had three, Maria, Santiago, and a third whose name I don't remember, who married Bernardo Salazar.
Q.-- Do you know where these three children of Santiago Bone are at present?
A.-- Yes, sir, I am acquainted with their whereabouts. Maria and Santiago are here in Santa Fe today engaged in prosecuting this claim, the third child is dead.
Q.-- How long have you known Maria and Santiago, the children of Santiago Bone, to whom you have referred?
A.-- Since they were born.
Q.-- Are these children of Santiago Bone in possession of the land formerly owned by their father and if so, for how long have they been in such possession?
A.-- I have always heard that they were in possession, I don't know how long. I suppose they have always been in possession, they are now in possession.
Q.-- How far is it from the Mora river to the high rock (*pena alta*), which you state is the South boundary?
A.-- About four miles more or less.
Q.-- How far is it from the dam to the Junction of the Mora with the Sapello?
A.-- It is further than the distance from the Mora to the South boundary; perhaps five miles, I don't know accurately what a mile is.
Q.-- Have you any interest in this claim, or in the result of this investigation?
A.-- No, not at all.
Cross Examination for the Surveyor-General:
Q.-- You have stated that you saw the grantee, Santiago Bone, living on the land in question about the year 1842: now did you ever see him there after that time?

A.-- I do not remember positively whether I saw him there afterward or not, but I was told by hunters whom I met when I was hunting deer in that vicinity, that they had been to Bone's place and that he was still there.

Q.-- When was the last time that you were told he was still living on the land?

A.-- Perhaps about the middle of 1843, but I cannot be positive as in those times we didn't pay much attention to time or the years.

Q.-- Do you know of your own knowledge that Bone was placed in possession of the land by Juan Antonio Garcia?

A.-- Yes, sir.

Q.-- Were you present at the delivery of possession?

A.-- No, sir.

Q.-- How then do you know that possession was given?

A.-- I afterward saw a copy that my father-in-law had of the act of possession, which had been delivered to Bone by him.

Q.-- Did you read this copy?

A.-- Oh, yes, I read it, it stated what the boundaries of Bone's land were.

Q.-- Do you recollect what those boundaries were as given in that copy?

A.-- They were substantially the same as those I have already given in my evidence. There may have been some difference in the description, but practically they were the same.

Q.-- Do you know of your own knowledge whether or not Bone's family remained upon the land after his death?

A.-- I do not know of my own knowledge as I was young at that time, and lived some distance from there, but I afterwards heard it said that they had moved away.

Jose Ignacio de Luna

Sworn to and subscribed before me this 30th day of March, 1887.

Geo. W. Julian.
Surveyor-General.

Transcript of testimony of Juan Pomoceno Mora
March 30, 1887, since deceased.

In the matter of the Investigation of Private Claim, file NO. 206, in the name of Santiago Bone, for the "Junta de los Rios" tract testimony was taken at the Office of the Surveyor-General for New Mexico, in Santa Fe, on the 30th day of March A. D. 1887.

There were present, Fernando Nolan, Attorney for the claimants; and Will M. Tipton, the Translator of the Surveyor General's Office who appeared for the Surveyor-General and also acted as interpreter.

Juan Pomoceno Mora being first duly sworn on his oath declared in answer to interrogations:
Question by Fernando Nolan Attorney for claimants:

Q.-- What is your name, age, occupation and place of residence?

A.-- My name is Juan Pomoceno Mora, my age is 64 years, my occupation is that of farmer and I live at East Encinosa in San Miguel County.

Q.-- State whether or not you know the late Santiago Bone?

A.-- Yes, sir, I knew him from 1838 until he died, which to the best of my knowledge was in 1846.

Q.-- State whether or not you know in what time of the year he died?

A.-- He died in October, but I do not know what day of the month.
Q.-- At what place did you first see him in 1838?
A.-- In Mora, at the lower settlement (plaza).
Q.-- Where did he live at that time?
A.-- At Mora.
Q.-- In what other places did Bone live from 1838 up to the time of his death in 1846?
A.-- At the junction of the Mora and Sapello Rivers.
Q.-- State whether or not [*you know*] when Bone went there?
A.-- He went there about 1841 or 1842.
Q.-- Were you in La Junta in 1841 or 42?
A.-- Yes, sir.
Q.-- What was Bone doing there?
A.-- He was building a dam and ditch to irrigate his lands.
Q.-- What lands do you refer to?
A.-- The lands from the junction of the Mora and Sapello and between those streams.
Q.-- Did Bone have any other improvements there than the dam and ditch?
A.-- The only other improvements he had that I saw, were some "dug outs" and two log houses.
Q.-- How long did you remain at La Junta on the occasion you have referred to?
A.-- I was there about a month, working for Bone in the dam and ditch.
Q.-- Where did you go at the end of the month?
A.-- I went to Mora to the house of Bone's father-in-law, Miguel Mascarenas.
Q.-- Did you ever return to La Junta where Bone lived?
A.-- I returned there on various occasions to Bone's place.
Q.-- When was the last time that you saw Bone living at La Junta?
A.-- I am not absolutely certain, but I think it was in 1845 when I was doing some work for him there.
Q.-- What kind of work were you doing for him on that occasion?
A.-- I went with fifty yoke of oxen to a place called Tul on the Cimarron Seco [*words on material indistinct*], this side of the Napeste (Arkansas) river, to bring some wagons that had been abandoned on account of a snow storm, the mules belonging to the [*wagon*] train having died in the storm. The train belonged to a man named Spier.
Q.-- Did you ever see Bone after the time of rendering the service just referred to?
A.-- I never saw him alive after that time, but I saw him when he was dead.
Q.-- State whether or not to your knowledge the family of Bone remained on the land after his death?
A.-- No, the widow was left alone with a number of little children, and went to Mora where her parents were.
Q.-- Did Bone's widow move her effects from La Junta when she moved to Mora?
A.-- Yes, sir.
Q.-- How do you know that?
A.-- I know it because I helped move them.
Q.-- Did you have anything more than that to do with Bone's effects after his death?
A.-- Yes, sir, I had to collect his animals together.
Q.-- By whose order did you gather up his stock?
A.-- By order of the widow.
Q.-- What was the object of gathering up the stock?
A.-- To place them in charge of the widow's father.
Q.-- Are you acquainted with the boundaries of the lands claimed by Bone?

A.-- I am not perfectly certain, but I think I know about what they were although I may be mistaken in some slight particulars. On the North, the Mora River, on the East, the junction of the Mora and Sapello Rivers, on the South, some scattered rocks near the Sapello, on the ridge that begins above where the river comes out of the Canon, on the West, the dam belonging to the land, which is in the Mora River.

Q.-- Were there any other persons than Bone living within the boundaries you have mentioned, up to the time of his death?

A.-- No, sir, no one.

Q.-- What was the name commonly applied to this place?

A.-- The junction of the river (La Junta de los Rios.)

Q.-- Who if anyone was recognized by the people of Mora and that vicinity as the legal owner of the lands within these boundaries?

A.-- Don Santiago Bone.

Q.-- State whether you know if Bone had any children or not?

A.-- Yes, sir, Maria was the eldest, Santiago, the second, and Rafaelita the third.

Q.-- State if you know whether they are living or dead?

A.-- Two are living, Rafaelita is dead, she married Bernardo Salazar.

Q.-- State if you know whether she had any children?

A.-- I am not certain about that, in fact I don't know.

Q.-- State if you know if Maria and Santiago Bone are married or single, and if married, who did they marry?

A.-- They are married, Maria is married to Trinidad Lopez, Santiago is married to the daughter of a man named Jimenes, but I don't remember her name.

Q.-- State if you know where Maria and Santiago Bone are now living?

A.-- They are living at La Junta de los Rios, and have lived there about twenty or twenty-one years, but I am not very positive about the time.

Q.-- How far do they live from the land that belonged to their father Santiago Bone?

A.-- Maria lives about 150 yards above the old house of her father, and Santiago lives a little further than that below; all the houses are within the boundaries I have mentioned.

Q.-- How far is it from the dam to the junction of the Mora and Sapello rivers?

A.-- It is about three miles, probably a little less.

Q.-- From the Mora river, how far is it in a straight line to the boundary on the South?

A.-- About two miles, a little more or less.

CROSS EXAMINATION FOR THE SURVEYOR-GENERAL:

Q.-- How long have you lived at your present place of residence at Encinosa?

A.-- Some three or four months, only.

Q.-- Where did you live previous to that time?

A.-- On the Red River in San Miguel County, for some four or five years.

Q.-- Where did you live before that?

A.-- On the Vermejo River in Colfax County, about five years; before that I lived at San Francisco, in the Territory of Colorado, about 8 years in the County that Trinidad is in; and before that I lived at Mora.

Q.-- Do you recollect what year you went from Mora to San Francisco?

A.-- I don't remember the year, but it must be 15 or 17 years [ago] more or less.

Q.-- Do you know whether Bone's widow is alive or dead?

A.-- She is dead, having died at Mora before I went to Colorado.

Q.--Were her children living at Mora at the time you went to Colorado?
A.-- I think not; I think they were living at La Junta.
Q.-- Do you know when they returned to La Junta?
A.-- I don't know in what year it was, but I know they returned there.
Q.-- Do you know whether Bone's widow returned to La Junta or attempted to return with the intention of living upon the land?
A.-- She attempted to return but she fell sick and I think never returned, but her children went there after they married.
Q.-- How do you know that the boundaries you have mentioned are the real boundaries of Bone's land?
A.-- I know it from the fact that Bone and all the laborers there mentioned those places as the boundaries of his land.
Q.-- Did you ever see any documents that mentioned those places as boundaries of his land?
A.-- No, sir.

     his
  Juan Pomoceno x Mora
     mark

Witness.
 Will M. Tipton.

Sworn to and subscribed before me this 30th day of March A. D. 1887.

   Geo. W. Julian.
   Surveyor-General.

SECTION IV: LAUMBACHS IN NEW MEXICO

Chapter 16: A Bonney Ballad
by Jan Girand

Around 2000, I published this frivolous Bonney Ballad in my Roswell Web Magazine. It caught the attention of many, and afterward, at least one writer used its suggested premise—a possible connection between Billy and James Bonney—for his small project. Although various cuentos (stories passed down) of New Mexico Bonneys and some of my kinfolk say there is a genealogical connection, that has not been proven.

Once upon a time – well it was more than a century ago –
there was a boy called Billy in the Territory of New Mexico.
Now Billy wasn't his name back at the beginning of his life;
they say that it was Henry and he was born to one then not a wife.

His mama was named Catherine, and he had a brother named Joe.
His mama's last name was McCarty, so, too, was his and Joe's.
Some historians say Henry McCarty was born without a dad
in New York to an Irish lassie and the way they lived was sad.

Our Henry had arrived there on his birthing day
in an Irish slum in 1859, or so *some historians say*.
Still, little is known about him, back in his early years,
except "How am I going to feed him?" was his mama's greatest fear.

They lived a while in Kansas, made a stopover in Denver, too;
why they landed in New Mexico historians have no clue.
What was it drove them onward? Why did they end up here?
Were they searching for a better life? Or was it plain despair?

Some say their lives got better before arriving here
'cause Catherine took a partner to share her load with her.
At any rate, they came here, to live in this wild place,
Catherine, Joe, Henry – and Will, a guy historians trace
to Kansas on the plains, a place called Wichita.
Even then, young Henry called William "Pa."

So, long before they got here, they'd ambled other places,
frustrating historians by leaving few traces.
Census, courts and archives, even churches cast
few if any clues upon our mysterious Billy's past.

One thing they know for certain (at least they think they do),
the Santa Fe Book of Marriages holds their *first* recorded clue.

The widow, Catherine McCarty, in Santa Fe, New Mexico,
stood with Henry and Josie (what they called her boy Joe) –
as she said her wedding vows, the boys stood up with them
at First Presbyterian, with her and William Henry Antrim.
That was the first known record establishing when he –
our Bonney lad – was in New Mexico; that was in 1873.

Like his mom, Henry McCarty just then changed his name
to Antrim. "William or Will like my new dad, if it's all the same."
Confusing historians, he was Henry McCarty just the same
but William Henry Antrim right then became his name.

In Santa Fe the Antrims' days of roaming still weren't done;
they traveled to Silver City to bask in its arid sun.
It was there the young William Antrim, called "Will,"
took yet another name: "Just call me the Kid or Bill."

Then his beloved mother died of consumption or T.B.
It broke the heart of Billy, and a boy he'd no longer be
for it was then this childish lad began his criminality;
on a lark he stole some clothes from a Chinaman's laundry.

It was only for the fun of it, but the sheriff did not laugh.
The Kid was thrown in jail but his lock-up did not last.
Billy vowed a little space with just a cot and pail
was not to be the end of his, our cunning boy's, tale.

He conned the sheriff's deputy, and knew well how to shimmy
so he made quick his escape right up that red brick chimney.
That proved to him and all the rest his wiles and slippery ways
and that was just the beginning of his desperado days.
(What could you expect, since Billy's home-life wasn't sound?
And his step-dad didn't care much to have the boy around.)

He was a homely kid, buckteeth and prominent ears,
so he relied upon his ways of charm and lack of boyish fears
to win him loyal friendships, cause girls to think him cute.
Still, his winning way was because … boy could he shoot!

To cause more consternation, sometime after that,
to his aliases added he another, and not a simple "Mac."
As if he hadn't then enough, he took a whole new name –
this newest one was Bonney, and his life was changed again.

Have you heard of that one? From whom or where was it taken?
It had to come from somewhere; was his family line forsaken?
He was Irish, they'd said? And Bonnie Prince Charlie was Scot,
so that's not it … hmmm … "a *bonnie* wee lad" he was not.

"It is just a name," philosophers and poets will tell you;
the name is not the thing, they say, it is the deeds you do.
Well! It's certainly true that Henry/William/Billy the "Kid"
McCarty/Antrim/Bonney did not out-live the deeds he did.

And daring-do deeds he did, they say in books, movies and songs.
His multiple lives and legends through mighty tall tales live on.
Twenty-one killings, say they, one for each year of his life;
those "facts" of his shootings aren't true, perhaps, too, the years of his life.

His life, especially if shorter, was certainly filled with strife,
but too many killings were credited him, extolling a violent life.
On the 1880 census, said Billy, the year before he died,
he was born in Missouri and his years were twenty-five!

But historian, Herman Weisner, said Billy was nineteen instead
when Sheriff Pat Garrett shot him, and there declared him dead
in Pete Maxwell's Fort Sumner adobe that July night of '81.
Billy died in that darkened bedroom, a tragic end for Catherine's son.

~~

Twenty-one killings intended just wasn't the way that it was –
Four, maybe five altogether, only a few for sure were his.
One was Olinger in Lincoln who'd bullied the poor lad so
and made false accusations. Our Billy just had to go
for if he hung around there long, a hanging would be his fate.
He had to make fast his getaway before it was too late!

Billy made a run for it, armed Bell and Olinger stood in his way
so Billy had to shoot them to make good his getaway.
~~
So: Who was our Henry McCarty, William H. Bonney, "the Kid?"
Where did he come from, who was his ma, why did he do what he did?
Of his latter years, alas so few, we know his story well
because many, including Pat Garrett, his stories loved to tell.

His antics, shoot-outs, hot pursuits are documented well
in books, in movies and in songs stretched out so they would sell.
And sell they did, even in England, for folks there love a tale
of strife, romance and intrigue as they quaff their brew and ale.
~~
Now, about "the Kid" Billy Bonney too much had already been said;
I had no interest in him, I preferred reading gothics instead.
Although I live near Lincoln, I never gave him much thought;
intrigue and history were my choices, cowboy shoot-em-ups were not.

Now, stories that I really loved were ones my mama would tell
of her intriguing family history. Ah, those tales she told so well!
My mama, born in '09, had an uncle of whom she spoke,
he had babysat her when he was an aged cowpoke;

the bewhiskered old man had held her when she began to cry.
Ramon Bonney was his name; he later lived in a cabin nearby.
That place was in a desolate spot on the picturesque canyon rim
overlooking the *Yegua*, a lonesome place for him.

My mama was a child back then, her memories were vague, you see.
Ramon, her great-half-uncle, was lonesome for company
so often he rode his donkey to her parents' ranch for chats
and meals and recognition, and a rub by their sociable cat.
He was nearly blind by then and hungered for more company
than that of his decrepit old mules and his faded memories.

He spoke only in Spanish; English was not his tongue
so his nephew's wife, his hostess, tried to teach him some.
In exchange he taught her Spanish; she, a German, needed that
for she was in New Mexico now where *Español* was the format.

My mama's mama, Emma, smiled and cooked for him huge meals
so Ramon would go home replenished, his spirit and stomach filled.

Back then, the children thought of him as just a silly old guy;
they were bored by his retold tales, scared of his cataract-scarred eyes.
They didn't listen to his stories, thought they'd better ones of their own,
and they laughed when his mule hid from him behind the scrawny piñons.

He hated growing older and with odd things dyed his hair
so it blossomed in many colors until Emma pointed there,
gently chiding: "No shame in growing older, no need to despair,
for with age comes greater wisdom." Thus ended the blooming hair.

"Old Uncle Bonney" to them he was, even Emma and Dan.
An old man he was then, but he once was a virile young man
who had fathered many children. Still … he chose not a domestic life.
Husbandry wasn't for him; he was the nomadic type.

He had lit out for adventure, and excitement is what he got
as he roamed the hills and canyons and mountain lions he shot.
He had a wagon caravan, and he took it far and wide,
to St. Louie, Santa Fe, Denver and beyond the Great Divide.

He peddled pots and pans then, bolts of calico, tatted laces
and he pushed herds of cattle as he roamed about the places.

~~

Born of James Bonney and Bibiana Martín in May of '46,
Ramon was Bibiana's first-born but – we know – not his.
James Bonney was an Englishman who'd traveled far and wide;
Bibiana was not the first one he had taken for his "bride."
James had lived in Missouri prior to New Mexico
and before he met Bibiana; that's something we believe we know.

In Missouri he had a wife and kids (we think at least were two);
we think that Great-Great-Grandma Bibiana also knew.

After he came to New Mexico (there's still more to this story),
he had yet another family in the New Mexico Territory.
So when James took young Bibiana and fathered our Ramon,
He already had <u>two</u> other places he'd previously called home.

We think James was a rogue, but he was immortalized anyway.
Twitchell and early journalists had said Bonney saved the day
during the American Occupation. With his prime cattle he had fed
Kearny's and Doniphan's soldiers—that's what R.E. Twitchell said.

Ramon was born in May; in October his dad was killed
not far from his La Junta lands, James' English blood was spilled.

James Bonney was killed by Indians, our family stories say,
while he tracked his stolen horses early one autumn day.

James had been a land grantee, had lands with sheep and cattle;
his neighbors then took everything, even Bibiana's saddle.
With her man and properties gone, she, by wagon team
returned to La Cebolla, to her dad Bernardo Martín.

Since the lovely young Bibiana, along with her babe, Ramon,
lost everything she had then, she returned to her childhood home.

(Later, my great-great-grandma Bibiana had another relationship,
this one with Daniel Eberle, my great-great-granddad, who was a German Swiss.)

～～

Eventually Ramon grew up and his nomadic life began
as a wagoneer, a herdsman, a merchant-suppliers' man.
On a caravan trip to Denver, he met a man then unknown:
Henry claimed to be brother of James, the papa of Ramon.

Uncle Henry was quite wealthy, so the family stories told,
and he wanted to adopt Ramon and share with him his gold.
Ramon declined the offer, the strings to the deal too tight.
He was required to stay in Denver and quit the nomadic life
and never see his mother. He liked the life he chose
so he declined that offer his uncle had proposed.

Ramon never saw him again, that Englishman uncle he had—
Henry, brother of James—so he lost all known ties to his dad.

When Ramon was somewhat older, he like all the others,
had heard of bad boy Billy. He wondered if they were brothers;
since they had the same last name, he thought they might be kin.
When Billy was locked up in 'Vegas, there Ramon visited him.

Billy and Ramon found no connection so my embarrassed family said,
but other New Mexico Bonneys say, "Oh yes there is!" now that Billy's long dead.

～～

An Englishman named James Bonney and a connection with Denver, too!
Those caught the attention of a Billy historian who thought they might be clues.
Cousin Karl brought Herman Weisner to see my mama and me,
a southwestern history buff and a published writer was he.
He'd heard of our Ramon Bonney and he just had to come and see
if he could confirm the Billy connection he thought he'd found, said he.

"I think Billy and the New Mexico Bonneys have a common link –
the odds of it NOT being so are long, Verna, don't you think?"
He and my mama, Verna, made an intriguing pair,
their lifelong love of New Mexico history gave them much to share.

"Especially when I tell you all the things that I now know,"
said Weisner. "We know Billy's life didn't begin in New Mexico.
His mother was named Catherine, that part is true as well,
but that is where I depart from others when I continue with his tale.

Catherine wasn't a New Yorker, she came from Missouri instead,
and an Englishman named James Bonney had been Catherine's dad.
As a boy, young Billy, I've read, had lived in Denver a while
with an aunt, a close kin of his, when he was still a child.

Billy was born in Missouri in '61; he was nineteen when he was shot.
He wasn't born in New York in '59; a twenty-one-year-old he was not."

To the historian, Frederick Nolan, I spoke of the theories we had,
that Englishman James Bonney might have been Billy's granddad.
Mr. Nolan, an Englishman, too, was thoughtful when we spoke;
our theory did not surprise him, 'though he stood by what he wrote.

I think what he wrote was not in conflict. Catherine, Henry and Joe
might not have been from New York; most historians say they do not know.

So, my friends, it seems to me, Uncle Ramon Bonney and Billy's ma
might have had the same Bonney Englishman for their roguish roving pa!
We might never know for certain if Herman Weisner's theory was true
but I think it has great possibilities; what think you?

View from Uncle Bonney's Place overlooking the canyon; oil painting by Verna L. Sparks

    I shared this poem with BTK historian Herman Weisner in the last years of his life. It made him extremely happy because it reflected his views, which he thought few people believed.

    He believed he had found documentation in Missouri linking James Bonney and Billy, but in his last years, heart medications affected his memory and he died before satisfactorily proving his strongly held belief. He would have caused a major world-wide ripple of interest, even beyond the history community, if he had been able to prove what he believed. In fact, he thought he had proved it.

    Billy the Kid Bonney is one of the most recognized names and characters in the world. With the Internet and the tremendous amount of new data becoming available, it may be just a matter of time before Billy's origin is known.

    Butch Sanders independently spent years searching for Billy's roots. In fact, it was the "Brushy Bill" Roberts, Wilson, Miller and other Billy scams that first captured Sanders' interest in genealogy. Anyone with his right brain tied behind his back should see through all of those impostors, he thought. From then on, he began doing historical and genealogical research of western characters using the many tools now available.

    After due diligence—far beyond that done by most modern historical writers—Sanders has found no documentation showing Billy, his brother Joe and his mama had began their lives in New York. He has also found no documentation placing James Bonney in Missouri with a family and a daughter named Catherine, who might have been Billy's mama.

    As long as we have no proof to the contrary, I am an agnostic about Billy's mother being born to James Bonney in Missouri. An agnostic: one who believes that no proof of an existence does not necessarily mean one does not exist. I remain open-minded.

    There must be a reason why *cuentos* about Billy among the various James Bonney descendents have survived for more than a hundred years, long before Billy-wannabes had become a fad.

Remains of Ramon Bonney's cabin near my grandfather's ranch. 2010 photo.

SECTION IV: LAUMBACHS IN NEW MEXICO

Chapter 17: Bernardo Martin, 1848 U.S. Military Service Record
by José Antonio Esquibel

Military service among the men of New Mexico is a long tradition. During the 1600s, nearly all able-bodied males age 14 and older served as soldiers and participated in numerous campaigns against hostile Indians in defense of their property, families and livestock, and that of the Pueblo Indians. With the formation of a presidio at Santa Fe in the late 1690s, a formal structure was established for military enlistment and services. For many decades the *Presidio de la Exaltación de la Cruz* in Santa Fe consisted of anywhere from fifty to one hundred soldiers. The surviving military records for numerous New Mexico men spanning the period of 1732 to 1820 are a testament to the dedication of men willing to place themselves in danger for the protection of others in service to the royal crown of Spain.

It was during the 1700s that a formal militia system was put into place in outlying settlements as a means of rapidly organizing and deploying men for the purpose of defense until professional support arrived from Santa Fe. This system was still in effect during the Mexican Republic era of New Mexico's history (1820-1846), and at the time the military forces of the United States of America entered New Mexico in 1846. Even with the transition from the Spanish government to the Mexican Government to the government of the United States of America, New Mexican men continued to place their lives in danger through military service.

The arrival of the U.S. Army in New Mexico in 1846 heralded changes for New Mexicans as they became territorial citizens of the United States of America. Although it can be argued that some of the changes were unfavorable, there were those who saw benefit and opportunity in the change of sovereignty. It did not take long for some people to take full advantage of the emerging opportunities. Among these individuals was Bernardo Martín, one of my third-great-grandfathers. He is also a common ancestor for a very large extended family group that includes these family names: Ebel, Bonney, Andrada, Laumbach, Esquibel, Gallegos, Córdoba, and numerous others. A small number of his descendants gather annually for a family reunion in the Mora Valley, where Bernardo settled in the mid-1830s.

The opening of the Santa Fe Trail in 1821 created an economic and social link between New Mexico and traders operating out of Missouri. Economic ventures increased the number of individuals coming to New Mexico from the United States. Suspecting an interest on the part of the United States in acquiring New Mexico as a territory, the New Mexican leadership encouraged and supported active settlement of the eastern slope of the Sangre de Cristo Mountains as a measure of added protection. One of the areas settled was the Mora Valley, through a land grant established in September 1835. Bernardo Martín acquired a grant of land and moved his family into the valley by 1836.

By the 1840s, political and military leaders in New Mexico and the United States began to realize the potential that existed in a change of sovereignty in New Mexico. Politicians in the United States weighed the advantage of taking New Mexico and other northern provinces away from the Mexican government, leading to the Mexican War of 1846-1848. In August 1846, Colonel Stephen Watts Kearny entered New Mexico, encountering no military resistance at Las Vegas or Santa Fe. Subsequent negotiations brought New Mexico under the laws and government of the United States, which altered the social and cultural history of New Mexico.

Bernardo Martín was one of many of his generation born a citizen of the Spanish Empire, married and had children as a citizen of the Mexican Republic, and then lived as a territorial citizen of the United Sates of America. Born May 20, 1792, at El Potrero de Chimayó in the jurisdiction of Santa Cruz de la Cañada (modern-day Española area), Bernardo was a direct lineal descendant of Captain Luis Martín Serrano, the elder, who settled in the Chimayó area in the 1600s. On January 8, 1827, at Santa Cruz de la Cañada, Bernardo married Santa Fe native Apolonia Gutiérrez y Solano, age fifteen, nineteen years his junior. Seeking to improve the lifestyle of his small family, Bernardo took advantage of the opportunity for owning land in the Mora Valley soon after the land grant was made available in 1835. His immediate descendants through his daughter, María Viviana Martín, continued to reside in the Mora Valley throughout the nineteenth century.

Bernardo Martín joined the U.S. Army in April 1848 and briefly served under 2nd Lt. Ashley Gulley, transporting quartermaster supplies for the troops of Lt. Col. William Gilpin. He was among the earliest New Mexicans to serve in the U.S. military. A record of Bernardo's U.S. military service is preserved in a bounty land warrant application filed in 1857 and 1858, uncovered by a relative, Amanda Maestas Freiberg.

The first document of the application is dated July 9, 1857, and is a formal attestation of Bernardo Martín, a resident of "Lo de Mora," in the presence of a Justice of the Peace in Taos County confirming his military service. Bernardo testified that he served in the company of Lt. Gilpin and was "employed by the quartermaster of the command in the transportation of Quartermaster and Commissary stores for the command in the month of April 1848 on a campaign against the Comanche Indians during the Indian War of 1848." We learn that this particular campaign lasted 14 days. During two other expeditions, Bernardo stated that he was involved in fighting with Indians, the first incident occurring near Pawnee Fork (just north of modern-day Dodge City, Kansas) in June, and the second occurring on the plains near Ft. Mann (now Dodge City, Kansas) below Cimarron Springs in August 1848.

Bernardo provided additional details in his second attestation dated June 28, 1858. From this document we learn that he entered into the U.S. Military service on or about March 20, 1848, with the Master Battalion of Missouri Volunteers under the command of 2nd Lt. Ashley Gulley. Bernardo confirmed that he served as a packer and teamster "in transporting commissary subsistence and quartermaster supplies and stores to troops in the field under the command of Lt. Col. William Gilpin, who was the commander of U.S. forces on campaign against the Plains Indians." Bernardo again mentioned having engaged in a fight with Indians in June or July 1848, but could not recall the name of the commanding officer at the time, naming several captains as possible commanders—Captain J.C. "Griffin" (sic Griffith), Captain Thomas Jones, or Lt. Stremmel, each with the Missouri Volunteers. Bernardo also stated that he was "honorably discharged from duty in the field at Ft. Mann in either September or October 1848."

Although some bounty land records contain genealogical information, the warrant application of Bernardo Martín only provides basic details of his services as a quartermaster and teamster with the Missouri Volunteers, which in and of itself is valuable information. Copies of these documents are presented on the following pages as an example of a source of documentation for U.S. military service of New Mexican men during the early years of New Mexico's U.S. territorial history. The copies of the documents are accompanied by a transcription made by Amanda Maestas Freiberg. Bounty land warrant applications relate specifically to wartime service between the years 1755 and March 3, 1855. Bernardo's service occurred during a time identified as the Mexican War.

Bernardo Martín's direct paternal ancestors served the Spanish crown as soldiers of the northern frontier in New Mexico beginning in 1598 and throughout the 1600s. His earliest known paternal ancestor, Hernán (I) Martín Serrano, resided in the region of Zacatecas (now in north-central Mexico) in the 1550s, being among only a small number of Europeans inhabiting what was then the far northern frontier of the Spanish Americas. The line of descent from Hernán (I) Martín Serrano to Bernardo Martín spans nine generations and almost three hundred years.

Ancestry of Bernardo Martín

Hernán Martín Serrano = ?

Sargento Mayor Hernán Martín Serrano = ?
b.ca. 1558, Zacatecas, and came
to New Mexico in 1598

Captain Luis (I) Martín Serrano = Catalina de Salazar
died ca. Nov 1661, NM

Captain Luis (II) Martín Serrano = Antonia de Miranda
b.ca. 1628-1633, NM

Cristóbal Martín Serrano = Antonia de Moraga
b.ca. 1655, NM   md. prior to October 1681, NM

Antonio Martín Serrano = Ana María Domínguez
b.ca. 1698, NM   md. May 12, 1717, Santa Fe, NM

Salvador Martín = María Manuela Trujillo
b.ca. 1737-1740   md. February 26, 1756, Santa Clara, NM

José Guadalupe Martín = María Juliana Vásquez Borrego
b.a 1762, NM   md. December 5, 1786, Santa Cruz, NM

Bernardo Martín = Apolonia Gutiérrez y Solano
b. May 1792,   md. January 8, 1827, Santa Cruz, NM
El Potrero, NM

Territory of NM, County of Taos, On this 9th day of July 1857, personally appeared before me, the undersigned Justice of the Peace, for county & Territory aforesaid, Bernardo Martin, a resident of Lo de Moro who being duly sworn according to law declares and says that he is the identical Bernardo Martin who accompanied the command of Major Gilpin that he was employed by the quartermaster of the Command in the transportation of QuarterMaster & Commisary stores for the command in the month of April 1848, on a campaign against the Comache Indians during the Indian War in 1848 that the company to which he belonged was commanded by the Quarter Master of the command and accompanied the command of Major Gilpin that his services were accepted in the Military service of the US in conformity with the instructions of, and orders from Comd'g officer Fort Leavenworth, that he served on said campaign during said war, on said expedition for the term of fourteen days, that he accompanied the command, was subject to, and under the immediate orders of the a.a.q.m & a.a.ci & Maj Gilpin commanding the expedition; and that during said service he was actually engaged in a fight with said Indians on or about the 25th day of June 1848 near Pawnee Fork; on or about the 28th Aug 1848 on the plains by the QuarterMaster at Ft. Mann as will appear by his accounts.

He makes this declaration for the purpose of obtaining Bounty Land to which he may be entitled etc. and hereby constitutes and appoints J. Georges Jr, Esq. of Santa Fe his Attny etc.

Attest (witness): J. Woods & Francisco R. Duran
Signed Bernardo Martin (his mark)

Sworn to and subscribed before me etc. came Jose Sandoval and Jose Lobato, residents of NM who being duly sworn, etc. say they are personally acquainted with Bernardo Martin who

Courtesy of: Amanda Maestas Freiberg
Document obtained from Natl Archives, Washington, DC

Page 1 of 5 of the U.S. Military Service Record of Bernardo Martín

has made and subscribed the foregoing declaration; that they were present and seen him make his mark to said declaration and know that he is the identical Bernardo Martin who accompanied the command of Maj. Gilpin on a campaign against the Comache indians during the Indian war, and the said Bernardo Martin was actually engaged in a fight with said Indians on or about the 25th day of June 1848 near and on or about the 28th day of Aug 1848 on the plains below the Cimaron Springs and that they know his statements to be true, from having served on the same expedition with the applicant.

Attest:
J. Woods
Fr. R. Duran

Jose Sandoval (his mark)
Jose Lobato (his mark)

Sworn to and subscribed before me this day......etc.

Julio Martines, Justice of the Peace

I W.W.H. Davis, Sec of the Terr. of NM hereby certify that Julio Martines Esq who has subscribed his name was at the time a Justice of the Peace in and for the county of Taos and Terr. of NM duly elected etc.

This 14th day of Aug 1857.
W.W.H. Davis
Secty Terr. of New Mexico

Courtesy of: Amanda Maestas Freiberg
Document obtained from Natl Archives, Washington, DC

Page 2 of 5 of the U.S. Military Service Record of Bernardo Martín

Terr. of NM, County of Taos
On this 28th day of June 1858 personally appeared before me the undersigned Justice of the Peace, in and for County & Terr. aforesaid Bernardo Martin, a resident of Moro NM who being duly sworn according to law declares and says that he is the identical Bernardo Martin who was employed at Moro NM for Military Service in the quartermasterns Dept M.S.W. on or about the 20th day of Mar 1848 by 2nd Lt Ashley Gulley WA of Masters Bat. Missouri Volunteers "for the plains" and served as packer and teamster..(??) in transporting commisary subsistance and quarter masters supplies and stores to the troops in the field under Command of Lt. Col. William Gilpin, Commanding US Forces on campaign against the "allied hostile tribes" of Indians on the Plains. during the Mexican and Indian War of 1847 and 1848: that he served for the term of fourteen days, and was honorably discharged from duty in the field, at Ft. Mann, Indian Terr., in the month of Sept. or Oct 1848. Oweing to his services being no longer required, and was paid for 2nd Lt. Edward Col. Store. A.G.M. for command or 2nd Lt Ashley Gulley a.a.q.m. or Capt. Enos u.s.a. temporarily on duty; but cannot recollect by which one; therefore he refers to the returns of the above named quarter masters for proof of service (&a.&c) He further declares that during said service he was actually engaged in a fight with the indians, during the month of June or July 1848 under the immediate command of Capt J.C. Griffin or Capt Thomas, Jones or 1st Lt. Stremmell, Mo. Bat. Vols, but fails to recollect the precise date of the battles, or names of officers commanding; and that his claim No. 281313, for which John Georges, Esq.

Courtesy of: Amanda Maestas Freiberg

Documents obtained from Natl Archives Washington DC

Page 3 of 5 of the U.S. Military Service Record of Bernardo Martín

of Santa Fe NM is his Attny has been suspended for further proof of service: he makes this declaration for the purpose of furnishing the additional evidence required by Hon. Com. of Pensions; that he has never received Bounty Land under any act of Congress nor made any applications therefor. Other than the one herein refered to:

Attest: Jose Ma. Valdez
         Bicente Romero

Bernard Martin (his mark)

Sworn to and subscribed before me on the day and yar first above named, and on the same day and year before me personally came Jose Ma. Valdes and Bicente Romero..residents of Moro NM who I know to be credible witnesses; and who being duly sworn according to law, declare and say; that they are personally acauainted with Bernardo Martin who has made and subscribed the foregoing declaration, that they were present and saw him make his mark to the said declaration, and know that he is the identical Bernardo Martin who was employed for service in the quarter masters department at More NM on or about the 20th day of March 1848; and who served in transporting quartermaster and commissary stores for the troops in the field under command of Lt Col William Gilpin Bat: Mo. Vols 1848 and from our daily intercourse with him for the past ten years we believe he has never rendered any other military service in the US, other than the above mentioned.

Jose Ma. Valdes
Bicente Romero

Sworn to and subscribed before me on the day and year first above written, and I certify that I am per-

Courtesy of: Amanda Maestas Freiberg

Documents obtained from Natl Archives Washington DC

Page 4 of 5 of the U.S. Military Service Record of Bernardo Martín

sonnaly acquainted with the affiants, and know them to be credible persons that the claimant is the person he represents himself to be; and that I have no interest in this claim.

Francisco Rael
Justice of the Peace

United States of America
Territory of New Mexico

I Agustus DeMarle, Clerk of the NM Supreme Court for said Terr, do hereby certify, that Franciso Rael Esq before whom the foregoing declaration and affidavit were made, was at the time of so doing a Justice of the Peace in and for the county of Taos, Terr aforesaid, --ly elected but qualified to act as such, and that his above signature is genuine.

In testimony whereof I have hereunto set my hand and affixed the seal of said county on this 7th day of August 1858.

A.DeMarle, Clerk

Courtesy of: Amanda Maestas Freiberg

Page 5 of 5 of the U.S. Military Service Record of Bernardo Martín

SECTION IV: LAUMBACHS IN NEW MEXICO

Chapter 18: Ancestors
by Verna Laumbach Sparks 1909-1996

Editor's note: *We have acquired new information since Verna (editor's mother) wrote this many years ago. She also did not have access to the Internet and census records, etc. like we fortunately do today. Updated or new information is added in brackets.*

Frederick Metzger and Henry Korte are prominently featured in this chapter, although they are not Laumbach ancestors. Like James Bonney, they are interesting and important facets of our history.

My grandfather had papers brought from Germany that gave some information about our earlier family tree. Those documents were birth and marriage certificates, with the notation that no stamp was necessary because the parties were of the nobility.

These papers were given to my father, Daniel Laumbach. After he married, they put them in a box in a large homemade writing desk at Cedar Springs Ranch. Through the years, the box was pushed back, out of sight behind a drawer, and my parents believed the papers were lost. They were found when my folks were moving from the ranch to Roy some 45 years later. He had them translated and I had copies made, which I shared. The originals passed to my brother Joyce, who kept them in a bank vault in Roy. He still has them. *[When Joyce Laumbach died at Las Cruces, New Mexico in 1991, the originals passed to his daughter Vera Jane Laumbach Morris, who recently donated them to the New Mexico Farm and Ranch Museum near Las Cruces for archived preservation.]*

These old papers, recorded at St. Johannis in Germany, show that my father's grandmother's maiden name was Anna Koos, and she was born August 9, 1811. Her parents were Detlef Koos and Anna Christina (born Bindt).

Anna Koos and Andreas Detlef Lauenbach were married November 4, 1832 in the church of Haddebyer. The Andreas Detlef Lauenbach (1st) birth certificate shows he was born November 25, 1802, and was from Geltorf. His parents were Christian Rudolf Lauenbach and Catharina Margaretha (born Buhite) *[according to translator in Las Vegas, New Mexico. However, that was corrected in 2005 by Pete Laumbach to actually be "born Busch"]* from Grohs.

Notes from my father show the son, same name, of this first Andreas Detlef Lauenbach, was born December 2, 1833 in the province of Schleswig near the city of Kiel, Germany. *[Andreas 2nd and his wife were both from Jagel, near the city of Schleswig, within the province of Schleswig. Kiel was then actually in the neighboring province of Holstein.]* The second Andreas died in New Mexico on November 4, 1904, at age 70 years, 11 months and 2 days. He was my grandfather on my father's side. Today's spelling, Laumbach, differs from the original spelling on the old documents.

My grandfather Andreas Detlef Laumbach (2nd) came to this country as a young man, soon after his parents, Andreas Detlef and Anna Koos Laumbach, had come and settled near Goose Lake, Iowa.

Andreas, an officer, deserted the army at Frankfort because he did not want to serve three years. *[Andreas probably related this detailed information years later to his family; perhaps he named Frankfort because that was where he boarded ship for the U.S.]* There was a great deal of unrest in Germany in the 1850s, before and after; many aristocracy and others fled.

Andreas and his friend Fritz Eggert came to America by working their way over on a ship. [*Those details came from Verna's brother, Joyce, who knew some of Fritz's descendants. The long-held family tradition of Andreas and Fritz coming to America together is unconfirmed. Fritz's family does not know exactly when he came, and the ship's manifest list of passengers showing Andreas 2nd does not name Fritz. No manifest listing Fritz has been found. Because of that long-held tradition that they were stowaways, perhaps Fritz had stowed away on that ship.*] The captain allowed them passage, as he did many other dissatisfied Germans. The New World beckoned as a land of promise, and above all, as a land of peace and freedom.

Andreas and Eggert first went to Iowa, where Andreas' parents had recently settled. The young men might have filed claims there but, still restless, began to think about the country farther west. With its vast unclaimed lands, the west called them. Iowa was becoming too settled.

One story says Andreas mortgaged his Iowa property for oxen to bring him west. The two friends, because Eggert came, too, drifted along, prospecting mountain streams. At Denver they stayed awhile and homesteaded in what is now the heart of the city. But something still over the horizon kept calling. They left Denver.

The two men finally came to the beautiful Mora Valley, where Andreas was to meet his future wife. This valley was one of the oldest settled places in New Mexico, having been part of a Mexican land grant and the home of early Hispanic settlers, as well as more recent immigrants. Here Andreas finally settled down. Eggert later remarked that "after all our wanderings, we landed on a sand bank!"

Buena Vista

It proved to be a productive sand bank, however, as Andreas married, raised a large family and had a fairly prosperous ranch when he died.

After living in New Mexico a [*very short*] while, Andreas wrote back to Iowa urging his father to come west also. He promised that he would help him and together they could run a good head of cattle. The letter sounded convincing; his father [*Andreas Detlef 1st*] and brother Henry [*Marx Heinrich*] said goodbye to the rest of the family in Iowa and they, too, came west. Their families, left behind in Iowa, never saw them again. [*In recent years, we learned Henry wasn't then lost to his family in Iowa as those in New Mexico had believed. However, the Iowa family did "lose" him years later.*]

- Andreas' father joined him in New Mexico, but Henry decided to look around first, and going on alone, was never heard of again. According to Aunt Leonor, whether Henry was killed or whether he settled down and just neglected to write home, remained a mystery [*to the New Mexico Laumbachs*].

Andreas and his father were able to acquire enough cattle to run them along the Red River [*which the locals called the Canadian*], moving camp from one site to another. As there were no fences, the cattle roamed great distances—mostly from Buena Vista in the winter, to what is now Springer in the summer. Two or three men were kept with the cattle to herd them in the open country. The Laumbach men occasionally checked on them. On one of those checking trips, Andreas' father was killed by a wandering band of Apaches.

Since he was killed far from home in a wild uninhabited country, his body was hastily buried [*there remains some mystery about who buried him*] on a hillside not far from the present town of Springer. His son, Andreas, wanted to move the body, but he could never find the grave. Once he and my father, then just a boy, spent a lot of time searching the area where it was supposed to be, but the rolling hills looked alike. They found no sign of the rock-marked grave. Andreas had to give up the search and return to Buena Vista. [*Those rolling hills my mother describe, and also painted in oils, are on the north side of the bridge on the current highway near Farley. The Rock Crossing of the Canadian, where he is said to have died and was nearby buried, is on the south side. We will never know exactly where he died and remains.*]

My father never forgot about it. Years later we seldom approached Springer from Roy without him recalling the mystery of his grandfather's resting place. Perhaps someday someone will stumble upon the grave and wonder whose it is.

Mora Land Grant and Bibiana's First Husbands

Andreas married Elionor Ebel. Her grandfather was Bernardo Martinez, one of the original grantees of the Mora land grant. He was related to the then well-known politician Felix Martinez.

The Mora Grant was composed of land extending from Holman down through the Mora Valley, Buena Vista and Saboya. [*In this book, Saboya is most often written as Cebolla or La Cebolla, with basically the same pronunciation.*] The land grant was approximately 3/4 million acres (more than 800,000 acres) in size. As years went on, the original grantees gradually lost their land. [*Others just left, seeking an easier existance.*] Sometimes they sold or traded part of it for a few cows or burros, or labor. The people who bought it that way often had no legal title. Certain people (T.B. Catron, S.B. Elkins, et al.) were able to get most of it by inventing deeds, supposedly signed by illiterate and very old people who did not realize what they were doing. Some deeds concerned parties already dead, and through false witnesses declared legally signed. When some of this evidence was later brought out in court, most of the grantees or their heirs had no money to fight for their land so it was lost anyway.

Father [*Jose Francisco*[i]] Pinard, a priest, got a portion of the Mora Grant from the grantees themselves. This was a large and beautiful tract of partially wooded land in Buena Vista, which later Metzger, my grandmother Bibiana's third husband [*more accurately, her third "partner"*] bought from Fr. Pinard. After Veeder took it as a lawyer's fee, the ranch became known as the Veeder Ranch. (This story will be told a little later.) Through the years, many different people, including Riner and Thompson, owned this property. [*It is now owned by Hughs G. Abel.*] Andreas and Elionor Laumbach acquired part of this ranch land from Metzger, and built structures and their home on it. It became my father's childhood home, known as "the Laumbach family place at Buena Vista." More recently the Shocks, and currently the Allsups family, have owned the property that was first established by the Laumbachs.

Before taking up the story of my father's boyhood at Buena Vista, I'd like to tell you about his grandmother Bibiana—the daughter of Bernardo Martinez and his wife, the former Apolonia Gutierrez de Solono.

Bibiana must have been a woman of great charm and beauty because she married very well—not once but three times. [*There is no evidence she married; she kept her last name, Martín or Martínez her entire life. Martinez is on her headstone. The photo of her grave marker is in chapter 19.*]

First was James Bonney from England. His brother, Henry, settled in Denver and became wealthy according to family stories. James had been married before and had children; two daughters and one son named Santiago (Spanish for James), by his former wife. [*Records show Juana Mascarenas as both married and unmarried to James.*] James lived at his Los Cerritos Ranch[ii] part of the time, but his home and trading post were near the present town of Watrous, then known as La Junta. He had many cattle. Kearny mentioned Bonney supplying his Army of the West with meat near La Junta in his account of the *Occupation of New Mexico*. James Bonney and Bibiana had one child, Ramon Bonney, when tragedy struck them. On one of Bonney's trips back and forth seeing about his livestock, a band of Indians surprised his party. He and all of his men, save one servant, were killed. [*There are at least two more versions of his death told by other family and his Bonney descendants. All agree he was killed by Indians, in one case, his Indian servant.*]

This servant notified Bibiana who, with her baby, traveled to her father's place at Saboya [*La Cebolla*] to get help. With her father, Bernardo, they traveled to Las Vegas to notify military stationed there. When they finally returned to the ranch near La Junta, they found the Indians had taken all the livestock. In those days, settlers had little protection from Indians or acquisitive neighbors. Getting help was slow. Bibiana lost everything. Area settlers had taken the La Junta property and the ranch. Kroenig's place is said to have once been part of Bonney's property.

Sometime after this, Bibiana married Daniel Ebel [*I do not know why, within that first generation, the Eberle name was changed to Ebel, the name his children used*], a German from Switzerland. Ebel was wealthy and had ranch property and a store in Las Vegas. He traveled back and forth, sometimes to Naupeste or other places, and brought back provisions for his store. He carried his money in gold. Stories said he could fill a hat with gold coins and carelessly showed it off.

While married to Ebel, Bibiana lived in Las Vegas. [*This is what Karl, Pete and others also believe.*] They had three children—Elionor Ebel, Andreas Ebel [*this branch changed spelling and pronunciation of their last name to Ebell, with accent on the first E*] and Maria Marta Ebel. It was when the youngest, Marie, was born that their trouble began. Ebel accused Bibiana of being unfaithful; some say Bibiana had to appear in court to answer charges and show reasons why he should not leave her. Finally he gave her a choice—his money or the children. She chose the children.

Ebel did not live long after the separation. He was returning from Naupeste[iii] carrying a lot of gold, with an employee he should not have trusted, when they stopped at Begosa[iv] for a siesta. Ebel's companion hit him on the head and grabbed the sack of money. Ebel fired his gun at him, but the man escaped. Mortally wounded, Ebel was able to travel by horseback to Las Vegas. He arrived at his store at 5:00 p.m. and died at 6:00 p.m. [*There is a slightly different version of his death, related by Karl in his chapter.*] It was said that he was buried near the old Presbyterian mission in Vegas. When he died, there was no one to take charge of his store and property. His friends divided up everything among themselves.

Bibiana, Metzger and Korte

Bibiana's third husband [*relationship*] was a Prussian, Frederich Metzger. In the Mora Valley, Metzger was called "El Aleman" (the German) by the Spanish people. [*That is a curiosity considering there were other German or Prussian settlers in the Mora Valley and surrounding area at that time.*] Metzger originally came to the west from Germany with a good friend named Fraker. They settled in the Mora Valley, partly because there were other German settlers already there. Metzger came to Mora first, leaving his friend in Kansas City. Then Fraker and Henry Korte,[v] another acquaintance, started west on foot to join Metzger. When they got here, Fraker decided to go on to Ocate and try his fortunes there. Korte settled first in Watrous and worked for Kroenig. He must have done well, as his son, Eduardo Korte of Las Vegas, had notes that said Korte earned $12,000 there, and with that money went into the ranching business at Buena Vista.

Korte found Metzger already there; the two formed a business partnership and bought the large piece of property from Father Pinard and settled there. Metzger had bought part of it alone and then the two bought the rest together. The land ran from Buena Vista to Mora and extended to the Red River.

They added many improvements to the place. Metzger planted a big orchard, said to be the first of its kind in that part of the country. His laborers made the lake at Buena Vista and planted it with fish. (Eduardo Korte told a popular fish story about the lake: It had so many fish that a fisherman needed two teams of mules to pull them out.)

A large house was built on the ranch, and as time went on, the two partners, especially Metzger, became rich. They were shrewd and bought local cattle for $5.00 or $6.00 a head, had a round-up, drove them to Kansas City, and sold them there for $90.00 a head. It was a long, hard trip but paid well. Ranch cowboys handled the cattle drives.

Besides those, the partners sent regular caravans of goods to the States and back. Those caravans consisted of 25 to 30 wagons, with as many men to handle them. Since there was still Indian trouble, a guard was kept on duty at night. He slept in the wagon during the day, not minding the slow creaking wheels under his bed.

The men had plenty of food for the trip, mostly the kind that would keep, like *biscochuelo*, *carne seca* and *carne de cibola* (biscuit bread, dried meat and dried buffalo meat). Fresh game was usually plentiful. Eduardo Korte remembered one of the drivers was named Juanisidro Martinez.

These trips brought back needed supplies for the ranch and for Metzger's store in Mora. Some of the main items were clothes, sugar, coffee and tea. Sugar was expensive, and only wealthier families could afford it.

During those prosperous years, a legend began that Metzger and Korte had a secret gold mine since they had so much gold. This legend continued long after their deaths. Years later, some Laumbach family descendants, with some professors from Montezuma College, searched for the mine. There was no mine—their gold came from shrewd trade and cattle sales.

Some gold found its way into jewelry. Most gold-filigreed jewelry back then was made from gold coins. Some of theirs was made in Las Vegas by Teodoso Sandoval, mostly from $50 gold pieces. My great-grandmother Bibiana had many beautiful filigreed pieces—pins and earrings mainly—some of it handed down in the family. My great Aunt Marie had a pair of her beautiful gold filigreed earrings, which she sold to my mother.[vi] [*A photo of one of those earrings made into a pin is in Chapter 27, Verna's story, "Never a Road."*] My great-half aunt, Isabel Metzger Gallegos, had the most pieces of family gold filigree jewelry that I ever saw. I once took a picture of them.

[*One of Bibiana's many pieces of jewelry was a delicate gold filigree butterfly pin. It has an interesting history. It passed to Aunt Estefanita in Santa Fe. Uncle Sito's private bank was beneath the trapdoor in the floor of his store, where he kept many of their valuables in a well in the basement. When Sito died, to avoid taxes, his grandson and heir, John Candelario, hid the contents of the well. He took them to Sanchez, his cousin Tony Sanchez's ranch, and buried them. When he later retrieved them, he gave some pieces to Tony, including the butterfly pin. Tony sent that piece to Jan for her birthday in the 1960s.[vii]*]

After living at the large ranch awhile, Metzger left Korte in charge and lived at Saboya [*La Cebolla*], a smaller place. He made a wonderful wine from the plentiful chokecherries that grew at his place, and made another wine, called tisween, which was spicy.

Bibiana had three daughters from her relationship with Metzger. Dolores "Lola" married Manuel Cordova; for a while they had a ranch near ours. Josefita married Manuel Duran; they lived at Ocate. Isabelita married Jose Rafael Gallegos; they lived in Las Vegas. There was a half-sister, Juanita, who married Henry Korte[viii]; that marriage kept the Metzger ranch in their family.

The trouble that followed Bibiana followed her there. She and Metzger separated, and he moved to Mora to take charge of his store and saloon there. She moved [*back*] to Seboya [*La Cebolla*], and in her last years, moved to Buena Vista. She lived there in a small house in the family's orchard, later known as Mr. Wissler's place because he had also lived there. Wissler, a German friend of the family, had been a skilled carpenter. He is buried in the Laumbach family cemetery at Buena Vista. This small house of Bibiana's in the orchard was near the bigger house of her daughter and son-in-law, Elionor and Andreas. When she lived in that little house, her grandchildren came to know and love her. My father spoke of her with great admiration. Her beauty and charm, which attracted three wealthy men, still captivated the children of Andreas and Elionor Laumbach.

Starting out a Catholic when she was young, Bibiana later became a Protestant. After a long eventful life, my great-grandmother Bibiana died in 1897 and was buried in the Laumbach family cemetery at Buena Vista. [*Photo of Bibiana's grave marker is in chapter 19, Andreas 1 and 2.*]

Bibiana outlived Metzger by many years.[ix]

~~

When Bibiana and Metzger separated, he went to live in the village of Mora where he had a large store. It was in a long adobe building running from what was later the Pete Boland store to the Catholic Church. There was a small alley between it and the church, only wide enough for a wagon to pass between.[x]

Metzger returned to Apolonia, the mother of his daughter, Juanita. Apolonia lived with him at Mora, near his store. In their last years, they both lived at Buena Vista with their daughter, Juanita and her husband—Metzger's friend and partner, Henry Korte.

One day [*in 1885*], Metzger was in his store when he received word that his old friend Fraker was dead. He grieved so much that he died also, at 4:00 the same day. He just dropped dead in the store, probably from a heart attack.[xi] [*This was the story Verna heard many years ago, perhaps from Eduardo Korte, but newspaper articles and other records give different details of Metzger's death.*]

Meanwhile, Korte also had family troubles at the big ranch. He and his wife Juanita worried that her half-sisters [*Lola, Josefita and Isabelita*] and other relatives would try to claim part of their property after Metzger died. [*Court records and testimony show Metzger tried to move all of his assets into Korte's and Juanita's names before he died so his daughters by Bibiana would receive nothing. That effort to cheat them had begun with Metzger.*]

Korte was also concerned about a young hired man, William Naeglin, who was becoming too interested in their daughter, Anna. Naeglin's interest in Anna began when Metzger was still living. Korte fired Naeglin because the family thought he was too poor to court his daughter. Naeglin later returned and Korte rehired him, giving him a job as blacksmith.

Since there were then no banks in which to deposit and safeguard money, Metzger and Korte hid gold as they accumulated it. They put some behind an adobe brick in a tool house or barn. Another time Korte hid his savings in a box that he buried in a corner of the cornfield. He did not know Naeglin was watching.

Korte became ill and realized he was going to die. He tried to tell his family where the bulk of his gold was buried, but he died before he was able to tell them. [*Henry Korte died at age 50 in 1889, and his wife, Juanita, at age 40, died nine months later in the same year.*[xii]]

The night after the funeral, two of Anna's younger brothers saw Naeglin digging in the cornfield. When they came to watch, Naeglin allowed them to help him lift the heavy box out of the hole. He told them not to mention the box; it was to be a surprise for their mother. It was indeed a surprise for her the next morning. Naeglin had talked Anna into running away with him in the night. The box of gold went with them. [*Butch Sanders found documentation that shows this story told for decades among many family members cannot be entirely true. Anna and William Naeglin married after Metzger died, and remained in the Mora area for a period of time <u>after</u> both Korte and Juanita died. They adopted Anna's young brothers. Records also show they were both involved with the ongoing family lawsuit. They probably did not leave the area until after the lawsuit was finally settled and their Buena Vista home was lost to attorney, Veeder.*]

[*This story of the stash of gold found by Naeglin seems to have come from the Gallegos family in Las Vegas. Verna heard a great deal of family history from her Great-Aunt Isabel and her daughter, Isabel. The younger Isabel's brother, John Gallegos aka John White, was also the source of the tale about Metzger's gold mine. Verna's Great-Aunt Isabel was Isabelita, the youngest of three daughters by Metzger and Bibiana.]*

With the bulk of the gold gone, there was still the immense real estate to quarrel over. Metzger's children by Bibiana were also his legal heirs [*apparently he left no will*], and the main ranch property had belonged to him. Juanita Korte refused to settle their claims. Finally, the other heirs brought a lawsuit against the Kortes. [*Metzger had died the year before the suit was filed; Juanita and Henry both died within three years after it began.*] They hired an ambitious lawyer named Veeder.

What remained of Metzger's and Korte's money and assets was spent on decades of legal wrangling. When Veeder pressed for his fee, the losers—Juanita and her family—could only pay him by signing over the deed to the ranch property. [*Some of Verna's information about the family lawsuit is not totally correct. Frank Metzger died in February 1885. On March 29, 1886, a civil lawsuit, pertaining to his considerable estate, was brought against his son-in-law Henry Korte by "Lola" Maria Doloritas de Cordova and her husband, and Bibiana's minor daughters. The lawsuits and appeals—between Metzger's daughters by Bibiana and the heirs of Metzger's daughter Juanita—continued until the deaths of Korte and Juanita in 1889. But it did not end then. Suits and counter-suits continued between Anna Korte Naeglin and her husband William, and Bibiana's daughters. Louis Sulzbacher was the attorney for the defense—Henry Korte et al. The attorneys for the plaintiffs—Maria Doloritas de Cordova et al.—was T.B. Catron and J.W. Veeder. Veeder ultimately took the Metzger-Korte ranch for his fee. The Korte side lost and technically Bibiana's children finally won. But they all lost everything. The loser—which would have been Korte heirs—probably had to pay all court costs and attorney fees. I have a copy of the extensive court proceedings to be published in the next family history book in this series:* Bibiana and Her Children*. There will also be more about these family lawsuits in a later chapter of this book.* [xiii]*]*

This was a terrible blow to all concerned; the ranch was gone.

Veeder's Fee

When Veeder took over the ranch, he leased it to various people. The Shoemaker family was one of those. [*A family story said they specifically leased it to search for gold.*] They found a stash behind an adobe brick in the tool house that amounted to something like $20,000. In those days, that was a considerable fortune. With the money, Shoemaker bought the historic show place at Watrous [*formerly La Junta*], which had once been an inn on the Santa Fe Trail. [*There are also stories of other stashes of gold being found.*]

The Gerk family also rented the ranch. When they were there, an effort was made to find the fabled gold mine or stashed gold. My Aunties—the three Laumbach sisters still living at the Buena Vista home-place—good-naturedly joined the search, along with some professors and students from Montezuma College near Las Vegas. [*Leona Gerk was a college chum of Verna's. These two young ladies were among the "searchers."*]

One night in particular, they were sure they would find it. The Gerk children and their mother spent the night with Aunties while the men searched. Nobody slept much that night, but no gold mine or gold was found.

The Korte family of Buena Vista never saw their gold again. As for the Naeglins, it was said that he [*William*] lived in Arizona for a while where he spent and lost a great deal of money. He and his family later moved to Cherry Valley [*also known as Cherryvale*]. His wife, Anna Korte Naeglin, never seemed happy and stayed almost in seclusion. [*Alvin Korte has a photo of Anna, a gorgeous blonde woman when she was young. Anna predeceased William by many years.*]

The Naeglin family was described as both proud and peculiar. Some of the children died young. It was said that Naeglin lost $30,000 in a Las Vegas bank failure. One daughter, Nellie, married a man, Padilla, of whom the rest disapproved. When Nellie came home, they showed their disapproval by doing all the work she did over again; they rewashed the dishes, redid the laundry, remade the beds. This drove Nellie away again.[xiv] Whether Naeglin enjoyed his stolen wealth, he paid for it in many misfortunes.

There was a cemetery on the Metzger-Korte ranch with beautiful headstones. [*Based on what few now remain in that cemetery, she was mistaken or they were stolen and replaced with simple "poured stone" markers.*] Most of them probably came from Denver. Apolonia was buried there, and also Frederick Metzger. Apolonia's grave marker was said to have been a fine rose marble brought from Denver, stolen years later. [*Now, Frank Metzger, Henry and Juanita Korte are the only marked burials there; Anna was buried elsewhere.*] During the years of the treasure-hunting craze, stones were overturned and broken. Some of those graves were opened. [Ac*cording to Karl Laumbach and Chick Burney, who saw it years ago, Apolonia's marker is now hidden under an overgrown bush. It now is a plain "poured stone," fallen or lying flat, hidden under a bush in a corner of the cemetery. In its vicinity, along a wall under brush, as if discarded there, are two broken markers that may have once marked burials of two of Juanita and Henry's young children.*]

Some lasting results of the lawsuit were hard feelings among family members. The Kortes were unhappy, and Metzger's other daughters were bitter for many years. Not only were they bitter against the Kortes, but they also blamed their older half-brothers and half-sisters. Since the three Metzger sisters were young at the time, at least one of them a minor, they felt the others should have tried to help them more. My grandparents were included in that blame. There was little visiting between some of the families. I scarcely remember visiting them with my parents. However, poor transportation in the early days prevented frequent visiting with distant relatives anyway.

Buena Vista Days

Elionor was living with her mother Bibiana in Saboya [*La Cebolla*] when she met Andreas Laumbach. They married and [*later*] lived at the Buena Vista place, which had been part of the original Metzger-Korte property. This became a beautiful place, especially after the cottonwoods grew tall along the rock walls. They planted an apple orchard, which produced enough apples to later sell in Las Vegas. They also raised cattle and sheep, which grazed on the hillsides.[xv]

Most of the homesteads at Buena Vista [*within the Mora Land Grant that was platted this way*] were laid out in long strips to provide settlers with land that extended from the river through the valley and included part of the hillside. The valley portion was used for farms, and the hillsides for pasture. Some farms were strips, only one mile wide and two miles long. The Mora River ran through the east side of the farmland from La Cueva to the Pinard Place. [*The "Pinard Place" was the property Father Pinard sold to Metzger and Korte, a portion of which became Laumbachs' ranch at Buena Vista.*]

The community of Buena Vista was only about five miles from the community of Mora. La Cueva, another small settlement, lay between the two. Beyond Mora was Holman and other small villages laid out like a broken chain along the Mora Valley.

This land, originally part of the Mora Land Grant, had been settled for years. Most settlers were Spanish, though several men of French, German and other European nationalities wandered or migrated there and married into those Spanish families. Some of those were as follows: Frederich Metzger, M.J. Fraker, William Kroenig, Heinrich Korte, Andreas Detlef Laumbach and St. Vrain. After marrying into the local families, they assumed the language, old customs and traditions of their adopted land. Many Hispanic families still living there have German or French names. Others of various nationalities who settled in the area were John Scolly, Captain William S. French, Henry Connelly (later governor of the

Territory), Samuel B. Watrous [*a settlement later named for him*], William B. Tipton [*founder of Tiptonville*], William B. Stapp, John B. Dawson, Lucien B. Maxwell, Milnor Rudolph, Herman von Grolman, Antonio A. Sanchez, Cresencio Gallegos, Vicente Romero (who founded La Cueva) and his brothers Eugenio, Dolores, and Casimiro Romero, Goke, Eberle, Bonney, Blattman, Des Marias, Branch, Maes, Abreu, Valdez and Quintana. Wealthy Spanish families included Luna, Otero, Baca, Lopez, and Romero as well as some with Anglo or German names.

My father listed M.J. Fraker and William Kroenig as one-time commissioners of Mora County. J.H. Koogler was a San Miguel county commissioner. Margaret Ellen Fraker was an early family acquaintance. The *Las Vegas Daily Optic*, dated September 13, 1881, mentioned early pioneers of the Mora and Cherry Valleys including W.B. Tipton, James T. Johnson and Captain W.R. Shoemaker, the latter in command of the ordnance department and arsenal at Fort Union; these three located claims in Mora in 1856 and 1857.

Trading centers for these settlers were as far away as St. Louis and Fort Leavenworth. At first, they did not trade with Denver. Later, however, Ramon Bonney, Bibiana's first-born, freighted from Denver, Las Animas and La Junta, Colorado. He brought supplies to the Mora Valley and later to Fort Union.

The factory-made Murphy wagon was popular with the freighters. Each wagon required three to six pair of oxen, but sometimes mules and horses were used. An oxen-pulled wagon could go 25 to 30 miles a day. Horses not pulling wagons could travel 40 to 45 miles a day, and if ridden in emergencies, were known to cover 75 miles in one day. That was a killing pace and seldom done. For ordinary travel the poor sometimes rode in ox-carts while the rich rode in carriages.

Food differed a great deal, too, depending upon the family circumstances. The wealthy could afford the most costly and scarce items brought west by wagon trains. The poor had enough to eat, but theirs was simpler fare.

One of the most important items was meat—wild, domestic, dried or fresh. Bread was baked in outdoor earthen ovens called *hornos*, or cooked flat as tortillas. It was made of wheat or cornmeal, ground in the local gristmill. *Atolé* was a popular and nourishing drink. Gardens yielded pumpkins, peas, *chile*, potatoes and *avos*. Orchard fruit was scarce. As far as my father knew, the Metzger orchard was the first to bear fruit in the area. It mostly had apples. Later my grandfather's orchard also began to produce.

My father talked of going to Doña Romero's gristmill at La Cueva.[xvi] You can still see it. Trambley had one in Vegas. [*Ceran St. Vrain also had a gristmill at Mora, and there was one at nearby Cleveland. Most early small settlements in the Mora area had their own grist mills.*]

Houses in the valley were made of logs and rock and sometimes adobe. They had flat roofs, and the poorer homes had dirt floors. Furniture in the beginning was simple and homemade—like tables, benches, and bunks. Some people preferred to sleep on the floor and used beds for home decoration. The well-to-do had bedsteads made from lumber cut in the first saw mills. Nearly every room had a small corner fireplace for heating.

Most clothes were still homemade when my father, Daniel, was a boy. His mother Elionor made his shoes, or *tewas*, which had rawhide soles and buckskin uppers. Men sometimes wore buckskin pants and coats. Wool was woven at home and made into blankets and clothes. The wealthy bought cloth from the wagon trains.

Families made candles out of tallow and even molded bullets for their guns. Money was usually scarce, and most of it was in gold. There was still some gold panning in the area when Papa was young.

It was expensive to send a letter east, as much as $10.00 or $15.00 a letter. Few Laumbach letters were sent back to relatives in Iowa.

Shinney was a popular amusement and taken about as seriously as our football games today. Bets were placed on the side expected to win; sometimes the single men played against the married men. The losing side might give a dance. Once begun, the game lasted until sundown, when whichever side had the ball won. Papa said there were no fences across those lands then because they played shinney ball up and down the valley without fence interference.

Canutes, which could be played indoors in the winter, was another popular game. It involved a hollow stick, closed on one end with a nail inside. I do not know the objects and rules of that game.

Dances were popular in the neighborhood and old and young attended. Sometimes they came for miles on horseback or in wagons. Music was by guitar and violin.

When a man was interested in a girl, he usually saw her at a dance. Couples seldom dated, as we know it today, or went places together before they were married. They could attend dances, each with his or her parent, and couples could dance or talk together. A man asked her parents for her hand, or parents arranged the marriage themselves. Engagements were short and weddings were held in the forenoon so feasting could be done in the afternoon and evening. Papa remembered three big weddings at Buena Vista during his youth when his aunts married.

Aunt Isabel Metzger was married by a preacher because her husband, Jose Rafael Gallegos [*1854-1917*], was Protestant. He was first Presbyterian, and later became a Baptist. There was no dance at their wedding. Catholic priests performed the wedding ceremonies for Aunt Josefita Metzger, who married Manuel Duran, and for Aunt Marie Ebel, who married Felipe Esquibel in the home of my Papa's grandmother, Bibiana, in her little house in the orchard. Both Aunt Marie and Aunt Josefita had feasts and dances. Josefita's dance was held in the home of Andreas and Elionor, Papa's parents, because it was much larger.

Papa went to school first at Buena Vista, which was a Spanish school. Then he went to the Presbyterian Mission School at Mora. At the time, this mission school served the New Mexico Territory. Later it was discontinued and several small schools were formed. One rural Presbyterian mission school today is in Holman. [*Verna's notes were handwritten years before they were typed in 1991. That school may not still be operating.*]

The boys' dormitory [*in Mora*] was downstairs in the same building with the kitchen and dining room. This was handy; the kindhearted cook threw biscuits over the partition to the hungry boys on Sunday evenings when there was a light supper.

The girls' dormitory was upstairs in the building where the superintendent and six teachers stayed. This building was next to the one with the kitchen and dining hall.

The dining hall was long—the girls sat on one end, the boys on the other, and the teachers sat between them. Special dishes were served to the teachers, but the children's meals were filling. Papa remembered their good beef hash. He also remembered the large meat room with quarters of beef hanging in it. A favorite friend of his was killed there when the heavy-laden rafters fell on him.

A favorite song was "Where is my Wandering Boy Tonight?" Sometimes in the evenings they had games and long talks.

Most of my father's brothers and sisters attended this Presbyterian school in Mora. It was where my Aunt Estefanita first met Jesus Sito Candelario, whom she married. My father finished the eighth grade there, which was considered good schooling at that time. He must have acquired a good education because he was later adept in mathematics[xvii] and read a lot, especially papers and magazines.

Andreas and Elionor Laumbach had 12 children; three died very young. Those were Alexander, Cordelia and John; John choked to death on a piñon shell at age two. The surviving children were Margaret, Peter, Estefanita, Daniel, Anna, Henry, Crestina, Mary and Leonor.

Margarita [*1865-1958*] married J.E. Cruz [*José Emiterio 1855-1931*] and moved to Holman. Peter Joseph [*1867-1954*] married Fidelia Andrada from La Cinta and they lived on a ranch, first in the Montoya Pocket, and later in La Cinta Canyon. Estefinita [*1870-1938*] married J.S. Candelario [*Jesús Sito 1864-1938*] and moved to Santa Fe where they owned Candelario's Curio Store [*also known as the Original Trading Post*]. My father Daniel [*1872-1947*] married next; his bride was Emma Margaret Henkens of Nebraska. (This will be enlarged upon later.) Henry [*1874-1929*] married several years after my father. He was 45 years old when he married an 18-year-old girl, Natividad Hurtado. [*After Henry died, his widow with several small children married Emelio Korte.*] After Henry was another son, Alexander [*born 1876*], who died young. Crestina [*1881-1974*] married Manuel Antonio Sanchez, a widower, and she lived in Las Vegas. He had a large ranch at Sanchez, near Sabinoso, where he spent most of his time. The three other girls, our "Aunties"—Anna [*1878-1958*], Mary [*1884-1965*] and Leonor [*1888-1974*]—never married and stayed at the Buena Vista home place with their mother, Elionor. After she died, they continued to run the ranch until they were too old to take care of it. They sold it and moved to Las Vegas, where they lived in Old Town off the Plaza, about a block from their sister Crestina Sanchez.

Papa's Memories of His Youth

Papa had many interesting experiences during his boyhood days in Buena Vista. One was watching the soldiers drill at Fort Union. He climbed a hill or mesa, which separated his home from the plain, above Fort Union. It was then still an important fort, supplying all the other forts in the Territory. The smartly dressed and high-stepping soldiers fascinated Papa.

Sometimes wandering bands of Apaches came through the valley. They were usually dirty and stole anything they found unguarded. Papa said the women were especially unattractive, without clothes from the waist up, with long sagging breasts. He said that if they were on horseback and their babies, strapped on boards behind them, were hungry, the mother just tossed a breast over her shoulder. Papa told this story with a twinkle in his eye, letting us know he had "stretched" the tale a bit. Mama did not care for his tale. He did not care for the Apaches; they had killed his grandfather.

He remembered the Montezuma Hotel in its heyday. He was about 14 or 15 when the Santa Fe Railroad built it, and he went there once to see the races. J.S. Candelario, a small man, was a jockey there for a while, before he married Aunt Estefanita. Work on the hotel was begun in 1882, and it became a fabulous health resort, where people from all over the world, even royalty, came to try its mineral baths. A branch railroad line from Las Vegas brought guests to the hotel. It had beautiful parks with bear and deer. After it burned in 1885, it was rebuilt and flourished again until 1893, when it closed. As the years went on, it became a Baptist College in 1922, and later a Catholic seminary; more recently, it became a World College.

Another highlight for Papa, when he was very young, was going to Las Vegas when the railroad arrived in 1879. [*He would have then been six or seven.*] The story of the building of the railroad is interesting but too long to tell here.

Papa especially remembered one trip to Las Vegas when his father bought a beautiful clock with a pendulum; Papa held it carefully on his lap all the way home to Buena Vista. They could not risk the clock to ride safely in the back of the jolting wagon. That clock told time accurately for decades but finally stopped. Aunt Mary claimed that grandfather clock, and it moved with Aunties to Las Vegas. Mary later gave it to my sister, Frances.

When Papa was only 12 years old, he made his first trip, miles away, to the area where he would later establish his ranch. He made the trip with his father, delivering cattle to his Uncle Andres Ebel. The cattle were on shares with his father and grandmother, and his Uncle Andres took care of them with his own stock in the Encierro country.

Uncle Andres was married to a remarkable woman, Aunt Euvalda. She must have been a hearty woman, according to stories told about her. One story was that she often begged to go to Buena Vista to see her mother, but Andres kept putting it off. He finally said he would take her if she chopped a huge tough cottonwood log into pieces small enough for the fireplace. Since it was hardwood and tough, he did not want to tackle it himself. It had been lying around a long time. Euvalda was determined to see her mother; she picked up an axe and did not stop chopping until the log was in pieces. Andres was amazed. He had to take her to Buena Vista.

On Papa's trip to the Encierro, he visited his Aunt Marie and Uncle Felipe Esquibel who lived in Cañon de Agua. A trip to that ranch country took several days. The first night out of Buena Vista they reached Sweetwater, east of Ocate. The next day took them to what is now Springer. They reached their destination on the third day. The only fence Papa remembered seeing on his first trip was a new log one built the year before, between Roy and the ranch. It was called a drift fence; today only a row of cedars show where it had been. Birds sat on the fence and ate cedar [*juniper*] berries, dropped some, planting the straight row of cedars. Those cedars are all that is left to show where once had been a log fence, pulled down by land rivals.

Cattle Days

The Montoya Pocket was a name given to a section of canyon and "brake country" that was part of the original Pablo Montoya Grant. That land was taken from the Grant heirs, as were most grant lands in New Mexico. The new owners were known as the Red River Valley Cattle Company, though we called it the Bell Ranch. The name came from a bell-shaped formation near the ranch headquarters.

Other Montoyas, who lived on what would later become Papa's ranch, were squatters who never filed on the land. Nevertheless, they acquired considerable stock and made land improvements. Those improvements consisted mostly of rock and log houses, and rock walls. When they lived there, there were not yet any wire fences in that country.

Jesus Montoya and his family lived in two log houses when Papa first knew them. Papa later tore down one of those. The rock house, started by Jesus and added onto by Mrs. Montoya, was where our family lived for a while, later used as a bunkhouse, and later still, was the ranch school house. Uncle Pete finished the house when he lived in it when he was first married. The Montoya children were Juan, Ramon, Vincente and Isidorita. They lived at what later became our home place, but as the Montoya sons grew up, they built other houses around the country. Some of the places where they lived were Cordova, Carruco, Alamasitas, Gallinas, and the TV country. In some of those places, you still see their rock houses and rock walls, the remaining monuments they left behind.

The sons were not as careful as their father; when he died they gambled away his stock and became poor. However, while the Jesus Montoyas had property, they felt themselves superior to another Montoya family living at Calivetas. They called them los Montoyitos because they were poorer. The two families may have not been related.

An example of cheap labor in those days can be seen in the wages paid for building a rock wall. One fat beef was paid when the wall was finished. These walls took some time to build, as they were three to four feet wide at their base. But there was plenty of time in those days and nobody was in a hurry, for a rock wall or anything else.

Papa's father, Andreas Detlef Laumbach 2nd, had run cattle over a wide range of country ever since he had come west. In the beginning he had a summer camp near the present town of Springer. But after his father (Andreas 1st) was killed there by Apaches, he gradually moved his camp to the Encierro country, which was later the Esquibel site. Here Andreas ran stock, part of it on shares with his mother-in-law, Bibiana. His cattle ranged in many directions, as it was wild and unfenced country in those days.

Papa was 12 when he first came to the Encierro country with his father. As the years went on, Papa and his brothers, Pete and Henry, came to camp for a while and looked after the stock. Sometimes they came by turns. When Papa was about 17, his father told him that he and Henry could have the rest of the cattle in the Encierro on shares if they wanted to look after them. For a long time afterwards, Papa and Henry shared their property and worked together.

Papa told many stories of his experiences looking after the cattle in the wild canyon country. He camped at the Encierro for a while after his Uncle Andres had moved to Arminta and his house was empty. Papa even raised a small crop of corn and after harvesting it, he stored it in a dry cave. When he told that story, I thought of Robinson Crusoe. His only companions were his horse, the cattle, his burro and the plentiful wild animals. The corn was planted with the help of the burro and a crude plow.

Papa had a camp at the Yegua on what was later Uncle Henry's place. There he built a shack and camped several summers. That was where he waged a war on a prairie dog town and tried to get rid of the animals by closing their burrow holes with tin cans. He gathered the tin cans from where a chuck wagon had left them after a round up. I never heard whether the cans were effective.

He rounded up a herd of 20 wild cows that strayed off into the canyons. They were too wild to drive out so he tried to gentle them by degrees. He first got on his horse and let their tracks lead him to them. When they saw him they ran away. The next day he followed them again. For several weeks they ran from him. Finally, the cows got tired and just ran ahead of him and his horse, then scattered out to let Papa pass them. But he didn't pass them. He just "monkeyed around" not far away, where they could see him and get used to him. Finally, he was able to drive them where he wanted, and he took them to the Encierro. This took a month and a lot of patience, but he reclaimed 20 cows.

An odd item of food Papa had one winter was a keg of sauerkraut. It kept well, and he ate it with sugar. Papa liked sugar on things—he sprinkled it on fresh tomatoes and lettuce.

He attended big community roundups. Many ranchers—Romeros, Esquibels, Andradas, Montoyas, Ebells, and others—joined together. Each rancher had many cowboys who tried to keep track of their cattle, but with no fences, they drifted over wide areas, and often mixed with other herds despite the effort of the cowboys to keep their stock apart, separated in certain ranges.

At roundup time, the cowboys of all the area ranches drove the cattle to the chosen branding place. Each ranch furnished men; one ranch furnished a chuck wagon and the main food. Calves were branded according to the brand of their mothers. Maverick calves—those without mothers or brands—were branded for the rancher that furnished the meat.

Sometimes the branded cattle were driven together to Mexico or some other selling point. The remaining cattle were turned loose. Each ranch "cut out" its own bunch and drifted them home.

Some cattle and horses escaped. Cañon Largo had wild livestock. Sometimes a man could catch a wild horse for his own. Papa had a horse, Chum, which had once been wild. After many years of companionship, it broke its leg and had to be shot. Chum's descendant, Dolly, was Papa's favorite mare for almost 20 years.

Many rugged canyons had stories and signs that gave a hint of their past history. Dogs were used to herd cattle once in a place called Hell's Canyon. My father found old Indian signs in his early days. A sign to point out water was made by crossing gaps between the brush with rows of rocks 12 feet apart. A circle of rocks identified an old campsite. Indian writing was found on rocks in Alamacitas Cañon. At the ranch when we were young, we found many arrowheads and spear points signifying that was once a favorite Indian hunting ground.

[i] Verna said Frank Metzger had bought his extensive ranch property at Mora from "Father Pinard," who had bought it from grantees. She said Andreas later bought a portion of that land from Metzger. There were several Pinards, including families, who lived in the area, and two were priests. Alvin Korte said Metzger and Henry Korte bought their ranches from Frenchman Father Jose Francisco Pinard

[ii] Verna was the only one we know who mentioned a Los Cerritos Ranch, and we do not know its location. We did not know James Bonney owned other property besides that at La Junta. We know he had his own 6,000 acre grant. Documented evidence and his descendant Joe Lopez said James' father-in-law Miguel Mascarenas had given him some of his allotted Mora Grant land. It appears that his heirs lost their claim to his 6,000 private grant but were able to prove their rights to the land given to him by his father-in-law. Those two properties were basically the same land.

[iii] Naupeste was an unfamiliar name to me, and also to Karl, when my mom mentioned it in her writings like this one. I later found it mentioned in several places, including in the first of five first edition volumes of *Leading Facts of New Mexico History* by Ralph Emerson Twitchell (published by the Torch Press, Cedar Rapids, Iowa, 1911). Twitchell wrote: "In the early 1830s, Charles Bent, together with his brother, William, founded a fort on the Arkansas River (the Spanish called it Rio Napiste) in what is today's southern Colorado. The river marked the southern boundary between the United States of America and the Kingdom of Spain since the Otis-Anin Treaty of 1819. A couple years later—after Mexico's Independence from Spain in 1821—the river became the northern boundary of the Republic of Mexico with the United States. Bent's Fort was, therefore, located at a very strategic place for international commerce."
I think it is reasonable to believe that Daniel Eberle—living in northern New Mexico—traveled that distance to trade and purchase merchandise for his store. In those days that kind of trip was common and necessary to run a mercantile business on the frontier.

[iv] Begosa was another name mentioned by Verna unfamiliar to Karl and me, until he recently found it on the Internet. A place of that name is north of Las Vegas on the Llano Estacado—the Great Plains. The grasslands of the prairies and the evergreens of the foothills form meadows, for which Las Vegas was named. To the west and northwest are the Rocky Mountains, with the plains lying north and east, surrounded on three sides by steep wooded canyons. Vegosa (Begosa) Creek forms the canyon on the east and south, and the Gallinas River forms the canyon on the west. It was probably at the Vegosa Spring near Las Vegas where Daniel Eberle was hit. That location fits the story that says, after he was struck, he was able to reach his store in Las Vegas before he died. Vegosa/Begosa, now a 537-acre grasslands bird and wildlife refuge, is about three miles northeast of Las Vegas.
Karl tells a slightly different story of Eberle's demise; Aunties told him that Daniel Eberle/Ebel was killed at Cañon de Perro, which is near Wagon Mound.

[v] Verna and others, including Eduardo, pronounced the German Korte family name with two syllables: COR-tee or COR-tah. Alvin pronounces his name with one syllable: CORT.

[vi] Bibiana gave a pair of gold filigree earrings to her daughter, Maria Marta "Aunt Marie," who sold them to her nephew's wife, Emma Laumbach. They were featured in a poignant story, written later as fiction by Verna, "Never a Road," which appears in this book slightly unfictionalized. Emma had at least one of the earrings made into a pin; a photo of it accompanies Verna's *Never a Road* chapter.

[vii] Gold filigree butterfly pin, believe to have belonged to Bibiana, given to Janet by Tony in the 1960s.

[xi] I'm uncertain which of the New Mexico Frakers was Metzger's friend related in Verna's story. Butch Sanders found records of a Charles L. Fraker, born 1841, died 1922, but his dates do not fit this story. I also do not know her source for this detailed story of Metzger's death, but it is at odds with published newspaper accounts. Verna's source may have been Eduardo Korte, whom she knew when she attended college in Las Vegas New Mexico; she often quoted him in her writings.

[xiii] There will be more details about these lawsuits in a later chapter.

[xiv] This family information probably came from Eduardo Korte.

[xv] See watercolor sketch of the Buena Vista place by Verna L. Sparks in chapter 19.

[xvi] See watercolor by Verna L. Sparks of grist mill at La Cueva established by Vicente Romero in chapter 19.

[xvii] Albert and Anna Marie Ortega, granddaughter of Henry Laumbach, found a mathematics book—copyright J.W.C. Gilman & Co., 1879—that belonged to Daniel (born 1872). It has difficult math problems for any era for a lower grade level. (Daniel only completed the eighth grade.) They include: Common fractions, decimal fractions, the metric system, percentages, commissions, trade discounts, profit and loss, stock transactions, assessments and dividends, stock investments, simple, compound and annual interest, partial payments, bank discounts and true discounts, monetary exchange, insurance, taxes, ratios and proportions.

SECTION IV: LAUMBACHS IN NEW MEXICO

Chapter 19: Andreas 1 & 2
by Jan Girand

Based upon clues found in records, Andreas Detlef Laumbach 1st came from Iowa to New Mexico sometime after the middle of the year 1860 and before early spring of 1864, and died within that time frame. In his chapter, Karl Laumbach relates the versions told by family about his death. All versions agree he was killed by Indians near Taylor Springs at the Rock Crossing a short distance east of what is now Springer in northeastern New Mexico; only the details of how he died vary.

The German documents (images provided earlier in this book) are dated March 31, 1856. We think Andreas 1st and his family left for America soon after that date. A ship manifest found by Butch Sanders shows his son Andreas 2nd came only a few months later, departing mid-July of the same year. Both of their ships were probably at sea almost two months. After processing at the port of entry at Castle Garden, they spent more time, we don't know how much, traveling overland from the east coast to their Clinton, Iowa destination in middle-America.

In addition to his crossing to America, thanks to Butch Sanders for finding his ship's manifest, we have several pieces of documentation for Andreas Detlef Laumbach 2nd in New Mexico, but we do not have his German birth certificate.

The taking of U.S. census began with George Washington in 1790; thereafter, it was taken in the American households nationwide every ten years. The data in those census records is only as accurate as the hired impersonal census takers, and also of the persons in the households giving the information those particular days and hours. Early residents did not know the value of those census records, did not know how important they would become for us who came later. They did not know those records immortalized every one of those listed.

This Laumbach family's first appearance in a formal U.S. census, four years after their arrival in America, was dated June 25, 1860. It showed Andreas 1st residing in Deep Creek, at the Boon Springs Post Office location, in Clinton, Iowa. He was listed as "Andros S. Laumbar," given age 55, farmer, born in Denmark. In 1860, he—born November 1802—was actually closer to 58. Shown living with him was Anna, age 37. His wife Anna—born in August 1811—was actually about age 47. Relationships were not given on census reports in that era, but then like now, the first one listed was head of household, next is the spouse, then their children in descending order of age. Next are older parents, if any, in the household. Listed last are non-family residents, including boarders and servants. Listed in the Deep Creek census following Anna was "Mark C." age 21. We believe that was Marx Heinrich "Henry" (maybe Marx sounded like "Mark C") born March 1840, who would have been almost 20. Next listed was "Chautina" age 18; that may have been Catharina Margaretha, born March 1836; she was actually older than Henry. Then "Margaret" age 16, who was probably Margaretha, born March 1837, also older than Henry. Then "Ann," age 12; if the age was accurate, that was Anna Christina born 1848, destined to marry Peter Henkens. (The family repeated given names, making it confusing for researchers.)

For whatever reason, some of their children were not listed on that census. We know the son Andreas had already left them and arrived in New Mexico end of October, just months earlier. Marx Heinrich was their only other son. The other children were girls who would not pass on the family name, or even keep it themselves if they married. The absence of some of them on this census might indicate they had already married and left home. Denmark was the stated origin for everyone in that household, including the children and "Deoleff Skneck" (first name probably Detlef), listed as age 26, farmhand.

From 1870 on, most U.S. census records show the origin of the New Mexico Laumbach family—rather than Denmark—as Schleswig, once as Holstein, and curiously, the 1880 La Cueva New Mexico census shows Andreas' origin as "Wurtenberg." Most often, it is shown as Germany.

The 1865 IRS Tax Assessment for Deep Creek, Iowa indicates Anna Laumbach was then head of household, therefore known as a widow.

The April 10, 1864 entry recording the marriage of Andreas Detlef Laumbach 2nd to Elionor Ebel at St. Gertrudes de Mora, New Mexico states the groom's father was deceased.

These documented clues tell us the brief time period in which the elder Andreas was in New Mexico, where he also died.

In the west, the only early means of long distance communication was by overland mail—by Pony Express, stage lines or military transport. It was expensive, slow and unreliable. Then came the telegraph. Especially in the west, it was associated with the railroad—that also brought mail. It arrived in northern New Mexico in 1879. Then and later, telegraph messages, usually by Western Union and often bearing bad news, came by wire at railroad depots in the form of audible Morse code, translated by telegraph operators from dits and dahs into words and hand-delivered, sometimes with difficulty, to the addressees. (*My father, Dal C. Sparks, was a telegrapher for the AT&SF for more than 40 years, beginning as an apprentice in 1929; he retired in 1971. He often traveled distances to remote areas to deliver telegrams past midnight, after his working hours. Those messages usually had bad news, especially during the war years. In the earlier days documented in this book, important news deliveries were even more difficult.*) The telegraph, invented by Samuel Morse in 1830, soon became widely used in eastern U.S. and by the Union effort during the Civil War. However, that means of communication was unlikely available in northern New Mexico prior to 1864, even at Las Vegas, for the family in Mora to advise the Iowa family of the death of Andreas 1st. That message was probably sent by overland letter, taking weeks to reach its destination.

We have fading letters written in German (with translations) by the Laumbach family in Clinton, Iowa, later also some written by the Henkens family in Nebraska, to the family in Mora, New Mexico before and after 1879. There were more, including earlier ones, which did not survive. I especially wish we had outgoing letters from the New Mexico family. Some from Iowa begged those in New Mexico to write. One reason for rarity of outgoing letters was their cost. However, the Iowa family probably learned about the father's death as soon as was then possible. Many years later, my mother, Verna, remembered seeing or hearing about a letter from the Iowa family responding to that shocking news. It lamented, in essence, "Our father survived war-torn Europe and travel across the ocean and across America only to be killed by Indians in wild New Mexico."

My mother's brother, Joyce Laumbach (eldest son of Daniel and Emma Laumbach), said the elder Andreas arrived in America with money. That would have included cash from the sale of their German property and the possessions they had to leave behind. Joyce wrote, they "…came to America well-off financially." They must have converted all of their physical assets to money that they could take on their persons and in their "carry-ons." They, vulnerable immigrants who did not speak the language in a new land, were fortunate that—we presume—they were not robbed or taken advantage of while traveling.

When son Andreas joined them in Iowa, and soon thereafter headed west, his parents may have given him a grub-stake to enable him to buy land and cattle wherever he chose to stop wandering and settle down. Or perhaps Andreas found a little gold in Colorado before he settled in Mora. Anna and Andreas may have also intended to give him some German family keepsakes after he was truly settled somewhere. Since Andreas 2nd made a hurried departure from his homeland, he probably brought with him few if any possessions and little money. Some German family keepsakes that had likely come as "carry-ons" with Andreas and Anna and their children still exist. A few of those ultimately passed on to Andreas 2nd, then to our Aunties, his unmarried daughters who were the last at home.

After arriving in the U.S. at Clinton, Iowa, the elder Andreas no doubt invested in property, livestock, seeds for crops, farm implements and tools.

A major question for all of us has been: Why, soon after they arrived and had just begun to settle into a comfortable Germanic community among friends, did the elder Andreas leave his wife and family behind in Iowa and go to New Mexico? According to my Uncle Joyce, son Andreas (Joyce's grandfather) asked his father to join him in partnership and invest money in his ranching business. That his father did. I think the older man intended to ask his Iowa family to join him in New Mexico after he was settled and secure. However, before that happened, within three years of his arrival, he was killed. His wife, Anna—finally feeling secure, settled and comfortable in a welcoming community of compatriots—may have refused to move again, so soon after experiencing the major upheaval of leaving behind almost everything, including friends and family in Germany, and crossing the ocean to a new land. She may have thought she was too old for more adventures. She may not have approved of her husband Andreas going off to New Mexico—to what seemed like yet another country where yet another language was spoken. Women then had little say and influence in their husbands' decisions. Perhaps she never intended to join him. Maybe she hoped her husband and son would come to their senses and return to settled and stable Iowa after they had their little adventure.

The Mora Valley that Andreas chose had been one of the earliest settled places in New Mexico. Prior to settlement, Apache and Comanche Indians occupied the valley, with its high, wooded mountains that provided good hunting and fishing, and its close proximity to the plains filled with abundant buffalo and other game. Eventually the valley began to be settled by Hispanics and a few foreigners, and it became part of the huge Mora Land Grant.

On September 25, 1835, Don Albino Perez, Mexico's Political Chief of New Mexico, gave the vast lands to its 76 settled families. The more than ¾ million-acre-grant (827,000 acres) extended from Holman through the Mora Valley, Buena Vista and La Cebolla, and as far away as Wagon Mound. "Nourished by the Sapinero and Mora rivers that sourced in the Sangre De Cristo mountain range, it was some of the finest farmland in the Territory," Verna wrote. But the grantees were expected to fend for themselves and their environment and lives were difficult. For most, their means of livelihood was subsistence only, but it adequately sustained them when New Mexico belonged to Spain and was self-contained. However, after Mexico possessed it, that government's open-door policy brought an influx of Americans and Europeans, drastically changing their way of life. Many tracts of land have no clear titles in what had been the Mora Grant, even today after generations of subsequent landowners made major improvements on those lands.

We know Bibiana's father (Elionor's grandfather) Bernardo Martín had been one of the Mora Land Grantees, but our family history and stories never again seem to refer to his grant land. Some think the Laumbach place at Buena Vista was inherited from Bernardo. They are mistaken. Elionor and Andreas' lands were not inherited from him or from his daughter, Bibiana. According to Verna and Joyce, the Laumbachs purchased a portion of Frank Metzger's land. Metzger, and also Korte, had bought the land from Fr. Pinard; this was confirmed by Alvin Korte, who said it was Father Jose Francisco Pinard. Pinard acquired it directly from various grantees. It is unlikely Bernardo was one of those grantees who originally owned it when Pinard bought the land. Bernardo had first lived at Potrero—on the other side of the Sangre de Cristo range—and then lived a few miles from Buena Vista at La Cebolla in the Mora Valley. He lived there the rest of his life, except for a brief stint in the U.S. military.

Verna described the portion of the Mora Grant property that Father Pinard acquired from the grantees as "... a large and beautiful tract of partially wooded land in Buena Vista."

Pioneer Merchants of Las Vegas, by M.C. Gottschalk, page 51, shows a sketch of the Las Vegas Old Town Plaza in 1853; a Reverend Francisco Pinard had a presence—perhaps an office—on the Plaza, in front of the "Old U.S. Army Barracks," but Pinard is not named in a subsequent sketch of the Plaza in 1867. Perhaps he had moved to Mora sometime after 1853.

There was more than one Frenchman named Pinard in the Mora area during those decades; at least two were priests. In the *New Mexico Baptisms for Mora, 1861-1878*, edited by Armando R. Sandoval and Jill Montoya, published by the Hispanic Genealogical Research Center of New Mexico, a list of priests serving Mora included one Jean Francois Pinard.

The Frank Metzger/Henry Korte and the Andreas D. Laumbach properties, which included their homes, adjoined with only an orchard on Laumbach land between them, according to my mother. Elionor's mother, Bibiana, lived in a small casita in that orchard the last years of her life. She died in October 1897.[i] That orchard between the properties took on more meaning when the conflict began between Metzger's daughters—heirs of Apolonia's daughter, Juanita, and Bibiana's three younger daughters, "Lola" Dolorita, Josefita and Isabelita. By making Juanita and her husband—his friend and business partner, Henry Korte—the sole heir of his considerable estate, Frank Metzger tried to disown his daughters by Bibiana. Lola, on behalf of herself and her young sisters, brought suit against Henry Korte, filed in Mora in March 1886, a year after Metzger died. The complaint said and records show Metzger owned considerable lands, livestock, money and other assets, a value estimated in excess of $100,000; some records say his estate was more than double that. Regardless, it was a huge estate for that era. He tried to manipulate the system to prevent his younger three daughters from inheriting anything from him. The lawsuit caused deep, long-lasting chasms between the two family branches.

Daniel Laumbach forbade his children—Verna and her siblings—as children and young adults, from going into or beyond that orchard when they visited their grandmother, Elionor. Beyond it was what had been the Metzger-Korte place where their great-great-grandmother Apolonia had last lived with Frank Metzger, their daughter, Juanita, and her husband Henry Korte. It was also where she had died. The family lawsuit went on for decades. When it ended, the only winner was attorney J.W. Veeder. He took what remained of the Metzger-Korte assets—the ranch—as his attorney fee. When Daniel's children were young, that place belonged to Veeder, which was a bitter reminder of the family dispute. There will be more in this book about that major conflict between family branches that caused heartache for generations. Andreas and Elionor were not involved. Lola, Josefa and Isabel resented that the Laumbachs—Elionor being their older sibling—did not help with their legal battle.

To the end of her life, Verna longed to see the place where Apolonia had lived, so near her family's home place but out of her sight and reach. She also wanted to see the little Metzger-Korte family cemetery, near the road to Golondrinas, where Apolonia was buried. That, too, was nearby but inaccessible. (She didn't drive so even when she was older, it was out of her reach, and the cemetery was surrounded by property owned by strangers.) At college in Las Vegas she had heard about Apolonia's beautiful rose-colored marble gravestone that had been stolen. That probably happened when talk of buried treasures caused a gold rush in Mora and the two family cemeteries were vandalized. Verna never saw "the Veeder place" or the nearby little Metzger/Korte family cemetery.

When Verna was in college, she learned more of this story from Eduardo Korte, her Great-Aunt Isabel and her daughter, Verna's friend, the younger Isabel Gallegos, and also Aunties. She questioned her father, who never talked about it. Once home for a college holiday in Roy, she tried. Her papa was so upset, he went outside and walked up and down in the yard for hours, his pipe stem clenched so tightly between his teeth that she thought it or his teeth and jaws would snap. She learned to never again mention it in his presence.

~~

Andreas and Elionor built a fine adobe ranch place at Buena Vista where they raised their children.[ii]

I wish I knew when Andreas and Elionor moved from La Cebolla to Buena Vista onto the land they bought from Frank Metzger. Record shows both Elionor and Andreas lived at "La Cebolla" when they married in 1864. We also take clues from available baptismal records. Margaret was christened at the "plaza de Francisco Abajo de La Cebolla" in March 1865 (Vicente St. Vrain was her godfather). Peter Joseph ("Pedro Lambek") was born June 18, 1867 to parents from La Cebolla; his godparents were Henry Korte and Juanita Metzger. Estefana was born May 1871; her parents' address was not given. Jose Henriques (Henry) was born October 1874 to parents from Buena Vista; his godparents were Felipe Esquibel and Josefa "Evans"—as Ebel was often written. But who was this Josefa? (The accuracy of priests as scribes was no better than that of census-takers. Or as Trent Shue put it, in that era "spelling was an art.") This was probably Maria Marta Ebel, Felipe's wife.

Alejandro "Lumback" was born January 1877 to parents Andres Lumback and Maria Eleonor "Aban" (Ebel) from Cebolla. Godparents were Andres Ebel and Ubalda Lopez. Alejandro died young. Ana Lumback was born 1878 to Andres Lumback and Leonor Evans (Ebel) from Cueva. Crestina was born November 1881 to parents of La Cueva. Maria Gracia (our Aunt Mary) was born February 1884 to parents from Buena Vista. (For a time, La Cueva was their postal address when they lived at Buena Vista. For a while later, Buena Vista had its own post office; that may have been the one located on the Frank Metzger/Henry Korte ranch.)

Based on above records, both Elionor Ebel and Andreas Laumbach lived at La Cebolla before 1864, when they married, and their family continued to live there maybe for the first decade of their marriage, at least through 1867 and perhaps even to 1877. Perhaps their home at Buena Vista was being built and prepared for the family within that period and some of those years they lived at both places. It would help if we could see the abstract of what been Laumbachs' Buena Vista property. I conclude they fully moved to Buena Vista sometime after 1877, before 1878. Even after they lived for years at Buena Vista, their formal address was at nearby La Cueva. That was their designated precinct, a more established community with a mail station.

There has been an interesting debate about a fascinating vintage photograph between Karl and me, with input from Danny Chavez of Mora. Most of his life, Danny has worked part time at what had once been the Laumbach place.[iii] The photo had been taken at Laumbach's Buena Vista place. The original that Karl has is in sepia tones. According to what is written on the back of it,[iv] it was mailed, by whom we do not know, to our Auntie Mary after she and her sisters lived in Las Vegas. The photo had been taken decades earlier. Of the three adults in the center of the photo, Karl and I agree the woman on the right is Elionor. I think the Germanic fellow on the left is Andreas; Karl disagrees. He thinks the fellow in the photo looks too young. I disagree; I think the photo was taken in the 1800s; Andreas died in November 1904 at almost 71. In his last years, he looked older in photos because he was ill. We agree the younger woman standing between them is an older daughter, Margaret or Estefanita; the depicted young woman resembles both. The two little girls vaguely seen on the far left are younger daughters. The young fellow in the corral with the donkey, Karl believes, is Pete before he left home at age 21.

More than the people depicted, our debate is over the buildings seen behind them. Tradition among Karl's family (see his chapter on his grandfather, Pete) is that the larger adobe building with the pitched roof in the background may no longer exist and was built by Andreas 1st. I find that barely possible. The senior Andreas was in northern New Mexico for three years or less before he was killed some time before the spring of 1864. I doubt he had time to establish a place, much less build or have built, his own adobe home, especially at Buena Vista. Making adobe takes time and heavy labor, and then must aridly cure before use for construction. I know from first-hand experience that adobe blocks can only be made a few months a year, especially at higher elevations, during warm weather months. I believe, during his brief life in New Mexico, that the father Andreas lived with or near his son and family at La Cebolla.

Among old family photo collections of my mother and her brother, Joyce, is the same photograph as Karl's. That one is not sepia; it is a camera snapshot. Perhaps one had been made from the other. On the front margin, and also backside of hers, Verna had written: "behind Buena Vista house," as if the eye of the camera was east of the Laumbach home aimed west. That indicated camera angle cannot be correct.

Danny Chavez of Mora, and also Anna Marie, believe the depicted "adobe-stucco" structure in the background is the original, and still existing, structure of the home of Andreas Laumbach 2nd. If so, the corral in the photo would have then been in front of the house and not behind it. "Ike" Casimiro Laumbach (at past age 101) said the same thing about that photo. He thought, when that photo was taken, the corral and ditch seen in the foreground had been in front of the family's home.

I remember, in my childhood, the *acequia* (irrigation ditch) ran past one side of the house, a short distance away, and the public road ran along-side that ditch; they were lined by huge cottonwoods. We could see the house from that road.[v] My perceptions of that long ago time are cloudy. That road is now at a different location. You no longer see the house from the common road, only now seen from their private road.

When my daughter, Tracy, and I were at Buena Vista in June and also October of 2013, we saw an old, distinctly shaped log and rock building[vi] standing alone on an incline behind, east, of the main house. I believe the roof of that small structure can be seen, immediately behind and right of the house, in that "vintage photo." The camera's angle caused the two structures to appear attached or closer to each other than they were.

That outbuilding—a stable—is preserved and still in good condition. Tracy and I explored it in 2013. It appears to be a little barn, some portions with a low roof to shelter small animals. Both versions, Karl's and Verna's, of the "vintage" photo are sharp and show a lot of detail. Danny Chavez suggested that early era cameras did not accurately show depth perception. He believes that early photo made this small log and rock barn appear closer than it actually is to the main house. Danny said time, erosion and cultivation had also altered the lay of the land, even within his own lifetime. For that and other compelling reasons, Danny believes, as I do, that the primary adobe structure with pitched roof in the vintage photo was the origin of Laumbachs' and now Allsups' main house.[vii]

~~

Andreas 2nd planted a large orchard and a garden, and later sold fruit and vegetables at Fort Union and Las Vegas. He was a rancher, with herds of cattle and sheep; he also cultivated crops. Sometimes he took a son or two with him to the mill at La Cueva[viii] that was then run by Señora Romero, widow of Vicente Romero. My grandfather Daniel remembered meeting Sra. Romero when he went there with his father to grind their corn and wheat.

In addition to the early Hispanic natives who lived there for generations, the settlers of the valley included foreigners—trappers, traders and merchants who came from Germany, France, England and other European countries.[ix] Most early European settlers intermarried with the native population, resulting in many Hispanic residents with European names, as is the case throughout New Mexico.

Andreas Detlef Laumbach filed a preemptive claim for 40 acres on the Carruco on the Canadian River—miles from Mora—on May 12, 1903, towards the end of his life.[x] An image of that document is in the endnotes, courtesy of Karl Laumbach. Andreas acquired his naturalization to become a legal U.S.A. citizen in 1902.[xi] (I have the original.)

Andreas 2nd had been a handsome man, and he and Elionor had handsome children. Their photos are in Chapter 21, Children of Andreas and Elionor.

The cause of Andreas' death is not disputed among family. They say he deliberately shot himself.[xii] Some family stories say his family found him outside by the barn. Someone recently said he died in the house, in a bedroom just beyond the entry. A newspaper article of that time also indicates he died inside.[xiii]

More than one reason has been given why he took his life. Karl and his branch of family say he had been jealous, that he thought his wife, Elionor, paid too much attention to her son-in-law, Sito. When I asked my mother why he did it, she said he was a jealous man but she gave no explanation. In his last photos, he seemed older than his almost 71 years. My cousin, Vera Jane Laumbach Morris (daughter of Joyce Laumbach), said she heard he had been ill, that he had a weakened body and uncontrollable tremors. She believes he had what we now recognize as Parkinson's.[xiv] She found that particularly interesting because her brother, Bill, developed Parkinson's at an early age. Anna Marie Ortega, granddaughter of Henry Laumbach, said her aunt Clara also said Andreas had been ill, probably had Parkinson's, the reason he did it. We may never really know why he shot himself.

---

[i] Bibiana Martínez grave marker at Buena Vista cemetery, as it appears today, showing signs of damage. The second photo was taken about 30 years earlier. "Bibiana Martinez Died Oct. 27 1897."

Next are transcription and translation of a published notice about Bibiana's estate settlement.

"Aviso

Es dado a todas aquellas personas a quienes concierna, que habiendo los administradores de Maria Bibiana Martinez, finada, obtenido el permiso de la honorable corte de pruebas, en y por el Condado de Mora y Territorio de Nuevo Mexico, para dar aviso, que en el proximo termino regular, de dicha corte, de ser tenida en el primer Lunes de Mayo de 1898, la administracion de dicho estado sera cerrada. Por lo tanto, todos las acreedores que tengan reclamos en contra de dicho estado las presenten antes del ajuste final para su arreglo; de lo contrario quedaran borrados para siempre.

Andres Laumback
Andres Evel,
Administradores
Por Emilio Orniz Escribano"

Translation:

"Notice

Is given to all persons to whom this concerns, that having the administrators of Maria Bibiana Martinez, deceased, obtain permission from the honorable court of evidence, of Mora County and Territory of New Mexico, to give notice than in the next regular term of said court, to be held on the first Monday of May 1898, the administration of the estate will be closed. Therefore, all creditors having claims against the said estate be submitted before final adjustment for settlement; otherwise will remain closed forever.

Andres Laumback
Andres Evel,
Administrators
By Emilio Orniz Notary"

[ii] The Elionor Ebel and Andreas Laumbach home at Buena Vista; watercolor by Verna L. Sparks.

Photo taken in 2013 by Tracy Ikenberry of the same home, now owned by the Lonnie Allsup family. In the years since Laumbachs owned it, it was extensively remodeled and enlarged by subsequent owners including the Lorenz Shock family.

[iii] The interesting and controversial vintage photograph, courtesy Karl Laumbach. This one, that had been in sepia tones, had been mailed to our Auntie Mary Laumbach. Butch Sanders improved the resolution and changed the

246

image to black & white for this publication. Verna had a duplicate snapshot of this picture. On hers she had written that it was of the Buena Vista place, photo taken in the 1880s.

Back side of Karl's "vintage photo" taken of the Laumbach place at Buena Vista; it almost resembles a postcard.

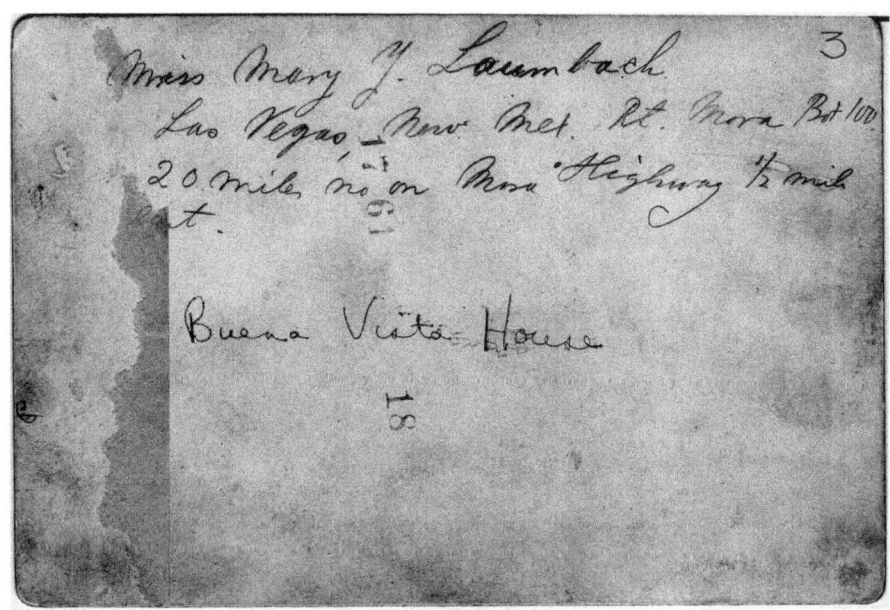

[v] Photo taken by my parents in the mid-1950s; the hand petting the horse in the foreground is mine. I stood on the public road, which ran beside the *acequia*, near the house. This photo shows the Buena Vista place before later owners extensively remodeled and made additions, and before the road was changed.

vi Unique-shaped log & rock building, probably a stable or barn for livestock, on a small rise east of the main house. Photo taken by Tracy Ikenberry in June 2013.

This view better resembles the structure that seems to be seen in the background of the vintage photo.

[vii] Danny Chavez did a study of the "vintage photo" and the current property. He sees a similarity in the distinctively cut ends of viga-like logs protruding from the corners of walls of both buildings. That similarity is just one of the reasons he thinks the primary structure seen in the "vintage photo" is the origin of the current main house.

[viii] Grist Mill at La Cueva established by Vicente Romero; watercolor by Verna L. Sparks

[ix] By chance and excellent luck, in the 1970s or early 1980s, Ruth Laumbach Fried (Karl's sister) found this document—see next image—in an uncataloged box in the National Archives at Washington DC. Ruth had an amazingly sharp eye to have noticed the notation and recognized its significance. Image provided by Karl Laumbach; its quality improved by Butch Sanders. We value this document. Except for the entry in the family

Bible saying he arrived in New Mexico on October 29, 1859, this is the earliest known documentation of Andreas Laumbach 2nd in New Mexico. As Karl said, we aren't even certain whether this document pertains to Andreas 1st or 2nd. It includes his signature, the only one we have for either of them. Various clues help us date it. It is a list of "strangers" or "foreigners" then living in Precinct 5, Mora County, Territory of New Mexico. Mora County was formed in 1860. Jesus Maria Montoya, *alcalde* (mayor) of La Cueva, certified the document with his signature on back. Sanders said if we knew when Montoya served as La Cueva mayor we could closer date it. Sanders found Montoya living elsewhere in an 1870 census. This document was written on both sides of one sheet of paper; the ink bled through. The men signed their names, and the alcalde wrote in Spanish the names he thought they said, and what each man told him. Andreas said he had lived in Precinct 5, Mora County for two years and nine months (*dos anos y nueve meses*) and that his prior country was Germany (*tierra antes era en la Alemania*). Assuming this pertained to Andreas 2nd and not Andreas 1st and comparing it to the date recorded in the family Bible of his arrival in New Mexico, this record indicates it was written about July 1862, according to Karl's calculations.

Karl's colleague Anselmo Arellano translated the document for him several years ago. He translated the "e" in the first line as foreigners, but Karl said the "e" is for the word "*estranjeros*" or strangers. The "e" was a common heading and section in the Mexican census (prior to 1846), apparently also used in this document. The document's purpose seems to be an early U.S. territorial census listing foreigners residing in Precinct 5 of Mora County. Anselmo translated "*pastor*" as a raiser of sheep; Karl translates it simply as a "herder," which could have also been of cattle, and that "*labrador y pastor*" means "farmer and herder."

Anselmo's translation: "List of foreigners, beginning with: Casimiro Pinard /s/, Juan Casimiro Pinnard from France whose occupation is farmer 33 years old and who lives in Precinct 5 Mora; Pierre Albin /s/, Pedro Albino de Francia whose occupation is freighter and foreman (overseer) at the time and who has lived in Precinct 5 Mora County since the year 1847 and in Mora County. Jacques Kinnel /s/, carpenter by occupation at the time and who has lived in Precinct 5 Mora one year and four months. Martin A. McMartin, Canadian /s/, Martin Alejandro from Canada whose occupation is merchant who lives in Precinct 5 Mora County, one year eleven days. Andreas Laumbach /s/, Andres Lomba, his occupation is farmer and sheep raiser who lives in Precinct 5 Mora County nine and one-half months. His country was before Germany."

Anselmo added: A few Germans and Canadians first entered the Mora Valley in the 1850s. A few Brizals are still there. [*Danny Chavez descended from that Brizal family through his mother.*] The Brazils who settled in Springer are of that same family from La Cueva. Blas Brazil of the Springer branch changed the spelling of their name. Anselmo thinks that family was in Taos before they settled in La Cueva. Casimiro Pinard was French. It was his son Saturtino Pinard who took Black Jack Ketchum into custody in 1900, wrote Anselmo.

/

Lista delos crembres delos e que resuretan son
los siguientes Jean Posimier Pinare
Juan Casimiro Pinar de Francia de oficio labrador
de agricultura tresaños vibe enel precinto cv:o 5° del
pierre albin Condado de mora

pedro albino de francia de oficio carro y maiordomo
el tiempo que tibe enel precinto del cv:o 5° desde el año
de 27 enel Condado de mora

Jacques Kinnel Jaquis Carpintero es su ficio
del tiempo que tibe enel precinto cv:o 5 un año y
cuatro meses

Martin. A. Mc Martin, Canadian, martin a
le Sandro de canada de oficio Comerciante el tiempo
que tibe enel precinto cv:o 5° del Condado de mora
un año onse dillos

Robert Garside, England,
Roberto angalatierra de oficio Comerciante el tiempo que tibe enel precinto cv:o 5° del Condado
demora un año onse dillos

Samuel Mc Martin, Canadian,
Samuel de Canada de oficio Comerciante
el tiempo que tibe enel precinto cv:o 5° del
Condado de mora un año onse dillos

Andreus Laumbuch
andres Lonba su oficio labrador y pastor
el tiempo que tibe enel precinto cv:o 5°
del Condado de mora dos años

This two-page document was written on one sheet of paper, front and back. The ink from the front of the sheet bled through to this back page. Butch Sanders improved, sharpened these images for the book.

nueve meses y medio
 subieron antes' eso. en lo
 alemanio

Jesus Mª montoyo
 Alcalde de La Cueva

x The May 12, 1903 preemption claim for 40 acres on the Canadian for Andreas Detlef Laumbach 2nd; courtesy Karl Laumbach. (Karl said it is "the place on the Corruco.")

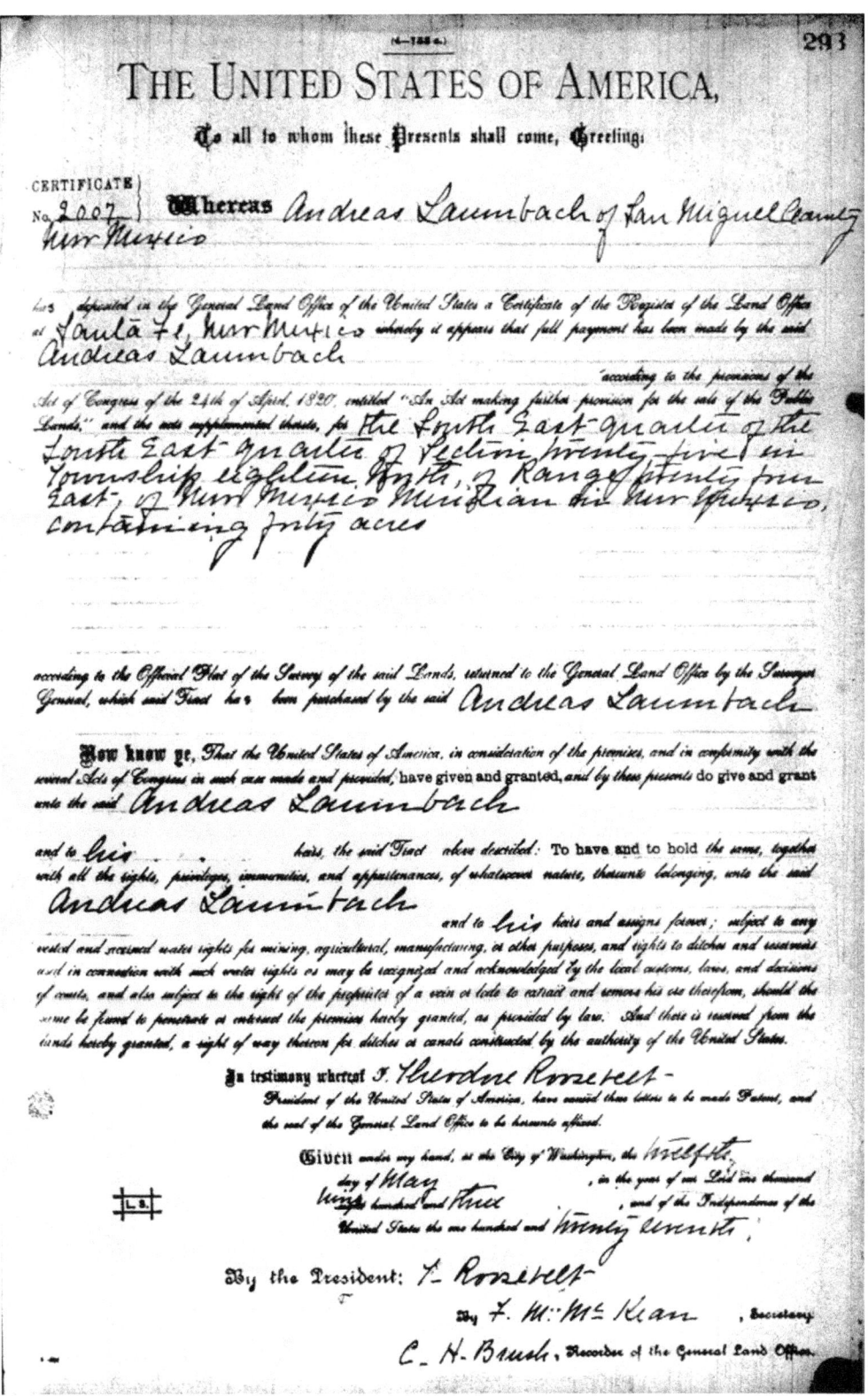

[xi] Andreas Detlef Laumbach 2nd became a naturalized U.S. citizen in November 1900, more than 40 years after he came to America, and just four years before he died.

United States of America.

Be it Remembered, That, at a regular term of the District Court of the Fourth Judicial District of the Territory of New Mexico, begun and held within and for the County of San Miguel on the 2nd Tuesday of November A.D. 1900, and on the 20th day of said term, the same being the 4th day of Dec, 1900, the following, among other, proceedings were had, to wit:

Now Comes Andreas Laumbach, an alien, and makes application to be admitted to become a citizen of the United States; and it being made to appear to the satisfaction of the Court, that, more than two years since, the said Andreas Laumbach declared, on oath, before F. W. Dancey, Clerk of the 4th Judicial District Court of the Territory of N.M., that it was bona fide his intention to become a citizen of the United States, and to renounce forever all allegiance and fidelity to any foreign prince, potentate, state or sovereignty, and particularly to William Emperor of Germany and it being further made to appear to the satisfaction of the Court, by the testimony, under oath, of Agapito Abeytia sr. and Jacob Stern citizens of the United States, that the said Andreas Laumbach has resided within the United States five years at least, and within the Territory of New Mexico one year at least, and that during that time he has behaved as a man of good moral character, attached to the principles of the Constitution of the United States, and well disposed to the good order and happiness of the same; and the said Andreas Laumbach declaring on oath that he will support the Constitution of the United States, and that he absolutely and entirely renounces and abjures all allegiance and fidelity to every foreign prince, potentate, state or sovereignty, and particularly to William, Emperor of Germany

It is Ordered By the Court that the said Andreas Laumbach be, and he hereby is, admitted to become a citizen of the United States.

Territory of New Mexico,
FOURTH JUDICIAL DISTRICT, } ss.
County of San Miguel

I, the undersigned, Clerk of the Fourth Judicial District of said Territory, hereby certify that the above is a true copy from the record of said Court.

In Testimony Whereof, I hereunto set my hand and the seal of said Court this ___ day of ___ A.D. 19__.

Secundino Romero

[xii] Andreas D. Laumbach 2nd remembrance cards. The first one was printed on heavy cardboard stock; image courtesy of Anna Marie Ortega. The second remembrance card image, courtesy of Vera Jane Laumbach Morris.

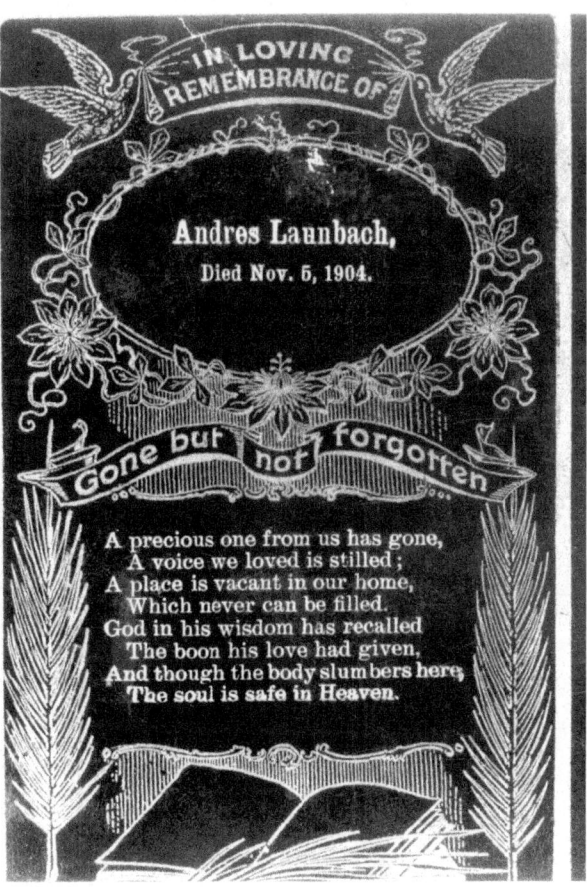

[xiii] Transcript of newspaper article found by Butch Sanders:

"Denver Rocky Mountain News
Denver, Colorado
Sunday, November 6, 1904
ACCIDENT COST LIFE.
Special to The News.
LAS VEGAS, N. M., Nov. 5.-Andres Laumbach, a ranchman at Lacueve, while cleaning a pistol accidentally discharged it, and the bullet passed near his heart. He was found lying dead on the floor."

This newspaper article indicates Andreas died in the house, probably in the front bedroom off the entry where Ned Walker, manager of Allsups' ranch, heard he had died. I had heard he had been found, shot, outside.

Both photos courtesy Karl Laumbach.

Portrait of Andreas and his eldest child, Margaret.

Portrait of Andreas and Elionor Laumbach (front row, sitting), with their children; (back row) Margaret and her husband, J. A. Cruz holding baby (probably Rosa), and Estefanita; (front row) Mary (perhaps) and Crestina. Verna wrote on her print of this photo that it had been taken in 1904. That was the same year Andreas died.

Portrait of Elionor Ebel Laumbach with her sons (from left) Henry (the youngest son), Pete (the oldest son) and Daniel. Photo from Verna or Ruth Laumbach collection, image sharpened by Butch Sanders.

SECTION IV: LAUMBACHS IN NEW MEXICO

Chapter 20: Fritz Eggert
by Trent Shue

Introduction

Various members of the Laumbach and Eggert families have said Frederick "Fritz" Eggert and Andreas Detlef Laumbach 2nd were friends and together came to America from the Schleswig-Holstein area in the 1850s. However, neither family has found documented evidence to establish that. Word-of-mouth accounts say they were both deserters from military service. They may have been the first of their families to come to America from that Germanic area. Did the young men meet while in the army, or later? How they met and exactly how far back goes the family relationship between the Eggerts and Laumbachs is unknown.

Laumbach records show the parents and siblings of Andreas Detlef Laumbach 2nd had come to America after March 1856 and settled in Clinton County, Iowa. Census records show an Eggert family—Adolph, Christena and a young boy, Christian—had come from Holstein and settled in Clinton County in 1857.

The 1900 New Mexico Census records indicate that Fritz Eggert immigrated to the U.S. in 1853, three years before the Laumbach family made their U.S. passage and four years before Adolph and Chistena Eggert's crossing.[1] Was the census record incorrect or was Fritz, at age sixteen, the family pioneer?

Charles O. Sanders, historian and genealogist, found a ship's manifest record establishing arrival of Andreas 2nd by steam ship from Hamburg in July 1856, but there is no entry for Frederick Eggert, or any Eggert with any other possible spelling or first name, traveling on that ship at that time. A manifest record for Fritz is still sought.

Frederick "Fritz" Eggert was born in 1837 in Prussia.[2] As a young man, Fritz Eggert was tall and good looking with gray eyes, light brown hair and strong hands, broad shoulders and a strong back. He was three years younger than his friend Andreas Detlef Laumbach 2nd, whose family was well established in Schleswig.

Census records show Adolph and Christena Eggert and their three children: August age 3; Christian age 4; and Margaret age 9—left Holstein in 1857 and immigrated to the United States.[3] They settled in Centre Township, Iowa in Clinton County. Their last name on the 1860 U.S. census record was spelled Agart.[4] In later censuses, family members spelled their name Eggert. It is common to find census records with names misspelled, or the spellings of names permanently changed at immigration. Was Adolph a relative of Fritz?

Based on the age difference of 13 years between Adolph and Fritz Eggert, could Adolph have been a younger brother of Fritz's father (name unknown), or a much older brother of Fritz's, or perhaps a cousin? Eggert family word-of-mouth accounts say Fritz may have come over with a brother. The Adolph Eggert family from Holstein, who settled in Iowa in 1857, is the only known Prussian family with a possible connection to Fritz Eggert, before he started his own family in New Mexico in the late 1860s. The parallel connection to families settling in Clinton County, Iowa implies that Fritz Eggert was somehow related to Adolph Eggert, and that the Eggert and Laumbach families were connected in Iowa and possibly acquainted before they left the areas of Schleswig and Holstein.

Transoceanic passage in steerage for two months was not something a family with three young children jumped into without a great deal of consideration. Adolph and Christena's decision to leave, if not prompted by the news from other emigrant families, was likely premeditated. Friends or family may have preceded the Eggerts and Laumbachs to Iowa, and may have discussed their plans before they left; perhaps sending letters back home describing their trip and their new life. Adolph and Christena Eggert of Holstein might have felt intrigued by news from Iowa as they planned their own trip. The imminent departure of that Eggert family in 1857 may have spawned Fritz's plan to depart, or Fritz's arrival in the U.S. in 1853 may have instigated theirs. Perhaps Fritz's family members boarding a ship gave him opportunity to slip aboard unnoticed and hide. We know Fritz settled in New Mexico around the same time as his friend, Andreas, according to both Laumbach and Eggert word-of-mouth. Their settlements in New Mexico were also less than ten miles apart by horseback.

The conditions aboard most emigrant ships at this time were difficult at best. There were cabin quarters reserved for the upper and middle class passengers; however, most passengers were confined in a lower level of the ship, below deck in steerage. In steerage, the ceilings were low and the sleeping area featured bunks fashioned from rough-sawn boards and arranged double-decker fashion from fore to aft with three to five people per bunk. Bunks were usually assigned to families. Passengers quickly learned that the best place to have a bunk was mid-ship, because the rocking of the boat was felt less there. Bunks were made of straw mattresses or mattresses stuffed with straw. The passengers had to bring their own pillows, blankets, etc. Rats, lice and fleas thrived in this environment. Travel in steerage was dirty, crowded and damp, with limited sanitation. There were almost always mortalities. Passengers were weekly provided food, which included staples like oatmeal, biscuits, flour, rice and sugar. There was a single community cooking-station and rough seas often made cooking impossible for days at a time.[5]

The Laumbach family had always presumed his friend Fritz was with him. What a journey it must have been from the Schleswig and Holstein areas, over the vast Atlantic, probably to New York, then overland, with stops between, and then to New Mexico.

Clinton County, Iowa

It was common in the 1850s for settlers in the U.S. to establish friendships and develop communities based on common connections with their past. The German immigrant community of Clinton County, Iowa, where the Laumbach family first settled, is a good example of that.

Eggert may have arrived in the United States in the summer of 1853. The weather during the colder months of the year was not conducive to trans-Atlantic sailing. His port of departure was probably Hamburg, but might have been Kiel. The name of Fritz's ship and where it docked in the U.S. is unknown, though if Fritz had followed the Laumbachs, he may have landed in New York. We think Fritz's targeted destination, like that of his friend Andreas, was the German farming community of Clinton County, Iowa, where there was a home base in the security of family or friends who preceded them to America. The trip to Iowa from the east coast was approximately 900 miles. I suspect that Fritz, at 16 years of age, had little money with him when he arrived. He probably had to find work and save some money to finance his overland trip. If Fritz made his ship passage later with the Adolph Eggert family, perhaps they arranged for transportation to Iowa soon after they arrived on the east coast of the U.S.

When Fritz finally arrived in Iowa, he spent some time recovering from the rigors of his journey and learning a little English. Since Adolph and Christena Eggert, like the Laumbachs, put down roots in Clinton County, Iowa, did both Fritz and Andreas 2nd stay there with or near their relatives for most of the next years? Or did they spend a large portion of that time—possibly three years between arrival in U.S. and arrival in New Mexico—by slowly working their way across the country?

The Pikes Peak Gold Rush

The year 1858 brought stories of a large gold strike in central Colorado; the Pikes Peak Gold Rush was on. Wagons rolled across what was then the Kansas Territory filled with men and women looking for fortune and a better life. Those prospectors were called "59ers," a play on the "49ers" moniker attached to the people of the 1849 California Gold Rush. The words "Pikes Peak or Bust" were often painted on the wagons of the potential prospectors. Pikes Peak is visible for miles from the open prairie lands to the east, making it an unmistakable target toward which the wagons rolled. During the Pikes Peak Gold Rush, over 50,000 people actually made it to Colorado; Eggert and Laumbach probably among them. However, gold was not found on Pikes Peak until 1890. There was some gold found in the area of Cherry Creek to the north. That gold rush was later more aptly renamed the Colorado Gold Rush.[6],[7]

The population growth and the discovery of a mineral-rich area in the Rocky Mountains prompted the creation of the Colorado Territory, passed by Congress and signed on February 28, 1861 by President Buchanan just before he left office.

The northern and southern states throughout the 1850s had been divided on issues surrounding the expansion of slavery and the rights of slave owners. In response to the Presidential election of Abraham Lincoln, seven southern states seceded from the union, including Texas, in February 1861. By April 1861, one month after Lincoln took office, the American Civil War had begun.[8] One year later, these same "59ers" would form the Colorado Volunteer militia and travel to Glorieta Pass, New Mexico, instrumental in supporting Union and New Mexico Volunteer Infantry forces in a battle that repelled the Confederate attempt to gain control of Fort Union, the Santa Fe Trail and the West.[9]

By the spring of 1859, we imagine the boys were culturally acclimated to the U.S., feeling adventurous and perhaps a little lucky. Seeing the gold rush in Colorado as their big chance, a small group of German friends packed their things and headed west. This group might have included Fritz and Andreas, perhaps also a man named William Frank.[10] We presume Adolph Eggert remained in Iowa with his family.[11]

There were three main routes they could have taken to Colorado from Iowa; the northern route was west across Iowa to Council Bluffs and then following the Platte River, taking the South Fork of the Platte south to Colorado. Clinton County, Iowa was along the northern route. Eggert and Laumbach may have witnessed a steady stream of wagons crossing the Mississippi River on barges and into Iowa headed west for Colorado. The other two routes went through to Kansas City via the Mississippi River to St. Louis and then traveled upstream on the Missouri River to Kansas City. From Kansas City, the direct route was due west, along the Smoky Hill River. The southern route followed the Mountain route of the Santa Fe Trail along the Arkansas River, west into southern Colorado to Bent's Fort and then north from there to the gold rush area. "The most popular northern route along the Platte was the most favored trail because of the good pasture for animals and the plentiful water supply for both man and beast."[12] The young men probably took the northern route.

From family lore, we think they made their way to the gold camp of Denver City. They found an area surrounded by beautiful mountains and crowded with people, most of them frustrated because, although thousands flocked to Colorado to find gold, only a handful actually did. Various Laumbach stories tell us that the young men spent several months panning for gold in the area of Cherry Creek. Perhaps disillusioned at the situation in Colorado and concerned about staying there through the winter, they decided to move south to the warmer climate of the New Mexico Territory, where there was a chance to own land and where there was also a growing population of Germans.[13]

Travel to the New Mexico Territory

From Cherry Creek in Colorado, they might have made their way along the eastern side of the Rocky Mountains, south to the Santa Fe Trail and the safety of Bent's Fort. The Santa Fe Trail was well-traveled by 1859. As the weather permitted, wagon trains regularly ferried goods from Kansas City to Santa Fe and back, crossing Indian country, where nomadic tribes were becoming edgy about the increasing numbers of white settlers moving into their area. At Fort Leavenworth, Kansas, large wagon trains were constantly staged for transport of military freight to New Mexico. Military escorts were commonly assigned to the mail wagons, government supply trains, wagon trains and merchant caravans traversing the plains for protection from marauding Indians.[14] Merchant traders established trading posts in the west and used mountain men as guides to secure the safe passage of their payloads to and from the population center of Kansas City. Settlers joined wagon trains for the security of military escorts, and the local knowledge the guides offered about the trails, people and the ways of the west.

From Bent's Fort, Fritz and Andreas might have attached themselves to a wagon train headed south toward Santa Fe. Making the journey to the south without the security of numbers that a wagon train provided would have been hazardous. The further south they traveled the more apparent it became that they would need to learn to speak Spanish.

William Kroenig of La Junta de Los Rios

An entry in the Laumbach family Bible said Andreas Detlef Laumbach 2nd arrived in New Mexico on October 29, 1859. Stories told by both the Laumbach and Eggert families say the two young men arrived in New Mexico together. Soon after they arrived, Fritz made the acquaintance of a local businessman and German immigrant, William Kroenig. Kroenig was well connected to the U.S. Cavalry, local Indian tribes and local merchant trade on both sides of the Sangre de Cristo Mountains and may have provided employment opportunities for Eggert, allowing him to get a foothold in the new territory.

Kroenig was an experienced veteran of the New Mexico Territory; his life was well documented. He was born on February 3, 1827 in Pataborn, Westphalia, Prussia. He left Europe in 1847 at 20 years of age, came to the U.S. for adventure, seeking fame and fortune, traveled around the United States from north to south, east coast to the mid-west, and eventually ended up in Independence, Missouri. In 1849, Kroenig ventured west based on news of the discovery of gold in California. On July 4, 1849, in the company of a young German doctor (name unknown), he arranged to join a wagon train that would take them as far as Santa Fe.[15]

Kroenig and his doctor friend wanted to leave the cholera-ridden city of Independence, Missouri. During their adventure-filled trip to Santa Fe, they would have passed through the town of La Junta de Los Rios (later named Watrous) in the New Mexico Territory, where he would ultimately settle.[16]

Before he settled there, Kroenig spent some time in the U.S. Cavalry and had some colorful encounters with area Utes and Apache Indians. Kroenig left the Cavalry to partner with a beef contractor named James H. Quinn of Taos (and of Santa Fe). He opened a store in Rio Colorado (now named Questa) and took a cut of the profit from the goods supplied to him by Quinn. Quinn was a well-connected cousin of Stephen A. Douglas and also the attorney for the southern district of the New Mexico Territory from 1846-1849.[17][18]

Business at the store was slow in 1849 until a group of Apache and Ute Indians, on their way to sign a peace treaty in Taos, came to town. "In total, 120 Apaches and ten Utes went to the house of the Alcade and asked for peace. The Indians were also well supplied with gold and in a short time they bought out all of the stock in Kroenig's store. Kroenig rode to Arroyo Hondo for more goods; in all, the Indians spent about $1200 in Rio Colorado—a small fortune."[19] Kroenig was so pleased with his newly found profit that he decided to close his store in Rio Colorado and start full-time trading with the Indians.

By 1853, the Vigil and St. Vrain Mexican Land Grants (originally more than 4,000,000 acres) were in jeopardy of being annexed by the U.S. expansion into Colorado. The railroad extending west focused interest in this land. The Mexican land grants awarded by Governor Armijo in 1843 were respected by the U.S., but only provided that the lands were occupied.[20] In a desperate attempt not to lose the land, Ceran St. Vrain persuaded Charlie Autobees, a well-known figure in northern New Mexico history and brother of the equally well-known Tom Tobin, to collect some settlers and establish a permanent colony on the grant.

In February of 1853, Charlie Autobees left Rio Colorado with 60 pack mules and 25 men for an area called Big Timber, the site of Bent's second fort. Big Timber was so named because a considerable body of gigantic cottonwoods grew there at the time; in fact, large timber was abundant along the river.[21] It was slow going as they started over the Sangre de Cristo Pass; the snow was deep on the western slopes. On the eastern side of the mountains the spring thaw was well underway, and they were able to make better time. Once they reached Colorado, they picked an area to settle in the vicinity of Greenhorn along the Huerfano River. The trip took three weeks. This group included the trader William Kroenig, and the French Canadian ex-trapper, mountain man, Indian trader and carpenter, William LeBlanc, as well as Marcelino Baca and J.B. Beaubien.[22] Along with Baca, who had abandoned his previous attempt to settle Greenhorn, LeBlanc and Kroenig also had plenty of experience in the area. In the early 1840s, LeBlanc worked for Ceran St. Vrain at Bent's Fort.[23]

LeBlanc and another French Canadian ex-trapper named Maurice LeDuc set up a trading post at an abandoned fort called El Nido del Cuervo, the Crow's Nest or Buzzard's Roost, on the junction of Mineral Creek and Adobe Creek in the Wet Mountains.[24] In 1849, Kroenig was heavily involved with the U.S. Cavalry, working with the territorial volunteer troop of Col. Benjamin Lloyd Beall in northern New Mexico and southern Colorado, acting in a peacekeeping capacity as a liaison between Col. Beall and Chief Chico Belasquez of the Ute Indians.[25]

"After a trip to Laramie, Wyoming to obtain cattle, Kroenig instead settled at the mouth of the Fountain River, the site of present day Pueblo, Colorado, where Marcelino Baca of Rio Colorado had already settled. Kroenig again established a store, but it was destroyed in the massacre at Pueblo on Christmas Day 1854. He went to La Costilla, where he established another store and a distillery, and then moved to Mora near present-day Watrous in 1856."[26]

La Junta de los Rios (now Watrous, New Mexico) is located where the Mountain Branch and the Cimarron Cutoff of the Santa Fe Trail come together. This is also the confluence of the Mora and Sapello Rivers, whose headwaters are in the Sangre de Cristo Mountains, the southern range of the Rockies. Historically, this location served as a trade area for the native Indian tribes; Comanches and Kiowas and Pueblo tribes from Taos met there to trade buffalo hides for corn and other goods.[27] Wagon trains on the trail to Santa Fe camped overnight there. The availability of trees, water and grass for grazing created a welcome paradise for the trail-weary travelers.[28] The area of La Junta de Los Rios was originally settled in 1825 by a brave soul, Irish or British farmer named James Bonney. Bonney was killed by Indians in 1846. He is buried in an unmarked grave in the Tiptonville Cemetery.[29]

By the late 1850s, the Santa Fe Trail was clogged with gold seekers and settlers. A British frontiersman named Alexander Barclay and his partner Joseph B. Doyle bought an interest in the John Scolly Land Grant, a 25,000-acre tract of land in the area of present day Watrous. Barclay had previously worked as a superintendent at Bent's Fort.[30] A business partner of Barclay's, an Indian agent named Thomas Fitzpatrick, had given him a tip that the government planned to build a fort in the area to protect the travelers on the Santa Fe Trail. Barclay hired Charlie Autobees from Mora to supervise the construction of a one-acre, walled fortified adobe building just west of La Junta, called Barclay's Fort. Barclay struggled to make his venture a self-sufficient and financially rewarding enterprise. If Indian raiders left his cattle and horses alone, and his post profited somewhat, Barclay hoped eventually to sell the fort to the United States government.[31] To his surprise, the government wasn't interested in Barclay's Fort, saying it was not worth the asking price.

In 1851, the U.S. Cavalry proceeded to build Fort Union at the foot of the mesa opposite the Turkey Mountains, a few miles north of La Junta on the Mountain Branch of the Santa Fe Trail. This area, called Los Pozos, was next to Wolf Creek and provided fresh pools of water up to 10 or 20 feet deep that were eventually stocked with fish.[32] As Fort Union developed, Los Pozos unfortunately disappeared. "The only disadvantage [of the site] according to Sumner was that there is not land enough for tillage." This problem was solved by locating a farm on Ocate Creek some 25 miles to the north.[33] Fort Union eventually became the largest military post in the Southwest, with a population of over 3,000 people. Alexander Barclay died alone in his failed fort in 1855.[34]

In 1856, William Kroenig and Morris Beilschowski bought the land and fort/trading post from Barclay's partner Joseph Doyle. Kroenig saw several opportunities that Barclay had missed. Kroenig was an enterprising merchant who had diversified his interests and investments. This allowed him to purchase land and establish the ranch sometime in the 1860s. He created nine artificial lakes on the land and stocked them with fish. The local topography was well suited to his purposes, a relatively low-lying area with a ready supply of water. He also developed an ice company and sold ice to Fort Union. Eventually, Kroenig went into partnership with Charles Ilfield, a long-time Las Vegas merchant, and together they operated the Ilfield & Kroenig Ice Company.[35]

"Mr. Kroenig's first wife was a Kincaid. She was married at age 15 and died at age 17, leaving one daughter. Later Mr. Kroenig married one of the daughters of Sam B. Watrous, a pioneer rancher in the area. Many of Mr. Kroenig's experiences are detailed in a diary, which was donated to the State Historical Society in Santa Fe. The diary is written in English; Mr. Kroenig and his descendants could also speak Spanish."[36]

In 1859, Kroenig was a successful businessman, running a store at the old Barclay's Fort and living in La Junta de Los Rios. Perhaps someone at Bent's Fort gave Fritz his name as a person who could help him get started in New Mexico. Or perhaps, while camping in La Junta, he may have visited his store.

For whatever reason, both Eggert and Laumbach decided to end their journeys and live in the area of northern New Mexico for the rest of their lives.

The Rise and Fall of Fort Union

With the annexation of the New Mexico Territory, the United States had a vested interest in developing the area and protecting the travelers along the Santa Fe Trail from attack by Indian warriors. Lt. Colonel Edwin Vose Sumner was assigned to the command of the Department of New Mexico on March 12, 1851 and was ordered to reorganize the distribution of troops and establish a quartermaster supply depot along the Santa Fe Trail to provide the protection travelers needed. He was accompanied by 642 marching dragoon recruits. Before his command could leave Fort Leavenworth, it would be plagued by an outbreak of cholera. Many came down with the disease, including several medical doctors. Thirty-five men died and many more deserted. At the time, the treatment was to plaster the patient with mustard from neck to heels until he resembled a bronze statue.[37]

Beyond the obvious military mission, the establishment of Fort Union in 1851 provided a boom to the local economy. Locals contracted with the Fort for the construction of administrative buildings, barracks, officers' living quarters, stables and corrals. Most commodities, such as flour, wool and grain, were obtained locally as much as possible. It was difficult for the local economy to keep up with the demands of the Fort. Oftentimes the Fort's demand created scarcities of certain commodities for the locals. Throughout most of the era that Fort Union was active (1851-1891), the army was the major business enterprise and the primary employer in New Mexico. Economic development of the region was thoroughly affected by military purchases of commodities, services, and labor.[38]

Fort Union served as a supply depot for the region during much of its occupation. It was the central storage and distribution center for equipment and provisions, as well as military transportation, for a large territory. It was also predominant in contracting for products and services and hiring civilians for numerous tasks.[39] Transportation had become the largest single item in the military budget, accounting for more than one-half of the entire army appropriation by the early 1850s.[40] The army had no choice but to import from Fort Leavenworth certain commodities that could not be obtained locally, such as medical supplies and uniforms, because New Mexico afforded so few of those required goods.[41] The military leaders of Fort Union desired to be self-sufficient, but eventually this position was abandoned as unpractical and they increased their reliance on local supplies and civilian workers. The troops were trained in combat, but many were inadequate and often unwilling to perform skilled labor or menial tasks that the locals were willing and able to do.

The poor quality of construction used in the fort directly related to its rapid deterioration. Between 1851 and 1853, Lt. Colonel Sumner employed only 29 civilians, but by 1856, when Colonel Garland took over, Fort Union employed approximately 250 civilians. Most of the civilians employed by Fort Union were teamsters.[42]

In 1861 when the Civil War broke out, the majority of officers at Fort Union were from the South. They resigned from the U.S. Army and joined the Confederacy.[43] This created a vacuum of leadership at Fort Union. A large portion of the Union forces were called east for redeployment from Fort Leavenworth to the battle fields in the southeast. This created a shortage of infantry soldiers in New Mexico and left the West vulnerable.

In the summer of 1861, concern about the potential of attacks from the Confederates of Texas caused the leadership at Fort Union to organize a local volunteer infantry. Lt. Colonel Kit Carson and Capt. Albert Pfeiffer, of the First New Mexican Volunteers, were sent to Taos to recruit Utes and New Mexicans to manage the herding, scouting and other non-combat duties at the Fort.[44] The enlistment of volunteers for combat proceeded quickly in New Mexico, although some companies had difficulty filling their quotas. The Colonel of the First New Mexico Volunteer Infantry, Ceran St. Vrain, was assigned to Fort Union, where the volunteers would be trained.[45] There were language difficulties between the Spanish speaking locals and the Union troops; this had to be accounted for in the organization and training of the volunteers and coordination of tactical maneuvers on the battlefield. Men who were bilingual in Spanish and English were placed higher in the chain of command.[46] Furthermore, "foreigners and stammerers must not be received, unless they can understand and speak rapidly."[47] When St. Vrain resigned, Lt. Colonel Kit Carson was promoted to take responsibility for this group and swiftly converted it to the New Mexico Mounted Volunteers.[48]

The Confederates felt that a successful campaign in New Mexico and along the Santa Fe Trail would secure the West for their cause. They probably had some support of the local slave owners in the New Mexico Territory. Slavery in the New Mexican Territory was primarily the product of warring Native American tribes, and typically involved the capture and servitude of children from enemy tribes. As white settlers began trading with the Native American tribes, slaves were a commodity to be traded.

In the summer of 1861, Confederate forces took the Union forts near the Mexican border, and the following winter 2,500 Confederate soldiers, led by Brig. Gen. Henry H. Sibley, a former Union officer who had served in New Mexico, defeated Union forces at the Battle of Valverde and occupied

Albuquerque and Santa Fe. Only an understaffed Fort Union, with approximately $300,000 in stores, stood between the Confederate forces and the goldfields of Colorado.[49] The combined forces from Fort Union engaged in a battle with the Confederates at Glorieta Pass on March 26-28, 1862.

Word of the Confederate conquest of Albuquerque and Santa Fe quickly spread. In response, the Territorial Governor of Colorado, William Gilpin, formed a small militia of strong-willed Colorado volunteers, many of them gold miners, who marched through the snow over Raton Pass and into New Mexico to reinforce the Union and New Mexican Volunteers.[50] They snuck into the Confederate camp and were instrumental in destroying the Confederate forces' supply stronghold. They burned 70 to 80 wagons full of ammunition, food, clothing, and forage; slaughtered hundreds of horses and mules; disabled a canon and took 17 prisoners.[51] The Confederates retreated and returned to Texas. As one Texan put it, "If it had not been for those devils from Pike's Peak, this country would have been ours."[52] In all, the death toll for the Battle at Glorieta Pass was 140 Federal, 190 Confederates.[53]

The Civil War was essentially over in April 1865 when Sherman surrendered to Grant at Appomattox. Fort Union resumed its mission to protect the Santa Fe Trail. The railroad made it to Las Vegas in 1879, and the requirement for protecting the travelers on the Santa Fe Trail became increasingly unnecessary. By 1883 Fort Union was falling into disrepair, and there was a growing sentiment that the Fort would be closed as the commanding officers refused to authorize repairs. Rain, hail and wind continued to batter the structures. Exterior plaster had disappeared and left the adobe walls exposed to the elements. Almost all of the roofs were leaking and some walls were falling down.[54] In the mid-1870s, retired Major General Benjamin F. Butler purchased the land surrounding Fort Union and felt some entitlement. He did not control his cattle, which created problems for the Fort as they encroached on the Fort's grazing areas.[55]

On February 21, 1891, the Tenth Infantry marched out from Fort Union for good.[56] Three years later, the Fort was returned to the original owners of the Mora Land Grant, who sold the fort to the descendants of General Butler who operated the Butler-Ames Cattle Company. "The Butler-Ames Cattle Company tried to utilize the abandoned fort for economic and social purposes. On January 12, 1895, Paul Butler, Blanches Butler Ames, and Adelbert Ames, owners of the company, entered into a contract with Dr. William D. Gentry of Illinois to lease the buildings to be used as a sanitarium."[57]

The importance of a military presence in New Mexico, which fueled an unprecedented economic growth and social impact on the New Mexico Territory, cannot be understated, nor can the importance of the successful battle at Glorieta Pass.

William Kroenig was in the right place at the right time. The purchase of Barclay's Fort in 1856 put him in close proximity (six miles to the south) to Fort Union in its heyday, where he could provide supplies to the U.S. Cavalry, then desperate to reduce their transportation costs of bringing supplies 728 miles from Fort Leavenworth, Kansas.[58][59] Over the years, Kroenig had diversified his estate. He had interests in farming, raising cattle and sheep, wool and lumber production, fish farming, ice and of course the trading post. Kroenig's Ice Company provided ice from his lakes to Fort Union. In his early years in New Mexico, Fritz Eggert hauled ice and other supplies for Kroenig to Fort Union and other local towns and settlements.

While this happened in his own backyard, Fritz maintained a relatively low profile. He knew all the right people in and around Las Vegas. The Germans were good at sticking together and supporting one another. They were also quick to recognize opportunities and many of the local stores and trading posts were owned and operated by Germans.

The LeBlancs from Arroyo Hondo

Soon after they arrived in New Mexico, Eggert and Laumbach went their separate ways, but the separation was only a few miles. Andreas married a local girl and acquired property near Mora, New Mexico, northwest of Las Vegas, and according to at least one Laumbach family story, Andreas 2nd recruited his father to move down from Iowa to join him.

Fritz's first property was in the area of the La Jara Creek off of the Sapello River.[60] This area is just west of La Junta (Watrous) and probably connected him on a regular basis with Kroenig. It is probably also fair to assume that Kroenig employed Fritz as a teamster or laborer during his early years in New Mexico between 1860 and 1870.

It was during this decade that Fritz was introduced to his future wife, Juanita Le Blanc. It is not clear how they met, but it probably happened because of Fritz's friendship/employment with William Kroenig. Kroenig's earlier trading post in Questa, on the western foothills of the Sangre de Cristo Mountains, made him a regular trading partner with other traders in the area, namely Juanita's father, William Le Blanc of Arroyo Hondo. Also, in 1853, they were both part of Ceran St. Vrain's effort to settle the St. Vrain and Vigil Land Grants in the area of Pueblo, Colorado.[61] Networking was very important to the trading community. Even though Kroenig had moved to the opposite side of the mountain range from Barclay's Fort, he kept his connections to traders on the western slope. Fritz, working as a teamster for Kroenig, would have managed the movement of wagons carrying food, ice, wool, and hardware with various traders with whom he did business. One of those would have been Kroenig's old friend William LeBlanc.

Juanita was the daughter of William Le Blanc, the retired mountain man and owner of the Arroyo Hondo gristmill and trading post, formerly owned by Simeon Turley.[62] Turley became famous for brewing "Taos Lightning" whiskey, as it was known at his mill in the canyon of Arroyo Hondo, north of Taos on the Kiowa Trail.[63] Turley was one of the richest men in the territory. He provided work for many men, including Charles Autobees and Tom Tobin, but likely his most loyal employee was William LeBlanc, who worked for him as a carpenter in the 1840s. Juanita's mother, Maria Alvina Vigil may have been Simeon Turley's illegitimate daughter,[64,65] but if not, she was surely his step-daughter. William LeBlanc would marry Alvina Vigil in November 27, 1844 in Taos County.

Two years later, Turley's Mill was one of the targets of the Taos Rebellion of 1847. William Le Blanc was present during the attack and somehow managed to escape along with Tom Tobin and a man named John Albert. Simeon Turley was killed after escaping from the attack on his trading post.[66]

William Le Blanc served on the jury trial of the perpetrators of the Taos insurrection that killed his friend and father-in-law, Turley. He later obtained the mill from Turley's common law wife, Maria Rosita Vigil y Romero. Rosita was awarded the bulk of Simeon's estate about seven months after his death.

William and Alvina would have eight children between 1845 and 1863. In the middle was Juanita Rosalia, born in February 3, 1851 in Arroyo Hondo, Taos County, New Mexico, just a little over four years after the Taos Rebellion had claimed her grandfather at Turley's Mill. She had three brothers: Jose Antonio, Jose de La Luz and Jose Gabriel, and four sisters: Maria Leucadia, Maria Rafaela, Maria Vincenta and Apolonia, who died at eight months.

Juanita LeBlanc and Fritz Eggert met each other between 1866 and 1868, probably when Fritz was on a trading trip to Arroyo Hondo with William Kroenig. She was in her late teens, and he was in his early thirties. Early in their marriage, she went by the name Juana Eggert, but later in life identified herself as Juanita LeBlanc. I have found no marriage record for Fritz and Juanita. It is possible that they were never formally married, as was then often the case. Fritz was probably Lutheran, which might have posed a problem because the LeBlancs were devout Catholics. Juanita's grandmother, Rosita, continued to live at the mill, and still lived there in 1883.[67]

William LeBlanc was away for a spell with Autobees and Kroenig at the settlement near Pueblo, and he later spent two years working on Bishop Lamy's ranch near Galisteo. LeBlanc was also a part of the party that rescued Fremont from the La Garita Mountains. He always managed to return to Arroyo Hondo where he and Alvina and family lived until 1870. Then they moved to a farm on the Rio Grande, a mile above Del Norte, Colorado, where he died on January 1, 1872, aged 68.[68][69]

Alvina was living with one of her children in Capulin, Colorado when she died (year unknown). Since she had moved from Del Norte, it is safe to assume she outlived her husband.

(Photograph of Fritz Eggert and Juanita LeBlanc taken about 1880.)

Homesteading in the Village of Sapello Ranch

Sometime during this decade, Fritz Eggert homesteaded 160 acres just west of La Junta de Los Rios by the southern bank of the Sapello River, along the road from Las Vegas to Fort Bascom. This area was known as The Village of Sapello Ranch. There Fritz and Juanita built a seven-room stone house with a corral.

In early 1869, Juanita was pregnant with their first child. Charles, or Carlos as he is listed in the 1880 census, was born in November 1869 in Sapello Ranch.[70],[71] Almost immediately after Charles was born, Fritz transferred the following property to Juanita's name:

"On November 9, 1869 Fritz Eggert husband assigned and transferred to his wife Maria Juanita Rosalia LeBlanc in consideration for assistance, care and other domestic help, 30 cows, one wagon, 6 mules and harness, 20 pigs, and all household items including kitchen and other furniture."[72]

It is unclear why Fritz felt the need to transfer his personal property to his wife's name. Perhaps he was concerned about his status as an alien, or maybe he was protecting his assets from a lawsuit.

The 1870 U.S. Census shows Fritz and Juanita living in the area of Los Alamos in the Village of Sapello Ranch, San Miguel County, New Mexico, and they had a six-month-old son, Charles. Fritz Eggert was listed as a farmer with estimated property value of $3,000. Juana was listed as a housekeeper, unable to read or write. Eggert incorrectly indicated that he was a U.S. citizen. He did not become a U.S. citizen until he was naturalized in 1873.[73] Juana or Juanita was inconspicuous in the 1870 census (her maiden name was not listed).

They would soon welcome a second child; Rosita Felicitas Eggert was born on February 6, 1871 also in Sapello Ranch.[74] Rosita was named for Juanita's maternal grandmother, Maria Rosita Vigil y Romero, whose mother was also named Rosa, Maria Rosa Quintana.

The Settlement of El Monton de Los Alamos

In 1878, Fritz bought 300 acres of land with a house at Jolla Larga from a rancher named Andres Sena for $960.[75] The property was referred to as the Plaza de San Luis at La Jolla Larga. Sena acquired his property from his wife, whose family name was Baca. The Bacas had a large stake in the Las Vegas Land Grant. Sena was known for raising large quantities of corn, wheat and cattle on the property.[76] This property was near El Monton de Los Alamos, a little further west than his other ranch, again along the Sapello River.

Before the coming of the railroad to this area in 1879, people traveled the Santa Fe Trail in wagons and by stagecoach. El Monton de Los Alamos was about nine miles outside of Las Vegas and three miles east of Sapello. It was a stage stop for the Barlow-Sanderson Stage Line, which went into Las Vegas. The merchant Charles Ilfield rented a store there from Las Vegas old-timer, F.O. Kihlberg in 1870, which he later purchased in 1872.[77] Today, the old buildings of the stage stop can be found just north of the Las Vegas airport, on privately owned property known as Ruby Ranch.

La Placita at El Monton Del Los Alamos

El Monton de Los Alamos was a beautiful little oasis sitting below the prairie, along the sleepy meandering Sapello River. The appeal of this area was similar to the appeal of La Junta de Los Rios area enjoyed by Kroenig. A very large white barn, which appears to have withstood the test of time, is the most prominent structure there today. About one hundred yards west of the barn is a shaded L-shaped Placita that was once the Barlow-Sanderson Stage Stop. Behind the stage stop is a small cemetery with the names of many of the former residents of the area. The Los Alamos, San Miguel County Post Office was also once located here.[78]

On the prairie hilltop, overlooking the old stage stop is a small Catholic church named La Capilla de Nuestro Santo Nino. Juanita LeBlanc was raised Catholic and likely spent time there worshipping.[79] The church is still actively used. There is a larger cemetery just south of the church. The children of William Frank are buried here.[80]

Juanita would bear two children in succession that did not live to adulthood. The reasons for their deaths are unknown. Maria Emilia Eggert was born on 21 January, 1874 in Wagon Mound, Mora County, New Mexico. She was christened on 5 April, 1874. A son was also lost to them, Solomon Amado Eggert, who was born on 28 February, 1876 in Wagon Mound, Mora County, New Mexico. He was christened on 16 April, 1876.

On August 10, 1881, Fritz and Juanita were blessed with another son, named Frederick or Fred, after Fritz, which was his nickname. Another daughter followed Frederick in 1885.[81] The name they chose for her, Margaret, is the same as that of the daughter of Adolph and Christena Eggert who emigrated from Holstein to Clinton County, Iowa in 1857.

In July 1886, Fritz sold all 200 acres of his Sapello riverfront property in El Monton de Los Alamos, and 160 acres in the Village of Sapello Ranch, to Charles Ilfield and his partners Adolph Letcher of Baltimore and Letcher's son-in-law, William Frank, for $4,000.[82]

The Charles Ilfield Connection

Charles Ilfield was born in Homburg Vor der Hohe, Prussia. He, presumably like Eggert and Laumbach, had escaped the Prussian conscription, and sailed to the U.S. In 1865, he was eighteen years old and had made his way to Taos with little money to his name. He went to work as a storekeeper for an older German gentleman named Adolph Letcher. His dedication to his business and his likeability were his trademarks. He quickly learned Spanish and became popular with the local Spanish-speaking people. Letcher soon made him a partner. According to O'Grady, Ilfield was "... a man who was willing to sleep under the counter of his store in its earliest beginnings to protect it from thieves."[83]

By 1867, the landscape of New Mexico was changing rapidly. Taos and Santa Fe were falling out of favor as the hot trading areas. Las Vegas had become a boomtown near the Santa Fe Trail, where eventually the Atchison, Topeka and Santa Fe Railroad would pass through town.

Ilfield and Letcher saw Las Vegas as a good opportunity. They packed their merchandise on 75 burros and made their way to Las Vegas, where they started the "Letcher and Ilfield, General Merchandise" in the Plaza of Old Town Las Vegas. In 1874, Letcher decided to move back to Baltimore. He sold his interest in the business to Ilfield for $36,000. Charles partnered with his brothers, Noah and Ludwig, and later with brother-in-law Max Nordhaus. Between 1882 and 1890, he built a four-story department store on the Old Town Plaza in Las Vegas, which was then the largest department store in the Southwest. It became the home of the Charles Ilfield Company, dubbed the Great Emporium by the locals.[84] Today it is the Plaza Hotel and has been used for the backdrop of several films, including *Easy Rider* and *No Country for Old Men*. The Ilfield name can still be seen on the east side of the building.

La Capilla de Nuestro Santo Nino

As Las Vegas grew, it became the home to a number of immigrant Germans and German Jews. The ability to share culture, worship and to communicate in one's native tongue smoothed the transition for non-native, non-English speaking people to New Mexico. Ilfield was supportive of the immigrant community, providing jobs and financing new business ventures. He partnered in the establishment of several county stores in the surrounding areas, the first of which was established in 1870 at El Monton de Los Alamos.[85] The outlying stores provided convenient collection points for agricultural produce and an outlet for him to sell or trade his finished goods. Ilfield partnered with William Kroenig of Watrous to form the Ilfield Kroenig Ice Company.[86]

In 1881, Ilfield contracted to supply lumber to the Mexican Central Railroad, which was being extended south of El Paso. He bought the lumber from Kroenig of Watrous and sold it for a modest profit to the railroad.[87] William Kroenig and Andres Sena were two of Ilfield's biggest suppliers of raw goods and trading partners.[88]

It is not surprising to see the Eggert name associated with Charles Ilfield. Eggert sold the land he purchased from Andres Sena in El Monton de Los Alamos in 1886 to Ilfield's partners. In August 1887, after selling his property, Fritz was an agent for Ilfield in the execution of a court-ordered injunction for the collection of 236 head of cattle from Jesus Ma. Gallegos.[89] Gallegos lived in El Monton de Los Alamos.[90] The following letter is typical of the professional manner in which Charles Ilfield did business. Ilfield would often author legal documents for locals who could not read or write.

```
          Next to Plaza Hotel        Office of
                                     CHARLES ILFELD,
                                     Wholesale & Retail Dealer in
                                     General Merchandise

                                     Las Vegas, N.M.
                                     August 30th, 1887

Mr. Fritz Eggert
Los Alamosos, N.M.

       Dear Sir,

    I herewith appoint you as my lawful agent to collect of the
 Jesus Maria Gallegos herd of cattle 236 head of cows of the following brands
 50 S + G and 150.  If you con't find enough cows to cover the above amount
 due me, you will collect other classes of cattle instead of cows, and keep a
 correct tally of classes, number and ages.  This order is in accordance with
 an injunction granted to me by the court, and whenever you do any branding and
 one of Gallegos' man should be close to your camp, please have him called to
 be present, if not take some other person to be present, as to the amount of
 cattle received.

                                     Yours Resp'y,

                                     Signed:

                                     Chas. Ilfeld
```
[91]

The Ilfield-Eggert connection would continue for several more generations, as Fritz's first son, Charles Eggert and his son also worked for Ilfield.

It is not clear where the Eggerts were living between 1887 and 1889. I suspect they stayed in their home in El Monton de Los Alamos through August 1887. By 1889, they were settled some 60 miles away along the Canadian River in the area of Sabinoso.

The Settlements of Cañon Largo and Ancon

In a rugged area of northeastern New Mexico, the Canadian River flows east out of the Sangre de Cristo Mountains in its meandering quest for its confluence with the Arkansas River in eastern Oklahoma.

In an area 50 miles east of Las Vegas, New Mexico, nature carved a long, wide, u-shaped canyon known as Cañon Largo. The Canadian River winds its way southward through this area and meets the eastern end of Cañon Largo at a place known as Ancon. Cañon Largo makes a moderately steep climb to the west from the river. Its contribution to the Canadian is largely ephemeral, as it flows from canyon runoff. The level of the river and intensity of the flows vary widely with the seasons.

Josiah Gregg describes the Canadian River Valley like this:

"After three or four days of weary travel over this level plain the picturesque valley of the Canadian burst once more upon our view, presenting one of the most magnificent sights I had ever beheld. Here rose a perpendicular cliff in all the majesty and sublimity of its desolation; there another sprang forward as in the very act of losing its balance and about to precipitate itself upon the vale below; a lid farther on, a pillar with crevices and cornier so curiously formed as easily to be mistaken for the work of art; while a thousand other objects grotesquely and fantastically arranged and all shaded in the sky-bound perspective by the blue ridge-like brow of the mesa far beyond the Canadian constituted a kind of chaotic space where nature seemed to have indulged in her wildest caprices. Such was the confusion of ground-swells and eccentric cavities that it was altogether impossible to determine whereabouts the channel of the Canadian wound its way among them."

Ancon is defined by a general southeasterly flow of the Canadian River, which makes a wide u-turn, coming toward Cañon Largo from northeast then heading southeast and then to the northeast, as it negotiates its way around the steep canyon topography. About a mile downstream, the river meets the neighboring community of Sabinoso, as it continues its journey toward Texas and Oklahoma.

A view of Ancon, New Mexico looking north from Cañon Largo.

The residents of Ancon had a ready supply of water, but they needed to channel it in order to irrigate their croplands. In the 1880s, the first settlers of the Sabinoso built a ditch from the mouth of the Mora River, about a mile upriver from Ancon, down the west side of the Canadian River to the arable lands near the Sabinoso. In order to dig through the sandstone/quartzite terrain, they built huge fires to heat the rock and then dowsed the fire with water, which had the effect of fracturing the rock so that it could be more easily excavated.[92] When rivers turn, they tend to erode the outer bank and deposit fine silt along the inner bank. Over millions of years, the river has created a rich, fertile delta on the inner bank of the river. Its outer bank rises about 50 feet above the river, and for the most part is protected from the river's seasonal surges. The delta side is lower and relatively flat, rising only 20 or 30 feet above the river.

The delta land on the inner bank of the Canadian River in the farming community of Ancon, also known as Rincon Redondo, became the home base for four generations of Eggerts. Fritz and Juanita purchased land here in July of 1889 from Charles Beach for $200.[93][94] They may have moved here several years earlier, most likely immediately after they had sold the Sapello River ranch property in 1886, as their oldest daughter Rosita would marry a local rancher at nearby Trementina in late 1887.

By the summer of 1887, Fritz was 50 years old and Juanita was 36. They moved here with their four children: Rosita age 16, Frederico was almost six and Margaret was just turning two. Charles was nearly 18 and may have remained working in the Watrous/Los Alamos area, or soon after returned there. For some reason, they purchased this land only in Juanita's name. They had a fair amount of liquidity when they sold their property to Ilfield and perhaps looked for a slower and more peaceful existence. The property in Ancon represented a considerable downsizing from the nearly 400 acres of ranch property they owned along the Sapello River.

Property in Ancon is divided into long, narrow strips of land approximately one-quarter mile deep and only 108 feet wide. The Eggerts, Montoyas, Sacramento Bacas, Ebells, Gallegos, Lujans and Esquibels settled there.[95] A small pioneer community was established across the river, at the northern edge of the mouth of Cañon Largo. This included a schoolhouse, a store and a small church, all built from stone, timber and adobe by the settlers of the area. The Ancon dwellings were generally located at the far end of the property near the rocks away from the river. They built their homes of adobe bricks, which they made at Ancon. Their homes had dirt floors. There were small corrals for horses, sheep and cattle, and pens for chickens and a place for the hogs.[96] Fritz planted a small fruit orchard along the bank of the Canadian River opposite his property toward Cañon Largo.[97] There was never a bridge between Ancon and Cañon Largo. Their children had to cross the river to go to school.

Inside the ruins of the church at Cañon Largo

Ida Eggert, the last child born to Fritz and Juanita, was born in October 1889, a few months after the Ancon deed was recorded. They lived there, for the most part subsistence farming in the sandy soil of Ancon, for 12 years.[98] Fritz gained a reputation for his orchard, which grew well alongside the Canadian River. Juanita's siblings occasionally visited. Her sister Leucadia LeBlanc married a Montoya who owned land in the Sabinoso area.

Rosita Eggert, at age 16, married Manuel Antonio Sanchez on December 3, 1887 at La Yglesia de San Ysidro El Labrador at Trementina, New Mexico, about 16 miles south of the Sanchez Ranch and about 25 miles from Ancon.[99][100] They were married for 17 years and had no children. Rosita died in 1905 at age 33.

The Eggert and Laumbach families again loosely connected when Manuel Antonio Sanchez married again, to Crestina Laumbach, daughter of Andreas Laumbach 2nd and Elionor Ebel.

Charles "J.C." Eggert

In 1895, Charles Eggert, who went by J.C., short for Juan Carlos, married Kate Mumford, daughter of Harry Mumford from New York, a Lieutenant in the U.S. Cavalry who served as a quartermaster at Fort Union and later as a Spanish interpreter at Fort Wingate. Kate's mother was Josefa Marquez. Around this time, Charles worked as a cattleman on the 77 Ranch in Watrous and also for the Raynolds Brothers of Las Vegas. One of his tasks was to drive cattle to market in Kansas City.[101] In February of 1895, Charles Eggert delivered ice to the Sanitarium at the former Fort Union. The following was transcribed from a hand-written receipt copied from the research records of Wilbur Eggert.

"Watrous N.M. Feb 14, 1895
Received of Dr. William D. Gentry for the National Sanatorium Seventy Eight Dollars
being in full payment of ice delivered to said Dr. W.D. Gentry at Ft. Union, N.M.
$78.00 Received Watrous N.M. February 14, 1895 of Dr. Wm. D. Gentry for the
National Sanatorium [sic] at Fort Union Seventy eight Dollars ($78.00)
being the full payment for fifty two tons of ice delivered to the said Sanatorium.
J.C. Eggert"

Juanita LeBlanc died on May 14, 1899 at age 48. Ida was only nine years old, Maggie was almost 14 and Fred almost 18. Across the river at Cañon Largo is a small cemetery with the graves of many of the early settlers of Ancon and Cañon Largo. Juanita is buried there. The elaborate cast-iron grave marker and iron fence that Fritz had made to mark Juanita's grave are testimony to the love he must have felt for her.

Juanita Le Blanc's gravesite in Cañon Largo, photo taken in 2012.

Curiously, the grave marker spells her name Juanita "LaBlance" using La instead of Le, adding an extra E, which could represent Eggert. Spelling was an art in those days.

Margaret, Fred and Ida Eggert photograph shortly after their mother's death.

By 1900, Charles Eggert and Kate Mumford had two children and lived in Ancon with Fritz, Fred, Margaret and Ida.[102] Fritz, at age 66, still managed to be somewhat independent after Juanita died, but had the support of his two grown sons and his two teenage daughters living with him.

On July 5, 1902, Fritz took the wagon into Las Vegas and spent the night in town. Early in the morning of July 6, 1902, he was at the Bacharach Brothers General Merchandise Store, near the railroad tracks in east Las Vegas, probably to sell fruit and pick up supplies, when he suffered a heart attack. The following was published in the *Santa Fe New Mexican*:[103]

> *"Fritz Eggert, one of the well-known ranch men and orchard owners living at Canon Largo, was found this morning in the corral back of Bacarach Bros' store in an unconscious condition. Medical aid was summoned about 7:30, but Mr. Eggert died before the physician arrived. Heart failure was the assigned cause of death and the remains were taken home yesterday by his son."*

It is believed that Fritz is buried next to Juanita in an unmarked grave.

Bacharach Brothers' sign painted on brick building on Old Town Plaza, Las Vegas still visible.

Margaret Eggert would marry Domingo Aguilar and the couple would take in Ida Eggert, who was just 14 after Fritz passed away.[104] In 1902, the same year that Fritz died, Fred Eggert would marry a local girl from Sabinoso, Alcaria Chavez, daughter of Manuel Chavez and Terricita Trujillo. Fred and Alcaria would raise their family in Ancon.

The 1910 Census for Sabinoso shows Juanita LeBlanc's brother, Jose Antonio LeBlanc, a carpenter, and a widower, 65 years of age, was living in Ancon as a renter. Jose Antonio had learned the carpentry trade from his father, William LeBlanc. In his autobiography, Alfonso Esquibel mentions spending time with Antonio LeBlanc. In the same 1910 census record is Leucadia LeBlanc Montoya, Juanita's sister. Leucadia was a widow, age 61, and listed as a property owner in Sabinoso living with one of her two children, a daughter Josefina.[105]

Closing Thoughts

Time has a way of obscuring details of the lives of generations that have gone before us. Unfortunately, as historians, we are often only left with a few remaining pebbles that have survived. I trust that my attempt to tell the story of the lives of Fritz Eggert and Juanita LeBlanc, the people they knew, and the social, economic and political climate in which they lived will serve as a solid stepping stone for future researchers and genealogists attempting to retrace their histories.

---

[1] 1900 New Mexico Territorial Census, Sabinoso Precinct No. 22. Sheet 9.

[2] LDS Family Search™ International Genealogical Index Record
http://www.familysearch.org/eng/search/igi/individual_record.asp?recid=100381876007&lds=1&region=8.

[3] The 1900 U.S. Federal Census Record for Hampshire, Clinton, Iowa indicates that Christian Eggert, son of Adolph and Christena Eggert, was born in Holstein in 1853 and immigrated to the U.S. in 1857.

[4] 1860 U.S. Federal Census for Center, Clinton, Iowa.

[5] Smithsonian Institute Museum of American History. "Enterprise on the Water" http://americanhistory.si.edu/onthewater/exhibition/2_3.html.

[6] Edited by David Lindsey. "The Journal of an 1859 Pike's Peak Gold Seeker." *Winter, 1956 (Vol. 22 No. 4)*, p 305-320.

[7] Calvin W. Gower. Kansas Historical Quarterly – "The Pike's Peak Gold Rush and the Smoky Hill Route 1859-1860" Published summer 1959 (Vol. 25, No. 2), pages 158 to 171.Transcribed by Jeannie Josephson. http://www.kshs.org/p/kansas-historical-quarterly-the-pike-s-peak-gold-rush-and-the-smoky-hill-route/13151.

[8] Wikipedia, The Free Encyclopedia. "The Colorado Territory."

[9] National Park Service. Richard Greenwood, "Glorieta Battlefield" (Santa Fe County, New Mexico) National Historic Landmark Nomination Form, Washington, D.C.: U.S. Department of the Interior, National Park Service, 1978; and Charles Phillips and Alan Axelrod, "Santa Fe and Chihuahua Trail," and Alan Axelrod, Patrick H. Butler 2nd, and Charles Phillips, "Civil War," *Encyclopedia of the American West* (New York: Simon and Schuster Macmillan, 1996).

[10] Research by Wilbur Eggert. William Frank was a godfather to Charles Eggert, eldest son of Fritz Eggert and Juanita Le Blanc. He lived in El Monton de Los Alamos and operated one of Ilfield's satellite stores during the same years Fritz and Juanita lived there. He was also the son-in-law of Ilfield's partner Adolph Letcher.

[11] Patrick B. Wolfe. *Wolfe's History of Clinton County, Iowa, Volume 1*. The Town of Goose Lake was platted by Christ Eggert et al. in 1889.

[12] Wayne C. Temple. *The Pikes Peak Gold Rush*. Illinois History Digitization Project.

[13] In 1850 there were 229 Germans in New Mexico; by 1860 there were 569. Tobias, Henry J. "A History of the Jews in New Mexico." University of New Mexico Press, Albuquerque, 1990.

[14] Fort Union Historic Research Study. "*Military Operations Before the Civil War*." Chapter 3. http://www.santafetrailresearch.com/fort-union-nm/fu-oliva-3.html.

[15] Charles Irving Jones. "*William Kroenig, New Mexico Pioneer - from his memories of 1849-1860.*" University of New Mexico Historical Review Volume 19 July, 1944 No. 3. Page 17. http://www.ebooksread.com/authors-eng/university-of-new-mexico/new-mexico-historical-review-volume-19-hci/page-17-new-mexico-historical-review-volume-19-hci.shtml.

[16] Ibid.

[17] Judith Cuddihy. 2003. New Mexico Office of the State Historian. "Questa-San Antonio del Rio Colorado." New Mexico Historical Review (Volume 19).

[18] Blanche Grant. "*When Old Trails Were New*," p 156, p 303.

[19] Judith Cuddihy. 2003. New Mexico Office of the State Historian. "Questa-San Antonio del Rio Colorado." New Mexico Historical Review (Volume 19). http://www.newmexicohistory.org/filedetails_docs.php?fileID=21982.

[20] Eventually the size of the Grants were adjudicated by the U.S. Congress and reduced to about 97,000 acres.

[21] Charles W. Bowman. Otero County Genealogy and History. The History of Bent County – Chapter: Other Pioneers – Indians and the Military. http://www.coloradoplains.com/otero/history/bent1881_chapter3.htm. Accessed 09-23-2011.

[22] Janet LeCompte. Pueblo, *Hardscrabble, Greenhorn*. University of Oklahoma Press-Norman 1923. p 229.

[23] Maria Clara Martinez et.al. "Siero, Spain, to La Culebra-Some Descendants of Francisco Montes Vigil 2nd" – Third Edition. p. 69. Copyright 2001.

[24] Ibid, p 105-106.

[25] Tessie Rael y Ortega and Judith Cuddihy. *Another Time in This Place: Historia, Cultura y Vida en Questa* (2003) http://www.newmexicohistory.org/filedetails_docs.php?fileID=21982.

[26] With the discovery of gold in the Moreno Valley area in 1860, for which he was partly responsible, Kroenig became a wealthy man. He lost his fortune in a plan to construct a 40-mile ditch and flume and then regained it from a smelter he built in the Magdalena Mountains. - Tessie Rael y Ortega and Judith Cuddihy.

[27] Shirley Cushing Flint and Richard Flint. New Mexico Office of the State Historian – "Watrous" http://www.newmexicohistory.org/filedetails.php?fileID=21281.

[28] Watrous, New Mexico, Sangres.com.

[29] Forum post by Charles Sanders http://genforum.genealogy.com/bonney/messages/684.html.

[30] George P. Hammond, "The Adventures of Alexander Barclay, Mountain Man, From London Corsetier to Pioneer Farmer in Canada, Bookkeeper in St. Louis, Superintendent of Bent's Fort, Fur Trader and Mountain man in Colorado and New Mexico, Builder of Barclay's Fort on the Santa Fe Trail, New Mexico in 1848: A Narrative of His Career, 1818 to 1855, His Memorandum Diary, 1845 to 1850" (Denver: Fred A. Rosenstock Old West Publishing Company, 1976), p.91-92.

[31] Ibid p. 92

[32] "Historical Sketch of Governor William Carr Lane Together with Diary of His Journey from St. Louis, Mo., to Santa Fe, N.M., July 31 to September 9, 1852, with Annotations by Ralph E. Twitchell," Historical Society of New Mexico, No. 20 (Nov. 1, 1917): 47.

[33] Fort Union Historic Resource Study (FUHRS).Chapter 2: The First Fort Union. http://www.santafetrailresearch.com/fort-union-nm/fu-oliva-2.html.

[34] Robert Hixson Julyan. "The place names of New Mexico," Page 30.

[35] Shirley Cushing Flint and Richard Flint. New Mexico Office of the State Historian – "Watrous" p://www.newmexicohistory.org/filedetails.php?fileID=21281.

[36] New Mexico Farm and Ranch Museum, Research and Collections Oral History of George Meredith ("Dogie") Jones. http://www.nmfarmandranchmuseum.org/oralhistory/detail.php?interview=102. April 24, 2001.

[37] Fort Union Historic Resource Study. Chapter 2: The First Fort Union. Fort Union NM: Fort Union and the Frontier Army in the Southwest (Chapter 9) A Historic Resource Study. Leo E. Oliva.1993. Southwest Cultural Resources Center Professional Papers No. 41 Division of History National Park Service. Santa Fe, New Mexico. http://www.santafetrailresearch.com/fort-union-nm/fu-oliva-2.html.

[38] FUHRS. Chapter 9: Military Supply & The Economy: Quartermaster, Commissary, and Ordnance Departments. http://www.santafetrailresearch.com/fort-union-nm/fu-oliva-9.html.

[39] Ibid.

[40] AR of QMG Thomas S. Jesup, AR SOW, 1852, House Exec. Doc. No. 1, 32 Cong., 2 sess. (Serial 674), p. 109.

[41] Forts and Supplies: The Role of the Army in the Economy of the Southwest, 1846-1861 (1983) and Miller, Soldiers and Settlers: Military Supply in the Southwest, 1861-1885 (1989). 2-3.

[42] Ibid. FUHRS. Chapter 9.

[43] Fort Union National Monument "An Administrative History by Liping Zhu, Senior Historian." 1992 National Park Service Division of History Southwest Cultural Resources Center. Santa Fe, New Mexico. Professional Papers No. 42.

[44] Ibid. FUHRS. Chapter 5: Fort Union and the Army in New Mexico During the Civil War. http://www.santafetrailresearch.com/fort-union-nm/fu-oliva-5.html.

[45] Ibid.

[46] New Mexicans joined the Union forces primarily for the pay ($13.00 per month) and a bounty of $100 for those who signed up for three years. Peons in New Mexico Territory were essentially indentured servants, or slaves. They viewed their participation in combat alongside the Union forces as their opportunity to earn their personal freedom. Their owners insisted that the peons were still their property and should therefore be returned. A writ of Habeas Corpus was imposed which would ensure their freedom, but it was later dropped. – Source Ibid. FUHRS. Chapter 5.

[47] Instructions from the war department quoted in General Orders No. 21, July 17, 1861, HQ DNM, DNM Orders, v. 38C, np, USAC, RG 393, NA.

[48] Ibid. FUHRS. Chapter 5.

[49] National Park Service. Glorieta and Raton Passes: Gateways to the Southwest. http://www.nps.gov/nr/twhp/wwwlps/lessons/117glorietaraton/117glorietaraton.htm.

[50] Ibid. NPS. *The Confederates*.

[51] Ibid. NPS. *The Confederates*.

[52] Quoted in William Waldrip, "New Mexico During the Civil War," New Mexico Historical Review, Vol. 28, 3, 4 *(July-Oct., 1953), 256-257;* cited in Richard Greenwood, "Glorieta Battlefield" (Santa Fe County, New Mexico) National Historic Landmark Nomination Form (Washington, D.C.: U.S. Department of the Interior, National Park Service, 1978) 8/2.

[53] Ibid. NPS. *The Confederates.*

[54] Ibid. FUHRS. Chapter 7. Construction and Military Operations. http://www.santafetrailresearch.com/fort-union-nm/fu-oliva-7c.html.

[55] Ibid. FUHRS. Chapter 7.

[56] Fort Union National Monument. An Administrative History. Liping Zhu Senior Historian 1992 National Park Service Division of History. Southwest Cultural Resources Center. Santa Fe, New Mexico. Professional Papers No. 42.

[57] Fort Union and the Frontier Army in the Southwest: A Historic Resource Study Fort Union National Monument Fort Union, New Mexico Leo E. Oliva 1993. Southwest Cultural Resources Center Professional Papers No. 41 Division of History National Park Service Santa Fe, New Mexico.

[58] Ibid. FUHRS. Chapter 9.

[59] Albuquerque Citizen, Dec 22, 1900. Obituary for William Kroenig indicates that he was a government contractor.

[60] Wilbur Eggert's Research.

[61] Janet LeCompte. Pueblo, Hardscrabble, Greenhorn. University of Oklahoma Press- Norman 1923.

[62] Taos Baptismal Records, 1844-1847, p. 113, Chancery, Santa Fe. LeBlanc's name on New Mexican records is usually given as "Guillermo Blanco."

[63] Janet LeCompte. 1978. "Pueblo, Hard Scrabble, Greenhorn." University of Oklahoma Press: Norman.

[64] James E. Perkins. "Tom Tobin Frontiersman," p. 20, 74. Herodotus Press, Pueblo West, CO.

[65] Maria Rosita Vigil y Romero married Antonio Vigil on Feb 18, 1828. She became pregnant with Alvina one month after the marriage. At some point early in the marriage, she abandoned Antonio to live with Simeon Turley. It is likely that her first child, Alvina, who was born in December of 1828, was the legitimate daughter of Antonio Vigil. In any case, she was raised by Simeon Turley and Maria Rosita Vigil y Romero. In spite of the awkward family dynamics associated with his wife and Turley, Antonio Vigil was working for Simeon Turley as a whiskey runner as late as 1843. Source: Letter from Robert Fisher of Pueblo, a business associate of Turley's—as published in Janet LeCompte's book *Pueblo, Hardscrabble and Greenhorn.* p 100.

[66] Hafen Collection. Janet LeCompte. "The Mountain Men and the Fur Trade of the Far West," William LeBlanc v. 5 and Simeon Turley v. 7.

[67] James A. Crutchfield. "The Battle at Turley's Mill - It Happened in New Mexico" James Crutchfield wrote a series of 29 events that shaped New Mexico history.

[68] Ibid. Hafen Collection, Janet LeCompte.

[69] Many of the LeBlancs descendants still live in southern Colorado.

[70] 1870 Federal Census for The Village of Sapello Ranch, San Miguel County, New Mexico Territory. p. 286.

[71] 1880 Federal Census for Jolla Larga, San Miguel County, New Mexico Territory. p. 286.

[72] San Miguel County, NM County Clerk's Office. Instrument: Transfer. Date 11/9/1869. Book 6. Page 168-169. Document is written in Spanish.

[73] INS-1 Immigration and Naturalization Service Office of the District Clerk in the County Courthouse Building, San Miguel County. Order of the Court. Title of Book: Cash, San Miguel CO. 1873-1875. Page 64 and 65. As researched by Wilbur L. Eggert.

[74] Ibid. 1880 Jolla Larga Census. p 286.

[75] San Miguel County, NM County Clerk's Office. Andres Sena-Fritz Eggert Warranty. 1/25/1878. Book 30. Page 11- 12. Recorded July 30, 1886, eight and a half years later, probably because there was no clear title after the initial transaction.

[76] William J. Parish. 1961. *The Charles Ilfield Company* p 370. Harvard University Press.

[77] Ibid. Parish. p 27.

[78] Ibid. p 40.

[79] There may be baptismal records available in Las Vegas church records.

[80] Wilbur Eggert's Research.

[81] 1900 U.S. Federal Census for Sabinoso, San Miguel County, NM. Precinct 22. p. 167.

[82] San Miguel County, NM County Clerk's Office. Andres Sena-Fritz Eggert Warranty. 1/25/1878. Book 29. Page 80-81.

[83] O'Grady, Janet. 1982. "The Pioneer Ilfields: Working Hard, Long, and Smart." New Mexico Magazine.

[84] Sophia Truneh. Winter 1995. Southwest Jewish History Volume 3, Number 2. "The Ilfields: A Family Story of Jewish Pioneers in New Mexico."

[85] William J. Parish. 1961, "The Charles Ilfield Company." Page 198. Harvard University Press.

[86] Ibid.

[87] Ibid. p 41.

[88] Ibid. p 59.

[89] Wilbur Eggert's Research.

[90] There are several Gallegos graves in the cemetery at La Capilla de Santo Nino.

[91] From Wilbur Eggert's Research. This document was transcribed by Wilbur from the records that he was able to find at the San Miguel County Courthouse, in Las Vegas, NM.

[92] Karl W. Laumbach of Human Systems Research, Inc., Las Cruces, NM. "Archaeological and Historical Resources in the Area of the Sabinoso Wilderness: A Narrative." Prepared for the Bureau of Land Management Taos District. Sept, 2010 HSR Report No 2009-26.

[93] San Miguel County, NM County Clerk's Office. Charles Beach-Juanita Eggert Warranty. 5/18/1889. Book 40. Page 560-561. For a sum of $200.00 USA money, Beach sold agriculture land to Juanita Eggert located on the left side of Rio Colorado beginning at a place called Ancon Redondo of Canon Largo, lines running North on Rio Colorado and South of Rio Colorado and East with land of Roman Montoya and West by Rio Colorado.

[94] There is often a delay, sometimes years, in the recordings of property transactions, getting clear title to lands that were homesteaded was a problem that Fritz encountered when he sold out to Ilfield.

[95] A number of the original families still own the property here. San Miguel County Records for Sabinoso District. Township 17 Range 24 Section A11.

[96] Interview with Virginia Eggert Green. 10-05-2011.

[97] October 28, 2009 Interview with Willie Eggert, local rancher.

[98] Assumes that they moved in 1887.

[99] From the book *New Mexico Marriages Chaperito La Yglesia de San Ysidro El Labrador.* Aug. 1876 Dec. 1898. Luis Gilberto Padilla y Baca. Published by The Hispanic Genealogical Research Center Of New Mexico. Page 21.

[100] Dec. 3, 1887. Manuel Antonio Sanchez, soltero hijo legitimo de Antonio Sanchez y de Candelaria Cortez, con Rosa Felicita Eggert, soltera hija legitima de Frederico Eggert y de Juana Blane, De Alamitos. Padrinos: Jose Aguilar y Juana Cisneros, tambien, D.F.Allen y Firenna Ceroa. Jose Aguilar and Juana Cisneros are the parents of Domingo Aguilar who married Margaret Eggert.

[101] *Albuquerque Journal.* May 10, 1938. Obituary for "J.C." Eggert.

[102] 1900 U.S. Census for Sabinoso, New Mexico. Ida was missed in this census.

[103] *Santa Fe New Mexican.* Monday, July 7, 1902. Page: 1 Column: 6. Las Vegas, July 6.

[104] Interview with Cecilia Maes. 2002.

[105] 1910 U.S. Census for Sabinoso, New Mexico.

SECTION IV: LAUMBACHS IN NEW MEXICO

Chapter 21: Children of Andreas and Elionor
by Jan Girand

Andreas and Elionor married in the spring of 1864 at La Cebolla, where they both were living at that time. Elionor was almost 15 years old, living there with her grandfather, Bernardo. (He died at La Cebolla on December 18, 1873). Elionor's home life had been complex, and confusing to us looking back trying to understand her family's dynamics. We are uncertain whether her mother or her grandmother was living in the same household with her in 1864. We have clues in census records, but those only give us a glimpse, sometimes an inaccurate look at one day, even just a peek at one hour when the census-taker came. In this case, we have the 1860 census taken four years earlier. We must also consider birth dates and other bits of data, and to those add inexact family tales to try to get a better picture. It's a jigsaw picture with missing pieces. Also many changes occur within the ten years between each census-taking.

Page 426 of La Cebolla census recorded on August 11, 1860, lists those present in the household number 3755 when Pedro Valdez came that day in the newly formed county of Mora. Those in the Martín household at the hour Mr. Valdez knocked were as follows: Elionor's grandfather, Bernardo Martín, the first one listed signifying head of household (listed as Martinez age 50, he was actually about 68); her mother Bibiana Martín (listed as Martinez, age 28, she was actually closer to 33); her half-brother Ramon Bonney (listed as Martinez, his age 14 was accurate); herself an adolescent (listed as Leonor Martinez, her age 11 was accurate); her younger brother Andres Ebel/Eberle (listed as Martinez, his age 8 was accurate); her little sister Maria Marta Eberle (listed as Martinez, age 5); plus a child, Elionor's half-sister, Doloritas Metzger (listed as Martinez, age 3, she may have been a little younger). Apolonia was absent. Bernardo's last name was assigned to everyone present.

By 1860, Metzger and Bibiana had been keeping company for at least three years, but not necessarily under the same roof. Their first child, Doloritas, was born at La Cebolla in 1858; we don't know where Metzger then lived. There were indications that he lived at Mora. If not together, they were on good terms at least until nine months before Isabel was born in 1864.

Just five days earlier, on August 6, 1860, the same census taker found Bibiana at her mother's home in Mora, at location number 3134, not far from Frank Metzger's store. She was probably just visiting. (See the next chapter for that census.)

Besides her grandfather, in April 1864 Elionor may have been living at La Cebolla with her mother Bibiana. Her mother had previously been with her father, Daniel Eberle, or had children by him, indicating a span of several years. Bibiana and her children may have lived with him in Las Vegas from 1848 through at least a portion of 1856, but some records show she had also lived at La Cebolla during at least part of that time. Bibiana and Eberle had Elionor, Andres and Maria Marta. Family tradition says they separated before or after the birth of Maria Marta, who was born in 1856. Then Bibiana and her children again (or still) lived with her father at La Cebolla. From about 1857 through some time in 1864, Bibiana and Metzger either lived together—but we don't know where that had been—*or* they just spent time together while she lived at La Cebolla and he lived at Mora or Buena Vista. Their three daughters were born in 1858, 1863 and 1864. We think Bibiana split with him before or after the birth of their third child, Isabel, in 1864. Sometime after they parted, Metzger and Apolonia were again together.

We don't know exactly when Apolonia had separated from her husband, Bernardo, but we know she and Frederick Metzger had Juanita, born in 1849, the same year Elionor was born to Bibiana and Daniel Eberle. We don't know when (or why) Apolonia and Metzger had separated earlier; we only know Bibiana and Metzger had their first child, Doloritas, in 1858, and their last in 1864. Court records about the later family lawsuit and what transpired before the suit began show their parting had not been amicable, at least not where Metzger was concerned.

The census shows Apolonia lived in Mora in 1860; she may have still lived there in April 1864. Records indicate Bibiana lived at La Cebolla with her father for at least a portion of the years she was having children by Frank Metzger. He originally lived at his ranch and home place that he established at Buena Vista. He later gave that property to his daughter Juanita and her husband Henry Korte. Where did he live while he and Bibiana were having children? Did he also live a portion of that time at his second ranch at La Cebolleta (aka Cebollita and La Cebolla), as indicated by Verna?

In the 1860 census, Bibiana's brother Manuel Gregorio lived at Mora with his mother, Apolonia. Did he leave his family again by 1864? He first disappeared in the late 1830s or early 1840s, returned in the late 1850s. Tradition says he again disappeared and was never again seen or heard from by his family. He also was never again mentioned in census or other records.

~~

There is a question for me as to when Andreas and Elionor moved from La Cebolla to what became their home place at Buena Vista. Their first children, Margaret and Pete, were born at La Cebolla. I believe Karl's story of his grandfather Pete's birth and early childhood indicates Elionor lived at La Cebolla with or very near her mother in the first years of her marriage. I wish we knew exactly where their home at "La Cebolla" was located, where Bernardo and Apolonia established their home that became home to Bibiana and all of her children. Rito de Cebolla meanders around Mora County lending its name to several small valleys and settlements, both west and east of Buena Vista. Records show a large number of people had resided at "La Cebolla" in Mora County, New Mexico. That name probably represented a composite of several small settlements along Rito de Cebolla. The *New Mexico Baptisms of Mora 1861-1878*, and the *New Mexico Baptisms of Mora 1879-1899*—both volumes edited by Armando R. Sandoval and Jill Montoya, published by the Hispanic Genealogical Research Center of New Mexico—list Cebolla, Cebolla Abajo, La Seboya, San Antonio Cebolla and San Jose de Abajo Cebolla. I believe the home Bernardo established at "La Cebolla" was less than 3 miles west of Buena Vista, off the highway near where a road heads to Ledoux (formerly the community of La Cebolla). Bernardo died at La Cebolla in 1873, and was buried in La Cebolla (now Ledoux) cemetery. That and other records point towards them living at that "Cebolla" area.

On the road to Ledoux, there remains, barely discernible, ruins of what had once been a fairly large hacienda with outbuildings. Even a large ceiling *viga* is still there. That is the location Karl and his cousins indicated was Bibiana's place, where their grandfather Pete (Peter Joseph) had been born, with the Cebolla Creek nearby. (Karl wrote that his grandfather, Pete, as a child at his grandmother's, had run out in the snow to bathe in the creek.) However, that is the same place and ruin Alvin Korte said his grandfather pointed out to him as a boy, when a portion of the adobe ruin still stood. He was told that was where Frank Metzger had lived.

Metzger's La Cebolla ranch and headquarters was secondary, a different tract of land, to his first established ranch and home at Buena Vista. Alvin had copies of Frank Metzger's land records, archived in Santa Fe, that provide descriptions and land coordinates. When my daughter, Tracy Ikenberry, and I were there with Alvin in the summer of 2013, he had a hand-held GPS unit. Using the coordinates in those documents, he zeroed in on that location, confirming it was the site of Frank Metzger's ranch house. He also pointed out the extent of Metzger's large ranch property, an expanse we could see while standing there; Henry Korte's lands adjoining his, said Alvin.

Perhaps the following newspaper article, found by Butch Sanders, reflects a portion of the affidavit Alvin had used that day that describes Metzger's Cebolla ranch. The sentence that says "known as the Metzger & Pinard Ranch of Buena Vista" seems to describe what we now know as Abel's Buena Vista Ranch.

El Hispano American
October 13, 1906

Veeder & Veeder - Land in Precinct No 5, acreage not given; one tract of land F. Metzger, Sebolla ranch, n. by the hill, s. by another hill or mountain on the other side of the Sebolla river, e. by land belonging to Henry Korte in the month of June, 1873, and known as the Metzger & Pinard ranch of Buena Vista, and also bounded by lands of one Jose Ignacio Martin and west by the mountains; also that tract of land known as the Frank Metzger, and also as the Pinard ranch at Buena Vista, n. by the Mora river, s. summit of the mountain, w. by the summit of the mountains of Buena Vista and Golondrinas.

Taxes $66.22
Penalty 3.34
Printing .... .70
Total $70.26

Maybe the home of Bernardo, Apolonia, Bibiana, and where her children grew up at La Cebolla was *near* Frank Metzger's property, also at Cebolla. The exact location of "Cebolla" where Bernardo establish his family's home remains uncertain to us.

I had multiple queries out asking about location(s) of "Cebolla." In October 2014, Danny Chaves responded: "I visited with several 'old-timers' over the last few days regarding La Cebolla. All seem to agree with what I've learned over the years. La Cebolla is the entire area above [*north of*] Mora. La Cebolla was several townships to include North and South El Carmen and El Oro. Due east from El Carmen is the valley I have always known as Cebolla or San Jose de la Cebolla (along the Rio Cebolla). Further along the valley and about 1/2 mile from where we visited the site with Chick [*we visited two sites that day; I believe he is indicating the one on the road to Ledoux*] are the remains of the old San Jose Church. Between this church and the site we visited is where rock corrals and a well are located (rock cliff). Beyond this rock cliff, further east, to include the [Henry?] Laumbach site is what has always been known to me as La Cebollita. North of La Cebollita is Buena Vista and east is the Buena Vista Ranch [*on which is*] the dissolved remains of what Chick suggested could be another related home." The "dissolved remains" Danny mentions is a barely discernable site Chick showed us in October 2013 that is in what he called the Veeder pasture, not far east of Abels' Buena Vista Ranch headquarters. Chick indicated the area east of Abels' ranch house, perhaps including the Veeder pasture, is also called La Cebollita (or Cebollcta). Rito de Cebolla also meanders through that area.

~~

The document Karl's sister, Ruth, found in Washington DC, probably dated spring 1862[i], states that Andreas D. Laumbach (presumably the son and not the father of that name) lived in Precinct Five in Mora County, Territory of New Mexico. I have found records that place Cebolla, as well as Buena Vista, in Precinct Five.

I wish we knew exactly where the census-taker's assigned household number for Bernardo, Bibiana, et al. was located. We only know the U.S. Census for 1860 places it in La Cebolla.

Apparently Bibiana and her mother were—at least in 1860—on good social terms with each other despite the relationship both held with Frank Metzger. We assume their bond began to come unglued long before 1886 when Bibiana's daughters filed the lawsuit against the heirs of Apolonia's daughter, Juanita. Metzger had transferred all of his assets to his son-in-law Henry Korte in 1873 to prevent access to it by his daughters by Bibiana. In March 1875, he basically disowned those daughters in court by paying off, with $3,000, any possible future claim to his estate by them and their mother. That was probably also to remove any claim by Bibiana and her daughters to her mother's—Apolonia's—estate.

Apolonia, who had lived with Metzger, her daughter Juanita and Henry Korte prior to her death, died before December 1873. She was gone when the suit began. Perhaps she had earlier been unaware of the extent of Metzger's intentions of later disinheriting a portion of her family.

~~

Several of Andreas and Elionor's children or their spouses became Presbyterian missionaries. Margarita Laumbach Cruz (1865-1958) and her husband, the Reverend Jose Emiterio Cruz (1855-1931) were active with the Presbyterian Church in northern New Mexico. Margaret had been educated in the church school at Mora, and then at the mission school in Las Vegas. She returned, for a while, to Buena Vista and resided with Alice Blake in a home converted to a Presbyterian teacher's home, school and meeting place. The two young women became life-long friends. Later Margaret worked at the mission school in Las Vegas, where she met the tall, handsome man who would become her husband, the Rev. Jose Emiterio Cruz. He was a widower with three small children: Robert, David and Lucrecia. They married in 1896 and the family lived in a nice home at Holman (which was originally named Agua Negra) in the Mora Valley. She became mother to them as well as the six she and J.E. had: Andreas, Juan, Alejandro, Bernardo "Barney," Rosa and Eleanor. She did her missionary work from home while she was responsible for all of those young children.

The Reverend Cruz was also a fine carpenter and built many area homes. After they married, he was assigned to Trementina. Margaret did not want to move there with their children, to a place with primitive conditions, but nevertheless she did. They served together there with Miss Alice Blake for five years. The two women were the only medical help the people had within a 60-mile radius. In addition to missionary work and providing medical assistance, they taught the residents domestic skills. The two women assisted at the births of many area children. Margaret and her family returned to Holman where they lived most of their remaining years.[ii] In her last years, Margaret lived with her daughter Rosa and husband, the Reverend Julián Duran. Margaret died June 16, 1958. Mother and I visited her in the Presbyterian Hospital in Albuquerque shortly before she died.

Margaret's son-in-law, the Reverend Julián Duran (1898-1995) was born in Dixon, New Mexico; his parents were some of the first to join the Presbyterian Church when its missionaries arrived in that area. Julián attended the Menaul Mission School in Albuquerque, and then the Coe College in Cedar Rapids, Iowa, and the College of Emporia at Emporia, Kansas, where he acquired his degree, and then graduated from the San Francisco Theological Seminary in San Anselmo, California. Thereafter he was ordained in Santa Fe and assigned to various churches and mission schools. Rosa Cruz had attended Hastings College in Nebraska. After he and Rosa married in 1929, they, too, were assigned to Trementina and worked with Miss Alice Blake. Like her mother had done, Rosa assisted Miss Blake with missionary work, teaching the people domestic skills, providing medical help and delivering babies. Julián also worked at Chimayo, Cordova and Truchas. They were later assigned to Trinidad, Colorado for a number of years and finally Albuquerque. Rosa died April 10, 1986 and Reverend Duran died at home on January 9, 1995 at age 97. They had three children: Julián Henry (middle name for Rosa's Uncle Henry), Eleanore Evelyn and Tomás Leonides "Leo."[iii]

Jesus Sito Candelario (1864-1938), born Jesus (HayZUS) but called Jesusito as a child, gave himself the middle name of Sito. His family was from Santa Fe, but as a young adult, he settled in Mora where he joined the Presbyterian Church. In 1888, he was assigned to and opened a little school in Rociada where he, and a few of his students, struggled to persevere in a predominantly Catholic setting. While Sito was assigned to the Chimayo Presbyterian mission church, he donated the church's bell.[iv] Years later when that church closed, Sito, with help from his brothers-in-law, transported that bell to his wife's family home at Buena Vista, where it resided for decades. When Aunties sold that place in 1948, they gave the bell to Tony, who transported it to his ranch at Sanchez. Tony built a tower to house it, where it remains at his ranch, now owned and operated by his heirs, the Martinez family.

Sito probably first developed his entertaining personality as a Presbyterian missionary, attempting to draw men's hearts and souls to his faith. He met Estefanita Laumbach in the Mora area. After they married, they moved to Santa Fe where he eventually, sometime *after* 1900, established his curio store. One of the many tall tales Sito told a gullible public was that his curio store had been established by his family in 1603, which would have even been before the founding of Santa Fe a few years later. Amazingly, there are still some who believe that tale today, and that "claim" is still seen on the old building that had once been his. His flamboyant personality drew considerable business to his store.[v] It was that and his acute business sense that made him financially successful and, during his lifetime, world-renowned.

~~

Andreas and Elionor had 12 children, nine of whom lived to adulthood: **Margaret** (born March 21, 1865, died June 16, 1958); Pedro, also known as **Peter Joseph** or Pete (June 29, 1867, died 1954); **Estefanita** (born January 28, 1870, died May 2, 1938); **Daniel** (born January 28, 1872, died August 5, 1947); **Henry** (born September 29, 1874, died September 10, 1929); **Anna** (born July 11, 1878, died May 10, 1958); **Crestina** (born September 30, 1881, died November 9, 1974); Maria Gracia "**Mary**" (born January 22, 1883, died November 5, 1965); and **Leonor** (born August 10, 1887, died August 16, 1974). Three died young: Alexander (born December 28, 1876); John A. (born May 23, 1886); and Cordelia (born November 20, 1891).

Margaret Laumbach photo; George Laumbach collection from Aunties, courtesy of Karl Laumbach.

Margaret Laumbach Margaret Laumbach Cruz at about 90 years old. Photo from Aunties' trunk; Anna Marie Ortega's collection. Courtesy of Karl Laumbach.

Estefanita and Crestina Laumbach photo from George Laumbach collection; courtesy of Karl Laumbach.

J. S. Candelario and Estefanita Laumbach. AnnaMarie Ortega collection; courtesy of Karl Laumbach.

Jesus Sito Candelario, Estefanita and Alice. John & Loris Candelario collection.

Eleanor Allison "Alice" Candelario, daughter of Estefanita & Sito Candelario.

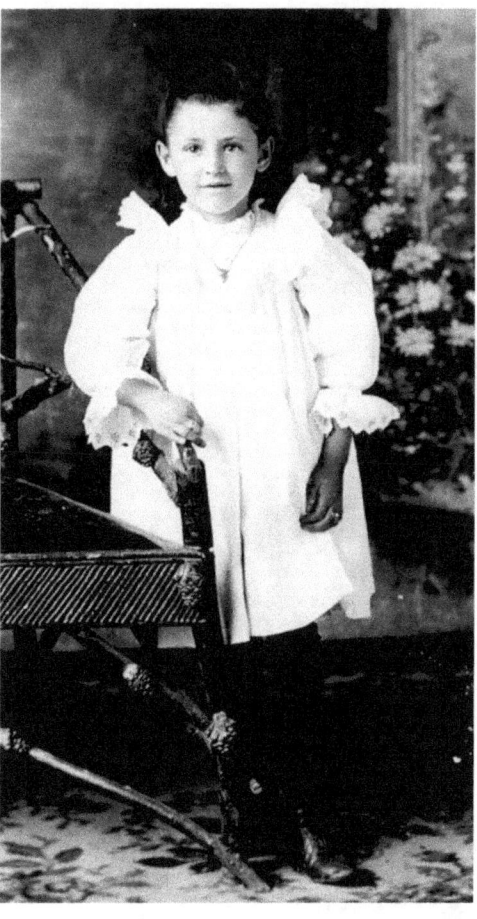

Note: Photos of Peter Joseph "Pete" Laumbach are absent from this chapter because many photos of him and his family are included with his chapter written by his grandson, Karl Laumbach.

Henry Laumbach and Natividad Hurtado on their wedding day. Verna L. Sparks collection.

Henry Laumbach. Verna L. Sparks collection.

Henry Laumbach at Buena Vista. Courtesy of Karl Laumbach.

Anna Laumbach. Duran collection; courtesy of Karl Laumbach.

Anna Laumbach and Rosa Cruz. Duran collection; courtesy of Karl Laumbach.

Daniel Laumbach. Verna L. Sparks collection.

Daniel with Alice Candelario. Verna L. Sparks collection

Crestina Laumbach. Duran collection; courtesy of Karl Laumbach.

Crestina Laumbach Sanchez. Duran collection; courtesy of Karl Laumbach.

Mary Laumbach. Duran collection; courtesy of Karl Laumbach.

Young Mary Laumbach. Verna L. Sparks collection.

Mary Laumbach in orchard at Buena Vista. courtesy of Karl Laumbach.

Mary Laumbach. George Laumbach collection from Aunties; courtesy of Karl Laumbach.

Leonor Laumbach. Courtesy of Karl Laumbach.

Leonor Laumbach. Duran collection; courtesy of Karl Laumbach.

Mary and Leonor with horses at Buena Vista. Courtesy of Karl Laumbach.

Leonor Laumbach. Duran collection; courtesy of Karl Laumbach.

Aunties Mary, Anna & Leonor with Adelina (daughter of Henry, raised by his sisters) at Buena Vista. Anna Marie Ortega's collection, courtesy of Karl Laumbach.

Rosa Cruz Duran (daughter of Margaret Laumbach Cruz), Adelina holding her son Albert, Aunt Anna holding Adelina's baby daughter Anna Marie.
Anna Marie Ortega's collection from Aunties, courtesy of Karl Laumbach.

Anna, Mary & Leonore among their flowers at Buena Vista. One of a series of photos taken by John Candelario. From collection of John and Loris Candelario.

I love the photos taken by John, especially because he made Aunties laugh! His are rare photos of Anna smiling and laughing. She was a beautiful girl and young woman but too often seemed sad in photos.

Margaret, Leonore, Mary, Crestina and Anna. The only Laumbach sister missing from this photo was Estefanita, who died in 1938. This was taken at Aunties' home on Hot Springs Boulevard at Las Vegas, near the Old Town Plaza. Anna Marie Ortega's collection from Aunties; courtesy of Karl Laumbach.

Once the home of Crestina Laumbach Sanchez on Valencia, off Old Town Plaza, Las Vegas.

Once the home of Aunties—Anna, Mary & Leonor Laumbach—on Hot Springs Boulevard, off Old Town Plaza in Las Vegas New Mexico.

Aunties themselves spelled Auntie Eleanor's name two ways, with and without an e at the end.

[i] Image of that document, courtesy Karl Laumbach, appears in chapter Andreas 1 & 2.

[ii] Presbyterian Missionaries in Rural Northern New Mexico, by Dale B. Gerdeman, published by the Menaul Historical Library of the Southwest, 1999.

[iii] Ibid.

[iv] Ibid.

[v] Ibid.

SECTION IV: LAUMBACHS IN NEW MEXICO

Chapter 22: Metzger and Korte
by Jan Girand

This vintage photo of Korte cowboys branding is in several family albums. It may have been taken in the 1880s. One thing is certain: The huge brand applied to the steer in the foreground is Henry Korte's. Based upon photos they've seen of Andrés, Karl Laumbach and his uncles believed the man squatting at lower right was Andrés Ebell. In that era, extended families and neighbors shared branding and other major ranching tasks. The man holding the branding iron is said to be Henry Korte. An older Korte kin of Alvin Korte's identified at least one man in the foreground as a Laumbach, but that is unconfirmed.

    Alvin thinks, because of information from his father or grandfather, that the branding scene was at a place locally called Arroyo de los Yutes (not to be confused with another place of that name, he said). He did not know where this scene was located. Chick Burney, manager of Abels' Buena Vista Ranch, is convinced he knows where this photo was taken and pointed it out to me. He believes it was within sight and walking distance east of the current ranch headquarters. Those headquarters would have been at the approximate same location as the Kortes' main house that burned. Chick showed me what he thinks is the same terrain as that depicted in this vintage photo. It does appear the same and seems logical, especially considering the woman standing on the upper right outer edge of the photo.

Was that Juanita? If that was the location where the photo was taken, it would have been an easy walk for her, in her long dress, from the house to where she stood that day. This photo was sharpened by Butch Sanders.

Frederick "Frank" Metzger, known as a Prussian emigrant called *El Aleman*, "the German" by locals in Mora, was believed to be of Jewish heritage. That seems to be confirmed by a period Jewish Ohio newspaper that reported happenings of his and Henry Korte's families in Mora.

Metzger arrived in New Mexico around 1846, the year New Mexico became a U.S. territory; he would have been about 27. He was born in Prussia. His burial marker says he was 66 years old at his death in 1885; therefore, he was born in 1819. An Ohio newspaper said he had come to New Mexico from St. Louis, Missouri.

Soon after his arrival in the Mora area, about 1848, Frank Metzger began establishing his presence there by buying property and beginning business enterprises. He was presumed single—that is, we know of no prior marital relationship before his arrival in New Mexico—when he met and joined with Apolonia. She was still legally married to but separated from Bernardo Martín. We do not know when they joined, but it must have been fairly soon after Metzger arrived in Mora because their daughter Maria Juanita Metzger was born in 1849. We are also uncertain whether they lived together under one roof, or just spent time together.

Verna said Metzger had bought a large parcel of land from "Father Pinard" at Buena Vista where he established his ranch and his home. Alvin Korte said Metzger bought his ranch from Father Jose Francisco Pinard, and that Henry Korte bought his property from the same priest. By all descriptions, it became a fine home[i] where Metzger initially lived, and also lived his last years with Apolonia, their daughter Juanita and her husband, Henry.

In his earlier years, Metzger had a profitable trade business running caravans of merchandise between Mora and St. Louis. He, later along with Henry Korte, also drove large herds of cattle great distances to market, where they sold them for many times more than what they would have sold locally. He was well compensated with huge profits for those weeks and months of considerable effort and risk. He began amassing his wealth by those enterprises and subsequent investments in large properties. He was also a shrewd and ruthless businessman. That was his "gold mine."

We do not know exactly when Metzger established his store on the St. Gertrudes Plaza de Mora, near the Santa Gertrudes parish church, but as he grew older, running trade caravans and herds of cattle to distant markets was replaced by sales of merchandise in a territory still starved for goods. He—and/or Henry Korte—also had a store, blacksmith shop and post office at their Buena Vista Ranch. (That historic, long adobe building has been preserved by its subsequent owners. Photos taken of it in 2013 are in Chapter 39.)

The U.S. census for Santa Gertrudes, Mora, New Mexico Territory, taken at Metzger's store, location 3128, on August 6, 1860 lists Frank Metzger, merchant, with three clerks, including one named I. T. St. Vrain. Metzger may have lived in an apartment in his store at least part of the time; his clerks may have also lived there. However, he and/or they may have instead lived nearby.

The numbers assigned by the census enumerator that August 6, 1860 day indicate that he found Apolonia living with her family six doors from the store at 3134. Apolonia "Gutierres" (listed as age 48); her daughter Maria Bibiana Martinez (listed as age 27, but she would have been closer to 33); her son Manuel Martinez (listed age 21, but he would have been about 30); and her daughter Maria Juana Metzger (listed as born at Mora, age 11, which was accurate). This time—unlike the census he took at La Cebolla five days later (see the previous chapter)—the same enumerator, Pedro Valdez, got the last names right. Also recorded in their household was a 20-year-old Indian servant named Sofia Gutierres. (It was then common for families to give their own surnames to their servants and slaves when they had them christened.) Since Bibiana was recorded in two different households on this year's census, she was probably just visiting her mother in Mora that day, and her residence was with her father and children at La Cebolla, even though her relationship with Metzger had already begun. Her appearance in her mother's home at Mora that day indicates the two women had a friendly relationship, at least then.

By 1860, Metzger and Bibiana had been keeping company for at least three years, but not necessarily under the same roof. We don't know where Metzger lived in 1860; there were several indications that he lived at Mora. If not living together, Metzger and Bibiana were on intimate terms at least until nine months before Isabel was born.

Exactly where was Apolonia's Mora household in 1860? The census-taker's assigned number does not necessarily mean she resided on lo de Mora plaza. There is a question about her exact location because of Metzger's current relationship with Bibiana. His and Bibiana's first daughter, Doloritas Metzger, was born in 1858 at La Cebolla according to her christening record. They would have two more daughters: Josefita Metzger born in 1863 and Isabelita Metzger born in 1864. The other two girls may have also been born at La Cebolla. Verna said Bibiana and Metzger split after the birth of Isabel.

Years later, a witness' court testimony said Metzger and Bibiana had been together 17 years, that Metzger divided his time between his La Cebolla ranch and Mora. They could not have been together for 17 years.

After Bibiana and Metzger had split—it was apparently a mighty rift—he was again with Apolonia, along with their daughter Juanita. The 1870 census shows them living together at Mora. Census and other records, and family, say Apolonia and Metzger spent their last years together living with Juanita and Henry Korte at the Buena Vista Ranch. That is where both of them died. Both were buried nearby in the little family cemetery.

~~

Henry Korte had arrived in Mora several years after Metzger came. He was not listed on an 1860 Mora census. We think he arrived in Mora sometime between 1860 and 1867. He would have been about 21 years old in 1860, younger than his friend, Metzger. In July 1867, Henry Korte married Juanita Metzger, age 18, his friend's daughter. One year later, their first child Anna Korte was born.

After his arrival in Mora, Henry had also bought land, adjoining Metzger's, from Fr. Pinard. Korte became Metzger's business partner. Later court testimony by witnesses said Metzger had given Juanita the money for Henry to buy a half-share of his businesses.

Soon after Juanita's and Henry's marriage, Frank Metzger began to dissolve—or make it appear that he dissolved—his partnership with Henry Korte. Metzger seemed to move *all* of his assets to Juanita and her husband. Metzger's estate was in excess of several hundred thousand, a huge sum for that era. He owned a successful store and mercantile business, a fine home, extensive properties stocked with cattle, and a considerable amount of liquidity in gold.

In 1872, Frank Metzger formally adopted his illegitimate daughter Juanita, when she was a married adult, to be sure she and her husband were the "sole and absolute" heirs of his estate. That was his first big step towards assuring that only she and Henry would benefit from his huge estate. Was that before Apolonia died?

We do not know exactly when Apolonia died; her burial marker is not visible in the little cemetery near the road to Golondrinas in Mora County. All we have is the entry recording Bernardo Martin's death in December 1873 that states Apolonia was then already deceased. Bibiana—living with her father when he died—must have provided that information to the officiating priest.

I first saw a copy of this photo when it was given to me by Faye Romero, mother of Mary Louise Maestas. Mary Louise had sent it and other material to her mother not long before she, Mary Louise, died. The studio's name imprinted on this photo, and the dates the studio's partners were in business in Las Vegas, set a time parameter for when it must have been taken. James N. Furlong arrived in Las Vegas, New Mexico from Massachusetts in 1875, and sometime after that, Theron Crispell joined him and they became partners. Their studio was located at Douglas Avenue and 7th Street. Even while Furlong was away for five years, 1885-1890, operating as a cattleman in Texas and California, Crispell continued the photographic business under their partnership. Some of their studio's famous photos

302

included Billy the Kid's pal Charles Bowdre and his wife Manuela; Pat Garrett; and photos pertaining to the Pancho Villa raid on Columbus, New Mexico. Their studio continued in Las Vegas until 1905.

The only person in this photo positively identified is Juanita Metzger, the darker haired young woman standing on the right. Her identity is certain because of the mole on her forehead, seen in other photos of her. According to the way the photographer arranged them, the man seated in front of her was her husband Henry Korte. He was ten years older than Juanita. Groups of people photographed together like this are connected. They are family or business associates or good friends; they are not strangers. This is most likely a family group photo. But who are the other people?

If living, Frank Metzger and Apolonia would have then been in a family photo with Juanita and Henry Korte. Some believed the older woman seated in front was Apolonia; she resembles her. However, she died before 1873 and would not have still been living when this photo was taken. Frank Metzger died in early 1885. If living when this photo was taken, he would have been much older than the young man standing in this photo. Some of our family believed the standing, pretty blonde woman was Bibiana because her description fits this woman. However, Bibiana had a daughter, Elionor, the same age as Juanita. Bibiana would have been about 58 when this photo was taken, and she would not have been in the Korte family photo anyway. The young blonde woman does not resemble Elionor. She is not young enough to be Anna Korte Naeglin, pretty blonde daughter of Juanita and Henry. Who was this pretty young woman? We believe this photograph was taken after February 1885. Aunties had also told Karl there never had been a photo of Bibiana, who died in Oct. 1897 at almost 70. No one has tried to guess the identity of the standing young man.

Most of the people in this photo are too young to have been those we wish they were. Except for Juanita and probably Henry Korte, we may never know the identities of all of the handsome people in this photo. We wish we did.

In May or June 1873, Frank Metzger formally retired, or made it appear that he retired, from his business partnership. He gave all of his assets and signed over all of his properties to his son-in-law Henry Korte.

In March 1875, Maria Bibiana Martinez signed an agreement in court giving up her legal right, and the rights of her children, to Metzger's estate in exchange for $3,000 from him. (Mary Louise Maestas, great-granddaughter of Maria Marta Ebel Esquibel, equated that "pay off" to the Biblical 30 pieces of silver.) That agreement was signed by Bibiana and witnessed by Ramon Bonney, Andres Ebell and Leonor (aka Elionor) Laumbach. Years later, the court deemed that she/they had no right to sign away her children's inheritances, especially her under-age daughters. (See the next chapter.)

Witnesses to the transaction testified in court that Frank Metzger gave Juanita the money for Henry to buy his first half of the partnership. Testimony under-oath described how Metzger, in front of those witnesses, also "sold" his second portion of the partnership to Henry. They described it like a shell game. They described Korte coming into the room with a box of gold to pay Metzger for his half-share of the partnership. Duly noted and witnessed, Metzger then told Korte to keep his box of gold, put it back where he had it. In other words, Metzger wanted Korte to appear to own both halves of the partnership. Korte did not actually buy Metzger's first or second half of the partnership. Witnesses testified that Metzger continued to own and control his businesses until his death.

Edward/Eduardo Korte, third son of Juanita and Henry Korte, was born on the Metzger-Korte Buena Vista Ranch in October 1880; his godparents were neighbors Andreas and Elionor Laumbach. That indicates that not long before the family lawsuit began, the Laumbachs and Juanita Metzger Korte, who died in 1889, were still on friendly terms.[ii] Juanita's father Frank Metzger had died four years earlier, in February 1885 at age 66.

303

In 1886, one year after Metzger died, Doloritas "Lola" Martinez/Metzger Cordova and her husband filed suit on behalf of herself and her sisters against Henry Korte over Metzger's estate. A year after that, in 1887, Anna Korte, daughter of Juanita and Henry, married William Naeglin. Henry Korte died in early January 1889, and in early September of that year, Juanita Metzger Korte died. But the lawsuit continued. Anna, age 21, and her new husband William Naeglin, asked the court to grant them guardianship of Anna's younger brothers: Charles, age 18; Frank, age 15; and Eduardo, age 10.

The suit brought by Bibiana's daughters was appealed by Juanita's heirs in 1898.

Anna died at age 41 in January 1909 and was buried in a Las Vegas cemetery. Her husband William Naeglin became the estate's administrator after her death.

Why did Frank Metzger have no will? Why did he try to assure that his daughter Juanita and her husband, Henry Korte, were the only ones to benefit from his estate? Why was he determined that Bibiana and her three daughters—Dolorita "Lola," Josefita and Isabelita—would never inherit anything from him? Everything said or written about Metzger (Henry Korte, too) indicates he was ruthless and probably unforgiving of even the smallest slight. Multiple suits had been filed against him by other people. Family tradition says Metzger had driven Andrés, Bibiana's son, away from home. He may have also driven away Ramon. Metzger was not a man admired by Bibiana's family.

~~

Publications of the time, and also testimony provided by witnesses during the ongoing family lawsuit, energized tales of hidden gold mines and stashes of gold, leading to the "Mora gold rush."

These are examples of published articles and testimonies contributing to the frenzy.

THE CANTON DAILY REPOSITORY
CANTON, OHIO
THURSDAY, FEBRUARY 12, 1885
An Old Timer Drops Dead.

LOS VEGAS, N. M., February 12. - Last week Frank Metzgar, an old timer, dropped dead while at the breakfast table. He was a merchant and ranchman, and was known to be very wealthy. No will was found, and the deceased was buried in a small cemetery built several years ago to receive his remains. It was reported that his worldly effects consisted of $250,000 in gold which was buried somewhere around his late residence. Great excitement prevailed over the fact. Henry Korte, a son-in-law, dug down in Metzgar's cellar, but did not find the pot of gold supposed to be hidden there. Metzgar lived in St. Louis prior to coming here. He was fifty-six years old and started his fortune in freighting across the plains in the early days. It is believed his gold will be found.

An 1891 transcription of court testimony stated that Metzger and Korte had no faith in banks or the people who controlled them. They hid their considerable amounts of gold around their properties. "A fortune in gold pieces lies hidden away in the bosom of mother earth," said a witness.

The private Metzger-Korte cemetery near Buena Vista in Mora was vandalized and graves opened. Headstones were broken and stolen. The Laumbach family cemetery at Buena Vista was also disturbed, primarily Bibiana's grave. When Mary Louise Maestas (great-granddaughter of Maria Marta Ebel Esquibel) had been a 4th or 5th grade school teacher at Las Vegas, a student wrote a paper telling about riding with his parents in a car on a certain section of highway near Mora. His father was driving, his mother beside him in the front seat, the boy in the back seat. Suddenly a woman dressed in white appeared on the road in front of the car. His father panicked and wanted to swerve or pull over. His mother grabbed the wheel and mashed the gas pedal with her foot. Their car surged forward, passing through the woman. The amazed and frightened boy turned around and looked back; the woman, intact, still stood in the road. A few years later, that same boy was in 8th grade and wrote about a time, when he was much younger, when his parents had dug into "a lady's grave" searching for gold. That teacher showed the paper to Mary Louise. Putting the two stories together, along with other things she had heard, Mary Louise believed they were two parts of the same story. The "lady's grave" was Bibiana's. So was the ghost. In the early 1970s, Tony Sanchez—then the caretaker of the Laumbachs' cemetery at Buena Vista—returning from there, stopped to see my mother and me in Springer. I had never before or since seen Tony, a gentleman, so furious. Someone had dug into Bibiana's grave and opened it.

For generations *cuentos* (tales) and *corridos* (ballads)—some of which made their way into publications—were told about *El Alemans*, Metzger and Korte, sometimes including a Laumbach. They were about secret gold mines and buried gold, mostly belonging to Metzger, but also Korte, sometimes also Laumbach. Our family heard of several instances of gold stashes that were found. One, with more than one version, said hired-hand William Naeglin secretly watched Henry Korte bury a stash in the corner of a field. When Korte was dying, Naeglin dug up the stash and ran away with the gold and Korte's daughter, Anna. That is the story heard by at least two generations of our family.

The following voice of reason was expressed by Butch Sanders about that tale: "William Naeglin and Anna Maria Korte [had married before] William Henry Korte's death. [They] married at Mora 18 July 1887. Their first child, Emil Gustave Naeglin, was born 18 June, 1888. William Henry Korte (better known as Henry) didn't die until 5 January, 1889. If [they] eloped, which is possible, they did it about 18 months *before* Korte died. As to Naeglin digging out a package from the fence post-hole or in the corner of a corn field, he could have dug it up before Korte's death (or before the elopement if there had been one), or he could have returned after Korte's death and retrieved the treasure. Or it never happened. My guess," wrote Sanders, is that "over time as the story was retold, Korte, digging for his just-deceased father-in-law's (Metzger's) pot of gold evolved into Naeglin digging up his just-deceased father-in-law's (Korte's) package of wealth."

I have traced this buried gold story back to the Metzger de Gallegos family in Las Vegas.

Various pieces of documentation confirm Butch's correction of the family's long-held *cuento*. After her parents died, Anna and William Naeglin legally adopted her brothers. They remained in Mora and played active roles in the family lawsuit. They probably did not leave Mora until after the lawsuit finally ended and they lost their Buena Vista home.

A "lost" or "secret" gold mine ranked high among tales told by some family and outsiders to explain Metzger's wealth. Multiple versions of a folktale or *cuento* of a secret gold mine were repeatedly told in areas of northern New Mexico. That led a couple fellows affiliated with Highlands University to record, transcribe, translate and publish one of those: *The Lost Gold Mine of Juan Mondragón, A Legend from New Mexico Performed by Melaquías Romero*, edited by Charles L. Briggs and Julián Josuá Vigil, published in 1990 by the University of Arizona Press. It is in Spanish with English translation. Ballads and legends are not expected to be factual, but the section providing the ballad's historical background has inaccuracies. John G. White, born John Gallegos to Jose Rafael and Isabel Gallegos, provided Metzger family history and information for the genealogy chart to the book's authors/editors. White was a grandson of Bibiana and Frank Metzger. The White/Gallegos family also provided information about "the lost mine" to Xanthus Carson. Carson's folktales composite was even more convoluted. Carson's published piece added frenzy to the Mora area gold rush. Additional stories about the fabled gold mine were published in various magazines.

Verna and I always doubted Metzger or Korte had a gold mine. I believe Metzger's wealth came from his business shrewdness. Tales of his gold mine evolved from his amazing wealth. Perhaps those tales were given credibility because there actually had been one or two mines in the Mora area with family connections.

The following two photos of J.S. Candelario's mine and winch came from Aunties' family album, courtesy of Karl Laumbach. The first one is of Uncle Henry with Uncle Sito holding the rifle.

(Butch Sanders observed how carelessly Sito held the rifle, at risk of shooting himself in the foot or filling the barrel with dirt. That indicates Sito's inexperience with guns.) The second photo is of Uncle Sito, still holding the rifle, with his son-in-law Arthur Weeks. Arthur's glasses obscure his eyes in the photo. J.S. Candelario's mine had been reported in a Santa Fe newspaper article.

Danny Chavez provided the next photo that he took in 2014 of the old Laumbach mine shaft on the Allsups' ranch. (This mine was probably Andreas Laumbach's "dig" because it was on his ranch.) Danny said he remembered, in the late 1970s, when Mr. Lorenz Shock (then-owner of the ranch) granted ingress to three Albuquerque TV stations for installation of their translator units near the mine site. Mr. Shock and his neighbor, Mr. Unger, were both retired geophysicists. They provided Danny, in his second year of college majoring in geology, the opportunity to learn local geology. Mr. Shock regarded "the Laumbach Mine" while the TV towers were being erected. Both men wondered what mineral the late Mr. Laumbach hoped to find in an exclusively sedimentary rock environment, certainly not gold. Whatever he sought, he was unsuccessful. There were no riches there.

Danny vaguely remembered a possible wooden framework to the mine, a vertical shaft. Time and elements took their toll; the shaft progressively caved in, he said.

Comparing the photos, this "Laumbach mine" was at a different location than Sito's, but both were in the Buena Vista-Mora area. Both the J.S. Candelario mine and the Laumbach mine were unsuccessful, regardless their intended purpose. Neither produced anything of value.

Following are ruins of Frank Metzger's large store on what had been the original plaza of Santa Gertrudes de Mora. Verna had described it as being very close to—with only a narrow alley between—the Santa Gertrudes church that burned in the 1960s. Photo taken by Tracy Ikenberry in June 2013.

There is no known photo of Frederich "Frank" Metzger. This is his grave marker in the private Metzger-Korte family cemetery near Buena Vista, Mora County, New Mexico. Photo taken June 2013 by Tracy Ikenberry. "Frank Metzger died Feb. 4, 1885 aged 66 years."

This photo of Heinrich "Henry" Korte, husband of Juanita Metzger, is from the family album of Daniel and Emma Laumbach, Verna L. Sparks collection.

Henry Korte's grave marker in the private Metzger-Korte family cemetery near Buena Vista, Mora County. Photo taken June 2013 by Tracy Ikenberry. "Henry Korte died Jan. 6, 1889, aged 50 years."

Below is Juanita Metzger's grave marker in the Metzger-Korte family cemetery near Buena Vista. Photo taken June 2013 by Tracy Ikenberry. "Juanita wife of Henry Korte died … aged 40 years." Juanita died in September 1889, within nine months of her husband, Henry. Years ago, the graves in this private cemetery were disturbed and stones broken. These markers for Henry and Juanita Korte were stolen and missing for many years. They were recently returned to the cemetery, repaired and reset, by Alvin Korte and Bobby Korte.

---

i The original Metzger-Korte home burned about 1975 when the Thompson family, then owner of the ranch, was away. Tony Sanchez, returning from a visit to Buena Vista, came by my mom's home at Springer to tell us about the fire. He was saddened for the Thompsons' loss and for the total loss of the Metzger-Korte home where Apolonia had last lived and died. The Thompsons were friends of Tony's. They rebuilt a different type home in approximately the same location. I have heard that the Thompson family buried their young daughter and her beloved horse near the Metzger-Korte family cemetery.

ii Butch Sanders found Juanita Metzger, age 11, listed on the 1860 census record for the Catholic mission school, Convent of Our Lady of Light, also known as the Loretto Academy, in Santa Fe. She was one of 33 students, including Maria St. Vrain also of Mora. Alvin said Metzger probably paid for Juanita's boarding and education at Loretto.

Verna L. Sparks' words on the back of the following original artwork: "Colored pencil sketch of blue flowers painted by Juanita Metzger. Juanita painted this while attending the mission school [Loretto Academy] at Santa Fe. Juanita married Henry Korte and lived at the Metzger-Korte Ranch (later called the Veeder Ranch) near my grandmother's home. She gave the picture to my Grandmother Elionor. Auntie Leonore gave it to me July 1966 because I always admired it when it hung in the old Laumbach home at Buena Vista."

Following is a letter dated October 1880 from Henry Korte and Juanita Metzgar (sic) de Korte to "Señor Don Andres Lomber y Doña Leonor Lomber." (Addressing someone by both Señor and Don shows high respect.) The letter requests Mr. & Mrs. Laumbach to be godparents for their child, to stand with them at his christening on October 17.

An archived sacramental entry shows that Eduardo Korte (Alvin's grandfather) was born in October 1880. Andreas D. and Eleanore Laumbach served as his *padrinos* at his baptism on October 17, 1880. This letter is Henry's and Juanita's formal request to Andreas and Elionor/Leonor to serve as their infant son's godparents.

Mora N. M. Oct 12 de 1880

Señor Dn Andres Somber
y Da Leonor Somber.

Muy Señores Nuestros.
　　　　　　En cumplimiento al
sacro deber a que estamos obligados
como padres, nos hacemos el honor
de solicitar a sus muy dignas y
honradas personas con el respecto
debido, para que se dignen venir
a sacar de tinieblas a la luz de la
Gracia por medio de las aguas
regeneradoras del Santo Bautismo
a un infante que Dios nuestro Señor
ha sido servido de darnos a luz.
Confiados que nos honraran con nuestra peticion, suplicamos de la bondad
de Vds. se sirvan venir para el Domingo

que contaremos diez y siete del corriente.

Con esto quedamos de Vds con alto respecto.

Henry Korte y
Juanita Nitzgar de Korte

SECTION IV: LAUMBACHS IN NEW MEXICO

Chapter 23: Henry Korte Civil Lawsuit

John D.W. Veeder and Thomas B. Catron were attorneys for Dolores "Lola" and her sisters. If Bibiana's daughters finally won the suit, why did their attorney, Veeder, end up with the Metzger-Korte ranch? William Naeglin was the final appelee/defendant—Henry Korte and his daughter, Anna, William's wife, had died before the case ended—who ultimately lost the case. Was this lawsuit filed on the contingency that the loser—the Metzger-Korte heirs, who had been in possession of the ranch—pay all court costs and attorney fees? Regardless, after years of wrangling in court, the ranch property was all that was left with which to pay attorneys and court costs.

When this civil case began, Henry and Juanita Korte—as Frank Metzger's heirs—were wealthy by inheritance of his estate. Dolores and her sisters had no wealth. They probably had no assets, but they and their attorneys believed they would win because they had right on their side. The case went on for years. In the end, the court found a.) Bibiana had no legal right to sign away her children's inheritance to their father's estate and, therefore, that "$3,000 document" was not legally binding. And b.) New Mexico law stipulated that, in the absence of legitimate heirs, illegitimate heirs inherit equally. The court found that all four of Frank Metzger's illegitimate daughters—Juanita, Doloritas, Josefita and Isabel—were equally entitled to his estate. All of Metzger's efforts to control his estate after he was gone were wasted. He had written no will. Regardless of his intentions, his chosen heirs lost everything.

The following court record was found by researcher Butch Sanders, who transcribed it.

Reports of Cases Determined in the Supreme Court of the Territory of New Mexico[i]
By New Mexico Supreme Court
Published by New Mexican Printing Co., 1897
Item notes: v.7 (1893: Jan. 3 1895:Aug. 24)
Original from Harvard University

Page: 678—685
[No. 582. August 24, 1895.]

DOLORITAS MARTIN DE CORDOVA Et AL.
Appellants, v. HENRY KORTE
Et al., Appellees.

Bill Of Discovery—Reference To Master—Presumption.—In a proceeding, by bill in equity, against an administrator, for a discovery and accounting, where the entire case was referred to a master, without objections, to take testimony and report his findings of fact and conclusions of law thereon, it will be presumed that the reference was made by consent of all the parties.

ID.—Conflicting Evidence—Findings Of Fact By Master—Presumption.—The findings of fact by a master, depending upon the weight of conflicting testimony, are presumptively correct, and are not to be disturbed, unless it clearly appears there has been error or mistake on his part, and any disregard of this rule by the court, acting solely on the master's report, is reversible error.

ID.—Admissibility Of Parol Evidence To Prove Partnership Name In Deed.—Parol evidence is admissible to prove that the name of a party, mentioned as grantee in a deed, is a partnership name.

Appeal, from a decree in favor of defendant, from the Fourth Judicial District Court, San Miguel County. Reversed.

The facts are stated in the opinion of the court.

T. B. Catron and J. D. W. Veeder for appellants.

Long & Fort for appellees.

Bantz, J.—This is a suit in chancery brought by Doloritas Martin de Cordova and others, as the natural heirs of Frederick Metzger, against Henry Korte. After the issues were made up, Henry Korte died, and the cause was revived against his heirs and representatives. The bill, briefly stated, avers that Metzger died in Mora county in 1885, possessed of a large real and personal estate, consisting of merchandise, cattle, horses, ranches, and farms; that Metzger, at the time of his death, was in partnership with Korte, under the name of Henry Korte; and that Metzger had made conveyances of all of his property to Korte, which were really intended for the use of the partnership conducted under the name of Henry Korte, and had contributed $100,000 to the firm, which was indebted to him in that sum at the time of his death. The bill further avers that Korte took out letters of administration upon Metzger's estate, and falsely and fraudulently inventoried the property as of the value of only $180, and that he had refused to account for the balance. It is also alleged that complainants are the children of Metzger, an unmarried man, and of one Viviana Martin, an unmarried woman, and that Metzger left surviving him, no other natural children or descendants. A discovery and accounting are prayed, and that the property of the firm, held in the name of Henry Korte, to which Metzger's heirs would be entitled, be decreed to complainants, and for general relief. The defendant's answer denied all of the material allegations of the bill, and alleged that Metzger left surviving him one Juana, the wife of Korte, a natural child of Metzger, by whom she had been adopted. The court below, without objection from either side, referred the whole case to a master, to take testimony and report his findings of fact and conclusions of law. A large amount of testimony was taken, and a great many witnesses were examined by the parties. The principal question of fact seems to have been in regard to certain conveyances made in June, 1873, by Metzger to Henry Korte, covering all of his visible property, real and personal, the consideration of which, as named, was $18,330 in money and $2,300 in book accounts. The complainants introduced a number of old and intimate neighbors and business acquaintances, who testified that, after these conveyances, Korte and Metzger, in the presence of each other, repeatedly said that they were in business together, as partners in equal shares, under the name of Henry Korte, and that both of them seemed to have control and direction of the business, as such partners. One of the witnesses introduced by the defendants, who was a subscribing witness to the deeds, testified that, when the deeds were delivered, Metzger said to Korte: "Henry, here is your papers. Hand me my money." This occurred in the store, and there was a little room adjoining, into which Korte went, and brought out a hat box which contained bundles of money, each having around it a white paper band, whereon was marked the amount of the contents. They looked over the figures on the bundles, and then Metzger told Korte to take the money and put it away again; and

Korte took the money, and put it back in the place where he got it from. On the part of the defendants, witnesses were introduced to show that Metzger ceased all control of the store and other property after the conveyances, and had repeatedly said that he had sold out to Korte, and a receipt for the consideration named was also shown in evidence. The answer avers that Metzger intended to go to Europe, and had sold out to Korte with that expectation, but that he afterward reconsidered his visit to Europe, and, being much attached to his daughter, Korte's wife, continued to live with her until his death. The master found that Korte had not in reality paid Metzger anything for the property, and that, in truth and in fact, Metzger and Korte were partners after the conveyances. The master expressly found that it was not the purpose of Metzger to disinherit his children, the complainants, and he recommended a decree in their favor. The defendants filed exceptions to the report of the master, and the court below sustained the exceptions, and entered a decree for the defendants, dismissing the bill; and this cause was brought here by appeal.

1. The findings of the master were upon disputed questions of fact, and were reached after weighing the conflicting testimony of a large number of witnesses. He had many opportunities afforded, by observation, for judging of the intelligence, character, and credit of the witnesses, which could not be obtained from the dry transcript of the testimony. The court below had, in the nature of things, no better facilities for weighing and judging that testimony correctly than an appellate court would have. It is not within the general province of a master to pass upon all the issues in an equity case, and it has been said that it is not competent for the court to refer the entire decision of the case to him, without the consent of the parties. Kimberly v. Arms, 129 U. S. 517. In the case at bar the court referred all of the issues to the master, without objection, and the parties united in executing the order. Consent is to be presumed where there is no objection. In Medsker v. Bonebrake, 108 U. S. 69, the bill was filed to set aside a deed to the debtor's wife, on the ground of fraud upon his creditors, and the issues were referred to a master without objection. The master found the issues for the defendants, but the circuit court overruled the master on the facts, and entered a decree for complainants. On appeal to the supreme court the lower court was reversed, and Mr. Justice Miller remarked: "The evidence taken by the master was reported with his findings, and the case seems to have been treated by the court below without much regard to the finding of facts by the master, or any special regard to the exceptions made to his report. This is not correct practice in chancery in the circuit courts of the United States, whatever may be the rule in the state courts. The findings of the master were *prima facie* correct." In Kimberly v. Arms, 129 U. S. 517, the rule is laid down that the report of a master upon disputed questions of fact should be treated "as so far correct and binding as not to be disturbed unless clearly in conflict with the weight of the evidence upon which they are made." And in Tilghman v. Proctor, 125 U. S. 149, Mr. Justice Gray says: "In dealing with these exceptions, the conclusions of the master, depending upon the weighing of conflicting testimony, have every reasonable presumption in their favor, and are not to be set aside or modified unless there clearly appears to have been error or mistake on his part." See, also, Davis v. Schwartz, 155 U. S. 633; Trow v. Berry, 113 Mass. 146; Howe v. Russell, 36 Me. 327; In re Murray, 13 Fed. Rep. 551; Greene v. Bishop, 1 Cliff. C. C. 186. The decisions on this subject by the Supreme Court of the United States are specially pertinent, in view of section 522, Compiled Laws. If the rule in regard to the effect of a master's finding of facts were otherwise, the service of the master, now so generally employed to pass upon all the issues of fact, would be of little aid to the administration of justice. Mason v. Crosby, 3 Woodb. & M. 269. If the findings of the master had been based upon illegal testimony, or he had misapplied the law of the facts, in drawing his conclusions as to them, there would undoubtedly have been good ground for setting his findings aside. Troy Iron & N. Factory v. Corning, 6 Blatchf. 332. But no exception was filed upon such ground, and none was urged here. It has been urged that the

presumptions in favor of a master's report apply only in the court below, and upon appeal from the district court, the presumption is in favor of that court's action. In Howard v. Scott, 50 Vt. 52, the court says, "Neither the court of chancery, nor the supreme court on appeal, will review the findings in regard to the weight to be given to the testimony." And in Medsker v. Bonebrake, Tilghman v. Proctor, and Kimberly v. Arms, the Supreme Court reversed the court below for overruling the master's finding of fact. The court below had, as we have, a mere dry transcript of testimony upon which to base conclusions of fact. It will be necessary to determine whether the findings of fact by a master, which have some evidence to sustain them, will be treated as unassailable in all respects as the verdict of a jury. It will be sufficient to say in this case that the findings of fact by a master, which depend upon the weight of conflicting testimony, have every presumption of correctness in their favor, and are not to be set aside or modified unless there clearly appears to have been error or mistake on his part, and that a disregard of this rule by the district court, acting solely on the master's report, and without any new testimony, is reversible error.

2. If this case had been one depending upon proof of an oral agreement, made at the time of the conveyance, to take and hold the real property conveyed by Metzger to Korte in trust for Metzger, it would seem that the statute of frauds would have been an insuperable bar, as such an express trust must have been manifested or proved by writing, although it need not have been so created and declared. 1 Perry, Trusts, sec. 79; Movan v. Hays, 1 Johns. Ch. 341. And the same result would probably have occurred, had the complainants' right depended merely upon proof that the consideration mentioned in the deeds had not in fact been paid by Korte to Metzger. Evidence will be received to contradict the recitals in the deed as to the considerations paid, in order to establish a debt from the grantee to the grantor, but not for the purpose of defeating the operation of the conveyance, or creating a resulting trust. To allow parol evidence for such a purpose would be to break in upon the express provisions of the statute of frauds. 1 Perry, Trusts, sec. 162. But in this case the bill, the proofs, and the findings of the master proceed upon the theory, and the point to which the evidence mainly directed was, that the name of Henry Korte was used in this matter as a firm name by the partnership composed of Metzger and Korte; and it was, therefore, a simple question of identity, and not a case of express trust, depending upon oral proofs, or a case of resulting trust, depending upon the nonpayment of the consideration named in the deed. And, indeed, that seems to have been the view of the learned solicitors for the defendants, as no point was raised upon either such ground. The absence of actual consideration was a fact to be weighed in connection with other testimony upon this subject, as equity naturally looks with suspicion upon conveyances made to strangers without consideration. Id. The name of one of the partners may be used as a firm name. Though a presumption may arise that it was a personal transaction, yet the proofs may show it to be one of partnership. Bank v. Monteath, 1 Denio, 404; Winship v. Bank, 5 Pet. 529.

It, therefore, appearing from the report of the master that the facts were with the complainants as to the ownership by the firm of the property held by Henry Korte, and the complainants, being the heirs of Metzger, became vested with his interest, it is therefore ordered that the cause be reversed and remanded, with directions to the district court to enter a decree in conformity with the findings and recommendations of the master, and for such further proceeding therein as the nature of the case may require.

Smith, C. J., and Collier, Hamilton, and Laughlin, JJ., concur.
Another edition of this can be found beginning on page 526 of the following:

The Pacific Reporter
By West Publishing Company
Published by West Pub. Co., 1895
Item notes: v.41 (1895)
Original from Harvard University

United States Supreme Court Reports
By United States Supreme Court, Walter Malins Rose, Lawyers Co-operative Publishing Company, LEXIS Law Publishing
Published by LEXIS Law Pub., 1901
Item notes: v.171-174 1901
Original from the University of Michigan

Page: 315—316

WILLIAM NAEGLIN, Annie Naeglin, Administratrix of Henry Korte, Deceased, et al., Áppts.,

v.

DOLORITAS MARTIN DE CORDOBA, Jose Manuel Cordoba, Josefita Martin de Duran, et. al.

(See 8. C. Reporter's ed. 638—641.)

Appeal from Supreme Court of Territory—release by mother of illegitimate children— when will not cut off inheritance.

1. On appeal from the supreme court of a territory, when no jury was had and there are no questions as to the admission or exclusion of testimony, the only question to consider is whether the findings of fact sustain the decree.

2. A release by the mother of illegitimate children, in her own right and for them, of all claims against the father, without the sanction of any tribunal, will not cut off a right of the children to inherit from him.

3. A natural guardian has no power to release the claim of a ward to an inheritance without the sanction of some tribunal.

[No. 35.]

Argued October 15, 1898. Decided October 24, 1898.

APPEAL from the Supreme Court of the Territory of New Mexico reversing the decree of the District Court of the County of Mora, Fourth Judicial District in said Territory, in favor of the defendants, and remanding the case to the District Court with instructions to enter a decree in favor of the plaintiffs, in an action brought by Doloritas Martin de Cordoba et al. against William Naeglin et al. to establish the right of the plaintiffs as the children and heirs of one Frederick Metzger. Affirmed. See same case below, 7 N. M. 678.

Statement by Mr. Justice Brewer:

On March 29, 1886, the appellees, Doloritas Martin de Cordoba et al., filed their bill in the district court of the county of Mora, fourth judicial district, territory of New Mexico, to establish their rights as the children and heirs of one Frederick Metzger. After answer the case was referred to a master, who reported findings of fact and conclusions of law in favor of the plaintiffs. Upon a hearing in the district court a decree was entered adversely to the conclusions of the master and for the defendants. On appeal to the supreme court of the territory that decree was on August 24, 1895, reversed, and one entered remanding the case to the district court, with instructions to enter a decree in conformity with the findings and conclusions of the master. Thereupon the defendants appealed to this court.

At the time of entering the decree, and also of overruling a petition for rehearing, no statement of facts was prepared by the Supreme Court, and no other determination of the facts than such as appears from the direction to enter a decree in conformity with the findings and recommendations of the master. But after the Supreme Court had adjourned, an application was made to have the findings of fact made by the master incorporated into the record as a statement and finding of facts by that court, for the purpose of an appeal, and upon that application the following order was entered:

And now the foregoing statement and finding as to the facts proven and established by the evidence in each of said causes are ordered to be incorporated in the record of said supreme court as part thereof as fully as we may be thereunto empowered, the July term of the supreme court having been adjourned on the 26th day of September, A. D. 1896, and this order made and signed by each of the judges while in his district respectively.

 Thomas Smith, Chief Justice.

 Needham C. Collier, Associate Justice, Supreme Court of New Mexico.

Signed at Silver City, in the third judicial district.

 Gideon D. Bantz, Associate Justice of the Supreme Court of New Mexico and Presiding Judge of the Third Judicial District Court.

Signed at Santa Fé, N. M., in the first judicial district.

 N. B. Laughlin. Associate Justice of the Supreme Court and Judge of the First Judicial District.

It appears from the bill, answer, and findings that Frederick Metzger, though an unmarried man, was the father of several children by different women, and this suit is one between the several illegitimate children to determine their respective rights to share in his estate. The counsel for appellants says in his brief: "The bill of complaint and the testimony present for determination of the court two questions: First, What estate and property did Metzger own at the time of his death? And, second, who is entitled to that estate?"

Mr. Harvey Spalding for appellants.
No counsel for appellees.

Mr. Justice Brewer delivered the opinion of the court:

No question is made in this record as to the admission or exclusion of testimony. There being no jury the case comes here on appeal, and the only question we can consider is whether the findings of fact sustain the decree. 18 U. S. Stat. 27; Stringfellow v. Coin, 99 U. S. 610 [25:421]; Cannon v. Pratt. 99 U. S. 619 [25:446]; Neslin v. Wells, 104 U. S. 428 [26:802]: Hecht v. Boughton, 105 U. S. 235. 236 [20:1018]; Gray v. Howe, 108 U. S. 12 [27:034]: Eilers v. Boatman, 111 U. S. 356 [28:454]: Zeckendorf v.

Johnson. 123 U. S. 817 [31:277]; Sturr v. Beck, 133 U. S. 541 [33:761]; Mammoth Min. Co. v. Salt Lake Foundry & Machine Co. 151 U. 8. 47 [38:229].

The order signed in vacation by the several members of the supreme court cannot be considered an order of the court. Assuming, however, for the purposes of this case, that, in view of the general language in the opinion of the court, we may take the findings of the master as its statement of facts, we observe that no doubtful question of law is presented for our determination. The master finds that Metzger was the father of the appellees, and that he owned certain property. These are questions of fact, resting upon testimony, concluded, so far as this court is concerned, by the findings, and into which it is not our privilege to enter.

While under the common law illegitimate children did not inherit from their father, the statutes of New Mexico introduced a new rule of inheritance (Comp. Laws New Mexico, 1884, 1435, p. 680): "Natural children, in the absence of legitimate, are heirs to their father's estate, in preference to the ascendants, and are direct heirs to the mother if she dies intestate." In other words, under this statute, there being no legitimate children, illegitimate children inherit.

It appears that on March 19, 1875, and while Metzger was living, the mother of these plaintiffs, then minors, in her own right and for the minors, receipted and relinquished all claims against him. Without stopping to consider what was meant by that release, and giving to it all the scope which its language may suggest, we remark that a natural guardian has no power to release the claim of a ward to an inheritance without the sanction of some tribunal. Woerner's American Law of Guardianship, p. 185, and following.

The decree is affirmed.

_____

[i] This court case among others can be accessed with a search engine via the Internet.

SECTION III—LAUMBACHS IN NEW MEXICO

Chapter 24: AUNTS, UNCLES AND EVENTS
by Verna Laumbach Sparks 1909-1996

Uncle Bonney

With nearly all her neighbors being Spanish-speaking people, Mama realized she needed to learn the language. With the help of a Spanish grammar book, she learned quite a bit the first year, but what most helped her the second year was having Uncle Bonney's son, Ramon, teach her. They taught each other; he wanted to learn English as much as she wanted to learn Spanish. They would point to a chair and each give a name for it. That sort of thing went on all day.

Mama even gave him spelling lessons. One day they came to a word, "lightning," which really bothered him. Mama repeated it several times, and finally Mabel, one year old, said "jightnihng," and young Ramon forgot to worry and laughed.

Uncle Ramon Bonney was Papa's great-half-uncle. He was Bibiana's son by her first husband, James Bonney of La Junta (Watrous). He loved his mother, but as he grew up, he left home to lead a wandering, adventurous sort of life.

He freighted out of Denver for Fort Union a few years, and had many interesting experiences. One time he learned there was an outlaw in jail nearby at Fort Union [*which was what Ramon had always said, but history says it must have been at Las Vegas*] also named Bonney. He went to see William Bonney (Billy the Kid) and talked to him through the bars, but they could not establish a relationship. Perhaps Uncle Bonney chose to not admit to his family or others that he had a kinship with the outlaw.

He *did* find a relative in Denver when he met his father's brother, Henry Bonney. His uncle was wealthy and offered to adopt Ramon if he would give up his freighting and go live with him. But Uncle Bonney thought about his mother, whom he might not see again, and refused. He never heard from his uncle again.

Later, Uncle Bonney married, had children, and seemed to settle down. He was acquiring cattle and horses and doing pretty well, but he found ranch life monotonous. He left his wife and children and began to travel around again.

As the years went on, Uncle Bonney seemed to wander from place to place to see his many relatives. He stayed quite a bit at our ranch because he liked Mama. He used to help her around the house and take care of the babies. He was gentle with them, perhaps remembering his own.

He had a marvelous appetite. Aunties at Buena Vista told of a time when he was leaving their home one morning after eating a huge breakfast. They handed him a lunch to take along to eat later. He looked at it a minute, went to the table, sat down, opened the lunch box and ate it all, every bit of it. He explained that it was too much trouble to carry a lunch around with him—it was easier to just eat it! His appetite had always been good at our house, too.

Sometimes the children, especially Joyce, called him Uncle Boney, the way some people pronounced his last name. That angered Uncle, who corrected him saying, "No! Uncle Bonney!" He did not like to be called Boney and thought they were teasing him.

He hated to grow old. When he began to get gray, he tried to dye his hair. It blossomed in strange colors. He finally stopped after Mama gently told him that it was no disgrace to grow old. It happens to all of us.

When he was getting too old to wander, Papa helped him patent a parcel of land near our ranch. [*Editor: When Uncle Bonney moved away, Daniel bought his parcel of land so he would have money to help with his support.*] With help, he built a small cabin and a pond with tiny pines sticking up out of the middle of it, and fashioned a cave corral on the hillside for his burro. His place was close to the road and a deep canyon. Tall pines lined the edge of the canyon, between it and his house.

He was proud of his little place and showed us all around when we went to see it.

About once a week he rode his burro to our place to fill his jug with drinking water, eat a good warm meal and have some companionship. He must have gotten tired of only his burro, and sometimes a dog, for company.

As careless as children are, we did not always talk to him or listen to his tales, and he spent long hours sitting alone in the living room, his watery old blue eyes weary and lost. But when someone took time to listen, he told wonderful stories of the old days.

As he grew old, his sight failed him. After a visit at our place, when Uncle Bonney was ready to leave, his burro stood behind a skinny pine tree as if to hide from him. That was a smart burro; he was easy for us to see, but hidden from Uncle Bonney.

[*Editor: One time one of Uncle Pete's sons—Casimiro "Ike"—was surprised to find him, with his burro, sleeping at the edge of a clearing not far from his cabin that was by the rim of the canyon. Uncle Bonney told Ike he was lost, could not see well enough to find his way home.*]

My folks worried about him when he became feeble and too blind to see, making it dangerous. Papa asked his family at Pastura to come for him. Knowing he had not been a good husband and father, he did not want to go. But he went. He died a few years later. [*Editor: He was buried at Pastura in an old abandoned cemetery, which is now on private ranch property.*]

There was never a time when we went by his cabin on the way to Roy that we did not think of him.

Other Uncles and Aunts, and Events

Papa had two aunts who lived near our ranch. Aunt Dolores "Lola" was his great-half-aunt, Bibiana's daughter by Metzger. I do not remember much of her except for the cool rock house on the edge of a canyon and the wonderful terraced orchard that her husband, Uncle Cordova, had built along the side of that canyon. When they moved away, the orchard died. [*According to his cousin, Alfredo, Daniel had bought the Cordova property from them when they moved away.*]

Aunt Marie [*Maria Marta Ebel Esquibel*] was a full sister of Elionor—Papa's mother. She and Uncle Felipe Esquibel lived in the Red River Canyon [*Cañon de Agua, one of many canyons made by the once mighty "Red River" named the Canadian*] about seven miles from our house. She might as well have lived a hundred miles away because we seldom saw her after she grew old. Her family never built a road down the side of the river canyon to her house below. The boys and men of her family rode horseback up the hill, got a wagon at our ranch on the top for the trip to town, and then took everything down the hill on horseback again.

Aunt Marie used to come up to see Mama in the early days and they visited. She, surrounded by men, hungered for female companionship. But as the years passed and she became too old to ride horseback up the steep trail, or walk it, she had to stay home. Her sons told us she hoped we would go visit her, but we girls were too busy or thoughtless; we seldom did. That is one of my major regrets. The men—Papa, Joyce and Daniel—occasionally saw her.

The last time I remember seeing her alive, I was ten and very sick with pneumonia, following whooping cough. She came into my bedroom, but the room was dim or I was too sick to see her clearly. I only remember her cool touch and soft voice saying, "*Pobrecita.*"

We went down to see her when she was dead—Mama, Frances and I—walking down that steep twisting trail to the little house by the river, where she had lived all those years without a way out. We saw the men carrying her casket, bought in Roy, on foot down that trail. We wondered at their ability to live that way, in that remote isolated canyon.

Laid out for the family, a tiny person, features fine and delicate, she had a little white lace at her throat. That may have been the last thing she had of her mother's. I've always believed she was the most beautiful old woman I had ever seen. She looked serene, lying there. I knew she had finally found a road…

[*Editor: I believe Aunt Marie's beauty that Verna saw and remembered the rest of her life was colored by her deep love for her great-aunt, and her strong regrets over their own neglect to go visit her. Not long before she herself died, Verna still remembered her Aunt Marie as a beautiful old woman, even in death.*]

After Papa married, he still had four unmarried sisters, so it was an exciting time when he and Mama went to Buena Vista once and found that one of them was getting married. Not knowing that then, Papa noticed handsome Manuel Sanchez in the yard when they arrived and stopped to speak to him. He knew Manuel was a well-to-do widower with a nice house in Las Vegas and a big ranch beyond the Red River country. Not knowing why he was there, Papa asked Sanchez if he had come to buy some livestock. Papa soon realized why the man looked embarrassed. Manuel and his father had come to arrange for a marriage with one of the Laumbach girls.

[*Editor: Family tradition said Manuel's interest was in Mary, the prettiest and sweetest natured of the unmarried Laumbach sisters, but their father chose to interpret that his interest was with his oldest unmarried daughter, Crestina. Manuel was too much of a gentleman to speak up and he "married the wrong woman." That story cannot be totally correct since Crestina and Manuel married in 1909, and their father Andreas 2nd had died more than four years earlier, in 1904. When they married, Uncle Sanchez was a widower; his first wife had been Rosa Eggert, daughter of Fritz Eggert.*]

They had a big wedding and most of the relatives came, some even shed a few tears, as is customary with weddings. Alice, Aunt Estefanita's stoic daughter from Santa Fe, thought the tears were unnecessary.

Aunt Crestina lived in Las Vegas and had two children—Antonio and Adelina. The girl died, still a child, of diphtheria. Uncle Sanchez reminded me of the early-day Spanish dons—always hospitable and polite, a fine, handsome gentleman. He lived at his ranch near Sabinoso; during most of their married life, Crestina lived in Las Vegas.

Besides Uncle Bonney, Uncle Sito Candelario was the most colorful of my uncles. He and Aunt Estefanita had only one child, Alice [*Eleanore Allison Candelario*]. They lived in Santa Fe where they had the nationally known Old Curio Store, where tourists from all over the United States visited, including some presidents. It was a fascinating place, with its beautiful jewelry, old *santos*, bells, stacks of Chimayo blankets and pottery. Uncle Sito himself made it an even more interesting place. His stories, which were often tall tales, could keep you breathless, but he was also a shrewd businessman. That was why he became rich.

Uncle Henry, my godfather, remained single until he was 45. He and Papa originally had all their Red River property on shares. When my grandfather died in 1904, my grandmother gave each of her three sons a share in Buena Vista land. Papa traded his Buena Vista share for Uncle Henry's cattle interest on the Red River.

Uncle Henry still had some land in the Yegua country that Papa leased. We enjoyed Uncle Henry's visits whenever he came to see us at the ranch; he had a jolly personality and brought us big sacks of candy. Store-bought candy was a rare treat for us.

Uncle Henry finally married a girl, Natividad. He explained to my Aunties that he wanted a young girl he could train, not one so old and set in her ways like them! He and Papa teased everyone.

The year 1904 was eventful. In September, after a long, heavy rain, a terrible flood swept down the Red River below the ranch and washed away many homes in small settlements. That day the folks heard a dull roar but did not understand why. Later, they knew it had been the flood. You can still see, along the sides of the canyon, the water's high water level marks.

That same flood caused damage at Springer, washing away the depot and the town's lower part, and destroyed Melvin Mill's orchard in Mill's Canyon [*a northern tributary canyon of the Canadian River Gorge*] as well as some of his property in Springer. Mill's orchard and house in the Mills Canyon were fabulous, according to stories, but he never rebuilt them. His big house [*known as Mill's mansion*] is still in Springer, unique in its size, style and many balconies. [*Editor: Mills, a business partner of Thomas B. Catron, had once been a powerful personality in New Mexico politics.*] After the flood, the community of Springer rebuilt further from the river.

My grandfather died in November of 1904, at almost 71 years of age. His death was a shock, sudden and unexpected. He accidentally, or so it was said, shot himself. [*Editor: Family says he took his life. I heard he had a health condition that made him weak and shaky, likely Parkinson's disease. Clara, daughter of Henry, who lived in California—she died in September 2014—also said he took his life because of an illness we now know as Parkinson's.*] After his death, three of his daughters—Anna, Mary and Leonor—stayed on at the old place in Buena Vista with their mother.

It was a wonderful experience to go to Buena Vista when we were children. In the beginning, we went by covered wagon and there was much preparation for the trip—getting the wagon ready, big lunches packed, and all of the children cleaned up.

It must have been even harder to prepare for a trip at Uncle Pete's house, because he had many children. He used to say they cleaned them up one at a time, then hung them on a nail or clipped them to the clothesline to stay clean until it was time to go. Pete was another teaser in the family.

My grandmother's house at Buena Vista was long, with many rooms. The rambling building framed a courtyard or square, which opened onto a shady lane with tall cottonwoods and running streams of water. Inside the courtyard was an old well [*Karl said his grandfather, Pete, dug that well in the hard rocky ground when he was still a teen-ager*] with a bucket, rock walls covered with woodbine and a flower garden. Surrounding the main buildings was a big apple orchard, ringed with streams and cottonwoods. It was a wonderful place to play.

We loved the house with its beautiful cool rooms and lovely old furniture. There was an apple cellar and a bedroom with a high ceiling that was always fragrant and cool. That was my favorite room where we usually slept; it had three beds with soft mattresses and beautiful quilts. [*Editor: My only memory, as a child, of the Buena Vista place when the family still owned it, is sensory. I remember with lingering nostalgia the scents and tastes of dried apples, plums and pears, of cracklings—the rich crunchy pork skins left after rendering lard—and the seasoned jerky—carne de vaca—Aunties kept in a certain cool room.*]

We enjoyed our gentle grandmother and the three beloved aunts who were always glad to see us.

In the year 1912, we saw the largest snowstorm at the ranch. It was later called the Big Snow.

We were still living in the rock house when Mama's father [*Peter Henkens*] and her youngest brother Claus came out to the "wilderness" to see us. They stayed most of the winter, even did a little trapping. I was just learning to talk. They taught me to say, "Shut your mouth." That got me into trouble.

The storm hit the ranch February 23, and it snowed so hard that just the top of the big corral showed. Everything was buried in snow, and it was difficult to take care of the stock around the house. The roads were impassable. Grandpa and Uncle Claus had to stay longer than they intended, but they spent some of the long hours indoors playing cards in the warm kitchen. Mama did a lot of baking for them. One time she made special doughnuts for her father. She probably realized she might never see him again. It was too far to Nebraska for her to often go there, and he was getting too old to travel so far.

The men were finally able to make the trip in a wagon to Roy on March 13 to begin their long journey home by train to Nebraska. My sister Frances was born on March 27.

Covered Wagon Trip

That summer of 1912, when Frances was a tiny baby and I was a little over two years old, we took a covered wagon trip through the mountains that lasted two months. Papa had not been feeling well, and the doctor thought he should get away from the ranch for a while and relax. It would be a nice break for him but not for Mama; it would be much more work for her.

Florencio Esquibel, Papa's trusted cousin, son of Aunt Marie, was hired to look after the ranch. Preparations were made. Uncle Pete and his family, living in La Cinta Canyon, decided to join us. The plan was to go to Buena Vista to pick up aunts Anna and Leonor. Mary would stay at home with their mother. Uncle Henry would later join us.

That was an ambitious undertaking in those days. The plans were to travel by wagon caravan, follow the mountains, fishing and camping as we went along. For the most part we'd be traveling in unsettled country; we had to take all needed provisions.

My mother was a brave woman to attempt such a trip, living in tents and roughing it, with a six-week-old baby and four small children. She had Mabel, Joyce, Alida, me and the baby Frances. She had to take enough clothes, soap, home remedies, bedding, cooking utensils, and food for all of us to last two months!

The bedding was put in the back of the covered wagon, some in rolls and some spread out so we could sit and lay on it. A huge wooden box contained the food, flour, sugar, lard, coffee, dried meat, dried fruit, jellies, some canned milk and other goods. When we got to Buena Vista, my aunts provided more food, including hams. The men expected to catch fish in the mountains.

It was lots of fun for the children sitting in the back of the wagon on quilts, watching the hills and canyons roll by. Uncle Pete's wagons followed ours. When we stopped, we played with his children. Mama had baked a lot before we left; in the beginning we had cookies when we were hungry.

The route followed our usual trip to Buena Vista, then up through the Mora Valley, through Holman where we visited briefly with Aunt Margaret, then into the wild, high mountains between Holman and Taos. The fir and spruce towered around us, and the mountain streams ran cold and swift and full of trout.

We stopped a while when we came to a good place, pitched our tents, built a good rock-sheltered open fireplace. Those who wanted fished.

Mama washed her baby clothes every day and kept them miraculously white and clean. She took care of her baby in a tent as well as she did at home; luckily Frances did not get sick. Sometimes Mama even felt inspired to climb a mountain.

Papa was a good fisherman; it seemed as if he only needed to throw a line in the water and a fish jumped on it. I was too young to really remember the trip, but I heard about the wonderful meals cooked over the open fires. There were the fish and biscuits baked in cast-iron Dutch ovens, and sometimes large *boñuelos*—yeast bread fried in deep fat until puffy [*Editor: what we now call sopapillas*].

Sometimes it rained, and we stayed inside our tents, but afterwards, the air was clean, cool and refreshed. Many of the older ones went off exploring and fishing and left the small children at camp. One of those times, when Mama and Aunt Leonor were left to take care of us, little George was fussy and Aunt Leonor spanked him. The next morning Uncle Pete's wagons and family left us and went home by a different route. My folks thought Uncle Pete was mad at Leonor for spanking George.

Mama still had Aunts Anna and Leonor, who were a great help. Uncle Henry had joined us, too, by then, so we went on—up through the high mountains and through the valley toward Santa Fe.

One day we arrived at the Indian village, Nambe, where the Indian chief welcomed us and allowed us to camp on his porch. Aunties, however, slept in our wagon. In the night they were awakened by hearing someone trying to open the big food box. When Aunt Anna rose up in the wagon and called out, the Indian took to his heels.

The "covered wagon tourists" finally arrived at Santa Fe where we visited our aunt and uncle, the Candelarios. From there, we went to Las Vegas and Buena Vista, where we left Aunties, and then we turned homeward. Arriving at the ranch, we found that cousin Florencio Esquibel had kept everything in good order.

It was a trip worth remembering.

SECTION IV: LAUMBACHS IN NEW MEXICO

Chapter 25: José Ramon Bonney (1846—1935)
With Short Biographies of Daniel Eberle (1826?—1856?) and Manuel Gregorio Martin (1830—1860?)
by Karl W. Laumbach

The 1900 census tells us Ramon Bonney was born in March 1846. Ramon was the first child born to Viviana Martin.[1] She was the daughter of Bernardo Martín and Apolonia Gutierrez de Solano, who were among the original grantees of the Mora Land Grant in 1835. Viviana was born in Portrero, New Mexico on December 1, 1827, before the family made the trek over the mountains to receive their portion of the Mora Land Grant.[2] Ramon's father was James (Santiago in Spanish) Bonney. A Santiago Bon(a) is listed as a foreigner living in Lo de Mora in the 1845 Mexican census. The same census lists an Enrique (Henry) Bon living in Mora with a wife and two daughters, ages 2 and 12. The presence of Henry Bon in the census has led to speculation that Henry was a brother of James. Research demonstrates that Enrique Bon was in fact one Henry Vaughn and not related to the Bonneys.[3]

An emigrant from Missouri who arrived in New Mexico in the early 1830s, James Bonney was living near La Junta de los Rios (now Watrous) when Kearney's Army of the West arrived there in August of 1846. The National Register nomination for the Watrous Historic District shows Jim Bonney was given a land grant by the Mexican government in 1835.[4] The land grant was located near the junction of the Sapello and Mora Rivers. James J. Webb reports that in 1844 Bonney was living in a one room dugout.[5] Webb states "I think he had a wife or housekeeper and three or four children, the eldest a son."[6] *[Editor: Census records show at that time their children were young; that "son" was likely an Indian boy. Records show they baptized an Indian youth around 1845. It was common to give their slaves or servants the family name at baptism.]* Bonney's common-law wife was Juana Maria Mascarenas, whose father was one of the 76 original grantees of the Mora Land Grant.[7]

In 1845, due to a rift in her relationship with James Bonney, Juana Maria and the Bonney children returned to Mora.[8] It is during this period that Bonney's acquaintance with 17- or 18-year-old Viviana Martin must have begun.

Lt. W.H. Emory, one of Kearney's officers, arrived at the La Junta de los Rios (now Watrous) on August 13, 1846. He noted: "The first object I saw was a pretty Mexican woman with clean white stockings, who very cordially shook hands with us and asked for tobacco."[9] Perhaps this was Viviana, perhaps not. Emory goes on to say, "In the next house lived Mr. Boney, an American, who has been some time in this country, and is the owner of a large number of horses and cattle, which he manages to keep in defiance of wolves, Indians, and Mexicans. He is the perfect specimen of a generous open hearted adventurer, and in appearance what, I have pictured to myself, Daniel Boone of Kentucky, must have been in his day. He drove his herd of cattle into camp and picked out the largest and fattest, which he presented to the army." *[Editor: The "pretty Mexican woman with clean white stockings" would not have been Bibiana if "in the next house lived Mr. Boney." She lived with him.]*

Lt. Abert, a surveyor who followed Kearny's soldiers into New Mexico, provides the only contemporary account of James Bonney's death, stating that Santiago Bonne (sic) was killed by "peons" in October of 1846 not long after Abert's departure.,[10] If so, the killing may have been a precursor to the Taos Rebellion, which flared early in 1847. The citizens of Mora and Las Vegas enthusiastically joined that rebellion and feelings would have already been strong in the fall of 1846. Local participation resulted in the destruction of the original plaza of Mora by American cannon fire, and a battle with American regulars in the Canadian River Gorge east of Watrous.[11]

Family oral tradition differs from Abert's account, holding instead that Bonney was killed by Indians in late 1846.[12] The story goes that the Indians raided the scattered settlement and stole a number of Bonney's horses. Determined to recover them, Bonney gathered what stores of bread and goods he possessed to trade with the Indians. Bread was a trade item held in high regard by the Indians and was regularly taken when the Comancheros ventured forth from the New Mexico settlements to deal with the Comanches and other plains tribes. James and a young Indian boy who worked for him caught up with the Indians in the vicinity of the Turkey Mountains west of present day Wagon Mound. They saw the Indians across a small stream bed and Bonney told the young man that he intended to cross and talk to them. The lad told Bonney not to do it, that the Indians would kill him. Ignoring the advice, James started toward them. As he did so, he was killed by a volley of arrows.

In light of James Bonney's untimely death, two things seem certain. Ramon was conceived without benefit of clergy, and he never knew his father. Ramon was raised by his mother. It is likely that after Bonney's death, they returned to the central Mora Valley or to the Rito de Cebolla where Viviana is known to have lived by 1860. Viviana's relationship with Bonney had not been blessed by her mother, Apolonia Gutierrez de Solano. We don't know what her father, Bernardo Martín, thought about it. Family tradition has it that Apolonia forbade Viviana to marry Bonney, and Viviana swore that if such was the case, she would never marry anyone.

By 1848, Viviana had met and possibly married a man named Daniel Eberle. Time and various alterations of the name (Eberle, Eble, Ebele, Ebel, Ebarley) have resulted in the name Ebell [*Editor: that spelling is used by only one branch*], which is still carried by a sizable clan in northeastern New Mexico. He and Viviana had one boy, Andres (1852), and two girls, Leonor (1849) and Maria Marta (1856). The duration of Viviana's relationship with Daniel Eberle implies stability and at least some family life. The current evidence for their marriage is found in the baptism record for their youngest daughter, Maria Marta, which states she was the legitimate daughter of Garlien Eberle and Viviana.[13] The name Eberle in this document is spelled Ebarley and scrawled in longhand, difficult to read, leading to the unfortunate publication of the name Ebarlem in a recent history.[14] Eberle's first name is Daniel in two post mortem documents[15] [*Editor: and also among the family*]; the first name of Garlien recorded in that entry is an error.

Surely Ramon must have seen Daniel Eberle as a father figure and role model. Unfortunately, we know little of Daniel Eberle. Family tradition says he was a Swiss-German. Whether or not he was from the old country or had relatives in the east is open to debate. Researcher Butch Sanders recently discovered the name of Daniel Eberle in the muster rolls of Artillery Company B, Missouri Light Artillery Battalion, Missouri Volunteers under the command of Lt. Woldemar Fischer.[16] Fischer's company was part of Col. Doniphan's expedition in support of Kearny's Army of the West and was primarily composed of Germans from St. Louis, Missouri.[17] Unlike the rest of the companies under Doniphan's command, Artillery Company B remained in Santa Fe and did not proceed to Chihuahua. Elements of Artillery Company B participated in the Battle of Taos during the Taos Rebellion of 1847.[18] A number of men from Fischer's company were mustered out in Santa Fe in June 1847.[19] Daniel Eberle was one of those who stayed in New Mexico.

Exactly what Eberle did after mustering-out in Santa Fe is uncertain. Verna Laumbach said Eberle had a store in Las Vegas and was relatively wealthy, showing off his hat filled with gold coins. [*Editor: Verna heard this story from her Aunties.*] He may also have owned livestock.[20] It is possible that Viviana, Ramon and the younger children lived with Eberle in Las Vegas during the early 1850s.

Using the sometimes inexact ages on the census records as well as the family Bible and baptism certificates, it seems likely that Daniel Eberle and Viviana were together from about 1848 to 1856. It was at the end of that uncertain period that Daniel Eberle met a violent death. Versions of the story vary depending on the source.

One version was told to me by Aunt Lenore Laumbach (sister of my grandfather Peter Joseph Laumbach and daughter of Lenore Eberle Laumbach). She said Daniel Eberle was in camp on the Santa Fe Trail in Cañon del Perro (Dog Canyon), a tributary running from the Turkey Mountains and emptying into the Mora River down-canyon from present day Watrous. The Santa Fe Trail crosses Cañon del Perro north of Watrous as it angles southeasterly towards the Mora River. Several men attempted to rob him at the camp and when he resisted, he was struck in the head. He was found unconscious and taken by wagon to Las Vegas where he died.

Verna Laumbach told a similar story. Sometime after Maria Marta's birth in February 1856, Eberle accused Viviana of being unfaithful resulting in a separation/divorce. Eberle gave her a choice between children or money. She chose the children. On a trip to Naupeste (research has not confirmed this location), Eberle was camped at a place called Begosa (probably near Begosa Creek, a tributary to the Gallinas River east of Las Vegas). His servant hit him on the head and took Eberle's sack of money. Mortally wounded, Eberle made it back to Las Vegas where he died and was buried near the old Presbyterian Mission.

Another version of the story, which corresponds well with that of Verna Laumbach, was told to Peter James Laumbach by Doña Carmen (Carmel) Ebell Naranjo, daughter of Andres Ebell and granddaughter to Daniel Eberle. Her father talked about being just old enough to remember a messenger arriving in Las Vegas and announcing at the Plaza that slavery was no longer legal in New Mexico. This news was possibly the result of the adoption of the Compromise of 1850 in which Texas surrendered its claim to New Mexico as far as the Rio Grande. Congress did not adopt the Wilmot Proviso, which would have admitted all territories gained in the Mexican Cession as free territories, but under the Compromise of 1850 both Utah and New Mexico could become slave territories by popular vote at a later date. In the meantime slavery was illegal.

According to Doña Carmel, Viviana and Eberle had two Indian slaves at their house in Las Vegas who were either Apache or Pima. They were set free and set out to walk to southern Arizona. Doña Carmel said Eberle offered them blankets and provisions but they refused, saying they didn't want Viviana to have any excuse to come after them. This suggests Viviana and Eberle lived together in Las Vegas.

Doña Carmel also related the story of Eberle's death. He was traveling but his destination is not known. He always carried a money belt under his shirt, and his traveling companion killed him in his sleep by crushing his head with a rock and then robbed him. His body was brought back to Las Vegas and buried "*en un camposanto cerca de la plaza.*" This must mean the cemetery just east of the river that now lies under the Highlands University campus. Many burials were disturbed and the remains collected there during various periods of construction at the university.

A second and very different version was told by Hilario Ebell, a grandson of Daniel Eberle who lives in Roy, New Mexico. According to Hilario, Daniel and Viviana become estranged and separated at some time after the birth of Maria Marta. Daniel decided to visit his family in the east and wished to take his son, Andres, with him. Viviana either objected or wasn't asked if Andres, then maybe six or seven years old, could go. Daniel came by the house and took him. When Viviana found Andres gone, she appealed to whatever men were in the area. They pursued Eberle and found his wagon along the trail. Daniel was under it greasing the wooden wheels. The men approached stealthily and one picked up the heavy wagon wrench that lay near the wagon. Daniel Eberle's skull was crushed with a quick blow and the boy was taken home to his mother. An alternate version told to me by Hilario's brother, Andres, has the men pursuing Daniel but, finding him already dead at the hands of others, they rescued the boy and returned him.

Daniel Eberle remains a man of mystery. The birth date of their first born, Leonor (January 1849) corresponds well with his presumed mustering-out in Santa Fe in mid-1847. Perhaps he received some compensation for his service and found a way to profit from the trade on the Santa Fe Trail that came through Las Vegas. The baptisms of his first two children by Viviana appear to have not been officially recorded. Ebell and Laumbach family tradition has them living in Las Vegas where Eberle had a store. Documentary evidence of Eberle's store has yet to be found. If he was in Las Vegas by 1850, he seems to have missed the census. His name appears in records of the day three times: once in Maria Marta's baptism in 1856, where he is mistakenly named Garlien Ebarley; then again in the wedding record for Leonor Ebel at her marriage to Andreas Laumbach in 1864, where her father is listed as deceased.[21] The third time is in the wedding record for Andres Evel and Maria Uvalda Lopez in 1874 at La Junta (Watrous), wherein Andres is named as the "natural" son of the deceased Daniel Evel and Maria Viviana Martin.[22] This indicates Daniel and Viviana were not married, at least at the time of Andres' birth. Louise Laumbach collected oral histories in the early 1970s that suggested a German or Swiss background for Eberle.[23] The Eberle name appears in several contexts during the 1840s in St. Louis.[24] Research has not yet found a link.

It was sometime in the 1850s and probably toward the end of that decade when Ramon's uncle, Manuel Gregorio Martin, returned to Mora. Manuel was the younger brother of Viviana and like her, had been born in Potrero, north of Santa Fe, on November 14, 1830. Like his sister, he was baptized at the church in Santa Cruz. Manuel and Viviana would have been about four and seven years of age when the Alcalde of Truchas, Manuel Antonio Sanchez, formally dedicated the grant to the original 76 grantees in 1835.

Growing up on the eastern New Mexico frontier must have been a challenge, but the new people and new concepts arriving via the Santa Fe Trail impacted the Mora/Las Vegas area more immediately than anywhere else with the exception of Santa Fe. The Santa Fe Trail was a two-way street, and many New Mexicans shipped goods back to St. Louis or found work with the trains of freight wagons that moved regularly back and forth along the trail. We do not know if Bernardo Martin had his own wagons or was simply working for such a train, but on one occasion he took Manuel with him, according to family tradition. It can be assumed Manuel was deemed old enough for such a trip (10 years or more); that assumption further suggests a date in the early 1840s for the fateful trip, although it could have been as late as 1847.

While in Kansas or Missouri, the boy found himself the focus of attention due to his light complexion (his sister Bibiana was described as light complexioned with auburn hair). Some of the Americans decided Manuel was too fair to be a Mexican and simply took him away from Bernardo. Perhaps their judgment was based on the great number of Anglo captives taken by the Comanche and other tribes and traded to New Mexicans. In this case they were mistaken. Bernardo was forced to return home without Manuel, which forever ended his relationship with Apolonia.

Bernardo lived with his daughter Viviana for the rest of his life.

Manuel, left in the Kansas/Missouri area, had been taken home by one of his abductors and raised there. As he grew older, he decided to return to New Mexico. Waiting until the man of the house was gone, he told the woman who had raised him that he appreciated what she had done for him, but he needed to return to his family. Taking a horse, he returned to New Mexico, probably by joining a wagon train headed west. Returning sometime after 1850, he must have been somewhat bewildered by the changes in the life he remembered. His parents were separated and his sister, now married to an Anglo, had two and possibly three or four children. And, of course, trade on the Trail and with Ft. Union had transformed Mora and Las Vegas from sleepy villages to thriving centers of commerce. That he did return is documented by his presence at Apolonia's home in the 1860 census for Mora. Then he disappears. One scenario has him going on a trapping or hunting trip and not returning. Another has him traveling to one of the high mountain villages, finding a wife and isolating himself from the goings on in Mora.[25]

What effect the death of Daniel Eberle may have had on Ramon Bonney is unknown. It is reasonably certain he shared his half-brother Andres' disdain for Viviana's next man. This man's name was Frederich Metzger "El Aleman" (The German), purportedly a German Jew. Metzger was very wealthy and owned a store and house in Mora [*Editor: at Buena Vista*] in addition to numerous other enterprises, including a ranch on the Rito de Cebolla. He had three girls by Viviana between the years 1858 and 1864. The girls were named Dolores (Lola 1858), Josephita (1863), and Isabel (1864). Metzger treated Andres badly and eventually forced him to leave home. His treatment of Ramon is not known. Metzger and Viviana eventually split up. In 1875, Viviana signed an agreement that yielded her right and her children's right to any inheritance Metzger might leave, in exchange for a cash settlement of $3,000. Ramon, Leonor and Andres also signed this agreement while Viviana signed for those underage.[26] Ramon would have been almost 30 years of age at that time.

His grandfather, Bernardo Martin, may have been the man who most shaped Ramon's life and attitudes. Bernardo lived with Viviana from the late 1840s to his death in the 1870s. Bernardo, born in New Mexico in the 1790s, was a proud *caballero* (horseman) and held traditional Spanish notions about proper language and behavior. My Uncle Casimiro (Ike), who learned to speak the Spanish language beginning in 1913, commented that he always thought Ramon spoke "funny" Spanish. It was not until Ike took Spanish grammar in high school that he realized Ramon had been using the old Castilian endings to words. Ramon was a very proud man and demanded respect and proper behavior from his younger relatives.

The 1870 census shows Ramon Bonne (sic), age 24; below that entry, Lenore, age 18. This Lenore is most likely his half-sister Lenore, although she is found in the same census in the household of Andreas Laumbach and is listed as age 21.

The church records document a marriage between Ramon Bonney and Concepcion Padilla on November 21, 1875.[27] They had two sons, Jose Firmino (1876) and Facundo (1878). Both boys were born in the Cañon del Encierro, an eastern tributary of the Rio Colorado [*"Red River"*] (Canadian River) near Sabinoso. Ramon was likely ranching in the area and working with his half-brother, Andres Ebell, who had also settled there. Andres is listed as the godfather to Jose Firmino on his baptism entry. The 1880 census shows a third child, Emilia, was born on May 13, 1880. Ramon's wife may have died in childbirth with Emilia. Both sons also died young, Firmino before 1880 and Facundo before 1890. According to Casimiro (Ike) Laumbach, the boys and their mother are buried in the extreme northeast corner of the Laumbach cemetery at Buena Vista. None of those graves are marked. They would be the earliest graves in the cemetery. I believe the earliest marked grave is that of Viviana Martin (1897).

Ramon's second wife was Anastacia Lucero, born in 1864. She was the daughter of Jose Lucero, who was married to a sister of Vicente Silva. Vicente Silva led a band of livestock thieves who operated all over northeastern New Mexico and southeastern Colorado.[28] In 1895, Vicente Silva was killed and his gang broken up. Tomas Lucero, Anastacia's uncle, spent several years in the State Penitentiary with other members of the group, including Jose Chavez y Chavez, a one-time companion of Billy the Kid. Jose and Tomas were twins known as "*Las Cuates de Mora.*"

Ramon and Anastacia were married in 1882. The 1900 census indicates they had 11 children, five died young. Those who survived were Roberto (1883), Abelina (1884), Maria Rafaela (1886),

Maria Viviana (1889), Ramon (1890), Juan J. Salomon (1893), Raphaelita (1896), Santiago (1898), Maria Amada (1901), and Emelia (1903).[29] Of these, Ramon, Salomon, Raphaelita, Santiago, Amada, and Emelia survived to adulthood. [*Editor: Records indicate, and Verna said, that Ramon did not live to adulthood.*] The later children are listed as born in Wagon Mound. Ramon and his family apparently continued to live in the Rio Colorado area for a while and are listed in the 1900 census for the Armenta Precinct.

Pictured below: Ramon Bonney (seated right), his wife Anastacia (seated next to him with child, probably Amada) and their three sons. Seated next to Anastacia are Mrs. and Mr. Jose Lucero (he was Anastacia's father), and possibly two of Mrs. Lucero's children from a prior marriage standing behind her. Aunties gave this photo to George Laumbach, its quality improved by Butch Sanders. From census records and other documents, Butch has concluded the two children standing behind Mrs. Lucero were not Ramon's, probably hers. See end note [30] for further explanation.

Armenta Plaza was a small farming community founded in the early 1870s. It was located in the bottom of the Canadian River Gorge between the Wagon Mound-Roy bridge and the mouth of the Mora River. The flood of 1904 washed it away. The Armenta Precinct included ranchers and farmers living both upstream and downstream from Armenta Plaza. Ramon was living two "doors" (as the census taker traveled) from Felipe Santiago Esquibel and Maria Marta Ebel/Eberle; three doors from Juan Andres Ebel/Eberle and Maria Uvalda Lopez; four doors from Pedro J. Lomba (Laumbach) and Fidelia Andrada; five doors from Conrado Andrada and Nicanora Ebel/Eberle; and 28 doors from Jose Nieves Gallegos and Isabel Ebel/Eberle. [*Editor: This Isabel was daughter of Andres Ebell.*] Ramon's proximity to these families indicates he was living near the Cañon Encierro where Andres Ebel made his home.

Sometime after the birth date of their last child, Emelia in early 1903, Ramon and Anastacia separated. One story says Ramon held the secret to the location of a gold mine in the mountains mined by Metzger. The Lucero relatives were after him to share the secret.[31] Finally, Ramon left to protect himself. The story goes that the gang mistakenly pursued another man and killed him.[32] An alternate family narrative says Ramon became extremely difficult and was hard on his wife and family. The older boys (Solomon and Santiago) were ready to leave when Anastacia's father and uncle, *Los Cuates de Mora*, Jose and Tomas Lucero, stepped in and advised Ramon to leave his family or risk a sound beating or worse.[33] The family moved to Pastura, a small community east of Las Vegas, between Santa Rosa and Vaughn. After the split, Ramon's later years were spent wandering northeastern New Mexico, visiting various members of his large extended family while occasionally visiting his children in Pastura. Jim Bonney, son of Santiago Bonney and grandson to Ramon, related that, when Ramon visited Pastura, he stayed with Anastacia until she tired of his company, then he moved to the house of one of his children and so on until all had been visited, at which point he departed.

It was during the period from 1910 to 1933 that Ramon often visited the homes of his nephews, Peter Joseph and Daniel Laumbach. Both men lived near the mouth of the Canadian River Gorge about halfway between Las Vegas and Roy, New Mexico. Ramon Bonney was quite a character and the children of Peter Joseph and Daniel developed strong impressions and memories of the man.

All remember him as a proud and neat man accustomed to people waiting on him, especially the children. It was their impression that Ramon had been raised like a young Spanish don and always had the best available. George Laumbach remembered his Tio Ramon calling into the next room for one of the children to pour him a glass of water even though the water pitcher and glass were next to him. When the children were slow to comply with a request, Ramon told my grandmother (in Spanish) that the children had no respect for him and should be punished. Ramon expected the children to present themselves each morning to the adults with a polite "*Buenas dias de le Dios, Tio. Como amanecio?*" (Good Day of our Lord, Uncle. How did you rise?) Although he did speak English, his normal conversation was in Spanish.

Peter James Laumbach recalled his father Rudolph giving an account of Ramon visiting Pete Laumbach's ranch at La Cinta. Ramon rode his burro to the gate, which was about a quarter of a mile from the house, and he sat there until someone noticed him. Then he expected everyone in the house to go meet him at the gate and escort him to the house. He expected to be, and was, treated royally. If he spent the night, in the morning he sat himself in a chair and received a line of all of the children who were required to wish him a good morning, one at a time. The required greeting was: "*Buenos dias, Tio. Como amanecio la noche?*" He would nod, and they were dismissed. Aunt Lucille (Rudolph's younger sister) was a little girl; when her turn came, she stood with her hands behind her back, her eyes closed, and she said it as fast as she could. When those ceremonies were completed, Fidelia Laumbach (Pete's wife) fried him some eggs according to his very specific instructions. On his departure, he expected and received the same escort to the gate.

Ramon was a large man, perhaps a little over 6 feet in height. He had reddish hair in his youth, which turned gray by old age. His face had a ruddy complexion, and he sported a large and bushy mustache. His eyes were very blue, a trait inherited from his father and passed down to numerous members of the Bonney clan.

He had a quick temper that manifested itself at any insult, real or imagined. He was also very proud of his strength. His grand-nephews recalled seeing rock walls he built that were capped by rocks of tremendous size. His hands were unusually large and powerful.

Two stories illustrate how Ramon felt about his strength. Pete (Peter Joseph) Laumbach was with his Tio Ramon at Fort Union when a cannon was to be lifted from a wagon bed. After Ramon attempted to lift it without success, a black soldier easily moved it. Ramon became upset and could not be consoled.[34] On another occasion, Ramon was helping his nephews brand at Uncle Dan's. Of the Laumbach brothers, Pete and Dan were tall, broad men while Henry was shorter but equally broad and powerful. An extra-large calf was roped and Ramon attempted to flank it so it could be branded. He grabbed the animal in the accepted fashion and tried to lift and throw it with sheer strength. When the calf didn't go down, he allowed that it couldn't be done. Henry stepped forward and declared he could do it. Henry grabbed the calf, and as he did so, kneed it in the belly. The calf jumped; while it was in the air, Henry flipped it to the ground. Ramon stomped off and would not speak to anyone for some time.

The Ebell family also remembers their Tio Ramon, who was their patriarch Andres Ebell's elder half-brother. Ramon occasionally visited their family when his homestead was near Ebell property. One story is that Ramon had a somewhat scrawny bull that was mixing with the Ebell herd. Not wanting its progeny, the Ebells grew tired of turning it back to Ramon's property and either dispatched or castrated the animal. Ramon, upon discovering his loss, berated them for the action. They told him of their dilemma and offered him a replacement bull. To this day, when one of the Ebells sees a scrawny bull, he comments, "*alli esta el toro de mi Tio Ramon.*" (There is the bull of my Uncle Ramon.)

Apparently the Laumbach brothers were not hesitant about teasing their uncle. Ramon had a big dog that followed him on his travels. Uncle Henry was a good roper and was always "fooling" with a rope. As the dog came within range, Henry roped it. Ramon was not far behind. It was all Henry could do to keep Ramon from whipping him.

In his earlier years, Ramon traveled horseback like most other men. My uncles remember him riding a blue "mouse-colored" roan with a light mane. Raised by the Esquibels and called El Dorado, the horse was given to Ramon by Daniel Laumbach. For many years Ramon traveled the country in a special wagon designed to be pulled by a single horse. Uncle Andreas (Red) Laumbach remembered Ramon kept the wagon well painted. The bed was green with a red stripe and the wheels were red. A black mare Ramon called "Blackie" pulled the wagon. As Ramon neared 80 years, he became nearsighted and abandoned the wagon in favor of two burros, Burro Pinto and Burro Pardo (the paint burro and the gray burro). He could find the pinto burro with greater ease than the black mare. He rode one of the burros and led the other. These burros frightened the horses. Uncle Frank Foxall (married to my Aunt Christina Laumbach) remembered coming back to the house at La Cinta after Ramon Bonney had arrived. Ramon's burro was tied near the gate and the boys could not lead their horses through it until the burro was moved.

Daniel Laumbach convinced Ramon that he should file on a homestead in the area. Ramon filed on a place near the head of the Poñiente Canyon, a tributary to the La Cinta, where he built a cabin and patented his claim in 1905.[35] The last time Casimiro (Ike) Laumbach saw Ramon was the morning after he had left the Pete Laumbach's La Cinta Ranch to go to his homestead. Ike was riding up the Poñiente Canyon and saw something on the ridge not far from Ramon's house. Investigating, he found Ramon and his burro. Ramon had become confused and camped because he could not see well enough to find his place. Soon after that, Daniel Laumbach helped Ramon move to Pastura, New Mexico to live with Amada, one of Ramon's daughters.[36]

Pictured is Amada Bonney Campos with her children. Photo courtesy of her daughter, Christine Campos Ortiz.

Ramon's wife, Anastacia, was a strong woman alone raising her family by Ramon. Much loved and admired by her children and grandchildren, she was also a well known herbalist, midwife and *curandera* (healer). Rudolfo Anaya based the character of Ultima on Anastacia in his *Bless Me Ultima* novel of a young Hispanic male coming of age in the Southwest. Her grandchildren did not appreciate Rudolfo's portrayal. Anastacia was a positive and compassionate force in the lives of her family and her community, and that is the way they want her remembered.

The grandchildren of Ramon and Anastacia remembered Ramon's visits to Pastura in his later years. His grandson James "Jim" Bonney remembered that Ramon demanded the same respectful greetings and behavior he required of the Laumbach children. He occasionally went to the back of the barn and sang like an Indian with no real words, just a booming voice carrying across the *llano*. He was conscious of being "white" and when a new baby was born to the family, the baby was presented to him. If the baby was too dark complexioned, he denied him, stating "that's not mine." His grandson Jim Bonney told me he was a dark complexioned baby, initially rejected by Ramon. However, when Ramon died, it was Jim who inherited Burro Pinto and Burro Pardo.[37]

For children growing up in New Mexico, Billy the Kid is either a hero or a villain, usually a hero. My father, George Laumbach, remembered reading a book on the life of Billy the Kid by Charles Siringo while growing up at the La Cinta Ranch. Because Ramon, and other members of the clan, spelled the name Bonney, it was natural for the children to ask if he was related to Billy the Kid. Fifty years or so later, I asked my father the same question. He remembered Ramon Bonney saying, "When Billy the Kid was in jail at Fort Union," he visited with him and attempted to establish whether or not a relationship existed. Although they had a cordial visit (in Spanish), they were unable to determine a relationship. Many of the relatives were somewhat relieved by that account. Others were disappointed. The odd thing about the "jail at Ft. Union" story is that there is no record of Billy the Kid being in jail at Ft. Union, yet Ramon told the story the same way to multiple relatives. Billy was briefly jailed in Las Vegas in December 1880; their encounter may have been there.

Several members of the other branch of the Bonney clan claim they are related to Billy. Maybe so, but no one has determined exactly how it happened. [*Editor: Herman Weisner believed he knew.*] It means little that Ramon was unable to establish a relationship with Billy the Kid. Ramon did not know his father and was not raised with James Bonney's older children by Juana Mascarenas. Ramon did tell Verna Laumbach that while working on a wagon train that took goods to and from Denver, he met an uncle, a brother to James Bonney, who said he was from Missouri. The uncle was satisfied that Ramon was his brother's son and offered him opportunities in Denver. Ramon refused, saying it was important to return to his family in New Mexico.

Amado (Leon) Bonney, the son of Santiago Jr., who lived in Watrous until murdered in the 1970s, claimed that after James Bonney was killed in 1846, Juana Maria Mascarenas and her children by Bonney moved to Mora.[38] [*Editor: Our family tradition, and Joe Lopez, descendent of James and Juana, said Bibiana came into his life after his first family moved away from La Junta.*] The three Bonney children are listed in the 1850 census: Maria Cleofas born 1838, Santiago born in 1842, and Maria Rafaela born 1845. When they returned several years later, much of the Bonney land grant had been preempted by claimants to the later Scolly Grant. The Bonneys were able to regain their land only after a court battle. All three of the children married and lived out their lives in the Watrous area. Maria Cleofas (grandmother of Benjamin and Joe Lopez) married Trinidad Lopez. Maria Rafaela married Bernardo Salazar. Santiago Jr. married Feliciana Jimenez. When Amado's sister, Vicentita, died in 1987 at the age of 102, her obituary claimed she was a relative of Billy the Kid. What is true is that Igenio Salazar, companion of Billy the Kid and resident of Lincoln, New Mexico, was indirectly related to Bernardo Salazar, husband of Maria Rafael Bonney. Given the ways of New Mexicans, that relationship would have sufficed for Igenio to call Billy *primo* (cousin) regardless of why Billy the Kid selected the name Bonney after arriving in Lincoln County.

Herman Weisner, a Las Cruces historian, became intrigued with the Bonney connection after talking to Benjamin Lopez, grandson of Trinidad Lopez and Maria Cleofas Bonney, in Ocate, New Mexico. Weisner's working hypothesis was that James Bonney had an even earlier family in Missouri. [*Editor: That was what Verna and La Junta Bonneys believed.*] Weisner believed that a daughter from that family, who would have been born around 1830, was the right age to be William Bonney's mother in the late 1850s. As the last name of Billy's father was McCarty and his step-father was named Antrim, Billy's use of the name Bonney after he arrived in Lincoln County might be explained as being his mother's maiden name. However, Weisner was never able to prove his theory.[39] The mystery and the possibility of a relationship remain.

Ramon Bonney died in Pastura in 1935. He is buried in an unmarked grave in the old cemetery that can be seen from the highway where the road to Las Vegas intersects with the road between Santa Rosa and Vaughn.

Pictured are Tia Anastacia Lucero Bonney, widow of Tio Ramon Bonney, with daughters; Amada is on right in photo. Photo courtesy of Pete Laumbach; photo quality considerably improved by Butch Sanders.

---

[1] Viviana's name is often spelled Bibiana and her grave marker spells it Bibiana Martinez. Her baptism record and her listing as mother of the bride for the marriage of Andreas Detlef Laumbach II and Leonor Ebel at the Santa Gertrudes Church in Mora has her name spelled "Viviana."

[2] Three years later, in 1830, Bibiana's brother Manuel Gregorio Martin was also born at Potrero.

[3] Luis Madrid, "Henry Vaughn becomes Enrique Boné" in Herencia, the Quarterly Journal of the Hispanic Genealogical Research Center of New Mexico, Volume 14, Issue 3, July 2006 pp. 23—24.

[4] The "Bonney Grant" was not upheld by the U.S. courts. A more detailed history of the Santiago Bone grant may be found at http://www.newmexicohistory.org/filedetails.php?fileID=24830.

[5] Another American, George Carter, lived with his housekeeper in a two-room house near the crossing. James J. Webb *Adventures in the Santa Fe Trade 1844—1847* edited by Ralph P. Bieber, University of Nebraska, 1995, pp. 74.

[6] James J. Webb *Adventures in the Santa Fe Trade 1844—1847* edited by Ralph P. Bieber, University of Nebraska, 1995, pp. 74.

[7] Rebecca McDowell Craver (1982) *The Impact of Intimacy: Mexican-Anglo Intermarriage in New Mexico, 1821—1846*, pp.54, Southwestern Studies, University of Texas at El Paso, Monograph No. 66.

[8] Santiago Bone (Bonney) and Maria Juana Mascarenas were living at La Junta de los Rios (Watrous) when an adult servant or slave of theirs (*famulo*) was baptized on Feb. 13, 1845. In Baptism Record 52, Taos. IN El Palacio, Volume 64, (1958) by Bruce Ellis and Paul A.F. Walter, Museum of New Mexico.

[9] Ross Calvin, editor nd. *Lieutenant Emory Reports,* UNM Press, pp. 46—47 reprinted version of *Notes of a Military Reconnaissance* by W.H. Emory, first published in 1848 by H. Long and Brother, New York.

[10] J.W. Abert, (1848) Report of Lieut. J.W. Abert of his Examination of New Mexico in the Years 1846—1847 IN Report of The Secretary of War to the 30th Congress, 1st Session, Executive No. 23. Pp. 27. Abert, arriving after Kearny on September 23, 1846, noted several corrals and several adobe houses, one of which was occupied by "Boney." The residents of the other houses were New Mexicans.

[11] Michael McNierney ed., 1980, Taos 1847: The Revolt in Contemporary Accounts. Pp. 35—40, 91—96, Johnson Publishing Company, Boulder, Colorado.

[12] Kenyon Riddle 1963 *Records and Maps of the Old Santa Fe Trail*. Pp 137—140 Southeastern Printing Company, Inc., Stuart, Florida.

[13] Curiously, baptism records for Leonor and Andres have not been found. The wedding entry for Andres Ebel and Uvalda Lopez states Andres was a "natural" child of Daniel Ebel and Viviana Martin, suggesting a marriage occurred after the births of Leonor and Andres, or not at all.

[14] Charles L. Briggs and Julian Josué Vigil ed. 1990. *The Lost Gold Mine of Juan Mondragon: A Legend from New Mexico* performed by Melaquias Romero pp. 181. University of Arizona Press, Tucson.

[15] Wedding entries for Leonor Ebel and Andreas Detlef Laumbach, and for Andres Ebel and Uvalda Lopez.

[16] John Taylor Hughes, William Elsey Connelley, Dewitt Clinton Allen, and Charles R. Morehead (1907) *Doniphan's Expedition and the Conquest of New Mexico and California* pp. 577—579.

[17] Joseph G. Dawson (1999) *Doniphan's Epic March* pp. 38, University Press of Kansas.

[18] Lt. Woldemar Fischer to the Adjutant General (February 16, 1847) In Michael McNierney ed., 1980, Taos 1847: The Revolt in Contemporary Accounts. Pp. 53—55, Johnson Publishing Company, Boulder, Colorado.

[19] Timothy L. Kimball "Fischer's German-American Artillery Volunteers on the Santa Fe Trail, 1846—1847." Presented at the 2011 Santa Fe Trail Symposium, Dodge City, Kansas, published in *Wagon Tracks*, the Santa Fe Trail Association Quarterly, Volume 26, No. 1, November 2011. Kimball provides considerable detail on the experiences of Fischer's company.

[20] Verna Laumbach said she had heard Eberle also had a cattle ranch.

[21] Church records on file at Santa Gertrudes de Mora Catholic Church. Roll 94, Frame 194.

[22] Luis Gilberto Padilla y Baca, compiler, *New Mexico Marriages, La Junta (Watrous), September 1873—April 1908* (Albuquerque, NM: Hispanic Genealogical Research Center of New Mexico, ca 2002), p. 5, p. 73, p. 84.

[23] Louise Laumbach 1970 Martin Family History unpublished manuscript in Karl Laumbach files.

[24] Correspondence with a Charles Eberle revealed that an Eberle family, including Hugo Jacob Eberle and several brothers, came to St. Louis from Germany in 1848. Since Eberle's first known presence in New Mexico was 1848, it is tempting to suggest a relationship to the St. Louis Eberle family of that time. Tim Kimball, New Mexico historian specializing in the Mexican War, has noted that the St. Louis city directory for 1844/45 shows a Valentine Eberle, cabinet maker located at 2nd & Spruce and that a St. Louis newspaper mentions a Mr. [no first name or initial] Eberle of the 2nd ward who served on the welcome home committee for the Fischer artillery company in 1847.

[25] Story of Manuel Martín was related to Karl Laumbach by his great-aunts Lenore and Mary Laumbach in their Las Vegas home sometime in the 1960s.

[26] Deed Records, Mora County, Volume C, Page 90, Sheet #66, conveyance from Viviana Martin to Frederich Metzgar, signed March 19, 1875, filed Feb. 16, 1885.

[27] Marriage Book #46 Santa Gertrudes Catholic Church, Mora, New Mexico.

[28] Tom McGrath, 1960 *Vicente Silva and His Forty Thieves: Vice Criminals of the 80s and 90s.* self-published.

[29] Emelia's son, "Lalo" Montano believes Emilia was born in 1907; the Record of New Mexico Births and Christenings list her as born in 1903.

[30] *Editor: The following information provided by researcher Butch Sanders: Census and christening records indicate Anastacia and Ramon had 13 children, 11 before the 1900 census and two after the 1900 census. In 1900, there were 4 children recorded in the family of Ramon and Anastacia: Ramon J. Jr., born Dec 1890, age 9; Juan J. S., born May 1893, age 7; Rafaelita, born May 1896, age 4; and Santiago, born Sept. 1898, age 1. Compare that info with these baptismal/christening records for the same four children: Jose Ramon, baptized 2 Mar 1891 at 2 months old; Juan Jose Salomon, born 24 May 1893, baptized 4 Feb 1894; Rafaelita, born 22 May 1896, baptized 26 May 1896; and Santiago, born 9 Sep 1898, baptized 20 Feb 1899.*

The census enumerator recorded Anastacia as born Jan. 1864. According to her baptismal/christening record, she was born 23 Jan 1865 and baptized 24 Jan. 1865. The enumerator got everything right except for Anastacia's birth year (off one year). This comparison of baptismal/christening records and census record demonstrates that the census enumerator recorded the right answers. Other questions asked: How many children did Anastacia have (answer 11), and how many were still living (answer 4). He recorded the four still living (three sons and one daughter). We also have the baptismal/christening records for four of the seven children who were no longer living, and we have the christening records for Ramon's three children by his first wife, Maria Concepcion Padilla, they and she no longer living. We also have the christening records for the two daughters born to Ramon and Anastacia after 1900—Maria Amada, born 8, Jul. 1901, baptized 22, Feb. 1902; and Emilia, born 8, Feb. 1903, baptized 13 Dec. 1903.

Ramon and Anastacia had six children who could be in the photo, depending on when it was taken: Jose Ramon, born Dec. 1890; Juan Jose Salomon, born 24 May 1893; Rafaelita, born 22 May 1896; Santiago, born 9 Sep. 1898; Maria Amada, born 8 Jul. 1901; and Emilia, born 8 Feb. 1903. There is only one baby girl in the photo; Emilia may have not been born yet.

The adults are identified beneath the photo as "Mr. and Mrs. Lucero," "Anastasia Lucero," and "Ramon Bonne." The "Mr. and Mrs. Lucero" label suggests the writer didn't know Mrs. Lucero's maiden name, and didn't know her and her husband's given names. He only knew they were married. Anastacia's mother, Maria

Refugio Velasquez, disappeared from records after the 1885 territorial census and the birth of her last known child Henrique Lucero on 14 Jul. 1885. In this photo, probably taken between 1901 and 1903, the woman with Tomas Lucero might be his later wife Filomena, and the two children behind her may be hers from a prior marriage.

Added comment by editor: Photographers arranged the subjects for the photos. Note the two children behind Mrs. Lucero placed their hands on her shoulders, indicating they belong to her.

[31] Mary Louise Maestas, personal communication to Karl Laumbach.

[32] Mary Louise Maestas, personal communication to Karl Laumbach.

[33] Christine Ortiz (granddaughter of Ramon and Anastacia Bonney) email to Jan Girand, January 2013.

[34] Interview with Ben Lopez and George Laumbach on file at the Rio Grande Historical Collections, New Mexico State University Library, Las Cruces.

[35] Ramon's homestead was patented on September 21, 1905 and consisted of 160 acres located in Section 15, Township 18N Range 24E.

[36] Christine Ortiz to Janet Girand.

[37] Interview with James "Jim" Bonney, grandson of Ramon, by Karl Laumbach, 2011, on file at the New Mexico Farm and Ranch Heritage Museum.

[38] Kenyon Riddle 1963 *Records and Maps of the Old Santa Fe Trail*. Pp. 137—140 Southeastern Printing Company, Inc., Stuart, Florida. Joe Lopez, a great-great-grandson of James Bonney and Juana Mascarenas, claims Juana and the children moved to Mora and married a Mr. Garcia.

[39] Herman Weisner 1990, "Billy the Kid's Roots" a paper presented at the Billy the Kid Symposium: In the Days of Billy the Kid, Violence and the Western Frontier, Ruidoso, New Mexico. Sponsored by the Lincoln County Heritage Trust. Manuscript in the Karl Laumbach files.

SECTION IV: LAUMBACHS IN NEW MEXICO

Chapter 26: Sunset—Uncle Bonney's Story
by Verna L. Sparks 1909—1996

Photo of Ramon Bonney with his wagon, on one of his many visits to ranch of Daniel and Emma Laumbach. This photo was taken in front of their "rock house." Photo from Verna's collection, provided by Karl, enhanced by Butch.

Editor: Verna wrote this story about her Uncle Bonney many years ago as a fiction. I gently unfictionalized it, but to keep Verna's writing as a good story, many fictitious portions remain.

When we were young, our family was close to Uncle Bonney. He was our great-grandmother Bibiana's child with an Englishman, James Bonney. Ramon Bonney grew up with the children from her second and third relationships, and he remained close to her even after he left home, did some wandering, married, and then went off on his own again.
Ramon had been a tall, handsome man with reddish hair and blue eyes, resembling his English father. He led an adventurous life, but eventually grew old. He then began visiting us at the ranch. He was fond of our mother who always found time for him in her busy days.

He was still independent enough in his later years to want his own place, so my father helped him patent some land, and he built a small log cabin a few miles from our ranch. He lived alone there for several years, but he came to see us every week. He came for a good meal as well as companionship. Sometimes he sat awhile and told us stories.

Today my memories of him are tinged with regret—regret for both the indifference of youth and the loneliness of old age. Perhaps my telling his story will help a little.

Uncle Bonney

He came down the road to the rock ranch house—a tired old figure on his burro. His hair was silvery under his old felt hat, and his eyes held the disillusionment of old age. An empty water jug hung from each side of his saddle, and the creak of their rise and fall against the leather kept time with the muddled thoughts in his weary brain. His main thought was that he was nearing a home again. There would be steaming dishes on the table in the long, dim dining room, a nice, soft armchair afterwards, and someone to talk to again. His was a pleasant thought after days spent alone, with just the burros for companionship.

He visualized the family—Doña Emma's smile, and the children frolicking about. They might not be too glad to see him, but they would put another plate on. Beggars are not choosers. After all, he was a beggar. He had come to beg a few hours of companionship and a real meal after eating cold hash and beans out of cans for many days. He was hungry in body and soul. But he would not bother them much. He would try to fill the aching emptiness in himself and then he would leave. Perhaps they would understand he was not always like this.

In the house, the children stood around in admiring and wondering poses, watching him eat the food in great platefuls. When he was through, the younger ones followed him to the living room where he sat in an armchair and lit his old pipe. Perhaps he would talk a little.

He was a gay caballero in his day. He had been a reckless, daring, adventure-loving character. As he looked about now at those living around him—ranchers and farmers—he wondered at the tameness of their lives. What would they have to think about, what experiences to relive, in the drab hours of old age? They would have a boring old age after a boring youth.

What memories lay hidden behind those sunken blue eyes still keen and piercing in their depths? Sometimes, when the mood was on him, he sat on Don Dañiel's porch in the evening, and held his audience breathlessly with his adventures told in Spanish. But he never told them everything. The

children thought there was much he would never tell. That must have kept his mind preoccupied when he also sat for hours in Doña Emma's cool living room, staring at nothing, or so the children thought. This southwestern country was unsettled when he was young. Spanish families predominated. There were also dangerous nomadic Indians, looting outlaws, and occasional American settlers. It was a country of fine large ranches and grants, with indefinite boundaries and indefinitely owned herds of cattle and wild horses roaming everywhere. There were small scattered settlements, where *tiendas* were restocked with eastern goods by the trade caravans from the States. It was an exciting time to be alive, for it was the days of the last frontier that would never come again. That was why there was sadness in his memories of the colorful times of cattle kings and the Santa Fe Trail. It was a time when some of the "lost" Spanish mines still operating had to be shut down because of isolated Indian hostility and encroaching Americans. Mines, never to be found again, lost color; their "tubes ... twisted and dried."
His father had been an Englishman who married a lovely Spanish young woman, and had a large place at La Junta. He was killed by Indians soon after Ramon was born, and his helpless wife, with a new baby, was unable to prevent the ranch from being looted by Indians and divided among neighboring ranchers. There was little law, only the survival of the fittest.

Then his mother had another man in her life. This one was a trader of Swiss-German descent; he, too, met a violent death, murdered for his gold.

Her third man was also a German. Ramon did not like him; neither did his half-brother, Andres, who left home at a young age because of him. That man, Metzger, had a large ranch and it was rumored he worked a secret gold mine. At any rate, he was known for having and spending gold. He was considered a very wealthy man. But he died without revealing his mine—if there ever was one. After his death, his family quarreled, litigated, and spent attorney fees until nearly everything was gone.

Then his mother, who was forceful as well as lovely, insisted the quarreling stop. She sent her sons out into the world to make their fortunes. She carefully married her daughters to ranchers, except for one, Marie, who ran away with a handsome young neighbor and seldom came home again. His mother kept Ramon, her first child, at home as long as she could. The others said he was her favorite; therefore, his half-brother and sisters did not like him. But he was young and did not care.

His blood was too hot to stay idly at home and dutifully attend responsibilities; he left. He ran away at night so he would not have to see his mother's sad eyes.

The overland freighting business seemed the most profitable and interesting life, so, by selling most of his possessions, he acquired a wagon and a pair of mules and started his business.
He made his first freighting trip to Denver, which was then a growing mining town. There he happened to meet his father's brother, Henry Bonney, whom he had never before heard of or seen. His uncle had been lucky in a mining venture and, being childless, offered Ramon a good home and education in the "States" if he would end his wandering ways.

Ramon thought of his mother and refused. He neither saw nor heard of his uncle again. He neglected to ask for an address, but his pride would have prevented any future contact with his uncle anyway.

When he returned from his trip, he learned that his mother had died. With her death, his home ties were broken, and he drifted away from his family.

Ramon continued with his freighting. He prospered and added more wagons to his caravan. He was commissioned to freight for Fort Union, the west's biggest fort at that time. It was an outdoor life—sleeping under the stars at night, and keeping an eternal watch for Indians and outlaws. He met many characters—including Billy the Kid, Kit Carson and Cerán St. Vrain.

When he married, his wife expected him to give up that wild, free life. He invested his savings in a ranch and bought horses and cattle. He had five children, three boys and two girls. After several years of domesticity, he could no longer stand the boring life. Giving everything to her and the children, he left home and them.

The days of freighting were passing. More Americans steadily arrived, Indians were being suppressed, outlaws hunted down. Law and order was near. The old way of life had changed. He did not belong anywhere anymore.

He still did a sort of freighting, from town to town. His wife learned to live without him. His children grew up, married and had their own homes and lives.

His business gradually dwindled. Eventually he began to go from relative to relative, for he now remembered he had relatives. If someone needed him, he would stay on awhile and help. Then he would drift on to another household. Always drifting…

He continued his round of visiting among his nieces in Buena Vista, his various nephews and cousins at La Junta and along the Red River. He wondered what had happened to the fine hospitality this country once had, but they fed him well, as if his stomach mattered most.

He liked best to stay with his nephew Dañiel; he liked his wife, Emma. She was a kind, motherly person who seemed glad when he came. He rocked and played with her babies and his hands were gentle. Perhaps he remembered his own he had deserted.

He decided to end the nomadic life. With Don Dañiel's help he filed on a claim, built a little log cabin, and got burros. He did not mind the burros now, though once he had owned fine horses. Doña Emma outfitted his cabin with furniture and dishes, and through the long days he made a pond. With it he watered his burro and the little garden he attempted to plant each year.

He really liked his little "rancho" as he called it. He felt happier and more independent there than he had felt for a long time. His log cabin was built up against the hillside, with pines around it. Extending along the edge of the hill was a corral for his burro, patiently built of rocks, and a cave or grotto for shelter. He was proud of that. He showed it to Don Dañiel's children when they visited him. On the western side was a sheer bluff that abruptly dropped away to a deep canyon below. Lining the top of this canyon were tall pines that moaned and sang when the wind rushed through them. On the eastern side was his pond, its perimeter dotted with little pines, and tiny ones beneath the water. When the sunset shone through the big trees, strange green and orange lights reflected on the water.

He lived there for five years, getting older and feebler all the time. He was getting careless with his appearance, and he did not attempt to cook much. He lived on the littlest amount of food possible. When he grew very hungry he went to Doña Emma's for a meal. That last year he went perhaps three or four times a week. He also depended on getting all of his drinking water there.

The children were growing up. They did not always seem glad to see him and seldom rushed out to welcome him, citing the respectful greeting he expected them to say, or wait on him as he thought they should. Sometimes the children were busy with their own thoughts when he visited. He sat in the living room for hours, gazing at nothing, his dim, blue eyes weary and lost. He now seemed to be living entirely in the past, and it was not always a happy past.

When they called him to the table, he ate carefully and slowly, as if he wanted to prolong the meal as long as possible. Then he filled his water jugs, painfully got on his burro, and began his lonely way home.

At first, he tried to hide that he was getting old. He dyed his hair and, ignorant of such things and clumsy, he mixed his dyes wrong. His hair bloomed in odd colors. Doña Emma gently told him that he was getting old and he might as well admit it. He needed a steady home. He should live with them, or go to his children and quit roaming—live his last days in peace. He refused.

Once he said to Don Dañiel's young son, as he was getting ready to leave: "Old people are not wanted. Nobody wants them, for what are they but a burden? Let me give you some advice, boy. Don't ever run away from home. Don't throw everything you have away on wild living. Stick to your family so your family will stick to you when you are old; so you won't have to go begging for a meal; so you won't hunger for a home with people who want you. Save something for when you are old. Save something besides memories. They are not enough to sustain you. Remember what I say."

He put a wrinkled, trembling hand on the boy's blonde head a minute, and a tear rolled down his cheek. Then he lifted himself with an effort onto his burro and went away. The boy remembered.

The day came when Doña Emma saw the old figure dozing in her armchair, and she had a feeling of foreboding. He looked so frail. She and Daniel worried about his staying alone any longer, and wanted to write to his family to come get him. But the old man kept refusing.

One day a nephew from a neighboring ranch found him lying asleep with his mule in an open meadow less than a mile from his cabin. He was too blind to find his way back to his home perched on the edge of the steep canyon.

He finally listened to Emma and Daniel and was willing to take their advice. Don Dañiel notified his family at Pastura and asked them to come get him. Ramon would have to humble himself to live with his children he had deserted. He expected them to never have a warm place in their hearts and homes for him. He was wrong; they did.

One day, the old uncle's family from Pastura came for him. He had to leave his burros behind.

Towards evening, Doña Emma looked out the window and saw her husband had come home after being gone for several days on ranching business. She left her work and went out into the yard to greet him. After he kissed her he said, "I see by his burros that Uncle Bonney is here."

"No," she said. She explained that the uncle's family had come, and that he had gone with them.

Don Dañiel was sad. He went into the house, turned and said, "We'll have to find someone to take his burros. I'm going to miss my old uncle."

They all did miss him. They remembered his visits and how, afterwards, he quietly rode away and disappeared into the sunset. They and their children remembered his stooped figure silhouetted against the bright sky. I, one of those children, later wrote a poem:

> The sun must set,
> though bright clouds flame against the sky,
> the old world knows that fires die,
> when men forget.
> Like the old pine, gnarled and bent by storm,
> we knew not the trials that bent that form.
> He, plodding now, seems wearily
> against that flame a mockery.
> To him the dawn and dusk are friends
> for he has learned all journeys end.
> The sun must set.

His burros were given away. But his log cabin still stands against the hillside. Visitors going to Don Dañiel's place might glimpse it among the vegetation and wonder what tales it could tell.

Sometimes the wind rushes through the tall pines and they moan and sing and bend over it. Sometimes the sunset throws strange colors on the pond's water, where the tops of little pines break its surface.

Still, sometimes in the evening Don Dañiel and his family are startled when the dogs bark, half expecting to see an old man coming down the road on his burro, an empty water jug tied on each side of his saddle—a tired, lonely, proud old figure, riding to the house, backlit by the sunset.

SECTION 4: LAUMBACHS IN NEW MEXICO

Chapter 27: Never a Road—Aunt Marie
by Verna L. Sparks 1909—1996

Editor: This is one of Verna's fictionalized stories that I gently unfictionalized. Some fictional portions remain in this poignant story I always loved.

Besides our grandmother, Elionor, and Aunties at Buena Vista, we occasionally saw other relatives.

There were at least two or three older ones who left us with lasting impressions.

One was my Great-Aunt Marie—Maria Marta Ebel Esquibel, my grandmother's full sister—who lived some miles west of us in the deep Cañon de Agua, its floor about 2,000 feet below our ranch. Over eons, the Canadian River, or Rio Colorado (Red River) as it was then called by locals, had created a huge gorge with a maze of deep canyons until it finally widened out into the more open land below the "mesa."

Aunt Marie's home was on the floor of Canon de Agua, where she lived the long years of her life after her marriage. Her husband, Uncle Felipe Esquibel, had been a handsome neighbor [*in Mora*] who swept her off her feet with his charm. She left an affluent home at La Cebolla to marry him, and they settled in this far off remote canyon. Marie made the best of her new life.

It was a hard life for her in many ways, and certainly a busy one with work, many sons, an easy-going husband, and no conveniences. Felipe was content to farm a little by the river. Having not had them, he did not miss the things Marie once had.

She saw her family a few times in her younger days. Occasionally they took the long trip by wagon, following the river's northern route, eventually arriving at Las Vegas, from there going on to the Mora Valley. After her mother, Bibiana, died [*in October 1897*], she seldom again made the trip north. My family did not live far away, and Aunt Marie had a special fondness for my father. She would have welcomed us if we visited her more often. We only lived seven miles across from the top of the river canyon. A steep trail ran up its side, but there was never a road.

The nearest town was 20 miles from our place and her sons traded there fairly often. They rode horseback up the trail, left their horses in our corral, borrowed a wagon and two draft horses from us to pull it; from there they went to town. After completing their trading, they came back to our ranch, packed their purchases on the horses, and went back home down the trail. They usually ate a meal with us, going or coming, so we knew that family fairly well. My parents were always glad to hear news about their Aunt Marie.

We seldom saw her, but I vaguely remember her one time when I was a child and had whooping cough that developed into pneumonia. News was handed down by the men on their trips. One day, Aunt Marie, then already an older woman, rode horse-back up that long canyon trail to see me. I woke once to see her standing by my bed. She gently touched my face and smiled. I heard her murmur, "*Pobrecita*," and I went to sleep again. That may have been the last time she came out of the canyon.

That was the last time I saw her alive. When she died, some of us went to her funeral. The men had gone ahead, but my mother, a sister and I walked down that trail to her little adobe house by the river. We looked at her lying there in a candle-lit room. I always believed she was the most beautiful, tiny old woman I had ever seen.

I remembered, too, the lovely gold filigree pin my mother had that was made from one of Aunt Marie's earrings. Years later I wrote her story.

Cañon de Agua (4 ft.) oil painting by Verna L. Sparks

Never a Road

Marie came outdoors again and stood still a moment, gazing up at the hill and the crooked trail. A tiny old woman in a black dress and shawl, she stood at the end of the long, low porch of the adobe house. When she turned back to old Felipe resting on the bench, her eyes were dim and strained.

She sighed. How quickly the sun went down behind the steep red canyon walls! Here in the bottom of the river canyon it was already in deep shadow.

She could see—not far from their front yard—a light, muddy thread. The Rio Colorado was at low ebb. In the spring she had seen it come down, sometimes like a mad, roaring thing. But it was sleepy tonight, whispering softly as it moved along.

"That river," Marie said. "It puts me to sleep, always talking to itself."

Felipe smiled at her. "I like to hear the river, *linda*. What is better than to sleep, when one is old?"

Her eyes came back to her husband. With the lazy dog at his feet he sat quietly, puffing on his corncob pipe. She shook her head slightly, stepped back on the porch, and sat down beside him. Up on the trail nothing was moving.

"He is late," she said. "He takes a long time to sell my earrings. Maybe Doña Emma did not have money to pay for them. Am I not her husband's aunt? They were Mama's earrings, his grandmother's."

She was still a moment, and then said, "That was a good home, Felipe, trees and a cool mountain creek. We had a big house, and it was where her father lived. My mother had beautiful things. How the years go! Nothing is left of that time, now not even the earrings."

"Then you should not have given them to our son," her husband scolded. "He could have worked for money to pay for his wedding feast. But no, he had to come to you for help. Now think of us. When I married you, Mariita, and took you away from that fine house at Saboya, I didn't ask help from anybody. People had more pride then. Those were better days." Then he said gently, "I have provided well for you, haven't I, Mariita? We have lived long and had many children, and, always, we have had plenty to eat."

She smiled gently at him. "We have lived well, and children are a blessing, even this son of ours. Sometimes I think I love him best, maybe because he is the last one."

"Well, he'll be married soon. I hope he brings his wife here. She would be good help for you. I think you are tired tonight, Mariita. What have you been doing today?"

"Nothing, always nothing—I just look at the trail, waiting for him. I look at it so much. *Santa Maria*, always looking and nobody ever coming! I think, maybe, if there was a road, Doña Emma and the girls would come see me. I'd like to see those girls; they must be grown by now."

Marie's words, "maybe, if there was a road," sounded empty, pointless.

Long ago she had argued: "You foolish ones—to always borrow a wagon from Don Dañiel at the top. You go to town and leave your horses. Then you come back, leave his wagon, and carry everything down the canyon on horseback. You should build a road."

But Felipe had laughed and shrugged, and went out to plow his field. If she pressed too hard, he might promise, "Don't fret, *linda,* I will build you a road someday."

The years passed by; he never did.

Later she thought, "The boys, they will do it. They won't be content to live this way."

But the boys grew up and were content to live the same old way, and then they left home.

Again Marie mused to herself, "Maybe, if there was a girl, just one, even, I would not be alone. A girl would think as I do."

But there were only boys. Marie finally gave up arguing. She gave up caring. There was no use quarreling with her men. The good Lord made them the way they were.

Tonight she only said, "Now that I am too old to ride horse-back out of the canyon, I never see Doña Emma anymore. And nobody comes here. But I still think, if there was a road…"

Patiently Felipe answered, "There never was a road. What does it matter now? We are old; pretty soon we will die and we won't need a road. Be content, *linda.*"

He stood up and pointed. "Look, he is coming now. He is almost here."

"He is coming alone." Marie stood up also, and turned to go into the house. "He will want his supper first, and then we'll hear about the earrings."

After their supper of beans, green *chile* and tortillas, the son pushed back his plate and looked at his mother. So far not a word had been said about his errand.

"Well," said the son, "I gave Doña Emma the earrings and she liked them very much." His eyes shifted to the floor.

As she watched him, his mother thought, "How handsome he is. But he looks uneasy. I wonder what's the matter? I hope he did not lose the money." She waited patiently.

After awhile, he continued. "She said she didn't have hardly any money at the ranch. She gave me four dollars."

"Just…four dollars? That is all?" Marie half rose, and sat down again.

Felipe frowned. "That won't pay for a wedding feast. You'll have to earn some money, after all."

"Yes," the son said, leaning back in his chair, still not looking at his mother. "She also said she didn't have any use for earrings. She could make pins with them."

Bibiana's gold filigree earrings were given to her daughter Maria Marta. Years later, Marie later sold them to her nephew's wife, Emma Laumbach, who had at least this one, pictured below, made into a pin.

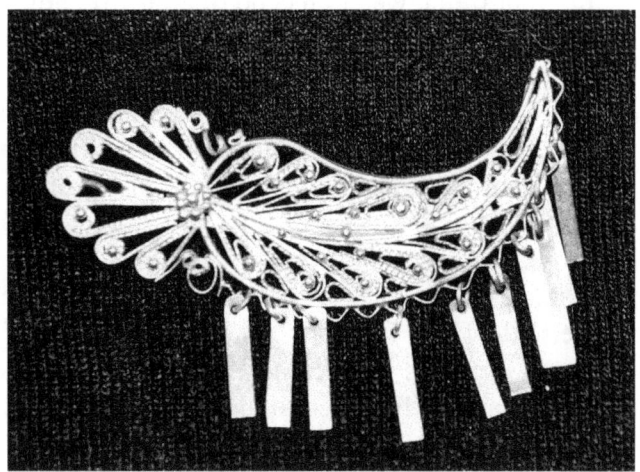

Marie shut her eyes. She remembered her own mother, Bibiana, as she stood late one day, young and very beautiful in the candlelight. She wore a long, soft-colored dress, and wore the earrings. They were fine gold filigree, with dangles that swayed and caught the light when she moved her head.

Marie recalled it well for that was on her wedding day, when she had married Felipe and left her home. Long afterwards, after her mother died, she received the earrings.

She remembered that day. She was making bread when Felipe came home from town and handed her a small package. Delicate like golden cobwebs, they lay inside a little white box.

She never had occasion to wear them but she looked at them often. She thought, if Santa Maria had blessed us with a girl, I would have given her my earrings and she would love them like I do.

Now they would be made into pins. The thought dismayed her.

She rose shakily and said to her son, "Please, you must take the money back to her and get my earrings!"

Surprised, her son turned to her, his eyebrows meeting in a frown. He shrugged and looked at his father. Old Felipe looked at the ceiling and said nothing.

Marie waited a moment. Then sighing, she picked up her shawl with trembling hands. The men watched as she wrapped it about her head and shoulders, but they still said nothing. She went to the door, opened it, and stepped out into the twilight.

She crossed the porch and turned down toward the river. More than ever before, she noticed the clear coolness of the night. She listened to the soft, whispering water below her. Could it be talking to her tonight? It never had before.

Above, the stars turned on their lights, as though an unseen hand touched them with a candle, lighting them one by one. It made her think of candles lit in church. It had been so long since she had been in a church. She often thought of the canyon as a mighty cathedral, the sound of the water beyond her rose and fell like a chant. For countless years, this had been her church.

She looked around and thought, "Why do I fret? I should know by now. What I want never matters to anyone but me."

Her men did not understand about the earrings, how she felt about them. It was now too late to worry about them. They were gone, like cobwebs in the wind. Maybe that was all they ever had been, just cobwebs of memories, without substance, just figments of her imagination.

She opened her hands; it seemed like all her cares and impatience fell away, swept downstream in the Rio Colorado. She wondered why she ever thought of this place as a prison. Something happened tonight. It was as if the high, steep walls were pushed aside, and she could breathe again.
The stars burned brightly, the murmur of the water an echo of a far-off choir.

She turned to go, almost stumbling over the dog at her feet. He had been lying beside her all the time, head on paws, sadly watching her. When he struggled slowly to his feet, she touched his up-lifted nose with a gentle finger and said, "Well, *mi compadre,* it's time for us old ones to go inside, to bed."

At the sound of her own voice, she realized the night air had turned sharply cold. It went through her thin shawl. The light coming from the kitchen window looked warm and inviting; she realized that she had been outside too long.

As she came near the house, she heard the twang of her son's guitar. She entered the kitchen and stood still a moment, before speaking to him.

"Do not worry, Son," she said. "Doña Emma may keep the earrings. *Da nada.*"

He looked up for a moment, shrugged indifferently as if he wasn't listening, and went back to his playing. His eyes had a dreamy look, and he hummed to himself.

Old Felipe, sitting by the stove, nodded over his pipe. She knew it was past his bedtime, but he had waited up for her.

In her bedroom, she said her prayers to the tired, suffering *santo, Jesu Cristo,* hanging on the wall. Then she looked at the empty box that had held her mother's earrings. That morning, when her son took them away, her heart had felt as empty as the box he returned to her. Now it no longer mattered.

She knew tomorrow would be another day, same as yesterday. *Chile ristras* would flame against the adobe walls, a red splash against dull monotony. She would go on, cooking, sweeping, praying a little. She did not care. Nothing mattered anymore. Lying in bed tonight, the years were heavy upon her. She would escape. Sometime soon there would be a road.

SECTION IV: LAUMBACHS IN NEW MEXICO

Chapter 28: The Letter
by Verna L. Sparks 1909—1996

Editor: Verna (my mother) first wrote The Letter when she was in college. Her professor encouraged her to submit it for publication but her Aunties were still living, and she did not want to offend them or Tony. This story first appeared in her little book, In Search of Springs, *in which she related some of her family history in fictionalized stories. She wrote this one about her Aunt Mary Laumbach ("Ramona" herein), and Manuel Antonio Sanchez ("Don Carlos" herein), who married Crestina ("Louisa") instead of Mary, as he intended. Verna and her sisters sincerely believed this story about their Aunt Mary's ill-fated love, but dates and data prove the story cannot be totally true.*

In real life, Manuel A. Sanchez[i] was a handsome rancher who, along with his father, owned a large cattle spread near Sabinoso at a place still shown on many maps as Sanchez because their ranch once had a post office and a store. He first married Rosita Eggert, she at age 16, daughter of Fritz Eggert, on December 3, 1887 at nearby Trementina. They were married 18 years, had no children of their own, but informally adopted some. Rosita died in 1905 at age 33. Four years later, in 1909, Manuel Sanchez remarried; his second bride was Crestina Laumbach. They had two children, Antonio "Tony," and Adelina, who died young.[ii]

The point of Verna's story was that the girl's father, "Don Henry," deliberately arranged for "Don Carlos" to marry his oldest unwed daughter instead of the one he probably knew was the man's intended. As the story told within the family goes, Manuel did not know he was marrying the "wrong" woman until his wedding day, when it was too late to speak up without loss of face and embarrassment for all. Manuel was always a gentleman.

In real life, the father, Andreas Detlef Laumbach 2nd, had died in 1904, five years before the marriage of his daughter Crestina in 1909. In truth, Andreas had nothing to do with this tale.

Was there any truth to it?

Except perhaps in the very earliest years when their children Tony and Adelina were born, Aunt Crestina and Uncle Sanchez were unhappily married. She lived most or all of their married life in Las Vegas on Valencia Street. She seldom visited the ranch where Tony lived with his father. It seemed to me that she was an unhappy woman. Perhaps sometime Crestina learned her husband had loved her sister. There were years when she and her three sisters—including Mary—who lived about a block from her in Las Vegas, did not visit, and we were cautious to not mention if we had first visited at the other house.

Even before I heard this story of The Letter, I thought Mary was the loveliest, sweetest-natured of all of our great aunts I knew. Regrettably, I did not know Aunt Margaret and Aunt Estefanita.

All of the Laumbach men and women were handsome and beautiful.

Because I know portions of this story cannot be true, I cannot undo her fiction without undoing the point of her story. I want to include it in this book because I always loved it, but to be fair I have left it in my mother's fictitious form. She fully fictionalized the girls in her story. Mary and Crestina also did not have red hair.

~~

I recently learned Mary was not the only Auntie with an unrequited love.

Anna Marie Ortega—her mother, Adelina Laumbach, daughter of Henry Laumbach, was raised by Aunties—ultimately inherited many of Aunties' things. That included a trunk that had belonged to her Great-Aunt Anna, but contained items that had belonged to all three Aunties. In it were fine, never-used embroidered linens with the initials "BB" stitched by Leonor. Anna Marie was told the initials were for Brad Bucker, Leonor's fiancé. He was drafted or enlisted in the U.S. Army during World War I and sent to fight in Europe. He never returned; he was killed or missing in action. Anna Marie and her husband Albert say they learned nothing more about Brad Bucker except that he had been Leonor's sweetheart and that they intended to marry. Those embroidered linens with the letters "BB" are all that remain to memorialize their love. Leonor never married, remaining single like her sisters Mary and Anna. Except for Aunties, Adelina, Anna Marie and Albert, I wonder if anyone else in the family, including my mother, knew of Leonor's love story. I only recently heard of it from the Ortegas.

Perhaps Anna also once had a love. I hope she did. She seemed so sad in her photos in her later years. She was always a wonderful, gentle and kind woman.

Manuel Antonio Sanchez

THE LETTER

We girls always enjoyed visits from our relatives, especially when they were women. Most of those who stopped by the ranch were men, and their talk concerned ranch matters. We casually listened to their "shop talk," but our Aunt Ramona's visit was different.

She came one day, riding up the river trail, after a visit with our Great Aunt Lola. [*In real life, that was Maria Marta Ebel Esquibel, known to us as "Aunt Marie," known to others in her family as Mariita.*] Ramona seemed old to us, but then, anyone over 30 seemed old. We did not know her age, but she had a warm and pleasant personality. We thought she was beautiful. There seemed to be a hint of sadness in her smile when she talked to Mama.

"How happy you must be," she said, "to have a lovely family like this—all these children growing up around you. It makes me realize how much I've missed by never marrying."

Why did she never marry? After she left, we asked Mama, who knew Ramona's story. It interested us then. Today it seems an almost impossible tale.

How could a letter, even one written that long ago, have so affected people's lives? Could it do that today? Probably not. When this story began, a man was still the undisputed head of household. It was a time when a disappointed husband-to-be felt bound by rigid rules of chivalry. There was also Ramona: She, too, respected the rules of honor and dignity, and kept her secret for many years.

It all began with a letter…

Their father said he would read the letter at 12:45. It was now 12:40. Ramona was the first of the girls to come into the living room; she hoped Papa would not think she was too eager.

He stood by the small marble-top table with the letter in his hand, staring at it. He glanced up as she came in and then he just stood there, pulling at his white mustache.

It was odd, Ramona thought, that a man so tall and stern had hands that now trembled a little. But then, letters like this were rare. Letters of almost any kind were rare, and they all knew this was a proposal of marriage.

The rareness of proposals in this household was not because of unattractive available daughters. The scarcity was suitable mates in this high, isolated north-central New Mexico valley. After all, they could not marry just anyone! It was a recognized fact in the valley that there were no daughters more handsome than Don Henry's. It would be hard to find their equal anywhere, even in Holman or Rainsville or Golondrinas or Saboya. Maybe even in Las Vegas. They were good cooks, too. Their little mother taught them well.

So far two girls in the family found good husbands and were happy in their own homes. Their oldest brother was married, too, but he did not really count when it came to marriage. It was easy for a man to get married.

But there were still four girls at home. Four girls—and just one letter! Each held her breath with suspenseful hope. The feeling was so strong that it made a faint wave of hostility quiver through the air above the dinner table. You could almost hear the vibration tinkle the water glasses.

The letter had come that morning, addressed to Papa, and had been put aside until he came in at noon. He picked it up and opened it before he started to eat. He read it through once, and then he read it again, more slowly.

It must be bad news, Ramona had thought.

Finally Papa looked up and said, "Mama, what do you think? This letter is a proposal for one of our girls!"

Then Papa laid down the letter by his plate and started to pass around the food.

"But who? Who?" Elena began.

Her mother slightly shook her head at her. "Papa will tell us," she said in Spanish.

Papa frowned a little. "As soon as dinner is over, and you girls have finished the dishes, you may come to the living room and we'll talk about it. By then it should be about 12:45."

Papa was so precise. You never could hurry him; it was no use to try. But now it was almost time.

As his other daughters came into the room, Ramona watched him study them one by one.

She tried to hide her excitement. She was sure she knew from whom the letter came, and what it asked. After Ramona, Louisa was the first to appear, nervously smoothing her skirt and brushing back her dark red hair. Although the smallest, Louisa was the oldest still at home, and she always seemed to know what everyone was thinking—even when they whispered to each other that she could not possibly hope to get married anymore, she was simply too old.

Then came the middle sisters, the silly ones their brother used to call them, Elena and Beatrice. They moved over to the organ stool and sat, heads close together, whispering.

Louisa frowned at them and moved closer to her father. He stood by the table, tapping the marble top with the letter. "How can Papa just stand there, holding that silly old letter?" Bea whispered to Elena but loud enough for all to hear. 'I can't wait any longer!"

Papa looked up from under heavy, white eyebrows and asked sharply, "Where is Mama?"

Louisa jumped. "I'll go get her, Papa."

Before she could go, Mama came hurrying in, wiping her damp hands on her apron, looking around.

"Ramona, why are you standing in the corner, child? If you didn't have red hair, we couldn't see you."

Papa stared, first at Ramona and then at her mother.

"Sit down, woman," he cried. "What are you waiting for?"

When Mama sat in the little rocking chair by Ramona, Papa still stood there, looking at the floor.

Ramona knew what was bothering him. It was not that he was stubborn or controlling; he was using his slowness to gain courage. He knew he would have one happy daughter and three disappointed ones after he finished reading the letter. She sent him a quick look of understanding that he did not see.

Finally Papa cleared his throat, held up the letter, and said, "Mama, I know all of you want to hear this letter. I think we ought to hear it together and decide about it. It's from Don Carlos."

He looked around proudly at his pretty girls, waited another minute—as long as eternity for them—and read:

March 23, 1904
Dear Don Henry:
It was my pleasure the other day to see one of your admirable daughters,
the one with the unusual red hair, in the store, and I feel I could care for her.
My house is lonely now. I hereby offer my hand in marriage to your daughter,
believing that I can give her a good home and hoping I will find favor in her
eyes. With regards to all your family, I remain
Your sincere friend and neighbor,
Don Carlos Santistevan

"But two of us have red hair!" Louisa exclaimed. She shot Ramona a look that crackled with emotion.

Ramona felt herself grow hot, but she ignored Louisa, kept her eyes down and waited.

Elena glanced at both of them and giggled. "Louisa, you goose, Don Carlos can't mean you—you're too old!"

Louisa flamed, "I am not too old! I am not much older than you! I know how you are, you and Bea always hiding behind things, whispering and talking about me!"

"Well," Elena said, "the last time one of us got a proposal it was Sophie, and she was younger than you."

"What makes me tired," Bea complained, "is that these proposals are few and far between. Nobody's left in the valley anymore fit for us to marry. At this rate, the rest of us will never get married!"

"As for Don Carlos," Elena said, wrinkling her nose, knowing it wasn't her he wanted, "I wouldn't want to marry him—he's awful old, and a widower, very dull, and no doubt cranky. I'm glad he doesn't want me!" she said, patting her long, dark brown hair pulled back and pinned at her neck.

Ramona stood, frowning. "Why Elena, he isn't cranky. And he's not old! He's a fine man. When he goes by on his horse, he sits so straight and tall, so handsome …"

Everybody looked at her in surprise. She blushed and turned away.

Papa cleared his throat. "Now girls, it will be easy for us to know which one he meant. Who was in the store lately?"

Ramona clearly remembered that day in the store. After Don Carlos had come inside, she caught him looking at her with interest and warmth. She was thrilled. Their eyes briefly met, she smiled at him, and then both looked away so they would not appear forward or rude. That was just three days ago.

"Why, all of us have been there in the past two weeks," Bea said. "That could mean any of us."
"But you don't have red hair, Bea and Elena," said Louisa, pointedly and smugly. "And you are both just too silly for any man to want!"

Papa got out his handkerchief and wiped his forehead. "It's getting hot. Open the door a little, someone."

"But the boys, the hired hands, Papa," Mama said. "They are in the kitchen and might hear."

"What? They ought to be back out with the stock by now. Never mind, leave the door shut then. Now, we have to think about Don Carlos. We should answer his letter today."

He studied the girls again. "You know Don Carlos is not a young man any more. He is a widower and has a large house in town and a ranch. He needs a steady, mature woman. He has been an honest neighbor and should make a good husband." The father knew Louisa had a sharp tongue. Could Don Carlos really mean her?

Louisa sat with her hands clasped tightly in her lap. She looked too hopeful to be proper, Ramona thought, turning her face to the window.

"What are you looking at, Ramona?"

"Nothing, Papa."

Elena laughed. "I suppose she's wishing she could leave and go for one of her walks. Every time she's supposed to be doing something, or something important is happening, she's out there walking in the orchard, or along the *acequia*, doing nothing."

Louisa turned gratefully to Elena and smiled. She said, "That's right, Papa. I never did see such a lazy girl as Ramona."

Papa knew Ramona wasn't lazy, that was just Louisa talking. He knew Louisa would be a hard one for anyone to live with.

He seemed lost in thought, then took a deep breath and spoke decisively. "Two of you Our Lord blessed with red hair. However, there is no doubt Don Carlos meant Louisa in his letter. He would want an older woman for his wife."

He looked at Louisa. Relief rouged her face as if she sat too close to the fire.

Ramona turned to leave the room, her back straight, her dignified head held high. Mama reached out and touched her hand as she passed by. Mama knew.

---

[i] The photo of Manuel A. Sanchez, "Uncle Sanchez," at the beginning of this chapter, and of his and Crestina's children below, are from Anna Marie Ortega's collection; courtesy of Karl Laumbach. Both of these photos were enhanced by Butch Sanders.

[ii] Photo of Adelina and Tony Sanchez. Tony looks embarrassed in that costume he had to wear.

SECTION IV: LAUMBACHS IN NEW MEXICO

Chapter 29: J. S. Candelario
by Jan Girand

This is one of many postcards Sito used to promote himself and his curio business.

Will the real J.S. Candelario please stand up? He invented himself. His tall tales about his family history and his store's origin were repeated by some of his family. I regrettably perpetuated some of his myths in a piece I wrote about him for the *New Mexico Magazine*, published March 2000. If other modern writers and I had done our homework, we could have separated some fiction from facts. My excuse is that my information had come from Sito's family, so it must be correct. Not! I knew, of course, as anyone should, that "the old curio store" had not been at that location and continuously owned by his family since 1603. As I wrote in the piece for the magazine, I believe "…curios are a fairly recent American concept; the possibility of a retail store of curios existing for nearly 400 years [*anywhere*] is as likely as that creature known to be part jackrabbit and part antelope." That date of 1603 was prior to the founding of Santa Fe. I doubt Sito intended that line to be taken seriously, but an amazing number of people did. Some still do.

Sito said his parents were Antonio Jose Candelaria (or Candelario) and Maria Altagracia Garcia. Researcher Butch Sanders found few records of his (probable) mother, even less on his father, and on his possible five siblings, all christened in San Felipe, Albuquerque, Bernalillo, Territory of New Mexico. Butch could not further trace Sito's lineage to his own satisfaction.

Then, said Sanders, "There's Sito—aka Jesusito, Jesus Sito, John S., J. S. and Jose Sixto. The first time I find him with absolute certainty is in the 1885 census when he is age 23, Jesus S. Candelario, occupation clerk, residing in the Santa Fe dwelling of his employer, merchant George E. Blain. In 1900 Santa Fe [*census*], he said he was 36, born March 1864 (he lost a couple of years). He stayed with the same birth-date through the next three censuses and on his death certificate. His photo caption and his other bios say he was born 10 March, 1864."

Sito said his curio store had been continuously owned by his family for generations. He had inherited, owned and managed it by 1882 or 1890 (date depends on source). He reportedly said he had left his friend Jake Gold in charge of running it while he attended Park College in Missouri, to become a Presbyterian minister. When he returned, he found Jake had commandeered his store; he had to fight to take it back. That is incorrect. Sito did attend Park College and graduated from there in 1888, but he did not become an ordained minister. Published newspaper articles and advertisements Sanders found show none of his claims about his store's origin are true. Also, Sanders does not believe Sito struggled with Jake over ownership of his store. They were friends. Sito remained a loyal friend to Jake, always. Any tale that Jake tried to claim ownership of Sito's store came from a source other than Sito.

Jesus (pronounced hayZOOS) Candelaria was called little Jesus or "Jesusito" when he was young. He was a small man. He adopted the middle name Sito but mostly went by the initials J.S. As I wrote for the *New Mexico Magazine*, Sito probably changed the spelling of his last name from Candelaria, fairly common in New Mexico, to Candelario because that spelling was as uncommon as he thought himself to be.

Sito received his education in private schools, including at Mora and then St. Michael's College in Santa Fe. When he was doing missionary work in the Mora area, he applied for and received a scholarship to attend Park College in Missouri to study for a Presbyterian ministerial degree. He returned to the Mora area to continue missionary work and teach, for a little while. There he met Estefanita Laumbach.

Sito said he and his brother Antonio Garcia had inherited from his father a meat market or general store on Santa Fe's San Francisco Street. That may or may not be true. If true, Sanders speculated that it might have been where Sito established his curio store, in the middle of that block, where it remains today.

Sito's family claimed he owned a large portion of Santa Fe property, including the city block from West San Francisco Street to Palace Avenue, bordered on one side by Burro Alley. Was all of that really once his?

Below is a young J.S. Candelario, from collection of John and Lores Candelario

A young Estefanita Laumbach; an original photography studio print was among the collection of Lores and John Candelario, as well as of Albert and Anna Marie Ortega.

Estafanita and Sito traveled extensively in their younger married years, promoting their store and marketing their wares. They often sent post cards to her parents and sisters. This is a postcard sent by Sito in 1909 from Guadalajara to her family at Buena Vista; note their mailing address was La Cueva.

~~

The majority of the following information, published newspaper articles and photos, were found and transcribed by Butch Sanders. They tell us a little of Sito's doings in the final decade of the 1800s.

Santa Fe New Mexican
Santa Fe, New Mexico
May 24, 1890
ROUND ABOUT TOWN.

J. S. Candelario, of Blain Bros.' store, who lately concluded his studies at Park College, Mo., is agitating the question among the young men of Santa Fe of organizing a literary and debating society.

~~

Santa Fe New Mexican
Santa Fe, New Mexico
Saturday, April 4, 1891
ROUND ABOUT TOWN.

J. S. Candelario, an energetic young man, formerly clerk for Blain Bros., has launched out into business for himself and has opened a second hand store just below Schnepple's.

~~

Santa Fe New Mexican
Santa Fe, New Mexico
Tuesday, April 28, 1891
ROUND ABOUT TOWN

J. S. Candelario, who has opened a new second hand store on lower 'Frisco Street, inserts a standing advertisement in this day's issue.

~~

Santa Fe Weekly Sun
Santa Fe, New Mexico
June 13, 1891

Otto Johnson of Lordsburg will open a first class boot and shoe shop in Mr. Candelario's second hand store on Lower San Francisco Street Monday morning, where he will be prepared to do all kinds of work in that line at lowest prices.

~~

Santa Fe Weekly Sun
Santa Fe, New Mexico
Sunday November 28, 1891

The store of J. S. Candelario, on lower San Francisco Street, was entered by burglars about 9 o'clock, last night. The thieves were evidently in a hurry, because they only took away about $20 worth of goods including some cheap pistols. Marshal Gray is an expert in matters of this kind, and will doubtless soon locate the guilty ones.

~~

J. S. Candelario and Estefanita Laumbach were married in the First Presbyterian Church at Mora in February 1892.

~~

El Mosquito
Mora, New Mexico
Thursday, February 11, 1892

El dia se unio para siempre por los lazos matrimoniales el joven J. S. Candelario, de Santa Fe, con la senorita Estefanita N. Laumbach, de Buena Vista, en ultima poblacion.
La ceremonia se efectuo en la Primera Iglesia Presbiteriana.
EL MOSQUITO desea a los recien desposados una eterna luna de miel.

~~

After they married, they lived in Santa Fe.

~~

Santa Fe New Mexican
Santa Fe, New Mexico
Tuesday, June 14, 1892

John Candelario, the second hand dealer, was standing near the post office at 8 o'clock this morning reading aloud an article in the El Mosquito, a penny-a-line publication from Mora. Jose B. Ortiz stood near and suggested that the reader would probably not have the paper in his possession if he had to pay for it. Candelario suggested that Mr. Ortiz was a liar. Then Mr. Ortiz drew up his cane and whacked Candelario over the head, spilling some little blood, and breaking a finger for the aforesaid Candelario. There was a tussle and the crowd rushed in and separated the combatants and two stalwart policemen were on hand promptly (!) to rush them off before the city magistrate. Both men were ordered to appear for hearing at 5 o'clock this afternoon.

~~

Santa Fe New Mexican
Santa Fe, New Mexico
Wednesday, June 15, 1892

Justice Vigil holds that when one man calls another a liar the man so addressed has a right to resent it. On this ground he discharged Jose B. Ortiz, accused of striking John S. Candelario yesterday.

~~

Apparently, Sito changed his name to John for a while, and thereafter implied the J in his initials represented John, which he seemed to prefer to Jesus.

~~

Estadarte de Springer
Springer, New Mexico
February 9, 1893
J. S. CANDELARIO
PAWN BROKER
DEALER IN
SECOND HAND GOODS,
AND
Sole Agent for the New Home Sewing Machine.
Also a Full Line of Supplies for All Kinds of Sewing Machines.
Buys, sells, rents and exchanges Furniture,
Sewing Machines, Stoves, Guns, Pistols,
Ammunition, Hardware, Tinware, Crockery,
Glassware, Clothing, Watches, Clocks, Jewelry,
Curtains and Fixtures, and Fine Carpet.
PROMPT ATTENTION TO CASH ORDERS BY MAIL.
POST OFFICE BOX, SAN FRANCISCO STREET, SANTA FE, N. M.

~~

I have an old book with Sito's "New Home Sewing Machine" advertisement rubber stamped inside the cover.

~~

There was a September 1899 article about a roof caving in, killing a Mora family named Cordova, said to be related to Sito's wife. A subsequent article ran a correction, saying the family involved in the roof accident was not Sito's family and did not live at Mora. The articles name Sito: "J.S. Candelario, the San Francisco Street merchant."

~~

Butch Sanders wrote: "We have a pretty good record of Jake Gold's curiosity shop location as it changed hands, but nothing on Sito's property, which supposedly stretched from his store on San Francisco Street, bordered Burro Alley on the west, and included the block facing Palace Avenue, where he and Estefanita lived in their brick home. That's a significant piece of property and should have made the news when he purchased it. Did he inherit it? Or did he ever actually own all of that property?"
Sanders said, we have records in newspaper articles and ads, as well as photographs of Jake Gold's curiosity shop during his "reign as curiosity king" in Santa Fe for the last decade(s) of the 1800s.

On Saturday October 11, 1890 the *Santa Fe Daily New Mexican* ran an article reporting that Jake Gold purchased, from the estate of Jose Leandro Perea for $5,000, the property where he would locate his "old curiosity shop." That location, on the corner of Burro Alley and West San Francisco Street was where Jake ran his successful trade business for a decade, with his landmark wooden *carreta* on the roof. Jake had opened his shop there in the early 1880s, but did not own it until he purchased it from the Jose Leandro Perea estate in 1890. Jake lost his shop in a foreclosure action in 1899 because of financial difficulties. *"In 1900 he [Jake] was sentenced to prison for violation of the Edmunds Act (adultery)."* Sito led an unsuccessful effort to get his friend Jake clemency.

Photo taken by William Henry Jackson in or about 1890.

If this photo was taken by William Henry Jackson in or about 1890 as reported, it was Jake Gold's Old Curiosity Shop. It was owned by Jake from about 1884/1885 until very near the end of September 1899 when Mrs. Lowitzki bought it, as reported in the *Santa Fe New Mexican* on September 30, 1899: *"Mrs. Solomon Lowitzki today bought the Old Curiosity Shop on San Francisco Street from Jake Gold, and reopened it with her sons in charge. The shop had been closed for some time by the sheriff on an execution in favor of J. G. Schumann. Mrs. Lowitzki paid the debt, costs and $50 for the stock, allowing Mr. Gold to retain his furniture."*

Less than a year later, Abe Gold bought the shop from Lowitzki—as reported in this newspaper article in the *Santa Fe New Mexican* on Monday, August 27, 1900: *"Bought the Old Curiosity Shop. Merchant Abe Gold today purchased the entire stock, fixtures and stand of Lowiztki curio store, Jake Gold's former place. He took possession at once and will add to the already large stock there the curios, Indian blankets, etc., now at his general store, making it the largest "old curiosity shop" and museum of curios anywhere in the west. Mr. Gold has also purchased the exclusive right to use the title 'Gold's Old Curiosity Shop.' He will conduct this business in connection with his general merchandise establishment which will be continued at the present stand on San Francisco Street."*

After Jake served his time in prison for adultery (imagine that!), he and Sito opened Sito's store four doors east of Burro Alley, at its present site, in curio competition with Jake's brother, Abe Gold, who had already acquired Jake's old shop on the corner of Burro Alley and San Francisco Street. That location later became the site of the Lensic Theatre.

Only after the turn of the century do we have newspaper and photographic evidence of J.S. Candelario's curio store, which became known as the original old trading post.

J.S. Candelario's Old Curio Store after 1901.

Sanders said, vintage photos of "The Original Old Curio Store" and "The Original Trading Post" are at the same location; that never changed from the time Sito and Jake Gold opened it for business in 1901. That little alley to the right of the store in post-1900 photos is not Burro Alley. To get to Burro Alley, you would have to walk west past three other businesses on that block. That alley on the right (east) side of Sito's (later called the Old Trading Post or the Original Trading Post) became an enclosed mall-type open entry corridor to restaurants and stores in that big building to the right, that is seen in some of the early 1900s photos.

Jake's mind was affected by venereal disease; he died in December 1905 in the Territorial Insane Asylum at Las Vegas. Sanders found a letter written by a Gold family member saying J.S. Candelario was the only true friend Jake still had in the world when he left it. Sito had corresponded with Jake until the very end. Therefore, Sito would never have said his friend Jake Gold tried to steal his curio store during his absence. That tale, later repeated, regrettably also in ignorance by me, was begun by someone other than Sito.

Jake's published obituary:

SANTA FE NEW MEXICAN
DECEMBER 20, 1905
[FRONT PAGE]
JAKE GOLD DEAD

First Indian Curio Dealer in Capital City Succumbs to the Inevitable.

Jacob Gold, the original old curio man of Santa Fe died Saturday last at the Territorial Insane Asylum at Las Vegas of progressive Paresis. He was 54 years of age and a native of this city, the son of Lewis Gold, one of the first Americans to settle in Santa Fe after the American occupation. For many years, and while his mental faculties were intact, he was very successful. He established an Indian trading and curio business on Lower San Francisco Street in the house purchased by his father, thirty years ago. His mental faculties then failing, the business was sold. Certain weaknesses, which overcame him on account of his mental afflictions, led him to the road that killed. While strong and healthy, he was a man of good moral character, considerable mental ability, good business habits and generous. He was his own worst enemy and suffered accordingly by being cut off before the allotted three score and ten years. Peace to his ashes and to his memory. The remains were interred in the cemetery of the insane asylum.

~~

Earlier, Jake's brother, Abe Gold, had a curio store on West San Francisco Street, probably on the opposite side of the street. His obit said he inherited the "Old Curiosity Shop" on San Francisco Street from his father, Louis Gold, who had established it in 1862. Perhaps it was the senior Gold, Louis, who first brought the concept of marketing novelties, Mexican and local Indian handcrafts to Santa Fe.

Abe bought his brother Jake's curio business that was located at the corner of Burro Alley and San Francisco Street after Jake lost it. While either Gold brother owned and ran it at that location, the old wooden *carreta* stood on its roof on the block's corner. Sito later adopted and used it at his location in the middle of the next block. In later years, the cart was replaced by a less dilapidated, not even wooden, *carreta* that does not even appear to be authentic.

~~

Following is partial published obit for Abe, who predeceased his brother, Jake :
SANTA FE NEW MEXICAN
AUGUST 14, 1903
ABRAHAM GOLD DEAD
End of the Eventful Life of a Well-Known Santa Fe Merchant
Abraham Gold, for many years one of the most prominent figures in Santa Fe affairs, died at his residence on San Francisco Street at 5:30 o'clock this morning after a lingering illness. The immediate cause of death was Bright's disease. Mr. Gold was 56 years of age, and came to Santa Fe over forty years ago, succeeding his father in business in this city. Mr. Gold is survived by a widow, Mrs. Mary Gold, and a brother, Jacob, who reside in this city, and two sisters, Mrs. F. MacFarland of St. Louis and Mrs. Morris Greenwald of New York.

"Uncle Abe" as he was affectionately called by many, was a man of sterling qualities and his friends were numbered by the thousands throughout the west. He was the owner of the "Old Curiosity Shop" on San Francisco Street, which his father established in 1862.

~~

This is the 1880 published obit for Louis Gold, the father of curio dealers Abraham "Abe" and Jacob "Jake" Gold:
SANTA FE WEEKLY NEW MEXICAN
JANUARY 10, 1880
Louis Gold, one of our well known citizens from Santa Fe and the territory, died last Monday from typhoid fever after being bedridden for several weeks.
Mr. Gold, who was German and Hebrew descended, resided in our city for more than 30 years, keeping busy with his business. He learned perfect Spanish, had many Spanish customs, had many acquaintances among the Spanish-American families of the territory and was most considerate of his fellow businessmen.
He also had considerable trouble with his business, which forced him to declare bankruptcy. Sometime later, with the help of his friends, he was able to open another store and regain a satisfactory level of solvency by the time of his death.
At the age of 60, he was one of the most active and intelligent merchants in the territory, an active and energetic man, who wanted a voice in the material details of his business.

~~

The curio stores—their ownerships and locations on West San Francisco Street—were deliberately confusing, Sanders believes. The *Santa Fe New Mexican* newspaper articles, ads and photos help sort them out. These advertisements ran, on the same pages, throughout most of 1903 for competing curio stores. One ad was Sito's: "The Old Curio Store, J. S. Candelario; Prop.; 301 and 303 San Francisco Street." Another was Abe Gold's: "Gold's Old Curiosity Shop, Abe Gold, Proprietor." A third ad: "Jake Gold, Manager; 311—317 San Francisco Street, Corner Burro Alley," with a photo of the shop and cart sitting atop it.

Sanders found similar ads that ran for the two stores in 1902—again, again both on the same page of the *Santa Fe New Mexican*. He said neither provided a San Francisco street number, but "Gold's Old Curiosity Shop" was listed as "San Francisco Street, Corner Burro Alley" with an odd photo of Abe Gold in costume and a wig. We know from the previous deed transfers/sales that Abe then owned Jake's "Old Curiosity Shop" at that location. Abe is his own manager at this time (1902) because Jake is managing Sito's: "The Old Curio Store, The Original 'Jake Gold' Curio Store, Jake Gold, Manager, J. S. Candelario, Prop."

According to The Historic Santa Fe Foundation, the old wrap-around building on the other corner of Burro Alley and San Francisco Street (across Burro Alley to the east, bordering Sito's store that was further east) was the house and business of Felipe S. Delgado. That was Juan Felipe de Santiago Delgado, older brother of Jose Felipe Benicio Delgado, aka Felipe B. Delgado, whose house is a historic landmark today on Palace Avenue, close to the site of Sito and Estefanita's home. Sito's home address was recorded as "136 West Palace Avenue" in the 1930 census. In that same 1930 census, the home of Lucia O. Delgado (Felipe B. Delgado's widow) was recorded as "124 West Palace Avenue," at the same location it is today.

The Gertrudis Barcelo house was an interesting neighbor, more than half a century earlier, to what would become J.S. Candelario property. The long adobe house with many rooms that had belonged to the famous Doña Tules was torn down in 1939 when the Santa Fe County courthouse was built. The famed Barcelo house, at the corner of Burro Alley and Palace Avenue, faced the Plaza. Diagonally across from it, on the southeast corner of Palace and Burro Alley, had been Madame Tules' gambling den. At one time Burro Alley was called Gertrudis Barcelona Street. On that street or alleyway, burros and their tenders sold their loads of firewood and other goods. The red-bricked two-story home of Sito and Estefanita on Palace Avenue was near that property once owned by Madam Tules. Candelarios' home later became the site of the Palace Restaurant, and then Señor Lucky's. The Candelario home was torn down and no longer exists. Mary Jean Cook, in her 2007 book, *Dona Tules: Santa Fe's Courtesan and Gambler*, wrote: [Doña Tules'] "...residence on Grant and Palace Avenues was demolished in 1938—39...The county courthouse may soon be sold or demolished. The property abutting her residence to the south was demolished when the Lensic Theater opened in 1931. The gambling sala at the corner of Palace and Burro Alley remained until the late 1940s. The fourth building to the east was demolished and became a brick house for the Candelario family."

Among their extensive J.S. Candelario collection, the Palace of the Governors Archives of the New Mexico History Museum has a 1904 photo of the "Mechanic's Baseball Team, J.S. Candelario manager, Santa Fe, New Mexico." Sito used that and many other postcards to promote himself and his business.

Another of Sito's postcards appeared in the 1912 *Representative New Mexicans, the National Reference Newspaper Book of the New State containing photographs and biographies of over four hundred men residents of New Mexico*. The caption under that postcard photo reads (verbatim): "J.S. Candelario, curio dealer; b. March 10, 1864, Santa Fe, NM; s. of Antonio Jose and Altagracia (Garcia) Candelario; educ. priv. schools and St. Michael's College, Santa Fe; grad. Park College, Parkville, MO 1888; returned to New Mex. succeeded to business of his forefathers, 'The Original Old Curio Store' estab. 1603 by the Candelario family and continuously in their possession. He is the only native born curio dealer in New Mex.; exhibits and ships Mexican and Indian curios and antiques to all parts of the world and holds largest collection on earth; city councilman 1899-1900; city treas. Santa Fe, one term; mem. I.O.O.F; K of P; Fraternal Union; Yoeman; Spanish-American Alliance. Address: Santa Fe N.M." That caption was obviously provided by Sito.

~~

Pictured, "Young Johnny Candelario, violinist at La Fonda." Photo courtesy Karl Laumbach, from Loris Candelario collection.

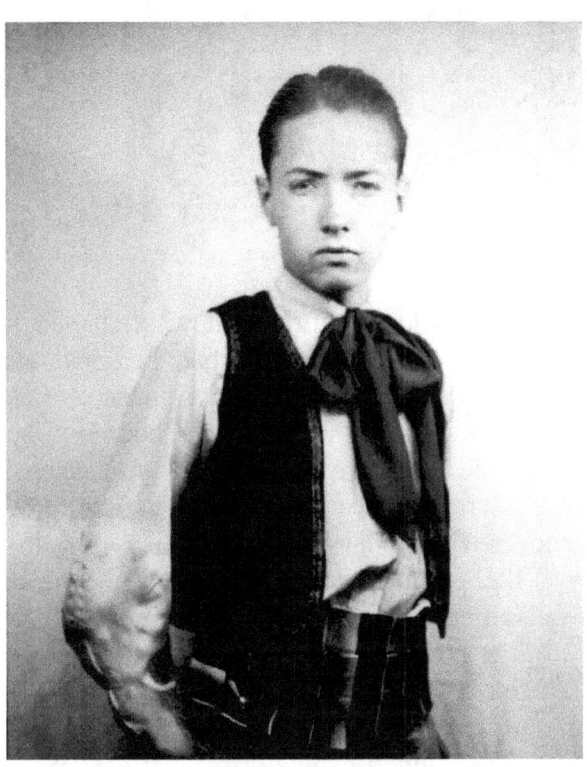

Verna Laumbach, as a college teenager visiting Santa Fe, wrote in a letter to her parents that young Johnny Candelario was the most polite, charming boy she and her friends had ever met.
Sito produced many postcards promoting himself and his tourist trade business. His postcards and other mass-produced material listed the tribes' and pueblos' feast days and other annual celebrations. While he promoted himself, he also promoted national, even international, interest in New Mexico natives, their important events, and their arts and crafts. This next photo with the Taos Indian Tribal Council, perhaps taken in the 1920s, was one of many of those.

When Sito and Estefanita grew old and infirm, they hired their handsome young nephew, Ike (Casimiro) Laumbach to stay with them and help with their personal and commercial businesses. Ike said that was his first paying job. He described entering the house on Palace Avenue, walking past the kitchen door and their bedroom. Looking in as he passed the bedroom, he saw large piles of money on the bed. He said the Candelarios did not have a bank account because they did not trust banks or bankers. When they had to write a large check to mail it somewhere, Ike walked Estefanita to the bank so she could deposit money and then immediately write a check for the same amount. (Banks would definitely not allow that today.) Ike's Aunt Estefanita allowed no one but herself to carry the heavy, cash-laden satchel when they walked down the street.

~~

Wednesday, May 4, 1938, Santa Fe, New Mexico
Obituary

[Rites for] Mrs. Estefanita Laumbach Candelario, wife of J. S. Candelario, who died Monday morning, were held this afternoon at the First Presbyterian church with Rev. A. G. Tozer and Rev. Uvaldo Martinez officiating. Interment was in the family plot in Fairview cemetery.

A host of sorrowing friends filled the flower-packed church and followed the long cortege to the cemetery. At the church services, Miss Olinda Rodriguez sang beautiful songs in both Spanish and English accompanied at the piano by Miss Margaret Scofield.

The Rising-Miller mortuary was in charge of the service.

~~

Jesus Sito Candelario died three months after Estefanita.

SANTA FE NEW MEXICAN
Santa Fe, New Mexico
Monday, August 1, 1938
J. S. Candelario Funeral Today
Rites Take Place at Presbyterian Church;
Interment in Fairview

Funeral services for Jesus Sito Candelario, prominent local curio dealer and property owner, who died early Saturday morning, were held at 3 o'clock this afternoon at the First Presbyterian church, with Rev. A. G. Tozer and Rev. A. V. Esquibel officiating.

The church was filled with floral offerings. Miss Olinda Rodriguez sang two beautiful hymns, "Saved by Grace," and "Nada De Sombras," with Mrs. D. W. Faw at the organ. Frank L. Wood and J. A. Poncel assisted as ushers.

Active pallbearers were Rudolph Laumbach, Antonio A. Sanchez, Elbert Wallace, Mariano Candelaria, Julian Duran and Joe Gallegos.

Honorary pallbearers were: Gov. Clyde Tingley, Mayor Alfredo Ortiz, Paul Gonzales, John E. Miles, Judge David Chavez, Jr., Miguel Leyva, Jose Larragolte, John McManus, Ben Luchini, Juan N. Vigil, J. O. Garcia, Robert Valdez, E. D. Trujlllo, Police Chief Tom P. Delgado, Tom Nicholson, Lorenzo Gutierrez, Sr., Diego Salazar, Luis Salazar, Biterbo Quintana, Cesario Ortiz, C. E. McGinnis, J. D. Kilkenny, Manuel Sanchez, David W. Carmody, Felipe Sanchez y Baca, Antonio F. Martinez, J. O. Seth, Paul A. F. Walter, Charles J. Eckert, Henry Dendahl, John Pflueger, Steve Anthony, Don Casados, Adolfo Ortiz, Tom Sanchez, Juan Olivas, Frank Billia, Ralph Rodriguez, Dan Rodriguez, Andres Gandard, Alfonso Duran, Sam Soza, Todosio Gonzales, Donaciano Gonzales, Lorenzo J. Sandoval and Patricio Olguin.

Interment was in the family plot at Fairview cemetery, with the Rising-Miller mortuary in charge.

~~

Many newspaper and magazine articles were written about J.S. Candelario after his death. On Saturday, July 30, 1938, the day he was found dead at home, 136 West Palace Avenue, at age 74, the *Santa Fe New Mexican* ran an extensive article. It said, when his housekeeper received no response, he entered his bedroom and found him. His grandson, his only immediate relative, had gone to Las Vegas the day before on a business trip. "Mr. Candelario, one of the most prominent curio dealers and property owners in the entire Southwest, had been in ill health for several years, but his death was unexpected." He had spent the day before at his auto camp on Water Street, and even attended a "picture show" that evening. His housekeeper, who was also his tourist camp manager, and his wife, Sito's secretary, were the only ones at home when he died. The article read, *"Upon graduation, he returned to the city and succeeded to the business of his forefathers, 'The Original Old Curio Store,' which was established by his family in 1603, and has been continuously in their possession since that date...Other than his business activities, Mr. Candelario had ventured into the political game but twice, having served as city councilman in 1899 and 1900, and as city treasurer for one term."*

Following that newspaper article in the *Santa Fe New Mexican*, Brian Boru Dunne wrote, *"New Mexico has lost one of its oldest citizens, perhaps its greatest salesman and its unique humorist."* And he wrote, *"Candelario [said] he had met tens of thousands of tourists from all over the U. S. A. and ... all over the world, and that he got 'intense pleasure' out of 'kidding' them. He said he 'kidded' everybody, even past presidents of the United States, and would-be presidents. He 'kidded' railway presidents and diplomats, and everybody—and they liked it. "Candelario seemed to know everybody and it was natural for visitors, famous and yet unknown to fame, to dash down San Francisco street to meet the genius who presided over the store under the ox cart. And it was the unique curio store of America, according to Vincent Massey, because its windows were of 'window, not plate of glass.' Dr. Durand, the philosopher, when in Santa Fe, said: 'Candelario is like the merchant of present-day Russia; he does not care whether he makes a sale or not.'"*

Dunne quoted several famous people, including William Jennings Bryan, who had visited Sito's store several times, and Vincent Massey, the millionaire poet and first minister from Canada to the United States. Massey had been widely quoted as saying, "I have spent a fine day in Santa Fe; I have called on the governor of New Mexico, the archbishop of Santa Fe, the Oldest Church, and finally on Candelario."

Many of Sito's quips about some of his "curios" became famous and were often repeated, including his bells that he claimed were dated 1500 years B.C., Ben Hur's trunk, and the skull of Henry Ward Beecher, small because it was "when he was a child."

Dunne wrote that Sito's store had been closed months before his death. He also wrote that one home visitor had seen Sito dump a barrel of rings of silver and gold and jewels and delighted over them.

The Historical Santa Fe Foundation had designated the Original Trading Post as a historical building. That explains why it has changed little in appearance in 100 years.

In 1999, a gracious Dennis Baca, then manager of the Post, took me down to the basement of the store to view the well being dug into and examined by archeologists. It has always amazed and confused me that the well was so far below ground-level. Had it, perhaps, hundreds of years earlier when Santa Fe was young, been in an inner exterior patio, and surrounding adobe melt of old structures and other conditions caused it to end up much lower than its surroundings, even with a building now above it?

The Historic Santa Fe Foundation had radio broadcasts of their "Fireside Chats." Copy of a transcription of one of those, from the spring of 1999, was given to Dennis Baca, who gave me a copy. During the broadcast, Mr. and Mrs. John Schroeder, owners of the Original Trading Post, were interviewed and conducted a tour of the building. The Schroeders had purchased the building in December 1987 without a building inspection. When they began to spruce it up—painting the storefront and shoring up the sagging front awning—they were inundated by complaining locals and media, because of its historical designation. They hired archeologists to excavate the old well, and David Snow, then the historian of the Museum of New Mexico, to research the building and its owners. They also paid the archaeologist to do extra digging, in anticipation of finding some of Sito's treasure stashes. They found none.

They later found an August 1944 newspaper article describing the collapse of a 15-foot section of ceiling that demolished cases of jewelry. The five or six feet of fallen debris blocked the store's front door. The needed repairs renewed much talk of J.S. Candelario's hidden treasures. Supposedly 35 pounds of gold was found at that time under floorboards, which the then-owner of the store was allowed to keep for making jewelry.

During their radio "chat," Schroeders described the well as having been beautifully constructed of river rock, no quarried stone. It had been "cleaned out" of any treasure stashes probably in the 1930s. (No doubt by John Candelario after his grandparents died.) The well was much older than most of what they found. Finds included ammo cartridges dating to 1873, and 1800s-era glass fragments. Pieces of bones were among the debris. They were mostly various kinds of animal bones, but some were human! They found pieces of bones from four different people. After some debate and consulting their priest from St. Bede's Episcopal Church, they reburied those mysterious remains in the store's basement in ground consecrated by their priest. In order to do that, they tried to dig a hole in the basement's dirt floor. They found—two feet below the dirt—a hand-quarried stone floor that appeared to be the basement's entire original floor.

During the broadcast, the Schroeders named several people who were present while the well and basement were cleaned up after the archeological examinations and excavations. That included Brian Lappe, a dowser who was also a "well-known *brujo*," who had expressed an interest in their activities. Witnessed by all present, Brian became aware of five different spirits present in the basement. He said one met his death there from a blow to his head. Another was an American Indian spirit guarding a corner of the quarried floor where an artifact of spiritual importance had been buried. Brian learned that artifact had been removed long before, but the Indian spirit did not know that. Those present that day moved piles of articles—trunks and packing crates—from the spot the Indian spirit guarded. There they found an open hole in the quarried floor where something appeared to have been dug up.

Brian believed his discovered spirits and findings were directly related to the "poltergeist(s)" that bothered some of the store's employees over a period of years. That included the Schroeders' own daughter. While she had worked at the store for a while, the daughter had an odd, chilling experience. She moved and rearranged a display of Indian fetishes, and then locked up the store for the night. She was also the one who unlocked the store the next morning. She was shocked to find the display moved back to where it had been, and the positions of the fetishes were changed. Dennis Baca and Robert Castillo, another gracious Original Trading Post manager, had told me about several employees' experiences, which included hearing a female Hispanic voice speaking and laughing inside the store after it had been locked for the night. Robert thought that voice might have been Estefanita's.

In my article published in the *New Mexico Magazine*, I wrote that my newly-wed parents visited Sito and Estefanita not long before they had died. Sito opened the trap door in his store, which is visible still, and took them into the cellar, where he opened trunks and showed them his best treasures too valuable for public display. He showed them huge amounts of gold filigree, rubies, opals and other precious and semi-precious jewels, heavy and ornate silver and gold antique pieces and valuable historical artifacts. Later in the house, their aunt and uncle showed them yet another private treasury. Under their mattress—surely creating an uncomfortably lumpy bed—were stacks of large denomination currency.

Sito had amassed a fortune by being a shrewd businessman, but he did not believe in banks. Instead, he stashed their valuables in hidden places.

A year after Estefanita's and Sito's deaths, a "bucketful of old gold coins and jewelry" was found by a workman in the old well in the basement of their store. It was buried about five feet above the bottom of the well, surrounded by broken pottery and other debris. Included was a small beaded bag filled with old gold coins. In June 1939, the value of the gold-weight in the bucket alone was set at $9,000, without factoring in the "intrinsic value" of the find. It was added to the Candelarios' estate, which was still being probated. The elder Candelarios had died without a will, but they had only one logical heir, their grandson, John. Their only child, John's mother, had died ten years before they did.

Sito and Estefanita's daughter, Allison Eleanor "Alice" Candelario, was educated at the Presbyterian mission school of Allison-James in Santa Fe. One time Sito dressed her like an Indian princess and placed her, seated on a blanket in front of a wigwam, in a New York Hilton hotel lobby, where she successfully sold many of her father's "curios" and Indian wares.

Alice married Arthur Weeks Match 5, 1912, and on September 7, 1916, their son was born, named Candelario Laumbach Weeks, called "little Lalo" by his family, according to John's widow, Lores. Estefanita's extended family believed Sito had undermined Alice's marital relationship. She filed for divorce from Arthur Weeks, son of a minister, after Christmas 1920. I do not know exactly when Sito took possession of the child, whom he renamed John S. Candelario, and adopted. Arthur Weeks tried unsuccessfully to keep custody of his son. Years later, John's widow, Lores, said John mourned the way his father had been treated and occasionally visited his grave.

Alice moved out of state and remarried; her second husband was named Mossman. She died in Kansas City, Missouri in 1928 at age 35. Her parents out-lived her by ten years.

This photo below might have been a publicity photo of Johnny Candelario because a newspaper article, when he was a college student in California, said he had tried out for the movies. Photo courtesy Karl Laumbach; it had been among Aunties' photo collection.

On June 9, 1938, the Santa Fe newspaper ran an announcement that John, a junior college student in California, would marry Gayle Holdsworth, another student, in September. By the date of that announcement, both of his parents were deceased; his grandmother, Estefanita, had died a month earlier. His grandfather, Sito, died two months later. A week after Sito's death, John and Gayle married in Albuquerque, but later held their preplanned large wedding in California.

Their engagement announcement in the Santa Fe newspaper said that John, still of college age, had become manager of his "grandfather's business interests, including real estate, finance, the unique curio store on San Francisco Street and the campgrounds."

John inherited an untold wealth and legacy, which he did not keep long. Unlike his grandfather, John had no business or money sense. He also married five times, and had four costly divorces.

Over the years, John dabbled at a variety of endeavors, including film-making and marketing Indian jewelry. He even tried his artistic hand at making jewelry himself. He received film awards. His still photography graced the covers of *Life, Look* and the *Saturday Evening Post*, and he was featured in the *New Mexico Magazine* and *Arizona Highways*. His lasting legacy is his photography. The many famous subjects of his photographs included Georgia O'Keefe and Mabel Dodge Luhan, and he worked with photography greats like Ansel Adams. He had said he was the most proud of his platinum printing process in photography for which he was elected to the Royal Fellowship of Great Britain.

In September 2000, the Museum of Fine Arts in Santa Fe ran an exhibit of his works for almost a year: "In his Native Land: The Early Modern Photography of John Candelario." The exhibition included 18 platinum prints, 17 gelatin silver photos and a bromoil photograph. His lovely widow, Lores, donated most of his artwork and worked with the museum on this exhibit. After that show ended, in the next year or two, the exhibit traveled around New Mexico and beyond, being displayed at various museum locations. It now resides at the Fray Angelico Chavez History Library and Photographic Archives at the Palace of the Governors, along with a huge collection of Sito's papers, letters, memorabilia, business records and ledgers.

John Candelario, photo taken in 1968 or 1969. Courtesy Pete Laumbach.

~~

Following are some pieces of Candelario memorabilia: Tin cup with "J.S. Candelario Indian & Mexican Trading Post" and his trademark *carreta* impressed inside; box printed with his carreta and J.S. Candelario, Santa Fe, N. Mex."; one of the many postcards depicting the Original Trading Post storefront; small Indian hand-beaded coin purse; Indian hand-beaded bag; comb with J.S. Candelario stamped on it; multiple silver and turquoise rings; turquoise and silver necklace (with signature "Eva" scratched on back); turquoise earrings with threaded screw-backs; two gold filigree pieces—pin depicting Sito's father-in-law Andreas 2nd and a cameo—both with "JSC" stamped on back.

~~

The following opened and flattened envelope, postmarked February 16, 1937, is typical of Sito's use of every available surface to advertise. This envelope contained a letter from Aunt Estefanita to my mother one month before her first child, my brother Jerry, was born on April 17, 1937. In it, Estefanita invited my mother to stay with them during her "confinement." This Candelario envelope was one of many like it that held correspondences between Sito, Estefanita and my mother. Below the envelope is a note written by Estefanita, dated December 22, 1936, mailed in a duplicate envelope, to my mother inviting her, and also my father if he was able, to spend the Christmas holidays with them. My dad, then on the Santa Fe Railroad's extra-board, worked erratic hours, dates and locations. They had not been married long.

THE ORIGINAL OLD CURIO STORE — J. S. CANDELARIO, Prop. Santa Fe, N.M.
THE ONLY EXCLUSIVE INDIAN AND MEXICAN WHOLESALE AND RETAIL CURIO STORE IN THE U.S.A. ESTB'D 1603

Mrs. Dalphen Sparks
422 Washington Ave.
Las Vegas, New Mex.

Beware of Fakes and Imitations
I sell genuine Indian and Mexican goods for lower prices than any other reliable house and send goods on consignment on receipt of responsible reference to any one in United States
J. S. Candelario, The Curio Man
Santa Fe, N. M.
U. S. of A

Balleta, Mexican and Moqui, Blankets, Silverware, Gold Filigree, Indian Pottery, Drawn Work, Sombreros, Jardiniers, Rain Gods, Bows, Arrows, Bead Work, Buckskin Work, Pillow Tops.

Navajo Blankets   *Chimayo Blankets*

Santa Fe the Sunshine City, The Heart of the Indian Country   *The Greatest Health Resort In the Southwest*

I am pleased to announce that at all times I carry the largest variety of Indian and Mexican goods and curiosities, and make a specialty of the better grades of their products and I am in a position to offer the best.

Owing to the well-known fact that the Indian goods will soon be a thing of the past, as the new generations are adopting our habits and abandoning those of their ancestors in weaving and pottery making, I am now reaching for more trade and can assure all my friends and customers that I shall continue with the assistance of my native brethren to treat them the same as in the past, if not better.

SEND 5 CENTS FOR PRICE LIST AND NAVAJO RUBY FOR LADIES

Santa Fe, New Mex.,
Dec 22nd, 1936.

Dear Verna;

This is a very informal invitation. We like to have you both come and spend Christmas day with us.

If for any reason your husband can't come, try and come yourself.

It will be nice if you can come since Thursday.

I am sending you two notes one to old town, the other to east Las Vegas, because I am not sure where you get your mail.

Lovingly,
Aunt Estefanita

One of Sito's many postcards had an image of his trademark carreta and this poem:

Candelario's

Do you know Old Candelario's,
Indian relics and curios?
In the ancient town of Santa Fe,
Anyone can show you the way
To Candelario's.

In the shop beneath the old ox cart
All the products of Indian art
Has Candelario.
Bows and baskets and pottery,
Beaten silver and filigree—
Every old kind of trumpery
Has Candelario.

For an Indian blanket you want to go
To Candelario,
He has zerapes and Chimayos,
Old beyettas and Navajos.
There are all the kinds that anyone knows
At Candelario's.

Should it be that you want a gem
Candelario also has them,
Sapphires, garnets, and turquoise blue,
Amethysts, rubies and opals too,
As good as you'd want he can furnish you,
Can Candelario.

In the ancient town of Santa Fe
Is Candelario's.
Anyone can show you the way
To Candelario's.
For anything you want to know—
For any old kind of a curio
Go to Candelario.

J.S. Candelario

~~

Someone in California had seen Sito's poem on one of many postcards, and responded with one of his own:

>Do You Know Candelario?
>No Señor! I'm not acquainted
>But if you have all you've painted
>Gladly would I steal away
>From Berkeley California by the Bay
>And hit the Trail for Santa Fe.
>Travel it by night and day
>'Till I found your magic store
>filled with wealth of Indian lore.
>
>Then safely on the desert sand
>I would camp quite near at hand
>Where long-tailed scorpions sing in glee
>And snakes keep busy as can be.
>Deep in Nature's torrid clime
>I shall have a glorious time.
>Unless the War God makes a start
>To Zeppelin your famous cart.
>
>By Author Unknown

SECTION IV: NEW MEXICO

Chapter 30: A Narrative History of the Sabinoso Area of the Canadian River Gorge
by Karl Laumbach

Butch Sanders enhanced and enlarged this BLM map. He "stitched" several maps together to show areas that affected many of the families mentioned in this book.

The rugged gorge and its tributary canyons made by the Canadian River, also known as the Rio Colorado or Red River in northeastern New Mexico, played a major role in the lives of families mentioned in this book, including: Fritz Eggert, Daniel Laumbach, Peter J. Laumbach, Andres Ebell, Felipe Esquibel, Ramon Bonney for a while, Manuel Cordova for a while, the Gallegos family, and three generations of Antonio Sanchez. It still plays a major role in many of their extended families.

The Canadian River runs south through Mora, Harding and San Miguel Counties. At Conchas Lake in San Miguel County, it turns eastward towards Texas. It is fed in Colfax County by the Vermejo River, the Cimarron River from Eagle Nest Lake, the Mora River at the top of San Miguel County and by the Conchas River as it fills the Conchas Lake.

The river extends southerly almost 100 miles in northeastern New Mexico before turning east to Amarillo. Eons ago it cut a dramatic, deep 30-mile long gorge through the prairie's flatlands. Nearly always, in our lifetimes anyway, the Canadian looks unremarkably mild, with muddy red, docile water, seldom wide or deep. The last memorable flood was in 1965 and before that 1904. But like the Grand Canyon of Arizona, the Canadian River Gorge is silent testimony to the mighty erosive power of a river that cuts deeply through underlying sandstone formations. There are places where the seemingly endless prairie dramatically opens up like a crack or fissure to become the awesome Canadian River gorge. One can drive on Interstate 25 and never realize that the deep canyon is, in some places, only miles away to the east.

People lived and toiled for generations on the dry land prairies on the tops of the flat mesas. Sometimes at the bottom of the gorge's canyons are places broad and open enough where generations of people also lived on vegas, grazed cattle and sheep, and grew crops.

~~

Karl Laumbach, an associate director for Human Systems Research, Inc. (HSR), and now also its principal investigator, did an initial archeological and historical study of the Sabinoso Wilderness for the BLM's (Bureau of Land Management's) Taos District. A BLM Cost Share Grant and the Barbara Roasting Ear and Henry Oliver III Family Foundation (of the HOBO Ranch) funded his five-day preliminary study conducted in mid-July 2010. Because the Sabinoso Wilderness is uninhabitable, Karl's study involved the areas surrounding the Wilderness. It provides a glimpse of some but not all portions of the Canadian River gorge. Following, with his permission, are excerpts from his written report. The area photos included here are also Karl's.

Below photo looks off the west rim of the Canadian towards Ancon and Sabinoso; the mouth of Cañon Largo is on the right.

Karl Laumbach's proposal was to perform a reconnaissance survey of the area, visiting with local people about the history, looking at archaeological sites and collections, and reviewing the known references…identifying local contacts…[studying] traditional life-ways of the area. He received permission to write his report as a narrative followed by a short but more formal referenced history of the area. This excerpt combines the two.[i]

Introduction

There is currently no public access to the Sabinoso Wilderness. It is composed of a chain of high mesas that overlook the Cañon Largo to the north, the Rio Colorado or Canadian River to the east, and the vast expanse below the cap-rock that encompasses the legendarily massive Bell Ranch to the south. Emanating from the high plains east of Las Vegas, New Mexico, the high mesas and adjacent canyons typify this little known and rarely traveled area of northeastern New Mexico.

The Sabinoso Wilderness consists of 16,030 acres in a remote area …The following description is found on the Bureau of Land Management web site: "The wilderness includes a series of high, narrow mesas surrounded by cliff lined canyons. Elevations range between 4,500 and 6,000 feet above sea level. The rugged country primarily supports piñon pine and juniper woodlands and occasional clusters of ponderosa pine, with a perennial warm season grass savanna on the mesa tops. Streams periodically flow in the canyon bottoms, supporting riparian vegetation including willow and cottonwood. The large deep canyon area surrounded by the wide open New Mexico plains is unique for this region. The deep incisions cut by Cañon Olguin, Cañon Largo, and Lagartija Creek create a striking topographical and geological contrast in this otherwise flat terrain."

I first heard of Sabinoso from my father, George Laumbach, who was raised on a ranch in the La Cinta Canyon located several miles to the east of the community of Sabinoso. The community of Sabinoso is located near the mouth of the Canadian River gorge in San Miguel County. My father told me how the first settlers, probably in the 1880s if not before, had worked together to build a ditch from the mouth of the Mora River down the west side of the Canadian River to the arable lands near the town. The ditch was built through the sandstone/quartzite deposits by building fires and then throwing water on the rock to break it up. My father also claimed there was a charter signed by all the original water right holders that was kept in the church at Sabinoso. The original community of Sabinoso was destroyed by the legendary flood of 1904, a torrent that also took out the community of Armenta Plaza located some 12 miles up the canyon. Sabinoso was subsequently rebuilt on higher ground and remains so today. The remnants of the original Sabinoso allegedly lie buried under a bank of sand.

The Canadian River Gorge was largely impassable to wheeled traffic from the *Vado de las Piedras* (the Rock Crossing) just below Taylor Springs east of Springer to the *Vado de las Carretas* (The Crossing of the Carts) located south of Sabinoso below the point where the cap-rock opens up. Native Americans, not dependent on wheels, used the natural avenues provided by the extensive side canyons. One of the most extensive of those, Cañon Largo, is immediately adjacent to the Sabinoso Wilderness Area. Cañon Largo was almost certainly a prehistoric trail and its utility was recognized by the U.S. Army when they needed to build a road to connect Fort Union to Fort Bascom, located near the present day Conchas Dam.[ii] Remnants of that wagon road should be visible today.

Many of the settlers in the Canadian River Gorge were disenfranchised Hispanics from the Mora and Las Vegas grants who had either lost land to the machinations of the Santa Fe Ring or whose families had expanded to the point that new land was needed for support. The Homestead Act of 1862 gave them opportunity to acquire land not at risk to the land grant politics of the day. A cursory review of the homestead locations within the townships that encompass the Sabinoso Wilderness Area shows the homesteaders were predominantly Hispanic and much of the homesteading occurred after 1900.

The remnants of many of these homesteads should still be visible as archaeological sites. Beyond that, many of the descendent families are still in the area. Prior to being claimed under the Homestead Act, many of these parcels were considered open range and, as such, were utilized by the Hispanic ranchers who claimed the rough canyon lands north of the storied (and Anglo owned) Bell Ranch.[iii] The stories relating to the interactions between these two ranching communities reflect the cultural conflicts of those times.

Two and one-half days of the study were spent on the north and west sides of the wilderness exploring Cañon Largo and its northern tributaries while conversing with local residents. One of the stops was an overlook that allowed an unobstructed view down Cañon Largo to its junction with the Canadian (Rio Colorado) and the communities of Cañon Largo and Sabinoso. A deep picturesque canyon, studded with junipers and piñon, Cañon Largo was a major avenue off of the Las Vegas Plateau and the steep canyon rims of the Canadian River Gorge. To the south are the mesas that compose a portion of the Sabinoso Wilderness. Steep slopes and an impressive rim-rock make them seem as impregnable as a medieval castle. Only an occasional canyon provides a break in the rim-rock where one might imagine access and then only on foot.

While on the HOBO ranch north of Canyon Largo we attempted to locate the grave of the young Naeglin boy. It is located in the bottom of a brushy canyon and difficult to find if you don't know exactly where to go. It interested me because of a Laumbach family story involving the boy's father, William Naeglin. It seems that at the turn of the last century, he worked for a Laumbach relative and neighbor, Henry Korte, near Buena Vista in the Mora Valley. Henry Korte [*as heir of his partner and father-in-law Frederick Metzger*] was a wealthy man, owning a store in Mora in addition to his ranch. Late one evening, unknown to Korte, William Naeglin watched his employer pull out a fence post, and after digging the hole out a bit more, dropped a package in the hole and replaced the fence post. At Korte's death, Naeglin remembered the fence post and dug out a package containing a portion of Korte's wealth. Thus financed, Naeglin eloped with Korte's daughter, Anna.[iv] The couple established a home at Cherryvale, which was a collection of homesteads located, in part, on [*what is now*] the HOBO Ranch.

The remainder of the day was spent attempting to locate the grave of the young Naeglin boy. It is located in the bottom of a brushy canyon and difficult to find (as we demonstrated) if you don't know exactly where to go.

Earlier that same morning, Harry Oliver (owner of the HOBO Ranch) had taken me to Cherryvale. It was not what I expected. Located in the rolling and almost treeless grasslands of the Las Vegas Plateau, just away from the beginnings of the "breaks" at the head of the Ciruelas canyon, all that is left of Cherryvale are low rock foundations. The first impression is that Cherryvale was a series of homesteads, each consisting of perhaps 160 acres. House foundations are usually small, containing only two to three rooms at most. Usually a well location was obvious, sometimes indicated by four posts in a small square. Sometimes artifacts are plentiful, sometimes not. Bottle fragments of purple and aqua glass, scraps of metal, a piece of sharpened slate and a shoe last are all that is left at the richest of the sites. One structure still boasts standing walls, the back wall bulging with an unusual chimney seems to have been a post 1900 homesteading effort. Robert Julyan, in his *Place Names of New Mexico*, states that it boasted a post office from 1910 to 1936.[v] The focus seems to have been farming, specifically pinto beans. Rancher Lillie Lester allowed me to make a copy of a photograph in her father's collection that depicts the bean harvest at Cherryvale in 1924. It was no doubt the drought and the economic depression of the late 1920s and early 1930s that brought an end to Cherryvale, leaving behind only the foundations and the Naeglin boy's grave.

The remaining portion of the third day involved travel around the western and southern sides of the wilderness through the communities of Trujillo, Trementina, and Sanchez, with a final destination of

Roy, New Mexico. Several miles north of Trementina and before Highway 104 turns to the east and crosses the Canadian River is the site of Sanchez. Sanchez was the ranch headquarters for three generations of Sanchez men. Our history is currently hazy regarding the early years, but the memoirs of Alfonso Esquibel provide some context.[vi] It seems that the first Manuel Antonio Sanchez, known to Esquibel as "Mito," was an early settler in Sabinoso and operated a store there.[vii] After the big flood of 1904, Mito moved to the present location of Sanchez, locally known as Ligartijas (place of the lizards). There he founded a store and a ranch. An early photo of the store showed it as an unplastered rock structure with the sign Antonio Sanchez y Hijo, La Tienda Barata (Anthony Sanchez and Son, The Trading Store). His son, Tio Manuel, and grandson Tony Sanchez operated the ranch until Tony's death in 1987. The Sanchez men were prominent in the area and connected through marriage with many of the local families.

Tio Manuel's first wife was Rosa Eggert, a daughter of German immigrant Fritz Eggert, an early settler of Sabinoso. After Rosa's death, Tio Manuel married Christina Laumbach. In the days of no fences and open range there was considerable mixing of stock between the herds of the Hispanic ranches in the canyons and, of course, the massive Bell Ranch to the south.[viii] Accordingly they held a communal round-up for branding. Representatives of all concerned parties participated. The gathered herd was held and branded at Sanchez with Tio Manuel running the show. There were no corrals. My father remembered that the *remuda* (horse herd) was held with a rope corral (ropes strung from tree to stake to boulder). The cows and calves were held night and day by cowboys riding the edges of the herd. Designated ropers were assigned to rope the calves and drag them to the branding area. As calves were branded according to which cow they were following, some of the ropers tried to pursue a particular calf into the herd instead of taking the easy one on the outside. That caused the herd to scatter, making it more difficult for the outriders to control. When that happened, Tio Manuel, watching the action, would sit back on his horse (Chorreado) and shout at the ropers, "*poco a poco, muchachos, poco a poco*" (little by little, boys, little by little). That recipe for making progress has followed me throughout my life.

The Sanchez Ranch would have abutted if not included the southern portion of the Sabinoso Wilderness. The steep slopes and rim rock of the mesas look no less daunting from the south. From Sanchez the road turns ever eastward and crosses the bridge on the Canadian near the site of the old crossing. Before the bridge, the crossing was referred to as "*el vado de las carretas*" (the crossing of the carts). The name dates to the days when the Hispanic buffalo hunters (*ciboleros*) sallied out from the settlements to hunt buffalo with a lance like their Native American counterparts. They took carts to carry the boxes of dried meat back to their families. Many of the same individuals were Comancheros (traders with the Comanche) and took hard bread and other items to trade for buffalo hides and other things, some of which had been purloined from Texas settlements.

The fourth day was involved with making oral history contacts in Roy and Mosquero, New Mexico and included a visit to the Mosquero County Seat. Descendents of many of the settlers from Sabinoso and Canon Largo currently live in Roy, Mosquero or their vicinity. While there, I visited with Casimiro "Casi" Esquibel about the possibility of pursuing an oral history project in the area. Casi's great-grandfather was Felipe Esquibel. Felipe and his wife, Maria Marta Ebel, and her brother (the original Andres Ebell[ix]) were some of the earliest settlers in the Canadian River Gorge. Felipe Esquibel, and very likely Andres Ebell, had first crossed the area as part of a buffalo hunting party (*ciboleros*). Felipe served as a meat cutter on these expeditions where meat was sliced, salted and dried before being transported home in big wooden boxes. My father and uncles remembered seeing some of the boxes, but they have all disappeared. Joyce Laumbach, my father's cousin, remembered watching Felipe cut meat from a beef round for drying.[x] Instead of cutting the narrow strips that are sold as jerky today, Felipe cut thin, broad sheets of meat in the manner of the old buffalo hunters.

One evening I stayed at the Mesa Hotel in Roy, owned and operated by Andres Ebell and his wife. Given the late hour, they shared their dinner with me, and I was treated to hearing Andres tell stories about the canyon country in the old days.

He remembered listening to old men in Cañon Largo tell stories when he was a boy in the 1930s. The men he named were Teodoro Gonzales, Nieves Coca and Raymundo Maestas. They spoke of seeing the ruins of a stone corral somewhere in Cañon Largo that they attributed to the Spanish period. They called it "*El corral de las mulas,*" the mule corral. Andres suggested that the men, who would have been boys in the 1870s and 1880s, might have heard about its use from their fathers and grandfathers, some of whom might have been born under the Spanish flag. Andres also told of a legendary round up and cattle drive that occurred in the late 1870s. Apparently the local ranchers were selling their cattle at the market in Las Vegas and getting only $6—$8 per head. Hearing of markets out on the plains where buyers were paying $22 per head, the first Andres Ebell organized the local *rancheros,* and they began gathering stock out of the canyons. Cattle living in rough country can become as wild as deer, and many of those animals were from two to five years old. It took good cowboys just to round them up. The round-up involved men from Cañon Largo, Sabinoso, Armenta Plaza and other areas of the Canadian River Gorge. Gathering 5,000 head of stock, they provisioned five wagons for the drive across the plains to the market. Other men involved were Felipe Esquibel and Ramon Bonney. Bonney was especially useful because he spoke the best English and could act as interpreter. One man served as the *cocinero* (cook); almost every day he picked out an animal to be butchered to feed the crew of from 50 to 70 cowboys. Everyone had to contribute animals for food on the drive; no one could complain about whose animal was butchered. Over the next several weeks they successfully took the herd overland to the market and received the going price of $22 per head. Bringing home over $100,000 in cash was as risky as the drive itself, but they made it home and the local singers composed a *corrido* (ballad) to tell the story. Andres remembers a number of verses to the *corrido* and recited them to me from memory. One stanza states that "they came to a big river [possibly the Arkansas] but they were not afraid because they were men from Sabinoso and Cañon Largo and they knew how to cross rivers."

During my visit with Andres Ebell, he told me of an incident involving his grandfather, the first Andres Ebell. No date was given, but it was likely during the 1870s or 1880s. He and his brother-in-law, Felipe Esquibel, were among the early ranchers along the Canadian. There were no fences, and cattle belonging to multiple owners were grazing well east of the Canadian where the Goodnight-Loving Trail passed on the way to Denver. One day another Hispanic rancher rode in from the east, warning that Texas cowboys were gathering all the cattle they found regardless of brands. Arming themselves and spreading the word, Andres and Felipe rode to the east, followed shortly by other Hispanic ranchers from the canyon. Displaying their weapons, they let the *Tejanos* know they would fight for their cattle, and when the reinforcements began to pour out of the canyons, their herds were saved.

On the fifth and final day of the project, I was guided to the community of Sabinoso by William Eggert and his son, Billy Eggert. The trip included the adventure of wading across the Canadian River to the abandoned community of Cañon Largo and an introduction to Chris Gutierrez, the *mayordomo* of the Sabinoso Community Ditch. That morning I woke to the sound of coyotes howling on the outskirts of town, and I went outside to view Roy's early morning traffic: a cottontail hopping slowly across the highway. William is a local rancher who was raised at Maes, a small community located on the north side of the Cañon Largo. The Eggert and Laumbach families go back to the 1850s when our respective great-grandfathers were unwilling soldiers in the German army. About 1857 [Editor: *July 1856 according to ship manifest listing Andreas 2nd recently found by Butch Sanders*], with their extended families already emigrated and settled in Clinton County, Iowa, Fritz Eggert and the somewhat older Andreas Laumbach decided to take "French leave" of the German army and inveigled a ship captain into letting them work their way across the Atlantic to the United States. Soon after their arrival in Iowa, the excitement of gold in Colorado spread through the region, enticing huge numbers of men to cross the plains to find their fortunes.

Unfortunately it was 1859, and the big strikes didn't happen until 1860. The two men staked a claim near the current location of the Denver railroad station but found little gold. Cold weather began to set in, and they decided to come south to New Mexico, arriving, according to the Laumbach family Bible, on October 29, 1859. Both men worked as farmers and herdsmen in the Mora area and married local girls. Andreas Laumbach settled [*editor: at La Cebolla*] near Buena Vista while Fritz Eggert lived first on the Sapello River north of Las Vegas and then moved to Sabinoso where he lived out his life.

Meeting William Eggert and his son Billy at the general store, we proceeded south towards Mosquero before turning west to descend the Burro Hill into La Cinta Canyon. Passing around Montoya Point, the storied location of seven burro loads of gold buried by Spanish priests, we were soon at the Sabinoso turn-off. Most of the road into Sabinoso is dirt but pavement has been applied to a particularly treacherous steep and winding portion. We passed the church in Sabinoso and proceeded upstream on the graded road. I quickly learned that, although the community is generally referred to as Sabinoso, there are, or at least were, three distinct areas of habitation. Sabinoso is the furthest downstream and currently boasts several houses, some of them occupied, limited amounts of farmable land, and the church. Upstream and on the other side of a ridge is Ancon, which contains most of the farmable land and is divided into the multiple long lots that I had seen from the north rim. Several landowners still farm the land there, some are residents; others drive in from outside the community to tend the fields. The third settlement was the community of Cañon Largo, located just across the Canadian from Ancon at the mouth of the Cañon Largo. Of the three villages, Cañon Largo is the only one that is entirely deserted.

I also learned that the original ditch was no longer in use. It was constructed from the mouth of the Mora River three miles upstream through sandstone that involved building big fires on or near the rocks, and cracking them with river water. The big flood of 1904 had taken that ditch out and with it much of the farm land on the west side of the river at Ancon and, just downstream, much of the original community of Sabinoso. After the big flood, those who stayed rebuilt Sabinoso in its present location and the farmable areas at Ancon were all on the east side of the river. Accordingly, water was diverted from the east bank of the Canadian upstream from Ancon and a second ditch was laboriously built to bring water to the community. Not only did they have to build a ditch through and around large blocks of sandstone but provision had to be made to prevent slope wash down the steep canyon sides from blowing out the ditch at multiple locations. The solution was to build *canales* out of hollowed logs. The *canales* were placed in areas where the side arroyos converged, there the *canales* catch the arroyo flow and carry it over the ditch.

William Eggert, born and raised in Maes on the north rim of the Cañon Largo, remembered going to the store in Sabinoso as a child. If he had any money he brought it to buy candy. Access off the rim was on impossibly steep roads laboriously constructed at an angle across the 1000 foot slopes. He told of bringing wagons down those roads and of horses pulling a Model A to the top of the rim just north of Ancon. He pointed to one house built on the top of a steep hill and said that anybody who went to visit there was required to bring a bucket of water from the well at the bottom of the hill.

Then he said "Let's cross the river." I thought he meant in the vehicle until he pointed to a place with riffles where the water was spread though a shallow area with lots of rocks. He pointed across the river to several rock houses on a ridge. "That's Cañon Largo and there's the church. I was baptized there in 1940."

At Cañon Largo, the top of the terrace is broad, allowing for multiple structures. A lower terrace that makes a southerly descent to the mouth of the Cañon Largo provides space for even more houses. Estimates of the population of the Cañon Largo community at its zenith range as high as 150 although that might have consisted of just 10 or 12 large families. Only in the rock-walled cemetery, located on the west side of the upper terrace, does one get a feel for the number of lives lived there. Without having made a count, it is likely that the census of the cemetery is between 100 and 200 souls. Most of the graves are marked with memorials of native sandstone, many intricately carved, others bearing a simple cross. An exception is the grave of Juanita Le Blanc and her husband, Fritz Eggert. An iron fence surrounds the plot and an ornate iron cross bears her name with birth and death dates (February 10, 1851—May 14, 1899). Juanita was the daughter of mountain man William "Guillermo" Le Blanc. He was an employee of Simeon Turley, who ran a famous distillery at Arroyo Hondo near Taos. Turley was killed in an epic battle between several mountain men and the insurgents during the Taos Revolt of 1847.[xi] William LeBlanc escaped the battle and was Turley's successor in the production of "Taos Lightning." The grave of Fritz Eggert, within the same plot, has no marker.

Precise beginning dates for the early settlements in the Canadian River canyon lands are difficult to ascertain. Several studies have approached the subject. A seminal work by Donald Meinig traces the broad outlines of Hispanic expansion in New Mexico. Meinig sees the 1860s as the zenith of Comanchero trade, an activity that ended when the United States military imposed their will on the Comanche with the Red River War of 1874 and the surrender of their great leader, Quanah Parker, in 1875.[xii] The old Comanche Peace had been generally upheld for the Hispanics, but Anglo ranchers trying to settle on the eastern frontier were at risk.[xiii] The Comanches were not the only threat, as the area was frequently raided by Navajos and other tribes. By the 1860s, even the Hispanics were increasingly at risk and it clearly wasn't safe to take families onto the plains. With the defeat of the Comanche and other tribes in the 1870s, it became possible to found actual settlements, usually small family groups. Meinig mentions several settlements east of the Canadian (Tramperos, Gallegos, Bueyeros) but does not mention any of the Canadian River communities.[xiv]

Just when the earliest settlements on the Canadian were founded is still a mystery. As discussed, most researchers believe it to have been in the 1870s but much earlier Comanchero period villages remain a distinct possibility. With one unreferenced exception, no one gives an exact date for any of the communities. The exception comes from the Master's Thesis of J.W. Wilferth, a gentleman I remember as an old, white haired man. His name graces the junior high building in Springer, New Mexico. His thesis was prepared for the Social Science Department at New Mexico Normal University, now New Mexico Highlands University, in Las Vegas.[xv] Focused on the economic history of Harding County, he briefly referred to the early history and states that Armenta Plaza (just up the canyon from Sabinoso) was founded by Pablo Romero in 1874.[xvi] We assume he was given that date by previous residents of Armenta Plaza, which was destroyed by the big flood of 1904.

Boyd C. Pratt and Jerry L. Williams explain the Hispanic expansion into eastern San Miguel County in terms of herding.[xvii] The wool market in St. Louis prompted expansion of sheep herds, and the sheltered canyon country was a great place to winter. The families of herdsmen who were working for wealthy owners on a "sheep-share" basis (*partidario*) found themselves clustering in small settlements along the bottom of the Rio Colorado (Canadian) gorge. These families were joined by former Comancheros and Ciboleros who were familiar with the area. With the buffalo and the Comanche gone, the resident population turned their hand to ditch building to irrigate land on the canyon bottom and to owning and expanding their own herds of both sheep and cattle.

With the Homestead Act of 1862, the canyon lands provided an opportunity to own land that had been severely reduced on the Mora Grant by political machinations and land grabbing by both outsiders and insiders.[xviii] Similar disenfranchisement occurred in the Maxwell[xix] and Las Vegas Grants[xx], pushing settlers out onto the plains. Pratt and Williams obtained information from interviews and church records that clearly identified the Mora and Maxwell Grants as staging grounds for the settlements in the Canadian and eastward.[xxi] Baptism and marriage records from the Holy Family Parish in Roy show 74 marriage partners had been baptized in Mora County while an additional 13 were baptized in Colfax County (Maxwell Grant). Only a few who were married in the 1930s had been baptized west of the Canadian River.

Beginning in 1885, baptisms were occurring in the canyon at the communities of Armenta Plaza, Cañon Largo and Sabinoso. Once these communities were established, residents and their descendants systematically homesteaded properties in the vicinity. Historians Pratt and Williams note that the success rate for "proving up" was significantly higher for the local Hispanic families than it was for Anglo families who arrived later.[xxii]

It should be noted that not all of the early settlers in the Canadian bore Hispanic surnames. The Las Vegas/Mora area was the first stop for trappers, then traders, and finally settlers from the east. Names like LeDoux, Branch, LeFebre, and LeBlanc came with the French trappers. Early day traders included Kortes, Metzgars and Ebels. Other pre-Civil War arrivals were Bonneys, Lesters, Eggerts and Laumbachs. These men did not bring families with them and as a consequence married local Hispanic women. Within a generation, the resulting families were culturally Hispanic, albeit with Anglo surnames. When opportunity beckoned, many joined their *primos* (cousins) the Romeros, Esquibels, Lujans, Gonzales, Bacas, Cocas, Gutierrezs and Andradas in the eastward movement into the canyons and onto the plains.

While the early Hispanic settlers located near springs and other water sources, the Anglo homesteader tended to be out on the plains, with little water and dependent on rainfall for irrigation.
The homesteads of Cherryvale epitomize the timing and situation of this effort. Most of these homesteads ultimately failed, and the land was acquired by merchants who had given credit or by neighboring ranchers who were expanding their range. My grandfather, Peter Joseph Laumbach, built up a ranch in this manner in the La Cinta Canyon east of Sabinoso. He had a neighbor who was also buying up all the land he could. When my grandfather asked him just how much land he wanted, the reply was…"just what neighbors mine."

The Hispanic families had two advantages: their early arrival allowed them to settle in areas with water; and their extended family support system encouraged homesteading in adjacent blocks, thereby consolidating property at least within the larger family group. Richard Nostrand provides a detailed study of how this worked for the Hispanic settlers of El Cerrito on the Pecos River south of Las Vegas.[xxiii] The Homestead Act of 1862 allowed only 160 acres; but in 1909, the acreage was doubled, allowing those with existing homesteads to claim an additional 160 acres. Subsequently, in 1916, 640 acre "stock-raising" homesteads were authorized, again allowing for the expansion of existing homesteads. Families with numerous children could, once the children were of legal age, expand their holdings by a square mile at a time. Finally, an additional 40 acres could be purchased from the government in an arrangement referred to as a preemption claim.

Nostrand points out that this situation did not always result in the formation of viable ranches but in some cases, Hispanic families were able to acquire sufficient land to make a living and to eventually keep it in the family.[xxiv] A perusal of "Harding County Family Histories" reveals that while many of the post-1900 homesteaders east of the Canadian River were Anglo/European, homesteads continued to be claimed by Hispanics with deep roots in the area.[xxv] The homestead records for the townships that encompass the Sabinoso Wilderness Area show much of the homesteading occurred after 1900. That most of those homesteaders were Hispanic reflects the strong family base created by the early settlements of Cañon Largo, Sabinoso and Armenta Plaza.

One near event that would have drastically changed the history of the area occurred in 1910 when authorities considered Sabinoso as a site for what later became Conchas Dam.[xxvi] Such a dam would have flooded the Canadian river gorge and all the side canyons for miles, including Cañon Largo. It would have created a huge lake, which would have been a recreational attraction but would have turned portions of the Bell Ranch into irrigated fields. Abelino Estrada, a resident of Trementina, recalled being a member of the local committee. "Me and two Quintanas, Pedro Roybal and his son, and Elvorio Lucero, five or six of us on this committee, we went to talk to people like Antonio Sanchez and Cipriano Lujan at Sabinoso." Of course they didn't want their farms flooded out, even if the government would give them new land outside the flooded area. "Oh forget it. I got the best orchard between here and California," Cipriano Lujan said to me. "I wouldn't trade it for nothing. I'm too old to start over again. Antonio Sanchez said he didn't believe the government would ever build a dam at the Canadian River or anywhere else. So we couldn't do any good at Sabinoso." Thus the area and its history and archaeology escaped the waters of what would have become Conchas Dam.

Below photo looks off the west rim of the Canadian towards Ancon and Sabinoso; mouth of Cañon Largo on the right.

[i] Laumbach, Karl W. 2010. Archaeological and Historical Resources in the Area of the Sabinoso Wilderness: A Narrative. Prepared for the Bureau of Land Management, Taos District. Human Systems Research, Inc. Report No. 2009—26.

[ii] D. Bradley Upton Nd. *Roads and Trails*. Self published, La Cinta Canyon, New Mexico.

[iii] Remley, David. 1993. *Bell Ranch: Cattle Ranching in the Southwest, 1824—1947,* University of New Mexico Press, Albuquerque.

[iv] Census data obtained by Charles (Butch) Sanders shows that William and Ana Marie were married about 1½ years before Korte's death in early January 1889, but why spoil a good story?

[v] Julyan, Robert 1996. *The Place Names of New Mexico*, revised edition, pp. 79, University of New Mexico Press, Albuquerque.

[vi] Esquibel, Alfonso. 1978. *Vaquero to Dominie: The Nine Lives of Alfonso Esquibel.* As told to J.A. Schufle, The Rydal Press/Printworks, Santa Fe, New Mexico.

[vii] Ibid pp. 27.

[viii] Culley, John H. (Jack). 1967. *Cattle, Horses, and Men.* University of Arizona Press, Tucson.

[ix] Editor: Using Andres's chosen spelling of their last name

[x] Laumbach, Joyce Nd. *Some History and I Remember.* Pp. 46. Self-published.

[xi] McNierney, Michael. 1980. *Taos, 1847: The Revolt in Contemporary Accounts.* Pp. 15—21. Johnson Publishing Company, Boulder, Colorado.

[xii] Meinig, Donald W. 1971. *Southwest: Three Peoples in Geographical Change, 1600—1970.* Pp. 33. New York, Oxford University Press, London, Toronto.

[xiii] Arellano, Anselmo F. 1990. *Through Thick and Thin: Evolutionary Transitions of Las Vegas Grandes and its Pobladores.* Pp 97—98, Ph.D. Dissertation in American Studies, The University of New Mexico, Albuquerque.

[xiv] Meinig, Donald W. 1971. *Southwest: Three Peoples in Geographical Change, 1600—1970.* Pp. 33. New York, Oxford University Press, London, Toronto.

[xv] Wilferth, J. W. 1933. *An Economic History of Harding County, New Mexico.* A Master's Thesis in Social Science presented to the faculty of New Mexico Normal University, Las Vegas, New Mexico.

[xvi] Ibid pp. 18.

[xvii] Pratt, Boyd C. and Jerry L. Williams. 1986. *Gone But Not Forgotten: Strategies for Comprehensive Survey of the Architectural and Historic Archaeological Resources of Northeastern New Mexico, Volume 1: History of Northeastern New Mexico.* Pp. 224. New Mexico Historic Preservation Division, Santa Fe.

[xviii] Shadow, Robert D. and Maria Rodriguez-Shadow. 1995. From Reparticion to Partition: A History of the Mora Land Grant, 1835—1916. IN *New Mexico Historical Review*, Volume 70, Number 3, pp. 257—298. University of New Mexico, Albuquerque.

[xix] Montoya, Maria E. 2002. *Translating Property: The Maxwell Land Grant and the Conflict over Land in the American West, 1840—1900.* University of California Press, Berkeley and Los Angeles.

[xx] Arellano, Anselmo F. 1990. *Through Thick and Thin: Evolutionary Transitions of Las Vegas Grandes and its Pobladores.* Ph.D. Dissertation in American Studies, The University of New Mexico, Albuquerque.

[xxi] Pratt, Boyd C. and Jerry L. Williams. 1986. *Gone But Not Forgotten: Strategies for Comprehensive Survey of the Architectural and Historic Archaeological Resources of Northeastern New Mexico, Volume 1: History of Northeastern New Mexico.* Pp. 224. New Mexico Historic Preservation Division, Santa Fe.

[xxii] Ibid pp. 219.

[xxiii] Nostrand, Richard L. 1990. *The Hispano Homeland.* Pp. 69—79. University of Oklahoma Press, Norman.

[xxiv] Ibid pp. 89.

[xxv] Harding County. 1998. *Harding County Family Histories.* Johnson Printing, Boulder Colorado.

[xxvi] Esquibel, Alfonso. 1978. *Vaquero to Dominie: The Nine Lives of Alfonso Esquibel.* As told to J.A. Schufle, Pp. 46. The Rydal Press/Printworks, Santa Fe, New Mexico.

SECTION IV: LAUMBACHS IN NEW MEXICO

Chapter 31: Census Records

All of the census records in this chapter were located by Butch Sanders.

1850 Census Northern Division Taos, page 128
11 Nov. 1850, Enumerator: E. (?) Williams

Household		property value	Origin
737	Rafael Garcia, age 60, male, farmer	800	Rio Arriba Co.
	Maria Juana Mascarenas, age 28		Taos Co.
	Maria Cleofas Bonne, age 12		"
	Santiago Bonne, age 8		"
	Maria Rafaela Bonne, age 5		"
	Maria Polequias (?), age 12		"

On the 1850 U.S. Census for the Northern Division of Taos County, Territory of New Mexico, Rafael Garcia's household #737—towards bottom of the following census sheet—lists Maria Juana Mascareñas, along with Maria Cleofas, Santiago and Maria Rafaela, her three young children by James Bonney, last name spelled Bonne on this census.

White race indicated for all in this household; only choices given were white, black or mulatto. The last entry of that household, name unreadable, may have been an Indian servant. It was common to give the family's last name to servants or purchased slaves in a household when they were baptized, and many were very young.

When Maria Juana left James Bonney, taking their children with her, according to their descendant, Joe Lopez, she returned to the home of her father, Miguel Mascarenas. However, he would not take her in. She had no choice but to go live with the man Bonney had accused her of being unfaithful with, Rafael Garcia. The man was more than double her age. They later married and had one daughter, who was not listed on this census.

A short while after Maria Juana Mascarenas left Bonney, Bibiana entered his life and home at La Junta.

SCHEDULE I.—Free Inhabitants in Northern Division in the County of Rio Arriba State of New Mex. enumerated by me, on the 14th day of Nov. 1850. C. Williams Ass't Marshal. 128

	Families numbered in the order of visitation.	The Name of every Person whose usual place of abode on the first day of June, 1850, was in this family.	Age.	Sex.	White, black, or mulatto.	Profession, Occupation, or Trade of each Male Person over 15 years of age.	Value of Real Estate owned.	Place of Birth. Naming the State, Territory, or Country.	Married within the year.	Attended School within the year.	Persons over 20 y's of age who cannot read & write	Whether deaf and dumb, blind, insane, idiotic, pauper, or convict.	
1	2	3	4	5	6	7	8	9	10	11	12	13	
731	731	Pedro Ahumada y Herrera	50	M	white	Farmer	400	Rio Arriba Co		1			1
		Juana Ma Cordova	40	F	"			Taos County					2
		Francisca de Herrera	15	F	"			" "					3
		Vicente de Herrera	12	M	"			" "					4
		Rafael de Herrera	10	M	"			" "					5
		Antonio de Herrera	8	M	"			" "					6
		Cristoval de Herrera	5	M	"			" "					7
		Jose Nicanor de Herrera	1	M	"			" "					8
		Maria Martina de Herrera	4	F	"			" "					9
		Maria Ifigenia de Cordova	25	F	"			" "			1		10
		Rafaela Antonia Cordova	7	F	"			" "					11
		Juana Maria Cordova	4	F	"			" "					12
		Ma Juana Cordova	1	F	"			" "					13
732	732	Jose Antonio Cordova	27	M	"	Laborer		Rio Arriba Co		1			14
		Ma Josefa Cordova	25	F	"			" "			1		15
		Ma Francisca Mestas	14	F	"			" "					16
		Ma Gabriela Mestas	11	F	"			" "					17
		Jose Desiderio Mestas	8	M	"			" "					18
733	733	Juan de los Reyes Pacheco	32	M	"	Shoemaker		Taos County		1			19
		Ma Apolonia Pacheco	13	F	"			Rio Arriba Co					20
		Ma Trinidad Pacheco	8	F	"			" "					21
		Ma Manuela Pacheco	6	F	"			" "					22
734	734	Juan Pedro Chacon	37	M	"	Farmer	100	Taos County		1			23
		Juana de Dios Martin	25	F	"			Chihuahua			1		24
		Jose Bibian Chacon	6	M	"			Taos County					25
		Maria Santa Chacon	5	F	"			" "					26
735	735	Luis Montoya	30	M	"	Laborer		" "					27
		Maria Clara Montoya	24	F	"			Rio Arriba Co					28
		Jose Felipe Montoya	10	M	"			Taos County					29
736	736	Maria Felipa Medina	40	F	"		50	" "					30
		Maria Nestora Bueno	16	F	"			" "					31
		Ma de Jesus Bueno	14	F	"			" "					32
		Maria Antonia Bueno	12	F	"			" "					33
		Maria Barbara Bueno	10	F	"			" "					34
		Jose Miguel Montoya	5	M	"			" "					35
737	737	Rafael Garcia	60	M	"	Farmer	800	Rio Arriba Co		1			36
		Maria Juana Mascareñas	28	F	"			Taos County					37
		Ma Clofas Bonne	14	F	"			" "					38
		Santiago Bonne	8	M	"			" "					39
		Maria Rafaela Bonne	5	F	"			" "					40
		Maria Peregrina Garcia	13	F	"			Rio Arriba Co					41
738	738	Jose Martin	60	M	"		150	Taos County			1		42

C. Williams
Ass't M.

1860 Census Santa Gertrudes Mora page 348 (Apolonia & family)
6 Aug., 1860, Enumerator Pedro Valdez

The last entry on the census page preceding this one lists Frank Metzger, merchant, heading location 3128. At the top of this page is listed:

Location		age	Occ.	Origin/born
3128	Wm Haehne	29	clerk	Oberkea Prussia
	I. T. St. Vrain	22	clerk	Kaskaskia Illinois
	A. B. Turley	59	clerk	Madison Co. Kentucky

Towards the bottom of the same page: Apolonia heads listing at her location; the given Value of Personal Property (*uncertain of number entered) indicates she was head of household.

Location		age	Occ.	Val. Prop	Va. Pers. Prop	Origin/born
3134	Apolonia Gutierres	48			1110 *	Santa Fe
	Manuel Martinez	21	laborer			Rio Arriba
	Maria Juana Metzger	11				Mora
	Sofia Gutierres	20	servant			unknown

Sofia Gutierres may have been an Indian servant or purchased slave given the family name.

This Manuel is Mañuel Gregorio Martín/Martinez, born 1830, brother of Bibiana. In 1860 he would have been about 30, not 21. He reappeared in this census after he was—according to family legend—missing for a number of years. Family tradition says he disappeared when he was a child or a boy. There are several *cuentos* explaining his disappearance. One was that he was stolen as a child by Indians during a raid of the Mora Valley. Another story was that he, a fair-complexioned boy, was stolen by "*gringos*" from his father, Bernardo, while together on a trip away from home. According to family stories, Bernardo's return home without their son caused Apolonia to angrily cast him out of the house and her life forever. (Bernardo, 20 years older than Apolonia, lived with his daughter, Bibiana, the last years of his life.) Manuel suddenly reappeared again to his family, prior to the date of this census, and remained with them a short while before again disappearing from his family for the last time.

Following is an image of this census page.

SCHEDULE 1.—Free Inhabitants in _the Precinct of Santa Gertrudis_ in the County of _Mora_, Territory ~~State~~ of _New Mexico_ enumerated by me, on the _6th_ day of _Augt_ 1860. _Pedro Valdez_ Ass't Marshal

Post Office _Fernando de Taos N. M._

Page No. 348

1	2	3	4	5	6	7	8	9	10	11	12	13	14
		Wm Hachine	29	m		Clerk			Oberhean Busid				
		I. S. St Vrain	22	m		"			Kaskaskia Ill.				
		A. B. Turley	59	m		"			Madison Co Ky				
3129	3129	Charles Raymond	39	m		Ind. Trader	100	400	Canada				
		Cesaria Trujillo	26	f					Taos Co. N. M.	1			
		Jose Silvestre Raymond	10	m					Mora		1	1	
		Ulino Raymond	3	m					"				
		Ma Jesus Maes	12	f					"				
3130	3130	Gaspar Gallegos	82	m		Farmer	400	500	Arriba "	1		1	
		Juana Catalina Soh.	49	f					Canada	1			
		Gaspar Luciano Gallegos	17	m		Laborer			Taos Co. N. M.				
		Jose Macial Gallegos	15	m		"			"				
		Luis Gallegos	13	m					Mora "				
		Jose Gr?. Gallegos	11	m					"				
		Margarita Gallegos	8	f					"				
		Jose Maria Gallegos	5	m					"				
		Ma Rita Gallegos	3	f					"				
3131	3131	Juan de Jesus Lujan	65	m		Laborer		100	Arriba "	1		1	
		Ines Gallegos	30	f					"	1		1	
		Margarita Lujan	10	f					"				
		Fran?? Ant. Lujan	7	m					Mora "				
		Ma Teodora Lujan	5	f					"				
3132	3132	Donacino Barela	25	m		Laborer		60	Arriba "	1		1	
		Carmel Medina	19	f					Taos "	1			
		Antonio Barela	2	m					Mora "				
3133	3133	Damaso Taladoid	41	m		R. C. Priest		2000	Madrid Spain				
		Juan Maes	30	m		Servant			Santa Fe Co. N. M.			1	
		Ma Josefa Torres	28	f					"			1	
3134	3134	Apolinia Gutierres	48	f				1440	"			1	
		Ma Albina Martins	27	f					Arriba "			1	
		Manuel Martines	21	m		Laborer			"				
		Ma Juana Metzger	11	f					Mora "		1	1	
		Sofia Gutierres	22	f	Ind	Servant			Unknown	1		1	
3135	3135	H. H. Green	38	m		Merchant		6000	Chicago Ill.				
		M. Chivion	28	m		Wheelwright			France				
		F. Hollier	25	m		Waggon Master			"				
		John Smith	50	m	B	Servant			Ky	1		1	
		Mary St Vrain	45	f	B	"			Madison Co. Mo.				
		Alexander Smith	7	m	B				"				
3136	3136	John Aarts	38	m		Carpenter		1000	Belgium				

No. white males, 23. No. colored males, 2. No. foreign born, ___ No. blind, ___
No. white females, 14. No. colored females, 1. No. deaf and dumb, ___ No. insane, ___
50 10200 No. idiotic, ___ No. paupers, ___ No. convict, ___

40

11 Aug., 1860 Census
La Cebolla precinct, County of Mora NM Territory
page 416, (Bibiana & family)
Enumerator Pedro Valdez

Location		Age		value of property	value of personal prop.	
3755	Bernardo Martinez	50	farm laborer	140	60	born Rio Arriba
	Bibiana Martinez	28				"
	Ramon Martinez	14				born Mora
	Leonor Martinez	11				"
	Andres Martinez	8				"
	Maria Martinez	5				"
	Doloritas Martinez	3				"

This household was in La Cebolla precinct, within the Mora County. The census enumerator assumed all of the family had the same last name as the head of household, Bernardo Martinez. Bernardo, born 1792, was actually about 68 years old; his daughter Bibiana Martin/Martinez, born December 1, 1827, was about 33. The cited ages for the remainder were basically correct, some off a little. Bibiana's son Ramon Bonney was born May 1846. Bibiana's daughter, Eleonor/Elionor Ebel was born in 1849. Her son Andrés Ebel was born in 1852. Her daughter Maria Marta Ebel was born in 1856 and was about four years old. Her daughter Doloritas Metzger was about two years old, born in 1858. Bernardo is shown as head of household.

Image of this actual census page follows, with entry of household #3755 about halfway down the page.

Page No. 410

SCHEDULE 1.—Free Inhabitants in the Precinct of La Cebolla in the County of Mora, Territory State of New Mexico enumerated by me, on the eleventh day of August 1860. Pedro Valdez Ass't Marshal
Post Office Fernando de Taos N.M.

Dwelling	Family	Name	Age	Sex	Color	Profession, Occupation, or Trade	Real Estate	Personal Estate	Place of Birth	Married	School	Read/Write	Infirmity
3752	3752	Antonio Esquibel	51	M		Farm Laborer		70	Rio Arriba Co N M			1	
		Rafaela Sanchez	40	F					" "			1	
		Juan And. Esquibel	20	M		Farm Laborer			" "			1	
		Juan Luis Esquibel	15	M		Do. Do.			" "			1	
		Tomas Esquibel	13	M					" "			1	
		Pablo Esquibel	11	M					" "			1	
		Ruperta Esquibel	9	F					" "			1	
		Jose Pablo Esquibel	7	M					" "			1	
		Pedro Esquibel	5	M					" "				
		Antonia Esquibel	3	F					Mora				
		Victoriano Esquibel	1	M					" "				
3753	3753	Juan Maria Ocaña	35	M		Farm Laborer	100	90	San Miguel			1	
		Josefa Estrada	28	F					" "			1	
		Tomas Ocaña	15	M		Farm Laborer			" "			1	
		Guadalupe Ocaña	12	F					" "				
		Pedro Ocaña	10	M					" "				
3754	3754	Jose Ma. Gonzales	33	M		Farm Laborer	96	100	Taos			1	
		Martin de J. Gonzales	10	M					Mora			1	
		Justa Gonzales	6	F					" "				
		Apolonia Gonzales	2	F					" "				
3755	3755	Bernardo Martinez	50	M		Farm Laborer	140	60	Rio Arriba			1	
		Biviana Martinez	28	F					" "			1	
		Ramon Martinez	14	M					Mora				
		Lemor Martinez	11	F					" "				
		Andres Martinez	8	M					" "				
		Maria Martinez	5	F					" "				
		Dolores Martinez	3	F					" "				
3756	3756	Guadalupe Mestas	38	F				25	Rio Arriba			1	
		Jose Tobias Mestas	14	M					Mora			1	
		Ma. Antonia Mestas	12	F					" "				
		Ramona Mestas	6	F					" "				
		Benino Mestas	4	M					" "				
		Josefa Mestas	2	F					" "				
		Jose Felis Mestas	4/12	M					" "				
3757	3757	Polo Carpio	39	M		Farm Laborer	40	50	Taos			1	
		Josefa Cortes	36	F					" "			1	
		Cecilia Carpio	28	F					" "			1	
		Eugenia Carpio	22	F					" "			1	
		Sabina Carpio	16	F					" "				
		Francisca Carpio	14	F					" "				

No. white males 20. No. white females 20. 376 395

1885 New Mexico Territorial Census
Precinct 5, Mora, New Mexico
Enumeration District: 15
Page: 27/C   15 Jul., 1885

282/282

Laumbach, Andres	W M	51	Farmer	Germany	Germany	Germany	
Leonore	W F	37	Wife	NM	NM	NM	
Margret	W F	19	Dau	NM	Germany	NM	**Margaret L. (Cruz)**
Peter	W M	17	Son	NM	Germany	NM	**Peter Joseph**
Stephina	W F	14	Dau	NM	Germany	NM	**Estefanita L. (Candelario)**
Daniel	W M	12	Son	NM	Germany	NM	**Daniel**
Emily	W F	10	Dau	NM	Germany	NM	**???**
Annie	W F	8	Dau	NM	Germany	NM	**Anna L.**
Crestina	W F	4	Dau	NM	Germany	NM	**Crestina L. (Sanchez)**
Mary	W F	1	Dau	NM	Germany	NM	**Mary L.**

Names in bold added, mostly by Butch Sanders, a few by Editor.

Dialogue between Jan and Butch:

<u>Editor Jan's</u> comment: Their daughter Leonor was not yet born; she's not listed. Henry is not listed but should be; maybe he was away from home that day? And who is Emily?

<u>Butch Sander's</u> response: "Emily," 10 year old daughter, is without a doubt 10 year old son, Henry; a census-taker error.

283/283

Bonney, Ramon	W M	47	Farmer	NM NM NM	**Ramon born 1846**
Anistacia	W F	20	Wife	NM NM NM	**Anastacia Lucero Bonney**
Facundo	W M	7	Son	NM NM NM	
Roverto	W M	2	Son	NM NM NM	
Martinez, Viviana	W F	60	Mother	NM NM NM	**Bibiana born Dec. 1, 1827**
Isabel	W F	21	Dau	NM NM NM	**Isabel Metzger, Bibiana's daughter**

Dialogue between Jan and Butch:

<u>Butch Sanders</u>: "Other than Ramon's age, which should have been 39, entries for his family are basically accurate. Anastasia was born about Jan. 1864. She married Ramon on 26 Feb., 1882, per entry in *Mora Marriage Book No. 3*: "February 26 of 1882. I married Ramon Bonny, widow [sic] of Maria Concepcion Padilla, from Buena Vista, with Maria Anastacia Lucero, single, legitimate daughter of Tomas de Aquino Lucero and of Maria Refugio Velasquez, from La Cebolla. Padrinos A. Chene and Maria la Roux.

Roverto/Roberto, age 2, is identified in *Baptisms Sacred Heart Church, La Junta de Los Rios (Watrous)*: "Today the 6th of January of 1883, baptized Roberto Boney legitimate son of Ramon and Anastasia Lucero, born on the 6th in La Junta. Padrinos Joaquin Sanchez and Adelaida Sanchez."

Another child born to Ramon and Anastasia before this 1885 census was Abelina, born 17 Jul., 1884, and baptized 27 Jul., 1884 at Santa Gertrudis, Mora, Mora Co., NM; that would place them in Mora not long before this 1885 census was taken. Apparently Abelina didn't survive to this census.

Facundo, age 7, was the second born child of Ramon and his 1st wife, Maria Concepcion Padilla. From *Baptisms Sacred Heart Church, La Junta de Los Rios (Watrous)*: "Today the 5th of October of

1878, baptized Facundo Boney born on the 20th of August in Encierro del Rio Colorado, legitimate son of Ramon Boney and of Concepcion Padilla. Padrinos Nabor Padilla and Espiridiona Baca."

From the same records, we have that couple's 1st born child with two familiar named *padrinos:* "Today the 22nd of January of 1877, baptized Jose Firmino Boney born in El Encierro del Rio Colorado on 3rd of November of 1876, legitimate son of Ramon Boney and of Maria Concepcion Padilla, from El Encierro del Rio Colorado. Padrinos, Andres Ebel and Ubalda Lopez." Jose Firmino Boney and his brother didn't survive to the 1880 census.

There is record of another child born to Ramon and Concepcion—Emelia, born 13 May, 1880. If it is accurate, it is likely that Concepcion and daughter, Emilia, died in or shortly after childbirth—at least before the census-taker visited a month later on 15 Jun., 1880.

Bibiana was born 1 Dec., 1827; she would have been 57 in this census instead of 60. That age is closer than listed in 1880 when she was 52, but recorded as 48. Isabel, age 21(accurate age given here), would be her daughter, Isabel/Isabellita Metzger, born about Jul. 1864.

Editor Jan: "This census indicates the Bonneys lived next door to the Laumbachs in Buena Vista in July 1885. I didn't know Bibiana lived with them for a while, but perhaps she and Isabel were just visiting. Enumerator gives wrong ages for Bibiana and Ramon; she was about 19 when he was born. I didn't realize Ramon was much older than his second wife, Anastacia."

Butch Sanders: "Ramon did live next door to Andreas Laumbach, or very close to him. Ramon's was the very next dwelling the enumerator called on after leaving the Laumbachs. In the 1880 census, only one dwelling separated Andreas Laumbach and Ramon Bonney, and that was Bibiana's. In 1900, Andreas and Ramon are some distance apart with Ramon recorded in the Armenta precinct."

~~

1885 New Mexico Territorial Census
Precinct 11, Mora, New Mexico
Enumeration District: 15
Page: 7/C   2 Jul., 1885

70/70
Bonney, Santiago	W M 47	Farmer	NM NM NM	**(James Jr. born about Aug 1841)**
Feleciana	W F 46	Wife	NM NM NM	**(Feliciana Jimenez born Feb 1849)**
Alvena	W F 18	Dau	NM NM NM	**(Alvina b: 10 Dec 1866)**
Juanita	W F 16	Dau	NM NM NM	**(Juanita b: 27 Jan 1869)**
Florenco	W M 15	Son	NM NM NM	**(Florencio b: 14 Mar 1871)**
Eacerido	W M 14	Son	NM NM NM	**(Isidro b: 15 May 1873)**
Pablo	W M 7	Son	NM NM NM	**(Pablo Albino b: 29 Jun 1877)**
Louisa	W F 5	Dau	NM NM NM	**(Luisita b: 21 Jun 1880)**
Adelia	W F 3	Dau	NM NM NM	**(Adela b: 20 Oct 1882)**
Agusta	W F 4/12	Dau	NM NM NM	**(Vicenta b: 13 Jan 1885)**

Editor Jan: This Santiago is James Bonney's son by Maria Juana Mascarenas. I think an earlier census showed him and his family living on the upper plaza, around Mora. He is incorrectly shown in this census as the same age as Ramon. James Bonney's three children by Juana: Cleofas (born around 1838); about 4 years later, Santiago (born around 1842, making him about 43 in 1885); and about 3 years later Rafaela (born around 1845). Juana and her three children had left James, leaving La Junta and returned to the "upper plaza" at least a few months before Bibiana began living with him. Bibiana's son Ramon was born in spring of 1846, just a few months before James was killed in October 1846.

Santiago and Feliciana ultimately had 12 or 14 children, including Amado Leon "Prim;" not all were yet born in 1885."

<u>Butch Sanders</u>: "Most of the above seems accurate. I've put their names (as I have them) with birthdates beside each entry. They also agree with the 1880 census (for those born by 1880). Their oldest child, Saturnina, born about Apr 1865, was recorded in 1880, but is not here in 1885—presumably because she already married Julian Gonzales and moved out. There is also a record of a child included in birth record abstracts that I've never been able to account for. He's Benito Bonney, born 14 Mar.; 1871, the same date as Florencio, and to the same parents, Santiago Bonney and Feliciana Jimenez. Ordinarily (considering occasional census inaccuracies) I would suspect they were one and the same child. However, these records have them baptized on different dates—Florencio on 19 Mar., 1871 and Benito, 4 days later, on 23 Mar.; 1871. If they were twins, only Florencio made it to 1880. I only included, above, the children born to Ramon and Santiago by dates of this 1885 census."

1885 New Mexico Territorial Census
Precinct 1, Mora, New Mexico
Enumeration District: 16
Page: 19/C   2 Jul., 1885

209/209

Name				Occupation				
Kourte, Henry	W	M	45	Merchant	Prussia	Prussia	Prussia	**(Henry Korte)**
Juanita	W	F	36	Wife	NM	Prussia	NM	**(Juana Metzger)**
Anna	W	F	17	Dau	NM	NM	NM	**(Anna married Wm. Naeglin)**
Henry	W	M	15	Son	NM	NM	NM	
Charles	W	M	12	Son	NM	NM	NM	
Frank	W	M	10	Son	NM	NM	NM	
Edward	W	M	5	Son	NM	NM	NM	**(Eduardo, Alvin's grandfather)**

After parents Henry and Juanita died four years later, in 1889, Anna and her new husband, William Naeglin, adopted her young brothers.

~~

1900 Census Precinct 14, Armenta pages 164 & 165 & 166,
Census taken June 23, June 25 & June 28, 1900 by W. H. Garner

The below information, with recorded misspellings, was taken from these three census pages; additional information provided. Images of these actual census sheets follow.

<u>Ramon Sr. Boney</u> (head of household, farmer, born May 1846), Maria (Anastacia Lucero, wife, born Jan. 1854), Ramon J. Jr. (son, born Dec. 1890), Juan (son, born May 1893), Rafaelita (daughter, born May 1896) and Santiago (son, born Sept. 1898).

<u>Felipe Esquibel</u> (head of household, rancher, born May 1849), Maria (Marta Ebel, wife, born June 1854), David (son, born Sept. 1877), Juanita (daughter, born April 1880), Aurelia (daughter, born Oct. 1881), Florencio (son, born Feb. 1885), Abelino (son, born July 1886), Marcelino (son, April 1889), Francisco (son, born July 1894) and Frutoso (son born Feb. 1900).

<u>Andrés Ebel</u> (head of household, stock-raiser, born Feb. 1852), Maria (Uvalda Lopez, wife, born 1860), Carolina (daughter, born July 1874), Carmelita (daughter, born July 1883), Maria E (daughter, born June

1884), Anita (daughter, born May 1887), Rafaelita (daughter, born June 1889), Zacarias (son, born Sept, 1891), Bonifacio (son, born June 1893), Andres (son born Aug. 1895), Maria V. (daughter, born Sept. 1898); plus Demetrio Lopez (father-in-law born Nov. ? 1816) and Maria (mother-in-law born Dec. 1830).

Pedro Lombar (Laumbach, head of household, stock-raiser, born June 1867), Fedelia (Fidelia Andrada, wife, born April 1881) and Cordelia (daughter born Sept. 1899).

Conrado Andrade, (head of household, stock-raiser, born Oct. 1869), Nicanora (Ebell, wife, born Jan. 1875), Casimiro (son, born June 1895), Guadalupe (daughter, born Dec. 1896) and Conrado Jr. (son, born June 1898).

C… Andrade (head of household), Pablita (daughter born Sept. 1882), Brijedo ? (son born Oct. 1889) and Reba/Rebeca ? (daughter born May 1890) Note: Karl Laumbach believes this is Casimiro Andrada, born 1837, father of Conrado. Conrado's daughters (matching those listed) were Pablita, Brijida and Rebecca, the younger sisters of Conrado and Leopoldo.

Towards bottom of page 166:

Nieves Gallegos (head of household, laborer, born ?) and Isabel (wife, born 1880?). This is Isabel Ebell Gallegos, daughter of Andres Ebell. She would live to 108 years old, spending her last years in Santa Fe.

TWELFTH CENSUS OF THE UNITED STATES.
SCHEDULE No. 1.—POPULATION.

State: Territory of New Mexico
County: Mora
Township or other division of county: Precinct No 14 Armenta
Enumerated by me on the Twenty Third day of June, 1900, W. H. Garner, Enumerator.
Supervisor's District No.: New Mexico
Enumeration District No.: 77
Sheet No.: 2 B — 170

Location		Name	Relation	Personal Description							Nativity			Citizenship			Occupation		Education			Ownership of Home				
31	34	Romero, Busaba	Daughter	W	F	Oct	1885	14	S			N Mexico	N Mexico	N Mexico						no	no	no					51
		— Porfirio	Son	W	M	Feby	1890	10	S			N Mexico	N Mexico	N Mexico						no	no	no					52
		— Federico	Son	W	M	July	1892	7	S			N Mexico	N Mexico	N Mexico													53
		— Deluvina	Daughter	W	F	Oct	1894	5	S			N Mexico	N Mexico	N Mexico						—	—	—					54
		— Felipa	Daughter	W	F	April	1896	4	S			N Mexico	N Mexico	N Mexico						—	—	—					55
		— Francisco	Son	W	M	Oct	1898	1	S			N Mexico	N Mexico	N Mexico						—	—	—					56
32	35	Valdez, Sleodoro	Head	W	M	June	1820	79	M	58		N Mexico	N Mexico	N Mexico				Farmer	0	no	no	no	R	anche	X		57
		— Refugia	Wife	W	F	Dec	1839	60	M	53	12 6	N Mexico	N Mexico	N Mexico						no	no	no					58
		— Angelia	Daughter	W	F	Feby	1888	11	S			N Mexico	N Mexico	N Mexico						yes	no	no					59
		— Carolina	Gr Daughter	W	F	Sept	1890	9	S			N Mexico	N Mexico	N Mexico						yes	no	no					60
		Bustamante, Antonio	Adopted	W	M		1888	12	S			N Mexico	N Mexico	N Mexico													61
33	36	Gomez, Quinto	Head	W	M	April	1854	46	M	23		N Mexico	N Mexico	N Mexico				Stock Raiser	0	yes	yes	no	O	F F	57		62
		— Refugia	Wife	W	F	Dec	1854	45	M	23	14 10	N Mexico	N Mexico	N Mexico						no	no	no					63
		— Vicente	Son	W	M	Dec	1877	22	S			N Mexico	N Mexico	N Mexico						no	no	no					64
		— Susan	Son	W	M	Nov	1879	20	S			N Mexico	N Mexico	N Mexico						no	no	no					65
		— Alvino	Son	W	M	May	1886	14	S			N Mexico	N Mexico	N Mexico						no	no	no					66
		— Guadalupe	Son	W	M	Feby	1888	12	S			N Mexico	N Mexico	N Mexico						yes	no	no					67
		— Juan	Son	W	M	Jan	1886	10	S			N Mexico	N Mexico	N Mexico						yes	no	no					68
		— Esteban	Son	W	M	Aug	1892	7	S			N Mexico	N Mexico	N Mexico													69
		— Hilario	Son	W	M	Aug	1895	4	S			N Mexico	N Mexico	N Mexico													70
34	37	Gomez, Francisco	Head	W	M		1830	70	M	50		N Mexico	N Mexico	N Mexico				Farmer	0	no	no	no	R				71
		— Maria D.	Wife	W	F		1828	72	M	50	10 2	N Mexico	N Mexico	N Mexico													72
35	38	Emry, Ramon	Head	W	M	Mar	1846	54	M	17		N Mexico	Missouri	N Mexico				Farmer		yes	yes	no	O	F F	52		73
		— Maria E.	Wife	W	F	Jan	1864	36	M	17	4 4	N Mexico	N Mexico	N Mexico						yes	no	no					74
		— Ramon Jr	Son	W	M	Dec	1890	9	S			N Mexico	N Mexico	N Mexico													75
		— Jose	Son	W	M	May	1892	7	S			N Mexico	N Mexico	N Mexico													76
		— Rafaelita	Daughter	W	F	May	1896	4	S			N Mexico	N Mexico	N Mexico													77
		— Santiago	Son	W	M	April	1898	1	S			N Mexico	N Mexico	N Mexico													78
36	39	Esquibel, Nicolas	Head	W	M	Jan	1855	45	M	7		N Mexico	N Mexico	N Mexico				School Teacher	8	yes	yes	yes	R	F F	53		79
		— Babarita	Wife	W	F	Dec	1871	28	M	7	4 3	N Mexico	Old Mexico	N Mexico						yes	no	no					80
		— Miguel A.	Son	W	M	Oct	1894	5	S			N Mexico	N Mexico	N Mexico													81
		— Victoriana	Daughter	W	F	Nov	1896	4	S			N Mexico	N Mexico	N Mexico													82
		— Luciano	Son	W	M		1900		S			N Mexico	N Mexico	N Mexico													83
37	40	Esquibel, Felipe	Head	W	M	May	1849	51	M	23		N Mexico	N Mexico	N Mexico				Rancher	0	no	no	no	O	F F	54		84
		— Maria	Wife	W	F	June	1854	45	M	23	11 8	N Mexico	N Mexico	N Mexico						no	no	no					85
		— David	Son	W	M	Sept	1877	22	S			N Mexico	N Mexico	N Mexico						yes	yes	no					86
		— Juanita	Daughter	W	F	April	1880	20	S			N Mexico	N Mexico	N Mexico						yes	yes	no					87
		— Aurelia	Daughter	W	F	Oct	1883	18	S			N Mexico	N Mexico	N Mexico						yes	yes	no					88
		— Florencio	Son	W	M	Feby	1885	15	S			N Mexico	N Mexico	N Mexico				At School	4	yes	yes	no					89
		— Abelino	Son	W	M	July	1886	14	S			N Mexico	N Mexico	N Mexico						yes	no	no					90
		— Marselino	Son	W	M	April	1889	11	S			N Mexico	N Mexico	N Mexico						no	no	no					91
		— Francisco	Son	W	M	May	1894	6	S			N Mexico	N Mexico	N Mexico													92
		— Fintoso	Son	W	M	Feby	1900	4/12	S			N Mexico	N Mexico	N Mexico						—	—	—					93
38	41	Ebel, Andres	Head	W	M	Feby	1850	50	M	23		N Mexico	Germany	N Mexico				Stock Raiser	0	no	no	no	O	F F	55		94
		— Maria	Wife	W	F		1860	40	M	23	12 12	N Mexico	N Mexico	N Mexico													95
		— Carolina	Daughter	W	F	July	1874	25	S			N Mexico	N Mexico	N Mexico						yes	yes	no	O	F F	55		96
		— Carmelita	Daughter	W	F	July	1883	16	S			N Mexico	N Mexico	N Mexico				At School		yes	yes	no					97
		— Maria E.	Daughter	W	F		1884	15	S			N Mexico	N Mexico	N Mexico				At School		yes	yes	no					98
		— Anita	Daughter	W	F	May	1887		S			N Mexico	N Mexico	N Mexico				At School		yes	yes	no					99
		— Rafaelita	Daughter	W	F	Jan	1889	20	S			N Mexico	N Mexico	N Mexico				At School		yes	yes	no					100

TWELFTH CENSUS OF THE UNITED STATES.
SCHEDULE No. 1.—POPULATION.

State: Territory of New Mexico
County: Mora
Township or other division of county: Precinct No 14 Armenta
Name of incorporated city, town, or village, within the above-named division: X
Name of Institution: X
Supervisor's District No.: New Mexico
Enumeration District No.: 77
Sheet No.: 12 (165 A / 170)
Ward of city: X
Enumerated by me on the Twenty-Fifth day of June, 1900. W. H. Garner, Enumerator.

#	Dwelling/Family	Name	Relation	Personal Description							Nativity			Citizenship			Occupation		Education			Ownership
1	38/41	Ebel Zacarias	Son	W M Sept 1891 8 S							N.Mexico	N.Mexico	N.Mexico									
2		— Bonifacio	Son	W M June 1893 6 S							N.Mexico	N.Mexico	N.Mexico									
3		— Ucheas	Son	W M Aug 1895 4 S							N.Mexico	N.Mexico	N.Mexico									
4		— Maria V.	Daughter	W F Sept 1898 1 S							N.Mexico	N.Mexico	N.Mexico									
5		Lopez Demetrio	Fa-in-Law	W M — 1846 84 M 54							N.Mexico	N.Mexico	N.Mexico					no no no			
6		— Maria B.	M-in-Law	W F Dec 1830 69 M 54 9 1							N.Mexico	N.Mexico	N.Mexico					no no no			4/2/2
7	39/42	Lombar Pedro	Head	W M June 1867 32 M 2							N.Mexico	Germany	N.Mexico				Stock Raiser	O	yes yes yes			O F F 60
8		— Fedelia	Wife	W F April 1881 19 M 2 1 1							N.Mexico	Old Mexico	N.Mexico						yes yes yes			
9		— Cordelia	Daughter	W F Apl 1899 2 S							N.Mexico	N.Mexico	N.Mexico									
10	40/43	Andrade Crispin	Head	W M Oct 1869 30 M 6							N.Mexico	Old Mexico	N.Mexico				Stock Raiser	O	yes yes yes			O F F 61
11		— Nicanora	Wife	W F Jan 1870 25 M 6 3 3							N.Mexico	N.Mexico	N.Mexico						yes yes no			
12		— Casimiro	Son	W M June 1895 4 S							N.Mexico	N.Mexico	N.Mexico									
13		— Guadalupe	Daughter	W F Dec 1896 3 S							N.Mexico	N.Mexico	N.Mexico									
14		— Conrado Jr.	Son	W M June 1898 1 S							N.Mexico	N.Mexico	N.Mexico									
15	41/44	Andrade Candelaria	Head	W F 1852 48 Wd 14 8							N.Mexico	N.Mexico	N.Mexico				Will not Say	O	no no no			
16		— Ysabela	Daughter	W F Sept 1882 17 S							N.Mexico	N.Mexico	N.Mexico						yes yes no			
17		— Brijida	Son	W M Oct 1884 15 S							N.Mexico	N.Mexico	N.Mexico						yes yes no			
18		— Rebeca	Daughter	W F May 1890 10 S							N.Mexico	N.Mexico	N.Mexico						yes no no			
19	42/45	Ballard Joseph R.	Head	W M Mar 1863 37 M 4							Arkansas	Alabama	Arkansas				Stock Raiser		yes yes yes			O R 62
20		— Catherine	Wife	W F June 1872 25 M 4 1 1							Texas	Tennessee	Texas						yes yes yes			
21		— Lucy	Daughter	W F April 1897 3 S							Texas	Arkansas	Texas									
22		— David L.	Son	W M April 1889 11 S							Texas	Arkansas	Texas						yes yes yes			
23		— George F.	Son	W M Oct 1887 12 S							Texas	Arkansas	Texas				at School		3 yes yes yes			
24		— Minnie	Daughter	W F Sept 1890 9 S							Texas	Arkansas	Texas									
25	43/46	Vigil Jose M.	Head	W M 1845 54 M 20							N.Mexico	N.Mexico	N.Mexico				Day Labor	O	no no no			O F F X
26		— Teodora	Wife	W F — 1860 40 M 20 2 2							N.Mexico	N.Mexico	N.Mexico						no no no			
27		— Jose de la Luz	Son	W M April 1890 10 S							N.Mexico	N.Mexico	N.Mexico									
28	44/47	Urioda Andres	Head	W M Jun 1306 9 M 23							N.Mexico	N.Mexico	N.Mexico				Day Labor	O	no no no			R 4
29		— Ramonita	Wife	W F Aug 1859 40 M 23 10 8							N.Mexico	N.Mexico	N.Mexico						no no no			
30		— Pablita	Daughter	W F April 1882 18 S							N.Mexico	N.Mexico	N.Mexico				At School	3	yes yes yes			
31		— Pilo	Son	W M Dec 1883 16 S							N.Mexico	N.Mexico	N.Mexico				At School	3	yes yes no			
32		— Candido	Son	W M Jan 1886 14 S							N.Mexico	N.Mexico	N.Mexico				at School	3	yes no no			
33		— Climaco	Son	W M Feb 1889 11 S							N.Mexico	N.Mexico	N.Mexico				at School	3	yes no no			
34		— Salvador	Son	W M July 1891 8 S							N.Mexico	N.Mexico	N.Mexico									
35		— Alvina	Daughter	W F April 1895 5 S							N.Mexico	N.Mexico	N.Mexico									
36		— Delvina	Daughter	W F Sept 1896 3 S							N.Mexico	N.Mexico	N.Mexico									
37	45/48	Garcia Jose	Head	W M April 1863 37 M 11							N.Mexico	N.Mexico	N.Mexico				Rancher	O	yes yes no			O F F 63
38		— Sedonita	Wife	W F April 1872 28 M 11 7 4							N.Mexico	N.Mexico	N.Mexico						yes yes no			
39		— Epimenio	Son	W M Mar 1891 9 S							N.Mexico	N.Mexico	N.Mexico									
40		— Jesus Ma	Son	W M July 1895 4 S							N.Mexico	N.Mexico	N.Mexico									
41		— Cleofas	Daughter	W F Oct 1896 3 S							N.Mexico	N.Mexico	N.Mexico									
42		— Florencia	Daughter	W F Dec 1899 m S							N.Mexico	N.Mexico	N.Mexico									
43	46/49	Garcia Maria R.	Head	W F — 1826 74 Wd 2 4							N.Mexico	N.Mexico	N.Mexico				Day Labor	O	no no no			O F H
44	47/50	Montoya Rosita	Head	W F Feb 1846 54 Wd 11 5							N.Mexico	N.Mexico	N.Mexico				Stock Raiser	O	no no no			O F F 64
45		— Adolfo	Son	W M Feb 1870 30 S							N.Mexico	N.Mexico	N.Mexico				Day Labor		yes yes yes			
46		— Candelaria	Daughter	W F Dec 1880 19 S							N.Mexico	N.Mexico	N.Mexico						yes yes no			
47		— Manuelita	G-Daughter	W F Jan 1884 16 S							N.Mexico	N.Mexico	N.Mexico						no no no			
48		— Miguel	G-Son	W M Nov 1888 11 S							N.Mexico	N.Mexico	N.Mexico									
49		— Reynaldo	G-Son	W M Nov 1891 9 S							N.Mexico	N.Mexico	N.Mexico									
50		— Aurelia	G-Daughter	W F April 1895 5 S							N.Mexico	N.Mexico	N.Mexico									

TWELFTH CENSUS OF THE UNITED STATES.
SCHEDULE No. 1.—POPULATION.

State: Territory of New Mexico
County: Mora
Township or other division of county: Precinct No. 14 Armenta
Name of incorporated city, town, or village, within the above-named division: X
Name of Institution: X
Supervisor's District No.: 170
Enumeration District No.: 77
Sheet No.: 13
Ward of city: X
Enumerated by me on the Twenty Eighth day of June, 1900. W. H. Garner, Enumerator.

Line	Dwelling #	Family #	Name	Relation	Race	Sex	Month/Year of birth	Age	Marital status	Years married	# children born	# children living	Birthplace	Father's birthplace	Mother's birthplace	Occupation	Own/Rent
1	57	63	Ornelas Francisco	Head	W	M	Sept 1844	55	M	12			N. Mejico	Old Mexico	N. Mejico	Stock & Ranch	O F F 69
2			— Leonora	Wife	W	F	June 1857	42	M	12	6	6	N. Mejico	N. Mejico	N. Mejico		
3			— Andres	Son	W	M	Dec 1888	11	S				N. Mejico	N. Mejico	N. Mejico		
4			— Francisco	Son	W	M	Oct 1890	9	S				N. Mejico	N. Mejico	N. Mejico		
5			— Alonzo	Son	W	M	July 1892	7	S				N. Mejico	N. Mejico	N. Mejico		
6			— Ricardo	Son	W	M	Mar 1894	5	S				N. Mejico	N. Mejico	N. Mejico		
7			— Josefita	Daughter	W	F	Sept 1897	2	S				N. Mejico	N. Mejico	N. Mejico		
8			— Jose	Son	W	M	Mar 1899	1	S				N. Mejico	N. Mejico	N. Mejico		
9			Montoya Rafael	S-in-Law	W	M	Nov 1871	23	M	3			N. Mejico	N. Mejico	N. Mejico	Farm Labor	
10			— Sanitas	Daughter	W	F	Nov 1879	20	M	3	1		N. Mejico	N. Mejico	N. Mejico		
11			— Anastacia	G-Daughter	W	F	Sept 1898	1	S				N. Mejico	N. Mejico	N. Mejico		
12	58	64	Sandoval Cayetano	Head	W	M	April 1853	47	M	26			N. Mejico	N. Mejico	N. Mejico	Stock Raiser	O L A
13			— Maria Dolores	Wife	W	F	Nov 1860	40	M	26	13	9	N. Mejico	N. Mejico	N. Mejico		
14			— Feliberto	Son	W	M	Jan 1882	18	S				N. Mejico	N. Mejico	N. Mejico		
15			— Socorita	Daughter	W	F	Nov 1884	16	S				N. Mejico	N. Mejico	N. Mejico		
16			— Enedelia	Daughter	W	F	Sept 1886	13	S				N. Mejico	N. Mejico	N. Mejico		
17			— Emilia	Daughter	W	F	Feb 1889	11	S				N. Mejico	N. Mejico	N. Mejico		
18			— Malario	Son	W	M	Dec 1892	7	S				N. Mejico	N. Mejico	N. Mejico		
19			— Trinidad	Daughter	W	F	May 1895	5	S				N. Mejico	N. Mejico	N. Mejico		
20			— Igumpito	Daughter	W	F	Sept 1898	1	S				N. Mejico	N. Mejico	N. Mejico		
21	59	65	Sandoval Estevan	Head	W	M	April 1852	46	M	6			N. Mejico	N. Mejico	N. Mejico	Stock Raiser	O F F 74
22			— Viviana	Wife	W	F	May 1875	25	M	6	4	4	N. Mejico	N. Mejico	N. Mejico		
23			— Cipriano	Son	W	M	Aug 1895	4	S				N. Mejico	N. Mejico	N. Mejico		
24			— Biseela	Son	W	M	June 1897	2	S				N. Mejico	N. Mejico	N. Mejico		
25			— Cecilio	Son	W	M	May 1898	2	S				N. Mejico	N. Mejico	N. Mejico		
26			— Mirenliqua	Daughter	W	F	Oct 1899	8/12	S				N. Mejico	N. Mejico	N. Mejico		
27	60	66	Vigil Jose	Head	W	M	Mar 1861	38	M	14			N. Mejico	N. Mejico	N. Mejico	Rancher	O F F 75
28			— Placida	Wife	W	F	1864	34	M	14	5	4	N. Mejico	N. Mejico	N. Mejico		
29			— Tomas	Son	W	M	Sept 1885	14	S				N. Mejico	N. Mejico	N. Mejico		
30			— Elaisa	Daughter	W	F	Oct 1888	11	S				N. Mejico	N. Mejico	N. Mejico		
31			— Santiago	Son	W	M	July 1890	9	S				N. Mejico	N. Mejico	N. Mejico		
32			— Fidencio	Son	W	M	Nov 1895	4	S				N. Mejico	N. Mejico	N. Mejico		
33			Romero Miquila	M-in-Law	W	F	1800	70	Wd		7	1	N. Mejico	N. Mejico	N. Mejico		
34			— Alvina	Niece	W	F	Mar 1886	14	S				N. Mejico	N. Mejico	N. Mejico		
35	61	67	Baca Emeneido	Head	W	M	Nov 1847	52	M	30			N. Mejico	N. Mejico	N. Mejico	Rancher	O F F 78
36			— Estafanita	Wife	W	F	Nov 1855	44	M	30	15	10	N. Mejico	N. Mejico	N. Mejico		
37			— Efremia	Daughter	W	F	June 1879	20	S				N. Mejico	N. Mejico	N. Mejico		
38			— Lotor	Son	W	M	April 1885	15	S				N. Mejico	N. Mejico	N. Mejico		
39			— Fleisma	Son	W	M	May 1887	13	S				N. Mejico	N. Mejico	N. Mejico		
40			— Rebeca	Daughter	W	F	May 1890	10	S				N. Mejico	N. Mejico	N. Mejico		
41			— Felicio	Son	W	M	1892	7	S				N. Mejico	N. Mejico	N. Mejico		
42			— Alberto	Son	W	M	Mar 1894	6	S				N. Mejico	N. Mejico	N. Mejico		
43			— Fidel	Son	W	M	June 1898	1	S				N. Mejico	N. Mejico	N. Mejico		
44	62	68	Pellegos Juliano	Head	W	M	June 1873	26	M				N. Mejico	N. Mejico	N. Mejico	Day Labor	O F F
45			— Manuelita	Wife	W	F	1877		M	1	1	1	N. Mejico	N. Mejico	N. Mejico		
46			— Emquil	Son	W	M	1892	8	S				N. Mejico	N. Mejico	N. Mejico		
47			Doloritas	Mother	W	F	1850	50	Wd	8	2		N. Mejico	N. Mejico	N. Mejico		
48	63	69	Gallegos Nicolas	Head	W	M	1858	30	M	3			N. Mejico	N. Mejico	N. Mejico	Day Labor	O F F
49			— Isabel	Wife	W	F	1880	19	M	3	1		N. Mejico	N. Mejico	N. Mejico		R H
50	64	70	Padilla Cruz	Head	W	M	May 1863	36	M	39			N. Mejico	N. Mejico	N. Mejico	Day Labor	

SECTION IV: LAUMBACHS IN NEW MEXICO
Chapter 32: Peter Joseph Laumbach (1867—1954)

by Karl Wayne Laumbach,
with Peter James and Rudolph Edward Laumbach

Known as Pete or Pedro throughout his life, Peter Joseph Laumbach was born June 29, 1867. His birthplace was an adobe house located in Cebollita Canyon, Mora County, New Mexico. The valley known as La Cebolla is located between the Mora and Sapello valleys two miles south [*and west*] of the community of Buena Vista. Pete's parents were Andreas Detlef Laumbach and Leonor Ebel. His father had come to the United States to escape the constant wars in which Germany was involved during the 1850s. His mother was the daughter of Daniel Eberle (Ebel), a Swiss German storekeeper and veteran of the Missouri Volunteers[1], and Viviana Martin.[2] Viviana's parents were Bernardo Martin and Apolonia Gutierrez de Solano, who were among the original 76 grantees to the Mora Land Grant in 1835.

When Pete's parents were married, his father, a Lutheran, agreed to raise their children in the Catholic Church. Accordingly, on September 1, 1867, Pete was baptized a Roman Catholic in the Santa Gertrudis Church, Mora, New Mexico, by the Reverend Jean Baptiste Guerin.[3] Pete's godparents were Henry Korte and Juanita Metzgar.

The original of the following photo was a large group of mostly unidentified people, taken at Buena Vista, perhaps in the 1920s. This is a cropped version of that photo with just those we can identify. From right to left: perhaps Mrs. Knaur, Pete Knaur, Ramon Bonney, Jose Cruz and Margaret Laumbach Cruz. The occasion and exact location for the gathering are unknown. From Karl Laumbach collection.

What exactly the Andreas Laumbach family was doing at La Cebolla in 1867 is not known. The most likely explanation is that Leonor was staying with her mother, Bibiana, for the duration of the pregnancy as the 1870 census shows Bibiana living at Cebolla. At some point during the 1860s, Andreas Laumbach purchased property in nearby Buena Vista, which became the headquarters for the Laumbach ranch until 1948. Prior to that time, they may have been living with or near Leonor's mother at La Cebolla.

Few memories of Cebolla have come down through the years. Uncle Red (Andreas Detlef III) said his father pointed out the ruins of the house and that he had been born in the corner bedroom nearest the road. A house mound (a nicely preserved archaeological site!) can still be seen approximately 200 yards west of New Mexico Highway 518. George Laumbach, a son of Pete, remembered his father telling of running from the house through the snow to bathe in springs located near the house. This story suggests the children spent considerable time with their grandmother.

In any case, the ranch at Buena Vista near the entrance to the narrow canyon that leads to the lower Mora Valley and the village of Golondrinas became the Laumbach home. The long adobe building with a pitched tin roof in this photo still stands at the ranch headquarters.[4]

Editor's note: Karl's family has this photo in sepia; it had been mailed to Aunties after they lived in Las Vegas but the photo had been taken decades earlier of their home place. Karl and family believe this house was built by Andreas 1st. Verna Laumbach had this same photo as a snapshot. She had written on hers that it was the (apparently still existing) Buena Vista family place, taken in the "1880s." Karl's uncle Ike (Casimiro) recently confirmed to me that this photo was of the still existing main house, and that this was the front view. The irrigation ditch can be seen in the foreground. A larger image of this photo appears in an earlier chapter of this book. Karl recently found a note that he had taken years earlier from a conversation with his Uncle Red (Andreas Detlef Laumbach III) who said the building built by Andreas 1st was a small building behind the family's home. Was that little stable, which is still there, the first building on the Laumbach's Buena Vista property, and was it built by Andreas 1st? We will probably never know.

That building is said to have been built by Andreas Detlef I, the father of Andreas Detlef II. If so, it is possible Andreas took over the location when his father was killed by Indians in the early 1860s.

The older man had been herding stock near the Rock Crossing (El Vado de las Piedras) on the Santa Fe Trail when his camp was attacked. Another man, Ruperto Aguilar, escaped and brought the news to Buena Vista. Andreas Detlef II and others returned three days later to bury the body. Attempts to relocate the grave many years later were unsuccessful.[5] Another family story of his death has Andreas I with a wagon train taking freight to Missouri. The wagons were pulled into a camp west of the crossing where they were attacked by Indians. One man was at the river getting water and was able to escape.[6] A variation of this account states that Andreas I was at the river getting water when he was killed.[7] In the 1920s and 1930s, Pete Laumbach's sons drove him from Roy to Raton. They invariably stopped on the hill immediately west of Taylor Springs, where Pete pointed to a hill across the Cimarron River just west of where it joins the Canadian River and said, "That's where your great-grandfather is buried."[8]

The Andreas Laumbach family built a fine house at Buena Vista near the banks of the Mora River. When the house was complete, Andreas asked [*young*] Pete to dig a well to supply the house with fresh water. Pete asked his father where he wanted the well. His father pointed to a spot on the sandstone bedrock immediately in front of the house and said he wanted it right there. The young Pete dug the well with pick, bar and shovel.[9]

The family grew quickly. Margaret, born in 1865, was the eldest, followed by Pete in 1867, and then Estefanita (1870), Daniel (1872), Henry (1874), Alexander (1876), Anna (1878), Cristina (1881), Mary (1884), John (1886), Leonor (1888) and Cordelia (1891).[10] Alexander, John, and Cordelia died in infancy. Cordelia is buried in the Buena Vista orchard, as the ground was too frozen for burial in the nearby family plot. [*Verna's story, remembered by her granddaughter, Tracy, was that baby Cordelia was buried very near the house because of inclement, frigid weather. When subsequent owners, the Shocks, expanded the house, Tracy recalled her grandma Verna fretting that the added house structure was built on top of baby Cordelia's grave.*]

Photo of Andreas Detlef Laumbach 2nd and family: (rear l-r) Margaret Laumbach Cruz, Jose Cruz (with baby) and Anna Laumbach. (Front l-r) Leonor, Andreas, Leonore Ebel Laumbach, Christina Laumbach.
[*Editor's note: Verna wrote, on her photographer's print of this photo, that it was taken in 1904. That was the year Andreas died.*]

All of the children spoke both English and Spanish, and at least the older ones spoke German. Uncle Red [*Andreas Detlef Laumbach III*] remembers his father occasionally speaking German to visitors. It is possible that Lenore Ebel had learned some German from her father, although he was killed when she was very young. [*Verna said she only heard her grandmother speak Spanish.*] Spanish was the language of choice for Margaret and Pete all of their lives. Pete was adamant that his own children speak Spanish without mixing in English words.

Although baptized a Catholic, Pete and his siblings were influenced by the founding of a Presbyterian Mission School at Buena Vista in 1875.[11] The founders, Jose Ynes Perea and John Annin, brought missionaries to teach the local children. Beginning when he was 16, Pete attended three six-month sessions of school, each lasting from October to April.[12] He received a Bible from his teacher in recognition of his scholastic achievements. That experience left Pete literate in both Spanish and English and knowledgeable of basic mathematics, amply demonstrated in his numerous business transactions in later life. He was keenly interested in local and world affairs and accumulated a small library that included an account of the sinking of the Titanic, a History of the World War (World War I) and Charley Siringo's *Life of Billy the Kid*.

It was an active life on the New Mexico frontier. Pete and his brothers worked hard from an early age. The 1880 census lists Pete, age 13, as a son and a laborer in the household. Pete worked at a sawmill in the mountains above Las Vegas for a couple of summers. His job was to trim branches from downed trees; he became quite practiced with an axe.

Peter Joseph Laumbach age 14—16. Karl said his hair had been cropped for hygienic reasons.

While spending time in the Canadian River area with his Uncle Andres Ebell when he was 15, he polished the skills of a cowboy learned at Buena Vista.

Uncle Andres Ebell and sons Andres, Bonifacio and Zacharias.[13]

The hard work put muscle on Pete's growing frame, and he grew into a tall, strong man.

Peter Joseph Laumbach, circa 1900? This may have been his wedding photo.

In his prime he was 6'2" tall and boasted a 48-inch chest and huge hands.[14] In those days, traveling athletes challenged locals to wrestle or race for money. On one occasion, Pete is reputed to have raced the challenger in his work shoes. Pete won all three races against the challenger, who was from Kansas. At the end of the last race, Pete was so far ahead that he turned around and ran backwards, taunting his opponent.[15] During an altercation later in life, Pete lifted his opponent over his head and threw him over a fence. Another feat of strength, picking up a 100-lb. sack of wheat with his teeth, eventually forced him to have his teeth pulled.[16]

Fort Union provided a huge market for local ranchers and farmers. Pete remembered accompanying his father to Fort Union to sell horses. Pete's father crossed a Steeldust (descended from Steeldust, a quarter-horse famous in 1840s Texas) stallion with Morgan mares to produce large, active horses suitable for cavalry mounts. A bill of sale has survived that documents the sale of one bay mare pony from Lt. A.W. Brewster, 10th Cavalry, by Andreas Laumbach on July 16, 1887. The bill of sale is stamped "*Office of Post Quartermaster, Ft. Union, N. Mex.*"[17]

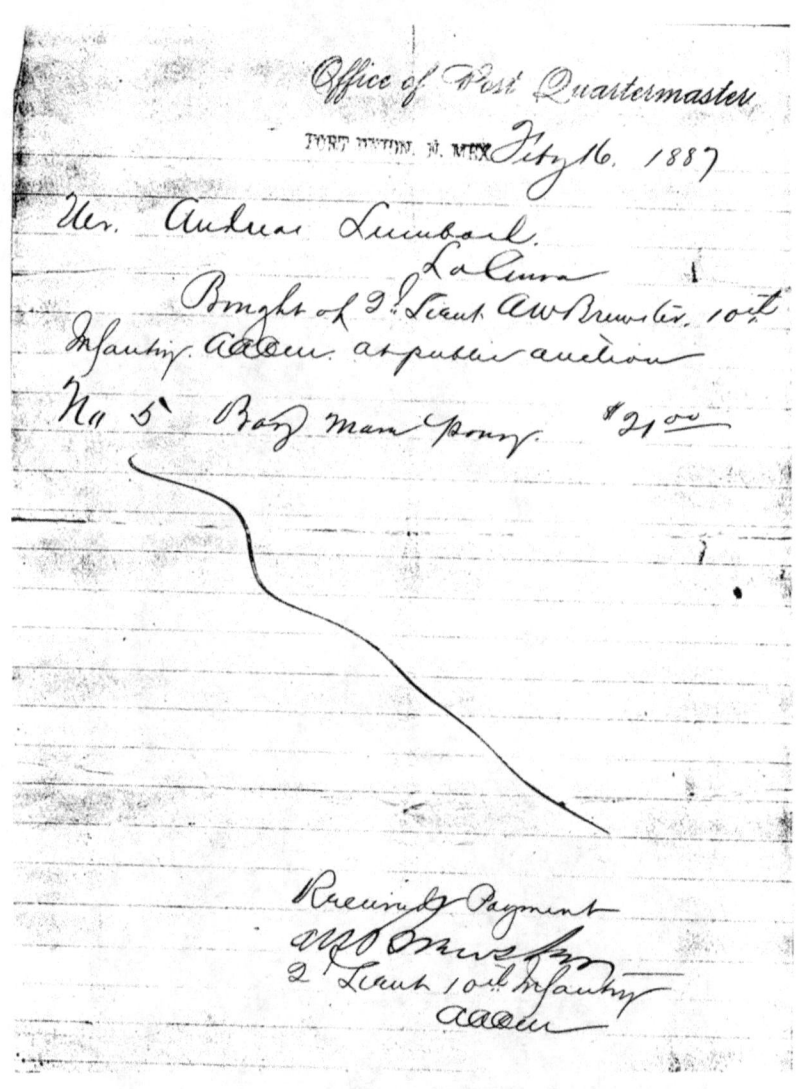

The news of the day is the stuff of western history. Custer met defeat at the Little Big Horn when Pete was nine. Billy the Kid fought in the Lincoln County War when Pete was 11, and was jailed in nearby Las Vegas when Pete was 13, and died in Ft. Sumner when Pete was 14. Pete and Rudy Laumbach [*grandsons of Peter Joseph*] were told that young Peter Joseph saw Billy escorted to the train when he was taken from the jail in Las Vegas by Pat Garrett.

The old men of that day could remember back to when the country belonged to Spain and then Mexico. Some had fought the hated *gringos* when Mora took an active part during the Taos Rebellion of 1847. Many had gone out onto the plains as "*ciboleros*," men who hunted the buffalo with lances and traded goods with the Comanche. One banty-legged old man told Pete that "the greatest satisfaction that he had known was the feel of hot blood hitting his leg after lancing a running buffalo."[18] The gush of blood meant the heart had been pierced and the kill was clean. Many years later, Joyce Laumbach recalled his Uncle Felipe Esquibel cutting jerky from a beef round in the manner of the old buffalo hunters by taking broad sheets of meat instead of the narrow strips we see today.[19] Felipe Esquibel had served as a meat-cutter on buffalo hunts, and some of the wooden boxes that had once been filled with salted meat were at the La Cinta ranch in the 1920s.[20]

An incident when Pete was still in his teens affected the course of his life. His father, Andreas Detlef, was a harsh taskmaster. He did not tolerate mistakes and vented his fury with a combination of curses, which included both Spanish and German phrases. On this day a fresh snow had fallen, covering the ground. Andreas was searching for a wagon chain and could not find it. He decided Pete had been negligent in putting the chain back in its proper place after use. Pete apparently protested and was soundly beaten. When the snow melted, his father found the wagon chain where Andreas, not Pete, had left it. When Pete reached the age of 21 (1888), he told his father that he was a free man and a citizen[21] and left Buena Vista to make his way in the world. He was large for his age and no doubt skilled in handling stock, so he soon found work.

A variation of this story has it that Pete got into an argument with "Old Man" Wissler.[22]

Peter Knaur, Mr. Wissler, Anna Laumbach, Leonore Ebel Laumbach, Nellie Knaur making cider at Buena Vista.

Wissler had been in the German cavalry and had known the Laumbachs in the old country. He followed Andreas to New Mexico and lived and worked at the Buena Vista ranch for the rest of his life. It is possible that it was Wissler who had left the chain out. In any case, Pete told his father that he wanted Wissler to leave. Andreas stuck up for Wissler, so Pete was the one to leave. Wissler is buried in the Laumbach cemetery at Buena Vista. His watch fob, made with an 1856 gold piece, is still in the family.

When Pete left the family's A+L Ranch, he penned a short poem:

Adios Rito de la Cebolla
Placita de Santa Gertrudis
Dondese tratan de firmezas
Y pagan con gratitudes

(Translation:)
Farewell little river of Cebolla
Village of Santa Gertrudis
Where we live in honesty
And pay with gratitude.[23]

He remembered that when he left: "*Mi mama me dio' la bendicion y mi papa dijo vete.*" (My mother gave me a blessing and my father said go). He left to find his fortune accompanied by a neighbor boy with a burro, a blanket, and carrying a silver dollar. They soon met a man selling whiskey and bought a jug for 50 cents.[24]

As he rode north from Buena Vista, he stopped at several ranches to inquire about work. At one ranch no one was home so he waited on the porch of the ranch house. He noticed a bag of jerked meat hanging from the rafters and helped himself as he waited. When the owner arrived, Pete commented on the tastiness of the dried meat and was informed that it was cougar.[25]

Pete found work at the Jerome Troy ranch located east of Raton, New Mexico. An 1892 obituary of a Troy child found in Aunt Mary Laumbach's trunk indicates regular communication at Buena Vista with that family. Several incidents that occurred during his tenure at the Troy Ranch have been preserved through stories told to his children. They offer the only glimpses we have of that period.

The first animal he owned was a horse encountered on the open range. Pete had stopped by a spring and noticed a horse grazing nearby. The horse was gaunt and still carried the remnants of a badly weathered saddle on its back. Rigging a brush corral at the water, Pete was able to catch the animal, subsequently gaining its trust. There was no indication of ownership, and he never learned where the horse had come from.[26]

Pete learned a lot about horses during his early years. Two stories illustrate Pete's knowledge of horses.[27] Pete stayed in the "Montoya Pocket" between La Cinta and the Canadian River during his first winter in the area with his herd. He had brought four horses from the Troy Ranch and kept one of them up while letting the others graze in the Montoya Pocket. He needed the extra horses, as he was planning to do some farming in the spring. One morning he discovered the three horses had taken off. After two days of searching, he found their tracks where they crossed the "*cerca divides*," a long log and rock fence that stretched from the caprock in the vicinity of the Encierro to the caprock on the Tequesquite Ranch north of Roy. The ranchers had built it to keep stock from drifting too far south in a driving winter storm. Pete's horses had returned to the Troy Ranch from whence they had come. Pete saddled up the next day and started on their trail. His horse gave out on him somewhere east of Mills, and Pete was forced to walk while driving the horse ahead of him to the Gillespie Ranch.

Arriving at Dave Gillespie's around 2 am, he was reluctant to wake up the house, so he and the horse, both of them worn out but too tired to sleep, stayed in the barn until daylight. When smoke began curling out of the chimney, Pete went to the house. Dave Gillespie asked him what the hell he was doing out at that time of day. When Pete told him that he was looking for his horses, Dave said his horses had come by and, recognizing them, he had put them in a pasture with his horses. Gillespie told Pete to sit and have breakfast and then they'd find a horse that Pete could use to pen his. As they talked, Gillespie told Pete that he had an outlaw horse, a big gray that no one could handle. He offered him to Pete if he thought he could handle him.

After breakfast, they went out to find Pete's horses and look at the gray. The horse had thrown everyone who had tried to ride it. After fore-footing and saddling the gray, Pete cut a slit in a fresh cowhide that was hanging on the fence. Jamming the slit down over the saddle horn, he released the horse. The big gray bucked and squalled and fought the cow hide for almost two hours. At the end, the horse was on its knees and turning to bite the cowhide with its teeth. When the horse was sufficiently exhausted, Pete took off the cowhide and mounted the horse. There was no more bucking and Pete commented to Gillespie about what a good horse he had given him. Pete kept the horse, which was big, strong and fast enough to catch a wild burro, something not all horses could do. He called him "Tin" (pronounced tēēn in Spanish) and later claimed that it was the best horse he ever had. After Tin died, Pete hung his skull in the corral, where it stayed for many years.

Later in life, when he was in his sixties, Pete's sons, Pete and Al, had a two-year-old filly that had not been broken and was difficult to approach. In Al's words, "Pete and I had a halter on her, and she was allergic to the hackamore and was jerking us around. Dad told me to give him the hackamore, and he walked down the halter rope and reached to put the hackamore on. She reared up, and he caught her front feet on the way up and held them while he walked the filly around the corral on her hind feet. When she gave it up, he "hackamored" her and we saddled her. Pete rode her, with me leading her from a gentle horse. Dad sure opened our eyes."

One of the cowboys he worked with was George McJunkin. He was a black cowboy who earned posthumous fame for his discovery of the Folsom early man site. George had noticed bones eroding from the base of an arroyo wall some 20 feet down. He was curious, took a look at the bones, and found the delicately flaked points we now call Folsom points. He commented on these at the local store and eventually his discovery came to the attention of Dr. Figgins from Colorado. Analysis revealed the bones were from an extinct form of bison, and the first direct evidence that man was in the New World 10,000 years ago was entered into the record.

Pete remembered that McJunkin was invariably teased when any of the local babies had a dark complexion.

Pete also remembered riding with a black cowboy (perhaps McJunkin) who used an extra long cotton rope that was much more limber than the manila ropes usually carried. They were together on the road near Folsom when they passed a school teacher driving a horse and buggy. The horse became frightened and ran away with the woman. Pete and the cowboy pursued the run-a-way. The cowboy built a huge loop with the cotton rope, and when he judged himself to be close enough, let it fly. Pete remembered watching the loop grow smaller and smaller as it took up the length of the rope. The loop was scarcely larger than its target when it settled over the horse's head. The cowboy then eased the horse to a stop.[28]

Pete probably stayed at most of the cow and sheep camps on the Troy Ranch at one time or the other. Years later (in the 1930s), Frank Foxall and his new bride, Christina Laumbach, lived at one of these locations. The place was located just a few miles south and slightly east of present day Raton. It had served the Troy Ranch as a sheep shearing location that was also near the railroad. A log shed was used to shear the sheep and was large enough for 20 shearers to work at a time.[29] Pete must have been thinking of starting his own ranch or perhaps already held a registered brand; Uncle Frank Foxall remembered a PJL burned into one of the logs that made up the shed.[30] The log shed was very old in the 1930s and no longer exists. During his time there, Pete planted a row of cottonwood trees. The tops of those trees could still be seen from Interstate 25 in the 1990s. Uncle Frank had a photo of both the trees and the log barn.

During his time working for the Troy family, an infectious disease began to affect the extensive sheep herds in northeastern New Mexico. A government inspector was sent to control the outbreak but required the services of someone who knew both the area and spoke Spanish. The Troy family loaned Pete to the inspector, and they traveled around inspecting sheep. The inspector was impressed and offered Pete a job, but the Troy family raised his wages to keep from losing him, making the raise retroactive for several months.[31] On another occasion, Pete had built a log cabin for the Troy Ranch and a neighbor, Mr. White, offered him $20.00 per month instead of the $16.00 the Troy family was paying. Pete asked him to put the offer in writing. When the letter arrived, the Troy family matched Mr. White's offer.[32] Pete worked for the Troy Ranch for seven years (1888 to 1895).[33] The Troy family sent Pete to buy livestock for them with a certain amount to spend. Any money left over became his commission. When Pete left, they paid him off in horses and cattle.[34]

The last three years Pete worked for the Troy family, they sold him the excess yearling rams for $1.50 per head. They were his to sell, and he made money selling the first bunch without having to move them too far.[35] The next year, he made it to the mouth of the Bueyeros east of the caprock where he sold the second bunch. The third year, Señor Don Francisco Gallegos,[36] a wealthy sheep rancher from Gallegos, New Mexico located east of Mosquero, sent a man to meet Pete at Gladstone. Gallegos offered to buy the entire 300 head of rams. The two men met and got acquainted. Gallegos wouldn't pay cash but would trade top quality ewes. So they traded, 2½ ewes for each ram. Pete was allowed to select his ewes and, to the consternation of the Gallegos sheepherders, he asked Señor Don Francisco Gallegos to bring in not one but two "*partidos*" of 3,000 head each so that he could make the best selection. Pete didn't say to whom he sold the 750 ewes, but if he received $2.50 per head, he would have cleared around $1,400. He may have traded the ewes for cattle at the rate of seven or eight ewes per head of cattle. In any case, his dealings with Señor Don Francisco Gallegos put him in good financial shape to get started in the cattle business.

Pete worked in the area for several years. It was not until 1897 that he left to start his own ranch south and west of Roy, New Mexico. He had last worked for the George Gillespie Ranch.

One story from this period of his life stands out as an illustration of the hardships endured by the cowboys of the day. A hard winter replete with blizzards had driven the cattle southward off of the plateau country. As the weather pushed them south, the cattle found shelter in the breaks and canyons below the Caprock. The Caprock overlooks the Canadian Gorge to the west and curves eastward, away from the mouth of the gorge, to overlook the short grass plains near the Oklahoma and Texas borders. The area is subject to long, hard winters, exemplified by the winter of 1889.[37] That year an intense blizzard hit northeastern New Mexico on October 31. The storm killed numerous cowboys and scattered not only local stock but also herds being driven north to Colorado.

In the spring of 1897, the cowboys were working the canyons and plains east of the Canadian River Gorge, gathering cattle that had drifted south in the winter.[38] The men were working with a chuck wagon and had no better quarters than their canvas bedrolls. A mild storm came through, showering the men with freezing sleet, chilling them to the bone. Pete developed chills and a fever, becoming delirious.

The other men wrapped him in his bedroll, placed him in the back of a wagon, and hitting the team of horses to get them started, sent him back to the headquarters. He traveled at least one and maybe two days before arriving at the home ranch. By the time the team arrived, his fever had broken. Pete remembered waking up and hearing a rooster crow. Mrs. Gillespie came out to see what was going on and brought him into the house. The doctor in Springer was sent for and Pete eventually recovered.[39]

Pete decided to use his homestead right to acquire 160 acres in Blosser Gap on the west side of Eagle Tail Mountain southeast of Raton. His experience with the inspector served him well, and he used the homestead as a holding area for his traded sheep and cattle. He acted as a middle man, selling sheep for the Troy family and investing his commission in both sheep and cattle. A man named Moore, who owned a nearby homestead, was a partner in this enterprise, and they soon had substantial herds of both sheep and cattle.[40] A letter Conrado Andrada sent to Pete during this period has survived. In the letter, Conrado gave Pete a very hard time about tending sheep.[41]

During his time at Blosser Gap, Pete shared his camp with a man who had a severe drinking problem. The man was overcome with a case of delirium tremens (referred to as the DT's). He began to scream that there were rattlesnakes crawling out of the roof of the camp house. Pete had to tie him up to control him and found him a new place to live.[42]

Pete occasionally traveled to Buena Vista to visit his family. (We don't know when or by what means he and his father reconciled.) On one such trip, Pete was on horseback when he joined company with a man driving a buggy as he crossed the Vado de Piedra (Rock Crossing) near Taylor Springs. Mr. Epimenio Martinez, the driver, invited Pete to tie his horse to the buggy and ride with him so they could talk. Epimenio was on his way to Black Lake near present day Angel Fire. The two men conversed in English all the way to the Agua Dulce (Sweetwater Valley), where Epimenio's friend lived. During the course of the conversation, Pete never let on that he spoke fluent Spanish. As they rode along in the buggy, Epimenio tried valiantly to use his limited English. When they arrived at the Sweetwater, Epimenio asked his friend if he and the "gringo" could stay the night. Both Epimenio and Pete produced a leg of lamb to add to the evening meal. Pete was introduced to the man's wife, and the host informed her in Spanish about the [extra] overnight guest. As she went into the next room, she inquired somewhat crossly where the guest was going to sleep. Pete's host replied in Spanish that the *gringo salado* (dirty gringo) could sleep on the floor.

Pete took his horse out to the pasture and when he returned, he noticed that the woman had placed some hot *atole* on the counter to cool. When dinner was ready, the woman asked Pete what he would like to drink, and he took pleasure in watching their expressions when he replied, "*Atole, si gusta.*" Epimenio exploded. "You've been laughing at me all day beneath that sloppy hat!" After Epimenio and his friends recovered from their surprise and embarrassment, they all had a good laugh.[43] The next day, Pete went over the mesa towards Buena Vista, and Epimenio continued on to Black Lake.

Just when Pete first visited the Canadian River gorge is speculative, but oral accounts indicate that it was in 1882.[44] His Uncle Andres Ebell and his Aunt Maria Marta Esquibel both lived in the area with their respective spouses. It is probable they had begun living there as early as the late 1860s. We do know the little community of Armenta Plaza was settled in 1874.[45] Thus Pete would have made boyhood trips to visit his relatives and work with his uncles.

Knowing both the area and its people, Pete decided to return to the Canadian in 1897, shortly after proving up on his Blosser Gap homestead (12/26/1896). He and his partner split the herds, with Pete taking the cattle and Moore taking the sheep. Pete arrived in the Armenta Plaza area with one hundred head of matched cattle.[46] Pete's brothers, Dan and Henry, had also acquired land in the area, so that was an added incentive for the move. It was upon his return that Pete wooed and won Fidelia Andrada. Or perhaps she was why he moved there.

Fidelia Andrada was the daughter of Casimiro Andrada and Carmelita Romero. She had been born near or at Bueyeros on what was later the Albert Mitchell Ranch. She had lived at Armenta Plaza most of her life. Armenta was isolated and extremely difficult to get to in a wagon. The plaza consisted of several rock houses, a church, a cantina, and a cemetery. It also boasted a school where Fidelia's older brother Leopoldo taught Fidelia and his future spouse, Manuelita Narvaez. Fidelia learned the skills required by pioneer life in New Mexico while growing up in Armenta. She sewed, baked bread in an *horno*, cooked beans in a clay bean pot brought from Taos or Picuris, roasted and dried green chile and other vegetables for the winter, and learned the medicinal use of native plants and herbs.

Fidelia's father, Casimiro, had been captured by Apaches during one of their frequent raids [in Mexico]. Of Yaqui descent, he and one of his sisters were captured near the village of Matape, Sonora, Mexico about 1844.[47] When captured, he attempted to leave a trail by tearing up his *corbata* (necktie) and strewing the pieces. He lived with the Apache for several years. No doubt he was a young boy when captured, as the older boys were generally killed. He may have been traded among different bands of Apaches because the group he was with ended up in northern New Mexico. He was eventually sold to the Romero family in the Taos area.[48] Our cousin Jose Esquibel found him in the Taos census of 1870 listed as a 36-year-old laborer from Sonora. It is likely that while with the Romero family, Casimiro met and later married the much younger Carmelita Romero, who had grown up in the Mora Valley on the eastern side of the Sangre de Cristos. The couple lived in Taos from 1869 to 1875, after which they relocated to the Mora Valley.[49] He worked for the Hall family, who ran a stage stop in the village of Ocate north of Mora.[50] He later herded cattle in the area of Albert, New Mexico (where Fidelia was born in 1880) and then established a place of his own near Armenta Plaza.

Casimiro remembered his upbringing because there are stories of an unsuccessful return to Sonora to see his family.[51] His son, Leopoldo, told Louise Laumbach Luft that they were also of Portuguese descent, so that detail must have been in Casimiro's memory. Andrada is a Portuguese spelling of the Spanish Andrade. Carmelita referred to Casimiro as "El Sonorense."

Fidelia Andrada was a very pretty girl in her late teens when she was betrothed to Pete Laumbach. They were married in Armenta Plaza on June 21, 1898.[52]

Fidelia Andrada Laumbach; perhaps her wedding photo.

According to Petra Laumbach, the Catholic ceremony was performed by a visiting priest. Uncle Ike (Casimiro) remembered hearing that the best man was John Howe. Nicanora Ebel, later the *madrina* for Fidelia's first born daughter, may have been the maid of honor.[53] A homemade wedding card sent by Mr. and Mrs. D.B. Sorrells is our documentary evidence of that ceremony.[54]

The wedding was almost postponed due to the Spanish-American War. In the spring of 1898, Teddy Roosevelt had recruited men from Arizona and New Mexico for his famed "Rough Riders." Pete Laumbach and his soon-to-be brother-in-law Conrado Andrada decided that they should join up. Riding all night to Las Vegas, they arrived to find the quota already filled. There is no word on what Fidelia thought about all this. Another version of the story is that Pete had already signed up and had acquired some equipment, including a saber.[55] When the call came to be in Las Vegas to board the train, he made it there too late. The saber was in the attic of the La Cinta house for many years.[56]

Peter Joseph Laumbach (seated) with unknown friend on left and Leopoldo Andrada on right, circa 1898. Pete may be dressed in his "Rough Rider" uniform.

Pete and Fidelia initially lived at his brother's place. Dan Laumbach had completed a preemption claim on a 40-acre homestead on top of the caprock east of Sabinoso in September 1900. (Dan was working on a sheep ranch near Animas, Colorado when he married Emma in January 1901.) Soon after Dan, Emma and their new baby daughter arrived at the place after Christmas in 1902, Pete and Fidelia moved to his father's (Andreas II) homestead (a cash entry in 1903) at the Coruco, which, like Uncle Dan's ranch, was up on the plateau overlooking the Canadian Gorge. Their first child, Cordelia, was born in 1899, followed by Alfred in 1900. Two more children were born, Peter Joseph "Pedro" (1902) and Rudolph (1903), but both of them died very young. Cancer claimed one and diphtheria the other. Both are buried in unmarked graves at the Coruco. The word *coruco* translates as bird louse or mite. According to one informant, it was the nickname of a local character.[57]

Pedro the first and Christina with their mother, Fidelia. Circa 1905.

Karl said this image of the first Alfred had been on something like a tin-type.

It was in 1902 that Pete bought land in La Cinta. He also purchased a herd of cattle from Sebron (Sebe) Sorrells. Sorrells had the reputation of a rough customer. When they drove the cattle to Pete's pasture, a third man helped them make the drive. Pete noticed bad feeling between Sebe and this other man; they consistently kept him between them as they worked the cattle. By the end of the day, Pete was nervous. When they finally drove the cattle through the gate, Sebe got off his horse so the horse was between him and the other man. Sebe laid his pistol over the saddle and told the man to get out. Pete never learned what the trouble was, but he was happy that day was over.[58]

Sebe Sorrells moved to Sierra County in southern New Mexico. In 1906, he was a member of the posse that killed the Apache Kid in the San Mateo Mountains. He is rumored to have been a local sheriff and is buried in a cemetery near Dusty, New Mexico.

Photo probably taken near Buena Vista place. l-r: unknown man standing; in carriage, top: Nellie Knaur and Leonor Laumbach; in carriage, bottom: Fidelia Andrada Laumbach and Pete Knaur; standing left, Mary Laumbach. Karl Laumbach collection.

La Cinta Canyon was an attractive place to settle, as it contained farmable land and, in those days, the creek held a steady supply of water. Building a two-story rock house at the headquarters, Pete soon moved his family to La Cinta. After trading the Coruco property for land in Gato Canyon (a tributary to La Cinta) where there was a good well, the family may have been living with Dan Laumbach's family for a time while the house was readied.[59] He slowly built up his land by acquiring homesteads from his neighbors. Over time, he put together a ranch of almost 35,000 acres. His brand, WAZ (later WΛZ) was acquired when the Wilson Company, a ranch located north of Mills, went out of business and Pete purchased the remnant of their herd (cattle still out in the canyons).[60] Later he changed the brand to simply ΛZ. The PJL brand belonged to his wife, Fidelia.

His family grew steadily. Christina (1905) was followed by Petra (1906), Rudolph (1908), George (1910), Andreas (1911), Casimiro (1913), Carmelita (1914), Bertha (1915), Lucille (1917), Alfred II (1920) and Pete (1923).[61]

Peter Joseph Laumbach family circa 1912. l-r: Petra, Cordelia, Christina, Fidelia, Peter Joseph, Alfredo 1st, Rudolph, George (below), and Andreas (Red) at 7 months, on the floor.

Peter Joseph Laumbach family circa 1926. Back row: Peter Joseph, Rudolph, George, a friend, Andreas (Red), Casimiro (Ike). Middle row: Fidelia, Petra, Cordelia, a friend (Ortiz), Christina, a friend, Bertha. Front row: Peter Joseph Jr., Alfred, Lucille.

Petra was likely the first child born at La Cinta. Carmelita and two unnamed babies died shortly after birth in the later years. Tragedy struck in 1918 when Alfred 1st was killed by lightning. As the oldest son, Alfred was a leader in the family and the bolt of lightning changed the course of all of their lives.

Pete and his family built a solid and largely self-sufficient life for themselves at La Cinta. Besides cattle, they raised horses, goats, hogs, and chickens. With good rainfall, fields of corn, millet, squash and watermelon thrived. A vegetable garden and orchard were watered from the well and creek. Prairie hay was cut and stacked for winter use. Goats and chickens provided meat during the warmer months, hogs were made into hams and souse, and beef was hung in cold weather, what wasn't eaten fresh was made into jerky. Corn and squash were dried for winter use.

Goods were acquired on overnight wagon trips to Roy and less frequently to Las Vegas. Staples such as flour, coffee, sugar and salt dominated the grocery list. Fruit and chile were bought in quantity and either dried or canned.

In the early years, numerous neighbors shared the work and harvest. As time went on, many of these homesteaders moved on, leaving empty dwellings, some of which became cow camps (e.g., Parker Wells Place). Many family members lived nearby, including Leopoldo Andrada (brother to Fidelia), Marcelino Esquibel, Manuel Sanchez (married to Pete's sister Cristina) and Pete's brother, Dan Laumbach. The families helped each other with branding and other tasks. There were occasional visits by other family members, notably Pete's Uncle Ramon Bonney. Well remembered neighbors from the early years included the Arnolds, the Kirkseys, Parker Wells and Bud Finch.

"Old Man" Finch, as he was known to the Laumbach children, lived in the northern plains during the latter years of the 19th century and was, among other things, an accomplished blacksmith. On July 4, 1912, Pete and Bud Finch attended the heavyweight boxing match between Jack Johnson and

"Fireman" Jim Flynn in Las Vegas, New Mexico. Pete recalled the blood spattering on the poles of the ring.[62]

Days were active, and the entire family was involved. Pete was up very early, making fire and putting on the coffee. The girls slept downstairs and the boys were upstairs. Dad remembered waking up to the sound of his father beating a raw egg and whiskey in a tin cup that would be soon filled with boiling hot coffee. Then they heard him call "*Muchachos*!" a suggestion that they should be up. The boys responded by picking up and dropping their shoes on the floor to make him think they were up and moving. He then went outside to do the morning chores, coming back in an hour or so for a full breakfast.

The older children helped with the smaller ones, with both boys and girls taking on greater responsibility as they got older. The boys worked in the fields, herded goats, milked cows, learned to rope and ride, broke horses, chopped wood, dug wells, butchered and processed meat and performed any other required tasks. The girls helped with the smaller children, cooked, sewed, made cheese, put up preserves and all the other domestic tasks of that time and place.

Fidelia organized the children and made sure all were tended to. Besides the usual domestic tasks, Fidelia was knowledgeable in the use of medicinal herbs. Small bags hung in the side room of the house, each containing herbs that she had selected and dried. When someone was ill, she went through the bags, sniffing until she found the right one for the occasion.

Pete sometimes had to defend his property against those who would take it from him. The public road ran through the ranch, but Pete noticed that one fellow purposely rode across country in an effort to check Pete's trap line and abscond with the trapped animal and the trap. Pete warned this individual but soon saw him wandering through the brush looking for Pete's traps. This time, Pete pulled out his .30-30 and fired a few rounds in the direction of a rapidly disappearing horse and rider. A few days later, Pete was talking to the sheriff on a Roy sidewalk when the culprit appeared. As he walked by, Pete told the sheriff, "*Este hombre tiene un caballo muy ligero.*"[63] (That fellow has a very fast horse.) His son Alfred Laumbach tells of another occasion where Pete used his rifle to discourage a neighbor from stealing a cow on the Romero Flats. He later met the man in Roy and commented on how fast his horse was.

Cattle theft was an ongoing problem. In 1917, a number of Pete's cattle came up missing. Marcelino Esquibel (a cousin) found the stolen cattle south of Wagon Mound. Pete and Marcelino went to recover the stock and were eating lunch when one of the accused arrived. Accosting Pete, the man told him that he had shamed him. When Pete responded that the man had no shame, he launched himself at Pete, who was cutting corn from a cob with a small knife. The knife stabbed into the man, wounding but not killing him. The man later died in the Spanish flu epidemic of 1918. His wife blamed Pete for his death. She followed him around Roy until he complained. When the sheriff stopped her, he discovered she was carrying a butcher knife hidden in her dress.[64] Pete was a member of the New Mexico Cattlegrowers Association until 1928, when the association refused to help him prosecute another cow thief.[65]

The following story by Peter James Laumbach provides the flavor for the time and place at Pete Laumbach's La Cinta Ranch.

~~

Calistro, Man of Mystery

"This story was first told me by my father, Rudolph Laumbach. The story was later refreshed and filled out somewhat by my uncle, Ike Laumbach and my brother, Rudy Laumbach. It all began, as my father told me, with my grandfather, Pete J. or Pedro Laumbach, riding with his brother-in-law, Leopoldo Andrada on my grandfather's ranch. They were horseback, of course, on the bottom country somewhere near La Cinta Creek, when they spotted a wisp of smoke curling up from near the top of the mesa. The top of the mesa was several hundred feet higher than where they were and a good climb. They decided to split up and approach the smoke from two different directions. They rode up the side of the mesa, and converged on the smoke to find a man camped out, as Uncle Ike said he had heard, in a cave. They hailed the man carefully before going in to talk to him. He identified himself as Calistro...that is the only name my dad or uncle ever heard. This was during the time when the Mexican Revolution was still raging below the border. Eventually they learned he had come up from Mexico, and had been in the Revolution, but he was not very talkative on the subject. Granddad offered him work, and he went back to my grandfather's ranch house and stayed on for several months as a ranch hand. He was an excellent horseman, and he broke and trained several horses for Grandded.

The next spring, Grandded and Calistro went to Buena Vista to help our great-grandmother, Leonor Ebel Laumbach, with the branding of her cattle. There was a woman from Mexico working for her who was called Señá Chon (Señora Chon) by all the children. After the work, when all the hands were gathered and seated around a large table for dinner, Señá Chon was helping with the serving. She walked into the dining room with a large platter of food, which she almost dropped when she saw Calistro sitting at the table. She exclaimed his name, and he looked thunderstruck. After dinner, Calistro quietly slipped away and was never seen again. If Señá Chon ever told anyone about how or where she knew Calistro, it was not shared with the younger members of the family. It always remained a mystery among my father's brothers."

~~

Having enjoyed an early education, Pete worked diligently to make sure his children received one as well. The first school was held in the Sebe Sorrells dugout, located immediately adjacent to the La Cinta headquarters.[66] Pete helped organize a local country school at the Luther Raines place a few miles away.[67]

Luther Raines school house, La Cinta Ranch, circa 1915.

In those years, the Spanish Presbyterian Church had become prominent in northern New Mexico. One of its leaders, Gabino Rendon, was a good friend of Pete's. As the country school only went to the middle grades, Gabino convinced Pete that the children should attend Presbyterian boarding school. At about age 12, the boys were sent to Menaul (Albuquerque) and the girls to Allison James (Santa Fe).[68]

Peter Joseph and Fidelia with older sons, mid-1920s: l-r: George, Rudolph, Peter Joseph, Fidelia, Andreas (Red) and Casimiro (Ike).

The ranch reached its full extent in 1927. The year 1928 was good in terms of rain and income, but it was followed by the Great Depression of 1929 and several years of drought. The depression killed the market, and drought made it more and more difficult to subsist on the land. Farming in La Cinta became a thing of the past. Making all of this even more difficult was the 1928 death of Fidelia, Pete's wife of 30 years.[69]

Peter Joseph and sons 1937, l-r: George, Alfred, Rudolph, Pete, Peter Joseph, Rudolph Jr. (Sonny, on Ike's knee), Casimiro (Ike) and Andreas (Red).

Laumbach brothers on horseback, 1932, l-r: Rudolph holding Sonny, Casimiro (Ike), Terry (a hired hand from Texas), George, Roscoe Latham (future husband of Petra Laumbach), Andreas (Red).

Pete again married, this time to the widowed Magdalena Garcia Trujillo in 1929. By then he was 61 years old. The pressures of the depression and drought forced him to sell the cattle and paved the way for the break-up of the ranch. Piece by piece it was sold, leaving only a 5,500-acre core, including the headquarters and land above and below the rim. Pete and Lena moved from the home place to a house above the rim in the early 1930s. Peter Joseph Laumbach passed away there in 1954.

Pete Laumbach was a man of few words and led a very active life. His life spanned from the frontier west to the age of the jet and the atom bomb. He saw open range turned into fenced ranches and a subsistence life-style become dependent on a cash economy. My aunt, Petra Laumbach Latham, when asked about her father, said, "He was a good man; he made sure we had clothes and food to eat. He took care of us."

Photo of grave marker by Pedro Laumbach of Colorado, son of Pedro and Lily Laumbach of Roy, New Mexico. Submitted by the senior Pedro for this book.

---

[1] See chapter on Ramon Bonney et al. for more details on the life and death of Daniel Eberle.

[2] Viviana is also commonly spelled Bibiana.

[3] http://www.guerinhistory.com/gen0-jeanbaptiste.php.

[4] Story attributed to Daniel Laumbach, son of Andreas II.

[5] Story told by Rudolph Laumbach to his sons Rudolph and Peter.

[6] Story told by Alfredo Laumbach, son of Peter Joseph.

[7] Memories of Casimiro (Ike), Andreas (Red) and George Laumbach.

[8] Story told to Karl Laumbach by George Laumbach.

[9] Dale B. Gerdeman in "Presbyterian Missionaries in Rural Northern New Mexico: Serving the Lord on the New Mexico Frontier". Pp. 22—37, Menaul Historical Library of the Southwest 25th Anniversary Edition.

[10] Alfred Laumbach Sr. to Karl Laumbach.

[11] According to Andres Ebell III, and the date of 1882 for Pete and Dan Laumbach's first experience in the Canadian River area is given in Wilferth, JW (1933). An Economic History of Harding County, page 18, MA thesis at New Mexico Normal University (Highlands), Las Vegas.

[12] Alfred Laumbach Sr. remembers his father wearing size 12 gloves and a size 19 shirt.

[13] Alfred Laumbach Sr. to Karl Laumbach.

[14] Alfred Laumbach Sr. to Karl Laumbach.

[15] George Laumbach to Karl Laumbach.

[16] Joyce Laumbach in "Some History and I Remember" page 46, self published, no date.

[17] Memories of George Laumbach.

[18] Alfred Laumbach Sr. to Karl Laumbach.

[19] Poem attributed to Pete by Carmen Ebell Naranjo.

[20] Memories of Casimiro (Ike) Laumbach.

[21] Memory of George Laumbach.

[22] Story told by Andreas (Red) Laumbach.

[23] Stories told by Alfred Laumbach Sr. to Karl Laumbach.

[24] Story told by George Laumbach. Ike remembered the story but in his version it was Mrs. Gillespie who was in the buggy.

[25] Alfred Laumbach Sr., Roy, New Mexico to Karl Laumbach.

[26] PJL eventually was registered to Fidelia Andrada.

[27] Memory of Andreas (Red) Laumbach.

[28] Alfred Laumbach Sr. to Karl Laumbach.

[29] Alfred Laumbach Sr. to Karl Laumbach.

[30] Rudolph Laumbach to Rudy and Pete Laumbach.

[31] Story from Alfred Laumbach Sr. to Karl Laumbach.

[32] Using the honorific title "Don" was a courtesy extended to many men, but when a man was considered to be very important the use of two titles "Señor Don" was used. Señor Don Francisco Gallegos qualified for that honor.

[33] http://www.newmexicohistory.org/filedetails.php?fileID=23326.

[34] The newspaper article puts their location in the side canyons of the Canadian near the Jaritas Ranch. Alfred Laumbach Sr. remembers that the cowboys were at a playa lake called Reunion located east of Roy, New Mexico.

[35] Andreas (Red) Laumbach to Karl Laumbach and article in Roy Newspaper (no date).

[36] Andreas (Red) Laumbach to Karl Laumbach.

[37] Letter from Conrado Andrada to Pedro Laumbach (1895). Original letter in Andreas (Red) Laumbach files, copy in Karl Laumbach files.

[38] George Laumbach to Karl Laumbach.

[39] Alfred Laumbach and George Laumbach to Karl Laumbach. George Laumbach would often point out Epimenio's house in Wagon Mound, which was built on top of a prominent hill. It can still be seen from the Interstate 25.

[40] Andres Ebell III to Karl Laumbach. The date of 1882 for Pete and Dan Laumbach's first experience in the Canadian River area is given in Wilferth, JW (1933). An Economic History of Harding County, page 18, MA thesis at New Mexico Normal University (Highlands), Las Vegas.

[41] Armenta Plaza was founded by Pablo Romero in 1874 according to J.W. Wilferth (1933). An Economic History of Harding County, page 18, MA thesis at New Mexico Normal University (Highlands), Las Vegas.

[42] Carmen Ebel Naranjo: "Pedro llego a la Armenta con cien vacas, todas igualitas." Alfred Laumbach Sr. remembers hearing that Pete's herd was composed of 92 cows and 12 bulls.

[43] Leopoldo Andrada to Alfred Laumbach. The date of 1844 makes the assumption that Casimiro was eight years old when captured. Jose Esquibel has located Casimiro as a 36-year-old laborer in the 1870 Taos census.

[44] Carmen Ebel Naranjo to Peter James Laumbach.

[45] Article on Carmelita Romero by a "double cousin" of Andrada and Esquibel descent, José Antonio Esquibel "Parientes" in La Herencia (Fall 2006: page 56).

[46] Memory of Rudy and Peter James Laumbach.

[47] Told to Karl Laumbach by Andres Ebell III and told to Peter James Laumbach by Carmen Ebel Naranjo. In the Ebell story, Casimiro arrived at a nearby village and asked about his family. He was told that his father had died and his mother had remarried. Unable to accept the remarriage, Casimiro came back to New Mexico without seeing his family. In the Naranjo account, Casimiro was simply unable to reconnect with his family.

[48] Peter James Laumbach.

[49] Card in the Karl Laumbach files, courtesy of sister, Louise Laumbach Luft, who found it upstairs in the La Cinta house.

[50] Casimiro (Ike) Laumbach remembered seeing the saber in the attic at La Cinta.

[51] George Laumbach to Karl Laumbach.

[52] Alfred Laumbach Sr., Roy, New Mexico to Karl Laumbach.

[53] Alfred Laumbach Sr. to Karl Laumbach.

[54] Andreas (Red) Laumbach to Karl Laumbach.

[55] Collective memories of Andreas (Red), Casimiro (Ike), Peter James and Rudy Laumbach. The accused was a Lucero who was married to Carolina Ebell. Carolina and Fidelia were *comadres*, making the whole affair that much more delicate.

[56] The archives of the New Mexico Cattle Growers Association in Albuquerque contain a written record of Pete's dispute with the association. J.B. McNeil, sheriff of Harding County, had found a man skinning a ΛZ cow. Despite the evidence, the New Mexico Cattle Growers Association would not assist in the prosecution.

[57] The dugout was destroyed when the current road to the La Cinta headquarters was built. It had been dug into the side of the hill overlooking La Cinta Creek.

SECTION IV: LAUMBACHS IN NEW MEXICO
Chapter 33: More Peter J. Laumbach
by Jan Girand

Below is photo of Pete and Fidelia Laumbach's rock ranch house at La Cinta. Ike (Casimiro) told us how his dad had built this large two-story home for his family with only quaint tools and a ladder he made. His children are rightfully proud of their father.

Pete and Fidelia Laumbach founded a dynasty. They may not have had many personal luxuries, but they were wealthy in family.

If you count Alfredo, who was struck by lightning when he was a teenager, 12 of their 17 children lived to grow up in an era when there were few if any doctors, preventive vaccinations or antibiotics available to combat the still-deadly illnesses of pneumonia, flu, diphtheria, chicken pox, or infections. Medicines and repairs of injuries and broken bones were dealt with at home with self-taught remedies or those passed on by older women in the families. It was still a time when babies were born at home, hopefully with capable women available to assist the mothers. Heaven help the poor woman and baby when something went wrong at birth or the baby had a problem. It was still a time of high mortality rates for women and babies. Men's lives and limbs were also daily at risk. They broke green horses, built amazing rock houses and walls with few implements, strung miles of barbed wire fences, dug wells by hand and built tall windmills.

Cowboys were in the saddle from dawn to dusk. They had to fight for their rights, their families and possessions against those who would take them or do them harm. Indians may have stopped being a danger, but there was still little law enforcement available. Wild animals and rattlesnakes remained hazards. It was a time when home canning—most foods were then still prepared and canned in the home kitchen—if done wrong could, and did, wipe out entire families.

All of this also applied to the Daniel Laumbach family and all the others who lived in remote areas on what had not long before been the wild frontier. They were self-sufficient and made do with what they had, which usually was minimal raw resources, their own experiences and common sense.

Pete and Fidelia, like Dan and Emma, raised strong healthy men and women with admirable ethics. Alfred said his father taught his children the most valuable thing they had was their word; don't squander it.

As Margaret Palladino, Ike's granddaughter-in-law wrote for her beloved Poppa's 100th birthday in June 2013, "Poppa worked hard all his life. So did his parents and siblings. His father and mother role-modeled hard work every day of their lives on La Cinta Ranch. Family needs were met and values were taught but life was tough. Everyone worked before dawn to after sundown. The boys, Poppa and his brothers, became cowboys; this meant more hard work utilizing every muscle and every bit of endurance they had. Getting sick or hurt did not mean you rested while you recovered. You worked through the pain. If there was a wound, they just poured kerosene on it, wrapped it up and went back to work. (I'm guessing they went through a lot of kerosene.)"

Try to imagine what was involved to bring food to the table, shoes and clothing for a growing family, sturdy homes to protect the family from elements and invasion, and sacrifices to provide children the luxury of an education. Hygiene we take for granted today then took considerable effort. Even in the early 1900s, life was difficult, especially for people living in rural isolated areas, which was much of New Mexico.

Left to right back row: Pete, Rudolph, Alfred, and Ike; middle row: Cordelia, Bertha and Lucille; front row: Peter Joseph Laumbach.

Red (Andreas Detlef 3rd), George, Lucille, Ike (Casimiro) and Alfred. Not present that day were Petra, Pete (Peter Joseph 2nd), and Rudolph (in attendance but not pictured). Photo taken in 1980, after Red's wife, Zulema, died. John Candelario was probably the photographer. Photo from John and Lores Candelario collection.

Cousins Tony Sanchez, Christine Laumbach Foxall and her husband Frank, and John Candelario. Photo by Lores Candelario. A note from Lores said she, John and Tony had gone to Durango, Colorado to visit "John's cousins."

Family gathering at Ross Ranch near Roy in 1983. Rear: Rudolph, Frank Foxall, Ike; second row: George, Petra, Lucille, Alfred; front row: Red and Pete.

Brothers Red (Andreas 3rd), Ike (Casimiro), Alfred and Pete Laumbach at the family gathering in Roy in June 2003, celebrating Pete's and Ike's birthdays. Jan Girand photo.

La Cinta Ranch, 1928.

Brothers Alfred and Pete Laumbach having an intense discussion. Butch Sanders found, posted on the Internet, this outstanding photo taken in 2009.

SECTION IV: NEW MEXICO

Chapter 34: Papa and Mama
by Verna Laumbach Sparks 1909—1996

Editor's note: this chapter is a composite of three or four pieces written by Verna.

A Dream Led West

Andreas Laumbach came west from Iowa in the fall of 1859. His father, Andreas Detlef, an older man recently settled with his family in Goose Lake, Clinton, Iowa had a restless curiosity about the great west. Soon after he had arrived in Iowa, he left his wife and children on their farm and went to New Mexico to join his son, Andreas 2nd. (The second Andreas became Daniel's father.)

When the father started off from Goose Lake, initially traveling with others, his family and neighbors bid him goodbye with heavy hearts. Andreas promised to return the next year, or send for his family after he was settled, but his wife and children remembered the wild tales they had heard about the West and were afraid to see him go. They watched the covered wagons move out and slowly disappear from view. The last they saw were the white canvas tops, like little clouds dropped onto the curving horizon.

In those first years, old friends and relatives seldom heard from either father or son after they went to New Mexico.

When he arrived, the father could see why the rich Mora Valley, with its old settlers and established ranches, had appealed to his son, who had met Elionor Ebel, the daughter of a rancher and store owner in Las Vegas who was also of German descent. This man had also come to America and headed west. *[Editor: We now know Daniel Eberle/Ebel came to New Mexico with Doniphan's Missouri Volunteers in 1846. Family tradition said he had been a Swiss-German immigrant.]* Elionor's mother, Bibiana, came from an old New Mexico Hispanic family. Elionor's grandfather, Bernardo, was a Mora land grantee.

After he arrived, Andreas' father went into cattle partnership with his son, and they were soon busy looking after their cattle that roamed over vast, unfenced land. The younger Andreas reported this to his mother [*Anna Koos Laumbach*], still patiently waiting back home in Iowa.

[Editor: The elder Andreas had joined his son in New Mexico within two years after his son had come. By the time Andreas 2nd had married Elionor in 1864, his father had come to New Mexico from Iowa, and had already died.] The father was killed by Indians.

Andreas had to write his mother to tell her the tragic news of his father's death, killed by a wandering band of Apache Indians while checking on cattle that had wandered many miles from the ranch. The older man's only companion, a servant, hastily buried him on one of the nearby sloping hills before going back to Buena Vista. Although Andreas and others looked for his father's grave, it was never found. (The town of Springer is now [*east*] below and beyond the hills that are west of the "lost grave.")

After hearing of Andreas' death, his wife, Anna, had no desire to come west. She died a few years later, in 1868.

After the younger Andreas married Elionor, they bought ranch land in Buena Vista, built a home, settled down there [*perhaps several years after their marriage*], and began raising a family.

The widely separated families tried to keep in touch with each other. In the early years, the cost of letters reduced their frequency from New Mexico, but there were a few.

As the years went by, the Iowa and Nebraska families knew Andreas had married and settled down in Buena Vista. *[Editor: their mailing address was nearby La Cueva, New Mexico.]* Emma's family now lived in Nebraska. Stories of the romantic west appealed to some of them.

More years went by and Andreas' children were growing up, as well as those in Iowa and Nebraska. Some of the younger generation began writing to each other. That was how it happened that Emma's brother, Claus, wrote several times to Daniel, one of Andreas' sons. Daniel responded. His letters were eagerly read and passed around. They were interesting to those in Nebraska, and told of a life entirely different.

Dan sent Claus a picture of himself seated on horseback, with a rambling rock wall and cottonwoods behind him. Dan's handsome face appealed to young Emma—his merry expression and the easy way he sat his horse. She tried to imagine the kind of man he was and the sort of life he led. It had to be more exciting than her ordinary life on the farm.

As time went on, Claus and Dan neglected to write each other. One evening when the family sat around the stove and the outside world was buried in snow, Emma's mother said, "I often wonder, while we're so comfortable here, how Andreas' family is getting along in New Mexico. We haven't heard from them in so long. Emma, why don't you write Dan a letter and ask how his parents are? You're better about writing letters than the rest of us."

So Emma carefully wrote a letter the next day and sent it to Daniel's mailing address at La Cueva, New Mexico. She received a reply a month later. The envelope was postmarked Folsom, New Mexico.

In the letter Dan told the news of his parents—they were well but busy, two of his sisters and one brother were married—and he was working on a ranch near Folsom. He inquired about Emma's parents in Nebraska and of his father's family in Iowa. He wished he could make a trip east to see them—especially now that train travel made the trip easier. Dan wrote that his father did not care for trains; he preferred his trustworthy horse and buggy.

The letter thrilled Emma and all the family enjoyed reading it. She answered it as soon as she thought it was proper. The correspondence between them progressed. That is how my mother became acquainted with my father. Her first letter from him, postmarked Folsom, told of his work on the sheep ranch. He sent a picture of himself and she studied it a great deal, thinking what a handsome man he was. The people of Buena Vista came alive for those in Nebraska as he told about his family and home place. At first the letters were eagerly passed around but as time went on, Emma was reluctant to share them. They continued writing to each other—far more often than Claus and Dan had written.

Meeting Daniel

Emma Margaretha Henkens was born in Goose Lake, Clinton, Iowa, the fourth in a family of six children, to Anna and Peter Henkens. Her family later moved to the rolling plains of Nebraska. Her father had a large farm and a spacious white house, with shade trees and orchard, and a creek running across the milk cow pasture. Along the creek, wild plums and elderberries grew, which the children gathered when ripe.

Their community of farmers was mostly of German origin, and they shared each other's fun and work like one big family. They worked hard but the tasks of harvesting were not as great with neighbors joining together, in turn, to put up each man's crop. Together, the tasks of husking corn and threshing wheat were not as big. In the same way, as needed, they worked together to build or repair someone's house.

In the long summer days, when men started work early in the fields, the women made them mid-morning lunches and carried them down to the fields. The men stopped work to eat and get refreshed. All the meals during the day were substantial and nourishing—juicy hams, puddings and cakes, all cooked with plentiful cream and butter from the farm.

Sometimes there was a barn dance and the young people, traveling to and from it, crowded together in wagons, singing and laughing in the moonlight. Courtships took place in the presence of chaperones. Parents were often present.

Emma had not taken any of the young men seriously, although one or two had shown interest in her by spending evenings popping corn in the kitchen with her family. She was smaller than the average girl, but she was a good worker and an excellent cook. She was called the runt of her family because all of her brothers and sisters were tall and sturdy. But Emma, with her delicate form and small hands could match the others in energy and endurance.

Years later Daniel said teasingly that it was her ability as a hard worker that appealed to him when he first met her, that and her good light bread. But listeners noticed his eyes resting on her shining blonde hair and her pink and white complexion.

Emma caught her breath remembering how it was only by chance that they had met each other. It happened because she had written a certain letter to New Mexico.

Both of her parents, and her mother's and father's families, had come from northern Germany. They may have been friends in Germany. Both families, Henkens and Laumbachs, settled in Clinton, Iowa.

After Daniel and Emma had been exchanging letters for a while, one bright spring day Dan arrived at the farm and found her baking bread. Most of the family was outdoors planting a garden. The orchard trees were in bloom and a mother duck went quacking by the kitchen door with ten bits of fluff waddling after her.

Emma looked up from the steaming fresh loaves and saw the tall, handsome young man standing in the doorway. Their eyes regarded each other for a long moment, and a singing went through her. It felt like all the warmth and fragrance of the spring day, like an apple tree had burst into bloom.

Dan laughed, came inside, and asked for a piece of bread.

The rest of the family came rushing in to see who the stranger was.

In the following days, Dan kept busy telling stories of New Mexico. A crowd of friends and neighbors often gathered around. Yet sometimes, when he talked, his eyes rested on Emma's and they felt as if they were alone.

Daniel was a dashing man when he was young—well-built, blue, blue eyes, brown hair and a mustache! He could sweep a girl off her feet, and his tales of adventures in the Wild West were added enchantment.

Emma was appealing, too, with her blonde curly hair, small trim figure, and blue eyes.

He was gone about a week visiting various family, friends and relatives nearby, then he returned to Emma's house to say goodbye. They stood alone by the garden fence and the sun turned her hair to gold. She was small beside Dan; he was tall and laughing and gay. But his eyes turned grave when he looked around the farm and then back to her.

He said, "I'd like to take you to my father's apple orchard someday. It has rock walls and the tallest cottonwoods you ever saw. My father planted them when he first went there to live. The Mora River runs below the orchard, and they have all the water they need. It is a lovely place, I think."

"I know it must be," Emma whispered, seeing it all in her mind.

"But," Dan said, "I don't live there anymore. I've been away, working on my own for several years. I've worked in different places. I am now foreman on a ranch near Folsom. Someday I'm going to have my own ranch and settle down. Just think: I'm 29 already. When a man gets to be 30 he should have a wife, don't you think?"

Evidently Emma did. She promised to wait a year for him, and then they would marry. He returned to New Mexico.

It was a busy year for her. Whenever her daily tasks on the farm were over, she spent long hours hemming tea towels and sheets and pillowcases. Her mother gave her two pillows of goose down and wished to give her a feather bed, but it would be too bulky to ship.

She made several calico dresses and aprons, and embroidered her underskirts and camisoles of fine, white lawn. There was one flowered muslin dress for dress-up wear—perhaps for when she visited his people in Mora.

She would marry in the wintertime instead of spring, and the wedding would take place in a town somewhere in Colorado instead of in her parents' home in Nebraska, as they first planned. He had left the ranch at Folsom and was now a foreman of Willard Wight's large sheep ranch in Colorado, near Las Animas. He expected to stay in this place and perhaps someday go into partnership with the owner.

He had a small cabin of his own on that ranch, and he was lonesome. He would be 30 in January and had already ordered a large set of dishes. Why wait for spring? Besides, he doubted if he could leave the ranch in the spring, the busiest season. They changed their plans. He suggested he send her ticket fare and she come by train as far as Trinidad, where he would meet her. Then they would get married and go together to the sheep ranch.

The following months were busy ones, preparing clothes and things for the hope chest. Emma's father tried to discourage her from marrying a man so far away, but she was determined. Her mother, a kind and understanding woman, helped her fill her trunk with towels and pillowcases, and all the other items necessary for housekeeping.

Aunt Emilie helped, too. Sometimes she went around the house baaing like a sheep, explaining she was just getting Emma used to the sound of a sheep ranch.

Toward the end of that year, Daniel kept writing about the nice little house he had for her, how lonesome he was, and the beautiful set of dishes he bought and had waiting for her.

So it was decided that she would take the train to Trinidad, Colorado in January and meet him there, where they would marry, and then go by wagon to the Wight Ranch. Willard Wight, who lived in Trinidad, promised to give them their wedding supper.

Emma's last things were packed, including her wedding dress. They had decided it would be warm and serviceable enough to wear afterwards, as well as beautiful. Made by a dressmaker in Fremont, it was pale gray, of soft, fine Henrietta wool, trimmed with lace, with leg o'mutton sleeves. *[Editor: The skirt portion of the wedding dress, with its many yards of fabric, was repurposed in later years. Jan had the top—the petite bodice portion of that wedding dress—hanging in her entry, preparing to take it to be encased in a shadow-box-type display for preservation. It was seriously damaged in her major home fire in July 2007.]*

This change of plan worried her mother, but she took comfort in what Dan had said about the country in Colorado. It was fairly well settled with good towns, and the danger of the frontier days was past.

They speeded up their preparations for her journey and had carefully packed her linens and clothes in a large trunk. Her mother tucked in numerous items, thinking perhaps they would come in handy on a sheep ranch far from stores. There were different kinds of medicines, threads and needles, and small household articles that took little room. When her mother thought of something else, she tucked it in, feeling she was losing her daughter to an unknown land and an almost unknown man.

Before she left, Emma was given her special wedding present—a set of silverware for six. She told her family she would remember them every time she used it. But now it was time to go. She had written Dan that she would arrive in Trinidad the 24th of January. She must not disappoint him.

She did not disappoint him.

Daniel met the train in Trinidad. When she came down the train steps, he caught and held her close. He exclaimed, "You've really come! I couldn't believe it until I saw you. You don't know how I've been longing for you."

Daniel and Emma Henkens Laumbach on their wedding day, January 24, 1902.

Later he explained that his boss and wife lived in Trinidad most of the time, and they invited him and Emma to be married in their home and eat a wedding supper there.

After their wedding, they had a wedding photograph made so they could send one to each of their parents, which Emma had promised her mother they would do.

They were married January 24, 1902. They ate their wedding supper at Wight's home. Mrs. Wight served them a special, unusual delicacy of oysters, which neither of them liked.

Daniel teased Emma afterward, saying she was in such a hurry to marry him that she arrived four days too early. He had wanted to wait for his birthday, January 28, so he would be 30 years old. But he always teased; nobody took him seriously.

They left Trinidad the next day by wagon and started the long trip to the sheep ranch. They stopped overnight in Las Animas and reached their destination the next day. To Emma the country looked somewhat like Nebraska, though not as fertile and settled. Except for the ranch buildings, there were no signs of nearby dwellings.

Dan said he preferred cattle and he really liked New Mexico better, but he had a good opportunity to work on this sheep ranch, and decided to stay. The owner lived in Trinidad because his wife was not strong. He had talked of turning management of the ranch over to Dan, of increasing his pay, and of building him a better house. Dan told her all this as he lifted his bride down from the wagon. The tiny, simply furnished cabin was a welcome sight to Emma after all her traveling, and she found a surprise on the table. Dan had proudly set out the dishes he had ordered for her. In the center of them was a new white porcelain chamber pot to match the set. Dan's eyes twinkled.

"I had to get even with you," he said, "because you came four days too early."

Emma blushed a little and thought how lucky she was to have Dan, a man with a sense of humor, even four days early.

At first she was busy and happy, unpacking her trunk and making curtains for the windows. The weather was cold, and she stayed inside most of the time, but she planned to spend lots of time outdoors when spring came, even riding the plains on horseback with her husband. In the long winter evenings, they spun dreams.

They lived in that Colorado ranch cabin on the windy cold plain, and Emma learned solitude. She was the only woman on the ranch, and there were no near neighbors. Daniel was gone during the day. She kept busy, sewing and mending her husband's clothes. After being a bachelor for many years, it was nice to have his socks darned neatly and buttons sewn on his shirts.

Toward the end of March, the cold weather seemed to be passing and they hoped for no more snow. Dan had been busy and away most of the time because it was lambing season. He and the hired men sometimes worked late at night. During these days, Emma tried to amuse herself with housework, mending, and hand-sewing. She even made him a shirt from material in her trunk. She cut it out carefully by taking an old shirt apart for a pattern. He praised it highly, but was privately skeptical of the color and print.

Once a month, the mail came from Las Animas by carrier. There were always letters from Emma's family in Nebraska and from Dan's sisters at Buena Vista, welcoming their new sister-in-law.
A mailman came out from Las Animas once a month, spent the night at the bunkhouse, going back to Las Animas the next morning. Dan and Emma sat up most of the night answering the letters so the mailman could take them the next morning. After the mail went off, they had to wait a month for answers.

Mail time was exciting, and Emma tried to pour out her happiness in letters home. She did not mention one concern.

She had not been feeling well. At first she thought she had just been staying indoors too much. She longed for warm weather so she could get out more and even go horseback riding. However, as the weeks went by she realized she was pregnant. She had not expected that so soon. But she remembered how other women had been similarly bothered by morning sickness and how they became increasingly unable to work hard. In Nebraska those women had neighbors and relatives to give comfort, advice and help, but on this sheep ranch there was nobody but Dan, and he had too many duties to stay with her.

She began to wonder how she could manage her pregnancy and birth of a baby in this isolated cabin. She began to hate the dreary plains and the spring winds. She longed for her old home and family, her security there, but she did not mention that to Dan. She knew she could not go home. Besides, Dan was getting thinner and at night he worried, too, wondering what he should do. He knew she could not stay on the ranch much longer. He even considered sending her to Las Animas, but there she would be among strangers. Finally, when the mail came again, he wrote to his mother, explaining the situation and asked if one of his sisters could come stay with them. He had four sisters still at home. If that was not possible, he wrote that it might be best for Emma to go to them until after the child was born.

After the mailman rode off with the letter, he felt more at ease. He knew his resourceful mother would think of some way to help them out of their difficulties.

In the evening he and Emma discussed the possibilities of her leaving the ranch. She did not want to leave him, but she realized he would be better off if she did. He was working too hard and also trying to take care of her. She thought, bitterly, that their marriage was not turning out the way they had planned.

They had been happy on the ranch until she became pregnant and was sicker and sicker. Dan worried about leaving her alone. They considered leaving Colorado. Also, Daniel was lonesome for the ranch country and his claim in New Mexico.

During the evenings, while waiting for an answer, they considered possibilities.

Dan thought of leaving the sheep ranch with Emma. They could first go to his parents' home and stay there until the baby was born. Afterwards he could try to get a job somewhere else.

Then he thought of his claim in New Mexico. It was about two hundred miles from the Mora Valley, a two or three days' trip by wagon. It was canyon country, with woods of pine, piñon, and cedar—as the juniper was called by the settlers. It had enough open places with plenty of grass, and there were springs and water holes, making it good cattle country. In the winter the cattle would have the protection of trees and canyons, and the scrub oak brush would give shelter to baby calves. He said the land was not settled much. Part of it had been ranged by "squatters" who built rock houses and a few rock walls here and there for protection but mostly just turned their cattle loose. Since there were no real fences dividing one man's land from another's, the cattle roamed free. That kept a cowman in the saddle. There were wolves and mountain lions to prey on the little calves if the owner was not attentive. Now the day of the squatter was over and the land was divided into claims and government land, which could be leased for a small amount of money. His brother, Pete, was living on Dan's claim now but he had his own close by.

That meant Dan's place was waiting for him, and he realized that was where he wanted to be. Just as their ancestors' dreams had led them west, he now knew his dream would lead him home. But first Emma would go stay with his family at Buena Vista until the baby was born. Until then he would work at the sheep ranch to make a little more money.

He wrote letters to his parents in Buena Vista and to his married sister, Estefanita Candelario, in Santa Fe.

Going To Buena Vista

During the spring months, Dan was especially busy with the lambing season, and Emma was still sick. When mail came again, Dan's folks at Buena Vista urged her to go there to stay until after the baby was born. Aunt Estefanita wrote that she would go to Las Animas to meet Emma and take her back to New Mexico.

Dan decided that he would take Emma to Las Animas by wagon with all her clothes and personal things packed in her trunk; from there she and Aunt Estefanita would take the train to Watrous. His father would meet them there, or they could hire a wagon to go the rest of the way to Buena Vista.

Dan, meanwhile, would pack up the household at the Wight ranch in Colorado to ship by train to Springer, where he could pick it up later to take by wagon to the claim in the Enciero. He would ride horseback from the Wight Ranch to his claim in New Mexico. At the claim he could get the log cabin ready to live in and see about the cattle Uncle Pete was taking care of for him.

He spent the rest of the summer and part of the early fall on the Wight ranch and then went to Buena Vista to see Emma.

Meanwhile, Emma and Aunt Estefanita had traveled by train from Las Animas to Watrous, getting acquainted on the way. When they arrived at Watrous, there was no one to meet them. They went to a café for a meal and bought some apples to eat on the road. A family friend there named Rankin found a man who would take them to Buena Vista in his wagon. Emma said the team of horses was frisky and the hard board seat got pretty tiresome, but they finally arrived at Buena Vista.

Everybody welcomed Emma into the family, and did everything they could for her. Under their gentle care she began to feel better. She never forgot how kind Dan's mother was, and also his younger sisters still at home. There were four then—Anna, Crestina, Mary and Leonor. Henry lived on his place nearby and also often visited.

The Buena Vista place was wonderful in the fall—the orchards ripe with fruits, the rock walls, the well, a little stream and the tall cottonwoods turning color in the fall and dripping yellow leaves in the water. Dan's father loved to show her around the place and took her some ripe fruit to eat before breakfast. There was plenty of fruit besides apples, like currants, plums and gooseberries.

Dan got to Buena Vista a short time before their first child was born. She was a beautiful brown-haired baby they named Mabel Anna Eleanore Laumbach. Anna and Eleanore were for her two grandmothers. She was called Mabel.

Going Home

They stayed at Buena Vista about two months longer, to give Emma and the baby time to get strong enough for the long trip. Daniel was anxious to get to his own ranch, so they left December 24, even though his father begged them to wait until after Christmas.

When they saw that Daniel would not wait, his sisters went to Emma's sacks and boxes and secretly hid a little present in each. Emma did not unpack and find them until she got home.

Daniel and Emma stopped in Las Vegas and borrowed $150.00 so they could get started at the ranch. Then they began the long road home. After riding in the wagon all day, they got to the little town of Wagon Mound the first night, which was Christmas Eve. Emma wondered what her family would think about her spending it in a strange little town, so far away. It was her first Christmas away from home and she missed her family. She thought about her folks all together in Nebraska with the Christmas tree and presents and rich food to eat. Probably Aunt Emilie would lead the singing and as they sang Christmas carols, they would surely think of Emma.

Daniel slept in the wagon that night to guard it, while Emma and the baby slept in the hotel. The bed had ruffles all around it and Emma dreamed there was somebody under it and the ruffles were moving. She was glad when morning came and they could be on their way again. That morning in Wagon Mound she heard, for the first time, the New Mexico custom of children crying, "Give me Christmas!" in the streets asking for treats, similar to what is done on Halloween today.

They traveled all Christmas Day, going over rolling hills and open stretches, with the mountains in the distance. *[Editor: From this physical description, they did not go east from Wagon Mound, which would have them cross the rugged Canadian River gorge. At that time, there probably was no safe wagon road across the gorge. Apparently they traveled across the prairie a distance north of Wagon Mound and from there turned east and then southward.]* It was all interesting country, and they felt happy and adventuresome, knowing they had a new baby, $150, and a wagon full of fruit, jelly, clean clothes, and even a small butchered pig.

Along the road, they ate lunches that the folks at Buena Vista had packed for them: a box full of fresh bread, butter, meat, *empañadas* (little meat pies), apples, cake and cookies.

The second night, they arrived at the newly founded town of Roy. This town was to be their shopping center in years to come, but then it was very small.

The Roy brothers, Bill and Frank, had a store, post office and saloon at what would become the site of Floersheim's store. Originally, The Roy brothers' store was west of the town of Roy, near the canyon, but they had moved to their new location in town because the railroad was expected to go through there. On this trip, the original building, although vacated, was still there near the canyon, and it was open. It even had a stove that was welcome on that cold night. They unhitched the horses, and Dan fed and watered them while Emma unpacked a few things in the room and got a hot fire going. When the room was warm enough, she unwrapped the baby a little and laid her on the bedroll. Mabel waved her tiny arms and seemed content. It probably felt good to stretch after being wrapped in blankets all day.

They had a hot meal and coffee and went to bed early. Emma worried about the hungry cats that were in the building and around the place. When the store was moved to Roy, the cats had been left behind. She never knew what became of them.

The next morning they left the old store site and started for the ranch. About ten miles from Roy began a canyon and wooded country. They rode through pines and piñon trees. This was the kind of country the ranch was in, very different from the settled farms of Nebraska that Emma knew. But it was thrilling to know they would soon be home in their own place—not on a sheep ranch on the prairie in Colorado, or the family home in Buena Vista, but a home all their own.

They arrived at the claim that evening where Uncle Pete and his wife waited for them. Aunt Fidelia could not speak English and Emma spoke no Spanish, but they managed to communicate. Uncle Pete and Aunt Fidelia already had two small children—Cordelia and Alfredo—and were expecting a third. Aunt Fidelia seemed cheerful and content. They were living in the rock house but planned to later move to the Curruco, not far away.

In the little log house Emma found her furniture and dishes that were brought from Colorado. There wasn't a stove or store-bought bedstead; Dan had ordered those but they had not yet come. They borrowed a little stove from Uncle Pete, and Dan brought the bedstead, made of ropes, from the Yegua.[i] Later, they got their own stove and a real bedstead, as well as six straight chairs [*Jan inherited three of those sturdy oak chairs*], one rocking chair and a treadle sewing machine. They had a good homemade cupboard and a homemade table.

The log cabin had a dirt floor, which was a new experience for Emma, but she learned how to keep it sprinkled and packed down. She put a blanket on the floor for Mabel when she learned to crawl.

One time, when she left Mabel alone to hang up clothes, she heard her screaming and ran to see about her. Mabel was scared of a big rooster that stood crowing on the doorstep.

The log cabin is on the right; the rock house—that later became the bunk house and school house—is on the left.

Their first house, that little log cabin, is still standing. From there, after Pete and Fidelia moved to their own place, they moved to the rock building that was later called the bunk house. It, too, remains.

To Emma, my mother who grew up in a settled farming community in Nebraska, this new home was strange and difficult. In the beginning, it took much work and willpower to make a living there. My father's brother, Pete, and his wife, Fidelia, had been helpful. When they moved to their place, they left behind various items for them to make their new life easier, like tools, dried foods, seeds, and even a few chickens. There were also a few head of cattle the brothers had accumulated in partnership.

That first winter was long and hard; some cows became so weak by spring that they were kept near the house, but had to go down the precarious trail for a drink. Later a pond was made on top to catch the summer rains. Many years later the pond was replaced by a well and water tank near the house.

Emma was a brave woman but that first year she shivered at night hearing wolves come howling down the hill, along the fence. As time went on, the wolves, like many other wild animals, disappeared from the ranch. The last wolf any of us saw came into the back yard one morning when we were living in the rock house. We never knew why he had come so close to our door and why he was so brave. Dan shot that big timber wolf and had him stuffed and mounted on a stand. He stood in the bunk house for many years. *[Years later, Alida's husband, Elbert, kept that preserved wolf at the Mosquero post office. Later still, it was taken to the Santa Fe Trail Museum in Springer.]*

Ranch Days

The rock house had a flat roof when they moved in. When the rainy season came, it leaked terribly. Once that spring, it rained five days in a stretch and they had to put a tent over one room to keep dry. Another time, a few years later, they had to put a tent over the bed and they all stayed in bed. Dan and Emma took turns getting up and moving around; one of them had to stay in bed to keep the kids in. (Joyce was born by then.) Whoever got up had to wear a slicker because the room leaked like a sieve.

It was hard to keep a fire going in the stove and it sizzled and popped. One time Emma was about to drink a cup of coffee when a stream of water poured into her cup. They even had company once in the rainy weather. A man named John Hine stayed there a couple of days, but decided the inside of the house was as wet as the outside, and he went on.

Dan finally made a trip to town and bought tin to make a new roof. Eventually the house had a peaked roof, with a low attic, which could be reached by an outside ladder. It was a good place to dry meat and apples. Another room was built later, which made the house into an L shape. A fence enclosed the small yard between the two wings of the house, and they transplanted a little cedar tree in the yard. Emma raised a few flowers and vegetables there, but scarce water was a problem.

Until a pond was built near the house, all the water had to be carried up the canyon trail from the spring. After the pond had water, the drinking and cooking water still had to come from the spring.

The first winter they traded 30 steers to Uncle Pete for old cows and calves. They got one cow and calf for each steer. By spring they had lost nine calves to wolves and coyotes. Quite often Emma woke in the night to the sound of wolves howling. They sometimes came down the hill, almost to the house.

The first cows traded for the steers got so poor that they could hardly walk down the trail to drink at the trough by the spring. Emma watched them, fearing they would fall down, for they wobbled so and their backsides were as thin as boards. During the summer they picked up and put on weight. The calves sold from this herd brought $9.00 each. In those days that was a fair price, as calves brought $8.00 to $13.00; cows sold for $25.00 to $35.00 and horses for $30.00 to $35.00.

In the beginning, the folks had four or five horses, and later got more. Aunt Marie Esquibel gave them three hens and a rooster. Emma set some of Uncle Pete's hens, and raised about 50 chickens on half shares. The coyotes were always ready to catch a chicken that wandered too far, and there were hawks and sometimes wild cats. As Dan said, "There were plenty of wild animals—wolves, lions, bears, and little varmints."

Ranching in those days was hard, endless work. Dan was in the saddle from early morning until dark, looking after his stock. There were so many canyons and woods for the cattle to hide in, and they roamed free because there were no fences in those years. They drifted as far as La Cinta, Sabinoso and the Red River. *[Area settlers called the Canadian River the Rio Colorado or Red River because the red clay soil turns the water red. The river runs through portions of several states. It enters New Mexico in the northeast. In places, it cuts a deep gorge through the caprock, exposing steep sandstone cliffs and rock formations. In the areas of the Laumbach ranches—Pete's and Daniel's—the rugged gorge has many deep canyons and pockets. Daniel's and Pete's ranchlands were vegas on top of the mesas and also on the floors of the canyons.]*

Dan also ran stock for his folks. In his herd might be cattle with brands belonging to his father, Uncle Pete, Uncle Henry, one of his sisters, and his own—the +VH. When it was branding time, Uncle Henry came from Buena Vista to help, and Uncle Pete came from the Carruco or La Cinta. There was often hired help from the river. As branding time usually lasted a week, it was a terrible job for Emma. She had small children to care for in addition to doing nearly all the cooking for the men. She handled it for several years, practically alone, until Uncle Henry realized it was too much for her. After that, when he came for branding, he brought someone to help her. Once he brought Aunt Leonor.

It always amazed me that Daniel let Emma do that tremendous job alone, hampered as she was pregnant or with babies. He hired so many men for *his* job but seldom thought about her.

Uncle Pete was an early riser, especially at round-up time. He got up at 4:00 and start shouting for the men to get up and go after the horses; the noise woke the babies. Emma did complain about that to Dan.

Karl calls this next photo: "Round-up at Uncle Dan's." Daniel is on Old Dolly, the horse with light colored mane and tail; his brother, Henry, is on horseback near him. Photo courtesy of Karl Laumbach. This photo was the basis, many years later, for an oil painting by Leon Shinn, husband of Daniel's daughter, Frances. That painting was later given to Daniel's eldest grandson, Elton Wallace.

One time Uncle Bonney's son, Ramon, helped Emma at branding. He kept the wood box full and carried water for her. Uncle Bonney thought it would be good for Ramon to stay with her awhile and learn some English. She felt badly later that the boy did not live to grow up. She had been fond of him.

Cattle buyers came to the ranch to inspect and buy the calves, sometimes at roundup time. When the calves were sold, it took Dan and his hired help from three days to a week to deliver them to Springer, Folsom or some other point to be transported by railroad. They slowly drove the cattle on horseback and then had to return.

One of the hardships living at the ranch was going so far to a town for provisions. Because Roy was small in 1902, they traded in Springer the first year. They tried to bring as much as possible each time, so they would not need to go so often. They had to bring corn for the livestock, as well as basic groceries like flour, sugar, lard, coffee, salt, baking powder, soda and cases of tomatoes.

One winter, perhaps 1903, Dan went to Springer for groceries, and coming home was caught in a terrible blizzard. When he did not come on the fourth day, Emma was wild with worry. Uncle Pete went out on horseback to see if he could find Dan and help him home.

Dan had been unable to keep traveling because of the heavy snow. The horses could not pull the wagon, and it was too hard to see where he was going. So Dan left the wagon and, unhitching a horse, rode it home; on the way, he met Uncle Pete. Dan was glad to get home, almost frozen. He went back for the wagon the next day because he was afraid wild horses, cows or deer might tear into the sacks of corn. He got the provisions home without more trouble.

Later in 1903, they started to trade more in Roy because it was only twenty miles one way, and the trip in a wagon could be made in two days, sometimes in one.
And so his dream came true. He, his wife and growing family made their home on the ranch and their experiences were many and varied. Some dealt mostly with the children's early years, but there were also the experiences of some of the elders who touched their lives.

Below is a photo of the ranch house when they had the pond in front for cattle and irrigation. After a well was dug near the house, the pond was filled in and the area became the "hospital pasture" for ill or expectant mother cows.

When we were old enough to think about books, one room in the bunk house was converted into a school room. Roy was the nearest town with a public school. As 20 miles was an impossible distance in those days of wagons and country roads, we had our own school at the ranch for eight years with several different teachers who lived with us and became part of the family. When Mabel, Joyce and Alida were ready for high school, a house was bought in town. Then we all went to school and graduated in Roy, except Mabel, who died the second winter in that house. She had attended Allison James,[ii] the Presbyterian boarding school in Santa Fe, the previous year.

She had been sick with pneumonia a long time that spring, and slowly grew weaker and weaker. Outside, the wind blew day after day. Now when I hear the wind, I recall that sad spring and the poem I wrote years later in the Dust Bowl days. I called it "Wind Storm." When I wrote it, I was again living in that house in Roy, but I was teaching school there.

Wind Storm

All day the black wind blowing in this land of little rain;
And all night the wind still blowing on this barren, barren plain.
All day we still keep dreaming—in new green fields we trust;
But all night the wind keeps screaming and all the world is dust.

As you can tell by the poem, the setting in Roy was entirely different from the ranch. We were never hurt as much by drought in the canyon country as those were who lived on the dry plains—especially during the Dust Bowl days.

A night wind can still bring an empty feeling for me, just as Mabel's death left an empty place in our lives. I know my mother missed her with a grief that never ended. Mabel was her first child and was more of a companion for her than the rest of us. I always thought Mabel was the prettiest and certainly the gentlest and kindest. She was small and looked delicate, brown hair with golden lights. Her complexion was fresh and clear and her eyes were the deep blue of wild flowers. If Mama was not available for comfort, we always had Mabel.

The children, in age order, were Mabel, Joyce, Alida, me, Frances, Ruth and Daniel. Joyce and Alida usually stuck together, and we three younger girls were inseparable. We had wonderful times with both our work and play. When our baby brother, Daniel, was old enough, we looked after him and let him join in our games as well. Ours was a childhood of many rich experiences.

Our family would not be complete without remembering the older ones. It could start with my father's grandmother, Bibiana, whom I never knew. She died October 27, 1897, before my folks married and moved to the ranch. The night she died, she appeared to my father in a dream, tiny, sitting in her rocking chair, shrouded in her black shawl, with her arms held out, calling Daniel to go to her. She had always been special to him. As soon as he had light to see, he departed on horseback for Buena Vista.

Sad tidings make me think about hearing a horseman galloping in at night. It's as unsettling as hearing your phone ring at midnight, thinking it brings bad news. I doubt anyone today has heard a horseman riding up to the house at night, but in those years, they knew nobody would do that unless there was an emergency. Horseback was nearly the only way to carry news back then.

I wish I could have known my great-grandmother Bibiana. She must have been a remarkable woman. She was a native of the Mora Valley; her father had been one of the original Mora Land Grantees. She grew up in her father's home, and it was said that she was fair complexioned and beautiful. She must have been, because she attracted three wealthy men, landowners who also owned stores.

Bibiana's first relationship was with James Bonney, a handsome red-haired, blue-eyed Englishman who owned his own private grant and a trading post on the Santa Fe Trail. He was killed by Apaches, leaving her, a single young mother with a baby, Ramon, whose story I will tell in "Sunset."

Bibiana's second relationship was with Daniel Eberle (or Ebel), a Swiss-German. He was killed by a servant for the gold he carried on one of his business trips. *[Editor's Note: In a chapter in this book, Karl Laumbach tells the family's various versions of his death.]* Bibiana and Daniel Eberle had two daughters and a son. One of those girls, Elionor, became my grandmother. The other, Maria Marta, married a local man and they lived in the river canyon; I will tell her story later, in "Never a Road." There was another aunt, Lola, their younger half-sister; for a while she and her husband had a ranch not far from ours. Lola was Bibiana's daughter with Frank Metzger.

Frederick Metzger, a German, was the most prosperous of the three men in Bibiana's life. He was wealthy by any account for those times. He acquired a large ranch in the Mora Valley and had a store in the village of Mora. He did so well with his trading and cattle drives that it was rumored he had a secret gold mine on his property. This third relationship produced three girls, Dolores "Lola," Josefita "Josie" and Isabel. Years later, when I was in college, I met and loved one of those great-half-aunts, Isabel Metzger Gallegos. She and her daughter, Isabel Gallegos, my friend, told me many stories of the early days. Among them was the tale of the buried gold in a cornfield on the family ranch. They said a hired man found it and ran away with the gold and the daughter. According to family tradition, years later a tenant[iii] at the ranch, when it no longer belonged to family, found more gold hidden behind an adobe brick in the barn. This new-found wealth made that ranch renter and his family well known property owners themselves. With their found wealth, they bought an historic property at Watrous (formerly known as La Junta).

My great-grandmother Bibiana lived out her old age in a little house in the orchard at my Grandmother Elionor Laumbach's place at Buena Vista.

After such an eventful life, Bibiana probably enjoyed living her last years in quiet surroundings. She left behind beautiful gold filigree jewelry, and many fond memories of her with her family.

It had been because of her son, Andres Ebell, and her son-in-law, my grandfather, Andreas Detlef Laumbach, that my father first became acquainted with the canyon country. The older men took up claims and homesteaded in that wild, empty land and ran cattle over vast areas. My father worked for them occasionally when he was young, even camped in a cave one winter when he was just twelve, with only a dog and a horse for company. When they were old enough, he and his brothers, Peter and Henry, filed claims. In the beginning, only Pete stayed and lived on them. He married, built houses and fences, and kept the claims safe for the others. Preferring Mora Valley, Henry never came back to live in the canyon country.

Daniel spent several years working on ranches in New Mexico and Colorado. It was only after he married that he decided to settle down on his own place where he had staked a claim on the river, and raise a family. Years later, my mother shared with us her impressions when she arrived there.

Homecoming

It was the day after Christmas, in 1902, when the weary horses drew the wagon over the rise of the last hill and the dim outline of a house, shadowed by trees, lay below them.

The man leaned forward and gave an impatient flick at the reins. But the horses did not need it; they seemed to know the journey was almost at an end. Below, they sensed, was a place to stop and rest. Their steps quickened. The rattle of the wagon over the rocky road grew sharper.

The man seemed to relax a little, but eagerness shot through him, almost making him tremble. After so many years of wandering, he was coming back to this land of his boyhood—this wild, untamed land of wooded hills and canyons, of wild game and lonesome silences, and a few isolated cattle ranches.

When he was only 12 years old, he visited this part of New Mexico with his father. He had been fascinated by the vastness of it. Later he had come again, still only a boy, to herd his uncle's cattle, and still later, when of age, he came to file a claim. Then he went away for nearly nine years.

But now, with his young wife and two-month-old baby, he was coming home. This land had always called him. He realized that now. These canyons, hills and woods were what had tugged at him all those restless years. They were the reason he could never settle down anywhere else. They would now hold him here most of the rest of his life.

"I have come home," he half-whispered to the dark pines and cedar, and then, suddenly, he corrected himself. "We have come home, Emma, you and I and the baby."

The small form beside him straightened, as if by great will power. Emma looked hopefully at her husband and smiled.

"Dan, are we truly almost there?"

"Yes, my little one, we are almost at our 'castle' and then you can get warm," he answered and urged the horses on.

As they rode along, the sun went down and the air grew colder. The trees and great walls of rock on either side almost grazed the wagon's sides. When a branch brushed against Emma's hat, she held the baby closer. The baby slept on, unmindful that her new home was near. To Emma, the trees in the darkening canyon looked like a shadowy marching army, but she did not mention this to her excited husband. He was intent on the road ahead, unaware the rugged country might frighten his wife. He preferred it to the rolling plains of her home in the sedate, settled German community in Nebraska.

They rounded a curve. The road led down into a hollow where the dim outlines of two buildings showed. A light spilled out from one.

As they drew closer, they heard a dog's furious barking. Then a door was flung open in the larger house. A tall, powerfully-built man with red hair came out and approached the wagon when it stopped. He smiled and shook hands with both of them at once.

"Hello, Dan. Hello! I'm glad to see you, and with a wife and baby, too. You're doing pretty well, I'd say. Get down and come in to the fire. How are our folks in Buena Vista?"

During this flow of words in Spanish, Dan looped the reins over the wagon brake and stiffly climbed down his side. He went around to Emma and gently lifted her down, while answering his brother in Spanish. "The folks are well in Buena Vista. We left them day before yesterday. They sent their regards to you and your family." In English, he said, "Emma, this is Pete. I guess his wife and children are waiting for us in the house. Let's go in."

Emma leaned against the wagon to let her stiff legs limber up again. It seemed an eternity since that early morning of December 24th when they had started out on the trek. But now they had reached their destination. This, then, was it.

She looked around, taking in the long, low rock house with lighted windows and close to it, a small log house. All around, the trees and brush gathered close, and a short distance beyond lay a deep canyon, dim and shadowy. It was strange to her. And scary. She wondered if she could go through with it, enter the house and take up life here. She knew it would be difficult, compared to what she had left behind. Could she ever get used to those silent hills and canyons?

The baby stirred in her arms and suddenly the house looked inviting after the long trip. The baby must be tired. She followed her husband as he and Pete went chatting into the house. They seemed to have a hundred questions for each other.

Pete opened the door and called, "Fidelia! Come here. Say hello to Dan and his new wife."

Emma entered. The fragrant warmth of the wood stove and the yellow light of the lamp filled the room. She saw a pretty young woman, heavy with child, standing shyly in the middle of the room. Two small children hid behind her skirts.

Dan shook her hand, patting each child's head, and brought Emma forward, saying, "Emma, this is my brother's wife, Fidelia. She will be your neighbor here for a few weeks until they move to their own place not far away. This is Cordelia and this is Alfredo," he said, touching each little head by turn. Emma smiled wanly and held out her hand. Fidelia took it in both of her warm ones and then, with motherly insight, took the squirming baby from its mother's tired arms. She laid it on the bed where it stretched and waved its arms.

Fidelia spoke in soft Spanish, *"La nina tan linda."* Her two little children crowded to the bed, wide-eyed and interested.

Dan looked at Pete and grinned. "Fidelia can't speak English and Emma can't speak Spanish, but they'll learn to understand each other."

The two men went outside to see to the horses and unload the wagon, while the women were able, through the universal understanding of mothers, to comprehend each other.

Fidelia, with warmth and kindness, sensed Emma's great weariness and motioned her to a seat by the stove. Then she started to prepare a meal for the travelers, shooing the little ones out of her way.

Emma looked about the room, realizing that this would soon be her home. Dan had said they would live in the log house until Pete and Fidelia moved to their own place, then they would move into this rock house. This, then, was her "castle."

The house was three rooms in a row plus one on the end that made it L-shaped. The rooms were low ceilinged with heavy beams, the walls whitewashed. Except for the stove, the furnishings in the kitchen were mostly handmade. There were some rough stools and a long table. There were also two cupboards, a small washstand with wash pan, soap dish, and water bucket on it. The floor was rough, wide boards. Dan had said this was better than the log cabin's dirt floor.

The room was filled with the fragrance of stewed beef, beans, and coffee; Emma realized she was very hungry. It had been a long time since their lunch on the road. She was glad when the men came in and they all sat down to eat. She could hardly remember when food tasted so good, especially the pinto beans. Since the baby was born she had a bigger appetite than she ever had before.

After their supper, Emma sat down on the bed and changed and fed the baby. Little Mabel looked at her with wide, blue eyes and smiled a brief angelic smile. Now that the baby was comfortable, Emma picked her up and cradled her until the tiny eyelids closed in sleep.

While she was preoccupied with the baby, the two men and Fidelia talked volubly in Spanish. She could not understand them. She resolved to learn that language as soon as possible. She did not want to be left out of anything that concerned Dan.

She looked at him, sitting at the table, talking eagerly to his brother. In the soft lamp light his face had lost its tired lines and his eyes were very blue. She thought again that he was the most handsome man she had ever known, and she knew she would follow him to the ends of the earth. She had begun to feel that she had—that this country truly was the end of the earth. But, she sighed, if she could do it again, she would make the same choice.

Fidelia talked some, but she smiled often. She had a happy, contented face. It puzzled Emma how anyone could be so serene with two tiny children, and about to have a third, in a place like this. Who would take care of her? A doctor or nurse here seemed out of the question, yet Fidelia must have managed twice before and did not seem worried now. Then a thought struck Emma: What of herself, if she also had to bear more children, here? Mabel had been born in the security of her husband's home, with his sisters attending her. In Nebraska, there were always people living close. But here in this unsettled place, there were no towns or neighbors for miles.

Resolutely, she pushed the thought away. She did not want to worry about that now.

It was decided that Emma and Dan should sleep in one of the bedrooms that night because the log cabin was cold. They could get it ready and move into it the next day.

In bed, Dan was tired from the long trip and soon fell asleep. There was a window by the bed; Emma saw the moonlight shining on a juniper and heard a far away quivering howl that struck her with a note of great loneliness. It was like the thin cry of the coyotes she had heard on the Colorado sheep ranch, but from its deeper tone, it was probably the howl of a timber wolf. Its forlorn echo widened the miles between her and her former home in Nebraska. Flashes of memory came from the past year. It was a year of many changes, and of joy, pain, and adventure. During it all, she had missed her own family with a deep, painful ache, but she didn't permit herself to dream of going home. She had known when she married that they could seldom make a trip to Nebraska. It was too far and they had no money. Perhaps they could go in a few years, providing they had luck in this new land. She tried to sleep but visions still came. The visions took her back to her old home and her German family, and all the things that had led her here to this wild, unsettled land of New Mexico.

~~

Pictured below: Daniel and Emma and their family at the ranch, in front of their new ranch home being built. From the left: Vernie, Mabel, Mama Emma with baby Frances, Alida and Joyce, with Papa Daniel on the porch in the background. Ruth and the younger Daniel were not yet born.

~~

Pictured below: Years later, a proud Daniel—pipe clenched tightly between his teeth—with Emma, sitting in his brand new horseless carriage.

Editor: Daniel never became fully accustomed to driving a car without horse sense. While driving down steep, curving, narrow canyon roads, a teenaged Verna would say, "Papa! You are on the wrong side of the road!" To which he would reply, "Don't be silly. The road is better over here." When he was driving her to Raton, the car missed a bridge and rolled over, pinning Verna underneath. Her papa was frantic. Years later she said he had ducked his head under the dash to light his pipe as they crossed the bridge. Someone must have come along to help him lift the car off of her. She was briefly hospitalized in Raton.

---

[i] Yegua—the canyon beyond Daniel & Emma's ranch house—is also spelled Llegua; the Spanish word (YAwah) means mare.

[ii] Mabel Laumbach's 1920 medallion from the Presbyterian boarding school, Allison James, in Santa Fe. She had attended there the year before her illness and death.

Next page: "The Match Maker" print "No. 6, copyright 1892" hung at Buena Vista; after the place was sold, it hung at Dan and Emma's ranch house and then at Roy. The little oak rocker was Aunties' at Buena Vista, later at Las Vegas; it was probably Elionor's. The oak pump Windsor organ was Emma's at the ranch, later at Roy; Mabel played it. Music book that came with the organ—lady dressed in leg-o'-muffin sleeves on the cover—and some of Mabel's World War I era sheet music are displayed. On the organ are photos of Andreas and Elionor in their vintage heavy brass frames that came from Aunties, a gift from Tony. These portraits, from Buena Vista and then Las Vegas, may have been one of the sets of original photography prints from which Daniel commissioned the large oval "studio portraits" of his parents when he and Emma lived at the ranch. On the organ's oak bench is Bibiana's kerosene lamp, "patent Aug. 29, 1876." Two butter churns came from Dan and Emma's ranch. On the left are a stack of Laumbachs' and perhaps some Henkens' vintage German and Spanish books, including Elionor's Santa Biblia, and the Lutheran Bible study book in German text that held the pictures of the Crucifixion and the Last Supper shown in Chapter 1. Hanging on the wall above the books is a small charcoal portrait of Daniel Laumbach by Betty Sparks, wife of Daniel's grandson, Jerry. Betty never knew Daniel; she did his portrait from a photo. Daniel died when Jerry and Janet were small so they had vague childhood memories of him. All Jan remembers of her grandfather is his rich speaking voice, his smiling blue eyes, and watching him brush his teeth at the granite wash basin with his forefinger and a bar of lye soap.

We are fortunate to still have Emma's kitchen cabinet with granite and enamel top from the ranch and then Roy. The open drawer with its metal, ventilated sliding cover shows that it had been a flour bin; it once also had a sifter. Displayed on top: Small, heavy cast-iron to-scale replica of a wood or coal burning cook stove, with moving parts, belonged to the Laumbach children. The small, pearl-like cover was Verna's 1928 Roy high school graduation announcement. (Not shown: The cover of her Roy high school diploma in soft kid-leather; her superintendent was J. W. Wilferth, mentioned in Karl Laumbach's chapter). The black folder holds Verna's 1933 graduation diploma from New Mexico Normal University in Las Vegas. The pearlescent cup (center, rear) with gold-leaf was Verna's christening cup, presented by her grandmother Elionor Ebel Laumbach at Buena Vista in 1909. Aunties said the dinner plate (with purple flowers) was carried by Emma's mother, eight-year-old Anna, on shipboard when she came from Germany to America. On it is a porcelain cup, with gold-leaf motif, carried to America by one of the Laumbachs when the family crossed the ocean from Germany, according to Aunties. Also displayed is an assortment of shoe button hooks, shoe horn, manicure tools, Emma's hair pins, wooden awls that Daniel whittled for Emma, a wooden darning egg, and just a few of the many perfect spear points and arrowheads the Laumbach children found at the ranch.

[iii] Named Shoemaker; the family believed he and his family rented the place from Veeder to search for Metzger's and Korte's secreted gold, and was successful. With the found treasure, the family bought and restored—as a showplace again—the historic place at Watrous, turning it into a palomino horse ranch.

Emma Henkens and Daniel Laumbach

The following picture was created from the above snapshot, which was taken at their ranch probably in the late 1930s.

Their son, Joyce, had commissioned someone to make a "studio portrait" from the snapshot. That was probably after Daniel died (August 1947), perhaps even after Emma died (April 1956). Vera Jane Morris of Las Cruces found this "portrait" among her father's keepsakes, and remembered seeing it hanging on the wall of his ranch house.

It is an early-day example of what we call "photo-shop"—images that are now electronically created or altered. Manually altering photos was, apparently, a common practice in New Mexico for at least two earlier generations of this family.

The person who created it was not artistic, especially with his applied coloring. Butch Sanders tried but was limited in what he could do to improve it. Notice the eyebrows, Daniel's especially; they look as if they had been drawn on cosmetically. Dan's hat was changed from straw to felt and repositioned on his head, and his clothes were changed. Emma's clothes also, but not as drastically. Making them look more formerly attired and changing Dan's hat was probably requested by Joyce so they would appear as if they sat in a studio for a photographer. However, Joyce had not bargained for poor workmanship.

Other examples we have were made from two small individual studio photos merged into one image as if the couple sat together for a family portrait. Those were recreated as large, tinted portraits in costly oval glass and frames. Some of the creators may have been itinerate door-to-door salesmen.

We have a large oval family portrait of Emma's parents, Peter and Anna Henkens, seated together. It is tinted and in oval glass and frame. It was commissioned by Emma while she lived on the ranch, homesick and missing her parents in far off Nebraska. It had been made from two small individual studio portraits. Butch—who considerably enlarged the photo of the picture on his computer to examine it—could see it had been "photo-shopped." It had been made from two individual photos, probably taken by different photographers at different times.

We have two large individual tinted portraits of Daniel's parents, Andreas and Elionor (Eleonore) E. Laumbach, in almost matching oval glass and frames. Those were commissioned by Daniel. They were created from two small black and white photography studio portraits. Clara, daughter of Henry Laumbach, had a colored "portrait" with Andreas and Elionor seated together. Butch studied it on his computer. Perhaps commissioned by their son, Henry, in Mora or Las Vegas, it had been made by merging the same two small studio photos we have, into one and tinting or colorizing it.

The three large oval portraits made for Emma and Daniel—Peter and Anna Henkens seated together; Andreas Detlef Laumbach and Elionor Ebel Laumbach in the other two— hung for years on their walls at the ranch and later in their home in Roy. Their daughter, Ruth E. Laumbach, inherited them. Toward the end of her life, she gave them to her niece, Vera Jane L. Morris, who has them in Las Cruces. When we tried to photograph them, their oval glass distorted the images. We have original small studio portraits of Andreas and Elionor, but do not have the originals used to make those of Peter and Anna. VJ took the large framed pictures to a photography shop to remove the portraits from the frames for reproduction, but they had bonded to the glass and could not be separated without damage. Butch Sanders spent considerable time working with a photographic copy, trying to remove the distortion (caused by the glass) of the Henkens' portrait, with excellent results.

The referenced portraits of Andreas and Elionor E. Laumbach are at the front of this book. An image of the large ("photo-shopped") portrait of Peter and Anna Henkens, seated together, is at the beginning of Chapter 9: Iowa and Nebraska.

SECTION IV: LAUMBACHS IN NEW MEXICO

Chapter 35: To Buena Vista by Wagon
by Verna L. Sparks 1909—1996

The day before our annual spring trip to Buena Vista, we children had to take a bath. Joyce, the oldest boy, went out to the wash-house under the shade of a big pine tree and built a fire in the stove. Then he had to fill the large boiler with water, and because the cistern was getting low, we girls got small buckets and helped carry water from the spring.

We did not mind going to the spring. Since all our drinking water came from there, we were used to it. Whenever Mama needed cold water for churning, or Papa came in tired from riding, we had to "run down to the spring" for water.

The spring was half-way down a little canyon, and the trail was soft with fragrant pine needles. On either side, among the rocks, the wild roses and wild raspberries began to bloom. When we got to the spring we lifted the wooden cover off the cistern and looked inside. In the water our reflections looked back at us, framed with cedar boughs and patches of blue sky. The illusion of terrible depths made me shiver, and I quickly plunged in my bucket.

A short pipe ran from the spring to a wooden trough, its sides green and slippery with moss and tiny black snails. The trough connected to the second spring, which was also kept covered. In turn it fed into a pipe that meandered down the canyon until it formed a shady pool. Wildlife and sometimes cattle came there to drink. On a slight level above the pool, some overflow of water trickled down through a wilderness of wild roses, spearmint and woodbine. The biggest cedars *[juniper]* on the place grew here, giving the ranch its name, Cedar Springs. There were a few fruit trees, too, but their blossoms were gone by this time in late spring.

We carried enough water to fill the boiler and have some cold water left over. Then we had to wait for it to heat.

We found Mama busy in the kitchen, but she was always busy. She was baking bread, cookies, and turnovers for the two-day wagon trip. She was also boiling a ham and baking a big beef roast. Potatoes boiled in their jackets on the back of the big wood-burning range, and a pot of beans was cooking for our next meal.

Soon after we were in the kitchen, we were sent out for firewood. The wood box was always empty, and so was the hungry stove.

"It's like the dragon in our reader," Frances said. "It keeps gobbling and gobbling the wood." We looked at its fiery tongue when the stove door was opened for another bite of wood.

"You'd better go out to see if your water is hot," Mama said.

After our baths, we left the wash house, feeling airy and cool, especially where the breeze touched the damp hair on our necks.

"I'm so clean I feel like peppermint candy," said Ruth, the youngest of us three girls.

"I'm so clean I feel holy," said Frances, the middle one of us, inclined to be saintly.

"Let's look out for snakes," I said. Being the oldest of the three younger girls, I had to look out for things.

One day, the summer before, Frances had started out of the wash-house door and almost stepped on a big rattlesnake coiled near the doorway below the pine tree. Her screams brought Mama from the house. She told us to keep back while she killed the snake with a hoe.

After that, when we stepped outside, we looked first at the crooked snake-like roots of the pine tree. It was best to be careful because, brave as Mama was, she might not always be available.

The rest of the afternoon went slowly because we were told, "Keep clean, for goodness sake!" We did not help Joyce and Alida fill the boiler again for the other baths because we might splash water on our clean stockings.

We walked out toward the shed where Papa was getting the wagon ready. He had put up the canvas top and was fastening the last bow in place. The inside of the wagon box looked inviting. A canvas and an old quilt had been spread on the floor for us to sit on. The bed roll against the front seat would make a comfortable leaning place.

"I wish tomorrow was already here," Alida said, trying to chin herself on a wagon wheel.

"It will get here soon enough," Papa said, "and you'll be tired before we get to Grandmother's. But I think this will be the last time we'll go by wagon. I plan to get a car this summer." Of course we were all excited, but we remembered he had talked for two years about getting a car.

"Uncle Henry got a car last summer," I said, hopefully.

Papa frowned at me. "Uncle Henry doesn't live in the canyons. That makes a difference. I don't know how we'd ever get out of here in a car after a heavy rain or snow. But I'm going to get one anyway, and just use it when the weather is good. That way it won't as likely die going up the big hill."

Frances looked worried. "My, I hope our car won't die after we get it."

"Oh, shucks," said Papa, going off to the shed for a piece of wire.

We hung around the wagon making plans until we were called to take care of the baby, Daniel. Then it was supper time, and after we did the dishes, it was bed time.

"You kids get straight to sleep," Mama said. "We have to get up early in the morning." In our large, high-ceilinged bedroom, we looked at our new dresses laid out for the morning. Then we got into our night gowns.

Ruth knelt to say her prayers, but Frances and I waited until we were in bed. We noticed our older sisters, Mabel and Alida, did the same.

I can think of much more to say lying down," Alida said. Mabel just smiled her gentle smile.

It was still dark when Mama woke us in the morning. She lit the lamp so we could see to dress. "Hurry and get up. Breakfast is almost ready, and they've finished milking." Half asleep, we stumbled into our clothes, buttoned up each other's dresses in the back, and made up our beds.

In the warm, bright kitchen, Papa and Bernal, the hired man, were splashing water at the washstand, and Mama was putting steaming dishes of food on the table.

"I want you girls to eat a good breakfast," she said, "so you won't get hungry right away." It was hard to eat the dish of oatmeal, and then the potatoes and egg, but with Papa's eye on us, we did our best.

The sky was beginning to get light above the hills in the east when we were finally settled in the wagon. We started off, leaving the place to the dogs and Bernal.

Joyce sat at the end of the wagon so he could jump out to open and shut the gates. The rest of us arranged ourselves against the bed roll, facing the open rear of the covered wagon. Mabel looked after the youngest ones, but I was big enough to look after myself.

The dark trees marched by us like a silent army. The cool breeze smelled of pine, and far away a sleepy bird woke up and began to sing. Behind our backs we heard the slap of the reins, the plod of the horses' hooves, and the murmur of grown-up voices. The baby Daniel slept in Mama's arms.

The road wound around the canyons and hills, and gradually came out into more open country. Occasionally we passed small scattered ranch houses of adobe or rock, with smoke rising out of chimneys and children playing in the yards. We met two men on horseback in the forenoon, and Father stopped to talk with them, the reins slackly held in his hands.

Around noon we reached a little piñon woods, where we stopped to eat. Papa unhitched the horses and led them to a water hole nearby, where they drank thirstily.

While Joyce and Alida gathered wood for a small fire to make coffee, Mama and Mabel spread a canvas on the ground, and arranged quilts for the baby at one end. Then we were told to watch him while they put out our lunch. Frances, Ruth and I sat close to little Daniel to make sure he did not crawl off the quilts. He looked around at the moving branches and laughed and clapped his hands.

We watched Mama get out a loaf of bread, a small jar of butter wrapped in a damp towel, the sliced roast beef and the turnovers. She poured each of us a tin cup full of milk from a bucket.

"I'm as thirsty as the horses," Frances said, immediately drinking her milk.

"You might as well drink all the milk you want," Mama said. "It may not be sweet tomorrow. But I hope it is still good for breakfast so Daniel can have some."

"It won't hurt him if he has to wait till tomorrow evening," Papa remarked. "We'll be at Buena Vista by then."

When we finished eating, Papa leaned back against a tree and filled his pipe. Joyce pointed to a row of small cedars in a clearing nearby and asked, "Why do they grow in a row like that?"

Papa looked far away and lit his pipe. "Well, Joyce, once there was an old drift fence there. When I first came to this country there were no fences. Later I remember there was a log fence built across here. I guess the birds carried berries and sat on the fence to eat them and sometimes dropped them. By and by little cedars grew along the fence. As the years went by, the log fence was torn down, but the cedar trees kept growing."

We sat listening to the conversation awhile and then jumped up and started chasing each other through the trees. Soon we were called to come back and get in the wagon again. The horses were hitched up and we were on our way.

Once in the afternoon Mama let Daniel sit in the back with us, and we played with him until the gentle rocking of the wagon put him to sleep. We covered him with a blanket, and then ate cookies. We told stories and watched the countryside move slowly past. Joyce whittled stick dolls for us, and we played with them until we, too, grew sleepy.

About sundown we came to a small, abandoned rock house, and Father decided it was a good place to spend the night. Inside we found the house was one long room, with a fireplace at one end. Soon Father had a big fire blazing, and the warmth felt good. The evening turned cool.

Mama had swept the dirt floor with a short, grass broom she carried in the wagon, and then spread the canvas at one end of the room to place the bed rolls on it.

By the time the fire had burned down, Mama had mixed biscuit dough, using the top of the wooden food box for a table. She put the biscuits in the cast-iron Dutch oven, replaced the heavy lid, and set the oven among the low coals. While the biscuits were baking, she put the tin coffee pot on to boil. We sat on the floor or bed roll and ate cold roast beef, hot biscuits, and canned tomatoes. We children drank milk while Mama and Papa drank coffee.

"When I get big," Frances said, "I'm always and always going to drink coffee and nothing else."

"Tomorrow the milk will be sour and maybe we can drink coffee," Alida suggested.

We were excited that night, lying on the floor of that little house. We were sure we could never go to sleep. An owl hooted in a tree nearby, and we could hear the horses snort and stamp their feet. Then a coyote howled a long way off, and we snuggled down under the warm covers.

Immediately it was morning and Papa was up, building a fire in the fireplace.

The second day we more often passed farm and ranch houses. About noon we met another wagon and stopped to visit awhile. The people were on their way to Ocate; we learned they were cousins. We had so many cousins that we children could not remember them all, but everyone was glad when we chanced to meet.

The road had followed the small stream that runs through the valley of the settlements of Shoemaker and Valmora. While the grown-ups talked, we were turned loose to play.

We took off our shoes and tried to wade, but the water was too cold. We watched Joyce cut willow branches and make whistles for us. The visit ended, and the wagons started up again, each going in an opposite direction.

I remembered an earlier wagon trip, in 1912, when I saw a cow out in a pasture and begged for fresh milk. Papa stopped the wagon and crawled through the fence with my tin cup. While he was at it, he got enough for everyone who wanted it. I was a big girl now; I saw what I thought were cows out on the *vega,* but I didn't ask Papa to stop.

We reached Watrous in the afternoon. Papa stopped at the store to see if any of his family was in town. He found some old friends from the Mora Valley who said Uncle Henry, Papa's brother, had been in the day before.

We went on, passing slowly by the old Inn, down the shady tree-lined lane leading away from town.

The road now led us toward the mountains. It was not long before we were among the pine trees. The low mountains crowded close on both sides of us, and we creaked along through the narrow pass. Occasionally, we saw an old adobe house with log corrals and an outdoor oven. We always waved at everybody in sight.

It was late afternoon when the pass opened into a valley. We saw the red cliffs of the mountain that rose above, east, of the little village of Buena Vista.

A thrill went through us when we came into sight of the old, old settlement of Mora. Here in this valley my grandparents and great-grandparents had lived. My grandfather had died a few years earlier, but my grandmother and three aunts were still on the old home place.

"Giddyap," said Papa, as we went a little faster down the crooked road that led to the heart of the village.

Then we came to Grandmother's lane. Cottonwoods towered over the rock walls on either side, and when we turned in at the big gate, we tried to see everything at once—the long, low adobe ranch house, the apple orchard to one side, the little streams of water running everywhere, and the old-fashioned well with its wooden bucket.

The wagon stopped inside the big, open courtyard and Papa gave a great shout. Down the steps and flagstone path from the house came Grandmother and my aunties hurrying to meet us.

We had a wonderful visit at Grandmother's. We always looked forward to another one.

The years went by, bringing many changes. After my grandmother's death and the place sold, it was never the same, but I remembered how attractive the old house and the village had been for me. Years later I wrote a piece about it:

"Old Spanish houses appeal to me. I remember such a house when I was a child. I used to play there. I still remember the long, cool patios; the rock garden with a profusion of rich color; the murmuring of pigeons in the eaves; rambling rock walls that went nowhere in particular, covered with dark green vines. There was a well and a mossy trough, small streams trickling everywhere, and the tallest cottonwoods I have ever seen dripping yellow leaves in the water. Most of the cottonwoods have since been cut down, and there are no more pigeons murmuring in the eaves. The place is not as beautiful as it had been, but not all the charm is gone. On long afternoons, I remember how blue the sky was there and dream—of Spanish houses." *[A piece Verna wrote, "Spanish Houses," was published in the* New Mexico Magazine *around 1932 when she was in college.]*

Jan found this poem among Verna's things after she was gone. She had written it as a college student at New Mexico Normal to accompany her ink sketch of a windmill for an art class. She wrote of windmills, once common on the open New Mexico prairies, now becoming specters of the past.

Weathered and worn and gray am I,
Years and ages have passed me by.
But at times when the midnight breezes play,
My old arms wave in a rhythmic sway,
Back and forth with a joyous creak
For that is the way I have to speak,
With the ghosts of folks who gather near
And prattle their tales of a bygone year.
Verna Laumbach, Art 113

A petite (4-11, weight 90 pounds) teenage Verna at college about 1928.

SECTION IV: LAUMBACHS IN NEW MEXICO

Chapter 36: Presbyterian Missions & Schools in Northern New Mexico
by Jan Girand

Dale B. Gerdeman of Las Vegas New Mexico wrote and edited *Presbyterian Missionaries in Rural New Mexico, Serving the Lord on the New Mexican Frontier*, published in 1999 by the Menaul Historical Library of the Southwest. Gerdeman wrote, "There were approximately 130 Presbyterian missionaries who served the Spanish-speaking people in rural northern New Mexico during the period from about 1869 until about 1950. This book tells about the lives of 27 of them and one lay leader. Eight of the missionaries mentioned attended or graduated from Menaul." That list included Rev. Julián Duran and Rev. Alfonso Esquíbel. Gerdeman's book's profiles include: Reverend Jose Emiterio Cruz (1855—1931); his wife Margarita Laumbach Cruz (1865—1958); Evangelist J.S. Candelario (1864—1938) who married Estefanita Laumbach; Reverend Julián Duran, (1898—1995), who married Rosa Cruz, daughter of Margaret Laumbach Cruz; and Reverend Alfonso Esquíbel (1899—1992).

Mr. Gerdeman and I had communicated in mid-2000; he was gathering more data for a second edition of this book with updates and additional information; I do not know whether he produced a second edition. In it, he intended to include a piece Tony Sanchez had written for him about his mother, Crestina, and a piece I submitted to him, written by my mother, Verna L. Sparks, about her Papa's experiences when he attended the Presbyterian mission school in Mora. Many Laumbachs and some of their kinfolk, because they had lived in rural areas and ranches, attended the Presbyterian mission boarding schools of Menaul in Albuquerque and Allison James in Santa Fe.

The first Protestant church established in New Mexico and Arizona was the First Presbyterian Church. Presbyterian minister, Rev. David F. McFarland, arrived in Santa Fe by stage coach in 1866, and registered for a room at the Exchange Hotel. Within two days he was holding worship services. He officially organized the church in the Council Chamber of the Palace of the Governors in 1867. (Coincidentally, on March 1, 1873, this same Rev. David F. McFarland performed the marriage ceremony in Santa Fe for Catherine McCarty and William Antrim; young Henry, later known as Billy the Kid, and his brother Joe were witnesses.)

Early Presbyterian John Knox of Scotland believed the church should provide regional, accessible school systems. That premise was brought to America by Presbyterians. McFarland opened a school in Santa Fe within days of his arrival. Eventually his school evolved into more than 40 schools throughout northern New Mexico. One of those, an industrial boarding school in Santa Fe for Hispanic girls, was run by a woman named Matilda Allison who arrived in 1881. A three-story brick dormitory was built to board the students near the Presbyterian Church, and a few years later a brick classroom building was built nearby. When Matilda Allison left, after 22 years of dedicated service, the school's name was changed to Allison School. A few years later, a new Mary James Missionary Boarding School for boys was begun. Eventually—by 1928—the two boarding schools in Santa Fe merged into one, named the Allison-James, which was a junior-high level boarding school primarily for Hispanic boys and girls who had already acquired their earlier education in the remote mission day schools of northern New Mexico. The Allison-James closed in 1958.

In 1896, Presbyterian minister Rev. James Menaul began a Presbyterian mission boarding school in Albuquerque with about 200 acres of land. Menaul was for Spanish-speaking boys primarily from northern New Mexico's rural areas, offering them education and life skills. A large percentage of those students pursued higher educations. Menaul began with primary and then included high school. They held their first class graduation in 1906. Years later it also admitted girls. Today it is an independent college-prep boarding and day school for sixth through 12th grade.

The mission day schools in rural northern New Mexico and the boarding schools of Allison-James and Menaul served important roles in providing education to generations of young men and women in the formative years of New Mexico's late territorial period and her early years of statehood.

Allison Mission School's new three-story brick dormitory for girls; photo taken in 1889.

The Presbyterian Allison Mission School; photo taken by Dana B. Chase about 1906.

THE SANTA FE NEW MEXICAN
Santa Fe, N. M. Wednesday, May 9, 1906

Interesting Commencement at Allison Mission School
Professor Hadley Delivers a Pleasing Address to Graduates.

The commencement exercises of the Allison Mission School were held in the spacious sitting room of the institution this morning in the presence of a large audience, composed of the friends and relatives of the members of the graduating class. The room in which the exercises were held had been prettily decorated for the occasion, apple blossoms, lilacs and foliage being used with artistic effect.

For the first time in the history of the school, the members of the graduating class, Allison Candelario, Sara Trujillo and Sarita Montoya, were presented with certificates showing that they had completed the course prescribed by the institution. A pretty coincidence in connection with the exercises is the fact that Miss Allison Candelario, daughter of Mr. and Mrs. J. S. Candelario, who was a member of the first class receiving certificates, was the first child ever baptized at the mission. She has spent all her school years at the Allison institution and was named after its founder.

The program given was an excellent one and comprised both musical and literary numbers. The graduating class address was made by Professor Hiram Hadley, superintendent of public instruction, and each of the members of the class participated in the exercises. Miss Sara Trujillo read an essay on "Our Territory" which was well prepared; Miss Allison Candelario gave a reading entitled "Gwen's Canon" and played a piano solo and Miss Sarita Montoya read an excellent essay on "What the Presbyterian Church Has Done for the Territory." The program in full was as follows:

Opening Prayer, Rev.............. Geo. F. Sevier
Anthem................................. By the School
Essay—"Our Territory"......... Sara Trujillo
Piano Solo—"Con Amore".... Ruth Rendon
Reading—"Gwen's Canon".... Allison Candelario
Chorus—"Now is the Month of Maying."..... By the School
Essay—"What the Presbyterian Church Has Done for the Territory"... Sarita Montoya
Piano Solo—"Fifth Nocturne"..... Allison Candelario
Address......Professor Hiram Hadley
Presentation of Certificates.... Supt. A. Breagle
Chorus—"Soldier's Chorus" ... By the School
Benediction........................... Rev. Gabino Rendon

The Allison school has had a successful year under the superintendency of Miss A. Breagle. She has been assisted in the work by the following teachers: Miss B. B. Bonine, Miss Grace Harris, Mrs. Harriet Campbell, Miss M. B. Morrow and Miss Eva Rupert.

Butch Sanders found these above two vintage photos of the Allison Mission School and the 1906 newspaper article with Allison Candelario's graduation commencement, which he transcribed.

~~

Rudolph "Rudy" Laumbach (son of Rudolph Laumbach) compiled the following documentation of Laumbachs who attended the boarding schools of Menaul and/or Allison-James. Included are the students' life dates and spouses, as well as the dates they attended the school(s).

Children of Peter and Fidelia Laumbach, Solano, Harding Co. New Mexico:
Alfredo Laumbach—(11/04/1900–8/28/1918), Menaul School (1913—1917);
Cordelia Laumbach—(9/10/1899–2/22/1942), married Fermin Maes, Allison-James School (1916—1920);
Christina Laumbach—(2/8/1905–6/19/1976), married Frank Foxall, Allison-James School (1920—1926);
Petra Laumbach—(11/16/1906–4/5/2000), married Roscoe Latham, Allison-James School (1922—1926);
Rudolph Laumbach—(7/23/1908–10/30/1989), married Leona Volk, Menaul School (1923—1929);
George Laumbach—(3/18/1910–12/23/1986), married Margaret Miller, Menaul School (1923—1930);
Andreas (Red) Laumbach—(10/12/1911–03/16/2013), married Zulema Tixier, Menaul School (1926—1931);
Casimiro (Ike) Laumbach—(6/09/1913-   ), married Irene Hurley, Menaul School (1926—1931);
Bertha Laumbach—(12/21/1915–4/24/1959), married Cecil Durham, Allison-James School (1930—1934);
Lucille Laumbach—(7/18/1917–11/1998), married Howard Schmalle, Allison-James & Menaul School (1930—1935);
Peter Laumbach—(6/10/1923—4/08/2015), married Guadalupe Gonzales, Menaul School (1940—1941)

Children of Daniel and Emma Laumbach, Roy, Harding Co. New Mexico:
Mabel Laumbach—(10//24/1902-04/05/1922), Allison James School (1919—1921);

Children of Henry and Natividad Laumbach, La Cueva, Mora Co. New Mexico:
Adelina Laumbach—(4/17/1927-1994), married Adolph Espinosa, Allison-James School, (1941—1943);

Children of Rudolph and Leona Laumbach, Las Vegas, San Miguel Co. New Mexico:
Rudolph Laumbach—(6/16/1931 -   ), married Joan McCune, Menaul School (1947—1949).

Additional children of Laumbachs who attended one of these Presbyterian mission schools—the Allison James in Santa Fe or Menaul in Albuquerque—included Allison "Alice" Candelario, daughter of Estefanita Laumbach and J.S. Candelario; Bernardo "Barney" Cruz, son of Margaret Laumbach and J. E. Cruz; and Antonio "Tony" Sanchez, son of Crestina Laumbach and Manuel Sanchez.

SECTION IV: LAUMBACHS IN NEW MEXICO

Chapter 37: Tony Sanchez
by Jan Girand

Oil pastel portrait of Tony Sanchez by Betty Sparks, wife of Jerry Sparks, son of Verna.

"Tony" Antonio A. Sanchez was born in 1911 to Manuel Antonio Sanchez and Crestina Laumbach Sanchez.

Tony's grandfather, Antonio Sanchez, was one of the early settlers in Sabinoso in northeastern New Mexico. With his son, Manuel, he operated a store—Antonio Sanchez y Hijo, La Tienda Barata—which was established in 1879 on their large cattle and sheep ranch. After a major flood in 1904 took out much of the settlement of Sabinoso, the Sanchez men moved their ranch headquarters and store to a place locally called Lagartijas (place of lizards) but commonly called Sanchez, partly because of the U.S. post office in their store. The white stuccoed gate entrance to the ranch, with inset decorative tiles from Mexico, is located past the bridge over the Canadian River on Highway 104 after coming down Corazon Hill from Las Vegas. You could also reach the ranch from Roy on Highway 419, and from Vaughn-Santa Rosa via Highway 129. The ranch is fairly isolated; the nearest communities are Roy, 35 miles north, and Las Vegas, about 70 miles west. At Corazon Hill, because of the Canadian escarpment, the elevation drops 1,000 feet from the high plains to desert grasslands below. The ranch is situated among a few uniquely shaped mesas—like the Flat Iron and the Bell—that rise up from the desert floor. A Sanchez Ranch neighbor is the well-known huge Bell Ranch, named for one of those formations.

Ultimately the Sanchez ranch was owned and operated by three generations of Sanchez men. At his death in March 1987, Tony became the last Sanchez owner when he—who never married and had no children—willed the central portion of the ranch to his long-time foreman, Alfredo Martinez and his wife, Paula, and their children. The Martinez children and grandchildren now own and operate it.

Like the front gate, the peaked roof buildings at Tony's ranch headquarters were white stucco adobe with turquoise painted trim. Above one portion of the older building, Tony had a tower built to house the bell that for years had been at the Laumbach's Buena Vista place. When Aunties sold the place, they gave that bell to Tony. The bell had been bought by J.S. Candelario for a small, rural Presbyterian mission church—one of my notes from a source said at Chimayo, another said Rociada. When the church closed, Uncle Sito and some of the Laumbach men transported the bell by horse-pulled wagon to Buena Vista.

The U-shaped structure at the ranch—the home of his grandfather and father that also had the store—remain. Tony built his unattached, more modern home nearby within the ranch headquarters' courtyard.

Tony's father, Manuel, born January 1, 1861 at Rociada, was educated in private schools. He was the only child of Antonio and Genoveva Sanchez. At the family ranch, Antonio, and also his son, Manuel, raised several children from poor families, providing them a good home.

In their times, the three Sanchez men had been affluent and influential area leaders. All three were staunch Republicans and active in the politics of their San Miguel County, and their neighboring community of Las Vegas. Tony's father, Manuel, was a member of the 32nd Legislative Assembly of the Territory of New Mexico. He was elected justice of the peace for his precinct in 1879, and appointed census enumerator by Mr. Pedro Sanchez in 1890. At his store—an isolated early era "convenience store" with a gas pump—Manuel daily met, visited with, and freely advised his neighbors. He also loaned them money. When they could not repay their loans, Manuel acquired their properties, which had been loan collateral. Thus the Sanchez ranchlands grew.

On December 3, 1887, Tony's father married Rosita Eggert, daughter of Fritz Eggert. They were married 19 years, until her death. They had no children of their own but raised several, giving them better lives than they would have had otherwise. A few years after Rosita died, Manuel married Crestina, one of the Laumbach girls from Buena Vista, in 1909. They had two children, Antonio "Tony" born in 1911, and Adelina, born in 1913; she died February 1920 of diphtheria.

Tony, age 2, and Adelina.

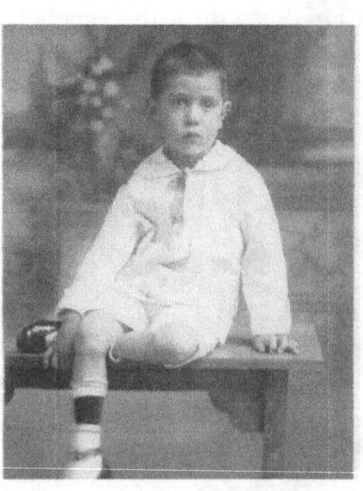

Most of her married life, Crestina chose to live in Las Vegas, only occasionally visiting the ranch. Tony wrote that while she was in good physical health and able to walk that far, she attended the Presbyterian Church at 10th and Douglas, and occasionally attended the Presbyterian Spanish Mission Church.

When he was old enough, Tony lived at the ranch with his father and—in Tony's early years—also with his grandfather, Antonio. Tony graduated from Menaul boarding school in Albuquerque, then attended public school in Las Vegas, and then New Mexico Normal in Las Vegas.

My mother had lived with her Aunt Crestina in Old Town during her college years at Normal. I have a letter her father had written to her saying he would pay his sister, Crestina, for Verna's room and board while she went to college. During those years, Verna and Tony became close. I have letters she wrote, including to her sisters, describing trips to Buena Vista with him to see their Aunties and grandmother. In one of Verna's girlish letters to her sisters, Verna described hers and Tony's daring adventure of climbing the rimrock behind the Buena Vista home place. In another girlish letter Verna wrote that her aunt Crestina had been annoyed to learn that she and Tony had attended a "moving picture show," an entertainment her aunt considered decadent. Crestina thought Verna, two years older than her cousin, was a bad influence on Tony.

While attending college at Normal, Tony studied German language and history. His college professor offered him an opportunity to visit Germany. Tony returned from there with several purchased German "trophies," including a World War I officer's helmet. After Tony's return, he became more involved with running the family ranch. Like Buena Vista having nearby La Cueva as its mailing address, when the Sanchez Ranch no longer had its own post office, their mailing address became Solano, their nearest post office.

In 1937, Tony and his friend planned to drive to Mexico City on the new Pan American highway that stretched from Laredo, Texas to Monterrey, Mexico. When they were nearly ready to depart, to their surprise, his mother announced that she was going with them. Tony wrote that she probably thought she would keep them from harm, but despite their misgivings, Tony said she was a wonderful traveling companion. They invited her to go with them on several subsequent trips to Mexico.

Tony Sanchez; photo courtesy Karl Laumbach.

Following his father's example, Tony was elected to the New Mexico Legislature representing San Miguel County. In the 1950s, he served as majority whip.

Letterhead on a letter from Tony to Verna.

ANTONIO SANCHEZ
MAJORITY WHIP
SAN MIGUEL COUNTY

HOME ADDRESS
SOLANO, NEW MEXICO

State of New Mexico
House of Representatives
TWENTY-FIRST LEGISLATURE
Santa Fe

COMMITTEES:
MEMBER:
AGRICULTURE, VICE CHAIRMAN
PUBLIC AFFAIRS
PUBLIC LANDS & LIVESTOCK
TAXATION & REVENUE
COMMITTEE ON COMMITTEES
JUDICIARY

January 2, 1954

After Tony died, state senators Alfred Nelson, Carlos Cisneros and Tom Rutherford introduced a senate memorial—number 101—to the 38th session in 1987; it was signed by Jack Stahl, president of the New Mexico State Senate. In the memorial, Tony's listed accomplishments were many, including:

Tony and his father owned and operated their ranch at Sanchez for many years, with the assistance of foreman, Alfredo Martinez. A dedicated Republican, Tony was elected to the State House of Representatives in 1952 and served as majority whip in 1953—1954; he was vice-chairman of the San Miguel Republican Party in 1952; chairman of the San Miguel Central Committee from 1952 to 1954; and an alternate delegate to the Republican National Convention from 1952 to 1956.

Tony served on the State Fair Board from 1956 to 1958; he was finance director of the New Mexico State Hospital from 1956 to 1959; was a board of trustees member of the Northeastern Regional Hospital from 1972 to 1980; was an FFA Board member in 1962 and 1963; was a member of the Las Vegas-San Miguel Chamber of Commerce Board for 20 years; he was appointed to the New Mexico State Agricultural Stabilization and Conservation Service on July 27, 1981 by the Secretary of Agriculture John Block, and had recently been reappointed. He was a long-time member of the NM Cattle Growers Association and the Farm Bureau. He was a founder, director and major share holder of The Bank of Northern New Mexico; was a corporate member of the Northeastern Regional Hospital; and served on the Board of Directors of the Bank of New Mexico, and in 1984 succeeded W.O. Culbertson as board president. Tony was also an active and contributing member of La Plaza Vieja partnership; he was a well-known benefactor in the Las Vegas area, having helped many people get started financially; and he most recently served on the Charles and Adele Illfeld Foundation Board.

Not mentioned in that memorial: For years Tony gave annual scholarships to Highland University students.

Tony and a few friends had founded a new bank in Las Vegas. He encouraged my mother, Verna, to buy stock; she did with limited money she had to invest. I also bought a small stock for my young son, Devin, as compensation for a financial slight by his paternal grandfather. Devin's was stock number 000001 (I don't remember the number of zeros). I suspect Tony was instrumental in that number's assignment. I do not now know the year THE BANK of Northern New Mexico was founded.

The earliest statement of condition my mother had for the bank was dated December 31, 1981. Named on it were: James Doolittle, chairman; Victor Quiroz, president; Irene Crespin, vice-president. Board Members were: Myles Culbertson; James Franken; Ralph F. Petty Jr.; Antonio A. Sanchez; Jeffrey Lane; James Doolittle; Michael Gregory; Alonzo Romero; W.O. Culbertson Jr.; Victor Valdez; and Victor Quiroz. For years, "Corky" George Fernandez had been the bank's president.

~~

I began corresponding with Tony when I was 10 or 12; I had initially written to ask for history of the bell at his ranch. From then on, we were regular correspondents. My brother, Jerry, and son, David, also occasionally corresponded with him. I have saved many letters from Tony, as well as from his mother and my other aunties.

I was amazed, when I was a pre-teen and teenager visiting the ranch, to recognize the significance of photos on the walls of Tony's little store. One was a huge photo of Ike—Dwight D. Eisenhower, that is. It was autographed, "Best wishes. To my friend, Tony. Ike." Another huge glossy photo print on a wall of his store was a full-length one of World War I General John J. "Black Jack" Pershing; that one, too, was personally autographed to Tony. Looking on the Internet at the many photos of Pershing, I do not see one quite like it. Pershing wore his general's military uniform; what, from my memory, made Tony's different was a long sword or saber Pershing held in his hand. In Tony's home, taped to the front of his fireplace, was a photograph of Tony Luhan, the Taos Indian chief husband of Mabel Dodge Luhan, famed heiress to the Dodge fortune. I only remember seeing Tony Luhan wrapped in his blanket in that photo; I don't recall Mabel in it, but it was personally signed to Tony by Mabel and "her" Tony.

Tony's *tienda*, where ranching neighbors continued to drop by to chat and share local news, was like a little museum. Inside his old oak and glass antique display cases below a worn oak counter were interesting items, many of an archeological nature. Included were baskets filled with Indian arrowheads and spear points. I think I remember seeing at Tony's ranch, and recognizing, the unique shape of a Folsom point. I wish I had asked about that, or taken a photo.

On a small table at Tony's front door home entrance was an Indian woven basket filled with calcified bone fragments, pieces of petrified wood, pottery shards—some seemed to resemble Mimbres—and perfect arrowheads and spear points. Most or all of those were an accumulation from an archaeological dig near his home. Archeologists from the Denver Museum of Natural History spent at least one summer there, as Tony's guests, excavating a prehistoric Indian site. Also seen as you came in the front door of his ranch house was a large, very old oil painting, dated by the crackled oils and pigment darkened by the passing of untold years and candle smoke. A distressed and wounded tonsured monk in a long brown robe stood in the foreground. In the distance was a burning adobe church. As I recall, it dated from the 16th or 17th century.

Tony had awesome and priceless artifacts at two different locations. One was upstairs in his mother's house in Las Vegas. That one held an amazing collection of rustic religious art, mostly *retablos* and carved *bultos*, most painted with natural pigments. Even back when I first saw them in the early 1950s, many were older than 100 years, most made by New Mexican Penitente *santeros*. I had believed his *santos* collection was as rare and valuable in antiquity as ones I had seen displayed in New Mexico history museums. That upstairs treasure trove also held Tony's collection of early rustic tools; some of those were hand-tools—perhaps used by *santeros*—and others were garden and field implements, most made of iron. There were also a few vintage household "tools."

His other collection, probably lesser-known among his friends and family because they were hidden away in trunks at his ranch and seldom seen, was his valuable art collection. He purchased those from museums like the Metropolitan Museum of Art in New York and other reputable sources. Each piece had a signed numbered certificate on the back, documenting its authenticity, guaranteeing it to be an original numbered print, some signed by the artist. Like people today who invest money in stamps or gold and silver coins and ingots, Tony invested some of his liquid assets in art. Those included two by Renoir (1841—1919); two by Rembrandt (1606—1669)—one of those an original ink sketch signed and dated by the artist in pencil; a Van Dyke, a Matisse; a numbered print of oil painting "The Gleaners," by Jean-Francois Millet, completed in 1857, that depicts three peasant women gleaning a stubble-field after harvest, plus another one by the same artist; at least one Picasso; two or three by Goya; one by Monet; a Gauguin; at least one by Salvador Dali; and at least one by J. McNeill Whistler. (I documented those when he showed me his collection in the 1970s.) He gave one of those pieces to my son, David, who was then a college student. On that Certificate of Authenticity: Title—Chapeau Epingle; Artist—Pierre-Auguste Renoir; Medium—Etching; and "Art Acquired by the Associated American Artists, it bears the artist's personal signature and is guaranteed to be an original print." Included on that certificate were a registration number and an authorized signature. Perhaps Tony's most valuable piece—the Rembrandt original ink sketch signed by the artist in pencil with the authenticated artist's original matting—hung on a wall of his ranch house. It was displayed beside a string art of nails and yarn made by my son Devin at age six or seven. I suspect Tony dared display it that way, in plain sight, because no one would suspect it's amazing value.

When Tony died at age 75 of a heart-attack, I asked his estate's executor, Alfredo Martinez—who knew I was tight with Tony—to let me go to the ranch and to the house on Valencia in Las Vegas, to document, under his supervision—Tony's valuable collections before they were hauled off. I hoped Alfredo would acquire itemized signed receipts for everything taken. He was understandably nervous about the responsibility suddenly thrust upon him. He locked up everything and permitted no one to come to the ranch in the ensuing days after Tony's death. Tony's family hopes documentation was made recording who came, what was taken and where it went.

Tony had no obvious heir, just many equally related cousins. He originally told Verna and me that he intended to bequeath the majority of his valuable artifacts, including the priceless *santos,* to the State of New Mexico. He later changed his mind and will. His last will stipulated that the majority of his considerable liquefied estate was to be used to build a museum and provide for its perpetual care and management. The museum was to house and display his collections and valuable family keepsakes.

Tony made a few bequeaths to individuals, including to one of John Candelario's ex-wives and to a ranch-hand who had been seriously injured in a car accident on Corizon Hill going to Las Vegas on a day off. Tony's real estate properties, including several in Las Vegas, were sold, and his other assets liquidated. That included a large portion of the Sanchez ranch. The ranch headquarters and some surrounding ranchlands were bequeathed to Alfredo, his wife Paula and their children, but not the contents. His will stipulated that all contents of his houses in Las Vegas—including his mother's house and what remained in Aunties' house—and his home and buildings at the ranch were to be collected and placed in that museum.

Tony worried that his will might be contested; he took measures to prevent that. One of those measures, per advice from his attorney, was to legally adopt his employee, Alfredo, as his son. Until he heard the will, that was unknown to Alfredo—age-wise, more like a brother than a son.

Alfredo's primary language was Spanish. After Tony died, Alfredo changed attorneys, choosing one who spoke Spanish fluently.

The formation of La Plaza Vieja partnership was fairly recent when Tony died in 1987.

Around 1984, Plaza area property owners formed the group called La Plaza Vieja partnership. Its purpose was to renovate, lease out and manage buildings they owned on and near the Old Town Plaza. They felt an urgency to do that work quickly to take advantage of Federal tax credits. The partnership began with financial contributions from its five primary general partners who owned the commercial buildings, plus a larger group of limited partners. Together they provided the initial amount of capital needed to begin. The historic Plaza Hotel headed the list for restoration.

Tony was a partner of La Plaza Vieja. He had co-signed a La Plaza Vieja banknote. Did that obligate his estate to pay for a major portion of that restoration?

The question remains unanswered: What happened to Tony's family memorabilia and keepsakes, including the old German family Bible, as well as his priceless artifacts and art collection? Some say a few pieces of his memorabilia, like books, are archived in Las Vegas' Carnegie Library.

SECTION IV: NEW MEXICO

Chapter 38: Visit to Emma and Daniel's Ranch in 2010
by Jan Girand

For her required continuing education as a teacher, one summer in her late forties, Verna acquired college credit hours on the Boulder, Colorado college campus. I went with her; we stayed in a nearby apartment. She took boxes of her lifetime accumulation of loose notes, stories she had written as a college student, and hand-written family history. In Boulder, she began to compile and write them into a cohesive paper, which she manually typed when she was in her seventies living in Roswell. She also wrote a little book, *In Search of Springs,* with slightly fictionalized stories from her memories and notes, with a limited number of copies printed.

This chapter describes my recent visit to her childhood home, Cedar Springs Ranch; much of my recollections had come from her descriptions. I'd only been there, briefly, once before in my memory. That had been with my mother decades ago, when owner Fern Hartley still lived there. This chapter also has memory vignettes provided by Alfredo Laumbach, born in 1921.

This panoramic view of La Cinta that looks three dimensional was taken perhaps three years ago by Alfredo's daughter, Christina Laumbach of New Zealand, used with her permission. Alfredo, with walking stick, leads the way across his ranch. It looks like they just had a nourishing rain, which is always a blessing in that arid land.

Roy

On Saturday, August 28, 2010, my husband, Dan Girand, and I traveled to Roy, New Mexico to see Pedro Laumbach, his wife, Lily, and his father, Alfredo "Al" Laumbach. (Al was my mother's first cousin, son of Peter Joseph Laumbach.) Pedro and Alfredo provided our guided tour.

From Roy, we set out, with permission from the current owner, to the ranch that had once been my grandparents, Daniel and Emma Laumbach. We hoped to also find the spot where our Uncle Bonney's cabin had once stood. My grandfather bought Uncle Bonney's place after he moved to Pastura and it then became part of Daniel's ranch holdings.

Al's wife, Eleanor, had recently died at age 86. They'd had 15 children; three died young, they raised 12, and within the last two years, their beautiful daughter Frances died. Alfredo still lives alone at his ranch south of Roy. "Why not? In my own house I built myself," he said. His son, Pedro, goes out to see him, and Lily sends food. "More food than I can eat," Al said, not complaining.

The year before, in the summer of 2009, a movie had been made with the setting of Roy, New Mexico, aka Ray, Wyoming: *Did You Hear About the Morgans?* starring Sarah Jessica Parker, Hugh Grant, Sam Elliott and Wilferd Brimley, among others. Alfredo was one of the local extras; he was the handsome white-mustached fellow in the background playing bingo in one scene.

On this day, Al was a remarkably spry 90-year-old man. He has thick white hair and mustache, still tall, slender, straight-backed, and strong.

I noticed he is missing a finger and thumb on his right hand; I asked how that happened. "I picked up a blasting cap," when he was about eight years old, he said. "This," he added, pointing to his right shoulder, "is from a horse falling on me" when he was 12. "I haven't been able to lift my arm higher than this;" illustrating, he raised his arm to mid-chest height. "It's sad; I haven't touched my head with that hand since I was 12." Without our modern medical miracles that we take for granted, his early-life injury healed badly. That is sad.

He said he had gone to see his doctor several years ago, perhaps when he was 85; his over-all good physical condition impressed her. She asked what he did to stay that way. He said he worked 40 miles of fence. He admitted to me that had been an exaggeration, it really wasn't 40 miles. He has a wonderful droll humor. In the back of his pickup, he showed me his well-used iron tools, including heavy sledgehammers, an ax, post-hole diggers and shovel, all probably older than he, which he still regularly uses to repair fences and other tasks. He said he had repaired some fence at his ranch earlier this day. I wondered how he, with a bum shoulder, worked fences—hard physical work requiring strength in both arms for anyone at any age. He is still a strong *hombre*.

This Alfredo, born in 1921, was the next-to-youngest child of 17 born to Peter Joseph and Fidelia Andrada Laumbach. Pete, born in 1867, was one of my grandfather's two brothers. My grandfather, Daniel (born in 1872) and all of his siblings were born in Mora County, mostly at the family home place at Buena Vista.

Uncle Bonney's Cabin

Ramon Bonney (born May 1846), son of Englishman James Bonney at La Junta, was the first-born son of Bibiana, then a teenager.

Uncle Bonney first married Concepcion Padilla, and they had two or three children. After they died, he married Anastacia Lucero, and they had many children, not all survived. He ultimately separated from his wife and children and became a wanderer, often visiting the homes of his various kinfolk. In his late years, he homesteaded and built a simple cabin near my grandfather's ranch.

My mother, Verna, was young when her father's Uncle Bonney lived nearby in his rustic cabin. She and her siblings remembered his visits to the ranch, riding to their place on his mule or burro after he was nearly blind.

I had made a print, a full-size giclee (SHEEclay) on canvas, of my mama's oil painting of "Uncle Bonney's Place." It depicted the cabin's overlook of the Yegua. I had taken that giclee print with us to Roy to give to Pedro. Before we left his house to go to the ranch that morning, I showed it to Alfredo. He looked at it and nodded, saying he knew exactly where the place was. The current ranch owner—descendents of the original buyer of my grandfather's ranch—had also described its location to Pedro the previous day when he called to ask permission for us to visit it and the Laumbach home place.

Alfredo asked, "What did you call him?"

I responded, "Uncle Bonney."

"You mean Ramon Boney?" (He pronounced the last name with a long O.) I had heard that Uncle Bonney, when visiting the ranch, was annoyed when Mama's siblings, especially Joyce, called him "Uncle Boney." He thought they were teasing him and sternly corrected them. "No! Tio Bonney!" Alfredo's father, Pete, had told him that his Uncle Bonney had been tough on his nephews and everyone else, even children. Once when Uncle Bonney visited the Laumbach place at Buena Vista, he was going to "whup up" on Pete, still a kid but already large and strong. To Uncle Bonney's surprise, Pete ably defended himself. Thereafter, said Alfredo's father, his uncle no longer bullied him.

Pedro and Al said the site of Ramon Bonney's place was near the state road, not far—around a curve—from Daniel and Emma's ranch house.

We parked alongside the county road, climbed over a fence and walked across a small clearing. Ahead, to the south, close to the rim-rock overlooking the canyon, were several tall pine trees that looked like those depicted in Verna's oil painting. "Very old pines, more than a hundred years old," said Alfredo. Most of the vegetation in the area was shorter and fuller bodied piñon and juniper evergreen. Pines were not common in the area, said Al. Perhaps an earlier settler had planted them, or maybe birds "planted" them long ago while eating pine nuts.

Uncle Bonney's Pines; 2010 photo

Across the small clearing, heading towards a wooded area of cedar and piñon, at a right angle from the county road, was a neat row of dirt and rocks on either side of a long slight indentation perhaps ten feet wide. Dan and I thought that was the remains of an early road that once passed Bonney's place. Perhaps Verna, in later years, had ridden on that road going to and from ranch and town and that was why she could years later recall the scene from her childhood memory and paint it with such accuracy. Al said no, it wasn't a road; Frank Hartley had made that with his big dirt-moving equipment for rainwater drainage. Perhaps to fill a shallow but broad pond, now dry, that we saw in a small clearing ahead. I wondered, could that be Uncle Bonney's pond described by Verna? She had written that Bonney had a pond near his cabin, and they could see the tops of baby pines sticking up out of the water. If that was it, said Al, Hartley made Bonney's pond bigger with his machinery, which took out the trees.

There was a huge, several-ton, thick slab of rock under one of the tall pines. I asked if that was a *tinaja* (TEEN-ah-hah)—a natural rock formation that catches rainwater, used by early settlers as a cistern. The rock had an indentation on the top surface like a basin, but it wouldn't hold much rainwater. Alfredo and Pedro said that huge rock was not naturally there under that pine. Frank Hartley had placed it there with his equipment. Hartley had moved several such rocks to select locations, perhaps "to make picnic tables and benches that would last better than wood ones." Alfredo said we would soon see two like that near what had been my grandfather's ranch house.

We walked around looking for evidence of Bonney's cabin.

Dan and I took photos from the rimrock of the huge open expanse of Yegua Cañon across from and below us—its bench formations pale pink and blue in the distance. What we saw resembled the Yegua overlook that Verna had painted from memory, which she had said was the view beyond Uncle Bonney's cabin. (*Pedro or Al may have said that day that this canyon was named Poñiente; but it was so close to the Yegua canyon behind my grandparents' place that I'm unsure which this is. I think Yegua was what my mom had called it. The word is properly spelled Llegua.*) Her painting did not depict the cabin, which she had thought was long gone; she had painted only what she thought was Bonney's rear view. *(Photo of giclee of Verna's oil painting is in Chapter 16, "A Bonney Ballad.")* The view also closely resembled her large four-foot oil painting of Cañon de Agua, at the bottom of which had lived her great-aunt Marie. *(Photo of that painting is in Chapter 27, "Never a Road.")*

From that view of the canyon and several tall pine trees, we were satisfied that we had found the place where Ramon Bonney lived, before he went to live at Pastura near the end of his life.

Nearby, to the west, was a thicket of piñon and cedar. Pedro climbed over a sagging fence of barbed wire and old bent wooden posts and walked into it, out of our sight. He soon reappeared at the edge of the woods and fence and beckoned us. He had found the ruins of Uncle Bonney's log cabin!

Alfredo at Uncle Bonney's cabin

    The rock foundation and the lower portion—four feet high in some places—remained. The corners had notched interlocking logs showing he had taken effort to build it. However, Alfredo observed that Ramon had not cared much about having a level house.

    We took many photos of the ruin that indeed did overlook the Yegua. Al pointed at a large nearby fallen pine, which he called "Verna's pine tree" that had once stood by Bonney's cabin.

    Al told us someone riding by (it had been his older brother, Ike) had found Ramon sleeping out in a clearing with his patient burro beside him, less than a mile from home. Uncle Bonney told Ike that he could not find his way to his cabin. "His burro wouldn't take him home!" said Alfredo in a peeved voice, reflecting Bonney's annoyance with his burro.

According to passed-down family stories among Laumbachs and Bonneys, Ramon was often annoyed with his burros. After that day when he was lost and confused and couldn't find his way home, Alfredo said, Daniel took Ramon to Pastura to live with his family. Actually, Daniel wrote to Ramon's family in Pastura, and they came to fetch him. His blindness made it too dangerous for him to continue living alone on the rim of the canyon. Ramon's granddaughter, Christine Ortiz, said she had heard that Daniel and Emma asked him to live with them but he refused.

When her parents were engaged, Christine Ortiz said, Anastacia may have asked Ramon to go to Pastura to meet his future son-in-law. At any rate, when Ramon was introduced to Guadalupe Campos, "Ramon took one look at [him] and told him to his face that he looked like a *tontolino* (dumbbell). Guadalupe just smiled at him." Years later, said Christine, "Anastasia received a letter from Daniel Laumbach telling her of Ramon's situation. Anastasia sent Guadalupe Campos (Amada's husband) and Santiago Bonney (Amada's brother) to pick up Ramon at Daniel Laumbbach's ranch. How ironic, Christine said; Ramon came to live with Guadalupe, the one he insulted when first introduced..." Amada and her husband took excellent care of Ramon at Pastura the remainder of his life.

My mother believed Uncle Bonney abandoned his wife and young children. According to Christine, however, Anastacia's father and uncle, brothers Tomás and José Lucero, told him to leave them because he was so hard on his family. And he did. He was considered, among those who knew him, as an ornery old man. He had been an ornery young man, too, according to many of his extended family. He was a character, perhaps not always a loveable one. Regardless, said Christine, his children loved him.

Christine—who never knew her grandfather—said Ramon had once lived near Wagon Mound with his wife, Anastacia, and their children. That was where her mother, Amada, was born. Ramon was often gone. When he was home, he was inconsiderate and hard on his family. The older boys finally told their mother they were leaving; they asked her to take the rest of the family and go with them. Instead, Anastacia complained to her father and uncle, the Lucero twins—known as *Los Quatos de Mora*. They made Ramon an offer he could not refuse. He left. He only asked to occasionally see his children. Anastacia and her children moved to Pastura.

Ramon then became even more of a vagabond. He occasionally went to Pastura. Christine described his visits, as related by her mother. Whenever Anastacia or any of the family saw Ramon sitting on his horse or mule on a certain hill, she bundled the children in their coats and sent them out to greet their father. He insisted they greet him with respectful formality, and they did. That was the case wherever he visited, including the Peter Laumbach place. Ramon expected the children of every household he visited to line up and greet him one by one. That included his family at Buena Vista, and his other extended families living at Roy and in the Canadian River Canyon country. According to Joe Lopez, Ramon's visits included his father's first New Mexico family at Watrous: the adult children of James Bonney and Maria Juana Mascarenas.

~~

On this visit this August day in 2010, I learned much from Alfredo. (I think he goes by Al or Alfred but I've called him Alfredo all my life, because my mom did.)

Our German documents show the senior Andreas was born in 1802. His son, the second Andreas, was born in 1833. The men were Germanic, born and grew to adulthood in the northern part of what would soon thereafter become Germany, but then was still part of Denmark and under its political control. From Alfredo I heard a tentative date and different version and details regarding the death by Indians in New Mexico of the elder (first) Andreas Detlef Laumbach.

Alfredo believed his great-grandfather, Andreas 1st, had been killed about 1860, and that his adult son, Andreas 2nd (father of Peter and Daniel), had witnessed it. The two men, father and son, had been in the area of northeastern New Mexico, east of where Springer is now, tending to their free-roaming cattle. The younger man had gone to get some water from the river when a band of Indians attacked his father. Out of sight, he helplessly watched the Indians kill and scalp his father. When he thought it was safe, he rode to the Mora Valley to fetch help to bury him.

When they returned, were they unable to find the body? Other family versions of this story, including from my mother, was that when family from Mora came, they could not find the spot, on a rolling hill, where the body of Andreas 1st had been hastily buried by a companion in the Taylor Springs area, east of where Springer is now. Mama had said it was on what would later become the ranch of the McAllister family, early Springer area settlers, where Ed, Matt, Viola and Lorena, our family's older neighbors on Maxwell Avenue, had grown up. What is not clear in that narrative is who had buried him. Taking time to bury him would have been dangerous if Indians were still in the area. From our perspective looking back, it seems more logical that whoever was present would have hastily taken his body back to Mora for burial. Grab the body, throw it over the horse in front of the rider and gallop away fast like in the movies. That scenario was not given in any version of his demise. My mother said that years later Daniel and Pete, as boys, returned to the area with their father, Andreas 2nd, to continue to search for the grave, but its location forever remained a mystery. According to Karl, his grandfather Pete, when passing by, always pointed out to his sons the area where his grandfather was supposed to have been buried. So, too, did Daniel. Their grandfather's death and his lost grave always troubled them.

Another conversation with Alfredo that August 2010 day brought up the subject of the Ebel family name. Alfredo firmly pronounced Ebel, his grandmother's name, the original German way, the way my family and Aunties said it, with a soft E without a hard accent on it. "I don't know why Andrés' people changed their name to Ebell," he said, referring to his uncle Andrés Ebell, Bibiana's son and full brother of Al's grandmother Elionor. I mentioned the oral family history recording in Spanish made, perhaps in the 1970s, by a descendant of Uncle Andrés', also named Andrés Ebell. I received a copy of the recording from a friend in Denver in the 1980s and gave a copy of it to Karl, who had it translated and transcribed. Neither Alfredo nor his son Pedro had heard of that audio recording.

~~

Alfredo said his father Pete went to school in Mora a total of 18 months, three six-month terms, at age 16, 17 and 18, until his teacher said he didn't need to come anymore; he had learned everything she knew. Alfredo spoke of his father with pride. He said Pete had left the Buena Vista home place with only a $1 silver piece, a burro and his mother's blessing.

In 1888, Pete had gone seeking work at a ranch owned by Oscar and Jeremy Troy, and was hired to do certain labor for a certain amount of pay. He worked hard and did the job well. The man told him he'd certainly earned his pay, he did have the money, but it was buried deep with maybe $20,000, his life's savings, somewhere over on some hill. He was too old to go dig it up. Therefore, he told Peter, he'd pay him instead with his choice of 250 rams. Alfredo said his dad was paid well. Peter took his time and picked out the best rams from the man's large flock. Peter then traded some of those rams for 750 ewes. In a year's time, he had much more—with his large flock of sheep—than what he would have had if he had been paid with money.

Pete worked for several years for the man named Troy, who paid him $16 a month. One day, a neighboring rancher, White, rode by and saw Pete building a rock wall. Pete's energetic labors impressed White, who made him an offer after asking how much money Troy was paying him. He said he'd pay him $20 a month if he'd go work for him. Pete asked White to put that offer in writing and send the letter to him at Troy's ranch. The man did. Pete showed that letter to Troy, who said, "Well then, *I'll* pay you $20 a month if you stay with me." In fact, Troy retroactively paid him $20 a month, including for the earlier months he'd worked for him. Peter continued to work for Troy for years.

Alfredo said his father, Pete, a large and powerful man, had always been a hard worker. He taught that ethic to his children, and also to keep their word—no matter how hard that might be to do. He taught them that their word was the most valuable thing they possessed, and to never squander it. People knew Pete Laumbach was an honest man, and his word was gold. He had Carte Blanc at the bank in Raton, where he could sign a note and go pay it off the next month.

Alfredo said he thought his father had arrived in this area about 1892 or 1895. His father first made an 80-acre claim at the Carruco in 1896. Before he died, he had amassed a ranch of approximately 30,000 acres, some of which was state-lease land. In arid New Mexico with sparse prairie grass, it takes many acres to nourish one beef. Alfredo said his father accomplished much in his life, especially considering that he had set out on his own at a young age with only a $1 silver piece.

After Pete died, Alfredo eventually bought out his brothers' shares of their father's estate; it was very hard, he said, with two mortgages and raising 12 kids. He built his own strong house, and still owns his father's ranch house that Pete had built with strong foundations. Both homes are still as solid as the rocks they were built with, Al said. His father's house "will be there another hundred years."

A wide canyon separated the two Laumbach brothers' ranches. When I said I hoped visiting his father's ranch with a camera would also be on our agenda, Alfredo asked, "How many days you going to be here? You can't get there today." It was then late afternoon. To go there we would have to go back to Roy and leave it heading in another direction. I agreed that visit would have to be some other day.

~~

My grandfather, Daniel, had worked for men named Wight. After the winter of 1897, Dan worked four years for Edward Wight who had a ranch on the Carrumpa[i], near Folsom, New Mexico that had a post office on it called Veda. He originally went there to work for a man named F.D. Wight, but worked for that man's nephew. Daniel next worked on a cattle ranch on the Dry Cimarron, "below Folsom" and stayed in the home of "that nice rancher's family," Verna said. (The 1900, June 14, U.S. census for "Cimarron, Union, New Mexico" shows boarders of Jose and Nestora Trujillo were: Frank Korte, born 1873; Charles Korte, born 1876; and Dan "Lambach," born "1873." (He was born in 1872.) Census entries show the fathers of all three young men were from Germany. Frank and Charles were sons of Henry and Juanita Metzger Korte. The three young boarders were not only from Mora, they were acquainted and related. Apparently they were also friendly despite on-going strife between their families at that time.) Eventually, Dan went to work for Willard Wight on his sheep ranch in southern Colorado, where he still worked when he married Emma Henkens in January 1902.

Dan's wife, Emma Margaretha Henkens, was born in a settled German community in Clinton County, Iowa in 1876. When a child, she moved with her family from Iowa to Nebraska, where Daniel, as a young man, met her years later when he traveled there by train to visit family. A courtship by letters followed, and they decided to marry. After Emma's mother and sisters helped make her wedding dress and linens for her new home, she traveled alone by train and was met at the Trinidad, Colorado train station by Daniel, his boss and the boss' wife, Mr. and Mrs. Willard Wight. Daniel was then foreman on the Wights' Colorado sheep ranch. The Wights witnessed their marriage in Trinidad that day—I believe Verna said the ceremony took place in their home—on January 24, 1902, and they served the newly-weds a fine meal that included oysters—an unfamiliar treat they did not fully appreciate.

After their marriage, Dan and Emma briefly lived at the sheep ranch in southern Colorado, 50 miles south of Las Animas where Daniel worked, until Emma was pregnant and ill. He took her to his family home at Buena Vista where his four sisters—Anna, Crestina, Mary and Leonor—could tend to her. (Crestina didn't marry and leave home until 1909.) Dan and Emma began their journey to their home-place two months after their baby, Mabel, was born. When mother and child were strong enough to travel by train from Animas, Colorado to Watrous, New Mexico, Daniel's married sister, Estefanita

Candelario of Santa Fe, came to make that train journey with them. Daniel traveled from the Colorado sheep ranch to Watrous by wagon, transporting the young couple's meager household furnishings. From Watrous, the new family traveled by wagon to Dan's claim, arriving the day after Christmas, almost one year after their marriage.

The area he settled on at the Encierro had once been part of the private Pablo Montoya Land Grant. As happened with most New Mexico grants, the Montoya family soon lost their land. A large portion of it became known as the Bell Ranch, because of the bell-shaped mesa formation on it. The Jesús (heyZUS) Montoya family had earlier squatted on what would become my grandfather Dan's ranch, and built log cabins and rock structures including walls, but never filed a claim and had abandoned the area. When Daniel reached the required age of 21 to file a claim, he filed on this land that he had coveted for years because of the nearby springs. Some of the Jesús Montoya structures remained. The Montoyas had built the original log cabin, which Daniel later torn down, and the rock house that is still there in 2010.

Little by little over the next years, Daniel and Emma developed and expanded their property until it became a large ranch by most standards even in New Mexico. My mother wrote that he eventually owned 10,000 acres, and leased more than 700 additional acres.

For several reasons, Daniel had to sell his ranch around 1945. His health was failing and, according to several recent sources, he could not keep hired hands on the ranch because of external influences that undermined him when he was too old and ill to run the ranch alone. He finally had to sell it. Daniel and Emma, hoping the ranch would remain in their family, wanted their sons and sons-in-law to buy it, to be managed by those with ranching experience. They had envisioned, like most ranchers and farmers do, that the land they worked hard to develop would pass on in perpetuity within their family, from their children to their grandchildren. Times were tough and Daniel's children could not buy the ranch, even at the offered bargain price. Besides, only one had ranching experience; the others did not want to be ranchers. In the end, he sold the ranch by the acre, with all the cattle, horses and other livestock, tools, implements, home and outbuildings on the land thrown into the deal. Daniel only lived a couple years after that. He died in 1947 at about age 75.

Aunties—Daniel's maiden sisters—had likewise hoped some of their nephews would together buy their home place at Buena Vista so it could remain in the family, but that place, too, sold to outsiders not long after Daniel had sold his ranch.

There is a great distance, now perhaps 200 miles by car, between the family home at Buena Vista in Mora County and the remote Encierro where Daniel settled in San Miguel County. It was an especially great distance then, even without fences, traveling by horseback or in wagons pulled by teams of horses. In my mother's early youth, as she described it in her writings, it still took two days by wagon. Yet, the Laumbach men, Andreas 2nd and his three sons, Peter, Daniel and Henry, rode horseback all over that Canadian River canyon country and the open prairies within and above it, and ran cattle there, before the turn of the last century.

Daniel had first come to that area with his father, running cattle when he was ten with his uncle, Andres Ebell. When he was about 12, he spent a summer there alone with his father's cattle.

In the late 1960s or early 1970s, my mother and I went to the old family place at Buena Vista, then owned by the Lorenz Shocks, a Texas family. The Shocks were gracious, hospitable people. Before our visit, they had extensively remodeled and added onto the house, and added an unattached six-car garage. When workmen tore into the adobe walls of the main house, Mrs. Shock said, they found a letter written by Daniel in formal Spanish to his mother, Elionor, at Buena Vista. Mrs. Shock gave my mother the letter Daniel had written, when he had stayed alone, as a boy, in the Encierro.

Daniel had just his horse and his dog, tending his father's herd of cattle in the remote area where, years later, he proved up on the land that would become his ranch. Perhaps part of the deal with his father then had been that he would thus earn ownership of some of those cattle with which he would one day begin his own herd. That summer, Daniel lived in a cave, ate sauerkraut from a keg, and practiced his shooting skills by aiming at old tin cans left behind by earlier campers.

Daniel grew to love the area during his stay that summer, the beautiful canyon country and the open prairies on the mesas where he envisioned his cattle would someday freely roam and feed on the abundant gamma grass. Years later, he homesteaded the land, which eventually became his extensive ranch holdings, a large portion down in the canyon floor and a larger portion on the prairie of the mesa above. Before that, however, Daniel and his brother, Peter, and even Henry in those early days, ran cattle there, and his maiden sisters homesteaded a portion of the land, building rustic cabins to comply with the Homestead Act. Daniel later bought his sisters' claims. In earlier years, Daniel's Uncle Andrés Ebell ran cattle in that country and sometimes Daniel worked for him.

Karl had found a court record showing Andreas Detlef Laumbach 2nd, father of Pete and Dan, had filed a pre-emptive claim in 1902—1903 on the Carruco, in the area that his son Peter later owned, so even their father had been interested in owning land in this area. (A pre-emptive claim enabled a man, by paying a certain sum to the government, to buy a parcel of federal land on which he'd been living or making improvements.)

According to Verna, for a while brothers Pete, Daniel and Henry, sometimes also their uncle Andrés, owned the cattle pastured there on shares. Eventually Daniel bought out his brothers' shares.

Before Daniel arrived with his new family, Peter was living there, with Fidelia and their first-born little ones, watching over Daniel's cattle with his own. Verna said her father later built another small log cabin, between Montoya's original log cabin that Dan tore down and the rock house that Pete and Fidelia had improved. Pete first lived in the original log cabin. After he married, he and Fidelia lived in the rock house while their own ranch home was being built. That was where Pete and Fidelia were living when Daniel arrived with his new wife, Emma, and baby Mabel the day after Christmas 1902. Those first months, Daniel and his new family lived in that first log cabin, and Pete and his family lived in the rock house. Daniel, Emma and baby moved into the three-room rock house after Pete and Fidelia moved to their own claim on the Carruco. They lived there with their growing family for 13 years, until their newer rock house, which became their final ranch home, was built.

At the Ranch

That day in 2010, we returned to the car, leaving Uncle Bonney's place, and drove a short distance down the private ranch road to what had been Daniel and Emma's home place. When we approached and I saw it, I was almost overwhelmed with nostalgia. For more than half a century, the ranch had not belonged to family. Because of poor health, my grandfather reluctantly sold it in 1945, when I was about four, to Frank Hartley. Members of that family still own it. This was the first time I had been there, except as a wee child with vague memories, and once when Mama and I briefly visited it in the 1960s by Fern Hartley's invitation.

On this August day, the home place was unoccupied and looked as if it had been uninhabited for years, no doubt for lack of water. Its springs and well had dried up years ago. However, Alfredo and Pedro told us a younger member of the Hartley family had lived there not too long ago, and we saw a few abandoned children's toys outside.

Dan parked the car, Pedro opened the gate, and we walked into the front yard. Dan commandeered the camera. The first picture he took was of the outhouse! To the left and behind the main dwelling was an old, small rock cabin-like structure, still in fairly good shape, which I could not identify. Apparently all of the old Laumbach ranch buildings remained. This was the only one I did not recognize from Mama's descriptions and paintings. I guessed it had been the family's washhouse where they bathed and did their laundry.

Laumbachs' bath house?

The other structures were easy for me to identify. First, or in the foreground to the left, was a long rock building with a porch, one of the earliest structures on the ranch, according to Mama, confirmed today by Alfredo. That was where the Daniel Laumbach family had lived and later used as the bunkhouse and schoolhouse.

A photo had been taken of an elderly Uncle Bonney standing in front of this rock building, beside his mule-pulled wagon, which was green with red trim. In his last years living near the ranch, when he was nearly blind, Uncle Bonney no longer used his wagon; he rode his mule or donkey between the ranch and his cabin.

Root Cellar

Behind the rock house was a structure, still roofed, half below ground, with steep cement steps leading into its dark subterranean interior. "That was my grandmother's cellar," I said with certainty, "where they kept their food—apples, potatoes and other root vegetables, her jars of canned stews, vegetables, fruit, tomato-lemon preserves, jerky and cracklings. This was also where they hung their fresh meat." Being partially a dugout, it was naturally insulated from extreme temperatures, used as a cold room—a necessity for keeping foodstuffs edible year round in those days of no refrigeration. Alfredo said he remembered Daniel's family had an icehouse where they packed straw around chunks of winter ice from the pond. "Because they knew how to do it, they had ice cream in August." That dugout was probably also their icehouse. Throughout her life, Mama had a weakened wrist, which she said was from a childhood fall down steep cellar steps at the ranch.

They had a good orchard, Alfredo said. Daniel was particular about his apples. "I picked apples for him twice as a boy. If an apple fell or was bumped, Daniel said 'throw it on the ground'; he wanted none that were not perfect. He was also particular about how those apples were stored so they would keep, carefully packed in straw, crisp and juicy for a year."

My only childhood memories—for I must have been little more than a toddler when those places were sold—was sensory, of both my grandfather's ranch and the home place at Buena Vista where grandfather's maiden sisters lived until they grew too old to keep it. Those memories were of the wonderful aromas of garlic and *chile*-spiced jerky (dried meat), dried slices of apples and pears, dried plums, grapes and currents, and cracklings—pieces of pork skins, high in cholesterol by today's standards—fried to a delectable rich, crispy crunch. They were the tasty and useful by-products after rendering lard to fry foods and make lye soap.

To the right in the foreground was a small log cabin structure, which Alfredo said was one of the two oldest buildings on the ranch. That was the one Daniel built to replace the original log cabin built by the Jesús Montoya family; it was where he and Emma and their baby first lived before they moved to the rock house.

Alfredo told us two stories he had heard regarding that earlier log cabin, now long gone.

The second log cabin at the ranch, this one built by Daniel.

Peter, as a young single man, lived there in 1897. He was riding home from the Yegua Canyon with his starving dog, and came upon 25 wild burros. Peter shot two of them, and went to the log house to get a knife to butcher them. When he rode up to the place, he saw two strangers sitting there in the shade. "Howdy," was all they said. Peter cut open the burros for his hungry dog, and cut off and skinned a hind leg and brought it back to the cabin. That night he fed the strangers supper. They were gone early the next morning. "Guess they didn't want burro for breakfast," said Alfredo dryly, probably quoting his father.

Peter had first lived in the original log cabin before he married, said Al. Before Pete went to bed one night, he tied his burro with a rope and staked him outside near the cabin and his horses so he could find him in the morning. A racket, the burro's loud urgent braying, woke him in the night. "That burro thought he was a gonner," said Alfredo, probably quoting his father. Pete stood in the doorway of the cabin with his 55-70 caliber rifle and saw a wolf hunkered down close, staring at the burro with her golden eyes. With only moonlight to see by, Pete fired at the wolf once. The wolf ran off into the trees. Peter thought he had missed. The next morning, in the daylight, he followed a blood trail into the trees and found the wolf dead, gut-shot. Not a bad 100-yard shot with peep-sights by the light of the moon, said Alfredo, of his father's accuracy.

He asked me, "Did you hear about Daniel waltzing with a wolf?" I had not. "Daniel was riding a green yearling—a barely broke horse. He sees a wolf eating a live calf. He fired his rifle, shot all eight shots at the wolf, later wished he hadn't. He figured he'd seriously wounded or killed the wolf. He got off his horse, tied him good with a rope he had with him, and went into the trees on foot after the wolf.

No wolf. He returned to where he had tied his horse, saw the injured, furious wolf hunkered down on his belly, ready to jump on the terrified horse jerking at the rope. Daniel fired his gun again; it just clicked, didn't fire. The wolf jumped Dan. He grabbed that wolf by both ears and hung on for life, with the wolf's gaping jaws inches from his face. He said that was the biggest mouth of teeth he'd ever seen. Daniel hung onto that wolf's ears until it bled out. He'd gut-shot him when he'd first fired his rifle."

Behind the log cabin, we saw the house, stucco over rock, with a pitched roof of weathered wooden shake and small gabled windows that gave summer ventilation to the attic where the Laumbachs' smaller children had slept. The well—windmill missing its blades—and an old collapsed wooden water tank stood near the kitchen door, a little aside of the house. Mama said the family had first dug a pond to catch rainwater in front of the house. Later, her papa dug that well. One of her oil paintings shows the pond; a subsequent painting shows the pond filled in, with that well conveniently near the kitchen door. Al said the driller dug several wells on the ranch for Dan, all dry. Finally he offered to dig one more, for free, near the house where he was certain he would hit water from the spring. Alfredo said he believed Hartley had decades later dug the well we saw that day, on the opposite side of the house and kitchen door, replacing my grandfather's that had probably run dry. The lawn and flowers Fern Hartley wanted required a lot of water. Soon thereafter, the well and all the springs dried up; so, too, the newer well. They were already dry when Mama and I visited there almost 50 years ago. The dried up spring down the trail had saddened her.

Further to the right of the house were the stables, barn and sheds surrounded by a metal pipe fence that, in the Laumbachs' day, had been wooden.

Inside the barn, its front wall or doors missing, we saw a small green, with red trim, open horse-drawn wagon with one seat or bench wide enough for two people and a boxed space behind to haul feed, groceries, and children—an early-day pickup. It had large wooden-spokes, iron-clad wheels, and a wooden wagon tongue. The entire conveyance was in surprisingly good shape. Alfredo and Pedro thought it was in too good of shape; it could not be old enough to have belonged to our Uncle Bonney, or to my grandfather and his family before they had motorized vehicles. If it had been carefully preserved and kept in the barn out of weather, they conceded to my hopeful wish, it might be that old, but they clearly doubted it. I said, perhaps it had been refurbished for Roy events and parades. I like to think it had been Uncle Bonney's, or the one Mama described in which her family traveled to and from Roy for shopping in their early ranch days. One of those trips was for the wow factor of seeing an airplane, but it never materialized.

The rimrock of the canyon began just yards behind the house. A trail wandered steeply down the canyon wall to the left, probably the original trail described by Mama that led to the springs below the house. Beside that trail was a deep, sharply defined gouge cut into the mountainside, too steep and deeply cut to be a trail, unless it once had steps. Beside it, edges almost level with the rimrock, was a rock-lined deep boxy hole, maybe six feet across and at least that deep, with a couple buried pipes leading into or out of it, which probably fed water to it from the spring. One pipe may have gone from there to the house. This, I knew, was the cistern of Verna's childhood. It was now a gaping hole without a cover.

Looking up at the house from the steep spring trail.

While we stood there, Alfredo had his back to the canyon and that cistern. I reached out, touching his arm, cautioning him to not take one step back because the rim-rock ledge was just behind him.

"I'll only do it once," he said.

Another example of Alfredo's droll wit: I told him there was a big bug on the crown of his hat, and to my husband he said, "Well, shoot it with your .45, Dan."

We picnicked on a huge, oblong flat-topped rock under a piñon, one of two large rocks in the yard that Alfredo and Pedro said Hartley had mechanically hauled in and placed there for Fern. The one we used was large enough for all four of us to sit upon and spread out a tablecloth and food, with ample space left over.

I asked Alfredo about the "TV country" that had been a portion of my grandfather's ranch on the prairie, which my Uncle Joyce later bought from him. That TV became Joyce's own ranch where he lived with his wife, Vera, and their small children until Vera died. After she died, three of their children, Bill, Fay Ann and Vera Jane, were raised by Vera's sister. Their fourth child, Jack, was raised by Emma until her death. Then Jack lived with his father at the ranch. Joyce continued to live at his ranch, and later also in Roy, until the last years of his life.

Alfredo said the name "TV" had come from the brand used by people who had earlier settled the area. In his booklet, *Some History and I Remember*, Joyce wrote that the TV valley or area was named for the brand used by a family named Tipton who dug the TV well and lived here for a time before moving to Tiptonville near Watrous. They were the same family for whom that community was named.

We walked around the old ranch buildings that August day in 2010, while I identified them from my mother's stories and paintings. I imagined what it had been like when my mother and her family had lived there.

I also recalled the story Al and his brother Pete had told me several years earlier about my grandmother: It seemed that every Monday, which just happened to be the day their mail was delivered at the ranch, Dan and Emma's hens laid no eggs. One Monday morning, Emma saw the mailman go into the hen house. She sneaked up, slammed the door shut and put a horseshoe nail through the hasp, locking it from the outside. Many hours later, when Daniel came home to supper, Emma said casually, "Daniel, there's a man in the chicken house." Daniel said, "What man? Let's go see." They went to see. Dan unfastened and opened the door to the chicken house; out rushed the embarrassed and miserable mailman. From then on, their hens laid eggs every day, even on Mondays, said Alfredo and Pete.

Alfredo, remembering when he was a boy visiting his uncle Daniel's ranch, said he watched a hired hand work on construction of the family's new house. As he watched, the rock wall began to topple. The nimble worker, said Alfredo, walked right up the wall as it came down. He ended up on top of the wall instead of it on top of him.

Alfredo said families didn't socialize in those days. The families of the two brothers, Daniel and Peter, seldom got together. However, the men gathered for shared ranch work like roundup and branding. As the crow flies, their ranches were maybe seven or ten miles apart, but La Cinta, a deep rugged canyon, lay between them. Pete's ranch was down in La Cinta Canyon. It was a long, hard ride on horseback in those days. To illustrate distances and the breadths of the canyons: From where we stood that day, looking east, Alfredo pointed at a distant blue point against the far horizon and said, "That is Poñiente Point, at the end of Poñiente Canyon."

Alfredo told a story that aptly describes the innards of the rugged Canadian gorge. Years ago, an easterner came; he was interested in buying some land. He was dismayed to find it was mostly steep, upended rock canyon walls. "Well," drawled the seller to the easterner, "you can use both sides."

When a traveler heads to Roy, going east from Wagon Mound, the floor of the fairly flat prairie seems to suddenly crack open into a deep, sharply cut gorge, with rugged, towering rock palisades cut by the Canadian River. It was called the Red River (*Rio Rojo or Rio Colorado*) by earlier settlers because the water turned red, when roiled, from the terracotta-colored soil and rock pigment. Alfredo firmly said it is a gorge, not a canyon. The canyons are all the large pockets that expand from the gorge. Even now, when crossing the gorge, heading east from Wagon Mound, driving on a good two-lane paved road, the descent is sudden and rapid from the top to the bottom, with sharp curves and hairpin turns. It ascends the same way up the other side. There are almost no shoulders on which to pull over to admire the view or catch your breath or take a picture. I can only imagine how difficult, even dangerous, crossing that gorge must have been in the early days of wagons and horses over rough-cut roads, and before that, on one-track trails that horses could barely navigate. Within the Canadian River gorge in that area are wide, deep canyons with unique names like the Encierro (AN-cee-A-rro), La Cinta (Lah-CEEN-tah), Llegua (YAH-wah), Poñiente (PO-nee-An-ta), Cuesta (Cu-AS-ta), Cato (CA-to), Cañon de Agua (Can-YON de AH-wah), and Cañon Largo (Can-YON LAHR-go)—which is "further down, the western part of the river, toward Sabinoso," said Alfredo.

When I was trying to pronounce Poñiente, Alfredo reminded me that in Spanish, "We don't waste letters, we use all of them." That is a good rule to remember when pronouncing Spanish words. They don't have silent vowels, unlike with English.

In the bottom of one of those canyons created by the Canadian had lived Daniel's Aunt "Marie," Maria Marta "Mariita" Ebel, who had married Felipe Esquibel. She was a full sister of Andrés Ebell and Elionor Ebel Laumbach—mother of Peter and Daniel. Aunt Marie's story is told in this book by my mother in her fictionalized story, "Never a Road." The canyon where Aunt Marie had lived was called Red River Canyon, and also Cañon de Agua. Aunt Marie lived about seven miles from my grandparents' ranch, but when my mother and her siblings were young, that distance might as well have been a hundred miles because of the difficulty of travel in those days, the rugged terrain, and where she lived at the bottom of that steep-walled canyon that had no road.

At Watrous, south and a little west of Wagon Mound, two rivers joined—the Rio Mora and the Sapello, the reason for the original name of La Junta (the "meeting" or joining of the two rivers). La Junta was also the meeting or joining of two branches of the Santa Fe Trail. It was the name of an early settlement at the river junction, perhaps 20 miles north of Las Vegas. Several rivers in northern New Mexico, including the Mora, flow into the Canadian.

Alfredo named two additional rivers that emptied into the Canadian "up the river a ways" from where we were that day. Did the emptying of rivers into the Canadian contribute towards its might, eons ago, that created that gorge? Mills Canyon, miles further north from where we were that day, is a better known picturesque canyon of the Canadian River. It was developed—with a fine home and orchards—by attorney Melvin Mills, a business associate of Thomas B. Catron. Mills' development was totally destroyed one of the few times in modern history when the Canadian River flooded.

The Canadian is the largest tributary of the Arkansas River, flowing from southern Colorado, passing through portions of several states. It flows approximately 100 miles through northeastern New Mexico. Its deep gorge begins southeast of Springer, zig-zagging where it had cut deeply through the caprock formation for many miles south to Sabinoso, where the steep cliffs end and the river flows onto the state's eastern plains.

~~

Alfredo told another story that August day. He said his father had heard his brother Daniel had made a deal with someone about the dry-ice gas wells on his ranch. Ranchers consider it a near-disaster if carbon dioxide is the only result when drilling for water. Carbon dioxide (CO_2) does not sustain life; it has no use to ranchers. Its only value is IF—a costly venture—it can be converted to dry ice, its solid, extremely cold form, for commercial purposes. Peter told his son, Alfredo, to ride to the ranch and ask Daniel what kind of deal he'd made for those gas wells.

After a long hard ride across the canyons, at last Alfredo knocked on the ranch house door late in the day. Emma went to the door. "Who are you?" she asked. "Pete Laumbach's son," he answered in the gathering darkness. She left him outside, closed the door, and called, "Daniel, there's a man at the door."

"Who is it?"

"Maybe one of Pete's boys."

"Well, tell him to come in!"

Alfredo explained to his Uncle Daniel why his father had sent him. Daniel said, "We talk business daytime, it's now nighttime. Emma, feed this boy." The next morning after a good night's sleep, Daniel and Alfredo talked a lot of business over a good breakfast.

Aunt Lola—Dolores Metzger, one of Bibiana's and Frederick Metzger's three daughters—married Manuel Cordova. They homesteaded on land near Daniel's place. Alfredo's older brother, Ike (Casimiro), had earlier told me that my grandfather bought the land, which adjoined his, from the Cordovas when they moved away.

I asked Alfredo about our Aunt Lola who had once lived near our families. He shook his head. "I don't know [*much*] about her." Alfredo was too young to have known her when she lived in the area. Pedro said there is a place nearby called Cordova on other privately owned land. Perhaps that is the place. "We can drive on the county road and see that land from there." However, we had no time to even do a drive-by this day.

Alfredo said his father and sons were at Daniel's place helping with roundup and branding when word came that his mother, Fidelia, was dying. Apparently knowing in advance that she was ill, Emma had already gone to tend to her. Alfredo said Emma was there, with his just-deceased mother, when their family arrived. (Karl said his uncles compared their hurried journey home that day to the opening scene of Bonanza: The Laumbach men rode hard, often at a gallop, in their rush home to La Cinta.) Fidelia, who had birthed 17 children and nurtured 12 who survived birth and childhood, died that August day in 1928.

Peter Joseph Laumbach, Alfredo's father, outlived her by many years, dying February 26, 1954. I remember sitting with family in the evening beside my great-uncle Pete's casket. That was still the custom—not leaving the deceased alone until burial. His funeral would be the next day in Roy. Even in death, Pete was an impressively large man, not only from my childish perspective; I would have just turned 13. Uncle Pete's hair was originally red. Lying there, he still had a head full of thick white hair and a white mustache. I remember his hands at rest on his chest, the biggest I had ever seen. He was known as a powerful man by anyone's standard, in his prime and even in his old age. He was that even in death.

Peter was the biggest of Elionor's three sons.

~~

Several times that August day in 2010, Pedro and Alfredo mentioned an unwanted tree or growth they called tamarack. That was an unfamiliar name to me. They explained it is also called willow or salt cedar, which especially grows along waterways, sucking up moisture desperately needed by residents, animals and crops. We in southeastern New Mexico are too familiar with the despised salt cedar. Not native to this country, it was accidentally or foolishly introduced like many other non-native species of the animal and plant kingdoms that later play havoc with the lives and livelihoods of man.

When we were leaving what had once been my grandparents' place, Alfredo asked if I would like to see where my uncle, Joyce, first lived. He said originally that was the only place where a drilled well hit water. Joyce chose that location for his first home because of the well and its nearness to his parents. Alfredo said Dan and Emma's orchard and garden—near that well now also dried up—had been where Joyce later established his first place. That interested me. Mama had written about walking—she, her mama and her sisters—to that garden to plant, weed, water, and gather produce. We drove the short distance up the road to where Ray Hartley's widow Ruth lived. Her house had fine rockwork facing. It was a short drive that day but would have been a long walk from my grandparents' home for the young family to spend hours daily tending to a garden there during many months of each cultivating and growing season.

Returning from the ranch to Roy late that day, we saw, fairly close on the wooded flatlands, a large beige-colored Barbary ram with curling horns beside his face. We also saw a magnificent bull elk with a huge rack, and his harem. Then, within minutes, we saw rattlesnakes lying flat out, stretched across the gravel road absorbing its warmth. Being ranchers and kin of ranchers, we stopped. Pedro killed the first one with a well-aimed rock to the head. We deliberately ran over the second one. With a shovel from the trunk, Pedro cut off the rattles of both snakes for trophies. The first one had twelve buttons. Alfredo explained that you don't count the black ones, so officially it was ten buttons. The second had nine buttons not counting the black ones nearest the snake's body. Alfredo said, "They always have the black ones." A snake has another button every time he sheds his skin, which might be more than once a year. Therefore, he said, the number of buttons does not necessarily tell you his age in years, but it comes close. He added, "Sometimes if you open a dead snake quick, out crawls a bunch of baby snakes. They are born alive, crawl out of an egg sack."

In addition to the types of critters we saw that day, Pedro and Alfredo said the area still has wolves, mountain lions, bobcats and deer. And bears! Pedro worked for the county; he had recently left his grader beside the county road. When he returned to it the next morning, he saw large bear tracks, "size twelve," he quipped, that circled the grader. Pedro had not realized—until Hartley described the location of the Bonney place we wanted to visit that next day—that he had parked the grader by the clearing near Uncle Bonney's cabin.

(In June 2014, Alfredo shot and killed a 200-pound, eight-foot-long—counting tail—mountain lion near his ranch house at La Cinta.)

Besides the unique treat of visiting my grandparents' ranch and finding Uncle Bonney's cabin, on our return to Roy, we had sighted an impressive ram, a noble elk, and rattlers basking in the sunshine.

~~

I told Pedro I hoped this visit would trigger more memories for his father. I want this Laumbach book to have input from him, from his point of view, as well as his brothers.

"You know they will be different. You listen to all of them. Then you pick the one you like best," Alfredo said.

"No," I said. "I want all of them; all are equally important. I want your stories as you tell them your way. Our stories all came from different sources and at different times in our lives. That, I think, is the importance of oral history, recognizing how family history evolves down through generations, and as told by a variety of storytellers. Each will be different. All of these stories need to be preserved for future generations.

~~

This book was to end with our grandparents' generation, but I could not resist adding a little about Pete's grown children in an earlier chapter. Here is a brief overview of Dan's.

Joyce (born February 4, 1905, died December 20, 1991), married to Vera Walker until her death in August 1945, had a ranch near his parents' in the TV country. His was on the grasslands below the mesas. He wrote, and Floersheim's Press in Roy printed, several little booklets. *Some History and I Remember* and *Newspapers Etc.* have, for me, informative bits of family and local history. Joyce personally typed those on an old upright typewriter in his later years at the ranch and Roy, despite having only a thumb and forefinger to type with on one of his hands.

Alida (born March 23, 1907, died November 8, 1994) married Elbert Wallace; she was a teacher in Mosquero for a little while; most of her life and most of her teaching years were spent in Roy. When she retired, the little Roy community gave her a big send-off. They turned out the lights in the filled gym and each of her students lit a candle. The entire gym was aglow.

Verna (born October 8, 1909, died May 23, 1996) married Dal Sparks from Oklahoma. She taught in Springer for many years and moved to Roswell in her later years. She painted New Mexico scenes in water colors and oils, wrote poetry when she was young, and always loved family history.

Frances (born March 27, 1912, died December 24, 1992) married Leon Shinn, a World War II veteran of the Battle of the Bulge, with two small boys from a prior marriage. Frances and Leon made many moves during their marriage but finally settled in Bosque Farms south of Albuquerque where they, especially Leon, painted in oils and had an art gallery.

Ruth (born May 13, 1914, died November 14, 1995) was an army nurse during World War II and served overseas. Her sweetheart was missing in action during the war. She never married. I wrote an essay about her, which was published in the Roswell Web Magazine. I provide a small overview below.

Daniel Chester (born January 15, 1916, died April 16, 1996) married Juanita of Las Lunas, and they had three children. They lived a while in California where Daniel worked on the dairy farm of actor Fred McMurray. He lived a few of his later years in Oregon. Most of his life was spent in New Mexico, primarily the Las Lunas area. Daniel was a dairyman most of his life.

~~

Ruth had been a surgical nurse in California. Then Pearl Harbor happened. Ruth was 27 years old. Her medical training and experience made her valuable at that time of war.

She took her oath on June 30, 1941, joining the U.S. Army at Letterman General Hospital, appointed to the Army Nurse Corps. One month later, she was assigned to active duty as a 2nd Lieutenant. On December 31, 1941—24 days after Pearl Harbor was bombed and we entered the war—she was assigned to an "extension of active Federal service for the period of the war and for the six (6) months immediately following its termination, unless sooner relieved by the President." She was issued a steel helmet, a gas mask and subsequent training; "gas chambers completed." Her assignments initially included being an attending nurse traveling between hospitals with some of the war's first casualties shipped stateside. Then she qualified with weapons and prepared to ship out to an undisclosed destination, "per Secret Movements," according to her military records. Before she departed, her mother Emma, sister Verna and small nephew Jerry traveled by train from New Mexico to San Francisco to say goodbye.

Ruth crossed the continent by train and boarded a troop ship, departing USA shores from Boston Harbor. She tended to her first overseas patients in England, was later transported to the Philippines by troop ship. The ship convoy's roundabout journey took 43 days to avoid shipping lanes where torpedoes were a known hazard. She arrived in Panama in time to hear the news of the Japanese surrender. In the Philippines, she and other nurses were taken to a staging area where they were fenced in for their safety. Daily, someone with a sense of humor played a cowboy recording of *Don't Fence Me In* over the loudspeaker. (That same song was played at the funeral of Ruth's father, Daniel, in 1947 in the little prairie town of Roy.) Ruth and her fellow Army nurses cared for survivors of the Bataan Death March and other casualties of war. Some snipers did not know or chose to ignore news of the war's end; they remained a danger in the area. A sniper shot and killed a fellow nurse.

Ruth became a casualty while stationed in the Philippines. She was also shot, but the gun that disabled her was an unexpected kind; it could even be called "friendly fire." She was shot with an inoculation gun. Decades later, I read in her military papers that, while in Luzon Philippines, she received "0.5 cc plague inoculation," and a little more than a week later, she received "1.0 cc plague inoculation." I thought that was the shot that did her in. Ruth said, no, not that one. In the Philippines, the Army asked volunteers to take a new experimental vaccine for the influenza that was killing tens of thousands. She had an immediate reaction after receiving the shot; she could not walk or use her arms. She was transferred to various hospitals until she was flown to Hawaii, then to stateside, ultimately ending up back at William Beaumont General, as a patient instead of a nurse. She spent months there flat on her back. She had been a trained and experienced surgical nurse, requiring her to daily stand for hours. She could no longer do that. She was retrained as a public health nurse while still under a doctor's care in the Army. She remained on sick leave until she received her final Army retirement, separation and medical discharge with the rank of Captain in May 1947.

Flu, like many other illnesses and diseases, is no longer as dreaded as it once was, thanks to medical technologies and those who risk their health and lives for experimentation to save others—reflecting the heroism of uniformed people serving their country.

Over subsequent years, Ruth's chronic illness from that shot was diagnosed as various nerve disorders, including sciatic neuritis and peripheral neuropathy, a degenerative disease of the nerves. Although she was a disabled World War II veteran, she received little Army compensation other than being retrained as a public health nurse. She was a self-sufficient wage earner for decades while living in Bernalillo and Albuquerque.

She lived her last decade in Roswell near me; her final years in a small apartment in a retirement facility. I was her caregiver and first responder in times of crisis. She had several. At age 81, while in a deplorable nursing home for temporary convalescence, a therapist carelessly broke both bones below one knee. An employee told me she and other staff clearly heard her bones snap. So did Ruth. Despite knowing their responsibility for her injury, the nursing home unkindly and severely neglected her that day and the following days, weeks and months. Thereafter she was often in crisis. Because of her lack of care there, I stayed with her non-stop many days and nights. At the same time, my mother lived with us. I felt I was neglecting her for Ruth, but Mama was doing well and was still fairly independent.

I was finally able to get Ruth out of that nursing home, back to her little apartment with full-time home health care. But that added considerable cost and soon her money was gone. She would soon be on Medicaid and could no longer live there. Her only option would be a nursing home.

Ruth was having one of her good days when I had to give her this news. I cried. She calmly patted my hand and said, "It will be okay, you'll see."

I know she asked God to let the choice be hers. And He did. A few hours later, she went to sleep and never woke up.

My mother, Verna, died six months after Ruth. Between them, their brother, Daniel, died. The last three children of Daniel and Emma were gone within six months.

Except Mabel (born October 24, 1902, died April 5, 1922), all seven of their children lived at least 80 years.

---

[i] Corrumpa is the more commonly accepted spelling, an Indian word meaning wild. Located in northeastern New Mexico in Union County, it was an early settlement on the Corrumpa Creek. The FDW Ranch was later established there by Frederick D. W. Wright, according to Google, and had a post office from 1905 to 1919. The creek flowed into the Canadian. It was first named McNees Creek by travelers on the Santa Fe Trail for a young man named McNees who was murdered there in 1828, six years after William Becknell had crossed it. McNees, and another man who died soon after, were attacked there by Indians, the first known deaths on the Trail.

SECTION IV: LAUMBACHS IN NEW MEXICO

Chapter 39: Buena Vista, Mora, La Cebolla 2013
by Jan Girand

In mid-summer 2013, my daughter Tracy Ikenberry and I visited Mora, the community of La Cebolla now known as Ledoux, and I presume also La Cebolleta (La Cebollita), which I think is what Alvin called that small valley en route to Ledoux. That was a brief one-day-excursion. We went with Alvin Korte, grandson of Eduardo Korte—who was a son of Juanita Metzger and Henry Korte.

From State Road 518, we turned west onto a narrow two-lane gravel road to a little valley before heading on to La Cebolla/Ledoux. Almost immediately after turning onto that road, before us was a high open valley with a cleared *vega*. The small Cebolla River—aka Rita de Cebolla, about the size of an *acequia* accented by brush—geographically runs several miles mostly west and east of Buena Vista. Alvin told us that Frederich Metzger had owned ranch land on both sides of La Cebolla River to the top of a mesa to the northeast, which he pointed out to us that day. At that crest and down the other side and beyond, the land had belonged to Henry Korte, he said. That was according to an archived affidavit with land description he found in Santa Fe, confirmed by his hand-held GPS device.

In the middle of the aforementioned *vega* (grassland or meadow) was what appeared from our distance as a patch of dirt, a grassless area. It was adobe melt. When he was a boy of 10 or 12, back when more of that adobe ruin remained, it was pointed out to him by his father or grandfather (I don't remember which of them he said). Alvin said that was where Frank Metzger had his ranch house, where Apolonia might have lived with him for a while.

Below, camera aimed westward toward Ledoux. Foreground is some of the "adobe melt" that was once a home. Three dying trees seen at left are all that remain of an apple orchard. This photo was taken later, in October 2013, by Tracy Ikenberry when accompanied by Chick Burney, manager of the Buena Vista Ranch, which included this property. Is that the Gap of the Crestón seen in the distance?

"Originally?" I asked, "Or when?" Juanita was born to Apolonia and Metzger in 1849; they later separated. He was with Bibiana for at least seven years, and then returned to Apolonia.

Alvin had found an 1846 Santa Fe newspaper article that mentioned Metzger. Records show Frank Metzger was in the Mora area no later than 1848. Based upon the birth of Maria Juana "Juanita" in 1849, he and Apolonia were probably together, the first time, soon after he arrived in Mora.

Metzger established his fine ranch home at Buena Vista (now the Abel ranch property). Verna said Metzger's home had been a large, two-story adobe with balconies, perhaps what would now be called New Mexico's territorial style. Apolonia probably lived there with him for several years, before and after 1849, until they separated. Metzger later gave the Buena Vista place to his daughter and her husband, Henry, and he lived at his rancho at Cebolla,

We have few clues. We can only speculate about times and places and situations during this period of their lives. We don't know how long Apolonia had been separated from Bernardo before she and Metzger joined together. We do not know how long Apolonia and Metzger were first together, or exactly when or why they separated. Our only clue was the date 1858 when Doloritas Metzger was born to him and Bibiana.

Census and other records seem to indicate that Bibiana lived with her father and family at La Cebolla, where Apolonia had also lived a while with Bernardo after they moved across the mountains. I wish we knew exactly where that particular La Cebolla was where Bernardo settled, where he and three generations of his family, including Bibiana and Elionor, had lived. New Mexico genealogy records show multiple places with the name Cebolla within the Mora area. Bernardo and his family could have lived at any of those places, presuming they were different locations, or at the still existing settlement or village of Ledoux, which was known as La Cebolla until around 1906.

To add to the confusion, Karl and his branch of family indicate that the same ruin site identified by Alvin as being Metzger's was where their grandfather Pete was born. They believe his mother, Elionor, stayed with Bibiana, at least during her "time of confinement."

At this time, all that remains—like that slight mound of adobe dirt—is a confusing, unsolved mystery.

~~

I cannot believe Metzger lived at Cebolla in the home of Bibiana, her father and children. Did Bibiana live with Metzger at his Cebolla ranch, as Karl believes? Or was her home place near his at Cebolla? Did they spend time together but live separately, nearby? We only know Metzger and Bibiana had three daughters: Dolorita "Lola" born 1858 at La Cebolla, she would marry Manuel Cordova (together they lived several places in northern New Mexico); Josefita born 1863, perhaps at La Cebolla, she would marry Manuel Duran of Ocate; and Isabelita born 1864, perhaps at La Cebolla, she would marry Rafael Gallegos of Las Vegas. Family tales and some records indicate Bibiana and Metzger parted company before or soon after Isabelita was born. She was born in 1864. His subsequent actions show their parting was contentious with lasting effects.

We use their children's dates of birth to guesstimate that they were together or spent time with each other for at least seven years. Verna wrote that at their separation, Metzger "went to live near his store on the Mora plaza."

The 1860 census taker for Mora would have gone to Metzger's store during work hours, while he and his clerks were present. Metzger or one or more of his employees may have lived in an apartment at the rear of the store, but maybe not. He and/or they may have lived nearby. Census records provide imperfect clues. They do not show the whole picture, and sometimes we are misled by what we see in them.

The 1860 census shows Apolonia (at location #2134) just doors—as the census taker traveled—from Metzger's store (at #2128). Verna wrote that after Metzger and Bibiana separated, he and Apolonia lived together near his store at Mora. Census records confirm that.

The 1870 Mora census shows Metzger "retired merchant of general merchandise," and Apolonia together, with three young servants—two recorded as Indians, the third, Josefa, age 12, "white female," who was likely Hispanic.

The 1870 U.S. census for La Cueva, Precinct 5, lists Bibiana first, indicating she is head of household and "farms on shares." Apparently the other share was her father's. Bernardo is shown on this census as age 80 (he was actually about 77) nearly at the bottom of the household's list, named after Bibiana's seven children. He was no longer shown as head of household. He may have been in failing health. This census was taken about three years before he died at "La Cebolla," according to his sacramental death and burial record. Does that indicate that "La Cueva, Precinct 5" was the legal description of their home-place at La Cebolla?

~~

Henry Korte was not shown on an 1860 census so we presume he had not yet arrived in New Mexico.

Several things happened in the 10 years between the 1860 and the 1870 censuses. Henry Korte, also a Prussian, arrived in Mora. Verna said he and Metzger were friends before they came to New Mexico; we presume that friendship is what brought Korte here, about two decades after Metzger. In July 1867, Korte married Metzger's daughter, Juanita. After Korte's arrival, before or soon after his marriage to Metzger's daughter, they became partners in multiple enterprises and properties.

Subsequent court procedures and Metzger's actions show that his split with Bibiana had lasting effects because thereafter he made major efforts to disinherit her three daughters with him. She accepted his drastic actions as if she wanted to sever all connections with him.

By the time Frank lived with Apolonia the second time, he was old for his years, not in good health, and determined to disown his three youngest daughters. According to Verna and records, Frank and Apolonia lived their last years with their daughter Juanita and her husband Henry at the Buena Vista home place, Metzger's first one that he had given to them. Apolonia and Frank Metzger were buried in the Metzger-Korte family cemetery on their ranch. Four years after Metzger died, Henry died, and Juanita died nine months after her husband. They too were buried there.

Evidence of Metzger's chicanery, subsequent actions and related events set in a timeline:

1. On May 6, 1872, Frank Metzger filed in Mora County Court to legally adopt Maria Juana "Juanita," his natural daughter by Apolonia. By then, Juanita and Henry had been married about five years. Metzger's obvious reason for doing that was to assure Juanita and Henry inherited his estate.
2. In 1873, Frank Metzger tried to make it appear that he had dissolved his business partnership with Henry Korte. He tried to show that he had no remaining estate by seeming to give or "sell" all of his businesses, properties and assets to his son-in-law. However, later court testimony said Metzger continued to control his businesses the remainder of his life.
3. End of 1873, Bernardo died, on December 18. Although they had been separated, his death record stated that his wife, Apolonia, was already deceased. That information was probably provided to the priest by Bibiana, who lived with him. If correct, Apolonia was not living in 1875 when Metzger proceeded to try to eliminate Bibiana's three daughters—and their mother—from any possible inheritance. Apolonia may have never known his full intentions.

4. In 1875, Frank Metzger gave Bibiana $3,000 to quiet any claim to his estate by her and her three youngest daughters. Bibiana signed, and several of her family witnessed, the court document agreeing that she and her daughters would never claim any of his assets.

5. The 1880 census shows Metzger living with his daughter Juanita and her husband Henry Korte at their Buena Vista place. Apolonia was not listed only because she had already died. She had lived her last years there, and died there, and was buried in the nearby Metzger/Korte cemetery.

6. A June 10, 1882 Las Vegas Optic newspaper article said Henry Korte struck it rich with a potentially high-yield gold mine near Mora. The Optic was prone to publish sensational exaggerations (like claiming to have Billy the Kid's trigger finger). That mine was never again mentioned in newspapers, only obliquely in folklore. Did Henry Korte fabricate a rich mine as a cover for his new-found wealth acquired from Frank Metzger?

7. Early February 1885, Frederick Metzger died at age 66.

8. A year later, in 1886, Lola Cordova on behalf of her sisters filed a civil lawsuit against Juanita and Henry Korte, claiming they, as Metzger's daughters also, had equal legal rights to his huge estate.

9. In January 1889, Henry Korte died at age 50.

10. In September 1889, Juanita died at age 40, less than nine months after Henry. Their deaths did not end the lawsuit. It was continued by their daughter, Anna Korte, and her husband William Naeglin.

11. Ultimately, after years of wrangling the matter in civil court, the state Supreme Court decreed that all four of Metzger's daughters were equally entitled to his inheritance. Metzger, Juanita, Henry and Anna had already died. By the time the case was finally closed, and its legal costs paid, no assets remained to be inherited by any heirs.

～～

On this 2013 summer day, Alvin pointed out the bald spot in the distance from the road, where he was told Metzger's ranch house had been. He commented, "That's the beauty of adobe houses, they go back to where they came." From our vantage point that day, nothing now remains there except a spot bare of vegetation. I wanted to get closer, but the location, like the small valley, was on private posted property. We did not venture off-road.

We continued west down that road to the small Hispanic community once named La Cebolla, now Ledoux. In Santa Fe, Alvin had found Bernardo's archived record of his death at La Cebolla and his burial at La Cebolla (Ledoux) in December 1873. (*"Bernardo Martin 80 años esposo de Polonia dif. y enterro en la Cebolla el dia 18 de Dic 1873." Roll 95 Frame 197, Mora St. Gertrudes.*) Bernardo, age 80, died December 1873. His wife, Polonia, had already died. He was buried at La Cebolla on 18th December, 1873. The New Mexico Genealogical Society also has this record.

Alvin said there were three cemeteries in the Ledoux area. We briefly searched the community's old, primary cemetery, the most likely one; we did not find Bernardo's marker. However, we only saw a portion of the cemetery, which was large, and Bernardo may have had no marker, or his was not durable.

Bernardo's son, Mañuel, was three years younger than Bibiana. According to family lore, he was only briefly in his family's life. At Bernardo's death, Bibiana was his only living child and natural heir. She would have inherited her father's La Cebolla home and lands after he died, or perhaps it was already hers. The 1870 census indicates she was by then running the family's farming operation, was a partner but head of household.

La Cebolla Creek meanders a number of miles creating several small valleys and little settlements named for the creek. Records show La Cebolla was where Elionor/Leonore was still living with her mother Bibiana when she met Andreas Laumbach. He first lived at La Cebolla when he came to New Mexico, according to their 1864 marriage record. An earlier document, probably created in 1862, lists several area foreigners, including Andreas, who resided at Precinct 5. Margaret and Pete Laumbach were born at La Cebolla. Sometime after the Laumbach marriage, the family built their permanent home on a portion of Frank Metzger's Buena Vista ranch that they bought from him.

We don't know exactly when, after the Laumbachs' 1864 marriage, they bought that property from Metzger. They already had a family connection with him because of Apolonia's daughter, Juanita Metzger. By 1864, Metzger was either still in a relationship with Bibiana (Isabelita was born in 1864), or he had just departed from her and may have been back with Apolonia.

~~

I had multiple queries out asking about location(s) of La Cebolla. In October 2014, Danny Chaves responded: "I have visited with several 'old-timers' over the last few days regarding La Cebolla. All seem to agree with what I've learned over the years. La Cebolla is the entire area above Mora. La Cebolla was several townships to include North and South El Carmen and El Oro. Due east from El Carmen is the valley I have always known as Cebolla or San Jose de la Cebolla (along the Rio Cebolla). Further along the valley and about 1/2 mile from where we visited the site with Chick are the remains of the old San Jose Church. Between this church and the site we visited is where rock corrals and a well are located (rock cliff). Beyond this rock cliff, further east, to include the Laumbach site, is what has always been known to me as La Cebollita. North of La Cebollita is Buena Vista and east is the Buena Vista Ranch, *[on which is]* the dissolved remains of what Chick suggested could be another related home."

The "dissolved remains" of another site Danny mentions is the barely visible spot Chick showed us in October 2013. That is the one in what he called the Veeder pasture, east of Abels' Buena Vista Ranch house. I think Chick had also indicated that the area east of Abels' ranch house, including the Veeder pasture where Rita de Cebolla passes through, is also called La Cebollita (or Cebolleta). This indicates that the area called Cebolla or Cebollita is fairly extensive.

The 1865 birth record for Margaret Laumbach, eldest child of Elionor and Andreas, says her christening took place at the plaza de Francisco Abajo de la Cebolla. Pete was born at La Cebolla in June 1867. The 1877 christening record for Laumbachs' son, Alejandro (who died young), stated his parents were from Cebolla. Record shows Anna was christened in 1878 to parents from La Cueva—the same address and precinct that seemed to be given for La Cebolla in some records, and also for those who lived at Buena Vista. That may also indicate Andreas and Elionor and their young family had moved from "La Cebolla" to their new place at Buena Vista between 1877 and 1878. Building their home at Buena Vista may have taken several years, and for a time their address may have been both places—Cebolla and also Buena Vista (aka La Cueva). Record for Daniel, born in 1872, said he was born to parents from La Cueva. When he was a young adult still living at home, his address was shown as La Cueva on letters as well as on his pocket knife. The address or precinct La Cueva seemed to have sometimes been applied for those who lived at both Cebolla and Buena Vista. All of that data still leaves us with an inexact date the Laumbachs moved from La Cebolla to Buena Vista, and we still do not know exactly where in La Cebolla or La Cebollita they and also Bernardo's family had lived.

~~

That summer day in 2013, we pulled into an open courtyard in the center of the community of Mora, across from the Mora Valley Spinning Mill on the main thoroughfare (NM 518), just past the turn- off to Guadalupita. Describing Metzger's store, Verna had written: "When Bibiana and Metzger separated, he went to live in the village of Mora where he had a large store. It was in a long building running from what was later the Pete Boland store to the Catholic Church. There was a small alley between it and the church, only wide enough for a wagon to pass between." Verna described Metzger's store and saloon as being a long one-story adobe. Alvin said her description was good. State Road 518 now borders the east end of the block and plaza, with only an open lot of vegetation now between the road and remains of the store. West of the ruins are two old, vacant, boarded up buildings, which Tracy photographed. Where was the site of the Pete Boland store? Mora historians would know. It is obvious there had once been a structure east of Metzger's, where now is only vegetation. The church Verna described next to Metzger's store was the original St. Gertrudes church structure that burned, replaced in the 1960s.

Below is a brief article found by Butch Sanders. He wrote: "[*Below*] is the short 18 Jul 1908 newspaper article (published in the Spanish American in Roy) reporting the 'wrecking of the oldest building in Mora' on the 'old Metzger corner' purchased by 'Dan Casidy.' That 'oldest building' part echoes Gregg's 4 July 1874 centennial piece." Sanders also wrote: "The correct spelling of this fellow's name is Daniel Cassidy, Sr. One of the very few historic sites registered in Mora town was the Daniel Cassidy House Site – with no address [*given*]. That's a bit odd since Daniel Cassidy resided in Cleveland (aka San Antonio/upper plaza) from his arrival in NM in 1881 until his death in 1927. Another historical house site registered in Mora town is that of John Daugherty, who really did live in Mora town – and who was the ex-sheriff shot and killed there in his home in front of his children by Tomas Lucero. Daniel Cassidy, Sr. clerked for ten years for John Daugherty's brother, James Daugherty, in his store in Cleveland before he (Cassidy) and another of John Daugherty's brothers, Joseph Daugherty, bought the business (from James Daugherty). He later went into partnership with Harry Daugherty – and later with Charles U. Strong with whom he opened a store in Mora town – presumably the one that will be built on the 'old Metzger corner' referred to in [this 1908] article."

> Dan Casidy the Mora merchant has purchased the old Metzger corner and is wrecking tht oldest building in Mora only to replace it with a modern structure, which will be used for a merchandise establishment, this is one of the best locations in Mora.

Someone had said at least one historic building in Mora had been pulled down before the state or federal historic preservation of historic properties stepped in to halt further destruction. That explains why Metzger's adobe store structure is preserved, perhaps, too, why a "merchandise establishment" was perhaps not after all built on the site of the one too hastily torn down next to Metzger's.

The next photo shows the two abandoned but preserved buildings due west of the Metzger store's adobe ruin. June 2013 photo by Tracy Ikenberry.

Pictured below are ruins of Frank Metzger store. Photo taken by Tracy Ikenberry, June 2013. Half of the walls and a portion of the tin roof of Metzger's store and saloon remain. It was a large building.

Metzger's store—its ruin and lot now surrounded by tall vegetative growth—is on the south side of the Santa Gertrudes de lo de Moro plaza. The newer (that replaced the older) Santa Gertrudes parish church and its associated buildings now primarily fill the square.

Alvin confirmed this was Metzger's store with a copy of an affidavit that gave its legal land description and using his hand-held GPS device. Verna had known where it was. She probably saw the ruins in the early 1930s, perhaps with Eduardo Korte, or with Tony when they visited their grandmother and Aunties, when she attended college about 30 miles away.

The next photo, taken by Tracy in 2013, is the gate entrance to Santa Gertrudes (Santa Gertrudis) on the Mora plaza, across from ruin of store.

The plaza's open courtyard is now—and was 150 years ago—parking space for visitors to the church and its related buildings. The church structures dominate the plaza, with only the Metzger store ruins and those two derelict buildings historically preserved on the south side of the square. That day of our visit, I was amazed to discover that the "Catholic church" my mama had mentioned but not named was Santa Gertrudis. In the original church, many of our family's early church events occurred, and the sacramental baptism, marriage and death entries were recorded and kept. That was the church Verna would have seen when she was in college. (Vintage photos and a painting of the earlier Santa Gertrudis mission church are in Chapter 12—Potrero, Mora, etc.) The current church, the nearby chapel and related buildings, including the priest's home are modern structures.

I searched the Internet for history of the earlier church, but found little. Sometime after the Santa Gertrudis de lo de Mora Plaza was platted in 1835, the people requested a church. Mexican census records for this Santa Gertrudis parish began in 1845, and at least by 1851, there was a church building on that plaza. The first one may have been an even earlier structure. The archived baptismal records of the Archdiocese of Santa Fe, beginning in 1855, were translated and transcribed by the New Mexico Genealogical Society and the Hispanic Genealogical Research Center of New Mexico. The Santa Gertrudis church building that was on the Plaza in the 1800s—the site of many of our family's sacramental events—burned in the 1960s. The newer structures were built, if not on the same spot, they were built on the same square.

~

On June 14, 2013, Tracy and I met Albert and Anna Marie Espinosa Ortega to continue gathering family history. Anna Marie is a granddaughter of Henry Laumbach, one of three sons of Andreas and Elionor Laumbach.

Henry was born September 29, 1874 in Buena Vista and died September 18, 1929 also at Buena Vista. He died in the same house, perhaps the same room, where he was born. Henry married late, at age 45. His bride was young Natividad Hurtado; they had seven children and lived near La Cueva, a few miles from his family's home at Buena Vista.

Anna Marie said Natividad believed her husband was being unfaithful with a servant girl. She sent the girl back to Mexico and locked Henry out of the house. Exposed to wet, stormy weather and developing pneumonia, he went to his nearby childhood home. His mother Elionor (she lived until June 1933) and sisters took him in and nurtured him. But he died. Anna Marie said his family never forgave Natividad for locking him out. She remarried. Emelio Korte, her second husband, found a job in California, which required the family to relocate after at least some of their children were born. When Aunties learned they were moving away, they insisted on keeping Adelina, the oldest of Henry's daughters. Aunties raised her, and spoiled her according to Anna Marie. Aunties wanted all three girls but Natividad would only part with one, Anna Maria said. In California, Henry's other children, raised with an additional seven children fathered by Korte, were less fortunate.

Children of Natividad Hurtado and Henry Laumbach: Henry, Adelina, Juan, Marta, Carlos, Frank and Clara. Photo taken maybe 1933, a few years after Henry died, before the family moved to California. Did Aunties commission this photo of their brother's children before they moved away? Clara, the last of Henry's children, died in California on September 3, 2014.

Together, the Ortegas, Tracy and I first visited the Laumbach family cemetery surrounded by Allsup ranchland. The ranch manager, Ned Walker, expected us and left the gate unlocked.

Anna Marie placed fresh long-stemmed red roses on her mother's grave—it was Adelina's birthday—and on Aunties' graves. She said she had been fortunate to have had three grandmothers.

Gate to the private Laumbach family cemetery at Buena Vista.

Private Laumbach family cemetery at Buena Vista.

Anna Marie had her dog, Skippy, with her one of the times she stayed with Aunties as a child. Aunties said Skippy required a bath before he could stay indoors with her. They bathed Skippy in the wash tub and—because he was a white dog—they added bluing to the rinse water. Anna Marie's little dog, Skippy, was a blue dog for a while.

Greg Laumbach (son of Pete Laumbach, the youngest son of Peter Joseph), lives in nearby Rainsville. He is the current caretaker of the Laumbach family cemetery. His father, Pete, was the one most likely to know who was buried there, and the exact locations of the burials without markers. Pete recently died; we hope he shared all of that knowledge with Greg.

Karl said Mr. Wissler was buried in a corner; his site has no marker. He said Ramon Bonney's first wife and their young children were also buried in the Laumbach cemetery without markers. Those with markers in the Laumbach Buena Vista cemetery include:
- "Bibiana Martinez, died October 27, 1897";
- "Andreas D. Laumbach born Dec. 2, 1833 died Nov. 4, 1904";
- "Eleonor E. Laumbach 1849—1933";

- "Anna Laumbach 1878—1958" (Auntie);
  a double "Laumbach" stone for:
- " Leonore A. 1888—1974" and "Mary G. 1884—1965" (Aunties);
- "Adelina Laura Laumbach-Espinosa 1927—1994" (daughter of Henry, mother of Anna Marie Ortega);
- "Sanchez, Adelina C. Feb. 7, 1913—Jan. 26, 1921" (sister of Tony, young daughter of Crestina Laumbach and Manuel A. Sanchez);
- "Albert Espinoza" (name etched on a fieldstone, brother of Anna Marie. She said only a box of his memorabilia is there, his ashes were scattered on Taos Mountain);
- "Steven Armijo 1868—1942" (Anna Marie said this was her father's grandfather. She said he worked at the Laumbachs' Buena Vista ranch and died there in an accident);
- "Christina Laumbach Foxall 1905—1976" (daughter of Peter Joseph);
- "Frank Leeson Foxall 1903—1993" (husband of Christina Laumbach Foxall);
- "Barney F. Cruz born Feb. 3, 1903, died Oct. 21, 1983, age 80" (son of Margaret Laumbach Cruz and Jose Emiterio Cruz of Holman, he only has a temporary mortuary marker); and
- "William J. Laumbach, June 25, 1938—June 27, 2000" ("Bill," son of Joyce and Vera Walker Laumbach, brother of Vera Jane L. Morris).

Frank Foxall was the last full-size (with casket) burial in this cemetery. To do so required tearing down a portion of the vintage wall to provide a backhoe access to the hard, rocky ground. In the future, Greg recommends only cremains with small markers because of limited space and to prevent further damage to cemetery walls and graves. The most recent interment was Bill's cremains.

~~

From the cemetery we went to the Allsup family's ranch, which had been established by Andreas and Elionor Laumbach, and where most of their children were born and all of them grew up. After Aunties sold the ranch in 1948 and moved to Las Vegas, it had several owners, including Shocks, between Laumbachs and the current owners. It now belongs to the Lonnie Allsup family, owners of the Allsup convenience stores throughout New Mexico and beyond.

At the Allsup Ranch, Ned Walker, manager, and Danny Chavez, principal at the Mora public schools who has worked part-time at the ranch most of his life, were our gracious hosts. They showed us the front bedroom where they were told "Mr. Laumbach" had died. I didn't think that was the patriarch Andreas, because I heard he was found outside near the barn. More than one family story, including Clara's, said Andreas had taken his life because he had what is now known as Parkinson's disease. The story I heard that he died outside may be incorrect. Some family and a 1904 newspaper article indicate he died inside. I had told Ned and Danny that the "Mr. Laumbach" who died in that bedroom might have been Henry, based upon Anna Marie's story of her grandfather catching pneumonia and dying there, rather than at his home because of a quarrel with his wife. Both Henry and his father Andreas may have died in that bedroom.

Danny Chavez and Anna Marie said there was a Laumbach mine "on top" of La Cueva. Danny said the shaft, timbers and ladder are still there (photo in earlier chapter), but it was not in the right geological strata for gold. What were they seeking? We have two photos of J.S. Candelario, husband of Estefanita Laumbach, at his own mine shaft. In both he held a rifle. A Santa Fe newspaper article mentioned Sito's mine. Therefore, both Sito and Andreas—assuming Andreas was the proprietor of the "Laumbach mine"—had mines in the area. Neither was a gold mine and neither produced any treasure. However, those, along with the publicized (and perhaps fabricated) Korte "gold mine" were likely sources for local folklores that claimed *muy rico Alemans* (very rich Germans), including a Laumbach, acquired their wealth from a secret gold mine. A published book: *The Lost Goldmine of Juan*

Mondragón, edited by Charles L. Briggs and Julian Josué Vigil, is a folk ballad in Spanish with English translation of a fabled mine. It is a tale of a poor sheepherder from Cordova who stumbled upon a rich goldmine, but he could never again find it. Our family's genealogy and chart shown in that book have errors. The ballad is interesting if you remember it is fiction. John, son of Isabel M. Gallegos (daughter of Bibiana) was the source for much of the erroneous information in that book.

My mother and I believed that Metzger goldmine was pure fantasy. Frederick Metzger, and Henry Korte more indirectly, were wealthy Germans but their wealth came from shrewd and ruthless business practices, not a secret mine. In the frontier west, banks were few and the little currency available was sometimes in the form of gold and silver pieces, occasionally even raw gold nuggets. Metzger and Korte hide some of their wealth. Our family heard detailed stories of at least two found stashes. There may have been more findings not reported for obvious reasons. One said William Naeglin, a blacksmith on Korte's ranch, watched Henry Korte bury a stash in a cornfield. When Korte lay dying, Naeglin dug it up and ran off with Korte's daughter, Anna. Verna heard this story from her great-aunt, Isabel Gallegos and her daughter, Isabel. Details of this story cannot be true. Another story was that a man named Shoemaker rented the attorney Veeder's place (formerly Frank Metzger's and Henry Korte's home place) specifically to search for Metzger or Korte gold. The story says he found a stash behind an adobe brick in the barn. With it he bought and restored the showplace at Watrous that once belonged to Samuel Watrous. There Shoemaker raised prized palominos.

The story of buried gold, and its source—a lost goldmine—has been a tale, with multiple versions, repeated in northern New Mexico for a hundred or more years; a few people believed those tales and searched unsuccessfully. Some caused cemetery vandalism and desecration.

In the mid-1970s, my mother's cousin Tony Sanchez (son of Crestina Laumbach and Manuel A. Sanchez) came to Springer to see my mother and me after working on the family cemetery at Buena Vista. He discovered a family grave had been dug into and opened. Telling us about it, he was so angry he trembled. I had believed that was Bibiana's grave, but it might have been Apolonia's in a nearby cemetery. At any rate, Apolonia's marble headstone was stolen. The Metzger-Korte cemetery had been vandalized, graves opened and markers stolen. Tony had been friends with the Thompsons, then owners of the Buena Vista Ranch, formerly owned by Metzger and the Kortes. Because of that friendship, he may have been caretaking the Metzger-Korte cemetery. Graves in both cemeteries had been disturbed.

Mary Louise Maestas (great-granddaughter of Maria Marta Ebel Esquibel) said that when she'd taught public school in West Las Vegas, she had a student (fourth or fifth grader) who wrote of a family experience for a class assignment. He wrote that, when he was younger, he was riding with his parents, his father driving, down a Mora highway. He was in the back seat. Suddenly a woman dressed in white appeared on the highway in front of the car. All three car occupants saw her. His father panicked and hit the brakes. His mother was also scared, but she reached her foot over and mashed the gas pedal; the car surged forward. The shocked boy turned around and looked back; the woman in white still stood serenely on the highway. Everyone was shaken but they kept going. That same student wrote another paper, for a different teacher, in eighth grade. He wrote that when he was even younger, his parents had dug into a *señora's* grave in a little cemetery. He said they were searching for treasure. There have been other reported sightings of this lady ghost. I like to believe Bibiana and Apolonia haunt those who desecrate their graves.

Danny Chavez is familiar with the Allsup property that once belonged to Laumbachs. He has worked there most of his life, and his mother and others in his family know much of its history and knew some of the family. He said his mother and aunt, as children, had lived near the "other" Laumbach place, the one near La Cueva. He later pointed out the place where, we concluded, it was Henry who had lived with his wife and children. Danny's mother and aunt had lived "next door" to the La Cueva Laumbachs. His aunt remembered a childhood neighbor friend named Clara.

The Allsup Ranch headquarters. Photo by Tracy Ikenberry, June 2013.

After we toured the Allsup Ranch, we went to the nearby Metzger-Korte cemetery on Abel ranch property. The sky was overcast. The weather was becoming cold and windy and threatened rain. It felt like a front coming in. All her life, Verna wanted to visit this cemetery and the place Apolonia had last lived. I was now given opportunity to do both. I hoped inclement weather would not spoil it, but I knew it would be selfish to hope it would not rain. This area desperately needed moisture. The nearby lake was totally dry. It had been made by Frank Metzger, but named Riner for a family who later owned the ranch. Eduardo Korte had told Verna Laumbach—more than 85 years ago—a commonly told story about that lake: Frank Metzger stocked it with fish so huge that it took a wagon team to pull them out.

This is the Riner Lake, totally dry on this day in June 2013, on the Buena Vista Ranch near the Metzger-Korte cemetery. Lake was made by Frank Metzger but named for a subsequent ranch owner. Photo by Tracy Ikenberry.

The gate, usually padlocked, was left unlocked because ranch manager Chick Burney expected our visit. The cemetery is surrounded by a rock wall; the gated entrance has a now-precarious rock arch.

A large mesquite bush—the top barely seen in this next photo on the far upper left inside the stone wall—obscures the grave of Apolonia. Karl and Chick saw her marker in that corner years ago.

This cemetery has few burials; there are now only three visibly marked graves.
- "Frank Metzger died Feb. 4, 1885, age 66 years."
- "Henry Korte died January 5, 1889, 50 years." This stone was stolen years ago. It is broken across the center and a portion of the inscription is missing. Alvin Korte and his cousin Bobby Korte knew where it was located; they returned, repaired and reset it in 2010.
- "Juanita, wife of Henry Korte, died ___ aged 40 years." This stone was stolen from the cemetery, and also returned and reset by cousins Alvin Korte and Bobby Korte in 2010. It, too, was broken, the portion of the inscription giving her date of death missing. She died in September 1889, nine months after her husband Henry. She was born to Frank Metzger and Apolonia in 1849.

There had been a few other burials there:
- "Polonia Gutierrez" - Chick Burney, manager of the Abel Ranch, and Karl Laumbach remember seeing that name, years ago, inscribed on a flat stone marker in the southeast corner. Learning that confirms what my mother, Verna, had said: Apolonia was buried in this cemetery. A large mesquite bush now fills that area, hiding it. Perhaps someday someone will carefully cut off the main trunk of the bush near the ground (not pull it up, roots and all, which would disturb the stone and grave) to expose the marker. Verna had said Apolonia's grave originally had a fine rose marble headstone brought from Denver but it had been stolen many years ago. She may have heard of it being stolen more than 80 years ago when she was in college, when there was so much interest and vandalism. Therefore, the now existing stone—probably of man-made material—that Karl and Chick remembered seeing was a foot stone or replacement marker. I hope it has her legible date of death. We don't know when she died, only that Bernardo's December 1873 death record said she was then already deceased. At her death, she had been living with Frank Metzger in the home of their daughter, Juanita and husband Henry Korte, at their Buena Vista place. That property now belongs to the Hughes G. Abel family.
- In this same cemetery, along the south wall near Apolonia's grave, are two broken man-made stone markers. In 2013, Alvin Korte mentioned seeing them and thought they might be children of Juanita and Henry Korte—a little girl named Amalia and a boy named Henry, both died young. Those markers are broken in half. Juanita's and Henry's seem to have been deliberately broken in half. Why were their markers broken and not Metzger's? If these were the Korte

children's markers, were they also deliberately broken? Why? Inscriptions on those broken stones half-hidden along the wall—as if discarded there—had only been etched, and are no longer legible.

We carefully poured bottled water over one of the broken markers along the wall, attempting to read the inscription. Vaguely visible might be the word "memory."

Were there other burials in this cemetery that now have no markers?

Private Entrance to the Abel family's Buena Vista Ranch

The modern ranch house was built after 1975. The original adobe house—Metzger's home—burned when the Thompson family had owned the property. Tony Sanchez, after being at Buena Vista tending to the family's cemetery, came to see my mom and me in Springer. He told us the home had burned while the Thompsons were away. Tony was upset; they were friends of his. It was also the final home—now gone—of his great-great-grandmother Apolonia, where she had last lived and had died.

After the Korte family lost the ranch to pay the legal fees for the lawsuit that went on for years, it was known as the Veeder Ranch. Over the years, the property was owned by various others, including Riner and Thompson, and now the Abel family.

It is known as the Buena Vista Ranch. It is a beautiful, well-kept property.

Buena Vista Ranch entrance. Photo by Tracy Ikenberry, 2013.

Buena Vista Ranch House. Photo by Tracy Ikenberry, 2013.

Perhaps Chick Burney's home behind Abels' main ranch house. Photo by Tracy Ikenberry, 2013.

The ranch was twice used as movie settings: the remake of *True Grit* and *The Homesman*, a movie starring Tommy Lee Jones.

Prison wagon built for movie filmed at Buena Vista Ranch. Photo by Tracy Ikenberry, 2013.

Way Station built for filming the remake of True Grit. Meandering in the valley below it may be La Cebolla Creek. That is yet another valley named Cebollita or Cebolleta. Photo by Tracy Ikenberry, June 2013.

I had been confused by my mom's story that an orchard separated the Laumbach home and the "Veeder" place. As children, when visiting their grandmother and aunts, her father had forbidden her and her siblings from going beyond the orchard. Besides of the rift the suit caused between the two family branches, there was still much bitterness about the attorney, Veeder, acquiring the Metzger/Korte place for his legal fee. Bibiana lived her last years, and later Mr. Wissler also lived, in the little house in that orchard on Laumbach land that separated the two properties. The orchard and the little house within it are gone. I am uncertain of their location. My confusion was that the Metzger/Korte/Veeder place and the Laumbach place did not seem that geographically close. I could not see one from the other, at least not structures. Chick confirmed the two ranch houses are about ¾ mile apart. The terrain must obscure them.

Responding to my emailed query about La Cebolla in October 2014, Danny Chavez wrote: "What I am still curious about is who lived in an old house less that 1,000 yards south of the Allsup (once Laumbach) house in Buena Vista. One of my tasks a few weeks ago on Saturday took me to this place. Both this household and the Laumbach house appear to have shared a common well, as it is located midway between them." He said it is within or near where an orchard had been. Was that Casa de la Abuela, which later was also Wissler's final home? Karl said a former owner's employee had taken a bulldozer to the remains of that little house. Perhaps he searched for some of that fabled treasure. Danny Chavez said evidence indicates it had been a two-room house.

Our visit was prearranged; Chick Burney expected us that October day. Chick had called Ned Walker at the Allsup ranch to tell us he was away working cattle but would soon return.

Albert and Anna Marie Ortega were familiar with the place. They said the Buena Vista community store, post office and blacksmith shop had been on Frank Metzger's ranch. Albert and Anna

Marie led us to the long building with a rustic boardwalk and thick stucco adobe walls—evidenced by the deep windows and door openings.

Doorways and window openings show the thickness of the adobe walls. This and the next photos were taken by Tracy Ikenberry in 2013.

The building was unlocked. We went inside through one of several doors.

View from behind the structure with the early Buena Vista post office, store and blacksmith shop that had once been on Metzger's ranch. On the far right is a glimpse of the large red barn and stables.

Albert Ortega on the boardwalk in front of the Buena Vista store, post office and blacksmith shop.

The portion of the building we first entered had pieces of antique furniture, as if it had once been used as a dwelling, but they may have been for-sale items in the store from long ago. We climbed the inside stairs to what seemed to be a sleeping area.

Back downstairs, we found an apple cider press. Alvin Korte had earlier mentioned it, saying it may have been Juanita's.

We went into the blacksmith shop. It had an old billows attached to a contraption that changed its position. The billows stoked the fire on the other side of the wall to heat tools and pieces of iron to make horseshoes and other metal necessities.

Billows to stoke the fire ran through the adobe wall to the elevated fireplace on the other side. Subsequent owners carefully preserved the equipment but restuccoed surrounding walls.

Nearby was a vice to hold the heated iron to bend into horseshoes and other items, and an anvil for pounding the iron into shape. It is understandable that early-day blacksmiths were depicted in art and movies with tremendous upper body strength.

This blacksmith shop, Metzger's and later Korte's, was where William Naeglin (aka Naegelin), the blacksmith hired by Henry Korte, had toiled. It is understandable that he fell for the boss' daughter, Anna Korte, a gorgeous blue-eyed blonde from an affluent family. But so doing, he fell out of favor with his boss, Henry, who sent him away. Family stories say Henry Korte did not think a blacksmith without assets was a proper match for his beautiful daughter. Later, Naeglin returned and was rehired. He was still sweet on Anna. They eventually married.

At the west end of the long building was an attached stable with separate stalls for horses and mules. Once red, the very large barn had weathered to a soft pink. Inside one of those stalls was a deep concrete manger to hold hay and other feeds for the animals.

As we walked towards it, Chick arrived in a pickup towing a horse trailer; in it were beautiful working horses. We saw more horses in corrals.

Chick Burney; the old red barn is behind him.

Chick led us into what he called the bunkhouse at Buena Vista Ranch

Inside the bunkhouse at Buena Vista Ranch.

    Inside the bunkhouse, Chick showed us a large topographical map hanging on the wall with the huge expanse of the Buena Vista land holdings, including the recent acquisition of what had been most of the Salmon's 75,000-acre ranch. The Salmons kept the grist mill, store and their "berry patch," he said.

    Chick showed us copies of several vintage photos of Laumbachs that someone had given him. (I later learned those copies came from Karl.) One was of Peter Joseph's sons—the photo of cowboys on horseback; written on back were their identities. (This photo of the Laumbach cowboys is in Karl's chapter on his grandfather, Pete.) Another copy of a Laumbach family photo Chick showed us, with identities written on back, was: rear, Anna, J.F. Cruz holding baby Rosa, and Margaret; front, Crestina, Eleanore (the mother), Andreas Laumbach (the father) and Mary. (This photo is in Chapter 32.)

    Among Laumbach family photos Chick had collected was an enlarged copy of the "cowboys branding scene." I told him most of those were probably Korte cowboys or were working for the Kortes that day. I said we wished we knew where that picture had been taken. He said he was sure he knew. He pointed it out from where we stood in front of what he calls the headquarters office. The site is behind (east) and a bit to the right, looking past the Abel ranch house towards the rock cliffs. We were then preparing to leave and Tracy wasn't nearby with the camera. The area Chick indicated is an open *vega* and hillside with some exposed rocks; more rocks were hidden from our view by vegetation. He thinks that area is identical to the branding scene in the photo, including the unseen rocks. It is a smaller cleared area above a larger open clearing. That being the branding scene location seems logical. It was on Korte property and not far from the Korte's main house. On the far right in the vintage photo is a woman wearing a long skirt. Dressed that way, she probably walked to where she stood to watch the branding, an easy walk from the house. I like to think that woman was Juanita.

Chick Burney showed his interest in the place's early history and its people. Perhaps the Abel family is also interested in their property's history. That same interest was reflected by Ned Walker, the Allsup Ranch manager. Over the years, prior and current owners of both ranches carefully preserved many original features of their properties.

To Taos and Return to Mora and Buena Vista, October 2013
On this trip, Tracy and I first headed to Taos to visit the home of Albert and Anna Marie Ortega.

The distance from Las Vegas, where we stayed, to Taos is about 70 miles; from Mora to Taos is about 40 miles. We first stopped in Mora to refresh my memory of the setting of Metzger's store and the St. Gertrudis church. After passing through Mora and several small outlying villages, the winding highway began a steep climb with sharp hairpin curves, opening up magnificent vistas above and below: forests of evergreen pine, fall splashes of yellow quaking aspens and brilliant red oak brush. The mountain peaks had been whitewashed the day before when a front blew in dumping snow, hail and rain even on lower elevations.

Ortegas' home on the outskirts of Taos is set before the grandeur of the Taos Mountains. As soon as we entered their home, I was awestruck by their huge collection of priceless *santos*,[i] many fairly large, in every room of their home. Albert's parents, Zoraida and Eulogio Ortega, were renowned *santeros*, and also beloved mentors to younger *santeros*. Their collectible pieces are signed "Los Ortegas." Albert's father, Eulogio, carved *bultos* out of wood. His mother, Zoraida, painted those and the *retablos,* which were on flat pieces of wood. Los Ortegas had been long-established *artisans*, their work showcased in several published books. Albert's mother had died, but his father then still lived in the small village of Velarde, some miles from Taos. They have a little private chapel filled with *santos,* and an alter screen that took the two of them two years to complete. In addition to Los Ortegas' art, Albert and Anna Marie have several very old *santos,* a collection of other pieces of old and new folk-art and other objects, including multiple old wooden troughs similar to one of Aunties' from their earlier years at Buena Vista.

Tracy took many photos of their santos and other artifacts.

Late in the day we began looking at Anna Marie's large collection of Laumbach memorabilia from Auntie's trunk. Among those were albums filled with postcards Uncle Sito had mailed to his sisters-in-law in the first decade or so of the last century. He sent them cards from all over the United States, Mexico and Europe on his extensive travels advertising his curio store and marketing his southwestern merchandise. Included in Ortiz's collection were images of some of Sito's ledger entries in his or someone's fine penmanship.

Tomas Jaehn, archivist at the New Mexico History Museum at the Palace of the Governors in Santa Fe, had told me the Museum's archives collections include J. S. Candelario's extensive ledgers and other bookkeeping records and correspondence.

It was becoming late; we had almost no time left to look at other things including many pieces of Aunties' memorabilia.

This very large old print, with ornate gold-leaf frame, hung for perhaps a hundred years at the Laumbach home at Buena Vista and Las Vegas. It now hangs in the Ortegas' home at Taos.

Anna Marie got out her collection of photos that had once been in Aunties' trunks and we began scanning them. It was late and we had to rush. Then Tracy and I headed to a Taos motel for the night.

~~

After we had returned from our earlier June visit to the Mora area, Karl Laumbach provided that vintage photo showing what we first believed was the view behind the Laumbachs' Buena Vista ranch, but we later concluded it was viewed from the front. It shows a corral with a young man and a donkey in the foreground, a man and two women, and—barely visible on the left—two little girls. In an earlier chapter, I included that image and discussed it. On my mother's copy of it, she had written that it was of the Buena Vista place in the 1880s, which would have been at least 20 years before Andreas died. In 1880, he would have been 47; in 1885 he would have been 52. In those years before his illness, he was and would have looked younger than in our later photos. In that photo, on a small hill behind them, was an adobe-stucco building with pitched tin roof. In the photo is also a structure of logs and rock, which we now think was a separate building, a stable, which still exists, carefully preserved by subsequent owners. The terrain and ranch layout has changed, but the ditch (*acequia*) in the foreground is a landmark that gives us perspective, shows that the photo was taken in front of the property.

When we first visited the place in summer of 2013, even without knowing its significance, my daughter Tracy took several photos of what we later thought, especially after seeing the vintage photo, was an old structure that survived from Laumbach days. By comparing the vintage photo to our recent photos, the unique shape and construction of the "stable" seems the same. Was it that structure built by Andreas 1st? Construction of dwellings, especially with adobe in those days, takes time. This small building was much smaller and simpler. When he died, his son, Andreas 2nd—the reason he came to New Mexico—was still a single man living at La Cebolla. Why would the father settle in Buena Vista and build a home to live there, alone? Perhaps that small structure was only the beginning of his intentions and he was killed before he accomplished much. We will probably never know.

Tracy and I had returned to Buena Vista after our visit with Ortegas in Taos. Danny and I discussed that little log and rock stable on the hill. He said when he was a young fellow working there, he offered to tear down "that eyesore." ("What did I know? I was young," he said.) He was adamantly told by the owner to leave it alone. Thus that vintage structure has endured, saved and preserved by subsequent property owners.

The little unique rock and log stable behind Allsup's house; photo taken in 2013 by Tracy Ikenberry.

This building fascinates us because of its distinct shape and construction. We think this is the same one that appears in the background of Karl's and Verna's early photos of Laumbachs' home.

When we explored the possibilities of the "vintage photo" taken at Buena Vista perhaps 130 years ago, Danny commented that the terrain then was different than it is now. This little stable is actually a distance behind the main house, now elevated on a hill but perhaps was not then. Danny pointed out that the ends of logs at the corners of the little structure are similar to those that are exposed at the main dwelling.

Viga-like logs protrude from corners of the main dwelling's walls. One set seems smoothly cut with a saw; the other set is jagged, as if chopped with an ax and has unusual notches cut into the ends. Those same features seem to have been repeated in the logs of the little stable.

Those and other aspects of the original Laumbach structures were carefully preserved and left exposed by later owners when they remodeled.

~

We returned to the Buena Vista Ranch to resume our visit with Chick Burney. Danny went with us from the nearby Allsup ranch. By pickup, Chick took us to a place, in what he says is still called the Veeder pasture, east of the Abels' headquarters. He said that broader area and valley is also called Cebolla or Cebollita. He knew we were seeking the location where Apolonia may have lived her first years in the Mora area. He showed us a barely visible site of what had once been a homestead. Some bits of debris from that site had been collected and exhibited on a rock. Chick wondered if some of our family or Kortes, perhaps Apolonia, had once lived there.

Debris from an early homestead site that Chick first thought might have been where Apolonia had once lived, but this place does not fit our known family history. Photo by Tracy Ikenberry in 2013.

We stood that day east of the Abel Ranch headquarters. It was on the "upper plaza" of Mora, where once were many small settlements. That road took early travelers a few miles down to the "lower plaza" of La Junta (now Watrous), where it passed through Bonney lands.

Chick said that now barely visible early home site (seen in foreground of below photo) was conveniently located near the old road down the mountain to the settlement once called La Junta. He pointed out evidence of that road vaguely seen in the hillside between evergreens.

"Upper plaza" and "lower plaza" were terms applied to the community plazas set out when the Mora Grant was first platted. Those terms were also sometimes applied in records—as I do now—to distinguish La Junta (lower) and lo de Mora (upper), not far apart travel miles but at considerably different elevations.

~~

From that there, I directed Chick to drive some miles west to an area I had believed Bernardo, Bibiana and her children, including Elionor had lived, just off state road 518 west of Buena Vista, nearer the town of Mora. The site is off the road that leads to Ledoux, formerly the settlement known as La

Cebolla. This site is now Abel property, but Chick had been unaware of that evidence of a home site until I showed it to him. That is where Karl indicated his grandfather Pete was born at his grandmother Bibiana's home, near the Cebolla Creek where he had bathed as a child. "In warm water," Karl later told me he had heard. This is also the site Alvin Korte said was Metzger's Cebolla ranch headquarters.

Is that the Gap of the Crestón in the background? Are there some warm springs near that "gap"?

All that remain at this site just past state road 518 on the road to Ledoux are the vague ruins of a large homestead—rocks, wooden debris, a piece of a large viga, and adobe melt—plus three dying trees of a long ago apple orchard.

This was once either where three generations of Bernardo Martín's family—he, Bibiana and her children—had lived, or it was the site of Frederick Metzger's second, later, "hacienda" where he had lived a while. I don't think it could have been both. Records indicate this was Metzger's later ranch headquarters.

~~

When we returned to the Buena Vista Ranch, I asked Chick Burney to again point out for me, now that I had an available camera, where he believes the Korte cowboys branding scene had taken place perhaps 130 years ago.

Chick thinks the photo had been taken east of and within easy sight of the Abel headquarters, in a small open meadow area beyond and above a larger one.

The smaller clearing on a slight rise across center of this photo might be the site of the vintage cowboy branding scene. There now are some small trees within the clearing and Chick said trees obscured our view of some of the rocks seen in the early photo. Our vantage point and perspective was also different than that earlier day camera's angle.

---

[i] Santos are indigenous pieces of New Mexico folk art, primarily from regions of the Sangre de Cristo mountains. Depending upon the beholder, they are religious, artistic, collectable and valuable. In the 17th and 18th centuries, Hispanic people settled along the Rio Grande corridor and then migrated to the remote mountainous areas of northern New Mexico where religious accruements were few or none. *Santeros* fulfilled the peoples' desire to have and to hold images of their beloved Madonna, saints, *Santo Nino* and *Jesu Cristo*. The saint-makers used available material—wood and *jaspe* (gypsum)—to create facsimiles of popular saints. *Retablos* were painted on flat wooden pieces of wood, first coated with *jaspe*. *Bultos* were carved in three-dimensional form and sometimes painted over *jaspe*. *Reredos* or *tablas* were painted on walls or flat panels behind alters in churches and *moradas*.

SECTION IV: LAUMBACHS IN NEW MEXICO

Chapter 40: Finale
by Jan Girand

This book spans hundreds of years and several diverse places during the eras our families lived in Germany, Iowa and northern New Mexico. Most of its chapters focus on New Mexico. It includes some history of other families from which we were not directly descended but that affected or indirectly touched ours in compelling ways. This book should also interest non-kinfolk and historians because of its regional histories. Like any honest history book, it does not claim total correctness. It is only as accurate as the data and records currently available, or found. Also, as a family saga, the book relies on inexact oral histories passed down for generations, seen from different viewpoints, altered in retelling. I try to include known versions of specific events that differ.

Tales naturally evolve and change through the ages, depending upon the beholders and the tellers. Oral histories make this saga more interesting by adding personal glimpses of its characters and past ways of life. Hopefully this book is not just dry "names and numbers," but fleshes out people, showing their human sides and their experiences during times very different from ours.

It could not have been written—as accurately or as detailed or as interesting—without extensive research by Charles O. "Butch" Sanders and valued input from many others.

At the end, I am left with questions about at least two intriguing aspects of our history that, at least for me, remain unsolved mysteries.

- The first of those is the strong role Frank (Fredrick/Frederich aka Francisco) Metzger, and secondarily Henry (Heinrich) Korte, played that drastically altered the futures of our ancestors' and their cousins' families. What so angered Metzger causing him to do what he did? Why did Bibiana—who seemed to have been such a strong-willed person—accept it?
- The second is my continued, unsatisfied, curiosity of exactly where Bernardo Martín and his family had lived in the Mora area. I have provided documentation that *I* think proves Bernardo and his family lived at "Cebolla," where he established the home-place for three generations of his family: himself, his daughter Bibiana, and all of her children during their early years. Others disagree with my conclusion, and mine leaves me puzzled about the specific location of that three-generational home. Perhaps I will acquire more information when preparing the second book of this trilogy: *Bibiana and Her Children*.

Both of these intrigues will be expanded upon here, in this book's final chapter, including a recap of why I believe that family had mostly lived at Cebolla.

~~

Karl provided images of that history-changing March 1875 document—the instrument conveying $3,000 from Metzger to Bibiana—from the copy Mary Louise Maestas sent him years ago. Karl also provided his typed transcription of it to make it easier for us to read. Butch Sanders enhanced the copy of the legal-size document and fit most of it on one page.

Source: "Deed Records, Mora County, Volume C, Page 90, Sheet #66, conveyance from Frederich Metzgar to Viviana Martín, signed March 19, 1875, filed Feb. 16, 1885."

This is the document Mary Louise called the proverbial "thirty pieces of silver."

Viviana Martin et al.

Abstract of Instrument: March 19, 1875
Filed February 16, 1885 at 12:00 A.M.
Consideration $3000.00

Francisco Metzger.   Recorded in Volume -C-   Page 90

Deed------   Records, Mora County, N. M.

Mora
Abstract
Company

    This instrument conveys the following described real estate situated in Mora County, New Mexico, to-wit:--

    Know all by these presents: That we Viviana Martin, a resident of La Sevolla, County of Mora, Territory of New Mexico, and Ramon Bonne, Andres and (Eleanor wife of Andres Laumbach) sons and daughters of major age, of the said Viviana Martin, and Maria Martha Doloritas, Josefita and Pablita minor daughters of the said Viviana Martin, and represented by their mother, the said Viviana Martin, as natural Guardian for the said minors, all residents of the County of Mora, in the Territory of New Mexico, for and in consideration of the sum of Three Thousand Dollars ($3000.00) to us paid in hand by Francisco Metzger, a resident of the town of Mora, County of Mora, Territory of New Mexico, the receipt of which is and remains acknowledged, with these presents we have released and discharged and forever ex-honorated, and with these presents we release, discharge and ex-honorate, ourselves, for our heirs, administrators and executors, forever the said Francisco Metzger, his heirs, administrators and executors, against any action or demand, debt or debts, cause or causes, of any nature whatsoever, they may be, and principally against any claim, against or declared mother Polonia Guitierez, be it for her inheritance, or any other thing, cause, or reason, and also against any claim for personal service, of any nature whatsoever, done by the said Viviana Martin, or her sons or daughters, at any time, before, now, or time past, and

    Also release, discharge and forever exhonorate the said Francisco Metzger his heirs, administrators, and executors, against any claim demand, action, debt or debts, cause or causes, be it in law or equity, of any nature so ever, if existed before, now or in the future, and these presents are made, executed and sealed, with the purpose and principal object to serve the said Francisco Metzger his heirs, administrators and executors, as a receipt of all and entire of the reasons and considerations mentioned here.

    In Testimony Whereof, we have set our hands and seals this 19th day of March, Anno Domini, One Thousand Eight Hundred and seventy-five.

Mora
Mora County
New Mexico

```
Attested in Presence of                her
        his                     Viviana X Martin    (SEAL)
Jesus M. X Gallegos                   mark
        Mark                          his
        his                     Ramon X Bonne       (SEAL)
Felipe X Gallegos,                    mark
        mark                          her
Francisco Gallegos              Eleanor X Laumbach  (SEAL)
                                      mark
                                      his
                                Andres X Eberle     (SEAL)
                                      mark

                            Maria Marta  ) By their mother and
                            Doloritas    ) Natural Guardian.
                            Josefita     )
                            Isabelita    ) Viviana X Martin (SEAL)
```

Sheet No. 66

ABSTRACTER'S NOTE:-- This Instrument was translated by Abstracter from the Spanish language into English language.

*Courtesy of Mary Louise M. Maestas
Las Vegas, NM 87701-*

Mora Abstract Company   Mora, Mora County, New Mexico   Sheet No. 66

Viviana Martin et al.

Date of Instrument : March 19, 1875
Filed: February 16, 1885 at 12:00 A.M.

Consideration $3000.00

Francisco Metzgar.

Recorded in Volume   -C-   Page 90
Deed---------------   Records, Mora County, N.M.

This instrument conveys the following described real estate situated in Mora County, New Mexico, to-wit: --

Know all by these presents: That we Viviana Martin, a resident of La Sevolla, County of Mora, Territory of New Mexico, and Ramon Bonne, Andres and (Eleanor Wife of Andres Laumbach) sons and daughters of major age, of the said Viviana Martin, and Maria Martha, Doloritas, Josefita, and Pablita minor daughters of the said Viviana Martin, and represented by their mother, the said Viviana Martin, as natural Guardian for the said minors, all residents of the County of Mora, in the Territory of New Mexico, for and in consideration of the sum of Three Thousand Dollars ($3000.00) to us paid in hand by Francisco Metzgar, a resident of the town of Mora, County of Mora, in the Territory of New Mexico, the receipt of which is and remains acknowledged, with these presents wehave released and discharged and forever ex-honorated, and with these presents we release, discharge, and ex-honorate, ourselves, for our heirs, administrators and executors, forever the said Francisco Metzgar, his heirs, administrators and executors, against any item or demand, debt or debt, cause or causes, of any nature whatsoever, they may be, and principally against any claim, against or declared mother Polonia Guitierez, be it for her inheritance, or any other thing, cause, or reason, and also against any claim for personal service, of any nature whatsoever, done by the said Viviana Martin, or her sons or daughters, at any time, before, now or time past, and

Also release, discharge, and forever exhonorate the said Francisco Metsgar his heirs, administrators, and executors, against any claim, demand, action, debt or debts, cause or causes, be it in law or equity, of any nature so ever, if exsisted before, now or in the future, and those presents are made, executed and sealed, with the purpose and principal object to serve the said Francisco Metzgar, his heirs, administrators and executors, as a receipt fo all and entire of the reasons and considerations mentioned here.

In Testimony Whereof, we have set our hands and seals this 19th day March, Ano Domini, One Thousand Eight Hundred and seventy-five.

Attested in the Presence of
    his
Jesus M. X Gallegos
    mark
    his
Felipe X Gallegos
    mark
Francisco Gallegos

    her
Viviana X Martin   (SEAL)
    mark
    his
Ramon X Bonne   (SEAL)
    mark
    her
Eleanor X Laumbach   (SEAL)
    his
Andres X Eberle   (SEAL)
    mark

Maria Marta   ) By their mother and
Doloritas   ) Natural Guardian.
Josefita   )
Isabelita   )Viviana X Martin (SEAL)

ABSTRACTER'S NOTE:--- This instrument was translated by Abstracter from the Spanish language in English language.

Why would Bibiana agree to forfeit her children's rights to their father's considerable estate? Why did she, apparently, agree to relinquish hers and her children's rights to her mother Apolonia's estate? (This should not have affected Bernardo' assets, since he outlived Apolonia, still his legal wife.) This document was dated, and effective, March 1875, but filed by the court 10 years later. Apparently Frank Metzger drew up the document several years after he and Bibiana quarreled and separated.

Aspects of this document are confusing and mystifying.

It begins: "This instrument conveys the following described real estate…" That indicates specific land property would change hands, and it promises to describe that "real estate." However, the document describes no real estate or land, and no specific real estate seems to have been conveyed. The only thing conveyed was $3,000 cash from one party for a promise to ask for nothing—considerable unspecific properties and assets—from the other party. From our perspective reading the one-page document, we see it as Bibiana's promise that she and her minor daughters would make no claim on her mother's estate or on any Metzger assets. Only some of his assets were real estate. Webster's dictionary defines "Real Estate or Property: Lands, tenements, and hereditaments; freehold interests in land property; property in houses and land."

This document—presented sometime after death of her mother, Apolonia—appears to also block Bibiana and her younger daughters, Maria Marta, Doloritas, Josefita and Isabelita, from claiming any inheritance from her. As their natural guardian, Bibiana signed for *four* daughters, not only the daughters of Metzger, but also for Maria Marta, daughter of Daniel Eberle.

Why was Bibiana willing to accept the conditions of this document? Did she think she needed to distance herself and her daughters from Metzger? Why did her adult children—sons Ramon and Andrés and daughter Elionor—agree that doing this was in hers and her younger daughters' best interests? Karl speculated whether forfeiting inheritance from Apolonia could somehow apply to Bernardo's personal allotment of the Mora Grant. At their deaths, Apolonia and Bernardo were still legally married to each other. Was intent of this contract to also prevent Bernardo's estate, including his grant lands, from passing to Bibiana and her children? Bernardo died December 1873—about one year and three months before this document was written. Apolonia had predeceased him but we do not know how long before.

Joyce Laumbach, brother of Verna, had written on page 43 of his little booklet, *Some History and I Remember*, that his great-grandmother [*Bibiana*] had sold her property to her grandsons, Daniel and Henry, before she died. "As she had children by three husbands, she was afraid they would fight over her estate. Uncle Henry and Papa deeded it to their sisters who were living on the old home, taking care of their mother [*Elionor*]." That transaction Joyce described would have been when Bibiana was older and moved to the little house in the orchard near her daughter, Elionor. Exactly what was that property she sold to her grandsons? Where was it? What size? Was that the home-place at Cebolla that had been her father's? I think that is likely since that was where Bibiana lived most of her life.

Will we ever know exactly where in Cebolla that home-place had been, when it had passed from the family, and under what circumstances?

The 1870 U.S. Census shows Apolonia "keeping house" with Frank Metzger in Mora. Some data shows them together before that. Did Apolonia and Metzger move to the Buena Vista place soon after that 1870 census? Frank Metzger died at age 66 in February 1885, while he lived at the Buena Vista place with Juanita and Henry Korte. Family tradition said Apolonia also lived there with him when she died, which would have been years earlier, "before 1873." Bibiana was almost 70 years old when she died in 1897, living near her daughter, Elionor Laumbach. She must have known, and directly or indirectly experienced, the family strife that followed after she ended her relationship with Metzger.

After they separated, Metzger spent the rest of his life trying to undermine Bibiana and their daughters the only way he could, by blocking any inheritance to them from him. Metzger had begun doing that when he went to court in 1872 to formally adopt his illegitimate daughter, Juanita, after she had been married for three years to his friend, Henry Korte. At least by then, Metzger had begun trying to prevent all except Juanita and Henry Korte from inheriting his estate. It seems odd he went to all of that effort but had no will.

After Metzger's death, Henry Korte continued his plan of disinheriting Bibiana's youngest daughters.

Alvin Korte told me he believed Juanita—daughter of Frank Metzger, wife of Henry Korte—had opposed their intentions of cutting off her half-sisters. Alvin's grandfather and others had overheard many bitter private quarrels between Henry and Juanita far into the night. Juanita might have even been a victim of spousal abuse. Alvin said he believes this is a woman's story. He thinks Apolonia, Bibiana, her daughters, Juanita and Anna Korte were exploited victims of a time in history when women had little say or authority.

As Alvin began delving deeper into court records and other documents, he said he was dismayed to learn what scoundrels Frank Metzger and Henry Korte had been, not only to the extended family but also within the community.

~~

The suit against Metzger's estate presented by Bibiana's daughters stated that, when he died, he had a large estate of unknown value within the Territory of New Mexico and also in the state of Missouri that included lands, cattle, moneys, personal properties and monies owed to him.

Testimony in this lengthy suit said the filed probate of Metzger's estate was made to appear that his estate was only valued at $180.00. In fact, according to court testimony, within a year of his death, in 1885 Metzger paid $12,000 in taxes.

Sometime after Korte had entered the partnership with Metzger, assets that appeared to be conveyed to him were lands, a large amount of goods, wares and merchandise at the store in Mora. Their partnership included cattle, mules, horses, burros, hogs, sheep and other domestic animals valued to $40,000 or $50,000. There were also various farm implements, machinery, and large amounts of produce from orchards and fields. There were several thousand acres with houses and other improvements, including fencing, and lands under profitable cultivation, thousands of trees bearing fruits resulting in valuable produce. Korte's profits from sales of grains and fruit, alone, were at least $8,000. And, said court testimony in that suit, on another ranch were grazing cattle that increased the estate's value by at least $60,000 more.

Court testimony said that, in addition to produce and livestock sold, Henry Korte had deposited large amounts of funds in banks in Missouri and other states and territories, he had loaned or invested in real estate in his or other names, such as his minor children's, for his own benefit. This was done while Metzger was still living, with or without his consent or knowledge. The specific purpose of this was to cheat, defraud and deprive the plaintiffs (Bibiana's daughters by Metzger) of their father's estate.

Court records claimed Henry Korte had "become exceedingly dissipated and reckless in his habits and is very much addicted to the drinking of ardent spirits and during the greater portion of the time keeps himself so much under the influence of liquor that he is absolutely unfit mentally and physically to manage, control, or do business intelligently or properly." It was also claimed that Korte had been "squandering or dissipating large amounts of money and other property in a most reckless and extravagant manner without reference to the interests of [*the plaintiffs*]." The suit said Korte had been threatening to lose, destroy or hide the estate's assets, and his own. Under oath, Henry admitted that he liked the "juice of the corn, when good, that it frequently has an exhilarating and re-invigorating effect" upon him.

After the case was aired in court for years, the plaintiffs—Bibiana's youngest daughters—finally won, but there were no assets left. Both family branches lost.

A large portion of the lawsuit—copies of the official translated court transcripts—between Bibiana's daughters and Metzger's heirs will be included in the next book of this trilogy: *Bibiana and Her Children*.

~~

The 1875 document, dated several years *after* Bibiana and Metzger had split, stated "Viviana Martin" was a resident of La Sevolla (La Cebolla). That indicates that she—at least then—lived at Cebolla but not at Metzger's Cebolla ranch. (I believe she had never lived at his ranch.) This and other documents, including several U.S. census records, show she had lived at Cebolla most of her life with her father (who died two years earlier, in December 1873) and her children during their growing up years.

If Karl's belief—that Bibiana only lived at Cebolla while she was with Frank Metzger at his Cebolla ranch—was correct, why were Bernardo and all of Bibiana's children also residing there when the U.S. census taker knocked on their door in 1860? On that census, Bernardo was listed as head of household. Metzger was not mentioned in that household of that census. I am convinced they were living at Bernardo's place in Cebolla, the one he established for his family after moving from Potrero. By that 1860 census, Bibiana had one child by Metzger and would have two more with him. But he is not shown as a resident in that household.

I had put out queries because of my ongoing quest for an exact location of Bernardo's and Bibiana's "La Cebolla" home. I continue to want to know approximately where, in the Mora area, Bernardo had settled and lived with his family—except for his brief sojourn with the U.S. Army.

Karl said he had not seen adequate evidence that Bernardo settled at Cebolla, and that Bibiana had also mostly lived there. From information he has concerning the Mora Grant[1] he believes the original grantees, including Bernardo, settled around the grant's designated plazas. A source Karl has about the Mora Land Grant provides information on early grantee settlements. He continues to believe Bibiana only lived at Cebolla when she was with Metzger.

Butch Sanders said records he found indicate Frank Metzger continued to live in "Mora town"—instead of his Cebolla ranch—until at least 1880.

Neither of their perspectives exactly coincides with mine.

This is a recap of information from which I make my conclusions:

Bernardo's December 1873 death record said he died at Cebolla, and was buried at Cebolla. On that record, modern genealogical researchers inserted "Ledoux," the community's newer name, as his place of burial, reflecting their conclusion that he was buried in that community's old cemetery. The priest who officiated at the burial would have known where that took place; he probably also knew exactly where Bernardo had lived. (I believe it was daughter, Bibiana, living with her father at Cebolla, who provided the priest the data that Bernardo's wife, Apolonia, was already deceased. That record is our only way of knowing a time frame for her death. If her grave marker legibly provides her death date, we cannot see it.)

I believe the Cebolla cited as his residence was a less specific place-name than that of his burial. Cebolla was the name frequently given—even 150 years ago—for multiple places in the Mora area.

The 1875 court document said Bibiana was a resident of La Sevolla.

I had noticed Mora area census, baptism and marriage records covering a span of years in the second half of the 1800s showed many people resided at a place called Cebolla or something similar. That seemed an excessive quantity of people to have come from one little settlement.

In the *New Mexico Baptisms, Mora, 1861—1878* and its sister volume spanning *1879—1899*, both published by the Hispanic Genealogical Research Center of New Mexico, are the following place-names: Cebolla, Cebolla Abajo, La Seboya (just a different spelling), San Antonio Cebolla and San Jose de Abajo Cebolla. (Butch said San Jose de Abajo Cebolla was the settlement later named Ledoux.)

From that, Danny Chavez and other sources I have confirmed "Cebolla" was a large area, not just one specific place. The Cebolla River gave its name to several small settlements and little valleys through which it passed. Danny asked several Mora "old timers" about La Cebolla. He was told pretty much what he believed and I concluded: La Cebolla was a name applied to multiple places along the Rita de Cebolla in the Mora area.

Clifford Regensberg's family has lived in the Cebolla area for generations. He lives in El Paso but maintains a place at Cebolla. He confirmed that the town of Ledoux was once called Cebolla. On his Facebook page he posted: "I understand the whole valley is referred to as the Cebolla valley, this includes Ledoux, El Oro, El Carmen, Monte Aplanado, El Aguila, etc." The image of an August 26,

1865 document that Clifford posted on Mora's Facebook page names the village San Jose de la Cevolla (sic). Among his collection of vintage documents, Clifford said, is one naming 1885 Cebolla valley residents involved with creating Murphy Lake to irrigate their lands. That document listing area residents would be a valuable resource for people doing genealogy searches. Clifford also posted on his Facebook page that there was an old settlement above Murphy Lake, now called La Rinconada, that may have once been named La Cebolla, and the present village of Ledoux may have been Cebolla Abajo. That posting brought a response from Raymond Espinoza, now of Las Lunas, whose family had also been from the Cebolla area. He posted that La Riconada was originally called Corral de Los Alamos because early settlers found a large corral with very tall fences made of aspen trees.

Names of places, like names of people, can be elusive. Clifford said—but he has not found confirmation—that a teacher years ago said many villages were changed to Anglo names to give New Mexico a better chance of success when being considered for statehood. He thought that might have applied to Agua Negra now Holman, San Antonio now Cleveland and San Jose de Cebolla now Ledoux.

~~

Butch Sanders found an April 18, 1908 published notice of unpaid property taxes. It included an entry for "Veeder & Veeder" with a land description of property previously owned by Metzger. Butch first found it published in the Roy, New Mexico El Hispaño American on October 13, 1906, and again in 1908 with increased penalties because those taxes remained unpaid.

"To the delinquent taxpayers in the following tax list whose taxes are over the sum of $25 Greeting: You are hereby notified that I will on the 26th Day of May. A. D. 1908 apply to the District Court of the county of Mora in the Territory of New Mexico, as provided by law, for judgment against all of the parties named in the following delinquent tax list, and against the land, real estate and personal property mentioned and described therein, for the amount of said delinquent taxes, together with the costs, penalties, and interest due and unpaid thereon, and for an order to sell said property to satisfy such judgment, and within 30 days after the rendition of such judgment against the property described in said list and after having given notice by handbill posted at east front door of the building in which the District Court for said county of Mora is held, at least ten days prior to the date of the sale, I shall offer for sale at public auction in front of said building, the real estate and personal property described in said list against which judgment may be rendered, for the amount of taxes, penalties, and costs due thereon."

I do not know the outcome of this demand for payment of taxes or of the threat of forfeiture of Veeder property.

This next publication interests us because it includes a detailed description of Metzger's property. Here is the Veeder & Veeder portion of that tax list in Precinct No. 5:

"Veeder & Veeder - 1 tract of land known as the Frank Metzger Cebolla ranch, lying and being situated on both sides of the Mora river, in Mora county, N. M., bounded north, by the hills; south, another hill or mountain; on the other side of the Cebolla river; on the east by a ranch belonging to Henry Korte in the month of June, 1873; and known as the Metzger & Pinard Ranch of Buena Vista; and on the west by three springs at the Gap of the Creston.

Also tract of land, known as the Frank Metzger and the Pinard ranch, lying and being situated at Buena Vista, Mora, N. M.; bounded on the north by the Mora river; on the south by the summit of the mountains; on the east by the junction of the Mora and Cebolla rivers; and on the west by the summits of the mountains between Buena Vista and Golondrinas. This being the same tract of land which Frank Metzger purchased of J. Francisco Pinard.

Taxes. $110.13
Penalty. 5.50
Printing. 70
Total. . . . . . $116.23"

Danny Chavez responded to my question asking if he knew location of "the Gap of the Creston" in the above publication. Based on the descriptions I gave him, he said, he thought the Gap of the Crestón would be near what he calls the dissolved remains of a hacienda we saw after we turned off Highway 518 onto the road to Ledoux in October 2013. I had directed him and Chick Burney, manager of the Abel family's Buena Vista Ranch, to that site on Abel land. (Until I showed it to him, Chick had been unaware of that site.) Danny said *crestón* means rimrock. That could describe several places around Cebolla and Buena Vista that have distinctive gaps where a stream or river—the Cebolla or the Mora—cut through the rock, he said. He reminded me that, on that day we were there, Chick had said there are a couple springs just beyond the rock cliffs and the road—the gap and rimrock.

Danny said, "The only place I know where there are springs is in [*that valley*] we today call La Cebollita—La Cebolla then. There are a couple hot springs within [*that*] valley that feed into the Cebolla Creek." He said there are springs [*west of the "dissolved" adobe hacienda*] between El Carmen and Ledoux "where we visited with Chick." He thinks there is a third spring across that road, and all of them feed into the Cebollita Creek near the ruin site. "I would say the Gap of the Crestón would be where Chick had driven us that day," he said. "There are no springs in the Buena Vista area or adjacent to the Buena Vista Ranch headquarters."

I believe Metzger's Cebolla ranch house had been those barely visible ruins we saw that had once been a substantial homestead, what Danny Chavez calls the ruins or melt of a hacienda. That was also what Alvin had pointed out in the summer of 2013 as being the site of Metzger's Cebolla ranch house. And that fits published descriptions of Metzger's Cebolla ranch. The Rita de Cebolla runs through that little valley not far from those ruins. However, that same place fits Karl's description of where he believed his grandfather Pete was born at Bibiana's place in 1867. Karl had written that his grandfather Pete, as a very young child, had run from there through the snow to bathe in the river. The full story Karl heard was that his grandfather ran to bathe in *naturally warm water*. He had not mentioned that part because he had no substantiation. He was excited when he learned of Danny Chavez's comment about hot springs nearby. That makes me think Bernardo's home might have been *near* Metzger's later established Cebolla Ranch, perhaps closer to the Gap near those springs.

I believe Peter Joseph and at least two of his siblings were born in Bernardo's hacienda, where their grandmother Bibiana spent most of her life, and that it was *near* Metzger's place. I believe Bernardo was already settled there with his family when Gov. Albino Perez granted the Mora lands to area settlers in 1835. I think he and his family were well established in that small valley before Fredrick Metzger bought his tracts of ranchlands—the one at Buena Vista and the one at La Cebolla—from Fr. Francisco Pinard. If Bernardo had settled there first, logic says he would have chosen the best spot. That would have been near those hot springs. Perhaps the near proximity of their two properties in that little valley was why Metzger had become well acquainted with Apolonia and Bibiana.

Danny Chavez said Rudy (Rudolph "Sonny" Laumbach) once told him that the "Laumbach family" had lived in that Cebolla valley area before they moved to Buena Vista about a mile east. *[It would have actually been more than a mile away.]*

Danny wrote, in a more recent email, that he hoped to soon return to that area to confirm those nearby springs. He wrote: "That area beyond the "Crestón" was called El Guajalote (Spanish for salamander). There must have been salamanders inhabiting springs since they prefer wet marshy areas (springs would qualify)." He also wrote, "That small perpendicular canyon has seen" several different owners living there. The newest owners renamed the area Cebolla Springs. "Maybe when the weather warms up I can walk [to] El Guajalote, aka Cebolla Springs, and locate these springs."

Throughout the New Mexico section of this book, I pondered exactly where Bernardo, Apolonia initially, and Bibiana and her children had lived. Verna had told me they lived at La Cebolla (Seboya) long before I had a clue where that was. Much later I learned from maps and other resources that it is in the Mora area. (Cebolla is a fairly common name; there is at least one other place named Cebolla in a different part of New Mexico.) For most of my life I had heard and believed that Bernardo's family lived in La Cebolla. More recently, I also believed that had been, at least then, in Precinct 5. But exactly where? Some documents show Precinct 5 for both Buena Vista and La Cebolla. Perhaps Precinct 5 was large or, as happens today, redistricting caused precinct boundary changes.

Earlier the same day Chick drove to the site I wanted to show him on the road to Ledoux, he showed us that other less visible site. That one is east of the Abel Buena Vista headquarters, near where the remake of *True Grit* was filmed. That area is also called Cebolla because the small Cebolla River continues through there on its way to the Mora River. Later, Danny told me that area has no springs.

~~

That rare bit of information in Joyce's little book, *Some History and I Remember*, about Bibiana transferring her property in her later years, provides an intriguing possibility of Bernardo's grant lands. I had thought Bibiana may have still had her father's grant land after he died, that he had not lost it soon after it was granted, as happened with other Mora grantees. I had no proof but I thought that property may have remained with Bibiana, but perhaps ended with her. Maybe the property Joyce wrote of had been her father's grant lands and it had stayed with the family a few more decades, until Aunties sold all of their lands and moved to Las Vegas. I wish Joyce had specified that location of Bibiana's property and its approximate size. If Joyce was correct, that may have been in La Cebolla, just a few miles west of the Buena Vista place. That may also mean that Frank Metzger and Henry Korte—or their heirs—did not get the Martín ancestral place, even if they had tried. Will we ever know? There are too many missing pieces to the puzzle.

~~

The land the Hughes G. Abel family owns includes the Buena Vista Ranch that had formerly been the Metzger-Korte property. While researching for this book, Butch Sanders found an interesting irony of that family name, although genealogy shows no connection between that Abel family and the Abel in the following story.

Sanders wrote: "There was an early 'Abel' in Mora village: 'Stephen Abel of Clermont,' one of the priests described as 'the saintly men who heard the voice of God in their hearts' when Bishop Lamy went to France in 1854 looking for help. Among the other priests who answered that call were "Pieter John Munnecum" (aka Peter John Munnecom), and "Damaso Taladrid." These three priests would be sent to St. Gertrudis/Gertrudes Church in Mora village.

"Father Peter John Munnecom was the first to arrive at St. Gertrudis/Gertrudes. He was the 'Pedro Juan Munnecom' of 'St. Gertrudes de lo de Mora' who baptized Maria Marta Eberle in 1856 and Maria Dolores 'Martinez' in 1857.

"Father Stephen Abel *[aka Etienne M. Avel]* was sent to assist/replace Father Munnecom at St. Gertrudis/ Gertrudes. It would appear the two priests did not like each other," wrote Sanders. The *[archived article found by Butch]* Saturday, December 18, 1858 *Santa Fe Weekly Gazette* reported the outcome of Father Munnecom's trial for the murder of Father Abel:
The judge reviewed the entire evidence adduced at the trial.

"The deceased and the prisoner at the bar were at the time of the poisoning, 3rd of August last, both officiating clergymen of the Catholic church of Moro in this diocese. The former, father Abel, upon his deathbed persisted in accusing the prisoner as his murderer, after having been repeatedly warned by one of the witnesses of the importance of such an accusation. The bottle of wine containing the fatal poison was that used at the Holy Sacrament *[while]* saying mass at the altar, and the dying priest declared that no one but himself and the accused had or could have access to the wine. …though this was very probably true, the contrary was possible. So fixed did the belief appear to be in father Abel that father Monnicum was his murderer that when the latter was suggested as the priest to officiate at the deathbed, the former replied that he 'did not want his murderer to administer to him' *[and]* that he 'did not want Monnicum's name to be mentioned to him—for that the person who had poisoned him was unfit to administer the sacrament.' The evidence was entirely circumstantial, and we understand that in the opinion of most persons who heard the trial, it was not at all conclusive of the guilt of the prisoner, whom the jury after a short absence found not guilty by the following verdict: 'Nosotros, los miembros del pequeno jurado, unanimemente hallamos sin culpa al acusado.'"

Butch Sanders continued: "Father Damaso Taladrid was then sent to St. Gertrudis/ Gertrudes to replace Father Munnecom. Just prior to that, he had been sent to Taos to replace Padre Martinez, but hadn't been received with open arms by the Padre's flock. But to complete this part of the story, we find 'Damaso Taladrid,' age 41; occupation, 'R. C. Priest,' born 'Madrid, Spain' recorded in Santa Gertrudis (Mora village) in 1860. *[That census record shows he resided]* between Frank Metzger and Apolonia Gutierrez. Frank is recorded in dwelling 3128, Taladrid in dwelling 3133, and Apolonia *[when Bibiana visited her that day]* was next door in dwelling 3134.

Butch added, "Now back to Maria Marta's baptismal record: the godparents recorded on it are 'Faustin Aveita and Qiria Lidoe.' They are husband and wife. This 'Qiria Lidoe' is Maria Quirina de los Angeles Ledoux, daughter of Antoine 'Antonio' Ledoux and Maria Apolonia Lucero. It was this Antonio Ledoux for whom "San Jose Cebolla" was renamed "Ledoux" around 1903."

That tells us about when San Jose Cebolla became the settlement of Ledoux.

Butch continues: "Oddly enough, in the 1850 census, it is not Bernardo Martin we find residing near the Ledoux family (I haven't yet found Bernardo in 1850), but Miguel Mascarenas. Antonio Ledoux and Maria Apolonia Lucero are recorded in dwelling 2067, Miguel Mascarenas *[father-in-law of James Bonney]* and María Ygnacia Lujan in dwelling 2069, and Faustin Abeyta and Quirina Lidu (Ledoux) in dwelling 2080.

"Maria Apolonia Lucero (Antonio's wife and Quirina's mother) is interesting for other reasons as well. Her brother was Pablo Antonio Lucero, the father of Tomas de Aquino Lucero who married Maria Refugio Velasquez, parents of Anastacia Lucero, wife of Ramon Bonney. Before Maria Apolonia Lucero's marriage to Antonio Ledoux, she was married to Juan Bautista La Lande. Among their children was Maria Dolores "Doloritas" La Lande who married Gervais Nolin, parents of Fernando Nolan, the father of Jose Fermin Nolan who married Maclovia Lopez, daughter of Trinidad Lopez and Maria Cleofas Bonney." This string of connections illustrates Butch's amazing research abilities! His discoveries show many early families of New Mexico connected by marriage and other circumstances. There is no wonder why many New Mexico families called each other *primo*; they were!

"So in the early days we have two key villages: San Jose Cebolla (later Ledoux) and Santa Gertrudes (aka Mora village). Here's another to consider: on early maps there was *[yet another]* village named Cebolla … depicted at the top of the Cebolla Valley about halfway between Mora and San Jose. It appears to be in the same place Abuelo (aka Abuelo Cebolla) is on modern maps. There is also El Oro Cebolla in the Cebolla Valley. Folks seem to believe San Jose Cebolla/Ledoux was the parent Cebolla Valley village. My guess is that Abuelo/Cebolla is the Cebolla that folks referred to in the very early days. It is closer to Mora, and on the same side of the valley as Mora, a better place to be when Indians or Texans visited.

"Most of the early action seems to have been in Mora village and just south of it (less than an hour's walk). While various grants [*Mora's individually parceled grant-lands*] may have been much farther distant, I believe most owners of those granted lands in those early days resided in small groups clustered around and near Mora village. When they went farming, they went in groups together. Where their grants were located and where their residences were located may have not been in the same places until after 1860 or so," wrote Butch.

~~

Reading this book, readers will find some information I wrote earlier evolved and changed as I proceeded to learn new things. Valued input from Butch Sanders, Karl Laumbach, Danny Chavez, Jose Antonio Esquibel and others has given all of us new information and broadened our knowledge. Together we have learned new and interesting facets of our family history, while we are still left with speculations, unconfirmed facts and unanswered questions. When researching family history there are few absolutes. Documentations provide good evidence, but between those we are left with many uncertainties. There is much more to know, evidence yet to be found. It remains a matter of piecing together everything we know, discarding some pieces, inserting new ones, hoping they fit. This quest for knowledge shows the importance of documenting, for future generations, what we now know or believe.

Between now and the next two history books of this trilogy—both already more than half-written—our family's saga continues to evolve and change. It seems as if we are working on a giant jigsaw puzzle, trying to make the pieces fit. Some won't. There are also missing pieces, perhaps lost forever. The picture that comes together may not be the one we expected to see.

---

[i] *From Reparticion To Partition: A History of the Mora Land Grant, 1835—1916*, by Robert D. Shadow and Maria Rodriguez-Shadow. Robert D. Shadow is professor of anthropology at the Universidad de las Americas-Puebla and Maria Rodriguez-Shadow is researcher in the Department of Ethnology and Social Anthropology at the National Institute of Anthropology and History, Mexico.

"Men in their generations
are like the leaves of the trees.
The wind blows and one year's leaves
are scattered on the ground;
but the trees burst into bud
and put on fresh ones
when the spring comes around."

Homer

LAUMBACHS IN NEW MEXICO
And Those Who Went Before
In Germany, Iowa and New Mexico

Who were they? Therefore, who am I?

APPENDIX

Appendix I: Newspaper Articles Located and Transcribed by Butch Sanders
    A. **Laumbach**
    B. **Metzger, Korte, Naeglin**

Appendix II: Genealogy Charts Researched and Charted by Butch Sanders
    A. **Martin-Serrano** By Butch Sanders with oversight by José A. Esquibel
    B. **Laumbach, Including "Paper Trail"** By Butch Sanders

Appendix III: Bios & Photos of Major Contributors

The past is never dead ...Actually, it's not even past.

William Faulkner

APPENDIX I
Part A. Pertinent Laumbach Newspaper Clippings

Researched & Transcribed by Charles O. "Butch" Sanders

EL MOSQUITO
Mora, New Mexico
Thursday, February 11, 1892

El dia se unio para siempre por los lazos matrimoniales el joven J. S. Candelario, de Santa Fe, con la senorita Estefanita N. Laumbach, de Buena Vista, en ultima poblacion.

La ceremonia se efectuo en la Primera Iglesia Presbiteriana.

EL MOSQUITO desea a los recien desposados una eterna luna de miel.

~~

SANTA FE NEW MEXICAN
Santa Fe, New Mexico
March 17, 1897

MANUEL A. SANCHEZ, Member of the thirty-second Legislative Assembly of New Mexico, Representative from San Miguel County, was born January 1, 1861, at Rociada, San Miguel County, and received his education in the private schools of that county. At his home in Savinoso, he conducts a mercantile business, which was established in 1879, and is a large owner of cattle and sheep.

In 1879, he was elected justice of the peace for his precinct, and in 1890 was appointed census enumerator by Mr. Pedro Sanchez.

Mr. Sanchez is a staunch Republican, and as such was elected to the legislature last November. His services as a member of the House have proven very satisfactory to the people of his county. Ever attentive to business, careful of the interests of the territory, and by his frank, fearless position taken on measures of importance has earned the good will and respect of his fellow members.

On December 3, 1887, Mr. Sanchez was married to Miss Roseta Eggert, and they have one child.

~~

SANTA FE NEW MEXICAN
Santa Fe, New Mexico
November 17, 1897
CITY NEWS ITEMS.

The children of Andres Laumbach of Mora have gone to Santa Fe to attend different institutions of learning. - Las Vegas Optic. And the institutions of learning in this city being first-class they could not do better than attend them.

~~

SANTA FE NEW MEXICAN
Santa Fe, New Mexico
March 27, 1899
PERSONAL MENTION.

Daniel Laumbach and his sister, Miss Mary Laumbach, of Buena Vista, are in the city visiting with Mr. Laumbach's brother-in-law, J. S. Candelario. Mr. Laumbach returns north shortly, while Miss Laumbach will remain here for some time.

SANTA FE NEW MEXICAN
Santa Fe, New Mexico
June 28, 1899
PERSONAL MENTION.

Mr. and Mrs. P. J. Lombach, of Sanchez are the guests for the week of J. S. Candelario. Mr. Lombach is a cattleman and says that the ranchmen around Sanchez were unable to dispose of their cattle on account of the drouth.

SANTA FE NEW MEXICAN
Santa Fe, New Mexico
October 2, 1900
PERSONAL MENTION.

Mrs. A. Laumbach, mother of Mrs. J. S. Candelario, of this city, who has been visiting here for the past two weeks, left this morning for her home in Buena Vista.

DENVER ROCKY MOUNTAIN NEWS
Denver, Colorado
Sunday, November 6, 1904
ACCIDENT COST LIFE.
Special to The News.

LAS VEGAS, N. M., Nov. 5.-Andres Laumbach, a ranchman at Lacueve [sic], while cleaning a pistol accidentally discharged it, and the bullet passed near his heart. He was found lying dead on the floor.

EL HISPANO AMERICANO
Roy, Mora County, New Mexico
February 13, 1905

Mrs. D. C. Olds, our popular midwife, returned home on Friday morning from the ranches of Dan Laumbach and Peter Laumbach, where she was attending both wifes of the Laumbach Bros.

To the home of Dan a bouncing baby boy arrived and to that of Peter a pretty little daughter.

NEBRASKA STATE JOURNAL
Lincoln, Nebraska

Sunday, November 29, 1908

FREMONT - At 3 o'clock Friday afternoon Mrs. Anna Henkins died at her home from a paralytic stroke. She is survived by her husband and eight children, five of whom are living in Fremont. The deceased was the mother of Mrs. Robert McCann. The funeral will be held Sunday at 1:30 at the Salem Lutheran church. *[This was Emma's mother, married to Peter Henkens. Mrs. Robert McCann was Emma's sister.]*

SCHLESWIG LEADER
Schleswig, Iowa
February 16, 1912
Marriage license

Fourteen marriage licenses were issued at the clerk's office in Denison during the past week. In the list we notice the names of Julius Ernst and Anna Laumbach. *[This Anna was from one of the Heinrich "Henry" Laumbach family branches that remained in Iowa. There were two Henry Laumbachs born in Jagel, Schleswig: a brother of Andreas 1st and a brother of Andreas 2nd.]*

THE SPANISH AMERICAN
Roy, New Mexico
January 3, 1914

Pete Laumbach went to Santa Fe Monday to take his son and little daughter to school there. They will study in the Catholic Schools of the old city and the parents are seeing that they are started right. Mrs. Laumbach came in to town with them to see them off.

THE SPANISH AMERICAN
Roy, New Mexico
April 18, 1914

FOR SALE: My Pecheron Stallion, "Monarch" he is Thorobred, eligible to Registry, weight 1500 lbs. and a fine animal. Also some milch cows. Will sell them worth the money.
  See me at the Ranch or in Roy.
T.6pd.   P. J. Laumbach.

Pete and Dan Laumbach were in town Wednesday remaining over to Thursday. They are now both full-fledged Odd Fellows and the local lodge is jubilating over the acquirement of such men as members. Several other good men are on the way and Homestead Lodge is enjoying a substantial growth.

Joe Ballard came in Wednesday to attend lodge. He and Pete Laumbach negotiated a cattle deal while here to their mutual advantage.

THE SPANISH AMERICAN
Roy, New Mexico
May 23, 1914

Pete Laumbach returned from Mora last week bringing his children who have been attending school at Vegas and Santa Fe with him. He and his brother Dan delivered a lot of cattle here Saturday and were in town over Sunday. They are getting their herds fixed up for the coming season. Pete reports two miles of fence washed out and a house which had stood for forty five years in the canyon carried away by the worst flood ever known in La Cinta.

THE SPANISH AMERICAN
Roy, New Mexico
July 11, 1914

Pete and Dan Laumbach were in town Monday. The latter was filing application for re-lease of some of the school land in his pasture.

SCHLESWIG LEADER
Schleswig, Iowa
January 7, 1915
PROMINENT COUPLE ARE WON BY CUPID

Miss Laura Laumbach, daughter of Mr. and Mrs. Henry Laumbach of near Mapleton and Mr. Theodore Jochims, son of Mr. and Mrs. William Jochims of this place, were married Wednesday forenoon at nine o'clock in the home of the groom's parents. Rev. Wetzeler of the Schleswig Friedens church officiated. The bride and groom were attended by Peter Laumbach and Miss Alwine Jochims. The young couple will go to housekeeping on a farm near Lake Park, Ia.

The bride is well known in Schleswig where she is respected and has scores of friends. She was born in the vicinity north of town where she lived until young womanhood with her parents. They recently moved to a farm near Mapleton. The groom is a popular young man of good character and ability. He was born in Otter Creek township and is an industrious worker. Their many friends, among whom The Leader wishes to be observed, wishes them success and happiness in their new endeavor.

~~

THE SPANISH AMERICAN
Roy, New Mexico
Saturday, February 20, 1915

A little child of Mr. and Mrs. P. J. Laumbach died Sunday from pneumonia at their home in La Cinta Canyon.

~~

THE SPANISH AMERICAN
Roy, New Mexico
May 26, 1917

Pete Laumbach was in town Monday to meet his daughter, Miss Cordelia, who has been in school in Santa Fe the past term. Miss Laumbach visited her grandmother and other relatives at La Cueva and also friends at Holman and Las Vegas. She was accompanied home by her aunt, Miss Laumbach, of La Cueva and Miss Kanto.

~~

THE SPANISH AMERICAN
Roy, New Mexico
June 2, 1917

Pete Laumbach and Joe Lopez were in town Monday getting out a petition to charge the road down across the point of the mesa between La Cinta and Burro canyons. It will make a good road to the top of the canyon hill from there to the bottom a parachute would be practical. *[Note the paper editor's sense of humor.]*

~~

THE SPANISH AMERICAN
Roy, New Mexico
July 14, 1917

Henry Laumbach, of La Cueva visited his brothers Dan and Pete Laumbach here the first of the week. He drove over in his Ford and returned home Tuesday.

~~

THE SPANISH AMERICAN
Roy, New Mexico
October 6, 1917
NO TRESPASSING

All persons are hereby warned not to trespass on my ranch and range lands in the breaks of La Cinta Canyon.

Deer hunters are especially unwelcome and dangerous to cattle. There is no land in this vicinity not in private ownership.

Trespassers and Hunters will arrested if found on these lands.

Ml. pd.   P. J. LAUMBACH, Owner.

~~

THE DENISON REVIEW
Denison, Iowa
Wednesday, May 29, 1918
[Photo]

Mr. and Mrs. Peter Jepsen, [*photo included*] taken at the time of golden wedding anniversary.

DEATH CLAIMS PETER JEPSEN

A Resident of Crawford County for 40 Years, Peter Jepsen Passes to the Great Beyond.

WAS VERY LARGE LAND OWNER.

Ill for Past Year, but Was Able to be Up Until Week Ago—Cancer of Stomach Cause of Death.

Peter Frederick Jepsen, a resident of Crawford County for more than 40 years, died at his home in Denison on Monday, May 27th, at the age of 71 years, 4 months and 9 days. Mr. Jepsen had been in poor health a year prior to his death and for the past few weeks suffered intensely, although he was able to be up and around a week prior to his death. He was afflicted with cancer of the stomach and death came as a relief from his suffering shortly after 5 o'clock on Monday afternoon.

The deceased was born in Schleswig-Holstein, Germany, Jan. 13, 1847. He was reared upon a farm there and early became familiar with farming, to which he devoted a large part of his life. He received his education in his native land and being an ambitious young man he decided at twenty years of age to seek his fortune in America. He came to the United States in 1867 and settled in Clinton county, Iowa, but later spent one year on a farm in Dakota. In the fall of 1875 he purchased 160 acres of land in Goodrich township, Crawford county, which he improved to good advantage, making it one of the valuable farms of that township. As years passed he showed remarkable ability in the acquisition of land and he later owned 960 acres in Goodrich township, also 120 acres in Milford, township, 170 acres in East Boyer township and 640 acres in Hayes township. In addition to his holdings here in Crawford county he owned considerable land in other sections. He probably owned more Crawford county land than any other man. In 1904 he retired from active farm work and moved to Denison, where he has since resided.

On the 10th of October, 1867, Mr. Jepsen was united in marriage to Miss Anna Laumbach, also a native of Schleswig-Holstein, Germany. The union was blessed with nine children, five sons and four daughters, as follows: Mrs. Wm. Gehring, of this city; John, of Denison; Peter, of Otter Creek township; Mrs. John Saggau, of this city; Henry F., of Milford township; Mrs. Martin Saggau, of Denison; Jurgen and Julius, of Goodrich township and Mrs. Henry Nath, of Pipestone, Minn., besides thirty-eight grandchildren and eleven great grandchildren. Also three brothers. John, Jurgen and Fred, all residents of Schleswig, survive him.

Mr. Jepsen, by an industrious and straightforward life years ago, gained and established a reputation for integrity and fidelity to duty and his personal worth is fully demonstrated by the esteem in which he was held by a wide circle of friends and acquaintances in Crawford and adjoining counties.

Funeral services were held this afternoon at 2 o'clock at the home. Rev. Wm. Frese, pastor of the German Lutheran church, officiating, after which interment was made in Morgan cemetery.

The bereaved family has the sympathy of a large circle of friends in their sorrow.

~~

THE SPANISH AMERICAN
Roy, New Mexico
Saturday, June 15, 1918

Pete and Dan Laumbach returned Monday from Las Vegas, where they were called by the serious illness of their mother. She is much better and they returned to their pressing activities on the ranches.

THE SPANISH AMERICAN
Roy, New Mexico
August 31, 1918

Mrs. Dan Laumbach went to Las Vegas Tuesday and will visit relatives at La Cueva. Dan is looking for a teacher who can teach his private school this winter. His eldest is in the 9th grade and the younger ones scattered along down the line.

It is a fine place for some competent girl.

THE SPANISH AMERICAN
Roy, New Mexico
Saturday, September 7, 1918
Killed by Lightning

One of the most regrettable accidents that has occurred lately resulted in the death by lightning stroke, of Alfredo Laumbach, eldest son of Mr. and Mrs. Pete J. Laumbach, at their home in La Cinta Canyon, last Thursday, Aug. 29th.

Alfredo, who was almost a man grown, and would have been 18 years old Oct 4th next, was working at building fence about 200 yards from his father's house when a little storm came up. He gathered up an armload of firewood, tops from the fence posts, and started to the house when the bolt struck him. He pitched forward on his face, killed instantly. Julian Sandoval, who was with him, was knocked down and stunned but managed to crawl on his hands and knees toward the house till he met Pete and could not then speak for a time. He is fully recovered, however.

Alfredo was found with his clothing riddled as if torn by shot, and burning. He was borne to the house and restoratives applied but to no avail.

The body was scarred and burned from head to feet and his hat and shoes torn to shreds.

Following close on this disaster a baby was still-born to the bereaved parents. Messengers were sent to Roy and relatives in Santa Fe, La Cueva were notified, but none could come until after the funeral which was held at 6:30 P. M. Friday evening. A hundred or more friends and neighbors were present with sympathy and to assist at the obsequies. Eight Odd Fellows from Roy went to the top of the hill in cars with Rev. Hearn, climbed down over the many hundred feet of rocks and walked to the ranch house on La Cinta creek, to attend. Rev. Hearn conducted a short service in English and Spanish and the bodies were carried from the desolated home to a little cemetery nearby, where both were interred in the same grave.

The parents, five sisters and three brothers survive them, three other children having died in infancy.

The death of their first-born is the most bitter grief ever experienced by this worthy family and all that friends could do was done to soften their sorrow. Alfredo had been sent to school in Albuquerque and received a good education and was already his father's main dependence in the management of his large ranch, as well as his pride and joy.

Card of Thanks

We are deeply grateful to all the friends and neighbors, and especially the Odd Fellows, from Homestead Lodge, for the sympathy and assistance rendered us in our time of bitterest affliction in the death of our eldest son, Alfredo, and at the funeral obsequies. May you all be spared such grief.

PETE J. LAUMBACH and family.

~~

Mrs. J. S. Candelario, a sister of Pete and Dan Laumbach, came last Saturday, too late for the funeral of Alfredo Laumbach and visited her brothers and families here. She returned to Santa Fe Wednesday. Her husband is the proprietor of the old Curio Store, in the Capital and one of the staunch Democrats and most unique characters in New Mexico. The things he can tell you of the past in this state are interesting.

~~

THE SPANISH AMERICAN
Roy, New Mexico
September 21, 1918

TEACHER WANTED

For Private School at Ranch Home. Five Pupils, ranging up to 9th grade. If able to teach elementary music will be preferred. Room and board furnished.

Applicant must have 2d class Certificate or equal qualification.

Apply to DAN LAUMBACH, Roy N. M.

~~

THE SPANISH AMERICAN
Roy, New Mexico
October 5, 1918

Dan Laumbach, who accompanied us on the back seat, visited his sister, Mrs. J. S. Candelario, in Santa Fe, and came home with Cipriano Lujan and his company. Mr. and Mrs. Candelario were especially nice to us and their home as well as the old Curio shop were open to us in a special manner from the hospitality extended to tourists. Coming home the prosaic route of the Ocean to Ocean Highway furnished many interesting experiences but we are convinced that when the road by way of Taos is made fit for ordinary drivers and ordinary cars it will be one of the most famous roads in the state.

~~

THE SPANISH AMERICAN
Roy, New Mexico
February 1, 1919

Pete Laumbach drove in from his home in La Cinta Canyon Tuesday to meet his daughter, who has been visiting relatives at La Cueva. She arrived on the noon train. Pete has fared well with his cattle, the shelter of the canyon and the early melting of the snow on the slopes exposed to the sun gave them feed while all the grass up on the mesa was covered up for weeks.

~~

THE SPANISH AMERICAN
Roy, New Mexico
Saturday, March 15, 1919

A Tragedy

Modesto Andrada, a son of Leopoldo Andrada, was found dead from a gun-shot wound in his father's house in La Cinta Canyon Thursday Morning. The news was brought here by a messenger with a plea for officers to come and investigate but it is out of the Roy jurisdiction so they did not go.

The victim was a young man of about 20 years and a member of one of the best families in La Cinta and a nephew of Mrs. Pete Laumbach.

~~

THE SPANISH AMERICAN
Roy, New Mexico
June 14, 191

Pete Laumbach went to La Cueva last week, returning Monday. He took out lumber for a new house he is building on one of his ranches in La Cinta canyon.

~~

THE SPANISH AMERICAN
Roy, New Mexico
December 6, 1919

Pete and Dan Laumbach went to La Cueva Tuesday to visit their mother who resides there. They went by train to Las Vegas and by auto stage on.

~~

THE SPANISH AMERICAN
Roy, New Mexico
May 1, 1920

~~

Mrs. J. E. Cruz of Holman N. M., Misses Anna and Mary Laumbach of La Cueva N. M., sisters of Dan and Pete Laumbach, came to town last Thursday on the train. Dan Laumbach came to town to meet them and took them home. Misses Anna and Mary Laumbach are going to make proof on their additional homestead in May. Mrs. Cruz and her sisters will visit their relatives while they are here.

~~

THE SPANISH AMERICAN
Roy, New Mexico
July 3, 1920
Lost, Strayed or Stolen

A perfectly good front gate from my ranch home in La Cinta Canyon. $2.50 reward for its return or the apprehension of the thief.

PETE LAUMBACH.

We half expected something of the kind when that gang went down to Henry Stone's dance last week. If you see a strange front gate about town see Pete about it.

~~

THE SPANISH AMERICAN
Roy, New Mexico
July 10, 1920

Pete Laumbach's two little daughters came home from a visit with relatives at La Cueva Wednesday.

~~

THE SPANISH AMERICAN
Roy, New Mexico

July 31, 1920

Dan Laumbach has purchased 4 lots in the Montezuma addition and will build a house on them. Mrs. will bring the children to town winters to school.

THE SPANISH AMERICAN
Roy, New Mexico
August 14, 1920

Pete Laumbach has abandoned his plan of building a residence and has purchased the J. E. Wildman residence near the Christian Church, where the family will live this winter and put the children in school here. Mr. Wildman took the lots in the Montezuma addition in exchange.

THE SPANISH AMERICAN
Roy, New Mexico
September 4, 1920

J. S. Candelario, the big Curio man from Santa Fe, visited at the Lumbach homes last week. Mr. Candelario is a brother-in-law of P. J. and Dan Lumbach.

THE SPANISH AMERICAN
Roy, New Mexico
September 11, 1920

Dan Lumbach and family have moved to their new home which they recently purchased from Ed Wildman. We are glad to welcome Dan and family to our little town as we know they will be useful citizens to our community.

THE SCHLESWIG LEADER
Schleswig, Iowa
Thursday, February 10, 1921

The many former friends of Henry Laumbach will be pained to learn of his death, which occurred at his late home in Ute last Thursday, February 3, 1921, after a short illness. He was one of the prominent farmers of this vicinity for any years, where he was well and favorable known for his industrious habits and kindly disposition.

It was only last October that he moved from his farm near Mapleton to Ute, to make his future home, and where death came to end his earthly carrier at the age of 74 years.

Henry Laumbach was born at Jagel, Schleswig-Holstein, Germany on the 4th day of November 1847. He came to this country in 1866 and settled first in Clinton County. Here he was united in marriage to Martha Peters, on November 24, 1872. To this union 12 children were born. After residing in Clinton County for several years they came to Crawford County, this was 35 years, and here they stayed until they moved to Ute. Nine of his children are still living who together with their mother are left to mourn his death. The children are: Hy Laumbach, Presho, South Dakota, Mrs. Herman Luetjens, Denison, Alfred, Detlef, Jacob, and Peter of Mapleton, Mrs. Bernhard Andresen, Mrs. Theo Jochims both of Lake Park, Iowa and Mrs. Julius Ernst of Mapleton. He also leaves one sister, Mrs. Peter Jepsen of Denison and one brother Peter Laumbach of Germany, also 15 grandchildren.

The remains were brought to the Morgan Township cemetery Sunday for burial. The stricken family and the friends will have the heartfelt sympathy of all in their sad hour of affliction. *(This Henry was not the brother of Andreas Detlef Laumbach 2nd and great-grandfather of Dallas. That Henry, born in 1840 at Jagel, married Augusta Grantz. The Henry of this obit, also born in Jagel, was about 7 years* *younger and married Martha Peters. Both Henrys, often confused because of similarities, settled in the same area of Iowa. They were contemporaries and related. The Henry of this obit descended from the Henry/Heinrich Laumbach who was brother of Andreas 1st.)*

THE SPANISH AMERICAN
Roy, New Mexico
May 28, 1921

Henry Laumbach, reports several rods of his fence in a draw carried away by the flood of water and ice and drifts two feet deep in many places, still Tuesday noon. He had to shovel paths from the doors of his house to get out after the storm, and the Mora River, at the scene of the storm, was at high flood.

The road out from Mora is not in condition now to attract travel and we are staying at home pretty closely, unless obliged to drive.

The leading social event for the week was the marriage of Miss Refugia ("Cuca") Rudulph eldest daughter of Mr. and Mrs. Milnor Rudulph, to Mr. Jose Florence, of La Cueva.

THE SPANISH AMERICAN
Roy, New Mexico
September 3, 1921

J. S. Candelario the Curioman of Santa Fe has been visiting his brother-in-laws P. J. and Dan Lumbach and families the past few weeks. Mr. Candelario is a rich merchant at Santa Fe and always enjoys a few days vacation each year with his relatives near Roy.

THE SPANISH AMERICAN
Roy, New Mexico
December 24, 1921

P. J. Laumbach, a prominent La Cinta canyon ranchman, was in town Monday to meet his daughter, who has been attending school in Santa Fe, and has returned home for a holiday visit.

THE SPANISH AMERICAN
Roy, New Mexico
March 4, 1922

Pete Lumbach was up from La Cinta Ranch last Wednesday. Mr. Lumbach reports that his wife has been ill for the past two months. Mr. Lumbach delivered 279 head of cattle to Mr. Solt of Fort Morgan, Colorado.

THE SPANISH AMERICAN
Roy, New Mexico
March 11, 1922

Mable [sic] Lumbach is reported quite sick with a severe case of pneumonia at her home near the Christian Church. As we go to press she is reported some better and the chance for her recovery is good.

THE SPANISH AMERICAN
Roy, New Mexico
March 18, 1922

Mabel Lumbach who has been very low for the past several weeks with a severe case of pneumonia is reported improving nicely.

THE SPANISH AMERICAN
Roy, New Mexico
March 25, 1922

Miss Mabel Lumbach who has been quite sick the past several weeks is improving nicely and will soon be able to be in school again.

THE SPANISH AMERICAN
Roy, New Mexico
Saturday, April 8, 1922
TWO YOUNG LADIES PASS AWAY

Mary Laughter died at Plumlee Hospital Monday evening and Mable Laumbach passed away at the family home Wednesday morning.

Roy and Solano and vicinities have been saddened this week by the death of two prominent young ladies of the mesa. Miss Mary Laughter a student of Solano Schools died at the Plumlee Hospital Monday evening following a serious operation she had undergone a few days previous and Miss Mable Lumbach a student of the Harding County High School passed away Wednesday morning at 7:30 from a relapse of a severe attack of the flu followed by pneumonia. They both were well known on the mesa and many homes will be filled with sadness in the loss of these bright young ladies.

OBITUARY

Mabel Anna Eleanor Laumbach eldest daughter of Mr. and Mrs. Dan Laumbach was born at La Cueva, N. M., October 24, 1902 and in the latter part of the same year her parents moved to their ranch about 20 miles southwest of Roy and where she has lived the past 19 years. She attended the grades in a private school and in 1917 graduated from the grades and then took up High School work in the Allison James School at Santa Fe. She attended this school two years and was just completing the eleventh grade in the Harding Co. High School when she took a severe case of the flu which later developed into pneumonia and for several days her life was despaired of but she rallied and had improved so rapidly that she was considered practically well and would have soon been able to be in school again when she became suddenly worse last Sunday morning and within a short time spinal meningitis developed and altho everything possible was done for her she grew gradually worse and passed away at 7:30 Wednesday morning.

While attending school at Santa Fe she became converted and joined the Presbyterian Church and lived true to her faith. She was an ardent student in school and loved dearly by her classmates and teachers and she will be sadly missed not only by her classmates but by the whole Roy Schools.
Mabel's death is the third pupil's death in the Harding County High School this winter and the school is again plunged into mourning.

At the time of her death Mabel was 19 years, 5 months and 12 days old and she leaves to mourn her early death four sisters, Alida, Verna, Frances and Ruth, also two brothers, Joyce and Daniel with a sorrowing mother and father and a host of friends and relatives.

The funeral took place from the Christian Church, Rev. R. A. Price of Weed, New Mexico delivering the funeral oration and burial followed in the beautiful Roy Cemetery.

The Spanish American which has been in this home practically since Mabel was born extends the deepest sympathy to the bereaved family and relatives and to the school children who are mourning the loss of one they loved so dearly.

CARD OF THANKS

With our hearts filled and torn with grief from the death of our darling daughter and sister we want to thank those dear friends and relatives who were so kind to us during her long .sickness and her death and those who helped us with kind acts and words. They will never be forgotten by us and will help us to overcome the grief that is ours to bear. We want to especially thank the schools and the I. O. O. F. Lodge for their floral offerings and we ask God's richest blessings for you all.

Dan Laumbach and family.

J. S. Candelario of Santa Fe attended the funeral of his niece Miss Mable [sic] Lumbach [sic] in Roy last Thursday. Mr. Candelario is head of a large curio store at the State Capital.

THE SPANISH AMERICAN
Roy, New Mexico
July 29, 1922

Dan Laumbach is having two small rooms built onto his home in Roy. Contractor Kitchell is doing the work. The additions will give him a five room house.

THE SPANISH AMERICAN
Roy, New Mexico
August 26, 1922

J. S. Candelario, the Curio man from Santa Fe, is spending the week with the Laumbachs south of town. He has promised to send us some of his jumping beans for exhibition, a write up of which occurred in the Santa Fe New Mexican.

THE SPANISH AMERICAN
Roy, New Mexico
October 7, 1922

Dan Laumbach spent a few days in Roy this week visiting with his children.

Pete Laumbach of La Cinta canyon was trading with our merchants in Roy Wednesday afternoon.

THE SPANISH AMERICAN
Roy, New Mexico
November 18, 1922
NOTICE TO HUNTERS

Notice is hereby given that hunting and trespassing in any manner is positively forbidden on any lands controlled or owned by us. All persons please take notice and govern yourselves accordingly.

Pete Laumbach,
Dan Laumbach,
11-18-tfn

DALLAS MORNING NEWS
Dallas, Texas
Saturday, October 22, 1932
Farms and Ranches for Sale 148 New Mexico.

NEW MEXICO ranch for sale; 10,000 acres fee simple and 3,000 acres State leases. Well watered and good protection. One of the best cattle ranches in Harding County. Priced to sell. P. J. LAUMBACH, Roy, N. M.

LAS VEGAS DAILY OPTIC
Greater Las Vegas, New Mexico
Tuesday, June 27, 1933
Recent Deaths
MRS. ELEANOR D. LAUMBACH

Mrs. Eleanor D. Laumbach, 84, a pioneer resident of Mora County and New Mexico, passed away at her home in Buena Vista, N. M. this morning after a lingering illness. Mrs. Laumbach was the widow of the late Andreas Daliff Laumbach and was born and raised in Mora County. She leaves a host of friends who will be grieved to learn of her passing. She is survived by eight children. They are Mrs. Marguerite Cruz, Holman N. M.; Mrs. J. S. Candelario, Santa Fe N. M.; Mrs. Manuel A. Sanchez, Las Vegas N. M.; Misses Anna, Mary and Eleanor Laumbach of Buena Vista N. M.; Peter and Dan Laumbach, two sons, who reside in Roy N. M.; a sister, Mrs. Isabel Gallegos of this city, and a half brother, Ramon Boney of Pastura N. M., also survive her. She was a member of the Presbyterian church of Holman N. M.

The remains will lie in state in the slumber parlors of the Johnsen Memorial Mortuary this evening until 7 o'clock when they will be removed to the family home at Buena Vista.

Funeral services will be held from the family home in Buena Vista at 2:30 Wednesday afternoon with Rev. T. Atencio, pastor of the Presbyterian church of Mora, officiating assisted by Rev. A. Maes, pastor of the Spanish Presbyterian church of this city. Burial will be in the family plot in the cemetery at Buena Vista N. M.

ALBUQUERQUE JOURNAL
Albuquerque, New Mexico
May 3, 1938
CURIO DEALER'S WIFE DEAD

SANTA FE, May 2 (AP) - Mrs. Estefanita L. Candelario, wife of J. S. Candelario, Santa Fe curio dealer, died here Monday following an illness of several weeks.

SANTA FE NEW MEXICAN
Santa Fe, New Mexico
Wednesday, May 4, 1938

Mrs. Estefanita Laumbach Candelario, wife of J. S. Candelario, who died Monday morning, [*services*] were held this afternoon at the First Presbyterian church with Rev. A. G. Tozer and Rev. Uvaldo Martinez officiating. Interment was in the family plot in Fairview cemetery.

A host of sorrowing friends filled the flower-packed church and followed the long cortege to the cemetery. At the church services, Miss Olinda Rodriguez sang beautiful songs in both Spanish and English accompanied at the piano by Miss Margaret Scofield.

The Rising-Miller Mortuary was in charge of the service.

ALBUQUERQUE JOURNAL
Albuquerque, New Mexico
Monday, December 1, 1941

Manuel A. Sanchez Dies; was Republican Leader of San Miguel County.

LAS VEGAS, N. M., Nov. 30 (AP) - Manuel A. Sanchez, rancher and member of the territorial New Mexico legislature, died Sunday at the age of 80. He had been ill for a long time.

A member of the Republican state central committee at his death, Sanchez had held most of the San Miguel County offices and served as a member of the 32d territorial legislature.

He is survived by his widow and a son, Anthony, who had been associated with his father in ranching. Funeral services will be at 2:30 p. m. Tuesday.

ALBUQUERQUE JOURNAL
Albuquerque, New Mexico
February 26, 1942

Big Range Conservation Job Under Way on Ranch Southwest of Roy.

ROY, N. M., Feb. 25 (Special) - One of the biggest range conservation jobs ever attempted in Northeastern New Mexico was begun a little more than a year ago on the Dan Laumbach and Son ranch, 20 miles southwest of Roy.

Joyce Laumbach, the son, reported 13 miles of water diversion structures, 11,000 yards of earth fill-in erosion control dams, 4,000 yards of earth fill-in stock water pond dams, 3500 small gully plugs, and 7,000 trees planted for gully control and as wildlife cover help to make up a part of the work done during the first year.

Some of the land was eroded seriously.

Late in 1940, Dan and Joyce Laumbach, after observing some of the work done by the Mesa Soil Conservation District, petitioned to have their ranch included in the district.

There remains about 20 miles of water diversion structures to be constructed, more than 10,000 gully plugs to be built, and more than 40,000 trees to be planted. There are approximately 600 acres of range land that is yet to be contour furrowed, many silt traps to be built above the existing farm ponds and other items of general conservation work.

EVENING STAR
Washington, DC
Sunday, May 24, 1942

Miss Laumbach, H. W. Schmalle Are Married.

Couple Are [sic] United In The Columbia Heights Church.

The marriage of Lucille E. Laumbach of Mosquero, N. Mex., to Mr. Howard W. Schmalle of Oregon took place Thursday in the Columbia Heights Christian Church, with the Rev. Benjamin Melton officiating.

The bride, a secretary in the office of Representative Clinton P. Anderson, was given in marriage by Mr. Anderson. She wore a gown of white marquisette and carried a bouquet of lilies and lilies of the valley.

Her bridesmaid and only attendant, Miss Margaret Reiss, a cousin of the bridegroom, wore a gown of pale blue, Mr. Walter Vinson was best man, and Mr. John Gregory and Mr. Edward Bryant acted as ushers.

After the ceremony a reception was held at the home of Mrs. K. Spann.

Miss Laumbach came to Washington last November. Mr. Schmalle is employed by the Navy Department here. They will be at home after Wednesday at 4305 Kaywood drive, Mount Rainier.

THE OELWEIN DAILY REGISTER
Oelwein, Iowa
March 15, 1946

Mr. and Mrs. Harold Laumbach and family of Rochelle Park, New Jersey, are expected to come Sunday night for an indefinite stay at the home of Mrs. Laumbach's parents, Mr. and Mrs. Del Austin.

THE OELWEIN DAILY REGISTER
Oelwein, Iowa
March 20, 1946

Harold Laumbach, Harold Jr., and Vera went to Sac City Friday for a few days' visit with his relatives. Mrs. Laumbach and Dean remained with Mrs. Laumbach's parents, Mr. and Mrs. Del Austin.

THE OELWEIN DAILY REGISTER
Oelwein, Iowa
March 28, 1946

Mr. and Mrs. Mart Nixon spent Thursday afternoon at the George Austin home visiting Mr. and Mrs. Harold Laumbach.

Mr. and Mrs. Harold Laumbach returned to their home at Rochelle Park, New Jersey, Friday.

THE CLINTON HERALD
Clinton, Iowa
Wednesday, March 5, 1947

Goose Lake - Mrs. Lena Claussen, 80, died at 4:50 p.m. Tuesday in the home of her daughter, Mrs. Alfred Bielenberg, Charlotte. Services will be held at 2 p.m. Friday in the Goose Lake home, the Rev. A.G. Landhold of St. John's Lutheran church in Preston, officiating. Burial will be in Center Grove cemetery. The body will be in the Pape funeral home, Clinton, until Thursday afternoon when it will be taken to the Goose Lake residence. Lena Boken was born March 18, 1866, in Germany. She and Andrew Claussen of Goose Lake were wed Oct. 6, 1892. She was baptized in the Lutheran faith. Surviving are two daughters, Miss Georgianna Claussen of Clinton and Mrs. Bielenberg; a son, Arthur of Goose Lake; a sister, Mrs. A.S. Schmidt of Preston, and three grandchildren. Preceding her were the parents, husband, a son, a brother and two sisters.

WATERLOO SUNDAY COURIER
Waterloo, Iowa
May 10, 1950

Divorces Granted.

LAUMBACH, Lois N., 33, from Hans Andrew, 41; Married Oct. 5, 1941; separated recently; defendant deeds certain property to the plaintiff; defendant to make certain payments in connection with the property; plaintiff to have all household goods located on the premises at 1123 Mulberry and pay off the encumbrance; defendant to pay plaintiff $1,040, payable at $10 a week; defendant to pay all outstanding accounts; defendant to pay plaintiff's attorney fees and his own attorney fees; grounds cruelty.

THE NASHUA REPORTER
Nashua, Iowa
June 11, 1953

Decoration Day visitors in the A. N. Herzog home were Mr. and Mrs. Lee Huffman and son, Mr. and Mrs. H. Laumbach, Carolyn True, and Mr. and Mrs. M. Sprague, of Waterloo; ...

~~

LAS VEGAS DAILY OPTIC
Las Vegas, New Mexico
Wednesday, April 18, 1956
Pioneer of North New Mexico Dies.

A pioneer resident of northeastern New Mexico, Mrs. Dan Laumbach, 77, died Tuesday in Roy. She was the mother of Mrs. Leon Shinn of Las Vegas and the aunt of Rudolph Laumbach of Romeroville.

Funeral services will be held in Roy, Thursday. Mrs. Laumbach is survived by four daughters, Mrs. Shinn, Mrs. Alicia Wallace of Roy, Mrs. D. C. Sparks, Springer, and Ruth Laumbach of Albuquerque. Two sons surviving are Joyce Laumbach of Roy and Daniel Laumbach of Los Lunas. Four sisters-in-law in Las Vegas are Miss Ann Laumbach, Miss Mary Laumbach, Miss Lenore Laumbach and Mrs. M. A. Sanchez.

~~

ALBUQUERQUE JOURNAL
Albuquerque, New Mexico
February 4, 1958
State Senator Wallace Dies of Heart Attack.

ROY (AP) - State Sen. Elbert L. Wallace, 58, died here early Monday. Death was reported due to a heart attack.

Wallace, a Harding County Democrat, had long been active in real estate and in lodge circles. Survivors include his widow, Elida Laumbach Wallace, and sons, Elton R. and Albert.

Rogers Mortuary of Las Vegas will announce funeral arrangements.

~~

LAS VEGAS DAILY OPTIC
Las Vegas, New Mexico
Saturday, May 10, 1958
Anna Laumbach, Area Pioneer, Dies.

Miss Anna Laumbach, member of a well-known Las Vegas family, died at a local hospital this morning. Miss Lumbach had been ill for some time. She made her home with her two sisters, Miss Lenore Laumbach and Miss Mary Laumbach of 1917 Boulevard.

Miss Laumbach was born at Buena Vista, N.M., July 11, 1878. She spent most of her life at Buena Vista except the last eight years, which she had spent in Las Vegas. She was the daughter of the late Andres D. and Lenore Ebell Laumbach, pioneer residents of this section. Miss Laumbach is survived by four sisters, Mrs. M. A. Sanchez, Miss Lenore Laumbach, and Miss Mary Laumbach, all of Las Vegas, and Mrs. J. E. Cruz, of Albuquerque. Tony Sanchez, business manager of the New Mexico State Hospital, is a nephew of the deceased.

Funeral services for Miss Laumbach will be held Monday afternoon at 2 o'clock from the Chapel of the Johnsen Memorial Mortuary, Rev. Tomas C. Gonzales, assisted by Rev. O. W. Randall, all of the Presbyterian Church, will officiate at the services. Burial will be made in the family cemetery on the Laumbach Ranch at Buena Vista. Funeral arrangements are in charge of the Johnsen Memorial Mortuary.

~~

LAS VEGAS DAILY OPTIC
Las Vegas, New Mexico
Monday, May 12, 1958

Anna Laumbach

Memorial services were held last night in the Chapel of the Johnsen Memorial Mortuary for Miss Anna Laumbach, who died in Las Vegas Saturday following a long illness.

Rev. T. C. Gonzalez and Rev. O. W. Randall, pastors of the local Presbyterian churches, officiated at the services. Both pastors spoke of the long and useful life which Miss Laumbach had lived. Miss Marie Vasquez, accompanied by Mrs. E. C. Israel on the Chapel pipe organ, sang two solos: "I Need Thee Every Hour" and "Abide With Me." A beautiful floral offering was sent by Miss Laumbach's friends, attesting to the esteem in which she was held in the community.

Funeral services were held this afternoon at 2 o'clock at the Johnsen Chapel with many friends and relatives in attendance. The Rev. Gonzalez and Rev. Randall officiated at these services. Mrs. George W. White rendered as a solo, "Oh Think of the Home Over There."

The following were named as casket bearers for Miss Laumbach. Adolph Espinosa of Taos, George Laumbach of Springer, Barney Cruz of Mora, Joyce Laumbach of Solano, Rudolph Laumbach and Tony Sanchez of Las Vegas. The body was taken to Buena Vista, Miss Laumbach's former home, where burial was made in the Laumbach family cemetery.

~~

LAS VEGAS DAILY OPTIC
Las Vegas, New Mexico
Monday, June 16, 1958
Pioneer of Mora Dies in Duke City.

Another member of one of New Mexico's pioneer families, Mrs. Margaret L. Cruz, 93, a former resident of Holman, where she resided for over 65 years, died in an Albuquerque hospital where she had been receiving treatment for the past several months, this morning.

She was the daughter of the late Andreas and Leonore Evell Laumbach of Buena Vista. She is survived by a daughter, Mrs. Julian Duran of Penasco; two sons, Barney F. Cruz of Mora and Andreas of Pioche, Nev.; three sisters, Mrs. M. A. Sanchez and the Misses Mary and Leonore Laumbach of Las Vegas. She was a member of the Holman Presbyterian church. The body was returned to Las Vegas today and is in the care of the Rogers Mortuary. Funeral announcement will be made later.

~~

Clinton Herald
Clinton, Iowa
April 14, 1961
MRS. ELSABEA MILLER

Mrs. Elsabea A. Miller, 91, of 614 10th Ave. South, Clinton, Iowa, died in her home early this morning. She had been in failing health for the past year. The body is at Snell-Smith Funeral Home. Burial will be in the Springdale Cemetery. Elsabea Laumbach was born Dec. 24, 1869 in Goose Lake, the daughter of Henry and Augusta Grantz Laumbach, and had lived in Clinton most of her life. She was married to William T. Miller who preceded her in death in 1937. She was confirmed and baptized in the Lutheran faith.

Surviving are four daughters, Isabelle Miller at home, Mrs. Fred E. Kube of near Elvira, Elsabea W. Miller of Clinton and Mrs. Joseph (Anna) Story of New Castle, Del, Mrs. Mathilda Hawks of Seattle, Wash.

Besides her husband she was preceded in death by one daughter, Josephine in 1939, two brothers and two sisters.

~~

LAS VEGAS DAILY OPTIC
Greater Las Vegas, New Mexico
Monday, November 8, 1965
Mary Laumbach Services Held.

Mary Grace Laumbach, 82, pioneer resident of Mora County and a resident of Las Vegas for the past 18 years, died in a hospital Friday afternoon following an extended illness.

She was born in Buena Vista to the late Andreas and Lenore Laumbach. She attended the Presbyterian Mission School in Buena Vista and the Allison James Presbyterian School in Santa Fe. Shortly afterwards she and her sisters took over the management of the Laumbach Ranch at Buena Vista until 1947 when they moved to 1917 Hot Springs Blvd. here in Las Vegas.

She is survived by two sisters, Miss Lenore Laumbach and Mrs. M. A. Sanchez, both of Las Vegas; and a number of nieces and nephews including Tony Sanchez and Rudolph Laumbach of Las Vegas, Bernardo Cruz of Mora, Pete Laumbach of Rainsville, Mrs. Adelina Espinosa of Taos, Mrs. Alida Wallace of Roy, Mrs. Verna Sparks of Springer, Mrs. Frances Shinn, Mrs. Julian Duran, Miss Ruth Laumbach and Mrs. Frank Foxall, all of Albuquerque. Miss Laumbach was a member of the Mora Presbyterian Church.

Prayer services were conducted Saturday evening at 7 in the Chapel of the Rogers Mortuary. Funeral services were conducted Sunday afternoon at 1:30 in the Rogers Chapel with the Rev. F. F. Payas of Las Vegas and the Rev. Alfonso Esquibel of Mora officiating. Ronald Wynn and a duet from the Mora Presbyterian Church each sang two hymns accompanied by Doris Elliott on the chapel console organ.

Interment was in the Laumbach Cemetery in Buena Vista with the following nephews serving as casket bearers: Tony Sanchez, Joyce Laumbach, Rudolph Laumbach, Bernardo Cruz, Pete Laumbach and Andres Cruz.

The family has requested that those who wish may contribute to the New Mexico Heart Association, P.O. Box 1327, Santa Fe.

~~

THE CLINTON HERALD
Clinton, Iowa
Monday November 28, 1966

Miss Georgiana M. Claussen, 214 1/2 4th Ave. S., died Sunday morning in Jane Lamb hospital. Funeral services will be held at 1:30 p.m. Tuesday in the Pape funeral home, where friends may call. Rev. W.D. Tolson, pastor of Grand Mound Lutheran church, will officiate. Mrs. Virtus Petersen will be organist and Mrs. DaVarro Rickertsen will sing. Pallbearers will be Walter Grantz, Carl Lorenzen, Vernon Ploog, Donald Hughes, William Cox and Ernest Jensen. Burial will be in Center Grove cemetery. Miss Claussen was born in Clinton county, daughter of Andrew D. and Lena Boken Claussen. She was baptized in the Lutheran faith. She was a life member of Local 79 of the American Federation of Musicians. Surviving are one sister, Mrs. Alfred (Adeline) Bielenberg of Goose Lake; two nieces, Mrs. Carl (Kathleen) Lorenzen of Goose Lake and Mrs. Doug (Marile) Piercy of Holbrook, Ariz.; and one nephew, David Bielenberg of Waukon. Her parents and two brothers preceded her in death.

~~

ALBUQUERQUE TRIBUNE
Albuquerque, New Mexico
April 11, 1970

[Excerpt from "A Letter from the editor" titled "Sentiment runs deep in N.M. - more about Trementina" by George Carmack]

IN MY LETTER last Saturday I mentioned the Rev. and Mrs. Julian Duran, who headed the Presbyterian mission there in the early 1930s when the Depression and a drouth killed Trementina.

Mrs. Duran told me one particularly touching story. Prior to her marriage, Mrs. Duran was Rosa Cruz. She was the daughter of the Rev. Jose Miterio Cruz, who also had been a missionary. He was a missionary at the little Trementina church early in the century and Rosa was born there. A few years later the family moved to another area but when Rosa was 12, she and an older brother were allowed to go back to Trementina for a visit.

Rosa's father asked her to kneel and offer a prayer of thanksgiving when they entered the house where she had been born.

No one was living in the house when they arrived. It had only a dirt floor and there were centipedes and spiders inside it. Rosa's reaction was that of a 12-year-old girl.

"Daddy, I just couldn't kneel there and offer a prayer of thanksgiving," she told her father on her return home. "I'm so glad we don't live there now and I don't ever want to go back."

BUT THINGS SOMETIMES work out in strange ways.

A few years later, Rosa married Julian Duran, also a missionary. And—you guessed it—the Durans were assigned to Trementina.

Rosa found herself back as the minister's wife in the same little mission where her father had been.

And no one could feel more sentimental about the years they spent there than Mrs. Duran.

MR. AND MRS. DURAN - who went to Trementina in 1930 - told of the death of the town.

In the years of normal or above rainfall, there had been corn and beans and good grazing for sheep and cattle. The watermelons and the cantaloupes were delicious and the Durans particularly remember the molasses made from the sorghum cane that grew there.

Then about 1930 the same drouth which struck much of the nation in the "Dust Bowl" days came to Trementina.

Crop failure followed crop failure. The grass dried up. Ranchers tried to hold on to their cattle to the last. For a time there was a little money to buy cottonseed cake and some other feed - and then the money ran out.

Some farmers even tried to burn the spines off and feed cactus to their cattle.

But in the end - Trementina had to die.

~~

LAS VEGAS OPTIC
Las Vegas, New Mexico
Monday, August 19, 1974
L. Laumbach, pioneer, dies.

Leonore Laumbach, 87, a member of a pioneer Buena Vista ranching family and resident of 1917 Hot Springs Blvd., passed away in a local hospital Friday evening following a brief illness.

She is survived by one sister, Mrs. Christina L. Sanchez of Las Vegas; 14 nephews, Tony Sanchez and Rudolph Laumbach, both of Las Vegas; Pete Laumbach of Rainsville, C.R. Laumbach of Corrales, Andreas Laumbach of Albuquerque, Barney Cruz of Mora, Alfredo and Joyce Laumbach, both of Roy, Daniel Laumbach of Los Lunas, Johnny Candelario of Albuquerque, George Laumbach of

Springer and Henry, Carlos, and John Laumbach, all of Roseville, Calif., 10 nieces, Mrs. Verna Sparks and Mrs. Janet Ikenberry, both of Springer, Mrs. Alida Wallace, Mrs. Frances Shinn and Ruth Laumbach, all of Bosque Farms, Mrs. Martha Bustos of Roseville, Calif., Mrs. Adelina Espinoza of Taos, Mrs. Petra Latham of Bishop, Calif., Mrs. Rosa Duran of Albuquerque and Mrs. Christina Foxall of Durango, Colo.

Funeral services were conducted Sunday afternoon at 2 from the chapel of the Rogers Mortuary. The Rev. Alfonso Esquibel, assisted by the Rev. A.R. Jutterbock of the First United Presbyterian Church, conducted the services. Interment followed in the family plot at the Buena Vista Cemetery with the following friends and relatives serving as casket bearers: Pete, Alfred and Daniel Laumbach, Carlos Martinez, John Lopez and Ralph Cruz.

The family has requested memorials to the Intensive Care Unit Fund, in care of Las Vegas Hospital, P.O. Box 238, Las Vegas.

LAS VEGAS OPTIC
Las Vegas, New Mexico
Monday, November 11, 1974
C. Sanchez dies at 93.

Chrestina Laumbach Sanchez, 93, a resident of 314 Valencia and a member of a pioneer Mora County ranching family, passed away Saturday evening following an extended illness.

She is survived by one son, Antonio A. (Tony) Sanchez of Las Vegas; 12 nephews, Rudolph Laumbach of Las Vegas, Pete Laumbach of Rainsville, C, R. Laumbach of Corrales, Andreas and Johnny Candelario of Albuquerque, Barney Cruz of Mora, Alfredo Laumbach of Roy, Daniel Laumbach of Los Lunas, George Laumbach of Springer, Henry, Carlos and John Laumbach of Roseville, Calif.; ten nieces, Mrs. Verna Sparks and Mrs. Janet Ikenberry, of Springer, Mrs. Alida Wallace, Mrs. Frances Shinn and Ruth Laumbach of Bosque Farms, Mrs. Martha Bustos of Roseville, Calif., Mrs. Adelina Espinoza of Taos, Mrs. Petra Latham of Bishop, Calif., Mrs. Rosa Duran of Albuquerque and Mrs. Chrestina Foxall of Durango, Colo.

Prayer services will be conducted this evening at 7:30 from the chapel of the Rogers Mortuary. Funeral services will be conducted Tuesday afternoon at 2:30 from the Chapel of the Rogers Mortuary. Interment will follow in the Masonic Cemetery.

LAS VEGAS OPTIC
Las Vegas, New Mexico
Tuesday, June 22, 1976

Christina L. Foxall

Last rites held

Christina Laumbach Foxall, 71, a long-life resident of New Mexico, who had been making her home in Alamogordo, passed away at an Alamogordo hospital Saturday following an extended illness.

She is survived by her husband, Frank Foxall, of Alamogordo; two sisters, Petra Roscoe and husband, Latham, of Bishop, Calif., Lucille Schmalle and husband, Howard of Livermore, Calif., six brothers, George Laumbach and wife, Margaret of Springer, Rudolph Laumbach and wife, Leona, of Las Vegas, C.R. Laumbach and wife, Irene and A.D. Laumbach and wife, Zulema, all of Albuquerque, Al Laumbach and wife, Lenore, of Roy, Pete J. Laumbach and wife, Lupita, of Rainsville; and numerous nieces, nephews and cousins.

Funeral services were conducted this afternoon at 2:30 from the Chapel of the Rogers Mortuary with Father Dan Jones of "Our Lady of Rosary Chapel in Westcliffe, Colo., as celebrant of the mass.

Interment followed in the Laumbach Family Cemetery in Buena Vista with the following friends and relatives serving as casketbearers: Antonio A. Sanchez, Bradley and Jack Upton, Alfredo Martinez, Greg Laumbach and Leo Laumbach.

~~

CLINTON HERALD
Clinton, Iowa
May 13, 1985

School Teacher, Miller Dies

Elsabea Miller, 82, formerly of 614 10th Ave. S., died Saturday, May 11th in the Alverno. The funeral will be at 10 A.M. Tuesday in the Clinton Chapel of the Snell-Zornig Funeral Home with a nephew, the Rev. Roger Dierks of Noblesville, Indiana officiating. Burial will be in Springdale Cemetery.

Miss Miller was born July 10, 1902, in Clinton, Iowa, to William and Elsabea Laumbach Miller. She taught school many years in the Clinton public school system, most recently at Horace Mann. She was involved in Special Education for 17 years and helped pioneer the program in the Clinton area. She graduated from Clinton High in 1919, Moody Bible Institute, Los Angeles, Calif., in 1928, and Drake University, Des Moines, in 1956. She lived most of her life in Clinton and was baptized and confirmed in the Lutheran faith.

Survivors include two sisters, Mrs. Adele Kube of Goose Lake and Mrs. Anna Story of Millsboro, Delaware. She was preceded in death by two sisters.

~~

LAS CRUCES SUN NEWS
Las Cruces, New Mexico
Sunday, December 28, 1986

George W. Laumbach, of Springer, died Wed. at the home of his son in Las Cruces. Age 76. Services at United Methodist Church in Springer. Survived by his wife, Margaret of Springer; three daughters, Janet Andrews of Holbrook, Neb, Louise Luft of Salisbury, MD and Ruth Fried of Silver Springs, MD; son, Karl Laumbach of Las Cruces; five brothers, Rudolph of Romeroville, NM, Ike and Andreas, both of Albuquerque, Alfred of Roy NM; two sisters, Petra Latham and Lucille Smalley, both of CA; and eight g-children. Graham's Mortuary.

~~

CLINTON HERALD
Clinton, Iowa
October 15, 1990
Adele M. Kube Funeral Wednesday

Adele M. Kube, 89, of Rural Route 1, Goose Lake, died Sunday at her home. She was born Dec. 18, 1900 to Clinton to William and Elsabea Laumbach Miller. She married Frederick E. Kube Dec. 24, 1919 in Clinton. He died in April of 1955. She attended Clinton Schools and was a 1918 graduate of Clinton High School. She had lived in Clinton County all of her life and was a member of the Elvira Zion Lutheran Church. She taught Sunday School for 40 years at Elvira Lutheran and Chancy Chapel. She was active for many years as a 4-H leader. Survivors include two daughters, Mrs. Roger (Elsabea) Dierks of Carmel, Indiana, and Mrs. Peter (Adele) Kroeger of Long Grove, Iowa, three sons, Frederick A. Kube of Bryant, Llewellyn Kube of Rural Goose Lake and Dr. Kenneth Kube of Bad Axe. Michigan:

12 great-grandchildren; a sister, Mrs. Anna Story of Millsboro, Delaware. She was preceded in death by three sisters.

ROSWELL DAILY RECORD
Roswell, New Mexico
Tuesday, December 29, 1992
Frances Laumbach Shinn

Frances Laumbach Shinn passed away at her residence, 655 S, Bosque Loop in Bosque Farms, on Thursday, Dec. 24, 1992. She was 80 years old. Memorial services will be held at the First Baptist Church, 1350 Bosque Farms Blvd., on Thursday, Dec. 31, at 2 p.m.

Those interested may make contributions to the Frances Shinn Memorial Fund at the First National Bank of Belen, Bosque Farms Branch, 970 Bosque Farms Blvd., Bosque Farms, N.M. 87068. A scholarship, through a local art contest for senior high school students, will be awarded with the proceeds from this fund.

Frances was born, one of seven children, to pioneer ranchers Emma Henkens Laumbach and Daniel Laumbach on March 27, 1912 at her parents' Cedar Springs Ranch in Harding County.

Her parents preceded her in death, as did her sister Mabel at an early age and brother Joyce Laumbach, who spent most of his life in the area of Roy. Joyce died on Christmas Eve one year ago. She also was preceded in death by a son, James Michael Shinn, of Bainbridge, Wash., in 1989.

Frances is survived by her husband, Leon M. Shinn, of the home; a granddaughter, Anita Shinn; and daughter-in-law Gloria Shinn of Bainbridge, Wash.; and a son, John Morgan Shinn, of Dallas. Frances also is survived by sisters Verna L. Sparks and Ruth Laumbach of Roswell and Alida L. Wallace of Tucumcari; a brother, Daniel Chester Laumbach, of Deadwood, Ore.; numerous nephews, nieces and cousins, and countless friends.

Frances grew up on her parents' ranch and in Roy and worked for a while for the Atchison Topeka and Santa Fe Railroad as secretary in Hurley, New Mexico. On June 25, 1947, she married Leon M. Shinn and adopted his two small sons, John and Jim.

During the years, the family lived in several places, including Las Vegas, Santa Maria, Calif., and Albuquerque. They settled in Bosque Farms, where Leon and Frances have owned and operated the Bosque Art Gallery for many years. Frances was an artist.

ROSWELL DAILY RECORD
Roswell, New Mexico
Thursday, November 16, 1995

Ruth E. Laumbach

A memorial service is scheduled for noon Friday, Nov. 17, at St. Mark's Lutheran Church, for Ruth E. Laumbach, 81, of Roswell, who passed away Tuesday, Nov. 14, 1995, at Roswell. The Rev. John Orwig of St. Mark's Lutheran Church will officiate. She will be interred at Sunset Memorial Park in Albuquerque.

Ruth was born May 13, 1914, in San Miguel County, to Daniel and Emma Henkens Laumbach. Survivors include a brother, Daniel C. Laumbach of Albuquerque; a sister, Verna L. Sparks of Roswell; numerous nieces and nephews, including Janet and Dan Girand and Tracy Ikenberry, all of Roswell.

Ruth had been a Roswell resident since 1982, and was a member of St. Mark's Lutheran Church, a life member of the D.A.V. Post 4 of Roswell and a life member of Albuquerque D.A.V. Post 26.

She had served in the military, as a captain in the U.S. Army during World War II. She retired as a registered nurse, and had been the Bernalillo County health nurse.

Friends may make memorials to the Roswell D.A.V. Post 4 or St. Mark's Lutheran Church. Arrangements are under the direction of LaGrone Funeral Chapel.

ROSWELL DAILY RECORD
Roswell, New Mexico
Sunday, May 26, 1996
Verna Sparks Loved life.
[*caption under her photo*]

Verna Sparks

Graveside services are scheduled for 2 p.m. Wednesday, May 29, at. Fairmont Cemetery in Raton, for Verna L. Sparks, 86, of Roswell and formerly of Springer, who passed away Thursday, May 23, 1996, at a local hospital. The Rev. Bill Stamper of the First United Methodist Church of Springer will officiate.

Verna loved life and enjoyed good health until the last 10 days of her life.

Verna Laumbach was born Oct. 8, 1909, at the family ranch in San Miguel County, to Emma (Henkens) and Daniel Laumbach. Verna's family ranched in northern New Mexico for generations. Her parents and brothers and sisters—Mabel Laumbach, who died at 19; Joyce Laumbach of Roy; Alida L. Wallace of Roy and later of Tucumcari; Frances L. Shinn of Bosque Farms; Ruth E. Laumbach of Albuquerque and Bosque Farms and more recently of Roswell; and Daniel C. Laumbach of Las Lunas and Oregon and most recently of Albuquerque — all preceded her in death.

Verna was married to Dalphon Clinton Sparks, originally of Copan and Bartlesville, Okla. Verna was a public school teacher in Springer, where she and Dal resided for many years. Her beloved husband, Dal, preceded her in death.

Verna and Dal had two children, who survive her: Janet Girand and her husband, Dan, of Roswell and Gerald C. "Jerry" Sparks and his wife, Betty Miller, of Vienna, Va. Other survivors include five grandchildren—Dr. David Ikenberry of Bremen, Germany; Tracy Ikenberry of Roswell; Devin Ikenberry of Anniston, Ala.; and formerly of Roswell, and Lara "Larisa" (Sparks) Ajemian and Dan C. Sparks of Vienna, Va.; and great-grandchildren G. Brandon Gallagher of Roswell and Kaze Toyota and Zophia Ajemian of Vienna; sister-in-law, Mary (Sparks) Hethcoatt of Burny, Calif; a special friend, Mabel Ikenberry of Springer; numerous nephews, nieces, cousins and friends, including a helpful friend, Evelyn Sanchez of Roswell; plus hundreds of former Springer fifth grade public-school students whom she called "my kids."

Graveside services are scheduled at the Fairmont Cemetery in Raton Wednesday at 2 p.m., with the Rev. Bill Stamper of the First United Methodist Church in Springer officiating.

Professional services were provided by the LaGrone Funeral Chapel in Roswell.

MOUNTAIN DEMOCRAT
Placerville, California
April 29, 1998

Lucille Evangeline (Laumbach) Schmalle died at her Grizzly Flat home March 23. She was 80.

She was born July 18, 1917. She was a housewife for many years and actively participated in the Fire Department Women's Auxiliary and the S&B Craft Group. Years ago, she was secretary for Sen. Clinton P. Anderson of New Mexico and moved to Washington, D.C., to perform her job. There she met her husband of 56 years, Howard.

She is survived by her husband, her children Janice Verdugo and Dorothy Jean Chase, her sister Petra Latham of Hinesville, Ga., her brothers A.D. "Red" Laumbach, Casimiro "Ike" Laumbach, Alfred Laumbach and Peter Joseph Laumbach of New Mexico and three grandchildren.

A memorial will be held in Grizzly Flat in June. Her ashes will be buried in New Mexico this summer.

Donations may be made to the Scholarship Fund of Menaul School, 301 Menaul Blvd. NE, Albuquerque, N.M. 87107.

SANTA FE NEW MEXICAN
Santa Fe, New Mexico
Thursday, 14 September, 2000

Gertrude B. Cruz, age 92, passed away August 24, 2000. She was born in Roy, NM, but grew up and spent most of her adult life in Mora. Gertrude was a homemaker but had many outside interests, especially her love of the outdoors, she loved camping and fishing. She was preceded in death by her husband, Bernardo F. Cruz; her sons, Ralph A. and Albert R. Cruz; her parents, Luis Branch and Francisquita Martinez; sisters, Rosalie E. Branch and Adela B. Maestas; brothers, Ralph Branch, Alex Branch, Richard Branch, Octaviano and Ricardo Branch; and twin grandsons, Lloyd and Floyd Cruz. She is survived by her daughter, Frances M. Moya and husband Guadalupe; son, Barney F. Cruz, Jr. and wife Terry; daughters-in-law, Harvey Linda Cruz and Patricia Cruz. She is also survived by nine grandchildren: Margaret Beckman, Anita Martinez, Raymond Moya, Roselyn Turner, Patricia Cruz, Barney Cruz III, Richard Cruz, Albert Cruz and John Cruz; 13 great grandchildren: Randy, Ryan, Kristi, Carrie, Joslyn, Alyssa, Marisa, Kalina, Barney IV, Ann, Katherine, Zachary and Chloe; and many nieces, nephews, and numerous friends, both in the Mora Valley and Santa Fe where she spent her winters.

Cremation has taken place. A rosary will be recited at Cristo Rey Church on Friday, September 15, at 6:30 p.m. A Memorial Mass will be celebrated at St. Gertrude's Church in Mora on Saturday, September 16, at 10:00 a.m., with the interment of her cremains at Cleveland Cemetery following the Mass. Memorial contributions may be made in her name to a charity of your choice or The Hospice Center, 1400 Chama Ave., Santa Fe, NM 87505-3372. Arrangements are under the direction of Berardinelli Family Funeral Service, 1399 Luisa, Santa Fe, 984-8600.

THE RAPID CITY JOURNAL
Rapid City South Dakota
Monday, November 26, 2001

Earl Edwin Henkens

CHADRON, Neb. - Earl Edwin Henkens, 90, Chadron, died Sunday, Nov. 25, 2001, at his home.

Survivors include his wife, Loretta Henkens, Chadron; two stepsons, Donald Osborn, Omaha, and Stephen Osborn, Hemingford; one daughter, Anna Schmidt, Chadron; two stepdaughters, Theresa Blausey, Chadron, and Jeannette Gabel, Sidney; and 14 grandchildren.

He joined the U.S. Army in 1942 and served in World War II.

Services were Tuesday, Nov. 27, at Chamberlain Chapel in Chadron, with the Rev. Kelly McDowell officiating.

Burial with military honors by Veterans Honor Guard was at Greenwood Cemetery in Chadron. A memorial has been established for Dawes County 4-H at Chamberlain Chapel, P.O. Box 970, Chadron, NE 69337.

AMARILLO GLOBE-NEWS
Amarillo, Texas
Sunday, October 13, 2002

ROY, N.M. - Steven Monreal, 18, died Thursday, Oct. 10, 2002.

Rosary will be at 7 p.m. today in the Roy High School Gymnasium. Mass will be at 10 a.m. Monday in the gymnasium with Larry Brito and Guy Roberts officiating. Burial will be in Roy Cemetery by Hass Funeral Directors of Clayton.

Steven was born July 19, 1984, in Amarillo to Steve Monreal and Rose (Laumbach) Monreal. He moved to Roy four years ago where he lived with his grandparents and attended Roy High School.

Survivors include his parents; and grandparents, Alfred and Eleanor Laumbach and Rafael and Maria Monreal.

~~

COLUMBUS TELEGRAM
Columbus, Nebraska
June 12, 2004

Ruth Henkens Hull

The memorial service for Ruth V. Henkens Hull, 97, of Fremont will be 10 a.m. Tuesday at Moser Memorial Chapel in Fremont.

She died Wednesday, June 9, 2004, at A.J. Merrick Manor in Fremont.

Ruth Knapp was born Oct. 19, 1906, in Yutan. She grew up in Fremont and attended Fremont Public Schools. She married Henry E. Henkens on Nov. 14, 1925, in Council Bluffs, Iowa. The couple lived and farmed south of Fremont in Saunders County. She worked at the former Palace Ice Cream Parlor and the former Gold Key Drive-In in Fremont. The couple moved into Fremont in 1973. Her husband, Henry, preceded her in death March 26, 1975. She married Ralph W. Hull on Jan. 13, 1980, in Fremont. He died Sept. 1, 1986.

She was a member of Salem Lutheran Church in Fremont and the church circle.

Survivors include: a son, John (and wife, Judy) Henkens of Henderson, Nev.; two daughters, Patricia Johnson of Santa Paula, Calif., and Marcie Pettit of Fremont; two stepdaughters, Sharon (Mrs. Warren) Wolfe and Marilyn (Mrs. Jerome) Sokolovsky, all of Fremont; eight grandchildren, 13 great-grandchildren and a great-great-grandchild.

She also was preceded in death by 11 brothers and sisters.

The Rev. Michael Thomas of Salem Lutheran Church in Fremont will officiate Tuesday's service.

There is no visitation; however, friends may sign the register book from 9 a.m. to 5 p.m. Monday at the funeral home. Burial will be in Memorial Cemetery in Fremont.

A memorial has been established to the Cystic Fibrosis Foundation.

~~

ALBUQUERQUE JOURNAL
Albuquerque, New Mexico
Sunday, 31 July, 2005

LAUMBACH -- Judith Duriez Laumbach passed away on Friday, July 29, 2005 after a long battle with cancer. She was born August 6, 1944 to Philip and Janette Duriez in Lufkin, TX. Judy graduated from high school in Nacatoches, LA in 1962. She attended the University of New Mexico in 1962 until 1964. She then wed Andrew D. Laumbach on August 8, 1964 in El Paso, TX. She went on to graduate Summa Cum Laude from the University of Texas in El Paso with a Bachelors of Arts degree in Psychology in 1966 and a Masters degree in Psychology in 1969. She is survived by her husband of 41 years, Andrew and her children, Kara Laumbach Turey of Palm Bay, FL, and Paul Laumbach of Woodbridge, VA. She has four grandchildren: Nicole, Omar, Joshua, and Vanessa also of Woodbridge, VA. Judy is also survived by her father-in-law, Andreas (Red) Laumbach, and in-laws, John and Mary Anne Hess of Albuquerque, NM. In addition, she is survived by uncle, Van Davison of Austin, TX; aunt, JoNell Toole of Pleasanton, TX; uncle, George Duriez of Vallejo, CA; aunt Margie Weiss of Sun City, AZ; and numerous cousins and loving friends. Judy and her family lived in Vienna, VA for 28 years before retiring to Albuquerque, NM in April. She worked for the Veterans Administration in Texas and later as a Human Resource Manager in Virginia. She was a very happy, full of life, loving wife, mother, grandmother, and friend to many. Over the last 20+ years she was active in church, Girl Scouts, and craft groups. She also enjoyed gardening, cooking, traveling, shopping, making crafts, and spending time with her family, friends, and grandchildren. The immediate family will be holding a private service at Gate of Heaven Cemetery in Albuquerque, NM. There will be an announced Memorial Service at a later date. For additional information, please call 505-828-0296. In lieu of flowers, the family asks that donations be made to the American Cancer Society, 10501 Montgomery Blvd. NE, Ste, 300, Attn: Lorraine West, 87111, in her name. French Mortuary 7121 Wyoming Blvd. NE 823-9400

ALBUQUERQUE JOURNAL
Albuquerque, New Mexico
Saturday, August 20, 2005

Margaret M. Laumbach, 92, of Springer passed away Thursday, Aug. 18, 2005, in Raton. She was born May 11, 1913, in Eagle Tail, N.M., the daughter of Rudolph and Elizabeth Ferfes Miller.

Margaret was a librarian for the Springer Library, a Springer 4-H club leader, a Sunday school teacher at the Springer First United Methodist Church and had a life-long interest in the people and history of New Mexico.

She is survived by three daughters, Janet Andrews and husband, Ernest, of Cambridge, NE, Louise Luft and husband, Phillip, of Salisbury, MD, and Ruth Fried and husband, Dave, of Austin, TX; one son, Karl Laumbach and wife, Toni, of Las Cruces, NM; one brother, Norman Miller of Colorado Springs, CO; eight grandchildren and seven great-grandchildren.

A memorial service will be held at a later date.

Arrangements for Margaret M. Laumbach are under the direction of the Yaksich-Long Funeral Home of Raton.

FREMONT TRIBUNE
Fremont, Nebraska
June 22, 2006

Mabel Henkens

The memorial service for Mabel A. Henkens, 99, of Fremont will be 11 a.m. Thursday at Salem Lutheran Church in Fremont.

She died Monday, June 19, 2006, at A. J. Merrick Manor in Fremont.

She was born Dec. 15, 1906, in Telbasta to William and Sophie (Waterman) Borcherding. She was only 6 weeks old when her mother died, and was raised by her grandparents. She graduated from the eighth grade of a Washington County school, and then graduated from Fremont High School in 1925. She attended Midland College for a year. Mabel Borcherding married George W. Henkens on Feb. 20, 1929, in Fremont. He farmed south of Fremont for 60 years even though they moved into Fremont in 1944. Mabel was a homemaker but did work for Dr. Frank Williams in his dental office for 10 years. She also was a dressmaker. Her husband preceded her in death in May 1994.

She was an active member of Salem Lutheran Church for more than 75 years. In recent years, she lived in the Nye Retirement Center where she enjoyed her life crocheting, playing cards and joining all of the activities available there.

Survivors include: a daughter, Helen Lannin of Fremont; a son, Kenneth (and wife, Lou Ann) Henkens of Omaha; three grandchildren, Tom (and wife, Linda) Lannin and Bob Lannin, all of Lincoln, and Ann (and husband, Dr. Jay) Matzke of Sheldon, Iowa; and six great-grandchildren.

She also was preceded in death by an infant son.

The Rev. Michael Thomas will officiate Thursday's service. There is no viewing, however, friends may sign the register until 5 p.m. today at Ludvigsen Mortuary in Fremont. A private family committal service will be in Memorial Cemetery.

In memory of Mabel Henkens, memorials are suggested to Salem Lutheran Church, Fremont Area Medical Center Hospice and Midland Lutheran College.

Ludvigsen Mortuary is handling the arrangements.

~~

AMARILLO GLOBE TIMES
Amarillo, Texas
Friday, January 19, 2007

ROY, N.M. - Vincent James Monreal, 7 months, died Wednesday, Jan. 17, 2007, in Omaha, Neb. Rosary will be said at 7 p.m. Sunday in Holy Family Catholic Church. Mass will be at 10 a.m. Monday in the church with the Rev. Steven Imbarrato, pastor, and the Rev. Larry Brito, pastor of Our Lady of Guadalupe Catholic Church in Taos, officiating. Burial will be in Roy Cemetery by Hass Funeral Directors of Clayton.

Vincent James Monreal was born May 31, 2006, to Steve Monreal and Rose Laumbach Monreal. Born six weeks premature, he suffered many complications, but his strength and perseverance kept him with us for seven months.

Survivors include his parents of Austin, Texas; a twin brother, Johnathon Conrad Monreal of Austin; a sister, Selena Therese Monreal of Austin; and his grandparents, Alfred and Eleanor Laumbach, Rafael and Maria Monreal and Jim and Jan Faulkner.

~~

ALBUQUERQUE JOURNAL
Albuquerque, New Mexico
April 28, 2007

FOSSUM -- Esther Sondreal Fossum, aged 90, passed away in the presence of family on April 22, 2007, after a brief illness. She was born in Cooperstown, ND, on December 14, 1916, and after graduating from high school in North Dakota, joined the staff of the Griggs County, ND, County Agent's Office. She married Donald E. Fossum of Maxbass, ND, in Devils Lake, ND, on May 24, 1942, and moved with him to New Jersey during World War II, where their first daughter, Cheryl, was born. After the war, the family made their home in Cedar Rapids, IA, where their second daughter, Donna, was born. In 1949, Don, who was an electrical engineer, accepted a position at Sandia National Laboratories and moved the family to Albuquerque. Esther participated in many school, church, and community-based activities in and around Albuquerque during the next 58 years, including PTA, Girl Scouts, Bernalillo County Homemakers, Scandinavian Club, Good Sam RV Club, and Corrales Senior Center. She was an enthusiastic leader and tireless organizer of events and activities for every organization in which she participated. She obtained her real estate broker's license in 1972 and spent the next 15 years showing and selling homes to families all over Albuquerque. She and Don also spent a part of these same years exploring the countryside of New Mexico and beyond in their motor home. In 1992, she and Don celebrated their 50th wedding anniversary with friends and family. After Don's unexpected death in May 1993, Esther moved to the Vineyard retirement community.

She is survived by her life-partner of 10 years, Casimiro "Ike" Laumbach; a brother, Palmer Sondreal of Amery, WI; two daughters, Cheryl Fossum Graham of North Bethesda, MD, and Donna Fossum of Alexandria, VA; and two grandchildren, Annica Graham and Andrew Graham of Santa Fe, NM. Cremation has taken place with the assistance of the Daniels Family Funeral Services. The family held a private Graveside Service in the Rose Garden at Vista Verde Memorial Park. A Memorial Service celebrating Esther's life will be held on Sunday, April 29, 2007 at the Vineyard Clubhouse at 6118 Edith Blvd. NE from 3-4 p.m. In lieu of flowers, her family requests that donations be sent to the New Mexico Museum of Natural History Foundation, P.O. Box 7010, Albuquerque, NM 87194 in Memory of Esther Fossum.

ALBUQUERQUE JOURNAL
Albuquerque, New Mexico
Sunday, January 4, 2009

LAUMBACH -- Carmen J. "Connie" Laumbach, 69, a resident of Albuquerque since 1940, passed away on Friday, January 2, 2009. She is survived by her children, Juli Palladino and husband, Anthony Fischer, Nick Palladino and wife, Margaret, Tony Palladino and Laura Gray, all of Albuquerque; grandchildren, Michael and Anthony Palladino; her father, Casimiro "Ike" Laumbach, 95 years; sister, Barbara "Bobbie" Cesaretti and husband, Lester; nephew and niece, Michael and Amy Cesaretti. She was preceded in death by her mother, Irene Laumbach. Connie was born on the Bell Ranch near Tucumcari, NM and later moved to Albuquerque. A memorial service will be held in her honor on Wednesday, January 7, 2009, 11:00 a.m., at French Mortuary, University Blvd. Chapel.

Hass Funeral Directors Obituary
Clayton, New Mexico
Eleanor M. Laumbach
(August 24, 1924 - July 3, 2010)

Eleanor Laumbach, age 85, died Saturday, July 3, 2010, at her home in Roy, New Mexico.

Rosary was recited at 7:00 PM on Tuesday, July 6 and Mass of Christian Burial was celebrated at 11:00 AM on Wednesday, July 7 at Holy Family Catholic Church in Roy, New Mexico. Fr. Paul Nkumbi was the Celebrant. Burial was in the Roy Cemetery by Hass Funeral Directors of Clayton.

Eleanor Laumbach was born on August 24, 1924, in Roy, New Mexico to Alferino DeHerrera and Secundina (Romero) DeHerrera. A life long resident of the Roy community, Eleanor married Alfred C. Laumbach, Sr. on November 19, 1945 at St. Joseph Parish in Mosquero, New Mexico. She was a member of Holy Family Catholic Church in Roy, New Mexico. In addition to her parents, Eleanor was preceded in death by 3 children, Virginia Laumbach and John Laumbach as infants and Frances Chavez on June 23, 2008, by 2 grandsons, Steven Michael Monreal on October 10, 2002 and Vincent James Monreal on January 17, 2007, by 2 sisters, Vera Sandoval and Amilia Romero and by 1 brother, Ernest DeHerrera.

SURVIVORS:
HUSBAND: Alfred C. Laumbach, Sr. of Roy, New Mexico.
5 DAUGHTERS: Lucille Gonzales and her husband Jimmy of Amarillo, Texas, Christina Laumbach of New Zealand, Elizabeth Trujillo and her husband Joseph of Mosquero, New Mexico, Rose Monreal and her husband Steve Austin, Texas and Petra Laumbach of Roy, New Mexico.

6 SONS: Alfred Laumbach, Jr. Of Las Vegas, New Mexico, Enrique Laumbach and his wife Mary, Pedro Laumbach and his wife Lillian, and Michael Laumbach all of Roy, New Mexico, Ralph Laumbach and his wife Liz of Portales, New Mexico and Andrew Laumbach of Baltimore, Maryland.
25 Grandchildren ; 20 Great-Grandchildren
1 SISTER: Mary Agnes Esquivel of Albuquerque, New Mexico
1 BROTHER: Alfred DeHerrera of Denver, Colorado.

ALBUQUERQUE JOURNAL
Albuquerque, New Mexico
Sunday, March 24, 2013

Andreas "Red" D. Laumbach, age 101, a long-time resident of Albuquerque, peacefully passed away on Saturday, March 16, 2013. He is survived by his children Andrew Laumbach and Mary Anne Hess and husband, John; five grandchildren and seven great grandchildren; brothers, Casimiro "Ike", Alfred, and Pete Laumbach; and many nieces and nephews. He was preceded in death by his wife, Zulema T. Laumbach. Red was born in the Territory of New Mexico in 1911 at La Cinta Canyon. He was an alumni of Menaul High School and retired from Rio Grand Steel after many years of service. Red was a loving and special father, grandfather and great grandfather.

Cremation has taken place and a private memorial service will be held at a later date. Interment took place at Gate of Heaven Cemetery. In lieu of flowers memorial contributions may be made to the Menaul School.

Peter J. Laumbach, Jr. June 10, 1923 - April 8, 2015

Peter J. Laumbach, Jr. age 91, a resident of Los Montoyas for the past 2 years and formerly of Mora County and Roy, New Mexico passed away on Wednesday, April 8, 2015 at his home in Los Montoyas. He was born on June 10, 1923 in La Cinta, New Mexico to Peter Joseph Laumbach and Fidelia Andrada Laumbach. He was a member of La Sociedad de San Antonio in Los Montoyas, NM and The National Trappers Association. He enjoyed hunting and fishing; he was a leather smith and enjoyed making boot and saddles. He was preceded in death by his parents: Peter Joseph and Fidelia Laumbach; first wife and mother of his children Guadalupe C. Laumbach; numerous brothers and sisters—Peter was the youngest of seventeen siblings; and great-granddaughter: Miranda Coca. He is survived by his [*second*] wife: Donilia Laumbach of Los Montoyas; [*by his*] sons and daughters: Leo Laumbach and wife Helen of Springer, NM; Fidelia Maes and husband Roque of Sandia Park, NM; Pete R. Laumbach and wife Joyce of Hope, NM; Greg Laumbach and wife Belinda of Rainsville, NM; Gloria Griego and husband Alex of Albuquerque, NM; many grandchildren, great-grandchildren and several great-great-grandchildren; brothers: Casimiro Laumbach of Albuquerque, NM; Al Laumbach of Roy, NM; numerous step-children and their families; many nieces, nephews, other relatives and many friends. Rosary services will be held on Friday, April 10, 2015 at 7:00 pm at Immaculate Conception Church in Las Vegas, NM. Funeral services will be conducted on Saturday, April 11, 2015 at 10:00 am also at Immaculate Conception Church with Father C. John Brasher as Celebrant. Interment will follow at Los Montoyas Cemetery.

APPENDIX I
Part B. Metzger/Korte/Naeglin Newspaper Clippings

Researched and Transcribed by Charles O. "Butch" Sanders

LAS VEGAS GAZETTE
Las Vegas, New Mexico
Saturday, June 21, 1873
NOTICE

Is hereby given that the copartnership heretofore existing between the undersigned, under the name, firm and style of "Metzger and Korte," has this day been dissolved by mutual consent, Frank Metzger retiring from business.

Frank Metzger,
Henry Korte.
Mora, N. M. June 9th, 1873.   38 4t

~~

LAS VEGAS GAZETTE
Las Vegas, New Mexico
Saturday, June 28, 1873

~~

NOTICE

Is hereby given that the copartnership heretofore existing between the undersigned, under the name, firm and style of "Metzger and Korte," has this day been dissolved by mutual consent, Frank Metzger retiring from business.

Frank Metzger,
Henry Korte.
Mora, N. M. June 9th, 1873.   38 4t

~~

LAS VEGAS MORNING GAZETTE
Las Vegas, New Mexico
Saturday, March 12, 1881
Mora

Mora is on the eve of a big boom. With inexhaustible mica mines, her agricultural resources, and vast tracts of timber, enough to supply the territory for fifty years to come. As a resort for the tourist, it is unexcelled. Trout abounding in all the mountain streams and the scenery is splendid beyond description. All this country will be opened to the world by the narrow gauge railroad, which will branch from Embudo through Mora County to Las Vegas. To us who traveled through these woodlands, valleys and mountains, half of the pleasure was lost by having an old hack of a nag whose average rate of speed was two miles per hour. Still we got some revenge out of him through the medium of the spur, and we are not certain but that the livery man would find a half a dozen pair by examining his flank. Mora has six stores, all doing a good business, also a hotel which is passable. The big stone mill owned by Señor Gallegos, was built in 1864, and is run to its uttermost capacity, wheat being one of the staple products. After leaving Mora we meandered towards La Cueva, from there to Buena Vista, where we met Mr.

Myers, who is one of the pioneers, and is now living off of the fruits of years of hardship on the frontier. It was after we left this place that we came to the most pleasant reminiscence of our journey, that of being caught in a snow storm in the mountains, being found by a stranger and taken in by Henry Korte, Esq., who kindly invited us to partake of the hospitality of his ranche. We found it an Oasis surrounded on all sides by peaks which are snow-capped the year round. Orchards and grain fields reveled in luxuriant contrast to the pine trees and bleak looking rocks. About one-quarter of a mile from the house Mr. Korte has a private fish pond, or a mere proper term would be lake, where all kinds of fish are found in abundance, including trout and carp, the latter being transported from the States. Take it all in all there was an air of western geniality which reminded us of the Pacific States. Pleasure seekers and sportsmen should visit Mora County before leaving the territory, as it is the garden spot of the southwest.

~~

LAS VEGAS DAILY GAZETTE
Las Vegas, New Mexico
Saturday, June 10, 1882
GOLD.
Mora the Coming Camp.

One of the richest gold strikes yet made in the territory was made near the plaza of Mora a few weeks ago. The load is only about seven miles from Mora. The ore is exactly the same in appearance as that of the famous Homestake at White Oaks. It is rich in wire gold, and the specimens which were taken from the surface rock, are in no way inferior to the specimens from the Homestake. It is safe to say that if a specimen was taken from the Mora lead and placed beside one from the Homestake, the most experienced miner could not detect the difference. Wm. Henry Korte, an old citizen of Mora, is the lucky finder, and if proper steps are taken to develop this mine, one of the biggest mining booms this country ever witnessed will strike Mora. A mining boom in that locality means something. Water is plenty. Grain of all kinds is raised in abundance, and at cheap rates. These facts alone are sufficient to guarantee a rich camp when mining operations are once commenced.

~~

DECATUR DAILY REPUBLICAN
Decatur, Illinois
Wednesday, June 14, 1882
More Gold in New Mexico.

The Las Vegas Gazette, of June 10 says: "One of the richest gold strikes yet made in the territory was made near the plaza of Mora a few weeks ago. The lead is only about 7 miles from Mora. The ore is exactly the same in appearance as that of the famous Homestake at White Oaks. It is rich in wire gold and the specimens which were taken from the surface rock are in no way inferior to the specimens from the Homestake. It is safe to say that if a specimen was taken from the Mora lead and placed beside one from the Homestake, the most experienced miner could not detect the difference. William Henry Korte, an old citizen of Mora, is the lucky finder, and if proper steps are taken to develop this mine, one of the biggest mining booms this country ever saw will strike Mora. A mining boom in that locality means something. Water is plenty. Grain of all kinds is raised in abundance, and at cheap rates. These facts alone are sufficient to guarantee a rich camp when mining operations are once commenced.

~~

LAS VEGAS DAILY GAZETTE
Las Vegas, New Mexico
January 9, 1883

Henry Korte, of Mora, will bring in to-day about 40,000 pounds of apples grown in Mora county and a quantity of fresh fish.

~~

LAS VEGAS DAILY GAZETTE
Las Vegas, New Mexico
Wednesday, September 19, 1883

Henry Korte a merchant of Mora and the boss apple raiser of New Mexico, arrived in the city yesterday from a trip to St. Louis, where he purchased new goods and had a good time generally.

~~

LAS VEGAS DAILY GAZETTE
Las Vegas, New Mexico
Thursday, November 8, 1883

Henry Korte, a ranchman of the Mora, is pictured in one of the illustrated police papers as "one of the great cattle kings of New Mexico." A short biography of Mr. Korte accompanies the illustration and therein it is stated that he has recently sold his cows to a big company for $300,000. It sometimes occurs that we must go away from home to learn the news. Korte's friends will have the laugh on him.

~~

NEW HAVEN REGISTER
New Haven, Connecticut
Wednesday, February 11, 1885
AN OLD TIMER'S GOLD.

Searching For the Treasures Left by a Veteran of New Mexico.

LAS VEGAS, N. M., February 11. - Last week Frank Metzgar, an old timer, dropped dead while at the breakfast table. He was a merchant and ranchman and known to be very wealthy. No will was found and the deceased was buried in a small cemetery built several years ago to receive his remains.

Yesterday it was reported that most of his worldly effects consisted of $250,000 in gold, which was buried somewhere around his late residence. Great excitement prevails over the fact. Henry Korte, a son-in-law, dug down in Metzgar's cellar but has been unable to find the pot of gold supposed to be hidden there. Metzgar lived in St. Louis prior to coming here. He was 56 years old and started his fortune in freighting across the prairies in the early days. It is believed his gold will be found.

~~

THE CANTON DAILY REPOSITORY
Canton, Ohio
Thursday, February 12, 1885
An Old Timer Drops Dead.

LAS VEGAS, N. M., February 12. - Last week Frank Metzgar, an old timer, dropped dead while at the breakfast table. He was a merchant and ranchman, and was known to be very wealthy. No will was found, and the deceased was buried in a small cemetery built several years ago to receive his remains. It was reported that his worldly effects consisted of $250,000 in gold which was buried somewhere around his late residence. Great excitement prevailed over the fact. Henry Korte, a son-in-law, dug down in Metzgar's cellar, but did not find the pot of gold supposed to be hidden there. Metzgar lived in St. Louis prior to coming here. He was fifty-six years old and started his fortune in freighting across the plains in the early days. It is believed his gold will be found.

ROCKY MOUNTAIN NEWS
Denver, Colorado
Wednesday, February 18, 1885

Frank Metzgar, a wealthy stock owner at Mora, died a few days ago.

SAUSALITO NEWS
Sausalito, Marin County, California
January 12, 1888

An epileptic son of Henry Korte fell into a stream and was drowned a few days ago, near Mora, N. M.

LA CRONICA DE MORA
Mora, New Mexico
June 13, 1889

Last week, at a special session of the probate court, Agapito Abeyta Jr., squared up his accounts, and turned over the administration of the estate of Henry Korte, deceased. Much litigation had been going on, lawyers were employed on each side, about accounts presented and contested, but our efficient county clerk came out all right and was delivered receipts in full for everything under his charge while acting as administrator. It speaks volumes in favor of Don Agapito and the widow and heirs can now enjoy the benefits of the property to their hearts content.

LAS VEGAS FREE PRESS
Las Vegas, New Mexico
Wednesday, January 20, 1892
AN IMPORTANT CASE

The case of Doloritas Romero et al. against the Henry Korte estate, which has been pending for some time, and which involves $40,000 or $50,000 of property, was argued before Judge O'Brien at chambers last Saturday. The case is a noted one, and the decision of Judge O'Brien is looked forward to with a great deal of interest. The judge has not indicated when he will hand in his decision, but it is expected in a few days.

The questions involved in the case seem to be the right of illegitimate heirs to claim the property of an unmarried father. It seems that Frank Metzger, the father of these illegitimate heirs, deeded his property in his lifetime to Henry Korte, and also went through the form of legitimatizing the wife of Henry Korte as his only legitimate heir. The petitioners in the suit claim that Metzger never deeded his property to Korte in point of fact, but that he made a fraudulent transfer, and that he was the actual owner of the property when he died. They also claim that he did not comply with the law in legitimatizing the wife of Henry Korte, and that he had no right to prefer her as the only heir to his estate. The heirs of Henry Korte, on the other hand, claim that he bought Metzger's property, and paid for it, and that Metzger had a right, if he so chose, to make the wife of Korte, who was also an illegitimate child of Metzger, his sole and universal heir. Geo. W. Prichard represents the Korte heirs, defendants, and T. B. Catron, J. D. W. Veeder and Rafael Romero, the petitioners.

The case is of special interest, not only on account of the large amount of property involved, but also the fact of the bearing it has on other cases of like character in the territory.

LA VOZ DEL PUEBLO
Las Vegas, New Mexico
Saturday, February 1, 1908
Tendieron el Vuelo.

Al amanecer del mártes de esta semana emprendieron la fuga Santiago Padilla del barrio conocido con el nombre de Chihuahuita y una muchacha llamada Nellie Naeglin, hija de Mr. William Naeglin y esposa, viejos residentes del territorio que vivieron durante muchos anos en el condado de Mora. Parece que los dos pichoncitos estaban enamorados el uno del otro y deseaban ver realizadas sus ilusiones por medio de la bendición del cura, pero los padres de ella se opusieron redondamente y los prisioneros de Cupido rompieron las rejas de la jaula y volaron Juntos "hacia otro cielo", El Sr. Pablo Padilla, padre del muchacho se presentó en le oficina del escribano de la corte de pruebas para aplicar por una licencia para el casamiento, pero, según aserta el Optic, el escribano rehusó expedir la licencia debido a que habia sido prevenido de no hacerlo lo por el padre de la muchacha y por el procurador. El mismo periódico dice que la muchacha tiene 18 anos de edad. El escribano dice que el rehusó la licencia porque la aplicación no estaba firmada por los novios como requiere la ley.

El jueves fué presentada la aplicación debidamente firmada y el escribano la concedió, casándose los novios en laIglesia de la Inmaculada en ésta ciudad.

~~

SANTA FE NEW MEXICAN
Santa Fe, New Mexico
Friday, January 8, 1909
TERRITORIAL NEWS NOTES
AT LAS VEGAS

Mrs. Annie J. Naeglin, wife of William Naeglin, a well known ranchman, died at her home in Twelfth Street, Saturday night shortly after 10 o'clock after an illness of several days. Mrs. Naeglin was born in Mora county forty-one years ago, being a daughter of the late Henry Korte, in his time a financial power and leading citizen of the territory. Most of her younger days were spent on the plains.

~~

ALBUQUERQUE JOURNAL
Albuquerque, New Mexico
Tuesday, January 16, 1917
FORMER LEGISLATOR DIES AT LAS VEGAS.
(SPECIAL CORRESPONDENCE TO MORNING JOURNAL)

East Las Vegas, N. M., Jan. 15. - Rafael Gallegos, a member of the New Mexico state legislature several years ago, and who was a Baptist minister and later an attorney, died yesterday evening at his home here after a protracted illness. Mr. Gallegos was 63 years of age. He was born in Las Vegas. Twenty-eight years ago he was married to Miss Isabel Metzger, who, with eight sons and daughters, survives him. Mr. Gallegos was a brother of Acasio Gallegos of Torrance County, a well known New Mexican. The funeral was held here this afternoon from the Presbyterian mission in Old Town, Rev. Norman Skinner and Rev. Gabino Rendon officiating.

~~

LAS VEGAS OPTIC
Las Vegas, New Mexico
Monday, January 24, 1921
LAS VEGAS DEATHS

Laura Naegelin, 24, daughter of Mr. and Mrs. Wm. Naegelin of 1130 Sulzbacher Street, died Sunday morning at a local hospital following a short illness. Funeral arrangements will be announced later.

LAS VEGAS DAILY OPTIC
Las Vegas, New Mexico
Monday, April 13, 1925
Recent Deaths
FRANK KORTE

Funeral services for Frank Korte, well known rancher and merchant of Buena Vista, who died there Sunday morning after an illness of short duration. The deceased is survived by a wife and three small children and a brother, Edward Korte of Las Vegas.

Interment was held in the family burial plot near Buena Vista.

LAS VEGAS DAILY OPTIC
Las Vegas, New Mexico
Friday, May 1, 1925
Recent Deaths
ANNA MARY NAEGLIN

Miss Anna Mary Naeglin died at the home of her father, Wm. Naeglin, on Twelfth and Suizbacher this morning following an illness of several months' duration. Miss Naeglin was born in Las Vegas and was 16 years of age. Pending the arrival of relatives no funeral arrangements have been made.

LAS VEGAS DAILY OPTIC
Las Vegas, New Mexico
Monday, January 21, 1929

According to word from Miami, Arizona, William Naeglin, aged 72 years, of Las Vegas, died at the former place while visiting his son. Mr. Naeglin was a prominent cattle man and recently came to Las Vegas. Six children survive.

LAS VEGAS DAILY OPTIC
Las Vegas, New Mexico
Thursday, January 24, 1929
FUNERAL OF A FORMER LAS VEGAS RESIDENT HELD AT MIAMI, ARIZ.

Services were held late Sunday at Miami, Arizona, for the late William Naeglin, a well known blacksmith and former resident of Las Vegas, whose death occurred January 17th and of which mention was made in the Optic. A year ago Mr. Naeglin went to Arizona in the hopes of improving his health. He was a resident of Colorado for some years, going there at the age of 17 years where he was engaged as a prospector and later as a rancher. In 1887 he married Miss Anna Korte and nine children were born of the union, six of whom survive. The wife and mother passed away in 1909. One son, E. G. Naeglin, resides at Miami, Arizona, where the father passed away.

LAS VEGAS DAILY OPTIC
Las Vegas, New Mexico
Saturday, February 1, 1958

Nellie Naeglin Padilla, age 68, died yesterday afternoon at her home, 1114 2nd St., from an extended illness. Mrs. Padilla is survived by her husband Santiago Padilla, one daughter Anna Padilla, Las Vegas, two sons. John L. Padilla, teacher in the Las Vegas City Schools, Paul Padilla, Richmond Calif.; one sister, Miss Ellen Naeglin of San Francisco, four brothers, Otto and John Naeglin of San Francisco, Fred Naeglin, Glendale, Calif., Emil Naeglin, Miami, Ariz., one uncle Edwardo Korte of Las Vegas, six grandchildren and two great grandchildren.

Rosary service will be held tonight at 8:30 at the Gonzales Funeral Chapel and also Sunday night at 8:30. Mass will be held at IC Church at 11 a.m., Monday.

Gonzales Funeral Home in charge of arrangements.

LAS VEGAS OPTIC
Las Vegas, New Mexico
February 8, 1959

[Photo of Cowboys Branding Scene]

This picture was taken in the early 1850's. West of Fort Union National Monument [*caption*].

The brand H. I. K. was the late Henry Korte brand, a German; immigrated and settled at the old place known for years as the John D. W. Veder ranch on the Mora River, now owned by Roy B. Thompson. The man on the right is the late Rudolph Laumbach, also a German that immigrated on the Old Santa Fe Trail, and settled on the Mora River, later killed by the Comanche Indians at the Rock Crossing of the Canadian River on the Santa Fe Trail, great-grandfather of Rudolph Laumbach and Tony A. Sanchez, his old place is owned by Lorenz Shock today. In those days there were only four settlers in Buena Vista Valley, Henry Korte, Rudolph Laumbach, Estrada's and Capt. Vicente Romero, [of] La Cueva Ranch, the William Salamon Ranch at La Cueva New Mexico. The picture is part of the Tom McGrath collection. [*The photo that accompanied this article is what we call the "Korte Cowboy Branding Scene." Apparently Tom McGrath bought one of the existing studio prints of this photograph. His copy was later included in his collection donated to a Las Vegas historical group. Several Laumbach families have original prints of this photograph. Some of the above data provided to the newspaper concerning this photo is incorrect. We do not believe the man on the right was German immigrant Andreas (his name was not Rudolph) Laumbach. Some of the family believe the man squatting in the lower right corner of the photo resembles Andreas Ebel, a brother of Elionor E. Laumbach. In the Mora Valley in those days there were certainly more than the four settlers named above. The above cited approximate photo date is also likely wrong. This branding scene was probably near Buena Vista, on the Korte ranch.*]

LAS VEGAS DAILY OPTIC
Las Vegas, New Mexico
Tuesday, April 28, 1959
Korte Funeral Set For Wednesday

Joe Edwardo Korte, age 79, pioneer resident of San Miguel County, died Monday morning at a local hospital from an extended illness.

Mr. Korte was born in Mora, and for many years was engaged in farming and later was in the grocery business for 18 years. He had retired five years ago. His wife died a year and a half ago.

Mr. Korte is survived by three sons, Henry Korte employed by the High Land Company at Las Vegas, Fred Korte employed at New Mexico State Hospital, John C. Korte, manager and owner of the Korte Furniture Store in Las Vegas; one daughter, Mrs. Canuto Ortega of Albuquerque, 16 grandchildren and 16 great grandchildren.

Rosary services for Mr. Korte was held Tuesday evening at 7:30 at the Chapel of the Gonzales Funeral Home. Funeral services were held Wednesday at 9:00 o'clock from Our Lady of Sorrows Church. Gonzales Funeral Home in charge of arrangements. Interment was at San Jose Cemetery with the following serving as pallbearers, Paul Korte, Gene Ortega, Max Ortega, Tony Gallegos, Orlando Sanchez, Bobby Korte, Dick Escudero, Juan Gomez and Alvin Korte. A fitting address was delivered at the grave side by Orlando Sanchez. Gonzales Funeral Home in charge.

APPENDIX 2: Genealogical Book Reports
Part A. Descendents of Hernan Martin-Serrano

Report Created and Transcribed by Charles O. "Butch" Sanders

The origin of all of this data is from the extensive extraction, translation and compilation of Jose Antonio Esquibel

First Generation

1. **Hernan I Martin Serrano** was a resident of Zacatecas, Nueva Galicia (Mexico), around 1558. He had the following children:

+   2 M   i. **Hernan II Martin Serrano** was born about 1556-1558, Zacatecas, Nueva Galicia.

Second Generation

2. **Hernan II Martin Serrano** (Hernan I) was born about 1556-1558 in Zacatecas, Nueva Galicia.
Hernan married (1) **Maria Juana Rodriguez**.
Hernan had a relationship with (2) **Doña Ines**, a Tano Indian of New Mexico.
Hernan had the following son by Doña Ines:

+   3 M   i. **Hernan III Martin Serrano** was born about 1606-1607.

Hernan also had the following son:

+   4 M   ii. **Luis Martin Serrano**. He died in November 1661, New Mexico.

Third Generation

3. **Hernan III Martin Serrano** (Hernan II, Hernan I) was born about 1606-1607.
Hernan married (1) **Isabel de Monuera**.
They had the following child:

     5 F   i. **Maria Martin Serrano**.

Hernan married (2) **María de Madrid**.

4. **Luis I Martin Serrano** (Hernan II, Hernan I) was born about 1610. He died in Nov 1661.
Luis married **Catalina de Salazar**. Catalina was born about 1615.
Luis and Catalina had the following children:

+   6 M   i. **Luis Martin Serrano** was born about 1631, New Mexico.
     7 M   ii. **Pedro Martin Serrano** was born about 1635-1637, New Mexico.
     8 M   iii. **Antonio Martin Serrano** was born about 1643-1647, New Mexico.
+   9 M   iii. **Domingo Martin Serrano** was born about 1649-1658, New Mexico.

Fourth Generation

6. **Luis II Martin Serrano** (Luis I, Hernan II, Hernan I) was born about 1622-1633, La Cañada, New Mexico. Luis married **Antonia de Miranda**.
They had eight children, including:

+   10 M   i. **Cristobal Martin Serrano** was born about 1655, New Mexico. He died on 28 Nov 1736.

9. **Domingo Martin Serrano** (Luis I, Hernan II, Hernan I) was born about 1649-1658, New Mexico, and was buried February 27, 1735, Santa Cruz, New Mexico. Domingo married (1) **Maria Josepha de Herrera**.

They had eleven children, including:

+   11 M   i. **Blas Martin Serrano** was born about 1686-1687.

Fifth Generation

10. **Cristobal Martin Serrano** (Luis II, Luis I, Hernan II, Hernan I) was born about 1655 in New Mexico. He died on 28 Nov 1736.

Cristobal married **Antonia Moraga**. Antonia died on 5 Aug 1729 in Santa Cruz de la Canada, NM. They had several children, including:

+   12 M   i. **Antonio de Jesus Martin Serrano** was born about 1698.

11. **Blas Martin Serrano** (Domingo, Luis I, Hernan II, Hernan I). Blas married **Maria Rosa de Vargas Machuca**.

Blas and Maria had several children, including:

+   13 M   i. **Pedro Martin Serrano**.

Sixth Generation

12. **Antonio de Jesus Martin-Serrano** (Cristobal, Luis II, Luis I, Hernan II, Hernan I) was born about 1698 in Santa Cruz de la Canada, Nuevo Mexico.

Antonio married **Juana Ana Maria Gertrudes Dominguez** on 12 May 1717 in Santa Fe, NM. Juana was born about 1699.

They had several children, including:

+   14 M   i. **Salvador de Horta Martin** was born about 1730.

13. **Pedro Martin Serrano** (Blas, Domingo, Luis I, Hernan II, Hernan I).

Pedro married **Maria Margarita Luna**.

They had several children, inlcuding:

+   15 M   i. **Jose Antonio Gerbacio Martin Serrano**.

Seventh Generation

14. **Salvador de Horta Martin** (Antonio, Cristobal, Luis II, Luis I, Hernan II, Hernan I) was born about 1730 in Santa Cruz de la Canada, Nuevo Mexico.

Salvador married **Maria Manuela Gertrudis Trujillo** on 20 Feb 1756 in Santa Cruz de la Canada, Nuevo Mexico. Maria was born in Oct 1740 in Chama, New Mexico. She was christened on 8 Oct 1740 in Santa Clara Pueblo, New Mexico.

They had the following children:

+   16 M   i. **Jose Guadalupe Martin** was born on 12 Sep 1759. He was buried on 11 May 1827.
       17 M   ii. **Ygnacio Martin** was born on 22 Oct 1761 in New Mexico. He was christened on 8 Nov 1761 in Santa Cruz de la Canada, New Mexico.
       18 F   iii. **Maria Lorenza Martin** was born on 10 Jul 1764 in New Mexico. She was christened on 18 Jul 1764 in Santa Cruz de la Canada, New Mexico.
       19 F   iv. **Antonia Josepha Martin** was born on 24 Jan 1767 in New Mexico. She was christened on 27 Jan 1767 in Santa Cruz de la Canada, New Mexico.

20 F   v. **Maria Damiama Martin** was born in Oct 1773 in New Mexico. She was christened on 15 Oct 1773 in Santa Cruz de la Canada, New Mexico.

21 F   vi. **Maria Andrea de Jesis Martin** was born in Dec 1775 in New Mexico. She was christened on 3 Dec 1775 in Santa Cruz de la Canada, New Mexico.

22 M   vii. **Salvador de Jesus Martin** was born in Jul 1776 in New Mexico. He was christened on 2 Jul 1776 in Santa Cruz de la Canada, New Mexico.

23 F   viii. **Maria Catalina Rafaela Martin** was born on 2 Apr 1781 in New Mexico. She was christened on 7 Apr 1781 in Santa Cruz de la Canada, New Mexico.

24 F   ix. **Paula Guadalupe Martin** was born in Mar 1783 in New Mexico. She was christened on 10 Mar 1783 in Santa Cruz de la Canada, New Mexico.

15. **Jose Antonio Gerbacio Martin-Serrano** (Pedro, Blas, Domingo, Luis I, Hernan II, Hernan I). Jose married **Maria Juana Josefa Cortez,** daughter of Salvador Manuel Cortez and Maria Antonia Martin.

They had several children, including:

+   25 F   i. **Maria de la Concepcion Martinez** .

Eighth Generation

16. **Jose Guadalupe Martin** (Salvador de Horta, Antonio, Cristobal, Luis II, Luis I, Hernan II, Hernan I) was born on 12 Sep 1759 in Santa Cruz de la Canada, New Mexico. He was buried on 11 May 1827 in Santa Cruz, NM.

Jose Guadalupe married **Maria Juliana Vasquez Borrego,** daughter of Diego Felipe Vasquez Borrego and Maria Francisca Gurule, on 5 Dec 1786 in Santa Cruz de la Canada, New Mexico. Maria was born on 25 Dec 1772 in San Isidro, New Mexico. She was christened on 25 Dec 1772 in San Felipe Pueblo, New Mexico.

They had the following children:

26 M   i. **Antonio de Jesus Martin** was born in Oct 1788 in New Mexico. He was christened on 17 Oct 1788 in Santa Cruz de la Canada, New Mexico.

+   27 M   ii. **Bernardino Martin** was born on 20 May 1792.

29 M   iii. **Miguel De Guadalupe Martin** was born in Dec 1794 in New Mexico.

30 M   iv. **Pedro Ygnacio Martin** was born on 1 Aug 1797 in New Mexico. He was christened on 4 Aug 1797 in Santa Cruz de la Canada, New Mexico.

31 F   v. **Maria Encarnacion Martin** was born about 1800 in New Mexico. She died on 4 Apr 1848 in Picuris, New Mexico.

32 F   vi. **Antonia Abad Martin** was born on 17 Jan 1801 in New Mexico. She was christened on 20 Jan 1801 in Santa Cruz de la Canada, New Mexico.

33 M   vii. **Jose Felipe Martin** was born on 6 Feb 1804 in New Mexico. He was christened on 13 Feb 1804 in Santa Cruz de la Canada, New Mexico.

34 F   viii. **Maria Rosa de los Reyes Martin** was born on 6 Jan 1807 in New Mexico. She was christened on 10 Jan 1807 in Santa Cruz de la Canada, New Mexico.

35 M   ix. **Antonio De Jesus Martin** was born on 17 Oct 1808 in New Mexico.

36 F   x. **Maria Ygnacia Martin** was born on 11 May 1810 in New Mexico. She was christened on 14 May 1810 in Santa Cruz de la Canada, New Mexico.

37 M   xi. **Felis de la Trinidad Martin** was born on 28 Mar 1817 in New Mexico. He was christened on 1 Apr 1817 in Santa Cruz de la Canada, New Mexico.

25. **Maria de la Concepcion Martinez** (Jose Antonio Gerbacio, Pedro, Blas, Domingo, Luis I, Hernan II, Hernan I).

Maria married **Luis Paulin Cortes**.

They had the following children:

+ 38 M i. **Jose Manuel Cortes** was born on 18 Dec 1801.

Ninth Generation

27. **Bernardino Martin** (Jose Guadalupe, Salvador de Horta, Antonio, Cristobal, Luis II, Luis I, Hernan II, Hernan I) was born on 20 May 1792 in El Potrero, Nuevo Mexico. He was christened on 24 May 1792 in Santa Cruz de la Canada, New Mexico.

Francisco married **Maria Apolonia "Polonia" Solano de Gutierrez,** daughter of Miguel Antonio Gutierrez and Maria Ynes Solano y Valdes on 8 Jan 1827 in Chimayo, Nuevo Mexico. Maria was born on 11 Apr 1811 in Santa Fe, NM. She was christened on 13 Apr 1811 in Santa Fe, New Mexico.

They had the following children:

  29 F i. **Maria Bibiana Martin** was born on 1 Dec 1827 in Potrero, Nuevo Mexico. She was christened on 4 Dec 1827 in Santa Cruz de la Canada, Nuevo Mexico. She died on 27 Oct 1897 in Mora Co., NM. She was buried in Laumbach Cemetery, Mora Co., NM.

     Maria Bibiana married (1) **James 'Santiago' Bonney Sr.** James was born in England. He died in Oct 1846 in Mora Co., New Mexico.

     Maria Bibiana married (2) **Daniel Eberle** .

     Maria Bibiana had a relationship with (3) **Frederick 'Frank' Metzger**. Frederick was born about 1819 in Prussia. He died on 4 Feb 1885 in Mora Co., NM.

  30 M ii. **Manuel Gregorio Martin** was born on 14 Nov 1830 in El Potrero, New Mexico. He was christened on 21 Nov 1830 in Santa Cruz de la Canada, Nuevo Mexico.

38. **Jose Manuel Cortes** (Maria de la Concepcion, Jose Antonio Gerbacio, Pedro, Blas, Domingo, Luis I, Hernan II, Hernan I) was born on 18 Dec 1801 in New Mexico.

Jose married **Maria Manuela Sanchez** daughter of Felipe Sanchez and Juana Maria Martin. Maria was born on 20 Sep 1806 in New Mexico.

They had the following children:

  31 M i. **Jose de Jesus Cortes** was born about 1827 in Taos Co., New Mexico.

  32 F ii. **Maria Petra Cortes** was born in Mar 1836 in Taos Co., New Mexico..

     Maria married **Juan Francisco Valdez** son of Jose Manuel Valdez and Maria de la Luz Trujillo about 1854. Juan was born in Jun 1837 in Mora Co., New Mexico.

  33 F iii. **Maria Ascencion Cortes** was born about 1838 in Taos Co., New Mexico.

  34 F iv. **Maria Candelaria Cortes** was born in Jun 1840 in Taos Co., New Mexico.

     Maria married **Antonio Sanchez** son of Manuel Antonio Sanchez and Maria de la Concepcion Mondragon on 11 Sep 1855 in Las Vegas, San Miguel Co., NewMexico. Antonio was born on 17 Feb 1836 in San Francisco del Rancho, New Mexico.

  35 M v. **Jose Lucas Cortes** was born about 1841 in Taos Co., New Mexico.

  36 F vi. **Maria Lenor Cortes** was born about 1848 in Taos Co., New Mexico.

Appendix A - Notes

In related documents:

Sargento Hernan was assigned to a company commanded by Captain Juan Ruiz de Cabrera. In a document presented to and approved by the commissary general, Jaime Fernandez, Hernan indicated that he would be accompanied by his wife and listed his possessions as follows:

Two coats of mail, the one a jaco, a short military jacket with sleeves (mail was a flexible armor made of metal links or plates, loops of chain or scales);
Two pairs of cuisse (armor worm to protect the thigh) of mail;
One beaver (a moveable piece of armor attached to a helmet or breastplate to protect the face, mouth or chin), and casque (helmet);
One arquebus (a heavy, portable matchlock gun invented during the 15th century);
One pistol;
One gunner's ladle for making musket balls to be shot from the arquebus or pistol;
Three coats – one buckskin, the other two of gamuza (chamois);
One sword and one dagger;
Four fencing foils (a fencing sword with a flat guard for the hand and a thin blade);
Two bridles;
Two sets of spurs;
Some horse armor;
Two janeta (military type) saddles;
Fifteen horses and two mules;
Twenty horses, young and old;
Twenty mares, young and old;
Sixteen unbroken colts;
Twenty-two tames cows, young and old;
Two carts (a gift from don Juan de Oñate), with twenty-six oxen;
A half-dozen pair of horseshoes with nails;
Two pounds of gunpowder;
Six pound of shot;
Seven augers (a tool, larger than a gimlet for boring holes in wood) of different sizes;
Twelve cutting axes;
Three adzes (an ax-like tool with an arched blade at right angles to handle) used for shaping wood;
Two chisels;
One large bar;
One hoe;
One grindstone;
Three copper ladels;
One large comal (a flat pan for cooking)
One barrel, and two pails.

The statement concludes with the following: "All these things, I, Hernan Martin, am taking, as stated, to serve his majesty. I so swear by God in due manner." (signed) Hernan Martin

In San Bartolome, Santa Barbara, New Spain, December 6, 1597, Hernan Martin Serrano made the above declaration under oath before the commissary general, who accepted it. Hernan Martin (signed) and Jamie Fernandez, notary (signed). (Source: Archivo General de las Indias).

In the new land, Hernan Martin Serrano would become the ancestor of thousands and the Martin Serrano name would become known as Martin. This sizeable family was referred to as "Los Martines", the Martin Clan, and by the late 1800s "Martinez" had become commonly used in the formal records, including church records and census documentation.

Yunque, most likely referring to the settlement of San Gabriel del Yunque (see ONMF: 72).

Researcher: José Antonio Esquibel

Sanders found many additional genealogy studies and articles on the Martín Serrano family researched and written by José Antonio Esquibel for various genealogical publications, including Beyond Origins of New Mexico Families. They are too numerous to include all of them here.

Maria Bibiana Martin
LAUMBACH & MARTÍN FAMILIES
By Jan Girand
(excerpt)

"Roots of both Bernardo and Apolonia go deep in New Mexico soil; families of both have been here for many generations. Their branches can be traced back, and are recorded, to the late 1500s. Apolonia's family originated in Santa Fe, Bernardo's in El Potrero. They both lived in El Potrero near Chimayo when they married. They settled in an area called La Cebolla (Seboya, "Onion").

My great-great-grandmother Bibiana Martín had monogamous relationships with three men. Each was a wealthy, successful landowner and property owner. Each of the three owned a successful trading post or store:

- James Bonney had a trading post at La Junta along the Santa Fe Trail;
- Daniel Eberle owned a store in Las Vegas;
- Frederich Metzgar owned a store in Mora, and also one at his ranch at Buena Vista.

Bibiana had children with each of those relationships. In each case, the prior mate had died or she had separated from him before she began a new relationship, but it is doubtful she legally married any of them. That may have been because in those days priests and ministers were seldom available. However, she was a strong-willed, independent woman, unusual for that era. She kept the name Martín or Martínez her entire life. Bibiana Martinez is the only name on her burial marker."

APPENDIX 2: Genealogical Book Reports
Part B. Descendents of Johann Jacob Lauenbach

Researched and Transcribed by Charles O. "Butch" Sanders

Modified Register for Johann Jacob Lauenbach

First Generation

1. **Johann Jacob Lauenbach** of Ascheffel.
    He had the following children:
+   2   M   i.   **Christian Rudolph Lauenbach** was born about 1751. He died on 11 Jul 1820.

Second Generation

2. **Christian Rudolph Lauenbach** (Johann Jacob) was born about 1751. He died on 11 Jul 1820.
    Christian married (1) **Anna Margaretha Ehlert** daughter of Peter Ehlert on 24 Oct 1790. Anna was born about 1761. She died on 7 Jun 1796.
    They had the following children:
    3   i.   **Wiebke Laumbach.**
    4   M   ii. **Peter Laumbach.**
    Christian married (2) **Catharina Margaretha Busch** daughter of Andreas Petersen Busch and Anna Petersen on 28 Apr 1797.
    They had the following children:
+   5   M   iii. **Andreas Detlef Laumbach I** was born on 25 Nov 1802.
    6   M   iv. **Jurgen Laumbach** was born about 1810. Jurgen married **Anna** on 21 Nov 1872 in Clinton Co., IA. Anna was born in Sep 1827 in Germany.
+   7   M   v.   **Heinrich Laumbach** was born in 1815. He died in 1857.

Third Generation

5. **Andreas Detlef Laumbach I** (Christian Rudolph, Johann Jacob) was born on 25 Nov 1802.
    Andreas married **Anna Koos** daughter of Detlef Koos and Anna Christina Wasmuth Bindt on 4 Nov 1832 in Haddeby Kirch. Anna was born on 9 Aug 1811. She died on 24 Aug 1868 in Clinton Co., IA. She was buried in Center Grove (Ingwerson) Cemetery, Center Township, Clinton Co., IA.
    They had the following children:
+   8   M   i.   **Andreas Detlef Laumbach II** was born 2 Dec 1833. He died 4 Nov 1904.
    9   F   ii. **Catharina Margaretha Laumbach** was born on 2 Mar 1836 in Jagel (Schleswig-Holstein), Germany.
    10   F   iii. **Margaretha Laumbach** was born on 1 Mar 1837 in Jagel (Schleswig-Holstein), Germany.
+   11   M   iv. **Marx Heinrich Laumbach** was born on 26 Mar 1840.
+   12   F   v.   **Christina Margaretha Laumbach** was born on 6 Jul 1841. She died on 4 Feb 1883.
    13   M   vi. **Anna Margaretha Laumbach** was born on 15 Sep 1843 in Jagel (Schleswig-Holstein), Germany.

+	14	F	vii.	**Anna Christina Laumbach** was born on 13 Mar 1848. She died on 26 Nov 1908.
	15	F	viii.	**Catharina Laumbach** was born on 11 May 1852 in Jagel (Schleswig-Holstein), Germany.

7. **Heinrich Laumbach** (Christian Rudolph, Johann Jacob) was born in 1815. He died in 1857.

Heinrich married **Wiepke Utermann** daughter of Hans Utermann and Margaretta Herringsen. Wiepke was born in 1816. She died in 1864.

They had the following children:

+	16	F	i.	**Anna M. Laumbach** was born on 10 Oct 1842. She died on 11 Sep 1935.
+	17	M	ii.	**Heinrich Fredrick Laumbach** was born on 4 Nov 1847. He died on 3 Feb 1921.
	18	M	iii.	**Jurgen Laumbach** was born on 24 Aug 1854 in Jagel (Schleswig-Holstein), Germany. He died on 14 Feb 1912 in Crawford Co., IA. He was buried in Morgan Cemetery, Schleswig, Crawford Co., IA.
	19	M	iv.	**Peter Laumbach** was born in Jagel (Schleswig-Holstein), Germany.

Fourth Generation

8. **Andreas Detlef Laumbach II** (Andreas Detlef Laumbach, Christian Rudolph, Johann Jacob) was born on 2 Dec 1833 in Jagel (Schleswig-Holstein), Germany. He died on 4 Nov 1904 in Buena Vista, Mora Co., NM. Andreas married **Eleonore Eberle** "Leonore" daughter of Daniel Eberle and Maria Bibiana Martin on 10 Apr 1864. Eleonore was born on 10 Jan 1849 in Mora Co., NM. She died on 27 Jun 1933 in Buena Vista, Mora Co., NM.

They had the following children:

	20	F	i.	**Natividad Laumbach** was born about 1863 in Mora Co., NM. Natividad may have been adopted. In the 1870 census she was recorded in the family of Andreas and Leonore as Natividad Laumbach, age 6, but after their three younger children. In the 1880 census Natividad was recorded as Andreas' daughter, age 17, and recorded first before Andreas' and Leonore's other children.
+	21	F	ii.	**Maria Margarita Laumbach** was born 21 Mar 1865. She died Jun 1958.
+	22	M	iii.	**Peter Joseph Laumbach** was born 29 Jun 1867. He died 26 Feb 1954.
+	23	F	iv.	**Maria Estefanita Laumbach** was born Dec 1869. She died 2 May 1938.
+	24	M	v.	**Daniel Laumbach** was born on 28 Jan 1872. He died on 5 Aug 1947.
+	25	M	vi.	**Henry Joseph Laumbach** was born 2 Oct 1874. He died 10 Sep 1929.
	26	M	vii.	**Alejando Laumbach** was born in Dec 1876 in La Cebolla, Mora Co., NM. He was christened on 14 May 1877 in Church of Santa Gertrudes, Mora, Territory of New Mexico.
	27	F	viii.	**Anna Laumbach** was born on 11 Jul 1878 in Buena Vista, Mora Co., NM. She was christened on 16 Dec 1878 in Church of Santa Gertrudes, Mora, Territory of New Mexico. She died on 10 May 1958 in Las Vegas, San Miguel Co., NM. She was buried on 12 May 1958 in Laumbach Cemetery.
+	28	F	ix.	**Maria Cristina Laumbach** was born 20 Aug 1881. She died 9 Nov 1974.
	29	F	x.	**Maria de Gracia Laumbach** was born on 10 Feb 1884 in Buena Vista, Mora Co., NM. She was christened on 10 Mar 1884 in Church of Santa Gertrudes, Mora, Territory of New Mexico. She died on 5 Nov 1965 in

				Las Vegas, San Miguel Co., NM. She was buried on 7 Nov 1965 in Laumbach Cemetery.
	30	F	xi.	**Leonore Laumbach** was born on 10 Aug 1888 in Mora Co., NM. She died on 16 Aug 1974 in Las Vegas, San Miguel Co., NM.

11. Marx Heinrich Laumbach (Andreas Detlef Laumbach, Christian Rudolph, Johann Jacob) was born on 26 Mar 1840 in Jagel (Schleswig-Holstein), Germany.

Marx married **Augusta K. Grantz** daughter of Johann D. Grantz and Elsabea Thoensen. Augusta was born in Mar 1848 in Schleswig-Holstein, Germany. She died in 1933 in Clinton Co., IA. She was buried in Center Grove (Ingwerson) Cemetery, Center Township, Clinton Co., IA.

They had the following children:

+	31	F	i.	**Elsabea Anina Laumbach** was born 24 Dec 1869. She died 14 Apr 1961.
+	32	F	ii.	**Anna Marguerite Laumbach** was born on 26 Feb 1871. She died on 31 Aug 1955.
+	33	M	iii.	**John Andrew Laumbach** was born on 13 Oct 1873.
+	34	F	iv.	**Matilda D. Laumbach** was born about 1876.
	35	M	v.	**Henry Albert Laumbach** was born on 27 Oct 1879 in Clinton Co., IA. Henry married **Clara Johnson** daughter of Herman Johnson and Anna Anderson on 18 Jun 1906 in Lyons, Clinton Co., IA. Clara was born about 1882 in Minnesota.
+	36	F	vi.	**Josephine Laumbach** was born about 1882.

12. Christina Margaretha Laumbach (Andreas Detlef Laumbach, Christian Rudolph, Johann Jacob) was born on 6 Jul 1841 in Jagel (Schleswig-Holstein), Germany. She died on 4 Feb 1883 in Clinton Co., IA. She was buried in Center Grove (Ingwerson) Cemetery, Center Township, Clinton Co., IA. Christina married **Dierk Claussen** son of Henry Claussen and Lena in 1861 in Clinton Co., IA. Dierk was born on 31 Jul 1835 in Schleswig-Holstein, Germany. He died on 17 Oct 1919 in Clinton Co., IA. He was buried in Center Grove (Ingwerson) Cemetery, Center Township, Clinton Co., IA.

They had the following children:

+	37	M	i.	**Henry J. Claussen** was born in Sep 1862.
+	38	F	ii.	**Anna Claussen** was born in Oct 1865.
+	39	M	iii.	**Andrew D. Claussen** was born on 25 Oct 1866. He died on 25 Dec 1936.
+	40	F	iv.	**Caroline Claussen** was born in Dec 1868.
+	41	F	v.	**Magdalena Claussen** was born in Feb 1872.
+	42	M	vi.	**George W. Claussen** was born about 1873.
+	43	M	vii.	**John William Claussen** was born on 6 Apr 1877.
	44	F	viii.	**Johanna Claussen** was born in Aug 1880 in Clinton Co., IA. Johanna married Wallace H. Cramer about 1918. Wallace was born about 1889 in Pennsylvania.

14. Anna Christina Laumbach (Andreas Detlef Laumbach, Christian Rudolph, Johann Jacob) was born on 13 Mar 1848 in Jagel (Schleswig-Holstein), Germany. She died on 26 Nov 1908 in Dodge Co., NE. She was buried in Ridge Cemetery, Dodge Co., NE. Anna married **Peter Claus Henkens** son of Claus Peder Henkens on 3 Dec 1867 in Clinton Co., IA. Peter was born on 6 Nov 1840 in Schleswig-Holstein, Germany. He died on 13 Feb 1916 in Dodge Co., NE. He was buried in Ridge Cemetery, Dodge Co., NE.

They had the following children:

+	45	F	i.	**Caroline Henkens** was born in Jan 1869.
+	46	M	ii.	**August F. Henkens** was born in Feb 1871.

+	47	M	iii.	**John Delef Henkens** was born on 16 Jun 1875. He died on 30 Jul 1944.
+	48	F	iv.	**Emma Margaretha Henkens** was born on 14 Jul 1879. She died on 17 Apr 1956.
	49	F	v.	**Emilie C. Henkens** was born in Jun 1881 in Clinton Co., IA.
+	50	M	vi.	**Herman D. Henkens** was born on 13 Jan 1884.
+	51	M	vii.	**Edwin T. Henkens** was born on 11 Jun 1885.
+	52	M	viii.	**Claus Peter Henkens** was born on 9 Feb 1891. He died in Dec 1973.

16. **Anna M. Laumbach** (Heinrich Laumbach, Christian Rudolph, Johann Jacob) was born on 10 Oct 1842 in Jagel (Schleswig-Holstein), Germany. She died on 11 Sep 1935. She was buried in Morgan Cemetery, Schleswig, Crawford Co., IA. Anna married **Peter Frederick Jepsen** son of John Jepsen and Elsobao Petersen on 8 Oct 1867 in Clinton Co., IA. Peter was born on 18 Jan 1847 in Schleswig-Holstein, Germany. He died on 27 May 1918 in Crawford Co., IA. He was buried in Morgan Cemetery, Schleswig, Crawford Co., IA.

They had the following children:

+	53	F	i.	**Anna Henrietta Maria Jepsen** was born on 3 Oct 1868. She died on 26 Aug 1958.
+	54	M	ii.	**John H. Jepsen** was born on 4 Dec 1869. He died on 11 Feb 1960.
+	55	M	iii.	**Peter Jurgen John Jepsen** was born 31 May 1871. He died 6 Oct 1924.
+	56	F	iv.	**Ella Katherine Jepsen** was born 21 Mar 1873. She died 17 Aug 1949.
+	57	M	v.	**Henry F. Jepsen** was born on 28 Sep 1874. He died on 1 Aug 1944.
+	58	F	vi.	**Caroline M. Dora Jepsen** was born 22 Apr 1877. She died 2 Nov 1960.
+	59	M	vii.	**Jurgen Henry Jepsen** was born on 11 Oct 1878. He died on 22 Jun 1949.
+	60	M	viii.	**Julius Johann Jepsen** was born on 30 Jan 1880. He died on 25 Aug 1938.
+	61	F	ix.	**Emma Dorothea Jepsen** was born 1 Jan 1883. She died on 10 Nov 1969.

17. **Heinrich Fredrick Laumbach** (Heinrich Laumbach, Christian Rudolph, Johann Jacob) was born on 4 Nov 1847 in Jagel (Schleswig-Holstein), Germany. He died on 3 Feb 1921 in Crawford Co., IA. He was buried in Morgan Cemetery, Schleswig, Crawford Co., IA. Heinrich married **Martha Peters** daughter of Jacob Peters and Elsaba Christiansen on 24 Nov 1872 in Clinton Co., IA. Martha was born in Jul 1852 in Wisconsin. She died in 1928. She was buried in Morgan Cemetery, Schleswig, Crawford Co., IA.

They had the following children:

+	62	M	i.	**Henry F. Laumbach Jr.** was born 19 May 1875. He died 12 Nov 1957.
+	63	F	ii.	**Ella K. Laumbach** was born in Sep 1876.
	64	M	iii.	**Alfred Niclos Laumbach** was born on 17 May 1879 in Clinton Co., IA. He died on 22 Feb 1947. He was buried in Morgan Cemetery, Schleswig, Crawford Co., IA.
+	65	M	iv.	**Detlef Andreas Laumbach** was born on 22 Feb 1880. He died in Jul 1964.
	66	M	v.	**Jacob Orns Laumbach** "Jake" was born on 17 Jul 1882 in Crawford Co., IA. He died on 28 Oct 1981. He was buried in Morgan Cemetery, Schleswig, Crawford Co., IA.
+	67	F	vi.	**Anna Margaret Laumbach** was born 9 Jun 1888. She died 8 Nov 1975.
+	68	F	vii.	**Emma D. Laumbach** was born in Jan 1890.
+	69	M	viii.	**Peter John Laumbach** was born on 15 Oct 1891. He died in Dec 1983.
+	70	F	ix.	**Laura Christine Laumbach** was born in Feb 1896.

Fifth Generation

21. Maria Margarita Laumbach (Andreas Detlef Laumbach, Andreas Detlef Laumbach, Christian Rudolph, Johann Jacob) was born on 21 Mar 1865 in Plaza of Francisco Abajo de la Cebolla, Mora Co., NM. She was christened on 19 Apr 1865 in Church of Santa Gertrudes, Mora, Territory of New Mexico. She died in Jun 1958 in Albuquerque, Bernalillo Co., NM. She was buried in Holman Presbyterian Cemetery, Mora, Co., NM. Margarita married **Jose Emiterio Cruz** son of Juan Cruz and Rosa Paiz on 30 Sep 1896. Jose was born in Mar 1853 in New Mexico. He died on 25 Jan 1931 in Holman, Mora Co., NM. He was buried in Holman Presbyterian Cemetery, Mora, Co., NM.

They had the following children:

- 71   M   i.   **Andres E. Cruz** was born in Sep 1897 in Mora Co., NM.
- 72   M   ii. **Juan A. Cruz** was born in Apr 1898 in Mora Co., NM.
- 73   M   iii. **Alejandro C. Cruz** was born about 1901 in Mora Co., NM.
- 74   M   iv. **Bernardo F. Cruz** "Barney" was born on 3 Feb 1903 in Mora Co., NM. He died in Oct 1983 in Mora Co., NM. Bernardo married **Gertrude Branch** "Gertie" daughter of Luis Branch and Francisquita Martinez about 1926. Gertrude was born on 15 Mar 1908 in Mora Co., NM. She died on 24 Aug 2000. She was buried in Cleveland, Mora Co., NM.
- 75   F   v.   **Rosa M. Cruz** was born about 1906 in Mora Co., NM. She died on 10 Apr 1986 in Albuquerque, Bernalillo, NM. Rosa married **Rev. Julian Duran** son of Jose Leonires Duran and Crucita Martinez in 1929. Julian was born on 4 Jan 1898 in Rio Arriba Co., NM. He died on 9 Jan 1995 in Albuquerque, Bernalillo, NM.
- 76   F   vi. **Eleanor Evalee Cruz** was born in 1909 in Mora Co., NM. She died on 18 Aug 1933 in Las Vegas, San Miguel Co., NM. She was buried in Holman Presbyterian Cemetery, Mora, Co., NM.

22. Peter Joseph Laumbach (Andreas Detlef Laumbach, Andreas Detlef Laumbach, Christian Rudolph, Johann Jacob) was born on 29 Jun 1867 in La Cebolla, Mora Co., NM. He was christened on 1 Sep 1867 in Church of Santa Gertrudes, Mora, Territory of New Mexico. He died on 26 Feb 1954 in Roy, Harding Co., NM. Peter married (1) **Fidelia Andrada** daughter of Casimiro Andrada and Maria Del Carmen Romero in 1898. Fidelia was born on 28 Apr 1880 in Mora Co., NM. She died on 23 Aug 1928 in San Miguel Co., NM.

They had the following children:

- 77   F   i.   **Cordelia Laumbach** was born on 10 Sep 1899 in Wagon Mound, Mora Co., NM. She died on 22 Feb 1942 in New Mexico. Cordelia married **Jose Fermin Maes** son of Adolfo Maes and Maria Onofre Montano about 1929. Jose was born on 7 Jul 1905 in Las Nutrias, Rio Arriba Co., NM. He was christened on 10 Jul 1905 in St. Joseph, Park View, Rio Arriba Co., NM. He died on 7 Jul 1958 in Canjilon, Rio Arriba Co., NM.
- 78   M   ii. **Alfred Laumbach** was born on 4 Oct 1900 in Mora Co., NM. He died on 29 Aug 1918 in La Cinta Canyon, Mora Co., NM. The cause of death was lightning.
- 79   M   iii. **Peter Joseph Laumbach Jr.** was born on 22 Apr 1902 in Mora Co., NM.
- 80   M   iv. **Rudolf Detlef Laumbach** was born on 15 Aug 1903 in Mora Co., NM.
- 81   F   v.   **Crestina Laumbach** was born on 8 Feb 1905 in San Miguel Co., NM. She died on 19 Jun 1976 in Alamogordo, New Mexico. Crestina married **Frank Foxall**.

82	F	vi.	**Petra Laumbach** was born on 16 Nov 1906 in San Miguel Co., NM. She died on 6 Apr 2000 in Hinesville, Georgia. Petra married **John Roscoe Latham** son of John Sidney Latham and Vivian Norma Tibbetts on 20 May 1931 in Clayton, New Mexico. John was born on 28 Mar 1909 in Floydada, Texas. He died in Sep 1994 in Flemington, Georgia.
83	M	vii.	**Rudulph D. Laumbach** was born on 23 Jul 1908 in San Miguel Co., NM. He died on 30 Oct 1989. Rudulph married **Leona**. Leona was born on 23 Mar 1908. She died in Jun 1982 in Las Vegas, San Miguel Co., NM.
84	M	viii.	**George W. Laumbach** was born on 18 Mar 1910 in San Miguel Co., NM. He died in 24 Dec 1986 in New Mexico. George married **Margaret Miller** daughter of Rudolph Miller and Elizabeth Ferfes. Margaret was born on 11 May 1913 in Eagle Tail, New Mexico. She died on 18 Aug 2005 in Springer, New Mexico.
85	M	ix.	**Andres Detlef Laumbach** "Red" was born on 12 Oct 1911 in San Miguel Co., NM. He died on 16 Mar 2013. Andres married **Sulema Tixier** in 1940. Sulema was born on 5 Feb 1916. She died in Apr 1980 in Albuquerque, Bernalillo, NM.
86	M	x.	**Casimiro Laumbach** "Ike" was born on 9 Jun 1913 in San Miguel Co., NM. Casimiro married **Irene** on 20 Feb 1937. Irene was born on 20 Dec 1918. She died on 22 Sep 1992 in Corrales, Sandoval Co., NM.
87	F	xi.	**Carmelita Laumbach** was born on 16 Dec 1914 in San Miguel Co., NM. She died on 14 Feb 1915 in La Cinta Canyon, Mora Co., NM. The cause of death was Pneumonia.
88	F	xii.	**Bertha Belle Laumbach** was born on 21 Dec 1915 in San Miguel Co., NM. She died on 24 Apr 1959 in Lubbock, Lubbock Co., TX. She was buried on 26 Apr 1959 in Resthaven Memorial Park, Lubbock Co., TX. Bertha married Cecil **Barton Durham** son of Ernest Durham and Ida Pearl Barton on 23 Sep 1939 in Denton Co., TX. Cecil was born on 22 May 1917 in Denton Co., TX. He died on 16 Dec 1994 in Denton, Denton Co., TX.
89	F	xiii.	**Lucille Evangeline Laumbach** "Lucy" was born on 18 Jul 1917 in San Miguel Co., NM. She died on 23 Mar 1998 in Grizzly Flat, California. Lucille married **Howard W. Schmalle** 21 May 1942. Howard was born on 8 May 1915. He died on 30 Apr 2003 in Las Vegas, Clark Co., NV.
90	M	xiv.	**Alfred C. Laumbach** was born on 28 Mar 1920 in San Miguel Co., NM. Alfred married **Eleanor DeHerrera** daughter of Alferino DeHerrera and Secundina Romero on 19 Nov 1945 in St. Joseph Parish, Mosquero, New Mexico. Eleanor was born on 24 Aug 1924 in Roy, Harding Co., NM. She died on 3 Jul 2010 in Roy, Harding Co., NM.
91	M	xv.	**Peter Joseph Laumbach III** was born on 10 Jun 1923 in San Miguel Co., NM. Peter married **Lupita**. Peter married (2) **Magdalena** about 1929. Magdalena was born about 1891 in New Mexico.

23. **Maria Estefanita Laumbach** (Andreas Detlef Laumbach, Andreas Detlef Laumbach, Christian Rudolph, Johann Jacob) was born in Dec 1869 in Mora Co., NM. She was christened on 21 May 1870 in Church of Santa Gertrudes, Mora, Territory of New Mexico. She died on 2 May 1938 in Santa Fe, Santa Fe Co., NM. Estefanita married **Jesus Sito Candelario** son of Antonio Jose Candelaria and Altagracia

Garcia in Feb 1892. Jesus was born on 10 Mar 1864 in New Mexico. He died on 30 Jul 1938 in Santa Fe, Santa Fe Co., NM.

They had the following children:

92   F   i.   **Leonor Allison 'Alice' Candelario** was born in Nov 1893 in Santa Fe, Santa Fe Co., NM. She died on 11 Apr 1936 in Kansas City, Missouri. Alice married **Arthur Conklin Weeks** son of Rev. Frank Gaylord Weeks and Marietta Conklin. Arthur was born on 19 Nov 1883. He died on 11 Apr 1936 in Albuquerque, Bernalillo Co., NM.
Alice married (2) Stanley A. Mossman.

93   F   ii.   **Refugio Candelario** was born in May 1897 in Santa Fe, Santa Fe Co., NM.

94   M   iii.   [Adopted] **John S. Candelario** "Little Lalo" was born on 7 Sep 1916 in Santa Fe, Santa Fe Co., NM, to Arthur Conklin Weeks and Leonor Allison 'Alice' Candelario (daughter of Jesus Sito Candelario and Maria Estefanita Laumbach). He died on 5 Oct 1993 in Albuquerque, Bernalillo, NM. John had 5 marriages.

24. **Daniel Laumbach** (Andreas Detlef Laumbach, Andreas Detlef Laumbach, Christian Rudolph, Johann Jacob) was born on 28 Jan 1872 in Buena Vista, Mora Co., NM. He was christened on 13 May 1872 in Church of Santa Gertrudes, Mora, Territory of New Mexico. He died on 5 Aug 1947 in Harding Co., NM. Daniel married **Emma Margaretha Henkens** daughter of Peter Claus Henkens and Anna Christina Laumbach in 1902. Emma was born on 14 Jul 1879 in Clinton Co., IA. She was christened on 7 Sep 1879. She died on 17 Apr 1956 in Roy, Harding Co., NM.

They had the following children:

95   F   i.   **Mabel Anna Eleanor Laumbach** was born on 24 Oct 1902 in La Cueva, Mora Co., NM. She died on 5 Apr 1922 in La Cinta Canyon, Mora Co., NM. The cause of death was Pneumonia.

96   M   ii.   **Joyce Laumbach** was born on 4 Feb 1905 in San Miguel Co., NM. He died on 20 Dec 1991.

97   F   iii.   **Alida Laumbach** was born on 23 Mar 1907 in San Miguel Co., NM. She died on 8 Nov 1994. She was buried in Solano Cemetery, Solano, Harding Co., NM. Alida married **Elbert Lawton Wallace** son of William Lafayette Wallace and Myra Pancake about 1928. Elbert was born on 16 Feb 1900 in Hamilton Co., TX. He died on 3 Feb 1958 in New Mexico. He was buried in Solano Cemetery, Solano, Harding Co., NM.

98   F   iv.   **Verna Laumbach** was born on 8 Oct 1909 in San Miguel Co., NM. She died on 23 May 1996 in Roswell, Chaves Co., NM. She was buried on 29 May 1996 in Fairmont Cemetery, Raton, New Mexico. Verna married **Dalphon Clinton Sparks** son of Alfred Burton Sparks and Sally Henrietta LaPrade on 27 May 1936 in Hillsboro, Sierra Co., NM. Dalphon was born on 20 Jul 1908 in Copan, Washington Co., OK.

99   F   v.   **Frances Laumbach** was born on 27 Mar 1912 in Cedar Springs Ranch, Harding Co., NM. She died on 24 Dec 1992 in Bosque Farms, Valencia Co., NM. Frances married **Leon M. Shinn** on 25 Jun 1947. Leon was born on 22 Oct 1914. He died on 15 May 1994 in Bosque Farms, Valencia Co., NM. They had no children; he had two they both raised.

100   F   vi.   **Ruth E. Laumbach** was born on 13 May 1914 in San Miguel Co., NM.

She died on 14 Nov 1995 in Roswell, Chaves Co., NM.

 101 M vii. **Daniel Chester Laumbach** was born on 15 Jan 1916 in San Miguel Co., NM. He died on 16 Apr 1996 in Albuquerque, Bernalillo Co., NM.

25. Henry Joseph Laumbach (Andreas Detlef Laumbach, Andreas Detlef Laumbach, Christian Rudolph, Johann Jacob) was born on 2 Oct 1874 in Buena Vista, Mora Co., NM. He was christened on 2 Nov 1874 in Church of Santa Gertrudes, Mora, Territory of New Mexico. He died on 10 Sep 1929 in Las Vegas, San Miguel Co., NM. Henry married **Natividad Hurtado** daughter of Gavino Hurtado and Alejandra Blea in 1920. Natividad was born on 26 Oct 1901 in Mora Co., NM. She died on 17 Jun 1981 in Placer, California.

 They had the following children:

 102 M i. **Laumbach** was born on 15 May 1921 in Mora Co., NM. He died on 15 May 1921 in Mora Co., NM.

 103 M ii. **Henry J. Laumbach** was born on 10 May 1922 in Mora Co., NM. He died on 29 Jan 2004 in Reno, Washoe Co., NV.

 104 M iii. **John Andrew Laumbach** was born on 3 Jun 1923 in Mora Co., NM. He died on 12 Jun 2008 in Shingle Springs, El Dorado Co., CA.

 105 M iv. **Carlos W. Laumbach** was born on 9 Sep 1924 in Mora Co., NM. He died on 1 Feb 1975 in Placer, California.

 106 M v. **Frank William Laumbach** was born on 2 Dec 1925 in Mora Co., NM. He died on 11 Jun 1971 in Placer, California. Frank married **Florentina Maira Sanchez**. Florentina was born on 4 Jun 1933 in Las Vegas, San Miguel Co., NM. She died on 11 Sep 1974 in Placer, California.

 107 F vi. **Adelina L. Laumbach** was born about 1927 in Mora Co., NM.

 108 F vii. **Clara B. Laumbach** was born in 1928 in Mora Co., NM.

28. Maria Cristina Laumbach (Andreas Detlef Laumbach, Andreas Detlef Laumbach, Christian Rudolph, Johann Jacob) was born on 20 Aug 1881 in La Cueva, Mora Co., NM. She was christened on 27 Nov 1881 in Church of Santa Gertrudes, Mora, Territory of New Mexico. She died on 9 Nov 1974 in Las Vegas, San Miguel Co., NM. She was buried in Masonic Cemetery, Las Vegas, San Miguel Co., NM. Crestina married **Manuel Antonio Sanchez** son of Antonio Sanchez and Maria Candelaria Cortes about 1911. Manuel was born on 1 Jan 1861 in New Mexico. He died on 30 Nov 1941 in Las Vegas, San Miguel Co., NM. He was buried in Masonic Cemetery, Las Vegas, San Miguel Co., NM.

 They had the following children:

 109 M i. **Antonio A. Sanchez** "Tony" was born on 18 Oct 1911 in San Miguel Co., NM. He died on 11 Mar 1987 in Las Vegas, San Miguel Co., NM. He was buried in Masonic Cemetery, Las Vegas, San Miguel Co., NM.

 110 F ii. **Adelina Candelaria Sanchez** was born on 7 Feb 1913 in Las Vegas, San Miguel Co., NM. She died on 26 Jan 1921 in Las Vegas, San Miguel Co., NM. She was buried on 27 Jan 1921 in Buena Vista, NM.

31. Elsabea Anina Laumbach (Marx Heinrich Laumbach, Andreas Detlef Laumbach, Christian Rudolph, Johann Jacob) was born on 24 Dec 1869 in Clinton Co., IA. She died on 14 Apr 1961 in Clinton, Clinton Co., IA. Elsabea married **William Traver Miller** son of Henry Miller on 21 Jan 1892 in Clinton Co., IA. William was born in Feb 1869 in Schleswig-Holstein, Germany. He died on 12 Apr 1937.

 They had the following children:

 111 F i. **Isabella E. Miller** was born on 11 May 1893 in Clinton, Clinton Co., IA.

 112 F ii. **Josephine H. Miller** was born on 25 Oct 1896 in Clinton, Clinton Co., IA.

			She died in 1939.
113	F	iii.	**Adele Miriam Miller** was born on 18 Dec 1900 in Clinton Co., IA. She died on 14 Oct 1990 in Clinton Co., IA. Adele married **Frederick Ernest Kube** son of Charles Luther Kube and Mary Thomas Smith on 24 Dec 1919 in Clinton Co., IA. Frederick was born on 13 Nov 1888 in Franklin Co., IA. He died in Apr 1955 in Clinton Co., IA.
114	F	iv.	**Elsabea Wilhelmina Miller** was born on 10 Jul 1902 in Clinton, Clinton Co., IA. She died on 11 May 1985 in Clinton Co., IA.
115	F	v.	**Anna E. Miller** was born on 14 Jun 1905 in Clinton Co., IA. She died on 5 Jul 1994 in Millsboro, Sussex Co., DE. Anna married **Joseph Story**.

32. Anna Marguerite Laumbach (Marx Heinrich Laumbach, Andreas Detlef Laumbach, Christian Rudolph, Johann Jacob) was born on 26 Feb 1871 in Clinton Co., IA. She died on 31 Aug 1955 in Santa Clara, California. Anna married **Hubert Earl Rogers** son of Henry Brigmon Rogers and Sarah Derwent about 1891. Hubert was born on 17 Jul 1869 in Winnebago, Winnebago Co., IL. He died on 6 Apr 1945 in Los Angeles, California.

They had the following children:

116	M	i.	**Arthur H. Rogers** was born in Oct 1892 in Brule Co., SD.
117	M	ii.	**Franklin Earl Rogers** was born in May 1895 in Brule Co., SD. Franklin married **Margit Ingrid Bergsvik**.
118	M	iii.	**Vertus W. Rogers** was born in Sep 1898 in Brule Co., SD. He died on 12 Apr 1930 in Walla Walla, Walla Walla Co., WA. Vertus married **Faythe Irene Brown** on 11 Dec 1917 in Davison Co., SD. Faythe was born on 17 Oct 1899 in Iowa. She died on 15 Aug 1973 in Tacoma, Pierce Co., WA.
119	M	iv.	**Harold V. Rogers** was born about 1903 in Brule Co., SD.

33. John Andrew Laumbach (Marx Heinrich Laumbach, Andreas Detlef Laumbach, Christian Rudolph, Johann Jacob) was born on 13 Oct 1873 in Clinton Co., IA. John Andrew married **Alvina Katherina Greve** daughter of Hans Henry Greve and Catherina Greve on 26 Jan 1899 in Wall Lake, Sac Co., IA. Alvina was born in Sep 1879 in Schleswig-Holstein, Germany. She died on 8 Oct 1939 in Calhoun Co., IA.

They had the following children:

120	F	i.	**Alma Margaret Laumbach** was born on 7 Aug 1899 in Lake View, Sac Co., IA. She died on 17 May 1984 in Calhoun Co., IA.
121	M	ii.	**Heinrich H. Laumbach** was born about 1901 in Sac Co., IA.
122	M	iii.	**Harold John Laumbach** was born on 1 Sep 1903 in Lake View, Sac Co., IA. Harold married **Zella Elizabeth Austin** daughter of Delbert Austin and Mary Ann Bogart on 26 May 1928 in Nashua, Chickasaw Co., IA. Zella was born about 1904 in Sumner, Iowa.
123	M	iv.	**Justus Theodore Laumbach** was born on 26 Mar 1905 in Lake View, Sac Co., IA. He died on 2 Feb 1993 in Lake City, Calhoun Co., IA. Justus married **Alice Lillian Kral** daughter of Stephen A. Kral and Anna Freml on 21 Aug 1929 in Crawford Co., IA. Alice was born on 15 Nov 1908 in Crawford Co., IA. She died on 21 Dec 1989 in Lake City, Calhoun Co., IA.
124	M	v.	**Hans Andrew Laumbach** was born on 16 Oct 1908 in Sac Co., IA. He died on 14 May 1961 in Los Angeles, California. Hans married (1) **Lois** on 5 Oct 1941. Lois was born about 1917. Hans married (2) **Madalyn K.**

>
> **Herzog** daughter of Albert N. Herzog and Selma Bigelow. Madalyn was born on 19 Oct 1915 in Iowa. She died on 14 May 1961 in Los Angeles, California.

125	F	vi.	**Augusta K. Laumbach** was born on 16 Oct 1908 in Sac Co., IA. Augusta married Paul Stanfield .
126	F	vii.	**Vera Alvina Laumbach** was born on 13 Sep 1910 in Sac Co., IA. She died on 28 Sep 1988 in Alameda, California. Vera married **Olhausen**.

34. Matilda D. Laumbach (Marx Heinrich Laumbach, Andreas Detlef Laumbach, Christian Rudolph, Johann Jacob) was born about 1876 in Clinton Co., IA. Matilda married **Arthur Henry Hawkes** son of William Hawkes and Elisa Piner about 1902. Arthur was born on 27 Jan 1877 in Cook Co., IL. He died on 5 Sep 1955 in Los Angeles, California.

> They had the following children:

127	M	i.	**Arthur W. H. Hawkes** was born on 11 Nov 1903 in Douglas Co., SD.
128	F	ii.	**Lillie Leone Hawkes** was born about 1905 in Douglas Co., SD. Lillie married William L. Lester on 2 Jun 1930 in Douglas Co., SD.
129	M	iii.	**Earl Alden Hawkes** was born on 27 Jun 1907 in Douglas Co., SD. He died on 28 Aug 1981 in San Diego, California.
130	M	iv.	**Emerson W. Hawkes** was born on 27 Jun 1907 in Douglas Co., SD. He died on 14 Jan 2002 in San Diego, California.

36. Josephine Laumbach (Marx Heinrich Laumbach, Andreas Detlef Laumbach, Christian Rudolph, Johann Jacob) was born about 1882 in Clinton Co., IA. Josephine married **Albert Schmidt** son of Lorenz Schmidt and G. Schatzle on 20 Jun 1907 in Clinton, Clinton Co., IA. Albert was born about 1882 in Wisconsin.

> They had the following children:

131	F	i.	**Josephine Genevieve Schmidt** was born on 13 Apr 1908 in Rock Island Co., IL. She died on 2 Oct 1981 in Milwaukee, Milwaukee Co., WI. Josephine married Melvin Ferdinand Otto Gentz son of Wilhelm August Herman Gentz and Lydia Koch on 27 Dec 1941. Melvin was born on 12 Sep 1910. He died on 7 Oct 1972.
132	F	ii.	**Ruth E. Schmidt** was born on 4 Oct 1909 in Rock Island Co., IL. She died on 5 Jan 2000 in Menomonee Falls, Waukesha Co., WI. Ruth married (1) **Delbert Fredrich Franz** "Doc" son of John Franz and Johnna Karoline Aguste Magdalena Honeyager about 1928. Delbert was born on 12 Nov 1902 in Wisconsin. He died in Aug 1935 in Wisconsin. He was buried on 19 Aug 1935 in Prairie Home Cemetery, Waukesha Co., WI. Ruth married (2) **Thomas Coghlan**.

37. Henry J. Claussen (Christina Margaretha Laumbach, Andreas Detlef Laumbach, Christian Rudolph, Johann Jacob) was born in Sep 1862 in Clinton Co., IA. Henry married **Dorothy Ehlers** "Dora" daughter of Jacob Ehlers and Margaret Massen about 1888. Dorothy was born in Feb 1867 in Clinton Co., IA.

> They had the following children:

133	F	i.	**Hilda C. Claussen** was born in Aug 1889 in Nebraska.
134	F	ii.	**Lillian M. Claussen** was born in Jun 1891 in Madison Co., IA.
135	F	iii.	**Irene Claussen** was born in May 1898 in Madison Co., IA.
136	F	iv.	**Pet Claussen** was born in May 1898 in Madison Co., IA.
137	F	v.	**Margaret Claussen** was born about 1901 in Madison Co., IA.

        138   M   vi.   **Lawrence Claussen** was born about 1905 in Boone Co., IA.

38. Anna Claussen (Christina Margaretha Laumbach, Andreas Detlef Laumbach, Christian Rudolph, Johann Jacob) was born in Oct 1865 in Clinton Co., IA. Anna married **Henry Gloe** son of Marx Gloe and Catherine Bendtschneider about 1890. Henry was born in Sep 1867 in Clinton Co., IA.

    They had the following children:
        139   M   i.   **Arnold D. Gloe** was born in Apr 1891 in Iowa.
        140   M   ii.   **Harold H. Gloe** was born in Jul 1895 in Iowa.
        141   F   iii.   **Esther A. Gloe** was born about 1901 in Ida Co., IA.

39. Andrew D. Claussen (Christina Margaretha Laumbach, Andreas Detlef Laumbach, Christian Rudolph, Johann Jacob) was born on 25 Oct 1866 in Clinton Co., IA. He died on 25 Dec 1936 in Iowa City, Iowa. Andrew married **Kathlina Boken** on 6 Oct 1892 in Clinton Co., IA. Kathlina was born on 18 Mar 1867 in Schleswig-Holstein, Germany. She died on 4 Mar 1947 in Clinton Co., IA. She was buried on 7 Mar 1947 in Center Grove (Ingwerson) Cemetery, Center Township, Clinton Co., IA.

    They had the following children:
        142   F   i.   **Georgianna M. Claussen** was born on 26 Dec 1893 in Clinton Co., IA. She died on 27 Nov 1966.
        143   M   ii.   **Arthur Dierk H. Claussen** was born on 3 Sep 1895 in Clinton Co., IA. He died on 17 Apr 1947.
        144   M   iii.   **Andrew D. Claussen Jr.** was born in May 1899 in Clinton Co., IA. He died in 1911.
        145   F   iv.   **Adeline B. Claussen** was born on 26 May 1909 in Clarion, Iowa. She died on 7 Nov 1979. She was buried on 10 Nov 1979 in Center Grove (Ingwerson) Cemetery, Center Township, Clinton Co., IA. Adeline married **Alfred August Bielenberg** on 25 Dec 1933. Alfred was born on 4 Jan 1904 in Clinton Co., IA.

40. Caroline Claussen "Carrie" (Christina Margaretha Laumbach, Andreas Detlef Laumbach, Christian Rudolph, Johann Jacob) was born in Dec 1868 in Clinton Co., IA. Caroline married **Deering**.

    Deering and Caroline had the following children:
        146   F   i.   **Christene Deering** was born about 1905 in Illinois.

41. Magdalena Claussen (Christina Margaretha Laumbach, Andreas Detlef Laumbach, Christian Rudolph, Johann Jacob) was born in Feb 1872 in Clinton Co., IA. Magdalena married **Albert Haberer** about 1896. Albert was born in Oct 1865 in Illinois.

    They had the following children:
        147   F   i.   **Evelyn Haberer** was born in Apr 1897 in Cook Co., IL.

42. George W. Claussen (Christina Margaretha Laumbach, Andreas Detlef Laumbach, Christian Rudolph, Johann Jacob) was born about 1873 in Clinton Co., IA. George married **Maud**. Maud was born on 6 Sep 1881 in Iowa. She died on 15 Dec 1967 in Custer Co., OK.

    They had the following children:
        148   F   i.   **Gladys E. Claussen** was born about 1904 in Iowa.
        149   M   ii.   **George Lynn Claussen** was born about 1906 in Iowa.
        150   M   iii.   **Marvin L. Claussen** was born on 29 Jan 1915 in Oklahoma. He died on 3 Jan 1992 in Thomas, Custer Co., OK.

43. John William Claussen (Christina Margaretha Laumbach, Andreas Detlef Laumbach, Christian Rudolph, Johann Jacob) was born on 6 Apr 1877 in Clinton Co., IA. John married **Harriet Alexander**. Harriet was born about 1890 in Illinois. She died in 1926 in Dade Co., FL.

    They had the following children:

| | 151 | F | i. | **Harriet Claussen** was born about 1912 in Illinois. |

45. Caroline Henkens (Anna Christina Laumbach, Andreas Detlef Laumbach, Christian Rudolph, Johann Jacob) was born in Jan 1869 in Clinton Co., IA. Caroline married **Robert H. McCann** about 1887. Robert was born on 16 Apr 1845 in New York. He died on 14 Oct 1924. He was buried in Ridge Cemetery, Fremont, Dodge Co., Nebraska.

They had the following children:

	152	F	i.	**Annie Mae McCann** was born in Oct 1887 in Nebraska.
	153	M	ii.	**William Henry McCann** was born on 30 Jan 1889 in Nebraska.
	154	M	iii.	**Thona Robert McCann** was born on 28 Jan 1891 in Nebraska.
	155	M	iv.	**John A. McCann** was born in Jun 1893 in Nebraska.
	156	M	v.	**Phillips Elmer McCann** was born on 13 Dec 1898 in Colfax Co., NE.

46. August F. Henkens (Anna Christina Laumbach, Andreas Detlef Laumbach, Christian Rudolph, Johann Jacob) was born in Feb 1871 in Clinton Co., IA. August married **Emma Grantz** about 1894. Emma was born in Oct 1874 in Germany.

They had the following children:

	157	F	i.	**Annie P. Henkens** was born in Jan 1895 in Cedar Co., NE. Annie married **J. A. Duncan** son of John D. Duncan and Julia Knights on 9 Jul 1924 in Crawford Co., IA. J. A. Duncan was born about 1884.
	158	M	ii.	**Eddie W. Henkens** was born about 1902 in Cedar Co., NE.
	159	M	iii.	**Harry R. Henkens** was born on 4 Jul 1907 in Boyd Co., NE. He died in Feb 1986 in Saline Co., NE.

47. John Detlef Henkens (Anna Christina Laumbach, Andreas Detlef Laumbach, Christian Rudolph, Johann Jacob) was born on 16 Jun 1875 in Clinton Co., IA. He died on 30 Jul 1944. He was buried in Ridge Cemetery, Dodge Co., NE. John married **Wilhelmina** "Minnie" about 1895. Wilhelmina was born on 15 Nov 1875 in Nebraska. She died on 3 Jun 1949. She was buried in Ridge Cemetery, Dodge Co., NE.

They had the following children:

	160	F	i.	**Elma Henkens** was born in Feb 1896 in Dodge Co., NE.
	161	F	ii.	**Alice C. Henkens** was born in Feb 1900 in Dodge Co., NE.
	162	M	iii.	**George W. Henkens** was born on 25 Dec 1901 in Dodge Co., NE. He died on 25 May 1994 in Fremont, Dodge Co., NE. George married **Mabel Borcherding** daughter of William Borcherding and Sophie Waterman on 20 Feb 1929 in Fremont, Dodge Co., NE. Mabel was born on 15 Dec 1906 in Telbasta, Nebraska. She died on 19 Jun 2006 in Fremont, Dodge Co., NE.
	163	F	iv.	**Dora Henkens** was born about 1904 in Dodge Co., NE.
	164	M	v.	**Henry E. Henkens** was born on 10 May 1907 in Dodge Co., NE. He died on 26 Mar 1975 in Fremont, Dodge Co., NE. He was buried in Memorial Cemetery, Fremont, Dodge Co., NE. Henry married **Ruth V. Knapp** on 14 Nov 1925 in Council Bluffs, Iowa. Ruth was born on 19 Oct 1906 in Yutan, Nebraska. She died on 9 Jun 2004 in Fremont, Dodge Co., NE. She was buried in Memorial Cemetery, Fremont, Dodge Co., NE.
	165	M	vi.	**Raymond Adolph Henkens** "Ray" was born on 24 Mar 1909 in North Bend, Dodge Co., NE. He died on 3 Apr 1990 in Fremont, Dodge Co., NE. He was buried in Memorial Cemetery, Fremont, Dodge Co., NE.
	166	F	vii.	**Irma B. Henkens** was born about 1918 in Nebraska.

48. Emma Margaretha Henkens (Anna Christina Laumbach, Andreas Detlef Laumbach, Christian Rudolph, Johann Jacob) was born on 14 Jul 1879 in Clinton Co., IA. She was christened on 7 Sep 1879. She died on 17 Apr 1956 in Roy, Harding Co., NM. Emma married **Daniel Laumbach** son of Andreas Detlef Laumbach II and Eleonore Eberle in 1902. Daniel was born on 28 Jan 1872 in Buena Vista, Mora Co., NM. He was christened on 13 May 1872 in Church of Santa Gertrudes, Mora, Territory of New Mexico. He died on 5 Aug 1947 in Harding Co., NM.
They had the following children:

    167   F   i.   **Mabel Anna Eleanor Laumbach** (see #95.)
    168   M   ii.   **Joyce Laumbach** (see #96.)
    169   F   iii.   **Alida Laumbach** (see #97.)
    170   F   iv.   **Verna Laumbach** (see #98.)
    171   F   v.   **Frances Laumbach** (see #99.)
    172   F   vi.   **Ruth E. Laumbach** (see #100.)
    173   M   vii.   **Daniel Chester Laumbach** (see #101.)

50. Herman D. Henkens (Anna Christina Laumbach, Andreas Detlef Laumbach, Christian Rudolph, Johann Jacob) was born on 13 Jan 1884 in Boone Co., IA. Herman married **Mayme Parsons** "Mamie" on 5 Dec 1917 in Sioux Falls, Minnehaha Co., SD. Mayme was born on 24 Jun 1882 in Illinois. She died in Jul 1972 in Sioux Falls, Minnehaha Co., SD.

    They had the following children:
    174   M   i.   **Lawrence W. Henkens** was born in 1929 in Dawes Co., NE.

51. Edwin T. Henkens (Anna Christina Laumbach, Andreas Detlef Laumbach, Christian Rudolph, Johann Jacob) was born on 11 Jun 1885 in Colfax Co., NE. Edwin married **Wilhelmina Kruse** daughter of Peter Kruse and Anna Barrickson about 1910. Wilhelmina was born on 26 Aug 1883 in Iowa. She died in Dec 1974 in Dawes Co., NE.

    Edwin and Wilhelmina had the following children:
    175   M   i.   **Earl Edwin Henkens** was born on 27 Jan 1911 in Dawes Co., NE. He died on 25 Nov 2001 in Dawes Co., NE. He was buried in Calvary Cemetery, Chadron, Dawes Co., NE.
    176   F   ii.   **Bernice Henkens** was born on 22 Aug 1914 in Dawes Co., NE. She died on 19 Jun 1979. She was buried in Greenwood Cemetery, Chadron, Dawes Co., NE. Bernice married **Chamberlain**.
    177   M   iii.   **Lester P. Henkens** was born in 1916 in Dawes Co., NE.

52. Claus Peter Henkens (Anna Christina Laumbach, Andreas Detlef Laumbach, Christian Rudolph, Johann Jacob) was born on 9 Feb 1891 in Colfax Co., NE. He died in Dec 1973 in Sioux Falls, Minnehaha Co., SD. Claus married **Bertha** about 1924. Bertha was born on 26 Oct 1886 in Illinois. She died on 22 Jan 1971 in Sioux Falls, Minnehaha Co., SD.

    They had the following children:
    178   F   i.   **Ruth Henkens** was born about 1925 in South Dakota.

53. Anna Henrietta Maria Jepsen (Anna M. Laumbach, Heinrich Laumbach, Christian Rudolph, Johann Jacob) was born on 3 Oct 1868 in Clinton Co., IA. She died on 26 Aug 1958. She was buried in Morgan Cemetery, Schleswig, Crawford Co., IA. Anna married **William Charles Louis John Gehring** son of William Gehring and Dora Priefs on 14 Jan 1891 in Denison, Crawford Co., IA. William was born in May 1870 in Chicago, Illinois.

    They had the following children:
    179   M   i.   **William George Carl Gehring** was born on 5 Jul 1891 in Denison, Crawford Co., IA.

180	M	ii.	**Edward Peter Johannes Gehring** was born on 7 Nov 1893 in Crawford Co., IA.
181	F	iii.	**Adela M. C. Gehring** was born in Mar 1898 in Crawford Co., IA.

54. **John H. Jepsen** (Anna M. Laumbach, Heinrich Laumbach, Christian Rudolph, Johann Jacob) was born on 4 Dec 1869 in Clinton Co., IA. He died on 11 Feb 1960. John married **Maria Nath** about 1895. Maria was born in Jul 1875 in Germany.

They had the following children:

182	M	i.	**Peter John Jepsen** was born on 5 Mar 1896 in Denison, Crawford Co., IA.
183	F	ii.	**Anna E. Jepsen** "Annie" was born in Dec 1897 in Crawford Co., IA.

55. **Peter Jurgen John Jepsen** (Anna M. Laumbach, Heinrich Laumbach, Christian Rudolph, Johann Jacob) was born on 31 May 1871 in Clinton Co., IA. He died on 6 Oct 1924. He was buried in Morgan Cemetery, Schleswig, Crawford Co., IA. Peter married (1) **Margaretta Schroeder** about 1898. Margaretta was born in Dec 1872 in Iowa.

They had the following children:

184	F	i.	**Emma J. Jepsen** was born in Jan 1899 in Crawford Co., IA.
185	M	ii.	**Peter John Tom Jepsen** was born on 11 Aug 1900 in Crawford Co., IA.
186	M	iii.	**William Jepsen** was born about 1902 in Crawford Co., IA.

Peter married (2) **Dora** about 1906. Dora was born about 1888 in Germany.

They had the following children:

187	F	iv.	**Esie Jepsen** was born about 1906 in Crawford Co., IA.
188	F	v.	**Edna M. Jepsen** was born about 1908 in Crawford Co., IA.

56. **Ella Katherine Jepsen** (Anna M. Laumbach, Heinrich Laumbach, Christian Rudolph, Johann Jacob) was born on 21 Mar 1873 in Clinton Co., IA. She died on 17 Aug 1949 in Crawford Co., IA. Ella married **John Christian Saggau** son of Hans Hinrich Saggau and Christine Storjohann on 24 Feb 1892 in Crawford Co., IA. John was born on 1 May 1867 in Bad Segeberg (Schleswig-Holstein), Germany. He died on 18 Aug 1944 in Crawford Co., IA.

They had the following children:

189	M	i.	**Hans Henry Paul Saggau** was born on 30 Jul 1892 in Crawford Co., IA.
190	M	ii.	**Hugo Peter Martin Saggau** was born on 4 Oct 1894 in Crawford Co., IA.
191	M	iii.	**Martin Jurgen Julius Saggau** was born on 20 Mar 1896 in Crawford Co., IA.
192	M	iv.	**Carl Edward Saggau** "Eddie" was born on 27 Jan 1901 in Crawford Co.,
193	M	v.	**Harry August Saggau** was born on 25 Jan 1903 in Crawford Co., IA.

57. **Henry F. Jepsen** (Anna M. Laumbach, Heinrich Laumbach, Christian Rudolph, Johann Jacob) was born on 28 Sep 1874 in Clinton Co., IA. He died on 1 Aug 1944. Henry married **Marie Hallender** about 1905. Marie was born about 1885 in Germany.

They had the following children:

194	M	i.	**Walter P. Jepsen** was born about 1906 in Crawford Co., IA.
195	F	ii.	**Hilda G. Jepsen** was born about 1910 in Crawford Co., IA.
196	F	iii.	**Duretta H. Jepsen** was born about 1914 in Crawford Co., IA.

58. **Caroline M. Dora Jepsen** (Anna M. Laumbach, Heinrich Laumbach, Christian Rudolph, Johann Jacob) was born on 22 Apr 1877 in Crawford Co., IA. She died on 2 Nov 1960. Caroline married **Martin J. Saggau** son of Hans Hinrich Saggau and Christine Storjohann about 1894. Martin was born on 28 Mar 1870 in Schleswig-Holstein, Germany. He died on 26 Jun 1940.

They had the following children:

197	F	i.	**Emma C. Saggau** was born in Nov 1894 in Crawford Co., IA.
198	F	ii.	**Annie M. Saggau** was born in May 1897 in Crawford Co., IA.
199	F	iii.	**Caroline Wilhelmine Saggau** was born on 13 Feb 1899 in Crawford Co., IA. She died in Nov 1979 in Phoenix, Maricopa Co., AZ. Caroline married **Frank Otto Reyer** on 6 Jan 1918. Frank was born about 1896 in Missouri.
200	M	iv.	**Johannas Henry Martin Saggau** "Jack" was born on 10 Sep 1900 in Crawford Co., IA. Johannas married **Nellie Saylor**.
201	M	v.	**Bernhard Saggau** was born on 28 Sep 1902 in Crawford Co., IA.
202	F	vi.	**Marie Saggau** was born about 1905 in Crawford Co., IA.
203	M	vii.	**Martin Saggau** was born on 15 Jun 1910 in Crawford Co., IA.
204	F	viii.	**Irene Saggau** was born about 1913 in Crawford Co., IA.

59. **Jurgen Henry Jepsen** (Anna M. Laumbach, Heinrich Laumbach, Christian Rudolph, Johann Jacob) was born on 11 Oct 1878 in Crawford Co., IA. He died on 22 Jun 1949. He was buried in Morgan Cemetery, Schleswig, Crawford Co., IA. Jurgen married **Anna Johansen** about 1902. Anna was born about 1882 in Iowa.

They had the following children:

205	F	i.	**Wilhelmina Jepsen** "Minnie" was born about 1904 in Crawford Co., IA.
206	M	ii.	**Albert Jepsen** was born about 1906 in Crawford Co., IA.
207	M	iii.	**Johann Jepsen** was born about 1908 in Crawford Co., IA.
208	F	iv.	**Rosie Jepsen** was born about 1914 in Crawford Co., IA.
209	M	v.	**Hugo Jepsen** was born about Jun 1915 in Crawford Co., IA.

60. **Julius Johann Jepsen** (Anna M. Laumbach, Heinrich Laumbach, Christian Rudolph, Johann Jacob) was born on 30 Jan 1880 in Charter Oak, Crawford Co., IA. He died on 25 Aug 1938. Julius married **Anna Rassow** about 1902. Anna was born about 1884 in Germany.

Julius and Anna had the following children:

210	M	i.	**Martin Jepsen** was born about 1903 in Crawford Co., IA.
211	F	ii.	**Adela Jepsen** was born about 1905 in Crawford Co., IA.
212	F	iii.	**Malinda Jepsen** was born about 1907 in Crawford Co., IA.

61. **Emma Dorothea Jepsen** (Anna M. Laumbach, Heinrich Laumbach, Christian Rudolph, Johann Jacob) was born on 1 Jan 1883 in Charter Oak, Crawford Co., IA. She died on 10 Nov 1969. Emma married **Henry Nath** son of John Nath and Magdelina Solomon about 1901. Henry was born in May 1877 in Germany. He died in Apr 1955.

They had the following children:

213	M	i.	**Henry Nath** was born about 1903 in Minnesota.
214	F	ii.	**Edna Nath** was born about 1908 in Minnesota.

62. **Henry F. Laumbach Jr.** "Hy" (Heinrich Fredrick Laumbach, Heinrich Laumbach, Christian Rudolph, Johann Jacob) was born on 19 May 1875 in Clinton Co., IA. He died on 12 Nov 1957. He was buried in Presho Cemetery, Presho, Lyman Co., SD. Henry married (1) **Adele Emma Ernst** daughter of Christian Ernst and Doris Kortum on 13 Mar 1904 in Morgan Twp., Crawdord Co., IA. Adele was born about 1882 in Morgan Twp., Crawford Co., IA. She died in 1905.

They had the following children:

215	M	i.	**Adolph E. Laumbach** was born about 1905 in Iowa. Adolph married **Katie**. Katie was born about 1910 in Iowa.

Henry married (2) **Emma Marie Seehusen** daughter of Claus Seehusen and Marguerita Storms on 27 Mar 1907 in Mapleton, Monona Co., IA. Emma was born on 28 Aug 1886 in Schleswig, Crawford Co., IA. She died on 6 Apr 1966. She was buried in Presho Cemetery, Presho, Lyman Co., SD.

They had the following children:

- 216 F ii. **Hilma Laumbach** was born on 9 Aug 1907 in Cooper Twp, Monona Co., IA. She died on 12 Jul 2000 in Wall Lake, Sac Co., IA.
- 217 F iii. **Alice Martha Laumbach** "Allie " was born on 25 Aug 1909 in Iowa. She died on 22 Oct 1951. She was buried in Presho Cemetery, Presho, Lyman Co., SD.
- 218 F iv. **Irene E. Laumbach** was born on 30 Jun 1912 in Lyman Co., SD. She died in Oct 1991 in Crane, Stone Co., MO.
- 219 M v. **Walter Henry Laumbach** was born on 16 Jan 1915 in Lyman Co., SD. He died on 17 Nov 1953 in Jones Co., SD. He was buried in Draper Cemetery, Draper, Jones Co., SD. Walter married **Florence Adrine**. Florence was born in 1922. She died on 6 Oct 2010 in Rapid City, Pennington Co., SD. She was buried in Draper Cemetery, Draper, Jones Co., SD.
- 220 F vi. **Martha R. Laumbach** was born about 1917 in Lyman Co., SD.
- 221 M vii. **Henry Arlo Laumbach** was born on 18 Jan 1919 in Lyman Co., SD. He died on 9 Mar 1979. He was buried in Presho Cemetery, Presho, Lyman Co., SD.
- 222 M viii. **Raymond F. Laumbach** was born on 10 Apr 1922 in Lyman Co., SD. He died on 7 Jan 1972. He was buried in Presho Cemetery, Presho, Lyman Co., SD.
- 223 F ix. **Madeline Laumbach** was born on 17 Feb 1928 in Lyman Co., SD. She died on 15 Jan 1980 in Fontana, San Bernardino Co., CA. Madeline married **Ralph Burton Smith** on 6 Dec 1965. Ralph was born on 11 Sep 1924. He died on 29 Dec 1996 in Las Vegas, Clark Co., NV.

63. **Ella K. Laumbach** (Heinrich Fredrick Laumbach, Heinrich Laumbach, Christian Rudolph, Johann Jacob) was born in Sep 1876 in Clinton Co., IA. Ella married **Herman J. Luitjens** son of Tiark Luitjens and Hilke Jansen on 17 Aug 1898 in Denison, Crawford Co., IA. Herman was born in Mar 1871 in Germany.

They had the following children:

- 224 F i. **Martha Mattilda Luitjens** was born on 3 Nov 1899 in Goodrich Twp, Crawford Co., IA. She was christened on 7 Jan 1900 in Zion Lutheran Church, Denison, Crawford Co., IA. She died on 3 Jan 1992 in Coon Rapids, Iowa. Martha married **Henry Lackman** on 12 Jan 1920. Henry died on 3 Jan 1975 in Denison, Crawford Co., IA.
- 225 M ii. **Tiark Hy Luitjens** was born on 22 Jul 1901 in Crawford Co., IA.

65. **Detlef Andreas Laumbach** (Heinrich Fredrick Laumbach, Heinrich Laumbach, Christian Rudolph, Johann Jacob) was born on 22 Feb 1880 in Clinton Co., IA. He died in Jul 1964. Detlef married **Hilda Lille** daughter of Henry Lille and Carlena Johanna Ladendorf on 17 Mar 1925 in Mapleton, Monona Co., IA. Hilda was born on 22 Apr 1895 in Mapleton, Monona Co., IA. She died in May 1984 in Mapleton, Monona Co., IA.

They had the following children:

- 226 M i. **Dale Edward Laumbach** was born on 12 Sep 1930 in Clinton Co., IA.

He died on 30 May 2000 in Sioux City, Iowa. He was buried on 2 Jun 2000 in Mt. Hope Cemetery, Mapleton, Iowa. Dale married **Dorothy Brownlee** on 3 Jun 1951 in Ida Grove, Iowa.

    227   F   ii.   **Doris Laumbach**. Doris married **Harold Astleford**.

67. Anna Margaret Laumbach (Heinrich Fredrick Laumbach, Heinrich Laumbach, Christian Rudolph, Johann Jacob) was born on 9 Jun 1888 in Crawford Co., IA. She died on 8 Nov 1975 in Mapleton, Iowa. Anna married **Julius H. Ernst** son of Christian Ernst and Doris Kortum on 13 Feb 1912 in Schleswig, Crawford Co., IA. Julius was born about 1888 in Iowa. He died on 29 Dec 1972 in Mapleton, Iowa.

    They had the following children:

    228   F   i.   **Fern Martha Dorothea Ernst** was born on 27 Dec 1917 in Cooper Twp, Monona Co., IA.

    229   M   ii.   **Herbert Julius Ernst** was born on 6 Dec 1923 in Cooper Twp, Monona Co., IA.

    230   F   iii.   **Pearl Ellen Ernst** was born on 20 Jun 1926 in Cooper Twp, Monona Co., IA.

68. Emma D. Laumbach (Heinrich Fredrick Laumbach, Heinrich Laumbach, Christian Rudolph, Johann Jacob) was born in Jan 1890 in Crawford Co., IA. Emma married **Bernard H. Andresen** son of Henry Andresen and Katherine Bock on 29 Nov 1911 in Morgan, Crawdord Co., IA. Bernard was born about 1884 in Ida Co., IA.

    They had the following children:

    231   M   i.   **Elmer Henry Andresen** was born on 5 May 1912 in Crawford Co., IA.

69. Peter John Laumbach (Heinrich Fredrick Laumbach, Heinrich Laumbach, Christian Rudolph, Johann Jacob) was born on 15 Oct 1891 in Crawford Co., IA. He died in Dec 1983 in Monona Co., IA.

    Peter married **Alete Rye** daughter of Ole Rye and Mary Ulven on 26 Sep 1923 in Crawford Co., IA. Alete was born on 15 Mar 1899 in Iowa. She died on 1 Feb 1990.

    They had the following children:

    232   F   i.   **Ethel May Laumbach** was born on 3 Jan 1924 in Cooper, Monona Co., IA.

    233   M   ii.   **Lyle Arville Laumbach** was born on 1 Jan 1929 in Monona Co., IA. He died on 4 Jan 1929 in Monona Co., IA. He was buried on 19 Jan 1929 in St. Clair.

70. Laura Christine Laumbach (Heinrich Fredrick Laumbach, Heinrich Laumbach, Christian Rudolph, Johann Jacob) was born in Feb 1896 in Crawford Co., IA. Laura married **Jurgen Theodore Jochims** "Theo Ted" son of William Jochims and Annie Peterson on 6 Jan 1915 in Schleswig, Crawford Co., IA. Jurgen was born on 22 Jul 1894 in Schleswig, Iowa. He died in Apr 1975. He was buried in Silver Lake Cemetery, Lake Park, Iowa.

    They had the following children:

    234   M   i.   **Roy Jochims** was born about 1916 in Dickinson Co., IA.

    235   M   ii.   **Arlo Theodore Jochims** was born on 12 Feb 1918 in Dickinson Co., IA. He died on 31 May 1977 in Lakefield, Jackson Co., MN. Arlo married **Margaret Spang** on 7 Apr 1960 in Lakefield, Jackson Co., MN.

Appendix A - Notes

5S. Anna Koos
U.S. IRS Tax Assessment Lists, 1862-1918
Name: Anna Laumbach
State: Iowa
Tax Year: 1865
Roll Title: District 2; Annual, Monthly and Special Lists 1865
 ALPHABETICAL LIST of Persons in Division No. 3, of Collection District No. 2, of the State of Iowa, liable to a tax under the Excise laws of the United States, and the amount thereof, as assessed by Robert Spear, Assistant Assessor, and by Phiny Fay, Assessor, returned to the Collector of said District, for the month of May, 1865.
(No. 24.)

Line No.	DATE	NAME	LOCATION	ARTICLE	VALUATION	TAX RATE	TOTAL
34.	May	Laumbach, Anna	Deep Creek	Income	241	5pct	2.95

Center Grove (Ingwerson) Cemetery, Center Township, Clinton Co., Iowa:
LAUMBACK, Anna   9 Aug 1811   24 Aug 1868 (Anna Koos)
KOOS, Marx   7 Aug 1809   28 Aug 1864

6. Jurgen Laumbach
Iowa, Marriages, 1809-1992:
Groom's Name: Jurgen Laumback
Bride's Name: Anna Vogt
Marriage Date: 21 Nov 1872
Marriage Place: Clinton, Iowa

6S. Anna
Iowa, Marriages, 1809-1992:
Groom's Name: Jurgen Laumback
Bride's Name: Anna Vogt
Marriage Date: 21 Nov 1872
Marriage Place: Clinton, Iowa

8S. Eleonore Eberle
New Mexico Death Records:
Name: Eleanor E. Laumbach
Death date: 27 Jun 1933
Death place: Buena Vista, Mora, New Mexico
Age in years: 84
Estimated birth year: 1849
Spouse's name: Andres Detelf Laumbach

Father's name: Daniel Ebele
Mother's name: Biviana Martinez

11S. Augusta K. Grantz
Center Grove (Ingwerson) Cemetery, Center Township, Clinton Co., Iowa:
LASSEN AUGUSTA   1848   1933   Mother CENTER GROVE A 3
LASSEN FERDINAND   1851   11/24/1927 76 yrs Father CENTER GROVE A 3

---

12. Christina Margaretha Laumbach
Center Grove (Ingwerson) Cemetery, Center Township, Clinton Co., Iowa:
CLAUSEN, Christena M.   06 Jul 1841   04 Feb 1883
CLAUSEN, Dierk   31 Jul 1835   17 Oct 1919

12S. Dierk Claussen
The farm was formerly owned by Henry Laumbach and wife. The transfer was recorded 13 May 1861 in book 7, page 168, Clinton County Court House.
Clinton Obituary:

Dierk Claussen, who passed away at his home, 900 South Eighth Street, at 11:30 o'clock this morning, was born July 13, 1835, in Schleswig-Holstein. He came to this country in 1854 and settled in Davenport and in 1878 moved to Clinton County. He was united in marriage to Miss Christine Laumbach of Goose Lake in 1861 and to this union 10 children were born, two dying in infancy. Mrs. Claussen passed away February 1, 1883. October 28, 1885, he was united in marriage to Mrs. Catherine Gloe at Lyons and they lived on a farm near Goose Lake until 1892 when they moved to Lyons and have resided at their present home since that time. Mr. Claussen at the time of his death was 84 years, two months and seven days of age. About eight days ago he was taken ill with bronchitis which developed into pneumonia. Mr. Claussen was well known, an honest upright man and a valued member of St. John's Lutheran church since 1893. He leaves his wife, Mrs. Catherine Claussen of Lyons, four daughters, Mrs. Anna Gloe of Schaller, Mrs. Carrie C. Deering of Chicago, Mrs. Lina Haberer of Chicago and Mrs. Hanna Cramer of Akron, O.; four sons, Henry Claussen of Ogden, Andrew of Goose Lake, George of Thomas, Oklahoma, and John Claussen of Miami, Fla., and four step-children, Chris Gloe of Dell Rapids, S.D., Henry Gloe of Schaller, Mrs. Elizabeth Grantz of Manning and Mrs. Amelia Robinson of Denison. Seventeen grandchildren and seven great grandchildren are also left.

Center Grove (Ingwerson) Cemetery, Center Township, Clinton Co., Iowa:
CLAUSEN, Christena M.   06 Jul 1841   04 Feb 1883
CLAUSEN, Dierk   31 Jul 1835   17 Oct 1919
Inscription:
DIERK CLAUSSEN
BORN
JULY 31 1835
DIED
OCT 17 1919

14. Anna Christina Laumbach
Iowa Marriages, 1809-1992:
Groom's Name: Peter Henkens (Peter Claus Henkens)
Bride's Name: Anna Laumback
Marriage Date: 03 Dec 1867
Marriage Place: Clinton, Iowa

Ridge Cemetery, Fremont, Dodge Co., Nebraska:
Peter Henkens
6 Nov 1840 - 13 Feb 1916
Wife, Annie Henkens (Anna Christina Lauenbach)
13 Mar 1848 - 26 Nov 1908

16S. Peter Frederick Jepsen
U. S. Passport Application:

UNITED STATES OF AMERICA
State of Iowa
COUNTY OF Crawford

I, Peter F. Jepsen a NATURALIZED AND LOYAL CITIZEN OF THE UNITED STATES, do hereby apply to the Department of State at Washington for a passport for myself and wife, ...

In support of the above application, I do solemnly swear that I was born at Schleswig, in Germany, on or about the 18 day of Jan, 1847; that I emigrated to the United States, sailing on board the Hammonia, from Hamburg, on or about the 26 day of April, 1867; that I resided 36 years, uninterruptedly, in the United States, from 1867 to 1903, at Denison, Ia; that I was naturalized as a citizen of the United States before the District Court of Crawford Co Ia at Denison, on the 21 day of September, 1881, as shown by the accompanying Certificate of Naturalization; that I am the IDENTICAL PERSON described in said Certificate; that I am domiciled in the United States, my permanent residence being at Denison, in the State of Iowa where I follow the occupation of Farmer; that I am about to go abroad temporarily; and that I intend to return to the United States within one year with the purpose of residing and performing the duties of citizenship therein.

OATH OF ALLEGIANCE.

Further, I do solemnly swear that I will support and defend the Constitution of the United States against all enemies, foreign and domestic; that I will bear true faith and allegiance to the same; and that I take this obligation freely, without any mental reservation or purpose of evasion: SO HELP ME GOD.

Peter F. Jepsen
Sworn to before me this 29 day of May, 1903
Theo Rolwer. Notary Public.
DESCRIPTION OF APPLICANT.
    Age, 56 years.
    Stature, 5 feet, 9 inches, Eng.
    Forehead, Full
    Eyes, Gray

Nose, Roman
Mouth, Large
Chin, Full
Hair, Brown
Complexion, Blonde
Face, Full

History of Crawford County, Iowa: A Record of Settlement, Organization, Progress and Achievement, Volume 2
By F. W. Meyers, S.J. Clarke Publishing Company, S.J. Clarke Publishing Company
Published by S. J. Clarke publishing co., 1911

Pages: 248 - 250

PETER FREDERICK JEPSEN.

Thirty-six years ago Peter Frederick Jepsen came to Crawford County. He was then a young man of twenty-eight years and by education and experience well qualified to note the agricultural possibilities of this county. He applied himself diligently to his chosen occupation and today is one of the large landowners of the county and one of its most respected citizens. Born in Schleswig-Holstein, Germany, January 13, 1847, he is the son of John and Elsobao (Petersen) Jepsen. The father was a weaver by trade and followed that occupation in early life but later engaged in farming. Seeking to improve his condition he emigrated to the new world in 1869 and spent six years in Clinton county, Iowa. In the spring of 1875 he came to Crawford county and bought a section of land in Goodrich township, upon which he took up his residence, becoming one of the well known farmers of that section. He died in 1878 at the age of sixty-two years. The mother of our subject departed this life in 1865, being then forty-eight years of age. She and her husband were both members of the Lutheran church. He was greatly respected by his neighbors and friends and was mayor of the village of Jagel in Germany.

John Jepsen, the paternal grandfather of our subject, was a weaver and small farmer and devoted his attention to teaching during the winter seasons. He married Margaretta Jepsen and there were four children in their family: Jurgen, John, Claus and Margaretta. The maternal grandfather was Peter Petersen, a farmer in the fatherland, whose wife was Obel Petersen. He died in middle life but Mrs. Petersen lived to be about eighty years of age. There were seven children in their family, namely: Henry, Claus, Detloff, Peter, Elizabeth, Elsobao and Kathrina. Seven sons came to bless the union of John and Elsobao Jepsen: John, now living in this county; Peter Frederick, the subject of this review; Henry and Hans, both deceased; Frederick, of Goodrich township; August, deceased; and Jurgen.

Peter Frederick Jepsen was reared upon a farm in Germany and early became acquainted with the business to which he has devoted a large part of his life. He received his education in his native land, and, being an ambitious young man, he decided at twenty years of age to seek his fortune in America. Accordingly, in 1867, he crossed the ocean and settled in Clinton county, Iowa, but later spent one year on a farm in Dakota. In the fall of 1875 he purchased one hundred and sixty acres of land in Goodrich township, Crawford county, which he improved to good advantage, making it one of the valuable farms of the township. As years passed he showed remarkable ability in the acquisition of land and he now owns nine hundred and sixty acres in Goodrich township, also one hundred and twenty acres in Milford township, one hundred and seventy-eight acres in East Boyer township, and six hundred and forty acres in Hayes township. He has sold a farm of one hundred and twenty acres and in addition to land heretofore designated he owns one hundred and ninety-one acres near Dunlop in Harrison County. He now has all told two thousand and ninety nine acres. In 1904 he removed to Denison, where he has since lived retired.

On the 10th of October, 1867, Mr. Jepsen was united in marriage to Miss Anna Laumbach, who was born in Schleswig-Holstein, Germany, October 10, 1842, a daughter of Henry and Wiepke (Utermann) Laumbach, her parents being also natives of Germany. The father died in 1857 and the mother in 1864, aged forty-two and forty-eight years respectively. The maternal grandfather of Mrs. Jepsen was Hans Utermann, and his wife before her marriage was Margaretta Herringsen. The union of Mr. and Mrs. Jepsen has been blessed by the birth of nine children, five sons and four daughters, as follows: Anna married William Gehring of Hanover township and has three children, William, Edward and Otilla. Johan, a farmer of Goodrich township, married Maria Nath and has two children, Peter and Anna. Peter, also a farmer of Goodrich township, married Margaretta Schroeder, by whom he had three children, Emma, Peter and Walter and Hilda. Carolina married Martin Saggan and has seven children, to this union, Elizabeth and Edna. Elsobao married Joannas Saggan and they have five sons, Henry, Hogel, Martin, Edward and Harry. Henry, a farmer of East Boyer township, married Marie Hallender and they have two children, Walter and Hilda. Carolina married Martin Saggan and has seven children, Emma, Anna, Carolina, Joannas, Bernhard, Marie and Martin. Jurgen, of Goodrich township, married Anna Johansen and is the father of three children, Wilhelmina, Albert and Johan. Julius, also of Goodrich township, married Anna Rassow and has three children, Martin, Otilla and Malinda. Emma, now living at Denison, married Henry Nath and is the mother of two children, Henry and Edna.

Mr. and Mrs. Jepsen are consistent members of the Lutheran church and active workers in its behalf. Politically, Mr. Jepsen is in sympathy with the democratic party and gives his earnest support to its principles and candidates. He is a good friend of education and served for five years as member of the school board of Goodrich township and for a number of years as township trustee and school treasurer. By an industrious and straightforward life he years ago gained an established reputation for integrity and fidelity to duty and his personal worth is fully demonstrated by the esteem in which he is held by a wide circle of friends and acquaintances in Crawford and adjoining counties.

---

18. **Jurgen Laumbach**
Inscription on gravestone in Morgan Cemetery, Schleswig, Crawford Co., Iowa:

> HIER RUHT
> JURGEN LAUMBACH
> GEB. IN LOTTORF
> SCHLESWIG HOLSTEIN
> 24 AUG. 1854
> GEST. 14 FEB. 1912

---

21. **Maria Margarita Laumbach**
Record of Baptism, Church of Santa Gertrudes, Mora, Territory of New Mexico:
Apr. 19 of 1865, baptism of Maria Margarita Lambach born on the 21st of Mar. in the plaza of Francisco Abajo de la Cebolla, legitimate daughter of Andreas Lambach and Maria Eleonora Hibert, Padrinos: Vicente St. Vrain and Emilia Rohman. Off: Faure.

Women of the New Mexico Frontier, 1846-1912
by Cheryl J. Foote
Edition 2,
Publisher UNM Press, 2005

Page: 105 [Excerpt]

Numbers of converts, however, indicated success or failure to the Woman's Board, which closed the school at Rociada in 1894 and transferred Alice Blake to Buena Vista, a small community northeast of Las Vegas. The mission at Buena Vista boasted a school enrollment of fifty students and a church membership of thirty, and Blake found such prospects encouraging. Moreover, Buena Vista offered her an additional compensation in the form of an assistant, Margaret Laumbaugh. The two women became close friends, calling each other "Hermana [Sister] Blakey" and "Hermana Maggie." Although some unmarried women disliked being paired with other missionaries, Blake valued the companionship that made difficult living conditions easier. When Laumbaugh was transferred, Blake protested that this loss represented a greater hardship than living in a house with a roof "green with mould." The Woman's Board, however, had suffered financial problems as a result of the nationwide depression following the panic of 1893, and they had removed Blake's assistant as an economic measure....

21S. Jose Emiterio Cruz
Mora County Guardianships, New Mexico 1882-1885:
Pages 19, 20, 5 Sep 1882. Guardianship Appointment.
Jose Emiterio Cruz for Maria Josefa Martin, 15 yrs.
Surety: Maxwell Phillips.
Pages 106–108, 10 Sep 1885. Guardianship Appointment.
Jose E. Cruz, of Agua Negra, Pct. 9, for Juan Ant. Martinez, 17 yrs., and for Marcelina Martinez and for Maria Rita Martinez.
Sureties: Juan Andres de Luna and Santiago Valdez.

Mora County Marriages 1875-1890:
13 Dec 1882 CRUZ, Jose de Gs of Agua Negra, and CORDOVA, Maria de la Cruz, of El Rito de Agua Negra. By Rev. Maxwell Phillips. Wit: Tomas Cruz, Jose Emiterio Cruz.

9 Nov 1890 MARTINEZ, Juan Antonio, CRUZ, Jose E., and others, at El Rito.
[No further information extracted.]

[Excerpts from *Trementina, New Mexico* by Henrietta Martinez Christmas]
"Church: The church was built by Reverend Jose Emiterio Cruz, he was a master carpenter and builder. He had previous dealing with Miss Blake in Buena Vista. The church seated 150 and was started with $300. The church was also the schoolhouse. In 1916 the church/schoolhouse burned down. Because it was built from flagstone, large portions were reusable. This second reconstruction was done and soon the church was dedicated to Santiago and Juana Blea."
"Mission house: This is where Miss Blake eventually lived. It consisted of a fellowship hall, audience or parlor room, 2 classrooms and a kitchen. Again Reverend Jose Emiterio Cruz was asked to return and help with the construction."

The Church at Home and Abroad, Volume 19
By Presbyterian Church in the U.S.A.
Presbyterian Church in the U.S.A., 1896

NEW MEXICO. Rev. F. M. Gilchrist, Las Vegas:
[Excerpt]
An incident which has attracted the attention of the whole community was the arrest of our evangelist, Jose E Cruz, for refusing to take off his hat in honor of the Catholic procession on Corpus Christi Day, in the public streets of Las Vegas On the way to jail, Mr. Cruz told the police that they "had no more right to knock off his hat than to make him bow to their idols." This angered them and one of the police struck him with a club, inflicting an ugly bruise on his eye-brow and mashing his nose. A three-days' trial before a Mexican justice resulted in Mr. Cruz being fined five dollars, costs, and thirty days in the county jail. Nothing better was expected from such a court, and an appeal to the district court was immediately taken. The policeman, fearing prosecution before an American justice, went before the Mexican justice and plead guilty of assault. He was fined five dollars and costs. A heated discussion between La Revista Catholica and El Anciano, over this affair, has attracted a great deal of attention. Our vigorous defense of Mr. Cruz has had a good effect, as the evangelists have been better treated by the people since the trial than before.

New Mexico Death Records:
Name: Jose Emiteris Cruz
Death date: 25 Jan 1931
Death place: Holman, Mora, New Mexico
Age in years: 75
Estimated birth year: 1856
Spouse's name: Margarita L. Cruz
Father's name: Juan Cruz
Mother's name: Rosa Paiz

---

22. **Peter Joseph Laumbach**
Record of Baptism, Church of Santa Gertrudes, Mora, Territory of New Mexico:
Sept. 1 of 1867 baptism of Pedro Lambek born on the 29th of June, legitimate son of Andres Lambek and M. (blank), from Cebolla, Padrinos: Henry Korte and Juanita Metzger. Off: J. Guerin.

New Mexico Births and Christenings, 1726-1918:
Name: Pedro Lambak
Baptism/Christening Date: 1 Sep 1867
Baptism/Christening Place: Santa Gertrudis, Mora, Mora, New Mexico
Birth Date: 29 Jun 1867
Birthplace: Santa Gertrudis, Mora, Mora, New Mexico
Father's Name: Andres Lambak

22S. Fidelia Andrada
New Mexico Death Records:
Name: Fidelia A Laumbach
Death date: 23 Aug 1928
Death place: La Cinta, San Miguel, New Mexico
Age in years: 48
Estimated birth year: 1880
Spouse's name: Peter J Laumbach
Father's name: Casdinies Andrada
Mother's name: Carmalita Romero

---

23. Maria Estefanita Laumbach
Record of Baptism, Church of Santa Gertrudes, Mora, Territory of New Mexico:
May 21 of 1871 (sic), baptism of Ma Estefana Lumbach legitimate daughter of Andres Lumbach and Leonor Lumbach, Padrinos: (illegible) Korte and Fca Met(illegible). Off: J. Guerin.

New Mexico, Births and Christenings, 1726-1918:
Name: Maria Estefana Lumback
Gender: Female
Christening Date: 21 May 1870
Christening Place: Santa Gertrudis, Mora, Mora, New Mexico
Father's Name: Andres Lumback
Mother's Name: Leona Lumback

New Mexico Death Records:
Name: Estefanita Laumbach Candelario
Death date: 2 May 1938
Death place: Santa Fe, Santa Fe, New Mexico
Age in years: 67
Estimated birth year: 1871
Father's name: Andrew Lumbach
Mother's name: Eleanor Evelle

23S. Jesus Sito Candelario
New Mexico Death Records:
Name: Jesus Sito Candelario
Death date: 30 Jul 1938
Death place: Santa Fe, Santa Fe, New Mexico
Age in years: 74
Estimated birth year: 1864
Father's name: Antonio Jose Candelario
Mother's name: Altagracia Garcia

24. Daniel Laumbach

Record of Baptism, Church of Santa Gertrudes, Mora, Territory of New Mexico:
May 13 of 1872 baptism of Jose Danuel Lumbes (Laumbach) born on the 28th of Jan., legitimate son of Andres Lumbes (Laumbach) and Ma Leonor Evely, from Buena Vista, Padrinos: Jose Ramon Bone and Ma Viviana Martin. Off: Remuzon.

New Mexico Births and Christenings, 1726-1918:
Name: Jose Daniel Lumber (Laumbach)
Gender: Male
Baptism/Christening Date: 13 May 1872
Baptism/Christening Place: Santa Gertrudis, Mora, Mora, New Mexico
Birth Date: 28 Jan 1872
Birthplace: Santa Gertrudis, Mora, Mora, New Mexico
Father's Name: Andres Lumber (Laumbach)
Mother's Name: Maria Leonor Evely (Eberley/Evel/Ebel)

25. Henry Joseph Laumbach

Record of Baptism, Church of Santa Gertrudes, Mora, Territory of New Mexico:

Nov. 2 of 1874, baptism of Jesus Henriques Lumback born on the 2nd of Oct., legitimate son of Andres Lumback and Ma Leonor Evans, from Buena Vista, Padrinos: Felipe Esquivel and Ma Josefa Evans. Off: J. Guerin.

New Mexico Births and Christenings, 1726-1918:
Name: Jose Henriques Lumback
Gender: Male
Baptism/Christening Date: 2 Nov 1874
Baptism/Christening Place: Santa Gertrudis, Mora, Mora, New Mexico
Birth Date: 2 Oct 1874
Birthplace: Santa Gertrudis, Mora, Mora, New Mexico
Father's Name: Andres Lumback
Mother's Name: Maria Leonor Evans

World War I Draft Registration Cards, 1917-1918:
Name: Henry Lambach
Permanent Home Address: La Cueva, Mora Co., NM
Age: 43
Birth Date: 29 Sep 1874
Race: White
Occupation: Farmer
Place of Employment: La Cueva, Mora Co., NM

Nearest Relative: Lenora Lambach, La Cueva, Mora Co., NM
Signature: Henry Lambach
Height/Build: Tall/Medium
Color of Eyes/Hair: Blue/Lt Brown
DraftBoard: 12 Sep 1918

New Mexico Death Records:
Name: Henry Joseph Laumbach
Death date: 10 Sep 1929
Death place: Las Vegas, San Miguel, New Mexico
Gender: Male
Age in years: 54
Estimated birth year: 1875
Spouse's name: Natividad Urtado
Father's name: Andreas D. Laumbach
Mother's name: Leonora Evel

25S. **Natividad Hurtado**
California Death Index, 1940-1997:
Name: Natividad U Korte (widow of Henry Joseph Laumbach and wife of Emilio Korte)
Social Security #: 546403642
Sex: Female
Birth Date: 26 Oct 1901
Birthplace: New Mexico
Death Date: 17 Jun 1981
Death Place: Placer
Mother's Maiden Name: Blea
Father's Surname: Urtado

---

26. **Alejando Laumbach**
Record of Baptism, Church of Santa Gertrudes, Mora, Territory of New Mexico:
May 14 of 1877, baptism of Alejandro Lumback 5 months old, legitimate son of Andres Lumback and Maria Eleonor Aban from Cebolla, Padrinos: Andres Aban and Ubalda Lopez. Off: F. Boucard.

---

27. **Anna Laumbach**
Record of Baptism, Church of Santa Gertrudes, Mora, Territory of New Mexico:
Dec. 16 of 1878, baptism of Ana Lumback 5 months old, legitimate daughter of Andres Lumback and Leonor Evans, from Cueva, Padrinos: John Burch and Ma de la Paz Duran. Off: J. Guerin.

---

28. **Maria Cristina Laumbach**
Record of Baptism, Church of Santa Gertrudes, Mora, Territory of New Mexico:

November 27 of 1881. Baptized Maria Cristina Lombach born on the 20th of August, legitimate daughter of Andres Lombach and of Leonora Ebel. From La Cueva. Padrinos, Jose Kesler and Altagracia Blea.

28S. Manuel Antonio Sanchez
"New Mexico Marriages Chaperito La Yglesia de San Ysidro El Labrador Aug. 1876-Dec. 1898."
By: Luis Gilberto Padilla y Baca. Published by The Hispanic Genealogical Research Center Of New Mexico.
Page: 21.
 Dec 3, 1887 MANUEL ANTONIO SANCHEZ, soltero hijo legitimo de Antonio Sanchez y de Candelaria Cortez, con ROSA FELICITA EGGERT, soltera hija legitima de Frederico Eggert y de Juana Le Blanc, De Alamitos. Padrinos: Jose Aguilar y Juana Cisneros, tambien, D.F. Allen y Firenna Ceroa.

New Mexico Death Records:
Name: Manuel A. Sanchez
Death date: 30 Nov 1941
Death place: Las Vegas, San Miguel, New Mexico
Age in years: 80
Estimated birth year: 1861
Spouse's name: Christina L. Sanchez
Father's name: Antonio Sanchez
Mother's name: Candelaria Cortez

---

29. Maria de Gracia Laumbach
Record of Baptism, Church of Santa Gertrudes, Mora, Territory of New Mexico:
March 10 of 1884. Baptized Maria de Gracia Lumback born on the 10th of February, legitimate daughter of Andres Lumback and of Leonor Evens. From Buena Vista. Padrinos, Joseph Kesler and Maria de Garcia Blea.

New Mexico Births and Christenings, 1726-1918
Name: Maria de Gracia Lumback
Gender: Female
Baptism/Christening Date: 10 Mar 1884
Baptism/Christening Place: Santa Gertrudis, Mora, Mora, New Mexico
Birth Date: 10 Feb 1884
Birthplace: Santa Gertrudis, Mora, Mora, New Mexico
Father's Name: Andres Lumback
Mother's Name: Leonor Evens

32. Anna Marguerite Laumbach
California Death Index, 1940-1997:
Name: Anna Marguerite Rogers
[Anna Marguerite Laumbach]
Social Security #: 0
Sex: Female
Birth Date: 26 Feb 1871
Birthplace: Iowa
Death Date: 31 Aug 1955
Death Place: Santa Clara
Father's Surname: Laumbach

32S. Hubert Earl Rogers
California Death Index, 1940-1997:
Name: Hubert Earl Rogers
Social Security #: 0
Sex: Male
Birth Date: 17 Jul 1869
Birthplace: Illinois
Death Date: 6 Apr 1945
Death Place: Los Angeles
Mother's Maiden Name: Durwent
Father's Surname: Rogers

---

33. John Andrew Laumbach
World War I Draft Registration Cards, 1917-1918:
Name: John Andrew Laumbach
Permanent Home Address: Lake View, Sac Co., Iowa
Age: 44
Birth Date: 13 Oct 1873
Race: White
Occupation: Farming; For Himself
Nearest Relative: Alvina Laumbach; R.F.D. 1, Lake View, Sac Co., Iowa
Signature: John Andrew Laumbach
Height/Build: Medium/Medium
Color of Eyes/Hair: -/-
Draft Board: Sac City, Sac Co., Iowa 12 Sep 1918

34S. Arthur Henry Hawkes
World War I Draft Registration Cards, 1917-1918:
Name: Arthur Henry Hawkes
Home Address: R.F.D. #1, Armour, Douglas Co., South Dakota
Age: 41

Birth Date: 27 Jan 1877
Race: White
Occupation: Farming; self
Nearest Relative: Matilda Hawkes (wife), Armour, Douglas Co., South Dakota
Signature: Arthur Henry Hawkes
Height/Build: Tall/Stout?
Color of Eyes/Hair: Brown/Black
Draft Board: Armour, Douglas Co., South Dakota   12 Sep 1918

California Death Index, 1940-1997:
Name: Arthur Henry Hawkes
Social Security #: 539140204
Sex: MALE
Birth Date: 27 Jan 1877
Birthplace: Illinois
Death Date: 5 Sep 1955
Death Place: Los Angeles
Mother's Maiden Name: Piner
Father's Surname: Hawkes

---

35. Henry Albert Laumbach
World War I Draft Registration Cards, 1917-1918:
Name: Henry Albert Laumbach
Permanent Home Address: 1662 Ross, St Paul, Ramsey Co., Minnesota
Age: 38
Birth Date: 27 Oct 1879
Race: White
Occupation: Freight Inspector, St Paul, Ramsey Co., Minnesota
Nearest Relative: Clara Laumbach; 1662 Ross, St Paul, Ramsey Co., Minnesota
Signature: Henry A. Laumbach
Height/Build: Medium/Medium
Color of Eyes/Hair: Blue/Brown
Draft Board: Div. 2, St Paul, Ramsey Co., Minnesota   12 Sep 1918

---

43. John William Claussen
U. S. Passport Applications:

UNITED STATES OF AMERICA
STATE OF FLORIDA
COUNTY OF DADE

I, John William Claussen, a NATIVE AND LOYAL CITIZEN OF THE UNITED STATES, hereby apply to the Department of State, at Washington, for a passport.

I solemnly swear that I was born at Clinton County, in the State of Iowa, on or about the 6th day of April, 1877, that my father Dierk Claussen, was born in Denmark and is now residing at Deceased; that he emigrated to the United States from the port of Schleswig, Denmark on or about don't know, 1850;

that he resided 69 years, uninteruptedly, in the United States, from 1850 to 1919, at Iowa; that he was a naturalized as a citizen of the United States before the County Court of Clinton County, at Clinton, Iowa............... and that I am domiciled in the United States, my permanent residence being at Miami, in the State of Florida, where I follow the occupation of Insurance....................... and I desire a passport for use in visiting the countries hereinafter named for the following purpose:
Bahama Islands & Cuba   To investigate business conditions

I intend to leave the United States from the port of Miami or Key West, Fla. sailing on board the First vessel after receiving passport......

       John William Claussen
       NOV 13 1919

[Attached]

      BAPTISMAL CERTIFICATE

John William Claussen, son of Dierk Claussen and Christina Margaretha Claussen, born sixth day of April, 1877, in Clinton County, Iowa, and was on the twentieth day of May, 1877, baptized in the Lutheran Church at Charlotte, Clinton Co., Iowa.

       C. R. Riedel, Pastor.
        Lutheran Church, Charlotte,
        Clinton County, Iowa.

Witnesses:
John Grantz
Elzeb. Grantz
Peter Henkens

---

47. John Delef Henkens

World War I Draft Registration Cards, 1917-1918:
Name: John Delef Henkens
Permanent Home Address: R.F.D. 2, North Bend, Dodge Co., Nebraska
Age: 43
Birth Date: 16 Jun 1875
Race: White
Occupation: Farmer; myself; R.F.D. 2, North Bend, Dodge Co., Nebraska
Nearest Relative: Minnie Henkens (wife), R.F.D. 2, North Bend, Dodge Co., Nebraska
Signature: John Delef Henkens
Height/Build: Medium/Medium
Color of Eyes/Hair: Blue/Light
Draft Board: Fremont, Dodge Co., Nebraska 12 Sep 1918

48S. Daniel Laumbach

Record of Baptism, Church of Santa Gertrudes, Mora, Territory of New Mexico:
May 13 of 1872 baptism of Jose Danuel Lumbes (Laumbach) born on the 28th of Jan., legitimate son of Andres Lumbes (Laumbach) and Ma Leonor Evely, from Buena Vista, Padrinos: Jose Ramon Bone and Ma Viviana Martin. Off: Remuzon.

New Mexico Births and Christenings, 1726-1918:
Name: Jose Daniel Lumber (Laumbach)
Gender: Male
Baptism/Christening Date: 13 May 1872
Baptism/Christening Place: Santa Gertrudis, Mora, Mora, New Mexico
Birth Date: 28 Jan 1872
Birthplace: Santa Gertrudis, Mora, Mora, New Mexico
Father's Name: Andres Lumber (Laumbach)
Mother's Name: Maria Leonor Evely (Eberley/Evel/Ebel)

---

50. **Herman D. Henkens**
World War I Draft Registration Cards, 1917-1918:
Name: Herman D. Henkens
Permanent Home Address: Chadron, Dawes Co., Nebraska
Age: 34
Birth Date: 13 Jan 1884
Race: White
Occupation: Farmer; Self
Nearest Relative: Mamie Henkens, Chadron, Dawes Co., Nebraska
Signature: Herman D. Henkens
Height/Build: Medium/Medium
Color of Eyes/Hair: Blue/Light
Draft Board: Chadron, Dawes Co., Nebraska 12 Sep 1918

---

51. **Edwin T. Henkens**
World War I Draft Registration Cards, 1917-1918:
Name: Edwin T. Henkens
Age: 30
Home Address: Chadron, Dawes Co., Nebraska
Birth Date: 11 Jun 1885
Birthplace: Dawes Co., Nebraska
Race: Caucasian (White)
Occupation: Farmer; Self; Chadron, Dawes Co., Nebraska
Nearest Relative: Wife and children
Signature: Edwin T. Henkens
Height/Build: Medium/Medium
Color of Eyes/Hair: Blue/Light Brown
Draft Board: Chadron, Dawes Co., Nebraska 5 Jun 1917

---

52. **Claus Peter Henkens**
World War I Draft Registration Cards, 1917-1918:
Name: Claus Henkens

Age: 25
Home Address: 1520 S. 10th Ave., Sioux Falls, (Minnehaha Co.), South Dakota
Birth Date: 9 Feb 1891
Birthplace: Colfax Co., Nebraska
Race: Caucasian (White)
Occupation: Bridge builder, Western Bridge & Construction Co., Sioux Falls, South Dakota
Nearest Relative: Single
Signature: Claus Henkens
Height/Build: Medium/Medium
Color of Eyes/Hair: Dark Blue/Light Brown
Draft Board: Sioux Falls, South Dakota   5 Jun 1917

---

53. Anna Henrietta Maria Jepsen
Crawford County Marriage Records:
License No. 1402
Groom: Wm. Chas Louis John Gehring
Residence: Hanover Twp., Iowa
Occupation: Farmer
Age next Birthday: 21
Birthplace: Chicago, Illinois
Father: Wm. Gehring
Mother: Dora Priefs
Marriage No.: First
Bride: Anna Henrietta Maria Jepson
Residence: Goodrich Twp. Ia
Age next Birthday: 23
Birthplace: Clinton, Ia
Father: Peter Jepson
Mother: Anna Laumbach
Marriage No.: First
Marriage Date and Place: Jan. 14, 1891 in Denison, Iowa
Date of Return: Jan. 14, 1891
Witnesses: Ella Jepsen
When Registered: Jan. 14 1891
Certified by: Rev. F. Lothringer

53S. William Charles Louis John Gehring

Crawford County Marriage Records:
License No. 1402
Groom: Wm. Chas Louis John Gehring
Residence: Hanover Twp., Iowa
Occupation: Farmer
Age next Birthday: 21

Birthplace: Chicago, Illinois
Father: Wm. Gehring
Mother: Dora Priefs
Marriage No.: First
Bride: Anna Henrietta Maria Jepson
Residence: Goodrich Twp. Ia
Age next Birthday: 23
Birthplace: Clinton, Ia
Father: Peter Jepson
Mother: Anna Laumbach
Marriage No.: First
Marriage Date and Place: Jan. 14, 1891 in Denison, Iowa
Date of Return: Jan. 14, 1891
Witnesses: Ella Jepsen
When Registered: Jan. 14 1891
Certified by: Rev. F. Lothringer

56S. John Christian Saggau

History of Crawford County, Iowa: A Record of Settlement, Organization, Progress and Achievement, Volume 2

By F. W. Meyers, S.J. Clarke Publishing Company, S.J. Clarke Publishing Company

Published by S. J. Clarke publishing co., 1911

Pages: 115 - 116

JOHN SAGGAN.

John Saggan, one of the well known and prosperous residents of Denison, is a native of the fatherland, his birth having occurred in Holstein on the 1st of May, 1867. His parents, H. H. and Christina Saggan, who were also born in Germany, crossed the Atlantic to the United States in 1872 and during the first five years of their residence in the new world made their home in Chicago, Illinois. In 1877 they came to Crawford County, Iowa, spending the remainder of their lives on a farm here. H. H. Saggan passed away in 1910, while his wife was called to her final rest in 1907. They reared a family of three children, namely: Mary, the wife of Paul Rosburg, of Plymouth county, Iowa; John, of this review; and Martin, who is a resident of Denison, Iowa.

John Saggan, who was a little lad of five years when he accompanied his parents on their emigration to America, attended the common schools in the acquirement of an education and when not busy with his text-books assisted his father in the operation of the home farm. On attaining his majority he rented the place and was busily engaged in its cultivation for ten years. On the expiration of that period he took up his abode in Denison, where he has remained to the present time, being engaged in business as the proprietor of a saloon. He now owns a brick business block containing five store buildings on West Broadway and is widely recognized as a substantial and representative citizen of the community.

In February, 1892, Mr. Saggan was united in marriage to Miss Ella Jepsen, a daughter of Peter and Anna Jepsen, of whom more extended mention is made on another page of this volume. Unto our subject and his wife have been born five children, as follows: Henry P., Saggan Hugo, Martin, Edward and Harry.

Mr. Saggan gives his political allegiance to the democracy but has no desire for the honors and emoluments of office. Fraternally he is identified with the Independent Order of Odd Fellows, belonging to Lodge No. 393 at Denison. He well merits the proud American title of a self-made man, owing his present prosperity entirely to his own efforts.

---

62. **Henry F. Laumbach Jr.**
World War I Draft Registration Cards, 1917-1918:
Name: Henry Lumbach (Henry Fredrick Laumbach Jr)
Permanent Home Address: Presho, Lyman Co., South Dakota
Age: 43
Birth Date: 19 May 1875
Race: White
Occupation: Farmer
Nearest Relative: ?inina?; Presho, Lyman Co., South Dakota
Signature: Henry Laumbach
Height/Build: Medium/Stout
Color of Eyes/Hair: Gray/Light
Draft Board: Lyman Co., South Dakota   12 Sep 1918

---

64. **Alfred Niclos Laumbach**
World War I Draft Registration Cards, 1917-1918:
Name: Alfred Niclos Laumbach
Permanent Home Address: Presho, Lyman Co., South Dakota
Age: 39
Birth Date: 17 May 1879
Race: White
Occupation: Farmer
Nearest Relative: Henry Fredrick Laumbach; Mapleton, Iowa
Signature: Alfard N. Laumbach
Height/Build: Tall/Medium
Color of Eyes/Hair: Blue/Dark
Draft Board: Lyman Co., South Dakota   12 Sep 1918

---

65. **Detlef Andreas Laumbach**
World War I Draft Registration Cards, 1917-1918:
Name: Detlef Andreas Laumbach
Permanent Home Address: R.F.D. #2 Mapleton, Monona Co., Iowa
Age: 38
Birth Date: 22 Feb 1880
Race: White
Occupation: Farming, Himself; R.F.D. #2 Mapleton, Monona Co., Iowa
Nearest Relative: Henry Laumbach, Father; R.F.D. #2 Mapleton, Monona Co., Iowa
Signature: Detlef Andreas Laumbach
Height/Build: Medium/Medium
Color of Eyes/Hair: Gray/Brown

Draft Board: Monona Co., Iowa   12 Sep 1918

---

66. Jacob Orns Laumbach
World War I Draft Registration Cards, 1917-1918:
Name: Jacob Orns Laumbach
Permanent Home Address: R.F.D. #2 Mapleton, Monona Co., Iowa
Age: 36
Birth Date: 17 Jul 1882
Race: White
Occupation: Farming, Himself; R.F.D. #2 Mapleton, Monona Co., Iowa
Nearest Relative: Henry Laumbach, Father; R.F.D. #2 Mapleton, Monona Co., Iowa
Signature: Jacob Orns Laumbach
Height/Build: Tall/Medium
Color of Eyes/Hair: Gray/Brown
Draft Board: Monona Co., Iowa   12 Sep 1918

---

67. Anna Margaret Laumbach
November 10, 1975 Obituary:

Mapleton, Iowa—Mrs. Julius Ernst, 87, Mapleton, died Nov 8, in Mapleton after a brief illness.

Services will be at 10:30 a.m. Nov 11 in St Peter's United Church of Christ. The Rev. Homer Perry will officiate. Burial will be in Mt Hope Cemetery under the direction of the Walter Funeral Home.

Mrs. Ernst the former Anna Margaret Laumbach, was born June 9, 1888, near Schleswig. She was married Feb. 13, 1912, near Schleswig.

The couple farmed near Ricketts before moving to a farm near Mapleton where they lived for 34 years. They moved to town in 1947. Her husband died Dec 29, 1972 in Mapleton.

She was a member of the United Church of Christ and a charter member of the church. Mrs Ernst belonged to the women's fellowship of the church.

Survivors include two daughters, Mrs. Fred (Fern) Schnoor of Mapleton and Mrs. Norman (Pearl) Hahn, both of Mapleton; four grandchildren, a great-granddaughter; and a brother, Peter of Ute.

---

69. Peter John Laumbach
World War I Draft Registration Cards, 1917-1918:
Name: Peter John Laumbach
Age: 25
Home Address: Mapleton, Monona Co., Iowa
Birth Date: 15 Oct 1891
Birth Place: Denison, Iowa
Race: Caucasian (White)
Occupation: Farming; Himself; Cooper Twp.
Nearest Relative: Single
Signature: Peter John Laumbach
Height/Build: Medium/Medium
Color of Eyes/Hair: Grey/Brown

Draft Board: Cooper Precinct, Monona Co., Iowa   5 Jun 1917

75S. Rev. Julian Duran
World War I Draft Registration Cards, 1917-1918:
Name: Julian Duran
Permanent Home Address: Dixon, Rio Arriba Co., New Mexico
Age: 20
Birth Date: 4 Jan 1898
Race: White
Occupation: Student; Menaul School, Albuquerque, New Mexico
Nearest Relative: Leonires Duran, Dixon, Rio Arriba Co., New Mexico
Signature: Julian Duran
Height/Build: Medium/Medium
Color of Eyes/Hair: Brown/Black
Draft Board: Tierra Amarilla, Rio Arriba Co., New Mexico 12 Sep 1918

Social Security Death Index:
Name: Julian Duran
SSN: 525-82-8517
Last Residence: 87108 Albuquerque, Bernalillo, New Mexico, United States of America
Born: 4 Jan 1898
Died: 9 Jan 1995
State (Year) SSN issued: New Mexico (1954)

76. Eleanor Evalee Cruz
New Mexico Death Records:
Name: Leonora Evallee Cruz
Death date: 18 Aug 1933
Death place: Las Vegas, San Miguel, New Mexico
Gender: Female
Age in years: 24
Estimated birth year: 1909
Father's name: Jose E Cruz
Mother's name: Margarita Laumbach

77. Cordelia Laumbach
New Mexico Births and Christenings, 1726-1918:
Name: Cordilla Lumback
Gender: Female
Baptism/Christening Date: 10 Nov 1899
Birth Date: 10 Sep 1899
Birthplace: Wagon Mound, Mora, New Mexico
Father's Name: Pedro Lumback

Mother's Name: Fidelia Andrade

New Mexico Death Records:
Name: Cordilia Laumbach Maes
Death date: 22 Feb 1942
Death place: New Mexico
Gender: Female
Age in years: 43
Estimated birth year: 1899
Spouse's name: Jose F Maes
Father's name: P G Laumbach
Mother's name: Fidelia Andrada

77S. Jose Fermin Maes
New Mexico, Births and Christenings, 1726-1918:
Name: Fermin Maes
Gender: Male
Christening Date: 10 Jul 1905
Christening Place: St. Joseph, Park View, Rio Arriba, New Mexico
Birth Date: 7 Jul 1905
Birthplace: St. Joseph, Park View, Rio Arriba, New Mexico
Father's Name: Adolfo Maes
Mother's Name: Onofre Montano

---

81. Crestina Laumbach
U.S., Social Security Death Index
Name: Christina Foxall
SSN: 522-96-1209
Last Residence: 88310 Alamogordo, Otero, New Mexico
Born: 8 Feb 1904
Died: Jun 1976
State (Year) SSN issued: Colorado (1973)

---

88. Bertha Belle Laumbach
Texas Death Certificate:
Name: Bertha Durham (Bertha Belle Laumbach)
Death date: 24 Apr 1959
Death place: West Texas Hospital, Lubbock, Lubbock Co., Texas
Gender: Female
Race or color: White
Age at death: 43 years
Birthdate: 21 Dec 1915

Birthplace: New Mexico
Marital status: Married
Father's name: Peter Joseph Laumback
Mother's name: Fidelio Andra
Occupation: Housewife
Residence: Rt. #1 Lubbock Precinct #2, Lubbock Co., Texas
Cemetery name: Resthaven Memorial Park
Burial place: Lubbock, Texas
Burial date: 26 Apr 1959
Informant: Cecil Durham (Cecil Barton Durham)

88S. Cecil Barton Durham
Social Security Death Index:
Name: Cecil B. Durham
SSN: 463-07-1181
Last Residence: 76208 Denton, Denton, Texas, United States of America
Born: 22 May 1917
Died: 16 Dec 1994
State (Year) SSN issued: Texas (Before 1951)

92S. Arthur Conklin Weeks
World War I Draft Registration Cards, 1917-1918:
Name: Arthur Conklin Weeks
Permanent Home Address: 402 San Francisco St., Santa Fe, New Mexico
Age: 35
Birth Date: 19 Nov 1883
Race: White
Occupation: Salesman (Training); "In business for myself"
Place of Employment: 402 San Francisco St., Santa Fe, New Mexico
Nearest Relative: Mrs. A. C. Weeks; 402 San Francisco St., Santa Fe, New Mexico
Signature: A. C. Weeks
Height/Build: Tall/Slender
Color of Eyes/Hair: Blue/L. Brown
Draft Board: Santa Fe Co., New Mexico   12 Sep 1918

New Mexico Death Records:
Name: Arthur C. Weeks
Death date: 11 Apr 1936
Death place: Albuquerque, Bernalillo, New Mexico
Gender: Male
Age in years: 48
Estimated birth year: 1888
Spouse's name: Emily Marks

Father's name: Weeks
Mother's name: Conklin

---

94. John S. Candelario
Social Security Death Index:
Name: John S. Candelario
SSN: 565-16-9545
Last Residence: 87190 Albuquerque, Bernalillo, New Mexico, United States of America
Born: 7 Sep 1916
Died: 5 Oct 1993
State (Year) SSN issued: California (Before 1951)

---

96. Joyce Laumbach
Social Security Death Index:
Name: Joyce Laumbach
SSN: 525-82-8838
Born: 4 Feb 1905
Died: 20 Dec 1991
State (Year) SSN issued: New Mexico (1954)

97S. Elbert Lawton Wallace
World War I Draft Registration Cards, 1917-1918:
Name: Elbert Lawton Wallace
Home Address: Silverton, Briscoe Co., Texas
Age: 18
Birth Date: 16 Feb 1900
Race: White
Occupation: Student; U??? Tex State Normal, Canyon, Randall Co., Texas
Nearest Relative: H. L. Haecase?; Silverton, Briscoe Co., Texas
Signature: Elbert Lawton Wallace
Height/Build: Medium/Medium
Color of Eyes/Hair: Blue/Light
Draft Board: Canyon, Randall Co., Texas

Solano Cemetery, Solano, Harding County, New Mexico:
Wallace, Alida Laumbach   March 23, 1907   November 8, 1994
Wallace, Elbert L   February 16, 1900   February 3, 1958   Senator

---

98. Verna Laumbach
Social Security Death Index:
Name: Verna L. Sparks
SSN: 525-98-1563

Last Residence: 88201 Roswell, Chaves, New Mexico, United States of America
Born: 8 Oct 1909
Died: 23 May 1996
State (Year) SSN issued: New Mexico (1958-1972)

98S. Dalphon Clinton Sparks
New York Passenger Lists:
                    LIST OF UNITED STATES CITIZENS
S.S. PANAMA Sailing from Cristobal, C. Z., JUNE 1ST, 1941, Arriving at Port of NEW YORK, N. Y., JUNE 7TH, 1941.
Page Number: 144
Line: 9
Sparks, Dalphon C. Age 34; Male; Married; Born 20 Jul 1908, Copan, OK
Address: 1009, West Monkbridge Avenue, Albuquerque, NM

99S. Leon M. Shinn
Social Security Death Index:
Name: Leon M. Shinn
SSN: 527-16-0774
Last Residence: 87068 Bosque Farms, Valencia, New Mexico, United States of America
Born: 22 Oct 1914
Died: 15 May 1994
State (Year) SSN issued: Arizona (Before 1951)

---

100. Ruth E. Laumbach
Social Security Death Index:
Name: Ruth E. Laumbach
SSN: 557-24-1745
Last Residence: 88201 Roswell, Chaves, New Mexico, United States of America
Born: 13 May 1914
Died: 14 Nov 1995
State (Year) SSN issued: California (Before 1951)

---

102. Laumbach
New Mexico Death Records, 1889 – 1945:
Name: No Name Laumback
Death date: 15 May 1921
Death place: Cebolla, El Carmen, Mora County, New Mexico
Gender: Male
Race or color: white
Age in years: 0
Birthdate: 15 May 1921

Birthplace: El Carmen, Cebolla, Mora County, N. M.
Marital status: Single
Father's name: Henry Laumbach
Father's birthplace: Buena Vista, Mora, N. M.
Mother's name: Natividad Hurtada
Mother's birthplace: Cebollita, Mora, N. M.
Burial date: 16 May 1921

---

103. **Henry J. Laumbach**
Social Security Death Index:
Name: Henry J. Laumbach
SSN: 525-24-6879
Last Residence: 89511 Reno, Washoe, Nevada, United States of America
Born: 10 May 1922
Died: 29 Jan 2004
State (Year) SSN issued: New Mexico (Before 1951)

---

104. **John Andrew Laumbach**
Social Security Death Index:
Name: John Andrew Laumbach
SSN: 525-32-8724
Last Residence: 95682 Shingle Springs, El Dorado, California, United States of America
Born: 3 Jun 1923
Last Benefit: 95682 Shingle Springs, El Dorado, California, United States of America
Died: 12 Jun 2008
State (Year) SSN issued: New Mexico (Before 1951)

---

105. **Carlos W. Laumbach**
California Death Index, 1940-1997:
Name: Carlos W Laumbach
Social Security #: 572369337
Birth Date: 9 Sep 1924
Birthplace: New Mexico
Death Date: 1 Feb 1975
Death Place: Placer

---

106. **Frank William Laumbach**
California Death Index, 1940-1997:
Name: Frank W Laumbach
Social Security #: 525387164
Birth Date: 2 Dec 1925
Birthplace: New Mexico

Death Date: 11 Jun 1971
Death Place: Placer

110. Adelina Candelaria Sanchez
New Mexico Death Records:
Name: Adelina Candelaria Sanchez
Death date: 26 Jan 1921
Death place: Las Vegas, San Miguel, New Mexico
Gender: Female
Race or color: White
Age in years: 7
Birthdate: 07 Feb 1913
Birthplace: Las Vegas, N. M.
Marital status: Single
Father's name: Manuel A Sanchez
Father's birthplace: Roceada, N. M.
Mother's name: Christina Laumbach
Mother's birthplace: Mora Co., N. M.
Burial place: Buena Vista, N. M.
Burial date: 27 Jan 1921

118. Vertus W. Rogers
Washington Death Certificates, 1907-1960:
Name: Vertus W. Rogers
Death date: 12 Apr 1930
Death place: Walla Walla, Walla Walla, Washington
Gender: Male
Age at death: 32 years 7 months 11 days
Estimated birth year: 1898
Marital status: Married
Spouse's name: Faythe Brown
Father's name: Hubert Rogers
Mother's name: Anna Laumbach

118S. Faythe Irene Brown
South Dakota Marriages, 1905-1949:
Name: Vertus W Rogers
Age: 21
Gender: Male
Spouse: Faythe Irene Brown
Marriage Date: 11 Dec 1917
Marriage County: Davison
County of Residence: Davison

Post Office: Mitchell

---

120. **Alma Margaret Laumbach**
Social Security Death Index:
Name: Alma Laumbach
SSN: 479-16-5994
Last Residence: 51449 Lake City, Calhoun, Iowa, United States of America
Born: 7 Aug 1899
Died: May 1984
State (Year) SSN issued: Iowa (Before 1951)

---

123. **Justus Theodore Laumbach**
Social Security Death Index:
Name: Justus T. Laumbach (Justus Theodore Laumbach)
SSN: 482-22-8656
Last Residence: 51449 Lake City, Calhoun, Iowa, United States of America
Born: 26 Mar 1905
Died: 2 Feb 1993
State (Year) SSN issued: Iowa (Before 1951)

123S. **Alice Lillian Kral**
Social Security Death Index:
Name: Lillian Laumbach (Alice Lillian Kral)
SSN: 482-60-7931
Last Residence: 51449 Lake City, Calhoun, Iowa, United States of America
Born: 15 Nov 1908
Died: 21 Dec 1989
State (Year) SSN issued: Iowa (1964)

---

124. **Hans Andrew Laumbach**
California Death Index, 1940-1997:
Name: Hans A Laumbach (Hans Andrew Laumbach)
Social Security #: 479180252
Sex: Male
Birth Date: 16 Oct 1908
Birthplace: Iowa
Death Date: 14 May 1961
Death Place: Los Angeles

U.S. Veterans Gravesites:
Name: Hans Andrew Laumbach
Service Info: CPL US ARMY AIR FORCES WORLD WAR II
Birth Date: 16 Oct 1908

Death Date: 14 May 1961
Service Start Date: 21 Dec 1942
Interment Date: 22 May 1961
Cemetery: Ft. Rosecrans National Cemetery
Cemetery Address: P.O. Box 6237 San Diego, CA 92166
Buried At: Section V Site 852

124S. Madalyn K. Herzog

California Death Index, 1940-1997:
Name: Madalyn K Laumbach (Madalyn Herzog, wife of Hans A. Laumbach)
Social Security #: 483228358
Sex: Female
Birth Date: 19 Oct 1915
Birthplace: Iowa
Death Date: 14 May 1961
Death Place: Los Angeles
Mother's Maiden Name: Bigelow

---

126. Vera Alvina Laumbach
California Death Index, 1940-1997:
Name: Vera A Olhausen
[Vera A Laumbach]
Social Security #: 561460083
Sex: Female
Birth Date: 13 Sep 1910
Birthplace: Iowa
Death Date: 28 Sep 1988
Death Place: Alameda
Mother's Maiden Name: Greve
Father's Surname: Laumbach

---

127. Arthur W. H. Hawkes
South Dakota Births, 1856-1903:
Name: Arthur Hawkes
Birth Date: 11 Nov 1903
Gender: Male
County: Douglas
Father's Name: Arthur Hawkes
Mother's Name: Matilda Laumbach
File Date: 6 Feb 1940

129. **Earl Alden Hawkes**
California Death Index, 1940-1997:
Name: Earl Alden Hawkes
Social Security #: 568105894
Sex: Male
Birth Date: 27 Jun 1907
Birthplace: South Dakota
Death Date: 28 Aug 1981
Death Place: San Diego
Mother's Maiden Name: Laumbach

---

130. **Emerson W. Hawkes**
Social Security Death Index:
Name: Emerson W. Hawkes
SSN: 525-01-1655
Last Residence: 92198 San Diego, San Diego, California, United States of America
Born: 27 Jun 1907
Died: 14 Jan 2002
State (Year) SSN issued: New Mexico (Before 1951)

---

131. **Josephine Genevieve Schmidt**
Social Security Death Index:
Name: Josephine Gentz
SSN: 389-01-1731
Last Residence: 53211 Milwaukee, Milwaukee, Wisconsin, United States of America
Born: 13 Apr 1908
Died: Oct 1981 (2 Oct 1981)
State (Year) SSN issued: Wisconsin (Before 1951)

---

132. **Ruth E. Schmidt**
Social Security Death Index:
Name: Ruth E. Coghlan
SSN: 395-40-5371
Last Residence: 53051 Menomonee Falls, Waukesha, Wisconsin, United States of America
Born: 4 Oct 1909
Died: 5 Jan 2000
State (Year) SSN issued: Wisconsin (1958-1959)

Ruth E. Coghlan
   MENOMONEE FALLS - Ruth E. Coghlan (nee Schmid) of Menomonee Falls passed on peacefully Wednesday, Jan. 5, 2000, with her family at her side.
   She was the beloved wife of the late Delbert "Doc" Franz of Waukesha and the late Thomas "Bill" Coghlan. She will be missed by her children, Keith (Mary) Franz, Carol (Bill) Schneider, Thomas

(Barbara) and Gerald (Beverly) Coghlan. She was the loving "Grandma Coghlan" of Warren, Luanne, Carolyn, Owen, Gail, Lynn, Scott, Michael, Brian and Shelley, and great-grandma of Kurt, Kimberly, Meghan and Branden. She is further survived by nieces, nephews, other relatives, many dear friends and special friend Marie Baumgart.

Memorial funeral services will be held at 3 p.m. Saturday, Jan. 8, at Schmidt & Bartelt Funeral Home, 10121 W. North Ave., Wauwatosa. Visitation will be held from 1 p.m. until the time of the services. There will be a private interment.
Schmidt & Bartelt Funeral Home, 774-5010, is serving the family.

175. Earl Edwin Henkens
Social Security Death Index:
Name: Earl E. Henkens
SSN: 505-40-2940
Last Residence: 69337 Chadron, Dawes, Nebraska, United States of America
Born: 27 Jan 1911
Died: 25 Nov 2001
State (Year) SSN issued: Nebraska (1951)

219S. Florence Adrine
Obituary:

Florence Adrine McLaughlin, 88, Rapid City died Wednesday Oct. 6, 2010 at her residence. Florence is survived by her 2 daughters, Carol Ernster (Glen), Gayville, SD; Myrna Laumbach (Tom Burdick), Box Elder and 1 granddaughter, Lisa Laumbach, Sioux Falls. She is preceded in death by her first husband Walter Laumbach; her second husband LaVerne McLaughlin; son Veryl Alan Laumbach; daughter Linda Laumbach; 4 brothers and 1 sister.

Memorial services were 2:00 p.m., MST, Tuesday Oct. 12, 2010 at Emmanuel Episcopal Church, Rapid City with Father Rich Ressler officiating. Graveside services were 2:00 p.m., CDT, Wednesday Oct. 13th at the Draper Cemetery.

Behrens-Wilson Funeral Home is in care of the arrangements and condolences may be conveyed to the family at www.behrenswilson.com.

224. Martha Mattilda Luitjens
Obituary:
Martha M. (Luitjens) Lackman (1899 - 1992)

Martha M. Lackman was born on a farm in Goodrich Township, north of Denison, Nov. 3, 1899, the daughter of Herman and Elsaba Laumbach Luitjens. She was received into God's Kingdom of Grace through the Sacrament of Holy Baptism Jan. 7, 1900, at Zion Lutheran Church in Denison and confirmed into her Christian faith there Mar. 28, 1915. Martha was raised on the farm and received her formal education in the Milford Number 9 rural school.

On Jan. 12, 1920, Martha was united in marriage with Henry Lackman at her parents' farm home by Pastor Frehse. Their union was blessed with two children, Marvin and Helen. They made their home on a farm in Milford Township and later farmed and lived on other farms in Crawford County. In 1959 they moved to Denison. Henry died Jan. 3, 1975, and Martha continued to reside in Denison where she enjoyed her card clubs and attending the Senior Center for meals and fellowship.

In February of 1989 Martha moved to the Eventide Lutheran Home in Denison. Since January 30, 1991 she has resided at Thomas Rest Haven in Coon Rapids, where her death occurred Friday evening, Jan. 3, 1992. At the time of her death she had attained the age of 92 years and two months. She was a member of the First United Methodist Church in Denison and the Ladies Circle there.

Including her parents and her husband, Martha was preceded in death by four grandchildren, Marilyn, Ralph, Sally and Richard Lackman; one brother, Henry Luitjens and her son-in-law, Gerald Bull.

Those left to cherish her memory include her son and his wife, Marvin and Anna Lackman of Denison; her daughter, Mrs. Helen Bull of Coon Rapids; one granddaughter and her husband, Janice and Sami Mirza of Longwood, Florida and two great grandchildren, Farah and Shaun Mirza of Longwood, Florida. Also surviving are other relatives and friends.

Funeral services were held at 11:00 a.m. on Monday, January 6, 1992 at the First United Methodist Church in Denison, Iowa with Dr. Edward R. Peterson officiating. Music for the service was provided by the congregation singing three hymns with Glenn Rankin serving as organist. Selections included "Abide With Me," "Amazing Grace" and "Just A Closer Walk With Thee." Casket bearers were Sami Mirza, Elmer J. Lorenzen, Martin Schneider, Kenneth Aldag, Earl Olsen and Fred W. Schnoor. Interment was in the Lutheran Cemetery in Denison. The Pfannebecker Funeral Home in Denison was in charge of the arrangements.

---

226. **Dale Edward Laumbach**
Monona County, Iowa Obituary:
Dale Laumbach

Dale E. Laumbach, age 69, of Mapleton died Tuesday, May 30, 2000, at Sioux City, Iowa. Memorial services were held 2:00 p.m. Friday, June 2 at St. Peter's United Church of Christ in Mapleton with Pastor Bob Fritzmeier officiating. Burial was in Mt. Hope Cemetery, Mapleton with military honors by the Little Sioux Valley V.F.W. Post #9124 of Oto, Iowa. Kathy Johnson was the pianist for the service and music was 'How Great Thou Art' (duet with Dianna Hanna) and 'Amazing Grace' (soloed by Dianna Hanna). Arrangements were made under the direction of the Armstrong Funeral Home of Mapleton.

Dale Edward Laumbach was born September 12, 1930 at Clinton, Iowa. His parents were Detlef Andreas and Hilda (Lille) Laumbach. As a child, he moved to Mapleton, Iowa, where he graduated with the Mapleton High School class of 1949. He then served his country with the United States Navy, returning home to farm. On June 3, 1951, he married Dorothy Brownlee in Ida Grove, Iowa. In 1959, Dale began working for Kueny Electric in Mapleton until about 1962, when he started working for Jacobson Brothers Construction where he worked until his retirement in 1984.

He was a member of the Little Sioux Valley V.F.W. Post #9124 of Oto, Iowa.

Those survivors left to cherish Dale's memory include two sons, David and his wife, Betty Laumbach of South Sioux City, Nebraska and Doug Laumbach of Battle Creek, Iowa; two daughters and their husbands, Debra and Chris Tyler of Omaha, Nebraska and Dianna and Bill Hanna of Farnhamville, Iowa; six grandchildren, Brandon Cox and his wife, Tammy, Wendy Gents and her husband, Charles, Kevin Laumbach, Christopher Laumbach, Nathan VanNess and Charissa Laumbach; six great-grandchildren and one sister and her husband, Doris and Harold Astleford of Lake City, Iowa. He was preceded in death by his parents and one daughter-in-law, Marcia Laumbach.

---

235. **Arlo Theodore Jochims**
Minnesota Death Index, 1908-2002:

Name: Arlo Theodore Jochims
Birth Date: 12 Feb 1918
Death Date: 31 May 1977
Death County: Jackson
Mother's Maiden Name: Laumbach
Certificate Number: 011216

LAUMBACHS IN NEW MEXICO
Appendix 3: Bios & Photos of Major Contributors

Charles O. "Butch" Sanders

Charles O. Sanders, better known as Butch, lives near Dover, Delaware with his wife, Barb. Butch was born in northern Kentucky in 1943. Upon his graduation from the University of Kentucky in May 1967, he was commissioned into the Air Force. He completed Undergraduate Pilot Training (UPT) at Moody AFB, Georgia and T-38 Pilot Instructor Training (PIT) at Tyndall AFB, Florida.

His first assignment out of PIT was Laredo AFB, Texas as a T-38 Instructor Pilot. After three years at Laredo, Butch's long awaited assignment to Vietnam came down. But it wasn't exactly for one of the fighters for which he had volunteered. It was an AC-119 gunship—aka the "Flying Coffin." On the October 1972 day he completed the AC-119G phase of that training near Columbus, Ohio, a secret peace agreement was signed with North Vietnam. Butch's assignment was cancelled and he was reassigned (or "exiled" as he calls it) as the commander of an Air Force detachment on an Army Post in New Jersey (Fort Monmouth).

After two years in exile, he was rescued and sent to Dover AFB, Delaware where he flew the C-5 Galaxy for the next 24 years, until his retirement in 1998. He logged about 8,000 hours in the C-5 and was a squadron Chief Pilot and Chief of Wing Standardization/Evaluation. Butch flew the C-5 in support of military operations all around the world. Most were 24-hour crew duty days, but flown in comfort afforded by the C-5's two bunkrooms, two kitchens and two real flush toilets. He said it didn't get any better than that.

During his early Air Force years, Butch's passion was Maya archaeology and photography. He combined the two, spending his annual 30-day leaves traveling around the land of the Maya (Mexico, Belize, Guatemala and Honduras) taking photographs, and the other 11 months of each of those years, when he had the free time, developing, processing and printing them.

Butch said he became involved with genealogy, like most of us, by searching for his own family history. He then wandered into the research of old west personalities like Calamity Jane, Wild Bill Hickock, Buffalo Bill, Annie Oakley, Wyatt Earp, Jesse James, Billy the Kid and his imposters.

Butch's approach is a little different than most. He researches not only his subject, but also his subject's family history, neighbors, and—in the case of famous people—the biographers and sources the biographers used.

Butch was a major research contributor for this book. He not only provided genealogy research and what he calls "book reports" that include newspaper articles, obit and draft records about the subjects, he enhanced most of the photos and other images in this book, and in some cases, even provided the images. Without him, this book could not have been produced in useful form for those seeking information.

Karl W. Laumbach

Born in 1951, Karl was raised on a northeastern New Mexico ranch located between Springer and Cimarron. Without a television to run interference, Karl grew up hearing local history and family stories from his father, George Laumbach (son of Peter Joseph), and from his uncles, aunts and cousins. His interest in the family history led him to systematically collect both stories and photographs. Beginning in the 1980s, Karl took his photo stand and a 35 mm camera with a macro lens to the homes of individuals who owned the historic family photographs, making copies and archiving the 35 mm negatives. He is currently working to scan and catalog the several hundred photographs in the collection so that they can be easily shared with family members and interested historians. He is grateful to all the cousins, aunts and uncles who have helped with the photo project.

Karl has pursued an archaeological career in southern New Mexico since 1974. A graduate of New Mexico State University, he directed projects for the NMSU contract archaeology program for nine years before joining Human Systems Research, Inc. (HSR) in 1983. After serving as Executive Director of that organization for ten years, he is now an Associate Director and Principal Investigator for HSR.

His research interests are varied, including historical research in his native northeastern New Mexico, the pueblo archaeology of southern New Mexico, and the history and archaeology of the Apache. Fascinated with the history of south central New Mexico, Karl has been involved in recording sites and collecting history of that area for the last 30 years. His interaction with private landowners has been integral in the preservation of numerous archaeological sites.

Another major effort has been the Cañada Alamosa Project, a research program that explores the last 4,000 years of human occupation and environmental change in the Rio Alamosa drainage of Socorro and Sierra Counties.

Active with public education, Karl has co-authored a curriculum for New Mexico school teachers entitled "Capture the Past" published by Eastern New Mexico University. Another publication is *Hembrillo: An Apache Battlefield of the Victorio War* available through Human Systems Research.

Karl was a gubernatorial appointee on Cultural Properties Review Committee for the State of New Mexico from 1997 to 2003, serving as both vice-chairman and chairman as well as chairman for the archaeological subcommittee.

Active in the history of Sierra County, he has been affiliated with the board of directors for the Sierra County Historical Society and Geronimo Springs Museum since 1992. In January of 2002, he was inducted into the Dona Ana Historical Society's Hall of Fame "for his outstanding contributions to the history and culture of the Mesilla Valley."

Karl works in Las Cruces, New Mexico and lives with his wife Toni, Chief Curator and Deputy Director of the New Mexico Farm and Ranch Heritage Museum, and their son Kristopher.

José Antonio Esquibel

José Antonio Esquibel is a descendant of Daniel Eberle (Ebel) and María Viviana Martín. Juan Andrés Ebel identified the birthplace of his father, Daniel, as Germany. Juan Andrés married on January 26, 1874, Armenta (Roy), New Mexico, with María Uvalda López and they were the parents Nicanora Ebel, born January 10, 1875, at Armenta. Nicanora married Conrado Andrada on September 15, 1894, in Wagon Mound, New Mexico, and they were the parents of Inéz Andrada, born March 20, 1904, Roy, New Mexico. Inéz married Juan Isidro Esquibel and they resided in Las Vegas, being the grandparents of José Antonio.

José Antonio is a genealogical researcher, historian and author of articles and co-author of books related to Spanish colonial genealogy and history, with particular regard to New Mexico and northeastern Mexico. With John B. Colligan he co-authored *The Spanish Recolonization of New Mexico: An Account of the Families Recruited at Mexico City in 1693* (1999). With Christine Preston and Douglas Preston, he co-authored *The Royal Road: El Camino Real from Mexico City to Santa Fe* (1998). Most recently, he is a co-author with Marc Simmons, France V. Scholes and Eleanor B. Adams of *Juan Domínguez de Mendoza: Soldier and Frontiersman of the Spanish Southwest, 1627-1693* (UNM Press, 2012)

For years, José Antonio has been a regular contributor for *Herencia*, the quarterly journal of the Hispanic Genealogical Research Center of New Mexico, and for the *New Mexico Genealogist*, quarterly journal of the New Mexico Genealogical Society, and of *El Farolito*, the journal of the Olibama López Tushar Hispanic Legacy Center.

In 2009, Juan Carlos II, King of Spain, admitted José Antonio as a knight of the *Orden de Isabel la Católica* with the rank of *Cruz de Oficial* (Officer's Cross) for his dedication to preserving the history of Spain and Spanish heritage in New Mexico.

Peter James "Pete" Laumbach

Peter James "Pete" Laumbach was born in October 1941 in Las Vegas New Mexico to Rudolph and Leona Valdez Volk Laumbach. Leona's father, born Volk, was raised by a Valdez family in Colorado; to honor them, he kept Valdez as part of his surname. Pete's paternal grandparents were Peter Joseph and Fidelia Andrada Laumbach. Pete married Ophelia Naranjo Laumbach and they have four children: Patricia, Lara, Chloe and Rudy.

Pete served three years in the US Army, graduated from the University of New Mexico, and over the years worked for several construction and engineering entities including the New Mexico Highway Department, GMA Engineering Consultants, Associated Engineers & Surveyors, Inc., and Peter Kiewit Sons Construction Company. He retired in 2004.

Pete has been interested in his and his wife's families' genealogies for many years.

In June and July 2005, Pete and Ophie traveled to Europe. They went to visit their son, Rudy, and his family who were again living in Ansbach, Germany, 30 minutes from Nuremburg. Rudy had returned there after serving a year in Iraq with the Apache Gunship Battalion attached to the 1st Infantry Division.

Pete and Ophie took advantage of having family in Germany by visiting them there and seeing the area of his Laumbach family's origin. Taking with him copies of the three family documents dated 1856, Pete researched and extended backwards in time the known Laumbach family genealogy, and acquired confirming copies of original entries and documents of births, marriages and deaths, which he shares in this book. He and Ophie also created a large genealogical chart that includes several of our family's branches, extending from 1684 to 1891. This chart is an awesome work, but too huge to fit in this book; unfortunately reducing it to fit would render it unreadable.

Pete and Ophie live in Los Lunas, New Mexico, and own property near Las Vegas.

Our Laumbach family has many Petes and variations of that name, including Petra and Pedro, honoring their patriarch grandfather, Peter Joseph, the first-known "Pete." The Pete and "re-Petes" in the family make it necessary to often identify which Pete (this one) appears with frequency in this book, by giving his paternity.

Trent William Shue

Trent William Shue is a great-great-grandson of Fritz Eggert and Juanita Le Blanc. He is the great-grandson of Fred Eggert Sr. and Alcaria Chavez, and the grandson of Fred Eggert Jr. and Adeline Vigil. Trent's mother is Virginia Eggert, of Tucumcari, New Mexico and his father Thomas Wayne Shue, of McCrory, Arkansas. He has an adopted Japanese sister, Karen. A younger brother, Terrence, died at age seven in France. Trent is married to Lori Huseby, wife of 33 years, and is the father of three grown daughters and four grandchildren.

Trent was born in Blytheville, Arkansas in 1956. Before he was eleven, he had lived in Arkansas, Japan, the Philippines, France and Germany. Trent's father was a career Air Force man and, consequently, relocation was a normal part of his life growing up. Growing up an Air Force brat means never having a single place to call home. When Trent was young, home was many places and yet it was no place. Such is the transient nature of military life. When people asked, he told them that he was from New Mexico, because that is where the family he best related to lived, though he never lived there himself. His grandfather, Fred Eggert, nicknamed Trent "The Arkansas New Mexican." When Trent was young, he didn't see the humor in it. On the other hand, a part of him was honored to be acknowledged by his grandfather. Today, he is proud of the moniker.

Trent developed an interest in genealogy, family history and New Mexico's history twenty years ago when helping his teenage daughter research family history questions as part of a school assignment. He has since collected a wealth of information about his family's ancestors from both sides of his grandparent's family. From his research, he has discovered family connections to some of the most important events in New Mexico's history. This is the first time his writings are published.

Trent earned a Bachelor of Science in Forest Management from Northern Arizona University and worked for the Forest Service as a Fire Prevention Officer and Fire Lookout during and after college. After college he turned his attention to learning computer programming.

Today, Trent is a Software Development Manager where he works on database, open source software and Java applications. His interests are varied and include home remodeling, archaeology, lapidary, and jewelry making. His wife says he truly fits the definition of Renaissance Man. Trent is also the founder and first president of one of the largest youth soccer clubs in the country, SC del Sol, Phoenix, Arizona.

In his free time, he enjoys writing, researching New Mexico history and studying family genealogy. For fun, Trent likes to explore the back country roads of Arizona and New Mexico in his Toyota Land Cruiser.

Dallas Laumbach

Dallas Laumbach and his wife, Rosalie, were both born and raised in Lake City, Iowa, about 225 miles west of Clinton County, Iowa. Dallas has been in the energy business for most of his life. When he was seven years old his father, Justus, became the Mobil tank wagon agent and ultimately built and owned a Mobil service station in Lake City. Dallas' father was formally educated through the 7th grade and his mother was valedictorian of her high school class and went on to Normal Training and taught country school. We stand on the shoulders of those who have gone before us. Dallas' parents provided strong shoulders.

Justus Theodore Laumbach did not smoke, drink or gamble but with six children to raise and ultimately send to college, he needed to supplement his income and, being a hard and honest worker, many work opportunities came to him. As a consequence, in addition to teaching Dallas about the oil and gas business, he taught him how to build good, tight fence; dynamite stumps and boulders; install culverts and build good headwalls; form, run, deaerate, screed and trowel concrete; tear down a barn, recycle the lumber and build a new garage; build tall swing sets; cut cockleburs and sunflowers out of the soybean fields; mow hay and leave no standing corners; hunt pheasant, duck and geese; catch catfish, bass, crappies, bullheads and walleyes; and trap mink, muskrat, raccoon and beaver.

Dallas' mother, Alice Lillian Kral Laumbach, ensured that her children's education was high quality and comprehensive, particularly in literature, writing, mathematics, science, economics, history, government, spelling and phonics. She was a true Christian and sacrificed much so that her children would have what they needed. She saw to it that all of her children learned to play at least one musical instrument from trumpet, clarinet, violin and viola to piano. They all went to college after being either valedictorian or salutatorian of their high school classes. An illustration of her knowledge and commitment: One evening she helped Dallas with his homework assignment to list and define homonyms. By bedtime, they had compiled a list of 125 homonyms along with their definitions. The next day the student with the next highest number in Dallas' 6th grade class had 25.

Dallas holds a B.S. degree in mechanical engineering from Iowa State University, an M.S. degree in mechanical engineering from the University of New Mexico and a Ph.D. degree in mechanical engineering and applied mathematics from the Massachusetts Institute of Technology. He served eight years in the U.S. Marine Corps (three of those on active duty) and achieved the rank of captain. Following his active duty time in the Marine Corps, Dallas held managerial positions at Sandia Laboratories, Shell Oil Company and Contour Production Company. He and his wife, Rosalie, currently live on the banks of the Blanco River near Wimberley, Texas. They have two children and three grandchildren who continually enrich their lives.

Verna Laumbach Sparks
October 1909—May 1996

Verna was born to Emma Margaretha Henkens Laumbach and Daniel Laumbach on her family's ranch on the rugged Canadian River gorge between Roy and Wagon Mound. She had six siblings, half older, half younger, all of whom lived at least to 80 except for eldest sister Mabel Anna Eleanor, who died at home in Roy of pneumonia at age 19.

Verna and her siblings grew up on their family ranch, and also in Roy during the months of their school years. Teachers who lived on the ranch provided their earlier educations. Verna's parents, her siblings and she were close to their family living at Buena Vista. She knew many of her family's older generation, including her grandmother Elionor Ebel Laumbach, her great-aunt Maria Marta Ebel Esquibel (her grandmother Elionor's sister), her great-uncle Ramon Bonney (Elionor's older half-brother), her aunt Estefanita and husband, Sito, her aunt Crestina, her maiden Laumbach aunts at Buena Vista and later Las Vegas, and most of her Henkens aunts and uncles in Nebraska, etc.

While attending college at New Mexico Normal in the late 1920s and early 1930s, Verna lived with her aunt Crestina L. Sanchez in Las Vegas near the old town plaza, and met her great-aunt Isabel Metzgar Gallegos and her cousin Edwardo Korte, son of Juanita Metzger and Henry Korte, grandson of Frank Metzgar. She grew up listening to the old ones, born in the mid-1800s, talk. While attending college, she gathered more information and wrote additional details of her family history. She, in turn, became the family's historian and storyteller.

As a young teacher, Verna met Dal Sparks (July 1908—January 1975) at French, a community that no longer exists in northeastern New Mexico, when he, a telegrapher then on the extra-board, was assigned to that depot. They married in 1936 at Hillsboro, New Mexico, now a ghost town. They had two children, Gerald C. "Jerry" and Janet "Jan."

Verna wrote poetry and stories, some of which were published in the 1930s in the *New Mexico Magazine*. Her lengthy <u>Las Vegas Before 1850</u> was published in the October 1933 issue of the *New Mexico Historical Review*.

In 1956, Verna compiled her many notes and finished pieces into a cohesive family history, which Jan later typed up for her in a bound manuscript for her 82nd birthday. When about 80, Verna wrote some of her family stories in fictional form professionally printed in a little book, with just 100 copies: *In Search of Springs*. Jan included some of those stories—gently unfictionalized—in this book to provide characterizations of those who lived long ago. This book also includes chapters of family history written by Verna.

In addition to writing, Verna painted with oils, watercolors and oil pastels. Nearly all of her subjects were New Mexico scenes. She saw beauty in its colorful skies, in knurled old trees and nostalgic adobe ruins. Much of her artwork had personal family significance. A few of her pieces are reproduced in this book.

Jan Girand

Cook Photography, September 2014

Jan Girand lives in Roswell, New Mexico with her husband, Dan. She spent her first almost 39 years in a small community in northeastern New Mexico, where her three children, David, Tracy and Devin, were born. That was also where her parents, Verna L. Sparks and Dalphon C. Sparks, lived much of their adult lives.

Verna's parents, Daniel and Emma Henkens Laumbach, lived their last years in the small community of Roy after they grew too old to manage their large cattle ranch on the rugged Canadian River southwest of Roy.

Jan grew up knowing many of her mother's extended family, and hearing her mama tell her family history. As Jan told her mother, everyone has a fascinating family history, but not all are fortunate to have their stories passed down for generations. Verna talked about the "old ones," even those in Germany and Iowa, long gone before she herself was born, bringing them to life for Jan. She and Jan inherited some things that belonged to their forebears, including a few pieces from Germany. We are all only caretakers of family keepsakes for while, before they pass on. Through those, the people who once owned them live on.

Jan worked for independent insurance agencies, was a licensed insurance agent, and secretary in engineering department of a large manufacturing corporation.

She and Dan designed, and after they married in mid-1985, hands-on built their own adobe home. Jan—already a grandmother—assisted in the adobe construction of a nearby home for an elderly couple. Besides other tasks and responsibilities, she was *jefe* for making 10,000 to 20,000 adobe bricks the old-fashioned way. The next year, Jan and her small crew made more sun-dried adobes and built an efficiency apartment onto their home for her mother, Verna, where she lived the last three years of her life. Verna died at half-past 86.

Jan was a newspaper reporter. An avid reader since childhood, she loved to write and has file boxes filled with her writings, including published newspaper articles and multiple fiction and non-fiction partial book manuscripts.

She has a magazine on the internet with 20 archived issues; she wrote many pieces for, and produced, five issues of the *Outlaw Gazette*; she developed and owns a small independent publishing company, YellowJacketPress, which has thus far published five books, including for others. Her recent publications are *Enchanted Lands, New Mexico*—an epic poem with photos taken around the state, and the first issue of *PastWord, Access the Era of Billy the Kid.*

Laumbachs in New Mexico is the sixth book published by YellowJacketPress. It is intended to be one of three family history books that span many generations and hundreds of years. The next two of that series, already in progress, are *Bibiana and Her Children* and *A Bonney on the Santa Fe Trail*.

Copies of her books can be ordered by email directly from Jan or from her website yellowjacketpress.com. Jan can be reached at jan.yellowjacketpress@gmail.com Her website is: www.yellowjacketpress.com .